D1032720

THEREFORE, STAND

A Plea for a Vigorous Apologetic in the Present Crisis of Evangelical Christianity

BY

WILBUR M. SMITH

Department of English Bible, Moody Bible Institute
Editor of *Peloubet's Select Notes on the International Sunday School Lessons*

BOSTON

W. A. Wilde Co.

1946

NINTH EDITION
Fifth Printing

MADE IN THE UNITED STATES OF AMERICA

To

Mary Irene

Faithful companion and devoted wife, a constant encouragement to the author to do his best in every task

This volume is dedicated with love and gratitude

ACKNOWLEDGMENTS

Without the generous help of many publishers both in this country and in Great Britain, much of the value of this book, if its readers find it to be of value, would be lost. As the preface states, it has been the deliberate intention of the author to give many, and at times extended quotations to illustrate and substantiate the statements which will be found in these chapters. These quotations would not be possible were it not for the generosity of many publishing houses that have been so kind to the author in every way. Both the publishers of this book, the W. A. Wilde Company, and the author himself, wish to express their profound gratitude for their coöperation.

When brief phrases or sometimes single sentences have been quoted, especially from older works, it has not been thought necessary to secure permission for quotation; however, if any such permission should have been secured, and through the author's own carelessness, or oversight, such has not been solicited, he would appreciate his attention called to the matter, and hereby apologizes for any such errors, which will be corrected in the second edition of this work (he really has that much hope for the book, that he expects a second edition will be called for, within his own lifetime).

The following publishing firms have generously given permission for the author to use quoted material from their publications.

Abingdon-Cokesbury Press, New York and Nashville: *The Resurrection Fact,* by Doremus A. Hayes.

Augsburg Publishing House, Minnesota: *What Is Christianity,* by Dr. Norborg.

Chapman and Hall. Ltd., London: *Christianity and Communism,* by Dr. Julius Hecker.

The Christian Century Press, Chicago: *The Kingdom of God and History,* by a number of authors, and a large number of important articles appearing in their valuable religious weekly, *The Christian Century.*

Columbia University Press, New York City, N. Y.: *Popular Freethought in America,* by Dr. Albert Post.

F. S. Crofts & Company, New York: *The Human Enterprise,* by Max Otto.

Doubleday, Doran and Company, Inc., Garden City, New York: *Madame Curie,* by Eve Curie.

William B. Eerdmans Publishing Company, Grand Rapids, Michigan: *Systematic Theology,* by Professor Berkhoff.

Dr. Vergilius Ferm of Wooster College, for quotations from *Contemporary American Theology,* which he edited.

Harper & Brothers, New York City: *The Survival of Western Culture,* by Dr. R. T. Flewelling; and, *School and Church: The American Way,* by Dr. Moehlman.

Harvard University Press, Cambridge, Massachusetts: *The Religious Thought of the Greeks,* by Prof. Clifford H. Moore.

Longmans, Green & Co., London, New York: *The Resurrection and Modern Thought,* by Dr. W. J. Sparrow Simpson.

The Macmillan Company, New York City: *A Critical History of Greek Philosophy,* by W. T. Stace; *God in History,* by Dr. Otto Piper; *The Philosophical Basis of Theism,* by D. G. Hicks; *People, Church and State in Modern Russia,* by Mr. Paul B. Anderson; *Timothy Dwight: 1752–1851,* by Dr. Charles E. Cuningham; and, *Christian Doctrine,* by Dr. Whale.

John Murray Ltd., Publishers, London, England: *Pro Fide,* by the Rev. Charles Harris.

Thomas Nelson and Sons, Limited, Toronto: *Reflections on the Revolution of Our Time,* by Professor Harold J. Laski.

Oxford University Press, Oxford, England: *The Greek Genius and Its Meaning to Us,* by R. W. Livingstone; *A History of the Ancient World,* by Professor Rostovtzeff; and *The Legacy of Greece.*

Ronald Press, New York City: *The Course of American Democratic Thought,* by Professor Ralph Henry Gabriel.

Charles Scribner's Sons, New York: *Christianity and the Social Revolution,* by various authors; *Main Currents of Modern European*

Thought, by Rudolf Eucken; and *Human Nature in the Bible,* by the late Professor William Lyon Phelps.

The Pilgrim Press, Boston, Massachusetts: *Paths to the Presence of God,* and *The New Christian Epic,* both by President Albert W. Palmer.

University of Pennsylvania Press, Philadelphia, Pa.: *Religion and the Modern World.*

The Vanguard Press, Inc., New York City: *What Is Communism?,* by Earl Browder.

The Viking Press, Inc., New York: *Faith, Reason and Revelation,* by Professor Harold J. Laski.

Westminster Press, Philadelphia, Pennsylvania: *The Intention of Jesus,* by Professor John W. Bowman; and *What a Man Can Believe,* by Dr. James D. Smart.

John Wiley & Sons, Inc., New York: *Outlines of Historical Geology,* by Professors Schuchert and Dunbar.

Yale University Press, New Haven, Connecticut: *Science and Criticism: The Humanistic Tradition in Contemporary Thought,* by Professor Albert J. Mueller; and *A Common Faith,* by Dr. John Dewey.

CHRISTIAN AT THE HOUSE BEAUTIFUL

"The next day they took him and had him into the armoury, where they showed him all manner of furniture, which their Lord had provided for pilgrims, as sword, shield, helmet, breastplate, *all-prayer,* and shoes that would never wear out . . .

"Now, he bethought himself of setting forward, and they were willing he should. But first, said they, let us go again in the armoury. So they did; and when they came there, they harnessed him from head to foot with what was of proof, lest, perhaps, he should meet with assaults on the way . . .

"Now, in this Valley of Humiliation, poor Christian was hard put to it; for he had gone but a little way, before he espied a foul fiend coming over the field to meet him; his name is Apollyon. Then did Christian begin to be afraid, and to cast in his mind whether to go back or stand his ground. But he considered again that he had no armour for his back; and, therefore, thought that to turn the back to him might give him the greater advantage, with ease to pierce him with his darts. Therefore he resolved to venture and stand his ground; for, thought he, had I no more in mine eye than the saving of my life, it would be the best way to stand."

(From John Bunyan's *The Pilgrim's Progress.*)

CONTENTS

PREFACE

The main purpose which the author of this work has had in mind throughout its writing is that from its perusal some of the present generation of young men, whose faith in God and in the Bible has been shaken or destroyed, by the years spent in collegiate institutions and universities where the Christian faith is under constant attack and ridicule, and those who have come under the power of the spirit of skepticism and irreligiousness of our present unbelieving age, might be persuaded to consider fairly, without prejudice, as they would any subject offered in college, the evidences which support and confirm the great elemental truths of the Christian faith, and find, in this reconsideration, or perhaps new consideration, a solid foundation on which a real and abiding faith might be built. In the well-known phraseology of the Apostle Paul, this volume has been written for "the defense and confirmation of the faith."[1] The author believes that now, more than ever, the facts of life, the facts of history, and the facts of science, are not on the side of agnosticism and atheism, but on the side of Christian truth, and that our faith is definitely not contradicted by *facts,* but is opposed only by the *theories* of men, whether they be theories of philosophy, psychology, and sociology, or the hypotheses of science. Young men today are selling their souls (and minds) too cheaply in forfeiting their holy God-given privilege of independent thinking, and are too quickly and willingly yielding their minds to, and framing the deeper convictions of life from, the teachings of skeptical professors, and the rationalistic assertions of many of our leaders of thought, such as Bertrand Russell, John Dewey, H. G. Wells, Julian Huxley, etc. If this volume shall but arouse some young men to the reinvestigation of the *facts* of the Christian faith, a faith which they have been told can no longer be reasonably held, if this volume shall prove an incentive for men to emancipate themselves from the paralyzing consequences

1. Philippians 1:7. "The defence was made for establishment or confirmation, and resulted in it." Marvin R. Vincent, *in loco.*

of the deceiving and faith-destroying spirit of our age, the author will be abundantly satisfied. The reason so many of our young men today are not embracing the Christian faith, have no fellowship with God, and know nothing of redemption in Jesus Christ, is not because they are so well informed about the facts of the Christian faith, and find them impossible of acceptance, but because they are so ill-informed, or misinformed, due, principally, to the fact that during the most formative years of life, the years of study in high school and college, they have been almost exclusively under the tutelage of those who hold anti-theistic, agnostic, or atheistic views. Thousands of young people in our land have rarely, or perhaps never in all their life, even once heard clearly proclaimed the gospel of Christ as it is revealed in the New Testament.

In the second place, the author has desired in writing this volume to place in the hands of believers who seek to defend the faith, who desire either to save young men from unbelief, or guide them out of the morass of skepticism into which they have fallen, something which may provide adequate equipment for such an undertaking. Many evangelicals today do not have access to great libraries, and, furthermore, some who do have access to such libraries find the literature both of skepticism and of the Christian faith so vast that soon they are lost, as it were, in a bewildering labyrinth of books and articles, and when their time for reading in any one portion of this field has elapsed, they discover they have not acquired what they were really searching for. Many who really love the Lord, and yearn to see young men brought to a knowledge of Christ, do not have the time for prolonged research, either in the literature of unbelief, or in the great works of Christian Apologetics, and find themselves inadequately equipped for work which they long to do. A large number of ministers, especially in small towns, know the experience of having young men of their parish return from the university, who not only have lost all interest in church, faith in God, and confidence in the Word of God, but who seem to take pleasure in disseminating their own agnostic views among the young people of their acquaintance, who (the latter) worshipfully look up to their more educated friends as the prophets of a new generation who must be blindly followed. What should be said to these young people? If this volume should prove helpful in placing at the disposal of some Christian ministers and teachers material of an authoritative nature which they themselves can use in this great battle for the Christian faith, a battle in which we must all today be engaged, the author will indeed be grateful.

A third reason for writing at least the earlier part of this book, is that Christians might be awakened out of the present spirit of indifference, complacency, and compromise, which seems to rest so tragically upon the Christian Church today. For the most part, not altogether, thank God, but generally, the Christian Church seems either to be unaware of the dreadfully antichristian teachings of so many of our great institutions, or, which is far worse, seems to be willing to compromise with these agnostic and skeptical tendencies, even to the point of supporting men in such educational centres who never let a day pass but that they deny, in classroom and in their writings, the truth of the Word of God, the necessity of redemption through Jesus Christ, indeed the very existence of God Himself. The psalmist once said, "The floods of ungodliness made me afraid."[2] It would be a hopeful sign in the Church today if we could really begin to fear these awful tides of unbelief. Calvin truly exclaimed: "Those who are not touched when they see and hear God blasphemed, and do not only wink thereat, but also carelessly pass over it, are not worthy to be counted the children of God, who at least do not give Him so much honor as they do to an earthly father."[3] We have come to the time in American Protestantism when ecclesiastics are not even rebuked for the denial of any of the great fundamentals of the faith, but are allowed to keep their professorial chairs, and their pulpits, even though they have long ago abandoned the Christian faith. But let a man stand up and say anything in criticism of denominational boards, of some theological seminary, or of some skeptical professor, and at once he is pounced upon, and often ex-communicated. This is a tragic hour, when loyalty to a church is placed above loyalty to the Lord Jesus Christ. We need to be awakened to the conditions that are now prevailing in our land, and to be moved to do something about them.

2. Psalm 18:4.
3. John Calvin: *Commentary on the Acts of the Apostles.* II. 147.

Finally, it is hoped that the reading of this volume, for those who are already believers in Christ, will result in a reconfirmation of their own faith. It cannot be denied that there are many teaching Sunday school and other classes today, bearing faithful testimony to the Lord Jesus Christ, who, down deep in their hearts, often know the agony of troubling doubts, who seem to be almost afraid to look into the literature of modern philosophy and modern science, lest they might discover that which, if accepted, would mean the collapse of their own faith. Dr. Machen once said, "Obviously, it is impossible to hold on with the heart to something that one has rejected with the head, and all the usefulness of Christianity can never lead us to be Christians unless the Christian religion is true."[4] The Apostle Paul, in his last epistle urged Timothy to *hold fast* to the form of sound doctrine, and to *keep* securely that which had been committed unto him.[5] We frequently need our faith confirmed, especially in these days, when that which we hold most dear is under constant and terrific attack.

The argument of the book proceeds as follows: In the first chapter I have tried to give a careful, detailed, comprehensive survey of the powerful forces and agencies which, for the most part, beginning with the naturalistic philosophy of Kant, have multiplied and grown in power and intensity until from every side, by the proud battalions not only of philosophy but science, psychology, political theory, higher criticism, and even a false theology, our faith finds itself incessantly assailed. No man goes into battle without attempting to ascertain as accurately as possible the strength of the enemy and the nature of the weapons that the enemy will be expected to use. Following this I have devoted a chapter to some of the consequences which are already tragically evident, throughout protestantism in the western world, at the present time, which show the fearful havoc which these attacks have already wrought. I have tried to be as factual and definite as possible here, because I find too many evangelical Christians fold their arms in total forgetfulness of the injunction frequently found in the New Testament to contend for the faith. Discovering evangelical protes-

4. J. Gresham Machen, in Vergilius Ferm: *Contemporary American Theology.* New York. 1932. p. 261.

5. II Timothy 1:13, 14.

tantism to have suffered in the last half century one defeat after another, with hardly any justified hope that even more defeats will not follow, unless there is a radical change, I have thought it advisable to give some consideration to the deeper causes for the unbelief of men and their agelong antagonism to God and to His Christ. This first major division of the book, if we may so call it, concludes with a brief chapter on the pessimism of modern skepticism, showing that whatever be the learning and fervor and growing power manifested in these attacks upon our faith, one thing our enemies have confessed again and again, and that is that their abandoning any true faith has brought them nothing but despair and sorrow, and no modern man need expect to follow in the steps of contemporary agnosticism and come to anything else but a similar despair. The major part of this book is devoted to a detailed presentation of the three great themes which the Apostle Paul proclaimed to the most intellectual city that the western world has ever known, at the time of its glory, the university city of the world—Athens. The message which Paul presented to these learned Greeks in defense of the faith which he was affirming is, I believe, the very message which we as Christians need to present powerfully in this day of unbelief and scoffing intellectualism. Before actually considering these three major themes themselves, I have thought it wise to devote considerable attention to the civilization of the Athenians, that we might realize anew the similarity between the age of the glory of Athens and our own intellectual age, and that we might get it settled in our mind, never to be forgotten, that with all the brilliant, intellectual and artistic and political achievements of Athens, she nevertheless failed to discover an adequate power for a higher ethical life, she confessed she had failed to discover final truth and to find the true God, and, as a consequence, she ended without hope. Our own humanly limited intellectual efforts, however brilliant, will never lead us to anything beyond what the Athenians were able to achieve, and will leave us, as it left them, without hope, without moral power, without God, and without peace. Before considering the major themes of Paul's Athenian address I have given a brief introductory chapter on the address as a whole. The central argument of the book then follows: (1) a consideration of the creation of the world by God, as an apologetic for this age of scientific emphasis; (2) a chapter on the evidence for the resurrection of Christ from the dead, as an apologetic for this age so constantly demanding historical certitude; and, finally (3), a discussion of a righteous judgment to come, as the apologetic for such an hour as this when our ethical standards are fast disappearing. These three chapters are followed by a brief consideration of "peace and joy in believing," which will reveal a truth which even unbelievers can never deny, that, while atheism and skepticism inevitably and always lead to despair, faith in the great truths which have just been discussed does result in peace and joy abiding in the heart of those so believing. The last chapter is an attempt to offer some suggestions for an immediate vigorous offensive, on the part of evangelicals in the western world, for the defense and the advancement of the Christian faith, for the recapturing of much that has been lost, and the winning back to Christ, and to the faith that saves, this new generation of young men and young women which is growing up so almost totally ignorant of the great facts of the only redeeming message which the world has ever known.

In regard to the principles which have guided the author in the manner in which he has selected, arranged, and presented his material, he would like to say three things. First of all, he makes no apology for the size and length of the book. Probably some whom he desires to reach will immediately turn away from the volume, because of its bulk. It is necessarily large. We hear people say today, especially in regard to Christian literature, "It must be brief. It must be to the point. People won't read anything that is long." This is a delusion, and one of the faults of Christian literature today. People not only will read large books, but some of the largest books that have been published in the last few years have had the greatest sale. Gunther's volumes, *Inside Europe* and *Inside Asia,* are huge books. *Berlin Diary* and *The Autobiography of William Lyon Phelps* are volumes that run to over 300,000 words each. Julian Huxley's new work, *Evolution: the Modern Synthesis,* must contain at least 220,000 words; while in the field of philosophy, Professor Schilpp's *The Philosophy of Alfred North Whitehead,* e.g., runs to something over 300,000 words. More important than the books which people may read, and do read, being frequently of great size, is the indisputable fact that many of the textbooks which our young people are compelled to work with in our universities, even in freshman courses, are large volumes. A course of one year's length in the University of Chicago, and many other universities, masters Frederick L. Schuman's *International Politics,* running to 350,000 words. Only this week, as I am writing this Preface, a student beginning a freshman course at Northwestern University showed me three of the textbooks used in only two courses: Tracy I. Storer's *General Biology,* L. L. Woodruff's *Foundations of Biology,* and Richard's and Scarlett's *General College Chemistry,* the three together totaling over 850,000 words, all of which must be absorbed in the freshman year of this seventeen-year-old young person. In the face of these facts, what right have we to say that the great truths of the Christian faith must be presented to our college young people in ephemeral pamphlets, and short monosyllabic essays, if chemistry and psychology and biology and politics are important enough to require large volumes for study? If we are going to really make a study of some of the great truths of the Christian faith, subjects greater than any we have just mentioned—the truth of God, the creation of the world, the resurrection of Christ, a judgment to come, etc.—we dare not submit to the oft-repeated admonition that we must put trivial tract literature in the hands of our young people, with the expectation it will stem the tides of unbelief. After a young man has been through four years of college, and heard his teachers in psychology, and philosophy, and biology deny the very existence of God, day after day, week after week, and has been open to every conceivable device of collegiate life to crush the faith of that person's heart, *no twenty-page pamphlet will be able to answer the questions which are in this young man's mind.* If the hour is coming, and God grant it may come soon, when our young men are once again going to give serious attention to the facts of and the reasons for believing or disbelieving the Christian faith, how tragic it will be if in that hour we do not have volumes to put into their hands, as adequate and thorough and dependable as the textbooks they have mastered in geology or medicine or European history!

The author has been very careful, and has considered no trouble too great, no prolonged research too taxing, to support everything that is set forth in this volume with adequate, abundant, and dependable quotations and references. There is no use of saying, e.g., that certain theologians today are denying God, unless we have their actual words before us, for many people will simply shrug their shoulders and say, "It is an exaggeration." There is no use of talking about the atheistic philosophy of John Dewey, when so many are dominated by his educational theories, unless we can actually show from his own writings that he is definitely and constantly antisupernaturalistic. Nowhere in this volume, I hope, have I stooped to second-rate, or third-rate, or tenth-rate stuff, too much of which is now flooding our book counters, in the name of fundamentalism or orthodoxy, a heterogeneous mass of denial and denunciation, sentimental and sophomoric exudations, which, too often, turn educated men away from the very truths they attempt to defend. Quotations and footnotes are purposely full and elaborate, and whatever else may be said by those who read this book, I trust that no one, believer or unbeliever, Christian or atheist, will be able to say of a single statement, "This is not true," or "This cannot be supported," or "He has misunderstood the author."

It is with regret that I have been compelled, here and there, to enter into philosophical matters. I have never had any great passion for philosophy myself, and I believe that thousands of pages of philosophical literature contain nothing but the vain speculations of men, contradicting one another, and greatly varying within the lifetime of the philosophers themselves. But philosophy is exercising an enormous influence in contemporary thought, and it has been impossible to avoid some metaphysical subjects. It has especially been necessary to say something about the relation of Kant's philosophy to religion, and the philosophic implications of the denial and affirmation of the doctrine of creation. Having said this much, I must here add two convictions of my own. The first is that I do not believe when this war is over, and young men return to a life of study and intellectual pursuits, that they are going to discuss the great truths of the Christian faith, either affirmatively or negatively, in the complex and difficult phraseologies of Kant and Hegel. It is paramount that we as Christians present some *facts* of the Christian faith, and the *facts* of science, as they relate to creation; and the evidence of history, as it relates to the resurrection of Christ. Though we do not flee from the arena of philosophical discussion, we insist that this is not the only area in which the Christian battle is to be fought. Unbelief can easily entangle young men in a philosophical, technical nomenclature, and make them only realize that they are in a fog. I do not find, e.g., that unbelief today is talking much about the evidence for the resurrection and the necessity for believing in God, as a Creator, yet it is back to these great inescapable *realities* that we need to go.

It has been the author's deliberate intention to avoid an irritatingly technical phraseology. Though this volume concerns some of the profoundest problems that can ever engage the minds of men, he hopes that no reasonably educated person, with careful reading, will fail to understand a single sentence in these pages. One of the most justified criticisms of much of our modern theological and philosophical literature is that one frequently is not really sure what an author means. I regret that I have had to read thousands and thousands of lines which are not only vague and indefinite, but which, in themselves, cannot possibly communicate any vital truth. Let me illustrate what I mean. Canon Charles E. Raven, one of the recognized scholars of the Church of England today, in his new book, *Science, Religion, and the Future,* quotes with strong approval this sentence from the writings of the late Professor Oman: "When Oman summarized his conclusions in the words, 'Reconciliation to the evanescent is revelation of the eternal and revelation of the eternal a higher reconciliation to the evanescent,' he stated the principles of a theology in which there could be no ultimate antithesis between nature and grace or between science and religion, in which indeed the words of the scientist and the theologian were seen to be one and the same, their unity being sacramentally or incarnationally interpreted." [6] Now, frankly, I do not know what Oman meant when he talked about "the eternal a higher reconciliation to the evanescent." And I do not know what Canon Raven means when he talks about the language of the scientist and theologian being "incarnationally interpreted." What is more, I do not think a

6. Charles E. Raven: *Science, Religion, and the Future.* Cambridge. 1943. pp. 74, 75. The quotation is from Oman: *The Natural and the Supernatural.* p. 470.

lot of other people know what these phrases mean, and I am absolutely sure that even if they knew what the phrases meant, they would not, by using them, be able to persuade young men today of the truth and the reasonableness of the great facts of the Christian faith. It is this kind of language I have striven to avoid.

No one is more aware of the shortcomings of this volume than the author himself. Most of all, he realizes that if he had three, or five, or ten more years, to work for the perfection of this book it would be more complete, and probably more acceptable. But I cannot bring myself to delay its publication any longer. Soon the war will be over, we hope, and men are going to turn from the weapons of destruction to some of the deeper problems of life, and it is time for some of us to speak, and to offer what little help we are able to give to the great work of the defense of the Christian faith, in this day of conflict and increasing denial. Carl Sandburg said to his friend, Lloyd Lewis, of the *Chicago Daily News:* "If I had not faithfully plodded through every last piece of material I could lay my hands on that concerned the essential record, I would feel guilty."[7] I am sorry that I have not been able to read every single line in the literature of the last three centuries, pertaining to rationalism, agnosticism, and atheism, Greek civilization, the doctrine of Creation, the resurrection of Christ, and the judgment to come. However, I have tried to read everything that seemed important, and a great deal which proved unimportant. Some of this reading began twenty years ago. A great deal of it has been done in the last two years, during which time this book has been the chief task (apart, of course, from my work of teaching) of every day and some nights. Professor Lynn Thorndike, of Columbia University, began the preface of his remarkable volume, *A Short History of Civilization,* with these words: "When the war broke out in 1914, I determined to do what little I could to keep civilization alive. This volume is a contribution in that direction. I have written the book because I think it is needed."[8] I am under no delusion that I am going to "keep civilization alive," but I have tried to do in this volume what little I could to awaken this generation to a realization of the seriousness, the depth, the alarming growth, and the destructiveness of con-

7. Karl Detzer: *Carl Sandburg*. New York. 1941. p. 202.
8. Lynn Thorndike: *A Short History of Civilization*. New York. 1926. p. v.

temporary unbelief, and to offer to bewildered, and I trust, searching souls, some indisputable evidence which, believed, will form a solid foundation on which a structure of faith can be built that not all the storms and attacks of our day can sweep away. I have written this book because I thought it was needed.[9]

As this volume goes to press, I wish to express my deep appreciation to Dr. Will H. Houghton, president, and Dr. William A. Culbertson, dean of the Moody Bible Institute, where it is my great privilege to be a teacher, for graciously arranging for a three months' leave of absence in the spring of 1944, that I might give myself entirely to the finishing of this work. Without this brief relief from the burdens of teaching, I do not know when this book would have been completed. It would have been impossible, of course, for this volume to be as comprehensive as the author hopes it will be found to be, had not many librarians throughout our country given generously of their time and wisdom, and allowed me to use some of the treasures of their great collections. Especially do I wish to express my appreciation for constant help to Mr. S. Kingsley Miner, of the Harper Memorial Library of the University of Chicago; to Miss Mabel Gardner, of Garrett Biblical Institute, Evanston; to Dr. John Frederick Lyons, librarian of the Presbyterian Theological Seminary, Chicago; to Dr. Kenneth S. Gapp, librarian of the Theological Seminary in Princeton, New Jersey; to Dr. Jeannette Newhall, of the Andover Harvard Theological Library, where some books were found which, apparently, are not in any other theological library in this country; and to Dr. Eligin S. Moyer, and Miss Mabel Sprague, of the library of the Moody Bible Institute, who have always been so kind no matter how many requests I have made of them. I am deeply indebted to two friends who have been of inestimable help in the tedious task of reading proof, without whom this volume would have infinitely more errors than are now to be discovered.

9. Since writing the above, I have come upon a strong statement regarding the confusing phraseology of much of our theological literature, from a most unexpected source, a former Dean of Harvard Divinity School, Dr. W. W. Fenn. "Readers of current theological literature must often wish that every writer were obliged to furnish a glossary in order that his teaching might be fully intelligible . . . A smear of words and a smouch of ideas are reciprocally related." "Modern Liberalism," in *American Journal of Theology,* XVII (1913), p. 519.

ST. PAUL FROM THE PRISON IN ROME TO THE CHRISTIANS OF EPHESUS

"Finally, my brethren, let your hearts be strengthened in the Lord, and in the conquering power of His might. Put on the whole armor of God, that you may be able to stand firm against the wiles of the Devil. For the adversaries with whom we wrestle are not flesh and blood, but they are the Principalities, the Powers, and the Sovereigns of this present darkness, the spirits of evil in the heavens. Wherefore, take up with you to the battle the whole armor of God, that you may be able to withstand them in the evil day, and, having overthrown them all, to stand unshaken. Stand, therefore, girt with the belt of truth, and wearing the breastplate of righteousness, and shod as ready messengers of the glad-tidings of peace; and take up to cover you the shield of faith, wherewith you shall be able to quench all the fiery darts of the Evil One. Take, likewise, the helmet of salvation, and the sword of the Spirit, which is the Word of God."

Ephesians 6:10–17. (Translation of W. J. Conybeare.)

(The title for this book is taken from the opening phrase of verse fourteen of this passage, as it appears in the Authorized Version—"Stand therefore.")

ST. PAUL'S ADDRESS TO THE ATHENIANS FROM MARS HILL

Now while Paul waited for them at Athens, his spirit was provoked within him as he beheld the city full of idols. So he reasoned in the synagogue with the Jews and the devout persons, and in the market-place every day with them that met him. And certain also of the Epicurean and Stoic philosophers encountered him. And some said, What would this babbler say? others, He seemeth to be a setter forth of strange gods: because he preached Jesus and the resurrection. And they took hold of him, and brought him unto the Areopagus, saying, May we know what this new teaching is, which is spoken by thee? For thou bringest certain strange things to our ears: we would know therefore what these things mean. (Now all the Athenians and the strangers sojourning there spent their time in nothing else, but either to tell or to hear some new thing.) And Paul stood in the midst of the Areopagus and said, Ye men of Athens, in all things I perceive that ye are very religious. For as I passed along, and observed the objects of your worship, I found also an altar with this inscription, TO AN UNKNOWN GOD. What therefore ye worship in ignorance, this I set forth unto you. The God that made the world and all things therein, he, being Lord of heaven and earth, dwelleth not in temples made with hands; neither is he served by men's hands, as though he needed anything, seeing he himself giveth to all life, and breath, and all things; and he made of one every nation of men to dwell on all the face of the earth, having determined their appointed seasons, and the bounds of their habitation; that they should seek God, if haply they might feel after him and find him, though he is not far from each one of us: for in him we live, and move, and have our being; as certain even of your own poets have said, For we are also his offspring. Being then the offspring of God, we ought not to think that the Godhead is like unto gold, or silver, or stone, graven by art and device of man. The times of ignorance therefore God overlooked; but now he commandeth men that they should all everywhere repent: inasmuch as he hath appointed a day in which he will judge the world in righteousness by the man whom he hath ordained; whereof he hath given assurance unto all men, in that he hath raised him from the dead. Now when they heard of the resurrection of the dead, some mocked; but others said, We will hear thee concerning this yet again. Thus Paul went out from among them. But certain men clave unto him, and believed: among whom also was Dionysius the Areopagite, and a woman named Damaris, and others with them.

(American Revised Version)

Acts XVII, 16–34.

Chapter I

THE FORCES AND AGENCIES ENGAGED IN THE MODERN ATTACK UPON CHRISTIANITY

It is to be expected that evangelical Christianity should often be under attack. At first one would think that a religion which exalts and seeks to follow the only perfect and righteous man who has ever lived on this earth, who never harmed anyone, whose words delivered from superstition and fear, whose works redeemed from pain, and demons, and death, and hunger, whose life was as a great shaft of light shot into the murky darkness of the Roman world, in that sensual and skeptic century, who died because He loved us, and who always sought to bring men into communion with God, to bestow upon them eternal life and a home in heaven, one would have thought that such a character, and the religion which His life and work on earth established, would have been welcomed with open arms the first moment it was announced, and would, by its very message, the good works which flowed from it, and the hope which it established, never know opposition, or attack, or denunciation, except from the demons of hell, and Satan, who is a liar and murderer from the beginning. But such has not been its history. In fact, the New Testament, itself, from the records of the birth of our Lord down to the end of St. John's vision of the era of anarchy and persecution to come, testifies in the most startling way to the fact that Christ Himself was most viciously and constantly attacked, that His apostles suffered the same opposition, and that it was predicted by these very apostles that Christianity would continue so to suffer, down to the end of this age.

When Mary took her blessed babe to the temple at Jerusalem, the aged Simeon, taking the child into his arms, predicted, "Behold this child is set for the falling and rising of many in Israel; and for a sign which is spoken against."[1] As Professor Alfred Plummer has well said,

"It was the Divine purpose that the manifestation of the Messiah should cause the crisis just described; men must decide either to join or to oppose Him. The *an* indicates that in every case the appearance of the Christ produces this result: thoughts hitherto secret become known through acceptance or rejection of the Christ."[2] Both in the parables and the pronouncements of our Lord, persecution and death are repeatedly emphasized. In the famous parable of the sower we read that, after a certain man had sowed good seed in his field "while men slept his enemy came and sowed tares also among the wheat." What this means our Lord Himself revealed, "The enemy that sowed them is the devil."[3] At a later time, in what has been called the parable of the wicked husbandman, when those to whom the householder had intrusted his estate and vineyard beat some of his servants, and killed others, and the householder determined to send unto them his son, the husbandmen "when they saw the son said among themselves, 'this is the heir; come let us kill him and take his inheritance.'" Our Lord does not leave us in doubt as to what He meant by this parabolic instruction, for immediately afterwards, quoting Psalm 118:22, He informed them: "the stone which the builders rejected, the same is become the head of the corner."[4] Later our Lord reminds His Jewish listeners, many of them professed followers of Moses and worshipers of God, that they were the sons of those that slew the prophets, and that, being such, they likewise would kill and crucify, scourge and persecute the messengers whom He would send to them.[5] The experiences of all the apostles, everyone of whom died a violent death, and the line of martyrs extending from them to the latest Russian and Nazi persecution, witness to the truth of the Lord's words

When one closely reads the Gospels to discover what men did to Christ Himself, the holy, righteous, loving Son of God, one begins to get some conception of the awful depravity and perversion of human nature. Thus, for example, in the record of the briefest and earliest of all Gospels, that of St. Mark, we read that His disciples were *offended* at Him.[6] The Greek word here is *skandalizo,* from which comes our word *scandal.* When our Lord was under arrest Peter denied Him Judas betrayed Him, and then "all forsook Him and fled."[7] When we turn from His own disciples who really loved Him, except Judas, we find that the Jewish authorities spat on Him, covering His face, buf feted Him (the word means to strike with the fist), they struck Him with the palms of their hands in the palace of Pontius Pilate; He was scourged; the soldiers clothed Him with purple in mockery, they put a crown of thorns upon His head, and then saluted Him. This not being enough, they struck Him on the head with a reed, then again in mockery they worshiped Him, and then mocked Him (the word here means to play with, to trifle with). Those who passed by while He hung upon the cross reviled Him, the word here being *blasphemeo,* from which comes our word *blasphemy.* Finally, the two thieves on either side reviled Him.[8]

The Apostle Peter plainly told the Jews that their treatment of Christ was one in which they had set Him *at naught,* the word meaning, as Thayer says, "to make of no account, to despise utterly, to treat with contempt."[9] There is one particular word which seems to sum up all that mankind did to Christ, and that is the word generally translated *rejected,* which means not only to reject but to reject "as the result of examination."[10] In other words, these so-called "builders," the Jewish religious authorities of Christ's day who should have known the Son of God when He appeared, these men, after carefully examining the credentials of Christ, rejected Him.

Our Lord Himself, before He died, told His followers that if they were faithful to Him they would be reproached and, like Him, they would be persecuted, and that in their work they would find a great number of adversaries opposed to them.[11] The day of Pentecost is hardly over when we find the apostles assaulted by the authorities of Jerusalem. As the fourth chapter of Acts opens we discover the priests and the Sadducees laying hands on the apostles, putting them into prison because they preached the resurrection of Christ, and (for the time being) simply threatening them. Soon after this, however, many miracles having been accomplished, we find that the apostles are again apprehended, put into prison, and this time beaten, and then charged not to speak in the name of Jesus. This is not enough: the servants of Christ must die, and so these same authorities "not able to withstand the wisdom and the Spirit by which . . ." Stephen spoke, procured false witnesses, and condemned him to death. The great persecutor Paul himself now appears on the scene, rushing with ecclesiastical power hither and thither, dragging believers out of their homes, and condemning them to punishment. Soon James the brother of John is killed by Herod the king, which, pleasing the Jews, led Herod to apprehend the Apostle Peter.[12] With further sufferings of the apostles the book of Acts does not concern itself; in fact, the *death* of not one of the apostles is recorded in the New Testament, but all of them, if we can trust the best traditions of the early church, died a violent death.

When Paul came to the Island of Cyprus, now face to face with paganism for the first time, we read that at Paphos, where they proclaimed the Word of God, they found the proconsul Sergius Paulus, who asked the apostles to preach to him the Word of God. "But Elymas the sorcerer withstood them, seeking to turn away the deputy from the faith." There are two very powerful words here in the Greek text, one meaning, "to stand up against," and the other, "to turn away from."[13] This was the purpose of this evil man—to keep a seeking soul from embracing the Christian faith. The verse may well serve as a title for a great number of professors in educational institutions, who have gone out of their way to stand up against the Christian faith, and to turn their students from the Word of God. In so doing they deserve the condemnation which Paul uttered against this man Elymas—"enemy of all righteousness." In Antioch of Pisidia we read that "When the Jews saw the multitudes that came to hear the Word of God they were filled with jealousy and contradicted the things which were spoken by Paul, and blasphemed."[14] In writing to the Thessalonians Paul, in referring to his experience among them upon his earlier visit (in the translation of Conybeare), spoke of the Jews as those "who killed both the Lord Jesus and the prophets and who have driven many forth; a people displeasing to God and enemies of all mankind, who did hinder me from speaking to the Gentiles for their salvation; continuing to fill up the measure of their sins."[15] In writing to the Corinthians, Paul spoke of the many *adversaries* who were opposing his work;[16] in writing to the Philippians he identified many as *enemies of the cross;*[17] and in writing his Roman Epistle he spoke of those who were *enemies of the Gospel.*[18] When we come to the very end of the book of Acts we find that Roman citizens were admitting that this so-called Christian sect was known to them as one "that everywhere is spoken against."[19]

The Apostle Peter in his Second Epistle has a remarkable discussion of false prophets, who were then deceiving the people, like those who would follow in the days to come, to be engaged in the same evil work. "But there arose false prophets also among the people, as among you also there shall be false teachers, who shall privily bring in destructive heresies, denying even the Master that bought them, bringing upon themselves swift destruction. And many shall follow their lascivious doings; by reason of whom the way of the truth shall be evil spoken of. And in covetousness shall they with feigned words make merchandise of you."[20] In the Epistle of John we read of this opposition to Christ and the Christian religion constituted in the person of *antichrist* and he preceding spirit of antichrist. The words here will suffice without any additional interpretation, "Who is the liar but he that denieth that Jesus is the Christ? This is the antichrist, even he that denieth the Father and the Son. Whosoever denieth the Son, the same hath not he Father: he that confesseth the Son hath the Father also."[21] To this we would add the terrible words of St. Jude, "For there are certain men crept in privily, even they who were of old written of beforehand unto this condemnation, ungodly men, turning the grace of our God into lasciviousness, and denying our only Master and Lord, Jesus Christ."[22]

In the book of Revelation we are in the presence of constant war on he part of the evil forces, energized by Satan, against the servants of God. The Apostle John, probably the loveliest character of the first century apart from Christ, was, himself, on the Island of Patmos "for the Word of God and the testimony of Jesus," no doubt a slave, though n old man, in the famous stone quarries of that tiny dot on the Mediterranean Sea.[23] At the opening of the sixth seal, John says that he saw nderneath the altar "the souls of them that had been *slain* for the Word of God and for the testimony which they held."[24] The whole of ie twelfth chapter of the book of Revelation is a marvelously profound nd significant account of Satan's hatred of the woman who gives birth o the Lord Jesus Christ, terminating with the words: "And the dragon waxed wroth with the woman, and went away to make war with the est of her seed, that keep the commandments of God, and hold the estimony of Jesus." In the next chapter we read of the beast coming up out of the sea, who "opened his mouth for blasphemies against God, to blaspheme his name, and his tabernacle, even them that dwell in the heaven. And it was given unto him to make war with the saints, and to overcome them: and there was given to him authority over every tribe and people and tongue and nation." In the seventeenth chapter we are told that the ten kings appearing at the end of this age as enemies of the truth "shall *war against the lamb*." In the nineteenth chapter, preliminary to the battle of Armageddon, we read, "The beast and the kings of the earth and their armies gathered together *to make war against Him* that sat upon the horse and against His army."[25]

In fact so terrible was the antagonism of the world to the Christian faith and those who were faithful to it that the very Greek word *martus,* which means a *witness,* one who bears testimony, soon came to mean, and has continued to mean ever since, not one that simply bears witness, but who dies because of his testimony, a *martyr* of the faith he professes. Thus in this very book of Revelation, we find that Antipas of Pergamos who is spoken of as "my witness" is also referred to as the one "who was killed among you." Incidentally, what power was it that really opposed this witness to the Christian faith? Let us read the whole verse, "I know where thou dwellest, even where Satan's throne is; and thou holdest fast my name, and didst not deny my faith, even in the days of Antipas my witness, my faithful one, who was killed among you, where Satan dwelleth."[26]

I have emphasized this fact that Christ and His apostles suffered every form of persecution, the hatred of the world and of men and of Satan, and that both Christ and the apostles have united in warning us that we should expect the same antagonism, the same persecution, because by such a study we will be prepared to consider the tragic things which must now occupy our attention, as we enter into the subject of the attack upon our own precious faith, during these last two centuries. Before entering upon such a task, let me call my readers' attention to just one more verse, a clause of which I must confess I had scarcely seen in my Bible until recently: "Blessed are ye, when men shall hate you, and when they shall separate you from their company, and reproach you, and cast out your name as evil, for the Son of Man's sake."[27] Notice the four things which our Lord foresaw would be hap pening to many of His followers: they would be (1) separated from the regular religious groups of their day, (2) they would be hated, (3) they would be reproached, and (4) they would be cast out as evil. (I wonder why there is not in our language any important sermon on such a verse as this.) Half a century ago the late Professor Henry B. Smith, beginning his famous work on Apologetics, gave what we might call a prophetic utterance concerning the great conflict that Christianity was then entering upon, and with these words we close our opening section of this chapter. "The main characteristic of the attack upon, and lefense of Christianity is, that it is all along the line. Forces that have)een gathering for centuries are concentrating simultaneously. Forces)f science and philosophy hitherto at war have made peace with each other that they may attack the common foe, viz., Christianity."[28]

The Undermining Influence of Modern Philosophy. Philosophy, when it is true to its higher purposes, seeks that which revelation estows, namely, truth, and, specifically, truth about the greatest prob-ems that can confront the mind of man: the origin and nature of the niverse in which we live, the nature of God, the criteria by which we etermine what is good and what is evil, etc., etc. Of course, there re *some* problems prominent in philosophical speculation, as, for in-tance, the nature of the knowledge itself, which do not arise in the terature of revelation. The difference between philosophy and revela-on, however, is this: philosophy seeks to reach the truth exclusively y man's reason, and absolutely refuses to recognize as authoritative, r of *divine* origin, any document whatever, including the Bible; while evelation, and here we are particularly thinking of the Christian reli-ion and its documents, claiming to be the inspired product of a divine ommunication, insists that the truths therein set forth come with un-uestionable authoritativeness, and, proceeding from God, must be eter-ally true. In other words, philosophy is confined to the intellectual rocesses of man's being, together with, of course, some of his moral tuitions; it is all within the compass of human nature, whereas revela-on claims to come to man from God. Now it has always been true at philosophy, generally speaking, has been *opposed to the claims of ligion,* and often has opposed the truths which religion (and from w on we are speaking of the Christian religion) sets forth. It is not

necessary here to go back to the time when philosophy suddenly came
of age, through the marvelous work of Socrates and Aristotle, when
many philosophers set out to deny the existence of the gods, because
there is hardly any parallel to what philosophy then attempted to do
in destroying faith in the Olympian deities (and others), and what
philosophy in our modern age has attempted to do, in destroying faith
in the God and Father of our Lord Jesus Christ. Among the ancient
Greeks their philosophy must, sooner or later, have insisted that the
gods of the Greeks were fabulous and mythical beings, historically non
existent and, therefore, that faith in them deserved to be opposed. On
the other hand, the God and father of our Lord Jesus Christ is a living
Being: so we believe Him to be, so the Bible declares Him to be, and
in the reality of this truth, of course, Christ always lived, declaring God
to be our Father, praying to God, seeking the guidance of God, com
manding men to love God, affirming He was going home to the Father
and preparing a home for us that we might also be with the Father in
the age to come. Thus, we do not, in this particular discussion, go back
to the oppositions of philosophy to *Greek* religion, for in this we think
philosophy was right.

From the post-apostolic period of the Christian church down to, le
us say, the middle of the eighteenth century, philosophy was more o
less of a handmaid of Christianity, first in the powerful influence o
Plato, in those early centuries in which the doctrines of Christianit
were formerly set forth in the great doctrinal discussions of the church
This was followed by the supreme influence of Aristotle, in the geniu
of Thomas Aquinas, whose writings have had more influence over th
thought of Christendom than perhaps the writings of any other on
man since the days of Augustine. With the coming of the Reformation
and the Renaissance, and a new spirit of independence and freedom o
thought, which in itself, of course, is to be commended, philosophy w
no longer the handmaid of the Christian religion. Instead of coming
its dogmatic defense, it became its opponent, as Windleband remarks
the beginning of his monumental *History of Philosophy*. "The fre
individual thinking became in its relation to the Church, the more in
dependently philosophy began the solution of the problem which sh
had in common with religion; from presentation and defense of do

trine she passed to its criticism, and finally, in complete independence of religious interests, sought to derive her teaching from the sources which she thought she possessed in the 'natural light' of human reason and experience. The opposition to theology, as regards methods, grew in this way to an opposition in the subject matter, and modern philosophy as 'world wisdom' set itself over against Church dogma."[29]

No greater tragedy has ever happened, nor could ever happen, in the intellectual history of Europe, since the dawn of Christianity, than the fact that the four greatest philosophers, at least the four philosophers who have exercised more influence over modern thought than any other four, should all have been rationalists, that is, men who denied divine revelation, the Sonship of Jesus Christ, the finality of the Christian faith, and, generally speaking, a personal, transcendent God. I refer to David Hume (1711–1776), whose famous essay on "Miracles" published in 1748 proved to be the most powerful attack on the whole conception of miracles that has been delivered in modern times, claimed by some philosophers to have forever prevented any further belief in miracles—though significantly, he never speaks of any of the New Testament miracles nor the resurrection of Christ; Immanuel Kant (1724–1804), the greatest of all modern philosophers, of whose views we shall speak in detail shortly; the pantheist George C. Wilhelm Frederick Hegel (1770–1831), whose philosophic system probably held more brilliant men in its grip during his lifetime than that of any other thinker in Europe held during his own lifetime; and, August Comte (1798–1857), whose philosophy, terminating in the worship of humanity, we will later discuss. I repeat: no greater tragedy could have possibly happened to the intellectual life of Europe, in these last nineteen centuries, than the fact that these four great philosophers, all of whose principal works were published within a hundred years (1730–1830), were enemies of evangelical, orthodox, biblical, Christ-centered Christianity. It is impossible for Europeans and Americans today to escape the influence of these four men, and other philosophers of lesser importance, who held similar views. As Christians, of course, we reject what they said; we hold firmly to what we believe is the truth, as revealed in the New Testament, and count their works as perversions of the truth, the vain results of the speculations of minds which have rejected Christ as the revelation of God; but our rejecting their writings, and firmly holding to the doctrines of our faith, do not in themselves change the fact that European thought will continue to be guided by the work which these men did, and will be forced to wrestle with the problems which they presented. Just as modern Europe cannot possibly cut itself off from its earlier history, and escape from the influence of Greek philosophy, Greek art, and Roman law, so it is impossible for us in the twentieth century to escape from the influence of our intellectual ancestors in the realm of philosophy. Whether European thought, and this includes American, will ever be delivered from the chains of these revelation-denying and Christ-rejecting systems, I do not have the wisdom for predicting. I cannot help but feel that our thinking will get more pagan and chaotic, unless a great revival from heaven falls upon our western world, and men are omnipotently delivered from the power of this darkness.

In this section of our chapter I want to discuss only (and that briefly) the teachings of Kant in regard to the Christian religion. If this book should occasionally fall into the hands of young Christians who know little of Kant, and care less, the question might be asked, "Why do you trouble yourself with bringing up the speculations of this man who however brilliant, has been dead now for nearly a century and a half?" I will tell you why I speak of Kant. It is not because I have any love for Kant's philosophy, but because Kant is so tremendously important Many of the most important books in philosophy, and even in theology begin or end, even in their titles, with the writings of Kant. Thus, e.g. Professor Otto Pfleiderer's epochal, though rationalistic, history of theology, carries this title, *The Development of Theology in Germany Since Kant*. When a new series of volumes called *Studies in Theology* was being prepared some years ago, the two which covered the history of Christianity, written by two of our most distinguished theologians carried these titles, *Protestant Thought before Kant,* and *An Outline of the History of Christian Thought Since Kant*.[30] Well, you and I will never be able to produce any work in our generation which, by later men, will be considered so important as to mark a boundary line in contemporary thought. When you really think about it, this in itself is a tremendous tribute to Kant's influence.

The only work of Kant's which I would consider here, is the one which he issued late in life, in 1793, when he was almost seventy years of age, which in English carries the title *Religion within the Limits of Mere Reason*. The title itself is significant. It is impossible in this chapter, of course, to discuss all the different aspects of Kant's views of religious matters; I desire only to emphasize the more important. First of all, Kant utterly denies that there can be any final manifestation of religious truth in history, and, consequently, he refuses to recognize the importance of the historical appearance of the Son of God. In fact, he admits that he is not concerned at all with the historical data of our Lord's incarnate life. Let Kant, himself, express this idea: "Religion is either natural—whereof, once extant, everyone can become convinced by his own reason—or else a learned religion, whereof we can convince others exclusively by learning, in and by which last they must be led. This distinction is of extreme importance; for, from the bare original of a religion, nothing whatever can be inferred as to its fitness or unfitness for being the universal religion of our race; although such an inference can very easily be drawn from the characteristic of its being communicable only locally and partially, or communicable universally, which latter property is of the very essence of a religion obligatory upon all mankind.

"Agreeably to what has just been laid down, although a religion be natural, it may notwithstanding have moreover been revealed, always provided the revelation exhibit *nothing that mankind could not, and indeed should not, have arrived at by the natural exercise of his own powers,* although very possibly he might not so soon and in such wide extent have attained this knowledge. To promulgate religion, by a revelation locally and specially given at a certain time, may consequently have been a wise and salutary measure; and yet when the religion thus ushered in has fairly struck root and become publicly known, conviction of its truth is to be drawn from its own self-evidencing certainty in reason. A religion of this kind would objectively be natural, and only subjectively revealed; wherefore its appropriate style and title would be that of Natural Religion; for even if, in the sequel, it were to pass to oblivion that a preternatural promulgation of it had ever taken place, still would it not on that account lose one tittle of its certainty, its facility of comprehension, or motive force upon the mind. The very contrary holds true of that religion whose inner structure is such as to render it essentially revealed: were it not carefully preserved by accurate traditions, or entrusted to that guardian document—a sacred book—it would pass from the world, and must then from time to time be publicly renewed; or else, privately a continuous preternatural revelation must take place in each individual, since otherwise the faith could neither be spread nor kept alive." [31]

Although he does not mention the Lord Jesus in this particular passage, no one would deny that it is to Christ he is really referring, and, we think in most of his phrases, somewhat sarcastically, and even blasphemously, though it is not considered that Kant had totally lost any reverence for Jesus. The denial of the significance of the historical factors in the founding of Christianity led Kant to repudiate the value of miracles, and to insist that any religion in the future that is to appeal to men must put aside any appeal to such supernatural manifestation: "Thus have we found in Christ's tenets a finished sketch and outline of a religion that can be brought home to the convictions and conceptions of every one; and that, by force of his own reason, the practicability whereof has been set forth by an example, making intuitive the possibility and necessity of adopting that ideal prototype as the standard of our manners. The truth of those doctrines, and the authority and dignity of their teacher, require no foreign confirmation, such as miracles or biblical lore, which are not within the reach of all. When appeals are made to the legislation of an earlier age, and a secondary meaning given to the oracles of the Jewish sages, these are not to be understood as if they were intended to bear witness to the truth of his doctrines. They are designed only for an introduction or vehicle, procuring them an inlet among people blindly attached to whatever was ancient. To convey truth to those whose heads are besotted with the statute-articles of a creed, and consequently numb to the religion of reason, is always a far more difficult task than to impart instruction to understandings, which, though uninstructed, are unbiassed and disengaged. Hence we need not be surprised if a mode of exposition, adapted to the prejudices of the day, should now seem enigmatically dark, and stand much in need of a cautious and elaborate exegesis, although a religion everywhere shines through, that demands no effort or learning to become alike intelligible and convincing."[32]

In regard to salvation, as everyone knows who has read Kant, the philosopher really made man *his own saviour*. The whole foundation of the ethical and moral aspects of his vast philosophical system, both in the book we are discussing and in the other critiques, is that the voice of God for man is in the great moral law of his inner nature, the categorical imperative, the conscience. As one of his most capable interpreters, Professor Clement C. J. Webb, of the University of Oxford, has said: "The God whose voice was heard by Kant in the Moral Law tended to become in his thought more and more *immanent;* for this God could not be conceived without injury to our whole moral outlook as accessible otherwise than *through* the moral law. We might indeed with advantage represent what our conscience perceives of itself to be right, not merely as the commands of our own reason, but as those of God; but only on condition of seeing in God no other than a Reason identical with our own, as ours is with that of all rational beings, yet untrammelled by having associated with it a sensitive nature with its self-regarding appetites and peculiar point of view."[33] If man is, therefore, to save himself by obedience to the moral law, then he does not need any external work of atonement, performed for him by another. These are Kant's words, with which he begins the section called, "Of the Moral Principle which Reason Opposes to all Delusions in Religion." "I lay down the following preliminary position, as one requiring no proof. Everything mankind fancies he can do, over and above good moral conduct, in order to make himself acceptable to God, is mere false worship to the Deity. I say, whatever *man* fancies he can do; for that something, beyond all our exertions, may lie in the mysteries of supreme wisdom, possible to be performed by God alone, and making us acceptable in His sight, is not denied by me. But even if the church were to promulgate, *as revealed,* any such mystery, still the opinion, that to believe in this revelation, as taught in the sacred volume, and to confess, whether inwardly or outwardly, such belief, were in itself anything rendering us acceptable to God, would be a dangerous delusion in religion. For *this belief,* considered as the inward self-confession of one's stedfast conviction, is so certainly an act, extorted by fear, that an honest upright man would rather accept any other condition; because all outward ceremonial worship mankind need only regard as something supererogatory to be gone through; whereas here he violates his conscience, by declaring in its presence what he is not convinced of. The confession, therefore, with regard to which, he persuades himself, that it (*as the acceptance of a proffered boon*) will make him acceptable to God, is something he imagines he can do, in addition to the moral conduct that the law ordains him to execute in the world, and which is done for the worship of God singly."[34]

Kant denies the need of divine revelation, he does not believe that the Bible has a final word for man, in fact he believes that man by his own reasoning abilities would discover the same truths that are found given to him in the Scriptures, although he admits that because we have a Bible, mankind may have found these truths sooner than he would have, had the Bible not been in his hands. Denying then the value of the miracles, of the historical significance of the incarnation, of all need for atonement performed by another, and of the authority of the Word of God, Kant goes on to even deny the value of personal prayer and says that a man should be ashamed if found on his knees alone. "It is related of him that if a guest at his table remains standing to say grace he would tell him to sit down."[35] Kant's idea of a church is exactly the same idea that some men have today, which is that we should give up everything distinct in the church, abolish the idea of a visible church and recognize that "rational religion has for itself ministers in every honest minded person." In other words, the real church of the future will be made up of all men with a good mind who at the same time are perfectly following the moral law of God, apart from Christ, apart from atonement, apart from confession of sin, and apart from prayer—this is Kant's idea of religion—the mature conclusion of the greatest thinker, or at least the most influential thinker, of the past two centuries, whose difficult and intricate pages too many of our young men know far more intimately than they know the New Testament. It was said by one German contemporary, Rheinhold, that "within one hundred years Kant will have the reputation of Jesus Christ."[36] Well, the hundred years have passed, and Kant does not have that reputation, and he never will, but the tragedy is that hundreds and thousands of our university and college graduates can tell you more about the *Critiques* of Kant than they can about the Epistles of Paul. Even in theological studies, it has been said by a very careful student of religion that "The philosophy of both Barth and Brunner are based chiefly upon Kant . . . Brunner says frankly that he regards the critique of Kant as standing nearest in their basal tendency to the Christian faith."[37] After this brief survey of what Kant really signifies, one must confess astonishment that so many people have been thinking that from Barth and Brunner a true return to the incarnate Son of God may be expected in European thought. Thus we discover, even from the writings of this one preeminent modern philosopher, that philosophy, and that the most important, the profoundest, the most influential philosophy of modern times, is diametrically, in every important sphere, ***opposed to the great fundamental truths of the Christian faith by which alone man can ever be redeemed.***

The Economic Attack upon Religion—Marxianism. In 1875 the Bampton Lecturer, William Jackson, expressed a truth which no doubt has been similarly stated by a number of other thinkers, but which I have not seen quite as succinctly expressed elsewhere: "As a rule, every crisis of thought and feeling which shakes traditionary beliefs will make, if it does not find, a corresponding crisis in affairs. It so happens that, coincidentally with the spread of Atheism and Scepticism, there is going on a vast social rearrangement . . . It is felt by every civilized nation, from Russia, across Europe, to America, and so round the globe."[38] As the philosophies of Kant, and Hume, and Comte, were shaking the foundations of European thought, another movement was beginning to convulse the economic foundations of nineteenth-century Europe, at least Western Europe (for Russia was then not susceptible to most of the movements of European economic thought). I refer, of course, to Communism, called by different names, e.g., Socialism. That economic system was first vigorously set forth in the writings of Karl Marx (1818–1883), and Frederick Engels (1820–1895), and is thus called today Marxian Socialism.

Before we even discuss the radical, ethic-destroying, and God-hating economic scheme of these men, we should not forget the tragic fact that both Marx and Engels found the inspiration for their fierce opposition to the Christian religion in the writings of three men who were attacking the supernaturalism of Christianity and the preeminence of Christ, of whom two were professors in theological seminaries! These were (1) David Strauss, whose *Life of Jesus,* published in 1835, was the most powerful criticism of the trustworthiness of the Gospel records ever written, and which gave tremendous impetus to the whole rationalistic repudiation of the deity of Christ in Germany and Continental Europe; (2) Bruno Baur, whose radically critical work, *The Religion of the Old Testament,* was published in 1838; and (3) Ludwig Feuerbach, whose *Essence of Christianity* was published in 1831. Otto Ruhle, in an authoritative scholarly biography, *Karl Marx, His Life and Work,* recently published in an English translation, devotes a large portion of one chapter to tracing the origins of Marx's denial of Christianity to the writings of these men. Of course, Ruhle is an adherent of the Marxian philosophy, and, consequently, says e.g., that Strauss, "by strictly scientific methods of investigation, showed that the Christian tradition was but myth or saga."[39] There was at this time in Germany a so-called Doctors' Club, the members of which were head masters, men of letters, and instructors, who believed that Strauss' book had not gone far enough! It was Bruno Baur who carried on this controversy, and went on to say that not Jesus or Paul but Seneca and Philo were the creators of primitive Christianity. Because of his radical criticism, Baur was dismissed from his instructorship. But there now arose another man in this group, Ludwig Feuerbach, who was also forced to abandon his instructorship in Erlangen after the publication of some of his radical writings. Feuerbach's *Essence of Christianity* was exactly what it seems Marx was waiting for, and soon after the book was published, Marx exclaimed: "Who has annihilated the war of the gods which the philosophers alone knew? Feuerbach. Who has put man in place of the old lumber and in place of the infinite consciousness as well? Feuerbach, and no one else."[40] This is not the place to introduce a long discussion of Feuerbach's blasphemous work, but a summary may indicate his fundamental conception. We take these words from the *Preface* to the English translation: "If therefore my work is negative, irreligious, atheistic, let it be remembered that atheism—at least in the sense of this work—is the secret of religion itself; that religion itself, not indeed on the surface, but fundamentally, not in intention or according to its own supposition, but in its heart, in its essence, believes in nothing else than the truth and divinity of human nature. Or let it be *proved* that the historical as well as the rational arguments of my work are false; let them be refuted—not, however, I entreat, by judicial denunciations, or theological jeremiads, by the trite phrases of speculation, or other pitiful expedients for which I have no name, but by *reasons,* and such reasons as I have not already thoroughly answered." His last sentence of the long preface is this, "In these works I have sketched, with a few sharp touches, the historical solution of Christianity, and have shown that Christianity has in fact long vanished, not only from the reason but from the life of mankind, that it is nothing more than a *fixed idea,* in flagrant contradiction with our fire and life assurance companies, our railroads and steam-carriages, our picture and sculpture galleries, our military and industrial schools, our theatres and scientific museums."[41] Marx embraced Feuerbach's work with enthusiasm, and spoke of his conversion to these atheistic ideas in his now seldom read *The Holy Family,* which he wrote together with his fellow-socialist, Engels.

Without further discussion of these origins of the atheism of this increasingly famous economist and philosopher, let us proceed at once to the words of Marx regarding religion, and especially the Christian religion. The following appeared in his *Contribution to the Criticism of Hegel's Philosophy of Law,* "Religion is the general theory of this world, its encyclopaedic compendium, its logic in popular form, its spiritualistic *point d'honneur,* its enthusiasm, its moral sanction, its solemn complement, its general basis of consolation and justification. It is the fantastic realisation of the human being, inasmuch as the human being possesses no true reality. The struggle against religion is therefore indirectly the struggle against that world whose spiritual aroma is religion. Religious misery is in one mouth the expression of real misery and in another is a protestation against real misery. Religion is the moan of the oppressed creature, the sentiment of a heartless world as it is the spirit of spiritless conditions."[42]

In 1848 Marx and Engels issued their famous *Manifesto of the Communist Party,* which begins with these (may we say) prophetic words:

"A SPECTRE is haunting Europe—the spectre of Communism. All the powers of old Europe have entered into a holy alliance to exorcise this spectre; Pope and Czar, Metternich and Guizot, French Radicals and German police-spies. Where is the party in opposition that has not been decried as communistic by its opponents in power? Where the Opposition that has not hurled back the branding reproach of Communism, against the more advanced opposition parties, as well as against its reactionary adversaries? Two things result from this fact. I. Communism is already acknowledged by all European Powers to be itself a Power. II. It is high time that Communists should openly, in the face of the whole world, publish their views, their aims, their tendencies, and meet this nursery tale of the Spectre of Communism with a Manifesto of the party itself. To this end, Communists of various nationalities have assembled in London, and sketched the following manifesto, to be published in the English, French, German, Italian, Flemish and Danish languages." In the midst of this *Manifesto* is the famous condemnation of all religious beliefs, and in fact all ethical principles, that previously had been recognized as fundamental in European thought: "When the ancient world was in its last throes, the ancient religions were overcome by Christianity. When Christian ideas succumbed in the 18th century to rationalist ideas, feudal society fought its death-battle with the then revolutionary bourgeoisie. The ideas of religious liberty and freedom of conscience, merely gave expression to the sway of free competition within the domain of knowledge. 'Undoubtedly,' it will be said, 'religious, moral, philosophical and juridical ideas have been modified in the course of historical development. But religion, morality, philosophy, political science, and law, constantly survived this change. There are, besides, eternal truths, such as Freedom, Justice, etc., that are common to all states of society. But Communism abolishes eternal truths, it abolishes all religion, and all morality, instead of constituting them on a new basis; it therefore acts in contradiction to all past historical experience.' What does this accusation reduce itself to? The history of all past society has consisted in the development of class antagonisms, antagonisms that assumed different forms at different epochs. But whatever form they may have taken, one fact is common to all past ages, viz., the exploitation of one part of society by the other.

No wonder, then, that the social consciousness of past ages, despite all the multiplicity and variety it displays, moves within certain common forms, or general ideas, which cannot completely vanish except with the total disappearance of class antagonisms. The Communist revolution is the most radical rupture with traditional property-relations; no wonder that its development involves the most radical rupture with traditional ideas. But let us have done with the bourgeois objections to Communism."[43]

From Marx and Engels we pass on to Lenin, whose famous work, *Religion,* may be taken as the authoritative expression of the Communist party toward the Christian faith and religion itself. This whole question of Communism and the influence of Communistic ideas over contemporary thought, and especially over the thinking of our postwar world is so important, and so profoundly affects the whole present conflict of the Christian faith with the world powers of darkness, that we do not hesitate to quote with some detail from Lenin's pamphlet: "Religion teaches those who toil in poverty all their lives to be resigned and patient in this world, and consoles them with the hope of reward in heaven. As for those who live upon the labour of others, religion teaches them to be charitable in earthly life, thus providing a cheap justification for their whole exploiting existence and selling them at a reasonable price tickets to heavenly bliss. Religion is the opium of the people. Religion is a kind of spiritual intoxicant, in which the slaves of capital drown their humanity and their desires for some sort of decent human existence . . . Our programme is based entirely on scientific—to be more precise—upon a *materialist* world conception. In explaining our programme, therefore, we must necessarily explain the actual historical and economic roots of the religious fog. Our programme necessarily includes the propaganda of atheism. The publication of related scientific literature (which up till now has been strictly forbidden and persecuted by the autocratic feudal government) must now form one of the items of our party work. We shall now, probably, have to follow the advice which Engels once gave to the German Socialists—to translate and spread among the masses the enlightening atheist literature of the eighteenth century.

"But, in this connection, we must under no circumstances allow ourselves to be sidetracked into a treatment of the religious question in the abstract—idealistically—as a matter of 'pure reason,' detached from the class struggle, a presentation often given by radical bourgeois democrats. It would be absurd to imagine in a society based upon the unlimited oppression and degradation of the working masses that it is possible to dispel religious prejudices by mere preaching. It would be bourgeois narrow-mindedness to lose sight of the fact that the oppression exercised by religion on humanity is only a product and reflection of the economic oppression in society. No books, no preaching, can possibly enlighten the proletariat, unless it is enlightened by its own struggle against the dark forces of capitalism. The unity of that genuinely revolutionary struggle of the oppressed class to set up a heaven on earth is more important to us than a unity in proletarian opinion about the imaginary paradise in the sky.

"That is why we do not declare, and must not declare in our programme that we are atheists; that is why we do not forbid and must not forbid proletarians who still cling to the remnants of old prejudices to come into closer contact with our Party. We shall always preach a scientific world conception; we must fight against the inconsistencies of the 'Christians'; but this does not mean that the religious question must be pushed into the foreground where it does not belong. We must not allow the forces waging a genuinely revolutionary economic and political struggle to be broken up for the sake of opinions and dreams that are of third-rate importance, which are rapidly losing all political significance, and which are being steadily relegated to the rubbish heap by the normal course of economic development. . . . Marxism is material. As such it is as relentlessly opposed to religion as was the materialism of the Encyclopaedists of the eighteenth century, or as was the materialism of Feuerbach. This is beyond doubt. But the dialectic materialism of Marx and Engels goes beyond the Encyclopaedists and Feuerbach; it applies the materialist philosophy to the field of history, to the field of social science. We must combat religion—this is the A B C of *all* materialism, and consequently of Marxism. But Marxism is not materialism which stops at the A B C. Marxism goes further. It says: We must be able to combat religion, and in order to do this we must explain from the materialist point of view why faith and religion are prevalent among the masses.

"The fight against religion must not be limited nor reduced to abstract, ideological preaching. This struggle must be linked up with the concrete practical class movement; its aim must be to eliminate the social roots of religion. Why does religion retain its hold among the backward strata of the urban proletariat—among wide strata of the semi-proletariat and the masses of the peasantry? Because of the ignorance of the people!—answers the progressive bourgeois, the radical or bourgeois materialist. Hence—'Down with religion!' 'Long live atheism!' 'The dissemination of atheist views is our chief task!'" [44]

Referring to the words of Heraclitus, "The world, the all in one, was not created by any god or any man, but was, is and ever will be a living flame, systematically dying down," Lenin says, "A very good exposition of the rudiments of dialectical materialism." Some people today, either deliberately hiding the truth or because they, themselves, have been deceived by others, suggest that Communism is really not as antireligious, as antichristian as Marx and Engels would have desired it to be; but wherever you pick up Communistic literature of the last century, or this, you will find the same underlying tone of undeviating hatred of religion. A recent authority on Communism, Iva Levisky, in the invaluable volume which Scribners published in 1936, *Christianity and the Social Revolution,* expresses the continual antagonism to religion in the following words: "The Church is still an obstacle to Socialist advance in the rural areas. It persuades the peasants that the reconstruction of society is beyond human efforts, and that all the experiments of the Soviet power will be destroyed by God. 'Antireligious propaganda in the village must assume the character of exclusively materialistic explanations of the phenomena of nature and of social life, with which the peasants come in contact. The correct explanation of the origin of hail, rain, drought, the appearance of insect plagues, the properties of various soils and the action of fertilisers, is the best form of anti-religious propaganda.'

"'The school and the village reading-room, under the guidance of the party organisation, must become the centre of such propaganda.

Special care must be taken not to offend the religious sentiments of the believers, which can be overcome only by years and decades of systematic educational work.'

"Thus the Communists regard 'the struggle against religion as a delicate task, requiring gradual, patient explanation, teaching, enlightenment—the exposure of the lies and deceptions underlying religion, the elucidation of its origin, significance, and harmfulness without the use of coercion against the believing population. It means laying bare the social basis of religion and taking an active part in the task confronting the Party, and the working class, of annihilating the bases of religion and creating a new, a Communist society where there will be no room for religion.'"[45]

Yet, with all its hatred for religion, and its bitter antagonism to the Christian faith, the exponents of Communism at the same time present their social revolutionary philosophy as *a religion in itself,* something which will be for modern man what the Christian religion was for his ancestors, and what it still is, thank God, for many of our day. These are the concluding words of a chapter on *Christianity and Communism in the Light of the Russian Revolution,* by Professor Julian Hecker of Moscow University, "This does not mean that the new culture will not have any objects of reverence, and that the emotions of awe, love, and beauty will not find their channels of expression. In this transitional generation which had to do with grim fighting and the hard work, these subtler qualities are somewhat submerged; but they are not dead, and will reappear in later generations so much the more intensively.

"If concrete examples are wanted, they may be observed at every step; there is the profound reverence for Lenin and the martyrs and the heroes of the revolution; there is the dynamic of an almost apocalyptic expectation of the decisive and final struggle with the resisting forces of dying capitalism; there is a great creative activity in the development of the country's natural resources; there is a flourishing art—particularly in the theatre, which is becoming the vehicle for the teaching of the new spiritual culture; there is a deepening of the new ethical sense expressed in a profound loyalty to the communal life interests; there is a wide sympathy expressed in service to the weak and suffering toilers of the world; finally, there is an undaunted assertion of life which leaves little interest in the dead and dying past. This explains the rather striking fact that at present the negative aspect of the anti-god movement arouses so little interest among the young generation. The leaders of the atheist movement themselves calculate that their work is about done, and that their society will soon cease to exist unless it changes its tactics and takes up the task of teaching the young generation the correct way of life and its meaning. In other words, it has to cease to be negative and take upon itself positive functions.

"All this corroborates that the old orthodox Christian culture is dying. It must die before it can find a new life in the ascending Communist spiritual culture. But will it then be called Christianity? We hardly think so."[46]

The tragedy is that this opposition to religion is more than theory: it is a reality. This war has not shown the Russian people to be weak, or fearful, or unpatriotic; our age will never forget, and should never forget, the bravery of these people in this present war, the sacrifices of that country to preserve its government and the life of its people. When this war is over, the Communism of Russia will be speaking with greater power and influence in our world than ever before! We postpone to a later section of this chapter the carrying out of the anti-religious philosophy of Communism, by governmental edicts in a brutal, butchering attempt to suppress the Christian faith and establish godlessness in Russia. Here we are only discussing the fundamental philosophy of Communism which, however, cannot remain as a philosophy, but must, sooner or later, be transformed into action. Would to God the flaming *Manifesto* of Marx and Engels had fallen upon the European masses only soon to be extinguished! Instead of that, rationalistic Europe, having rejected the authority of the Word of God, ignored the commandments of God, forgotten to pray to God, ignorant of the real significance of the redemption that is in Christ, this Europe was a tinderbox, waiting for such a spark. In less than a hundred years from the time the *Manifesto* was issued, and in less than fifty years from the death of Marx, this vast, organized, philosophically-grounded atheism arose to confront Europe as a specter from the bottomless pit. Ay more! a specter is but a ghost that can be laughed at, but this was something in flesh and blood, ready to carry out its diabolical will at whatever cost, and with every conceivable torture. You and I may not like to acknowledge it, but we dare not close our eyes to the terrible fact that while evangelical Christianity is declining, this thing called Communistic Atheism is increasing.

The Theory That Christianity Is an Enemy of Man's Welfare. One of the most subtle and at the same time, one of the most untruthful arguments that we find increasingly used against Christianity is that the Christian faith is an enemy of mankind, that man will never be wholly free, attaining to fullness of stature, until he gives up his faith in a superior being, and his devotion to the Lord Jesus Christ. There was a time when only the most vicious enemies of religion, especially of Christianity, talked this way, while the great body of the church and the majority of better-informed people in the Western world could shrug their shoulders, aware that these unjustified indictments only proceeded from hearts of men who were determined to say anything and everything that religion might be destroyed. Today we are finding this false indictment being used by men who are in high places, in our largest universities, who are teaching our young men to believe that this business of religion has always been a hindrance to mankind. Professors in our universities are now saying the very things that once we shuddered at, when we came upon them, e.g., in the writings of Voltaire. It was this brilliant, sarcastic and strictly unethical Frenchman who wrote, whether he believed it or not he made many others believe it, "Religion is the chief cause of all the sorrows of humanity. Everywhere it has only served to drive men to evil, and plunge them in brutal miseries . . . it makes for history an immense tableau of human follies."[47] In the first volume of the most important of the American liberal journals at the close of the nineteenth century, the *Open Court,* the most influential antichristian writer of his generation, in our country, Benjamin Franklin Underwood, wrote: "To many liberals, Christianity appears an unmitigated evil; a superstition which although it had its origin in innocent ignorance and credulity, has been the greatest obstacle to human progress that mankind has had to encounter." One of the most blasphemous utterances that I have seen along this line is from Ingersoll himself, who said that the church for a thousand years had "extinguished the torch of progress in the blood of Christ." Now, however, we actually have men in the most prominent chairs of philosophy and even New Testament literature saying the same awful things. Thus, e.g., Kirsopp Lake—for many years Professor of ecclesiastical history in the Divinity School at Harvard University, denies immortality and the efficacy of prayer, and has lately gone so far as to question the existence of a personal God—Kirsopp Lake many years ago said, "In past generations to attain salvation was thought to be the object of existence. It is not altogether surprising that the people who argue in this way contributed little to the improvement of the world."[48] But to come to a greater man than Professor Lake and one far more influential, Dr. John Dewey of Columbia University, recognized by all as having, during the last thirty years, exercised more influence over the educational ideals of our country than any other one man, actually dared to say in some lectures at Yale University a few years ago that Christianity was opposed to the democratic way of life and to hold to the idea of anything supernatural was a hindrance to mankind in its modern progress and advancement. These are Professor Dewey's words: "The objection to supernaturalism is that it stands in the way of an effective realization of the sweep and depth of the implications of natural human relations. It stands in the way of using the means that are in our power to make radical changes in these relations. It is certainly true that great material changes might be made with no corresponding improvement of a spiritual or ideal nature. But development in the latter direction cannot be introduced from without; it cannot be brought about by dressing up material economic changes with decorations derived from the supernatural. It can come only from more intense realization of values that inhere in the actual connections of human beings with one another. The attempt to segregate the implicit public interest and social value of all institutions and social arrangements in a particular organization is a fatal diversion."[49] Because of the attitude of Communism in its bitter hatred of all religion and its determination to destroy it, and in this increasing vogue among many of our intellectuals to claim that Christianity has been a hindrance to man's own progress, I think it is important that I take time right here to present a few testimonials concerning this problem from some of the great leaders of thought and modern statesmen of the last three-quarters of a century. The argument will have to be met, and while the subsequent chapters of this book will, we hope, contain sufficient material for any necessary reply to the other anti-religious arguments presented in this chapter, this particular indictment should be replied to *here.*

Confining ourselves first to our own country, let us remind ourselves of the words of John Fiske, by no means a Christian, in his well-known work *The Beginnings of New England,* in which he pays such a glowing tribute to the primacy of religious faith in the lives of those who, by their sacrifice and labor, gave us this grand country in which we live. These are Fiske's words: "It is not too much to say that in the seventeenth century the entire political future of mankind was staked upon the questions that were at issue in England. To keep the sacred flame of liberty alive required such a rare and wonderful concurrence of conditions that, had our forefathers then succumbed in the strife, it is hard to imagine how or where the failure could have been repaired. (Had it not been for the Puritans, political liberty would probably have disappeared from the world.) If we consider the Puritans in the light of their surroundings as Englishmen of the seventeenth century and inaugurators of a political movement that was gradually to change for the better the aspect of things all over the earth, we cannot fail to discern the value of that sacred enthusiasm which led them to regard themselves as chosen soldiers of Christ. It was the spirit of the 'Wonder-working Providence' that hurled the tyrant from his throne at Whitehall and prepared the way for the emancipation of modern Europe. No spirit less intense, no spirit nurtured in the contemplation of things terrestrial, could have done it. The political philosophy of a Vane or a Sidney could never have done it. The passion for liberty as felt by a Jefferson or an Adams was scarcely intelligible to the seventeenth century. The ideas of absolute freedom of thought and speech, which we breathe in from childhood, were to the men of that age strange and questionable. But the spirit in which the Hebrew prophet rebuked and humbled an idolatrous king was a spirit they could comprehend. It is to the fortunate alliance of that fervid religious enthusiasm with the Englishman's love of self-government that our modern freedom owes its existence." We wonder if those who condemn Christianity as being a stumbling block in man's progress would say that the founders of our nation were stumbling blocks also.[50]

When the Pilgrims landed at Plymouth Rock, in 1620, they signed a declaration to the effect that they had come to found a colony "for the glory of God, and advancement of the Christian faith." The Puritans, a few years later, recorded their determination in similar terms: "We covenant with the Lord, and one another; and do bind ourselves in the presence of God, to walk together in all His ways, according as He has pleased to reveal Himself unto us in His blessed word of truth." In view of such testimonies as these, found on every page and in every undertaking of our forefathers, we see the fairness of Daniel Webster's conclusion, that, "The Bible came with them. And it is not to be doubted that to the free and universal reading of the Bible is to be ascribed in that age that men were indebted for right views of Civil Liberty."[51]

Henry Campbell Black in his standard *Handbook of American Historical Law* offers this clear testimony concerning the place of Christianity in the fundamental law of our land: "The saying (that Christianity is a part of the law of the land) is true in this sense, that many of our best civil and social institutions, and the most important to be preserved in a free and civilized state, are founded upon the Christian religion, or upheld and strengthened by its observance; that the whole purpose and policy of the law assume that we are a nation of Christians, and while tolerance is the principle in religious matters, the laws are to recognize that the existence of that system of faith, and our institutions are to be based upon that assumption. The prevalence of a sound morality among the people is essential to the preservation of their liberties and the permanence of their institutions, and to the success and prosperity of government, and the morality which is to be fostered and encouraged by the state is Christian morality, and not such as might exist in the suppositious 'statute of nature' or in a pagan country. The law does not cover the whole field of morality. Much that lies within the moral sphere does not lie within the jural sphere. But that which does lie within the jural sphere, and which is enforced by positive law, is Christian morality."[52]

I cannot close this part of our chapter, without quoting the words of President Theodore Roosevelt, which he uttered in an address given at the dawn of our century (in 1901). "Every thinking man, when he thinks, realizes that the teachings of the Bible are so interwoven and entwined with our whole civic and social life that it would be literally —I do not mean figuratively, but literally—impossible for us to figure what that loss would be if these teachings were removed. We would lose almost all the standards by which we now judge both public and private morals; all the standards towards which we, with more or less of resolution, strive to raise ourselves." [53]

To cross the Atlantic, let us first consider the verdict of one of the greatest philosophers of modern times, Rudolf Eucken. In his *Main Currents of Modern Thought* (Eucken was not a Christian, though he did believe strongly in the spiritual values of life), he says: "It was the Christian conviction that the divine had appeared in the domain of time, not as a pale reflection but in the whole fullness of its glory; hence as the dominating central point of the whole it must relate the whole past to itself and unfold the whole future out of itself. The unique character of this central occurrence was beyond all doubt. Christ could not come again and yet again to be crucified; hence the countless historical cycles of the Ancient World disappeared, there was no longer the old eternal recurrence of things. History ceased to be a uniform rhythmic repetition, and became a comprehensive whole, a single drama. Man was now called upon to accomplish a complete transformation, and this made his life incomparably more tense than it had been in the days when man had merely to unfold an already existing nature. Hence in Christianity, and nowhere else, lie the roots of a higher valuation of history and of temporal life in general." I would like to repeat Eucken's last sentence, "Hence in Christianity, and nowhere else, lie the roots of a higher valuation of history and of temporal life in general." [54] One of the most distinguished historians of modern times was Guglielmo Ferrero. In his *The Ruins of Ancient Civilization and the Triumph of Christianity,* he pays this tribute to the Christian religion —and I believe, coming from a lifelong and profound student of Ancient History it is worth infinitely more than the philosophical speculations of some men who have had little discipline in ascertaining the value of historic data: "Christianity brought about the most audacious, the most original, the grandest spiritual revolution the world has ever seen. The supreme object in life is the moral and religious perfection of the individual; . . . Man has only one real Master,—God; if he serves well that one and supreme Master, if he meets His love and praise, the rest does not count . . . It was this new conception of life by which Christianity revolutionized the intellectual and moral foundations of the ancient civilization from the top to the bottom and which triumphed finally over the awful disasters of the third century and produced a supreme reaction against disorder." [55]

The greatest modern statesman in Great Britain was, as everyone knows, William E. Gladstone. Gladstone was a classicist, a churchman, Christian, statesman, brilliant speaker, gentleman, gifted writer, intellectual giant, a man of great vision and flawless character, as men go. There was not a greater man in Europe during his premiership than Gladstone. He was emphatically a believer in every fundamental truth of the Christian faith, from the time of his youth to the time of his death. He spoke lovingly, humbly, and boldly, concerning Jesus Christ, and His salvation, and the truthfulness of the Word of God. Now there is one thing that Gladstone understood, and in which he played an enormous part, namely the affairs of state of a great empire. Gladstone certainly knew what was for the welfare of men, and what worked for their hurt and harm. A man of his vast knowledge, and his place in a great government, has a right to speak with authority on the value of any powerful influence playing upon his nation. Let us then carefully consider Gladstone's own verdict concerning the influence of Christianity upon men. A verdict like this coming from a statesman who knew the problems of government and who always sought the welfare of the greatest number is worth ten verdicts of sceptical philosophers, who have never had to wrestle with the intricate problems of modern government: "I say, then, choosing points of the most definitive character, that Christianity abolished (1) gladiatorial shows, and other spectacles of horrid cruelty to men; (2) human sacrifices; (3) polygamy; (4) exposure of children; (5) slavery (in its old form, and has nearly accomplished the work in its new); (6) cannibalism. Next, Christianity drove into the shade all unnatural lusts, and, indeed, all irregular passions. But the former it effectually stamped as infamous. Next, Christianity established (1) generally speaking, the moral and social equality of women; (2) the duty of relieving the poor, the sick and the afflicted; (3) peace, instead of war, as the ordinary, normal presumptive relation between nations. Here is a goodly list. I speak not of what it taught. It taught the law of mutual love. It proscribed all manner of sin. But the preceding particulars refer to what, besides saying, it did, besides trying, it accomplished. And in every one of these instances, except that of cannibalism, the exhibition of what it did is in glaring contrast, not with barbarous but with the most highly civilized life such as it was exhibited by the Greeks or Romans in the most famous ages of both. Now I think that is a fair statement, not easily shaken. I admit that many of these results are negative. And as to those of them which are positive, there are other and higher results in the excellence and perfection of the human soul individually; but I have taken such as are palpable, and I think undeniable." Speaking of Gladstone, I came the other day upon a remarkable tribute to his compassionate regard for men in need, in a volume devoted to the life and friendship of the rationalist John Morley, who, by the way, was the biographer of Gladstone. This is what the author of this volume says, "In Gladstone's lifetime he was the one statesman to whom oppressed peoples turned in hope."[56] I wonder what a communist has to say against something like that. I wonder how Professor Kirsopp Lake, and Professor John Dewey, can speak about Christianity hindering the progress of man, in the face of truths like these.

Let us reduce this now to one practical illustration of the influence of Christianity, to be exact, the influence of the gospel, over the people of a small village, as testified to by one who was definitely not a Christian. I refer to Charles Darwin. Ernest Gordon in his fascinating volume, *A Book of Protestant Saints,* tells a remarkable story, which I have not seen elsewhere but which, knowing Mr. Gordon's scholarly accuracy, I can confidently accept. He is talking about a certain Mr. Fegan, a pioneer of camps for boys who in the latter part of the nineteenth century had a camp in Down where Charles Darwin lived. This is the way Mr. Gordon tells it: "It seemed that the naturalist had established a reading-room in the village which, however, was little frequented. Fegan asked him if he might not have it for a week's mission and the request was more than granted in a gracious letter. 'Dear Mr. Fegan,' so it ran; 'you ought not to have to write to me for permission to use the reading-room. You have done more for the village in a few months than all our efforts for many years. We have never been able to reclaim a drunkard but through your services I do not know that there is a drunkard left in the village. Now may I have the pleasure of handing the reading-room over to you? Perhaps if we should want it some night for a special purpose you will be good enough to let us use it. Yours sincerely, Charles Darwin.' So the property was turned over to Mr. Fegan and for half a century meetings have been held there continually."[57]

Even in the present world-horror of Nazism, we should remember that it was the Christian church that first strongly opposed this brutal regime, as a recent authority on these matters reminds us. "While in Germany the political parties, the law, the universities, the Press, the trade unions capitulated, the first check to the triumphant onward march of Nazism was given by a small resolute body of Christian men—the Confessional Church. Many even of them thought they could distinguish between Nazism as a political system and its extraneous anti-religious manifestations. They stood for the purity of the Christian creed against the pollution of a 'positive' Christianity, and in defence of Jewish Christians. They fought on too narrow a front, but they saw the situation more clearly than the rest of us did at that time. They were the patrols of that Christian counter-attack that is now being offered by practically the entire Christian Church. They put up a costly and determined resistance that evokes our admiration and respect. And the resisting Christians in Germany, Roman Catholic or Protestant, have the unenviable task of opposing their own country's Government in the middle of a war of survival. The Churches of Norway and Holland and the rest face the Nazis as at once enemies of the Christian way of life and also foreign invaders or internal traitors."[57a]

Let me close this discussion concerning the energizing, ennobling, emancipating influence of true religion upon mankind, with the words of one of our greatest Essayists, who, probably, is not to be classified an evangelical Christian, but who had the wisdom to see clearly the value of that which men were, even in his day, trying to be rid of. These are the words of James Russell Lowell: "The worst kind of religion is no religion at all, and these men living in ease and luxury, indulging themselves in the amusement of going without religion, may be thankful that they live in lands where the gospel they neglect has tamed the beastliness and ferocity of the men who, but for Christianity, might long ago have eaten their carcasses like the South Sea Islanders, or cut off their heads and tanned their hides like the monsters of the French Revolution. When the microscopic search of skepticism, which had hunted the heavens and sounded the seas to disprove the existence of a Creator, has turned its attention to human society and has found a place on this planet ten miles square where a decent man can live in comfort and security, supporting and educating his children unspoiled and unpolluted; a place where age is reverenced, infancy respected, manhood respected, womanhood honored, and human life held in due regard—when skeptics can find such a place ten miles square on this globe, where the gospel of Christ has not gone and cleared the way and laid the foundation and made decency and security possible, it will then be in order for the skeptical literati to move thither and then ventilate their views. But so long as these men are dependent upon the religion which they discard for every privilege they enjoy, they may well hesitate a little before they seek to rob the Christian of his hope, and humanity of its faith, in that Saviour who alone has given to man that hope of life eternal which makes life tolerable and society possible, and robs death of its terrors and the grave of its glooms."[58]

The Depersonalization of God. We shall have a great deal to say in this chapter about the modernistic attitude toward God, and what many of our leading thinkers are trying to do to destroy the idea of any personal God in the minds of our generation. It is difficult to classify these various and widely different anti-theistic views. Let me speak first of the general tendency in contemporary thought of denying personality to God, together with the now commonly-repeated idea that God is something man has made, rather than the creator of man, and then pass on, in a subsequent section, to the inevitable corollary of this tendency, namely, the deification of humanity. Later in our chapter we shall have considerable to say about sheer intellectual atheism, the denial of everything called by the name of God. Here we are not concerned with the philosophical attempt to hold to the name of God while parting from all that the word has ever meant. Let me remind my readers as they begin this section of our chapter that, as Professor Hubert S. Box has recently said in his learned volume, *God and the Modern Mind,* "We must be prepared for some shocks when we come to read what many modern thinkers have written concerning the Supreme Being, the Almighty Lord of the universe."[59]

Professor Douglas Macintosh, one of the outstanding authorities on theism in our day, said a few years ago that there seems to be "almost nothing, upon the destruction of which, leading humanists seem so determined as any vital belief in God as a superhuman, intelligent Being worthy of human faith and fellowship."[60]

If I understand his words correctly, it is the conviction of Dr. Henry Nelson Wieman, Professor of Philosophy in the Divinity School of the University School of Chicago since 1927, that God cannot be considered as a person, but as a social force, a sort of pantheistic idea. This is his own conception of God, as he has recently phrased it: "God is that interaction between individuals, groups, and agencies which generates and promotes the greatest possible mutuality of good. This mutuality is not only with the living, but also with the dead and unborn. It is the largest possible body of favorable experience which can be accumulated through centuries, as individuals and generations contribute to it, appreciate it, refine it and make it more widely and profoundly sharable. God, like everything else in existence, a human person, a nation, a planet, is a process, having a distinctive pattern, the distinguishing pattern of God being that of promoting mutuality." Elsewhere he speaks of God as "that something, however unknown, which brings human life into the largest fulfillment when proper adjustment is made to it."[61]

This is also the view of Dr. James Bisset Pratt, for thirty years (and still) the Professor of Theology and Religion at Williams College, who, in an article appearing as late as 1942, says, "The whole theistic conception of the relation of God to the world must be considerably modified. I have given to this type of religious philosophy the title Spiritual Pantheism, because the all-inclusive God is not merely a pious name for the totality of everything, but the indwelling mind of the universe."[62]

Dr. Walter Marshall Horton of Oberlin, whose writings are having a great deal of influence in this country, in delivering the Ayer Lectures at Colgate (Rochester) Divinity School in 1935, said to the assembled students and professors, "Whatever may happen to the word, 'God,' the *idea* of God can no more perish than the idea of men or the idea of nature. . . . The idea of God then is eternal; but ideas of God are temporal . . . Yet one will lay hold upon the worthiest and mightiest deity he is capable of embracing, and may the best man's God come out victorious." I have looked at these words for some time, and the more I think on them, the more terrible they seem to me—"may the best man's God come out victorious."[63] I wonder if Dr. Horton would like the God of H. G. Wells to be victorious, or maybe the god of Hitler, or, why not, the god of the Japanese? That these men have wholly abandoned any conception of God as set forth in the Scriptures, or as revealed in Jesus Christ, it is not necessary to argue.

One of the most amazing pantheistic confessions is that of Dr. John Laird, Regius Professor of Moral Philosophy in the University of Aberdeen, who, in his Gifford Lectures, *Theism and Cosmology* (the Gifford Lectures for 1939), frankly states, after many pages filled with philosophic speculations, somewhat difficult to read, that, the "Notion of a God who is impersonal, rather than personal, might seem to be firmer and more easily creditable than a notion of a personal deity. God, for instance, might resemble a church rather than a man."[64]

Following these theologians, Julian Huxley expresses the view of a great many contemporary scientists, when he says, "It is impossible for me and those who think like me to believe in God as a person, a ruler, to continue to speak of God as a Spiritual Being in the ordinary way."[65]

From denying personality to God, it is not a far step to insisting that the idea of God was created by man himself. This is one of the fundamental tenets of the most influential of all modern scientists, Sigmund

Freud. In a now seldom seen volume of his, Freud says, "I believe that a large portion of the mythical conceptions of the world, which reaches far into most religions, is nothing but psychology projecting into the outer world . . . When human beings began to think, they were obviously compelled to explain the outer world in an anthropomorphic sense by a multitude of plurals in their own image."[66] We look upon Freud as an outstanding enemy of everything that Christianity stands for, as an unbeliever of the most radical type, but it becomes an altogether, infinitely more serious matter when we find professors in our theological seminaries saying the same thing, that man has made God. Thus, e.g., George Burman Foster, Associate Professor of Systematic Theology, and then Professor of the Philosophy of Religion in the University of Chicago, for twenty years, continually taught his students and emphasized in his books that, "A man creates whatever concepts and principles he may need in order to make himself master of the phenomena of his environment. To the same end were the gods created . . . Man made the gods to do for him what he could not do for himself . . . It is an inextinguishable need of human nature to create gods for itself and so ever to replace old gods by new."[67]

This is the view of Edward Scribner Ames, who likewise has been in the University of Chicago, as a Professor of Philosophy and Religion for over forty years, and was pastor of the University Church of the Disciples of Christ, and University Preacher at the University of Chicago. Ames has frankly expressed his opinion of this idea of a man-created God in the following words: "The idea of God, when seriously employed, serves to generalize and to idealize all the values one knows. Our actual interests move in the social world and within the vast order of nature. In the simplest reflections upon the facts of life one is led deep into the labyrinth of the natural and of the human worlds. The idea which gathers into itself the interests and values of our daily concerns must therefore signify what are for us the greatest realities in nature and in human experience. To the plain man as he uses the idea of God, in contrast with a passive formal attitude toward it, the idea involves a living process, law or movement, in the working of which human needs are satisfied, justice and truth established, and distant ideals attained. . . . The reality answering to the idea of God, it may be said, must include, at its best, all that is involved in the deep instinctive historical and social consciousness of the race. It signifies the justice which government symbolizes, the truth which science unfolds, and the beauty which art strives to express."[68]

"Ye Shall Be as Gods"—The Deification of Humanity. There is hardly anything more accurately indicative of the godlessness, the blatant arrogance, the sheer paganism of the last century, and increasingly so in the generation in which we are living, than a strange, profound, loudly-proclaimed tendency *to deify humanity,* or, to call *humanity* God. I suppose that many of my readers, who are not acquainted with ultra-modernistic philosophic and theological literature will, when they see such a statement as this, say to themselves, "Here our author is making to be a major tendency of our day something that is only very sporadic, found in the writings of only obscure men, or in the literature of Communism and may, consequently, not be seriously considered in our own lovely Christian land." The truth is, that it is in our own land that the tendency to deify humanity is more prevalent, and is found in a more extensive literature, than in any other civilization of the modern world. Even Russia, itself, says very little about deifying humanity, although it may live exclusively for humanity. While it has always been more or less of a tendency, even in the days of the Roman Caesars, to deify certain individuals, especially kings, the philosophical formulation of, and the attempt to logically justify the deification of mankind as a whole, and all men who participate in humanity, may be said to have begun with the philosophy of Auguste Comte (1798–1857). It was in his famous and extraordinarily influential *Positive Philosophy,* which he began to publish in 1830, that he developed the idea of the exaltation of humanity as the final state of a perfect society. "The main principles of the Comtian system were derived from the *Positive Polity* and from two other works,—the *Positivist Catechism; A Summary Exposition of the Universal Religion Is in Twelve Dialogues by a Woman and a Priest of Humanity;* and second, the *Subjective Synthesis* (1856), which is the first and only volume of a work upon mathematics announced at the end of the *Positive Philosophy.* The system for which the *Positive Philosophy* is alleged to have been the scientific preparation contains a polity and a religion; a complete arrangement of life in

all its aspects giving a wider sphere to intellect, worship and feeling than could be found in any of the previous organic types—Greek, Roman, or Catholic-feudal. A moral transformation must precede any real advance. The aim, both in public and private life, is to secure to the utmost possible extent the victory of the social feeling of self-love or altruism over egotism. The business of the new system will be to bring back the intellect into a condition, not of slavery, but of willing ministry to the feelings. The subordination never was, and never will be, effected except by means of a religion, and a religion to be final, must include a harmonious synthesis of all our conceptions of the external order of the universe. The characteristic basis of a religion is the existence of a power without us, so superior to ourselves as to command the complete submission of our whole life. This basis is to be found in the positive stage of humanity, past, present, and to come, conceived as the Great Being.

"The least amongst us can and ought constantly to aspire to maintain and even to improve this Being. This natural object of all our activity, both public and private, determines the true general character of the rest of our existence, whether in feeling or in thought; which must be devoted to love, and to know, in order rightly to serve our Providence, by a wise use of all the means which it furnishes to us. Reciprocally this continued service, whilst strengthening our true unity, renders us at once both happier and better."[69]

This idea of the deification of humanity spread rapidly to our own shores. In 1867, a group of radical Unitarians in our country organized a Free Religious Association, and soon had, as another has called it, their Magna Charta, in Frothingham's book *The Religion of Humanity*. Their influence, however, was temporary and probably few today know either of this earlier organization, or have seen the book to which we have referred.[70] Robert Ingersoll, who has said more terrible things than our generation has any idea, because no one now reads his writings, showed his own sympathy with this exaltation of humanity when he said, "We are laying the foundations of the grand temple of the future—not the temple of all the gods, but of all the people—wherein, with appropriate rites, will be celebrated the religion of Humanity."[71] Ingersoll is gone, and his writings have little influence today, but this antichristian, pride-encouraging tendency to exalt man to the throne of God, need no longer be propagated by some rationalist organization, or a little group of free thinkers, or by the popular, well-paying lectures of such a man as Ingersoll, for this is now what is taught not only in many of our universities, but actually in many of our theological seminaries, and is, indeed, one of the fundamental proportions of a vast amount of literature that has appeared in this country since the beginning of our century under the name of religious education! The most powerful single personality in this philosophy of a man-centered religion has been Dr. George Albert Coe. Dr. Coe was Professor of Philosophy at Northwestern University from 1891 to 1909, and then held the very important chair of Professor of Religious Education in Union Theological Seminary, New York City, for thirteen years. In the five years beginning with 1922, he was Professor of Religious Education in Teachers' College, Columbia University. No man can hold such professorships as these, and be the author of scores of books used extensively in academic institutions throughout our land, during half a century, without making disciples of thousands of students of religion, and, specifically, students of religious education. Dr. H. Shelton Smith, one of the outstanding authorities on this very subject of religious education, and at the same time the most powerful opponent of Dr. Coe now writing, speaks of him as, by common consent, "America's most distinguished, living philosopher of religious education." [72] In ascertaining Dr. Coe's views of religion we will discover what are the views of thousands of students and leaders in religious education in our country at the present time.

Dr. Coe's fundamental conception is that religion is to be found in the "discovery of persons." "The spiritual is present wherever persons are present; . . . To be utterly devoted to whatever in heaven or earth is perfect is to be religiously sacred." [73] This means that one can have religion without God, and this is exactly Dr. Coe's own belief. He even goes so far as to say that "The sovereign (that is, the sovereign for us) is just ourselves when we cooperatively insist upon *providing for ourselves what we want.*" [74] If anything could be more man-exalting, selfish, and God-denying than such a statement, we do not know what it is. Russia itself could nail a sentence like that over all of its atheistic institutions, and add the legend that the sentence is a quotation of a professor for many years in a theological seminary in Christian America! "What significance the idea of God is to have," says Dr. Coe in a recent confession of his own faith, "we cannot even forecast until we have commended ourselves unreservedly to the creation of the new order of society."[75] In other words, democracy is to be our religion, and whether some day we can have a God or not is after all not important. I do not know how my readers feel, but for myself, I must shudder to think that for fifty years our young people have been subject to the philosophy of this man, who can say, "God, who breathing Himself everywhere into the human clod makes it a spirit, a social creature, even the spirit of humanity, yes, the spirit of a possible world society. I bow my spirit before the Spirit of the world democracy that is to be."[76] He closes his famous work, *The Psychology of Religion,* with this confession: "The thought of God may indeed undergo yet many transformations, but in one form or another, it will be continually renewed as the expression of the depth and heighth of social experience and social aspiration."[77] Of course, this means that God is only the product of man's imagination, and this is exactly what Coe, and many others, believe. It is significant that Coe confesses himself that he is "in debt most of all to John Dewey,"[78] and John Dewey is an atheist, as we shall soon see, a bitter enemy of Christianity, who denies vigorously that there is any such a thing as a supernatural person or event. So the most influential leader of religious education in our country is the disciple of the most pronounced antisupernaturalist of our generation. That Dr. Coe's liberalism has destroyed the faith of many and made them social radicals, he himself boasts. "More young people are exposed to social radicalism by the churches than by all other agencies combined."[79] If an evangelical minister today said that, he would be called an obscurantist, a crank, narrow-minded, or medieval, but the words are Dr. Coe's, and one can only regret that they are true.

This social gospel which has so dominated the whole modernistic interpretation of Christian truth in the twentieth century, found its most popular exponent in Walter Rauschenbusch, who, in his *Theology for the Social Gospel,* dared to say: "The worst thing that could happen to God would be to remain an Autocrat while the world is moving toward Democracy. He would be dethroned with the rest (i.e., of the rulers of the universe)."[80] What a hatred for God there must be in the mind of man who can raise his fist in this blatant way against the Lord of heaven and earth. Dr. A. C. McGiffert, for many years the noted, liberal president of Union Theological Seminary, once said, our modern democracy "demands a God with whom men may co-operate, not to whom they must submit."[81] So man tells God what God must be!

This school of sociological interpretation in religion has been the dominant factor in the theology and religious philosophy of the University of Chicago for the last quarter of a century. Among its distinguished professors has been Dr. Gerald Birney Smith, Instructor and Assistant in Systematic Theology from 1900 to 1906, Associate Professor of Dogmatic Theology 1906–1913, and Professor of Christian Theology, 1913–1929. His abandonment of the idea of a personal God is undeniable. "The religious man will, under modern conditions, have many a doubt concerning the objective reality of what the theologians call God."[82]

Another teacher in the University of Chicago for many years, was Dr. R. W. Sellars, who, in his book *The Next Step in Religion,* with subtle words, but not hiding his real meaning, says that, "The humanist's religion is the religion of one who says yea to life here and now, of one who is self-reliant and fearless, intelligent and creative. It is the religion of the will to power, of one who is hard on himself and yet joyous in himself. It is the religion of courage and purpose and transforming energy. Its motto is, 'What hath not man wrought?' Its goal is the mastery of things that they may become servants and instrumentalities to man's spiritual comradeship."[83] Dr. Edwin A. Burtt, Professor in the Sage School of Philosophy of Cornell University, as late as 1939 let it be known frankly that, for him, man now takes the place of God: "God is no longer the central fact in religion or the controlling principle in theology. His place is taken by man's religious experience—by that selected phase of human doing and suffering which appears to be distinguishable from the secular phases of life and is emphasized in people whom all recognize as especially religious.

The religious experience of men and women becomes the decisive fact and the ultimate court of appeal by which we test the validity of any theological concept—the concept of God along with others." [84]

From the idea that man may now be spoken of as God, and that the only God we can know is mankind, we can easily pass to the idea that the only present conception of God we can have is one expressed in the term *democracy.* This is becoming more and more important in contemporary thought and needs our very careful attention. Dr. H. A. Overstreet, for many years Professor of Philosophy, and then Head of the Department of Philosophy in the College of the City of New York, in an article significantly entitled "The Democratic Conception of God," which he published some years ago in the *Hibbert Journal,* remarked: "A philosophy fashioned in the spirit of democratic-biological ideals will inevitably repudiate whatever of monarchic or oligarchic still lingers in the god-views of the present. We are well enough aware that these elements do still linger, that the conception of a supreme person ordained in the nature of things to be eternally perfect, as against the mass of beings struggling with imperfections, is still the prevalent thought. But the continuance of such a monarchic view means simply that the biological-democratic way of thought has not yet grown into a habit of our life. Eventually no doubt, it will do so . . . the conception of the god *that is ourselves,* in whom and of whom we literally are; the god that, in every act and intention, *we, with all our countless fellows, are realising* . . . It is a god that in one respect is in the making, growing with the growth of the world; suffering and sinning and conquering with it; a god in short, that *is* the world as the spiritual unity of its mass life." [85]

While some of the men we have been referring to were, and are, professors of philosophy in secular institutions, let us not forget that the same idea has been expressed by some of the most influential professors of religious subjects in our theological seminaries. This is the verdict of the late Dr. Arthur Cushman McGiffert, for a score of years President of the most influential theological seminary in the United States who in addition to the sentence we have quoted above, elsewhere said, "As the rights of men over against each other and over against their rulers were emphasized, and rights over against God received fuller recognition, His absoluteness and His responsibility only to His own character gave way to the notion of relativity and responsibility to men. They, too, have rights, and God is bound to respect them."[86]

From the conception that man is God and that democracy must determine for us our final conceptions of anything called God, we come naturally to the idea of what has been generally entitled the social gospel. It is acknowledged by the leading authority on the social gospel in this country that its chief proponents have been the more radical members of the Unitarian Church, men who have emphatically denied the great fundamentals of the Christian faith. The church, in the social gospel, turns from preaching a message that saves men from sin, from hopelessness, from darkness, and ignorance of God and wrath to come, to a message that has nothing to do with the life of the future, practically nothing to do with what the Bible calls sin, and is wholly divorced from anything that Paul considered the gospel. In fact, as Professor Gerald B. Smith said, a few years ago, "The triumph of democracy is now the chief concern of the church and all theological training should be to that end!"[87] We are afraid that a good deal of theological training during these last thirty years has been just that—a training in the problems of our economic order, sociology, and abnormal psychology. May we tarry for a moment with a personal illustration here? When living in the East we occasionally visited the library of one of the most outstanding modernistic seminaries of the Atlantic seaboard, and we can well remember the shock that first came to us, when we saw, spread out over the tables of the library, with students pouring over their pages, not commentaries, not lexicons, not church histories, not works on Christology and theology, but labor journals, volumes on economics, the literature of socialism. What can these men know about the Christian gospel, and the Word of God when they come out of a seminary like that? Nothing! One evening a graduate student of this school, which was less than fifty miles from my home, who had spent five years in this one institution, and now ready to enter a pastorate, could not find a church, came to see me to ask about uniting with my own denomination. We went for a drive in the car. I asked him, "What do you believe about the virgin birth of

Christ?" "Well," he said, "I am sorry, but I do not know what to say about that. We were not told anything about that subject." "What do you believe about the bodily resurrection of Christ?" "I am sorry but I do not know anything about that subject; our professor did not seem to tell us much about that." Finally, I said, "What do you believe about the inspiration of the Scriptures?" He said, "I do not know what I believe; I am all upset in everything." It was not his fault, it is not the fault of thousands of other young men in this country, who do not know what to believe, except that there is nothing believable in the Bible. It is the fault of the professors who, without faith of their own, have done everything within their power to prevent their own students from believing in God, and in the Gospel of the Lord Jesus Christ. There is an awful judgment awaiting men like that. It is to such teachers our Lord was referring when he told some of the ecclesiastics of his day, "Ye took away the key of knowledge: ye entered not in yourselves, and them that were entering in ye hindered." [87a]

And so this religion of humanity comes finally to be a practice of doing good, and that is about all. Some years ago no less a person than President Angell of Yale, in an address on, "Contemporary Youth and the World of Religion and Morals," frankly said, "Let us agree without cavil that we are living in an age of moral and religious hesitation and uncertainty. Does this mean that, in consequence, our spiritual life must be paralyzed? Certainly not. The gods of the Greek Pantheon may indeed be dead, and Isis and Osiris but faint voices from the tomb; yet the God that dwells in the heart of man is not dead and will not die. There is that in the human spirit which cannot be wholly smothered by the fumes of a purely self-centered philosophy, or choked by the tentacles of a smug materialism. You may teach that there is no God until many have come so to believe; you may ridicule as guileless, or as fools, all who put anything before the gratification of personal pleasure and worldly passion; but you can never wholly slay the ineradicable instinct for noble living, for daring spiritual adventure, for genuine devotion of self to the needs of society and to interests conceived as higher than this self and essentially sacred; *and that is true religion.*" [88]

Even men with some real faith, and members of conservative denominations, are found talking like this. Charles Stelzle, the outstanding worker among the laboring class in the Presbyterian Church, whon all of us thought, a quarter of a century ago, was almost a prophet o God, once dared to say that Christianity was not "a scheme to increas the population of heaven . . . but to bring heaven down to earth." Tha was in 1912; two years later we had the First World War. Thirty year have gone by since Stelzle wrote this, and we are in the midst of hel on earth instead of heaven on earth! And what of all the men, our ow flesh and blood, our American youth, who have died in battle, and th great multitudes that are going to die, what of them and the future, i they have not heard the Gospel that gives them eternal life? It seem almost as though God Himself had judged this social gospel, this ide of turning from Him and centering all our thought on the economi welfare of man, by really showing to the world, once and forever, wha humanity can be when it turns from God, and how wicked and bruta and devilish men can be, when let loose in such a holocaust as this Some years ago Professor Ames, of whom we have already spoken, Professor in a seminary and a minister in a Protestant church, wrot that, "Man the community is the source of salvation . . . I say that thi conscious spiritual community is the source of salvation."[89] It is best t leave the statement without comment.

Professor Robert Flint, in his monumental work on Theism rightl said, "Humanity must be blind to its follies and sins, insensible to it weaknesses and miseries, and given over to the madness of a boundles insanity, before it can raise an altar and burn incense to its own self."[9 It would appear that even here and there among our unbelievers a fev are coming to the same conclusion, for in a volume recently publishe by the Harvard University Press, with the significant title *Free Minds George Morley and His Friends,* a volume devoted exclusively to th fellowship enjoyed at the close of the nineteenth century by some o the outstanding free-thinkers and rationalists in England, who, them selves, were more or less worshipers of humanity, the author makes thi significant statement, "For us, facing the worst that human cruelty ca do, it is unthinkable that men could worship humanity, or even spel it with a capital H. We have to remember that these mid-victorian belonged, as it has been said, to the happiest class of the happiest coun try in the happiest period of the world."[91]

Some Phases of Contemporary Attacks upon the Deity of Christ. The one question by which the truth of all religious expression and discussion is determined is, "What think ye of Christ?" This has been the most debated single problem in the whole vast realm of theology, since our Lord was here upon earth, and will continue so to be until the end of this age. Everything pertaining to the destiny of a man's soul, the corporate strength of the church, the essence of that which is preached, the very character and hope of every man, are all determined by the answer given to this question. Without going back over the eighteen centuries of discussion of Christ's Sonship, His divinity or deity, whichever word one wishes to use, I would like to begin this section of our study of the forces attacking evangelical Christianity with the consideration of a new volume which was honored by being selected as the choice of the Religious Book of the Month Club, in May, 1943, a volume written by one who has been for some years a distinguished missionary of the Presbyterian Church in India, editor while there of the *United Church Review* (1930–1936), Professor of New Testament in the Union Theological Seminary at Saharanpur and, since 1936, the Professor of New Testament in Western Theological Seminary (Presbyterian) in Pittsburgh. I refer to *The Intention of Jesus* by Dr. John W. Bowman. We must recognize Dr. Bowman's work as the result of genuine scholarship, revealing a mastery of all the important literature, and the various problems of contemporary New Testament criticism, a book written in dead seriousness, and one which must certainly be accepted as the sincere and mature expression of one of our best trained New Testament scholars, now near the age of fifty.

It is important to see what Dr. Bowman makes of Christ and of Christ's "intention." Regarding Christ's virgin birth, the author says that ". . . if Jesus knew of the tradition of his virgin birth, he never pressed it. After all, who should have decided between him and any number of pagan demigods and heroes for whom such a birth was claimed! It was the Church that added these mundane traditions to its Gospels; . . ."[92] This is in the language of one who does not accept the doctrine of the miraculous conception of Christ by the power of the Holy Spirit. How can anyone claim any faith in the divine inspiration of the New Testament writings when such a holy theme as the virgin birth of our Lord is referred to as "a mundane tradition," which means, of course, a tradition proceeding from an earthly origin? It would seem to the ordinary reader that if ever there was a birth on this earth to which the word "mundane" could not be accurately applied, it would be the birth of Jesus—announced by angels sent from heaven, accomplished by the power of the Holy Spirit, ushering into the world not a mere man, but indeed the very Son of God now taking to Himself true humanity.

Regarding the deity of Christ, or rather Christ's own conception of His person and mission, Dr. Bowman says, ". . . Jesus knew himself to be the Messiah because of the great love for men that welled up within his soul: he knew himself to be the Messiah because he knew he possessed the only character that could make one worthy—he was man's utter Lover." ". . . He recognizes his right to Messiahship because of his awareness of a special relation to God as 'Son.' " ". . . He is the Messiah because he is at once God's Son and man's holy Lover."[93] One might judge from this that Dr. Bowman believes Christ was very God of very God, divine in a way in which other men are not divine, by His very essence, but this is not what one would gather from the author's later statements. He continues, "Because he was the Son of God, he possessed within him a 'spirit of holiness' that was equally unique, and because of that same spirit, he is the rightful Lord of life. It is in this high moral realm alone that Jesus ever claimed to be the true Messiah of the prophetic voice, and in this sense he is and always will be the Lord of men."[94] In other words, it is Christ's high, lofty moral life "alone" which makes Him the Son of God, not His eternally divine nature.

Dr. Bowman's phrase "spirit of holiness" leads us to carefully note his comment on the verse in which the Apostle Paul uses these words, found in the first chapter of Romans: "Declared to be the son of God with power, according to the spirit of holiness, by the resurrection from the dead." Dr. Bowman italicizes that part of the verse beginning "the son of God," and says that this portion of Paul's statement ". . . is not so much a theological dictum as a statement of an obvious historic fact for which there was plenty of testimony. Jesus' *power,* felt by all his contemporaries—friend and foe alike—was seen to lie in the crystal purity of his ethical character." [95] Now, if I am not greatly mistaken, the church has always taught that this passage of St. Paul's affirms that Christ was manifested to be the Son of God by the stupendous fact of His resurrection from the dead, and the phrase "according to the spirit of holiness" is recognized as subsidiary (and is in fact quite difficult to interpret). The author here, however, says nothing about the deity of Christ being proved by His resurrection from the dead, but asserts that Christ's Lordship is set forth by "the crystal purity of His ethical character." One would like to ask, Does not the resurrection have a direct relationship in this passage to the deity of Christ, and if so, why omit all reference to what Paul is emphasizing?

In regard to the cross, this is Professor Bowman's view: "The cross thus stands as the *symbol,* at once of the complete identification of our Lord's will with that of his Father, a fact of which the 'spirit of holiness' was the visible sign, and also of that love which welled up within him and which guaranteed his right to be the Messiah so far as his ability to represent man as his mediator before God was concerned." This conception of the cross is accompanied by a strange interpretation of the Lord's supper. Our author believes that this was not a fulfillment of the Passover feast, symbolizing deliverance, and involving a sacrifice, but was instead a ceremony of sanctification, "the Jewish Qiddush," and that what Christ had in His mind that night was a fellowship group called by the Jews, the Haburah. Therefore, as I understand Dr. Bowman, what we call the Lord's supper was not intended as a commemoration of the sacrificial work of Christ on the cross, but was rather a symbol of the communion we have one with another in Christ. Christ then was "One who had died to seal the love he bore his disciples with his blood." [96] Nowhere do I find in this book what St. Paul declares, that Christ Jesus came into the world to save sinners. Nowhere does our learned author say or hint that, "He who knew no sin became sin for us, that we might be made the righteousness of God in him." In fact, Dr. Bowman implies that Christ Himself needed repentance and even "a turning to God." These are his words, ". . . Jesus' coming to repentance-baptism, said the Church, was *his response* to the divine 'call' through the prophet to throw in his lot with the new movement, his *moral decision* to take his stand for the God of Israel," and that with Him this and other experiences "stand for of heart-searching, prayer, fasting, and a turning unto God." [97]

We believe that this book of the intention and work of Christ by Dr. Bowman is representative of much in contemporary theology, and is so subtle in its presentation of what we emphatically believe is a misrepresentation of the New Testament, that we would like to bring into this discussion two extended statements from two of the greatest Calvinistic theologians of the last generation to contrast with these pages. Let us take a statement concerning this type of Christology prevalent in Germany a hundred years ago from Dr. James Orr's challenging and scholarly work, *The Christian View of God and the World.* "Constrained by the evidence of Scripture, many theologians agree in ascribing 'Godhead' to Christ, whose views of the Person of Christ yet fall short of what the complete testimony of Scripture seems to require. Schleiermacher may be included in this class, though he avoids the term; of more recent theologians Rothe, Beyschlag, Ritschl, etc., who speak freely of the 'Godhead,' 'God manhood,' of Christ and of the 'incarnation' of God in Him. But what do these expressions mean? In almost all of these theories Christ has a high and unique position assigned to Him. He is the second Adam, or new head of the race, Son of God in a sense that no other is, sinless Mediator and Redeemer of mankind. This is a great deal and must be recognized in any theory of the incarnation. All these theories acknowledge further a peculiar being or revelation of God in Christ on the ground of which these predicates 'Godhead' and 'God manhood' are ascribed to Him. However, with Schleiermacher, Ritschl and others, Christ is an archetyped man, ideal man, sinless man, the central individual of the race, the founder of the Kingdom of God in humanity—but He is not more than man. His humanity may be a 'God-filled humanity'; still a God-filled man is one thing and God become man is another. There may be participation in the divine life—even in the divine nature—on the part of the ordinary believer; but the man in whom God thus dwells does not on this account regard himself as Divine, does not speak of himself as a divine person, does not think himself entitled to divine honors, would deem it blasphemy to have the term 'Godhead' applied to him . . . Incarnation is not simply the enduing of human nature with the highest conceivable plenitude of gifts and graces; it is not a mere dynamical relation of God to the human spirit, acting on it or in it with exceptional energy; it is not simply the coming to consciousness of the metaphysical unity all along subsisting between humanity and God; it is not even such moral union, such spiritual indwelling and the oneness of character and will, as subsists between God and the believer. The scriptural idea of the incarnation is as unique as the biblical conception of hell. It is not the union simply of the divine nature with the human,—for that I acknowledge in the case of every believer through the indwelling Spirit,—but the entrance of a Divine Person into the human."[98] Now these are profound words, but this is a profound subject, and we ought never to complain about the necessity of careful thought when we are discussing such a subject as the person of the Son of God, our Lord.

The title of Dr. Bowman's book is, as we said, *The Intention of Jesus*. Our Lord, Himself, had a great deal to say Himself, about His intention, and it is generally believed among practically all New Testament scholars, even the most radical, that there are eight specific different passages in which Christ speaks of His own intention. Let us just enumerate them. He speaks once of His mission of preaching (Mark 1:38; Luke 4:43); once of His coming to fulfill the law and the prophets (Matthew 5:17, 18); of coming, not to call the righteous but sinners to repentance (Mark 2:17; Matthew 9:13; Luke 5:32); of coming not to give us peace, but a sword (Matthew 10:34); of being sent to the lost sheep of Israel (Matthew 15:24); of having baptism to be baptized with (Luke 12:49–53); of giving His life a ransom for many (Mark 10:45; Matthew 20:28); and finally of coming to seek and to save that which is lost (Luke 19:10). Now nowhere does Dr. Bowman give any *adequate* consideration to any one of these declared intentions of Jesus, in coming into the world, though he does refer to some of them in a very hurried and obscure, and we believe, erroneous way.

Three passages in the Gospels relating to the intention of Jesus are brought together and commented upon. The passages are as follows:

". . . They that are whole have no need of a physician, but they that are sick: I came not to call the righteous, but sinners." "For the Son of man also came not to be ministered unto, but to minister, and to give his life a ransom for many." "For the Son of man came to seek and to save that which was lost." Of these pregnant passages, our author says, "All three of these sayings tell us the same story. The 'Son of man' has come to identify himself with sinners with a view to their becoming the new people of God. His consorting with such persons, therefore, was a *symbol or acted parable*." I repeat what I have said above, that I cannot find in this scholarly volume on the intention of Jesus, which means of course His purpose in coming into our own world, I cannot find any assertion that Christ Jesus actually came to offer Himself a sacrifice to God, nor that by His shed blood are our sins remitted, nor that through the cross alone are we reconciled to God. To me the author seems to have missed the two great truths concerning Christ—His deity and His work of vicarious atonement accomplished by the cross.

Some years ago, the greatest Calvinistic theologian of America of our century, Dr. Benjamin B. Warfield, wrote on the very subject which is supposed to engage Dr. Bowman in his new volume, an article which he called "Jesus' Mission According to His Own Testimony," in which each one of the passages we have just enumerated is carefully considered. At the end of his scholarly treatment of this subject of the purpose of Jesus, Dr. Warfield makes the following statement concerning Christ offering Himself a ransom to God, and we quote the passage only that our readers may discover for themselves what a vast chasm separates the conviction of Dr. Bowman concerning the intention of Jesus, and the mature conviction of this great Calvinist, Dr. Warfield. One of them is wrong; and one of them is right. Dr. Warfield's verdict is the conviction of evangelical Christianity; Dr. Bowman's is the voice of something else. These are Dr. Warfield's words: "Only living things can imitate anything. Dead things must be brought to life. Lost things must be found. Sinners must be saved. Even the heathen knows that he may see the good and yet pursue the bad. The awakened soul cries out, O wretched man that I am who shall deliver me out of this body of death? Jesus has done for us something far greater than set us a good example, and summon us to its imitation: something without which there could have been no imitation of His example; no transformed ethics; no transfigured lives. He has undoubtedly set before our eyes in living example the perfect law of love. But He has done more than that. He has written it on our hearts. He has given us new ideals. And He has given us something even above that. He has given us the power to realize these ideals. In one word, He has brought to us newness of life. And he has obtained for us this newness of life by His own blood.

"It is this that Jesus declares when He says, 'I came to give my life a ransom for many.' And therefore this is the greatest declaration of all. In it He shows us, not how He has become our supreme example merely, but how He has become our Saviour. He has set us a perfect example. He has given us a new ideal. But He has also given us His life. And in giving us His life, He has given us life. For 'He gave his life a ransom instead of many.' "[100]

After three careful readings of His book, unless I do not understand our English language, and unless now in middle life I have wholly failed to comprehend the elemental factors relating to the person of Christ, as set forth in the New Testament, I am compelled to believe that Dr. Bowman does not accept the Christ of the New Testament, the pre-existent Christ, the only begotten Son of God, nor that Christ offered Himself a sacrifice to God to deliver us from divine wrath, and shed His blood that we might have forgiveness of sins in Him. The Christ of the Christian Church, very God of very God, as well as true man, as far as I am able to discover, is not the Christ of this book. What grieves me most is that this is the conclusion of a man who has had the very finest theological training our country could give, for some years at Princeton Theological Seminary; later receiving, I believe, his doctorate degree under the late Professor A. T. Robertson, supported as a teacher for years in our missions fields, and now teaching young men in a seminary of the Presbyterian Church. This is what I cannot help but call an undermining of the foundations of evangelical Christianity. The cross of Christ, the crucifixion of Christ, the death of Christ, we admit are frequently referred to in this volume, but certainly there is no conception of our Lord's holy death such as He, Himself, expressed that night when He took a cup, and said that His blood was shed for the remission of sins; nor any conception of that death such as the Apostle Paul proclaims, in the first chapter of his Epistle to the Colossians, that Christ made peace "through the blood of His cross," and that "we" who were "sometime alienated, and enemies in mind by wicked works, yet now hath he reconciled in the body of his flesh through death."

This is approximately the same as the position of a man whose works have had considerable influence in contemporary theological thinking, Dr. Edwin Ewart Aubrey, a professor of religion and ethics at the University of Chicago, who in his widely discussed work, *Man's Search for Himself,* has said, "If God be love-in-a-dynamic-world, then Jesus is divine for He incarnates that. There will be some to question this and to ask whether Jesus is really God. To this one can but say that He is not the Creator who made heaven and earth, nor is He all of God."[101]

It is a somewhat similar conception of Christ that is held by Dr. Henry Pitney Van Dusen, for seventeen years Instructor, and, subsequently, Professor of Systematic Theology at Union Theological Seminary. This is the expression of his own conception of Christ: "In Jesus of Nazareth, God Himself was as fully present as it is possible for Him to be present in a human life. Jesus' thought, feeling, will, were identical with God's intention for Him. In and through Jesus' words and acts and attitudes and inmost spirit, the life of God spoke as fully as it was possible for the Sovereign of all reality to find expression through a man of Nazareth in the days of the Caesars.

"This is a very great claim. But it is a claim implying definite limitations. Limitations of knowledge—such knowledge as could normally have been available to a man of Jesus' time, place, and circumstances. Limitations of outlook—such breadth of comprehension and depth of insight as could occur in a genuine human spirit of that day. Limitations of divine indwelling, of incarnation. It is mistaken to claim that in Jesus, the whole Being of God was present, that God's purpose was fully expressed through Him. If we are to make earnest with the assertion of Jesus' humanity, we must recognize that only such of the Being and purpose of God found expression in and through Him as was appropriate and possible for one of His heritage, His era, His span of experience." Multitudes of people in the Christian Church today accept this view of Christ.[102]

Denying Any Unusual Divine Significance to Christ. At the beginning of our century, the noted and influential president of Harvard University, Dr. Charles E. Eliot, created a great furore when he began to write and talk about "the future religion." It is important that we recall his words concerning our Lord: "The true reformer is not he who first conceives a fruitful idea: but he who gets that idea planted in many minds and fertilizes it there through the power of his personality. Such a reformer was Jesus. He spread abroad, and commended to the minds of many men, the loftiest ethical conceptions the race had won. He vitalized them by His winning and commanding presence, and sent them flying abroad on the wings of His own beautiful and heroic spirit. In a barbarous age He was inevitably given the reward of deification, just as the Pharaohs and Alexanders and Caesars were; and His memory was surrounded by clouds of marvel and miracle during the four or five generations which passed before the Gospels took any settled form. The nineteenth century has done much to disengage Him in the Protestant mind from these encumbrances; and the twentieth will do more to set Him forth simply and grandly as the loveliest and best of human seers, teachers, and heroes. Let no man fear that reverence and love for Jesus will diminish as time goes on. The pathos and the heroism of His life and death will be vastly heightened when He is relieved of all supernatural attributes and powers. The human hero must not have foreknowledge of the glorious issue of His sacrifices and pains; He must not be sure that His cause will triumph; He must suffer and die without knowing what His sacrifice will bring forth. *The human exemplar should have only human gifts and faculties.*"[103]

The Christian Church *then,* vigorously repudiating Eliot's Unitarian convictions, felt that nothing less could be expected from a *Unitarian* center such as Harvard, that such expressions as these would soon be forgotten, and the great truths of Christianity would go on being proclaimed with power, unaffected from a source acknowledgedly heretical. Little did evangelical Christians, forty years ago, think that in our own generation we would have men of high position in the theological seminaries of so-called *evangelical* denominations, setting forth the same humanized Christ, as the only one we could now confidently accept. We will discuss with some fulness in the immediately subsequent chapter the absolute antisupernaturalism of Dr. Albert W. Palmer, for the last twenty years president of the Chicago Theological Seminary. Here may I simply mention his attitude to the virgin birth. Dr. Palmer asks, "Did Jesus have two parents or only one?" and then answers, "It is purely a historical question and has no bearing on the authority of Jesus . . . You may decide that the evidence for the virgin birth is so slender that it is imperative for you to think of Jesus as born like all the rest of us, of two human parents. Personally, I should welcome that conclusion, for it would only the more definitely make his divinity a moral and spiritual thing . . . and so Christ shall be reduplicated in a myriad of saviours." The newly elected president of Union Theological Seminary, for ten years the Roosevelt Professor of Theology in the same Institution, lets us know, though his language is a little involved, that he frankly does not believe in any such thing as the Godhead of Christ, but that only in Christ God was present with perhaps a little more fulness than he is in all the rest of men: *"The fact of Jesus Christ,* the determinative center of Christian faith, both its belief and its practice, *is—the total impact of Jesus Christ upon history*. That fact embraces various and successive phases of a single organic personal reality—*Jesus-Christ-in-the-life-of-the-world*. The reality which we actually confront, and which we seek more fully to comprehend and more adequately to interpret, is not merely the human career of a certain man in the first century of our era, Jesus of Nazareth. Nor is it a unique supernatural event occurring through the life or death or resurrection of a misty, mythical figure who trod the earth in the semblance of a man. Nor is it a stream of influence in history initiated somehow by that life or by events connected with it and then pursuing a more or less independent course down the centuries. Rather it is a continuous, coherent, consistent personal reality, rooted in and springing from a particular commanding human life, and persisting with powerful effectiveness through nineteen centuries. . . . The Christ of Christian history and of present experience should never be thought of except through the clear lineaments of the words, deeds, mind, spirit, faith of the man, Jesus of Nazareth. All that *is* truly Christ is unmistakably continuous with that life . . . If God be thought of in abstract metaphysical categories—infinity, immutability, impassibility, substance, essence—incarnation is impossible. But if God be thought of as intelligent, holy, purposeful Personality, he may become incarnate within the persons of men. Indeed, speaking quite strictly, God can indwell *only* intelligent, purposeful persons. This is the highest if not the only proper meaning of the immanence of God, incarnation. Immanence is the presence in human spirits of some measure of the Divine Vision and Purity and Purpose, that is of the Divine Life. Complete immanence would occur in a genuine human person who shared, as fully as is possible for a truly human life, the Vision and Purity and Purpose of God. That would be the Incarnation. Precisely this is what Christian faith affirms to have been true of Jesus Christ. The pith of its contention may be very simply put: *In Jesus of Nazareth, God himself was present, as fully present as it is possible for him to be present in a truly human life."* This is exactly the opinion of President Van Dusen's colleague, Dr. John C. Bennett, professor of Christian Theology and Ethics in Union Theological Seminary: "If one were to ask how did God act upon the human nature of Christ, the only answer that I can point to is that in form there was no difference between His action upon Christ than His action upon other men. The difference is to be found only in the responsiveness of Christ. The mystery of human freedom and divine initiative is no different in the case of Christ from what it is in the case of all men."[104]

Dr. Douglas Clyde Macintosh, who has been teaching now for nearly thirty years in the Divinity school at Yale University, going over to India some twelve or more years ago to deliver a series of lectures in that land of strange religious philosophies, coming with the authority of a great school like Yale, supposedly identified with the Christian faith, frankly told the Buddhists, and Hindus, and others of that benighted land, that they ought to retain practically all their own religion, and to recognize in their ancient religious leaders men of great spiritual potentialities to be equated with Christ. These are his words: "If it is true that God is revealed in the unselfish self-dedication of Jesus Christ to human well-being, it must be true that he is also revealed in the unselfish self-dedication of other great spiritual personalities to human well-being—in that of Gautama Buddha, for instance, even though Gautama's ideal may have been defined too much in negative terms and though he himself may have remained agnostic with reference to the being and nature of God. I would say to you, therefore, continue to appreciate and revere all that is of divine value and significance in your own great religious leaders; but consider also this other historic figure; try to understand him and whatever significance he may have for the individual and for the world to-day. To those of you whose religious traditions are those of Hinduism, I should like to say: Retain all of your traditional Indian religion that is in accord with the universal ideals of rationality, of beauty, of righteousness, and of truly spiritual love, but do not fail to adopt and incorporate into your faith all the additional values that are accessible in this new age."[105] I repeat—this is from one who has been teaching in the Yale Divinity School for over thirty years!

"Perfect Christ and Imperfect Jesus." It is difficult to logically classify each different writer on the person of Christ today; sometimes they seem to shift from one attitude to another, and to change their views from year to year. We cannot make too rigid a classification, but certainly among those who deny to Christ any supreme divine significance, must be included Dr. Hornell Hart, for some years a member of the faculty of Bryn Mawr College, and Hartford Theological Seminary, now professor of sociology and anthropology at Duke University, and a member of the faculty of the Duke School of Religion. In a recent article of his, which has created a great deal of discussion, with this very significant title, "Perfect Christ and Imperfect Jesus," Dr. Hart says that, "The gospel records, when studied by the methods which social scientists apply to any historical document, give evidence of a Jesus who was limited by the culture out of which he emerged, and whose behavior toward his opponents did not always show understanding and self-suffering love . . . Like many other religious innovators (in spite of the supreme act of forgiveness on the cross) he showed marked evidences of resentment against those who disagreed with him and opposed him. Like other prophets he went through periods of depression and

self-distrust. Like other founders of religions he displayed (according to the record) certain psychic powers. . . . To pretend that the historic Nazarene was perfect is to deny the Christ in order to glorify Jesus."[106]

Years ago Paul W. Schmiedel, Professor of Theology in Zurich, to whom had been assigned the important task of writing the article on the Resurrection of Christ in the *Encyclopedia Biblica* (which is recognized today as the most scholarly and powerful attack on the historicity of the Resurrection of Christ of the last century), said in a later work of his, *Jesus in Modern Criticism,* "My religion does not require me to find in Jesus an *absolutely perfect model,* and it would not trouble me if I found another person who excelled him, as indeed, in some respects, some have already done. Convinced as I am that he was human, if another should have more to offer me than he had, I should consider this simply another instance of God's bounty and favour."[107] The Doctors John Herman Randall of the Department of Philosophy in Columbia University, join in the same repudiation of the imperfectness of Jesus when they say, "Before most liberals can hope to face frankly the problems of moral reconstruction, they must rid themselves of the idea that it is enough to seek to embody in our social order the ethical precepts of Jesus . . . The moral precepts of Jesus show little concern with what have become the necessary conditions of human existence today."[108]

The Denial of the Importance of Historical Christ. Probably because after a hundred years of the fiercest kind of prejudiced criticism against the gospel, with scores of scholars of great learning in the universities of continental Europe, Great Britain, and our own country, attempting to strip the life of Christ on earth of its supernatural factors, only to find that the legitimate laws of literary and historical criticism fail to deny to Christ His supernaturalism and to the Gospel records their historical validity, we find today a tendency among some to turn away from the whole question of historical investigation, and say, with a carelessness and a presumed omniscience which is really quite astonishing, that, after all whether Christ lived or not is not so important, or at least, it is not important to know the historical facts concerning the life of Christ because, these say, they are beyond our reach. Now into the barren question as to whether or not Christ lived, we do not intend in this book to enter, for the question to us has always seemed one of the most foolish imaginable, just as foolish as the question "did Napoleon ever fight a battle?" But this business of repudiating the significance of the historical facts of Christ is something we are afraid might appear to weary men and women, who are not able to follow the intricacies of New Testament criticism and involved problems of Christology. So Schweitzer, looked up to by so many people during the last two decades as one of the great Christians of our day, frankly says at the end of his famous book, *The Quest of the Historical Jesus:* "In the very moment when we were coming nearer to the historical Jesus than men had ever come before, and were already stretching out our hands to draw Him into our own time, we have been obliged to give up the attempt and acknowledge our failure in that paradoxical saying: 'If we have known Christ after the flesh yet henceforth know we Him no more.' And further we must be prepared to find that the historical knowledge of the personality and life of Jesus will not be a help, but perhaps even an offence to religion.

"But the truth is, it is not Jesus as historically known, but Jesus as spiritually arisen within men, who is significant for our time and can help it. Not the historical Jesus, but the spirit which goes forth from Him and in the spirits of men strives for new influences and rule, is that which overcomes the world. Jesus as a concrete historical personality remains a stranger to our time, but His spirit, which lies hidden in His words, is known in simplicity, and its influence is direct."[109] All this may sound beautiful and almost pious, but when you get down into the meaning of it, the historical Christ has vanished like a ghost.

This is the attitude of Dr. Douglas Clyde Macintosh of Yale, to whom we have previously made reference, when he develops the idea in an article, the very title of which is significant, "Is the Belief in the Historicity of Jesus Indispensable to the Christian Faith?" that, if we had to give up the entire conception involved in a historical Christ, we would still have enough of the Christian religion left: "The disproof or rendering seriously doubtful of the historicity of Jesus would not mean the disappearance of any essential content from the Christian religion. As a religion it would remain what it was, discharging the same function as before in human life. The losses of a sentimental and pedagogical sort, while serious enough, would not be such as to render impossible the exercise of a Christian faith in God.

"Our conclusion, then, is that while the historicity of Jesus was indispensable to the rise of the Christian religion, and so to the Christian experience and faith of today, a continued belief in that historicity is not indispensable, though very valuable, to the Christian religion. Without belief in the historical Jesus, would Christianity have arisen? No. Without continued belief in the historical Jesus would Christianity collapse? No. Granted the historicity of Jesus as above defined, is belief in his unique divinity an expression of essential Christian faith? Yes. And yet this is not a return to the assertion that belief in the historicity of Jesus is religiously indispensable; saving faith is not dependent upon the outcome of the higher criticism. The upshot of all this, then, is that Christianity, while enjoying the advantage of historical verification, has this qualification for being the 'absolute' and universal religion, that its fate is not bound up with the actuality of any one reputed fact of history, even when that 'fact' is the one which surpasses any other fact in its value to humanity."[110] In fact, Professor Macintosh, in his famous lectures at Calcutta, spoke for all modernists when he said, "The Jesus of Christian tradition must die that He may live . . . The trappings of an ancient and outworn Christology . . . insofar as it is *outworn* . . . must be cast aside that the true Jesus of history may be clothed anew in robes of religious appreciation and interpretation which will better befit Him in the exalted place He is to occupy in the world of modern thought and life and, particularly in the universal religion of the future."[111] Giving up the Christ as presented in the Gospels, the only record of Christ's life on earth that we have, we really wonder where Professor Macintosh is going to find the historical data for the creation of a new Christ. The fact is when he talks about the exaltation of Christ in a new world religion we should carefully note that he is not talking about Christianity, he does not say when *Christianity* is accepted throughout the world, but when the Christianity of the last nineteen centuries is abandoned and in the pantheon of saviours gathered from the past and present of all the religions of the world and placed in a new temple of humanity, Jesus will then come into His deserved recognition. This is an altogether different thing than Paul was speaking of when he said that "God the Father had exalted Christ and given Him a name that was above every name, that at the name of Jesus every knee should bow and every tongue confess that He is Christ to the glory of God the Father."

The So-called Folly of Adoring Any Exalted Individual. Some years ago Dr. Harry Emerson Fosdick, without doubt one of the greatest enemies of evangelical Christianity of modern times, published his famous sermon, "The Peril of Worshiping Jesus," in which he asserted that the Lord Jesus did not want the worship of men, and that it was the one way of destroying Christ! This sermon was reprinted throughout the English world, and while considered blasphemous by the conservatives, was welcomed by many of the liberals as a brilliant though daring expression of their own position in which, long ago, they had abandoned any act of worship toward Christ.[112] This position has in a subtle way been reaffirmed by Professor Burtt of Cornell University, toward the close of his *Types of Religious Philosophy,* when he frankly says that humanism and the religion of science do "not approve devotion to any founder of religion, when this feeling strikes so deep as to suspend, as far as he and the ecclesiastical tradition which stems from him are concerned, our critical faculties, with the result that attachment to him becomes superior, in our experience and reflection, to open minded regard for impartial truth. From this viewpoint such devotion is bad on several accounts." Professor Burtt goes on to tell us why he considers such devotion to any founder of religion an evil one—one is sufficient for our purpose here: "It means that we become blind to real difficulties in the personality of our chosen leader, measured against the spiritual needs of contemporary life."[113]

Some Contemporary Manifestations of Hatred for Christ. Of course, none of us are surprised that in Germany, where everything relating to Judaism and the Old Testament is despised, there should develop a diabolical hatred for Jesus, as evidenced in the title of one of their recent books, *Jesus the Greatest Enemy of Mankind*. but that a man *in our own English-speaking world,* able to command the attention of millions of educated people, with his vast scientific, historical, and literary output, should at the same time be one who has often spoken bitterly, sarcastically, scoffingly of the Lord Jesus, is only an indication of the temper of our modern life, the willingness of men today to listen to those who blaspheme the Son of God, without any notable or vigorous repudiation. We refer, of course, to Mr. H. G. Wells (and there are many others whose words have been just as vicious). The growth of Mr. Wells' hatred for Jesus may be seen in considering three volumes of his written at three different periods of his life. This is his conception of Christ, as set forth in one of his earlier books, *First and Last Things,* first published in 1908, when Wells was forty-two years of age.

"I admit the splendid imaginative appeal in the idea of a divine human friend and mediator. If it were possible to have access by prayer, by meditation, by urgent outcries of the soul, to such a being whose feet were in the darknesses, who stooped down from the light, who was at once great and little, limitless in power and virtue, and one's very brother, if it were possible by sheer will in believing to make one's way to such a helper, who would refuse such help? But I do not find such a being in Christ. I do not find, I cannot imagine such a being. I wish I could. To me the Christian Christ seems not so much a humanized God as an incomprehensibly sinless being, neither God nor man. His sinlessness wears His incarnation like a fancy dress, all His white self unchanged. He had no petty weaknesses. Now the essential trouble of my life is its petty weaknesses. If I am to have that love, that sense of understanding fellowship which is, I conceive, the peculiar magic and merit of this idea of a personal Saviour, then I need some one quite other than this image of virtue, this terrible and incomprehensible Galilean with His crown of thorns, His blood-stained hands and feet. I cannot love Him any more than I can love a man upon the rack. The Christian's Christ is too fine for me, not incarnate enough, not flesh enough, not earth enough." [114]

Many thought when Mr. Wells had said some fairly decent things about the Lord Jesus in his later and famous *Outline of History,* that he was gradually coming to a more lofty, and somewhat reverent conception of the Son of God. In a rather extended discussion of the beginnings of Christianity, Wells spoke of "The lean and strenuous personality of Jesus (which is much wronged by the unreality and conventionality that a mistaken reverence has imposed upon His figure in modern Christian art). Jesus was a penniless teacher who wandered about the dusty, sun-bitten country of Judea . . . a being very human, very earnest, and passionate, capable of swift anger, and teaching a new, and simple, not profound doctrine—namely, the universal, loving fatherhood of God, and coming of the kingdom of heaven. He is clearly a person of intense personal magnetism. He attracted followers and filled them with love and courage."[115] But when, in 1934, at the age of nearly seventy, he wrote his *Autobiography,* he forever put an end to any hope that he was acquiring an increasing respect for the Founder of the Christian faith. This is his final verdict: "Jesus was some fine sort of man, perhaps, the Jewish Messiah was a promise of leadership, but our Saviour of the Trinity is a dressed up, inconsistent effigy of amiability and a monstrous hybrid of men, an infinity making insignificant promises of helpful miracles for simple souls, an ever absent help in times of trouble."[116]

Simeon, at the birth of Jesus, said that by Him, "The thoughts of many hearts may be revealed," and certainly when Mr. Wells comes to talk about Christ there is an awful revelation of what is in his heart. As Tholuck said long ago, "The appearance of Jesus Christ in the flesh is the test of the human heart which alone truly tries and brings to light what is in every man."[117]

The Spirit of Antichrist. In one of the precious smaller portions of the New Testament, the First Epistle of John, written by the one who probably knew more of the love of Jesus than any other single Christian of the first century, in his old age, toward the end of the apostolic period, St. John foresees coming into the world the spirit of antichrist, and at the end of the age, antichrist himself. Now this subject of antichrist is a very profound and difficult one, and most important, and has created a vast literature throughout the ages of the church, with which in this volume we are not directly concerned. But the words of the late Professor Robert S. Candlish, in what is probably the greatest single volume of expository lectures on the First Epistle of John ever composed in our language, has so perfectly expressed what the Apostle meant by the spirit of antichrist that we close this particular phase of our discussion of arguments antagonistic to evangelical Christianity by a quotation of his words, because they are an accurate description of the spirit which now prevails in the world, apart from the true church, regarding the person of the Lord Jesus Christ: "The essential characteristic of the spirit of antichrist is that it is, in the sense now explained, not of God. It does not look at the Saviour and the salvation as on the side of God; rather it takes an opposite view, and subjects God to man. It subordinates everything to human interests and human claims; looks at everything from a human and mundane point of view; measures everything by a human standard; subjects everything to human opinion; in a word, conceives and judges of God after the manner of man. This, indeed, may be said to be the distinctive feature of all false religions, and all corruptions of the true. They exalt man. They consider what man requires, what he would like, what is due to him. Even when they take the form of the most abject and degrading superstition, that is still their spirit. They aim at getting God, by whatever means of persuasion and prostration, to do the bidding of man. For it is the essence of our corrupt human nature, of which these corrupt worships are the expression, to care and consult for self, and not for God. This is pre-eminently the spirit of antichrist; the spirit that breathes and moves in the false notions that have gained currency in the church respecting Jesus Christ come in the flesh. Their advocates give man the first place in their scheme. Their real objection lies against those views of gospel truth which assert the absolute sovereignty of God, and put forward pre-eminently what he is entitled to demand,—what, with a due regard to his own character, government, and law, he cannot but demand. They naturally shrink from owning explicitly Jesus Christ as come in the flesh to make atonement by satisfying divine justice. They prefer some loose and vague way of putting the fact of his interposition, and the manner of it. Admitting in a sense its necessity, they are unwilling to define very precisely, either the nature of the necessity, or the way in which it is met. He came in the flesh, to redeem the flesh, to sanctify, elevate, and purify it. He came in the flesh, to be one with us, and to make us, in the flesh, one with him. So they speak and think of his coming in the flesh. Any higher aim,—any prior and paramount design as involved in this great fact, viewed in its relation to the nature and supremacy of God, his holiness and justice, a lawgiver and judge,—they are slow to acknowledge. Hence their gospel is apt to be partial and one-sided;—looking rather like an accommodation of heaven and heaven's rights to earth and earth's wishes and ways, than that perfect reconciliation and perfect assimilation of earth to heaven for which we hold it to have made provision;—our heavenly Father's name being hallowed, his kingdom coming, his will being done, in earth as it is in heaven. Their system is not 'of God' as the primary object of consideration; for they themselves are not out and out in this sense, 'of God.'[118]

The Non-necessity of the Bible. We are not attempting in this volume any survey of the tragical history of higher criticism in relation to the Holy Scriptures, in its destructive effects, nor do we intend to even mention the many wild, foolish, and unfounded assertions, said to be, in times past, "the results of unprejudiced scholars" which have now long been disproved; the truth is that there are more evidences today, of a factual nature, as the result of extensive philological research, and archaeological exploration, confirming the truthfulness of the knowledge of God, than have ever been available to theologians and laymen alike in any period of the Christian church. It is true that much criticism of the Scriptures was in the hands of radicals, of men who denied the deity of Christ, of rationalists, and, as such, it has been proved an enemy of evangelical Christianity. We are not opposed to true criticism, textual criticism, historical criticism, or any other kind of justified, unprejudiced, investigation of the Word of God. However all this must be left untouched for our chapter is already too long. The one argument of contemporary thought which I would emphasize in relation to the Bible itself in this chapter is that hardly understandable idea, proposed by many enemies of Christianity, that the Bible is no longer necessary, and can easily be dispensed with without any tragical consequences! In truth, it seems that now that those who have an innate antagonism to the Bible as the supreme Book of mankind, realizing that more and more its historical truthfulness is being confirmed by the advances of archaeology, philology, and the historical sciences, give up the idea of proving the Bible historically wrong, and sweepingly make the announcement that the Bible, after all, is not necessary.[118a]

The whole Western world was set agog when, in 1921, H. G. Wells the prophet of so many millions, in his now forgotten book, *The Salvaging of Civilization,* proposed the writing of a new Bible. He gave a number of reasons for this, one of which he stated in these words

"During the last century the Bible has lost much of its former hold, it no longer grips the community, and I think it has lost hold because of those eighteen centuries to which every fresh year adds itself, because of profound changes in the methods and mechanisms of life, and because of the vast extension of our educations by the development of science in the last century or so." Words similar to these we have heard for a quarter of a century now and we only quote them here without feeling compelled to enter into a discussion of these rather indifferent accusations. That a new Bible has not arisen Mr. Wells regrettably admits, "It has lost its hold but nothing has arisen to take its place. That is the largest aspect of this matter . . . It was the cement with which our Western communities were built and by which they were held together . . . It is no longer a sufficient cement . . . we need to get back to a cement."[119]

So important does one of the outstanding protagonists of the Chris-ion religion of our day, Mr. Julian S. Huxley, think this matter to be —the discarding of the Bible, that he has written an entire book devoted o this question, called *Religion Without Revelation*. With the addition of one word to this title, and he would have correctly described the contents of his book—"Without Revelation, Without Religion."[120] Why Mr. Huxley should insist that we can have religion without revelation, when he has no religion at all, and thinks everybody else is better without it, I do not know.

In 1923, Dr. James Bissett Pratt wrote in one of the outstanding in-ellectual journals of our country, *The Yale Review*, "Men can get on without the Bible, they can live good and religious lives without it, or without any sacred book. The man who does not know the Bible, or whose acquaintance with it has begun in an unimpressionable age, will probably never know that he is missing anything."[121]

Julian Huxley says that there is no more revelation in man's con-eption of God and his recording of that conception "than the revela-ion concerned in scientific discovery, no different kind of inspiration n the Bible from that in Shelley's poetry." Now in another direction, his has led to the compilation of a large number of anthologies of so-alled "Bibles of different religions," as Robert O. Ballou's *The Bible of he World*. All these men seem to want to call other religious books

after the name of our precious Book, *BIBLE*. Is it not strange that th
do not speak of the "Koran" of the world, etc., etc? Mr. Ballou,
his introduction, says, "A philosophy for today needs knowledge
mankind's many paths to God and . . . the all embracing vision
life, and next for other religions, for Hinduism and Buddhism, etc
As the pre-eminence of the book we know as the Bible is increasing
denied, how significant that many scholars are insisting on the suprem
value of religious books of other faiths which in themselves hav
as the faiths confessed, never brought anyone into the presence
God.[122]

This low conception of the Word of God is at the basis of Professo
Coe's vicious assertion that it is not necessary for our children to kno
anything particularly about the Bible. "The aim of instruction is no
to impose truth, but to promote growth. The instruction may be emp
tied of its traditional implications, of telling pupils what to believe. T
impose such beliefs upon a child is not to promote the growth of a fu
personality . . . What boots it if they know all Scripture, all doctrin
etc., if they have not both the forward look and a sort of desire tha
can reconstruct a world?"[123] In other words, the most important thin
for a man is not to know God, but to be engaged in the reconstructio
of a new earth. Incidentally, however, Coe denies to teachers of th
Bible and religion that which is insisted upon as fundamental in th
teaching of other branches of knowledge. Imagine a teacher of histor
being told that he must not impose beliefs upon his pupils! Imagine
teacher of Latin being told that his pupils must be allowed to deter
mine the laws of Latin rhetoric and grammar for themselves, and tha
they must not be held to any formulae for constructing Latin sentence
even though they were fundamental with the Romans of old!

The General Repudiation of Supernaturalism. In discussing super
naturalism we come to the very core of the whole problem of the plac
and acceptance or rejection of Christianity in the modern world. Chris
tianity is a supernatural religion, it proceeds from a supernatural Bein
—God the Father, who has revealed Himself in His supernatura
Son, the Lord Jesus Christ who, when He was on earth performe
supernatural acts, that is He performed miracles, He healed the sick
He subdued storms, He miraculously fed five thousand with a handfu

of food, He raised the dead, He, Himself, came forth from the dead. Supernatural Christianity claims to have a factual book, and believes that it was inspired by the Holy Spirit of God, the third Person of the Trinity. Christianity believes in a supernatural experience, i.e., in regeneration, a change of the inner man by the power of God through the work of the Holy Spirit; Christianity believes in a supernatural destiny, i.e., in the resurrection of believers, in a life of eternal glory and perfection in the presence of God in heaven. Every force attacking Christianity today repudiates supernaturalism. The corollary to this is that every philosophical, theological, sociological, and historical position which denies the reality of the supernatural, the possibility of the supernatural is, whether it admits it or not, antagonistic to true Christianity. This is the battle of our day. One who, himself, is not a supernaturalist, but one of the outstanding scholars of the twentieth century, Professor W. Macneile Dixon, of whom we shall speak later, in his Gifford Lectures, *The Human Situation,* delivered when he was seventy years of age, said: "Briefly and broadly the issue is what it has always been, and always will be, the age-long issue between naturalism and supernaturalism. In the end everything melts into the cosmic background. All enquiries lead to the one enquiry. The great debate circles round a few words—good and evil, the soul, immortality, God."[124]

"*A Humanist Manifesto.*" I do not know of any two-page document n the whole history of American thought that is such a revelation of amazing apostasy from the faith by men of some importance in conemporary American life than a declaration called, "A Humanistic Manfesto," which was first published in *The New Humanist,* May–June, 933, and has since separately been republished by the American Hunanist Association. It begins with this sentence, "The time has come or widespread recognition of the radical changes in religious beliefs hroughout the modern world." The second paragraph begins, "There s great danger of a final, and we believe fatal, identification of the vord *religion* with doctrines and methods which have lost their sigificance and which are powerless to solve the problem of human living n the Twentieth Century." The first affirmation of this Manifesto is a ery simple affirmation which needs no further explanation, "Religious umanists regard the universe as self-existing and not created." The fifth affirmation begins with this sentence, "Humanism asserts that the nature of the universe depicted by modern science makes unacceptable any supernatural or cosmic guarantees of human values." The tenth statement reads, "There will be no uniquely religious emotions and attitudes of the kind hitherto associated with belief in the supernatural." There are fifteen theses here, all of the same tone and tendency; the word God does not appear in this Manifesto, and a careful study of its statements leads one inevitably to the conclusion that none of those signing this Manifesto believe in God or anything at all higher than a man. Now, in itself, such a statement would not be so startling because one might expect this from any radical sceptic or any unbeliever or rationalist at any time in human history. It is not the Manifesto itself which is so startling as it is the position which the men hold who have signed it. Of the thirty-three names signed to this Manifesto, nineteen of them appear in the latest volume of *Who's Who in America.* (I have not attempted to trace biographical details concerning any of the others; what we find concerning the nineteen will be significant enough.) Leaving out all titles, this is what we find:

J. A. C. Fagginger Auer was educated in Meadville Theological Seminary, became pastor of a Unitarian church in Hyde Park, Massachusetts, as early as 1908, and continued in various pastorates until 1924. He was assistant Professor of Church History in the Theological Schoo of Harvard, 1928–1930; thus we have an atheist preaching in one of ou churches and teaching in one of our theological seminaries.

The career of Harry Elmer Barnes, we will have occasion to speak o later; let us here remind our readers, however, that after being a Pro fessor for some years at Clark University, he held a Professorship a Amherst, 1923–1925. Barnes is one of the greatest haters of Christianit in America, as the titles of his books indicate.

L. M. Birkhead, educated at Drew and Union Theological Semi naries, was a student preacher in the University of Illinois, 1904–191 an assistant minister at Grace M. E. Church in New York, 1910–1912 pastor of a Methodist Church in St. Louis, 1913–1916, and then entere the Unitarian denomination where he has held pastorates in a numbe of churches. Once again then we have an atheist trained in ou seminaries and preaching in our churches.

Edwin Arthur Burtt was educated at Union Theological Seminary, has been assistant and full Professor of Philosophy in Cornell University since 1924.

John Dewey, whom we have already discussed previously in this volume, and we will return to him later, is an atheist as everyone agrees. That one holding such atheistic beliefs should be at the same time the most influential single force in American education in the last forty years is a tragedy in the history of American thought.

A. C. Dieffenbach was educated in the Reformed Theological Seminary of Lancaster and in the Meadville Theological School. He served earlier in the Reformed church, and later he entered the Unitarian denomination and became editor of its outstanding magazine, *The Christian Register;* a chaplain in the United States Army with rank of Captain, and did special survey work in Europe for the Y.M.C.A. One wonders what an atheist can say to soldiers in a time of death.

John H. Dietrich was educated in the two seminaries in which Mr. Dieffenbach was also educated, he was ordained minister in the Reformed church, but some years later joined the Unitarian denomination. Significantly, he is the author of *The Religion of a Sceptic* and, later, *The Religion of Humanity.*

Frank H. Hankins was a Professor at Amherst College, 1923–1926, Professor of Sociology at Smith College for the last twenty years.

Albert Eustace Haydon will be considered in detail below. Haydon is not only an atheist but he has said some of the most terrible things about God that have dropped from the pen of any man in our country in this generation.

Llewellyn Jones was for four years, 1934–1937, an editor for the religious publishing house, Willet Clark & Company, and since 1937, Editor of the Unitarian paper, *The Christian Register.*

Robert Morss Lovett, who has been before the American public as one of the outstanding socialist agitators of this country and has frequently expressed himself as an opponent of the Christian faith, was a distinguished member of the English Department of the University of Chicago for a quarter of a century, being Dean of the Junior Colleges, 1907–1920.

Charles Francis Potter, of course, is a noted unbeliever in our country, who received his education at Newton Theological Institution, was ordained a Baptist minister in 1908 but united with the Unitarian denomination in 1914, was Professor of Comparative Religion in Antioch College 1925–1926, and the founder of the First Humanist Society of New York. His own signature on the Humanist Manifesto marks him as an atheist.

John Herman Randall, Jr., has been in the Department of Philosophy in Columbia University for twenty years and is notably an enemy of Christianity as all his writings clearly indicate.

Curtis W. Reese was educated in the Southern Baptist Theological Seminary of Louisville, Kentucky, and in the Meadville Theological School. After he moved to Chicago he was ordained to the Baptist ministry in 1908 but joined the Unitarian church in 1913; he became the Managing Editor of the Unity Publishing Company in 1933, and after nine years he was Editor of *Unity;* he is a member of the Board of American Unitarian Association, and for some years served as a trustee of the Meadville Theological School.

Roy Wood Sellars, educated at Hartford Theological Seminary, has been teaching at the University of Michigan since 1905, forty years an atheist teaching in the Department of Philosophy in one of our great State universities.[126]

Vivian T. Thayer has been engaged in teaching in Ethical Culture Schools for some twenty years and is a frequent contributor to educational journals.

Joseph Walker is a lawyer, candidate for governor on the Republican ticket in the State of Massachusetts in 1912. He identifies himself with the Unitarian denomination but is a humanist and a non-believer in God.

Frank S. C. Wicks was educated in Meadville Theological Seminary and the Harvard Divinity School, ordained to the Unitarian ministry in 1895.

David Rhys Williams was educated at Harvard Divinity School, ordained a minister in the Congregational church in 1914, but later changed his allegiance to the Unitarian faith.

As we go over this list we wonder how many graduates of our theological seminaries are today in their hearts atheists. There are probably scores and scores of them, few come into prominence, many of them remain without fame or wide reputation. We believe that if a true statement could be secured of the faith of men and women prominent in religious and educational work today in this country, the percentage of those who have denied the existence of God and rejected the Lord Jesus Christ would indeed be startling.[127]

Intellectual Atheism. We come now to the saddest of all tendencies in the study of the forces that are antagonistic to evangelistic Christianity, namely, the denial of the very existence of God, which is saturating so tragically the whole philosophic and religious thinking of our day. This is nothing less than atheism, let the devotees call it by whatever name they please. In 1926 Dr. Walter S. Athearn, the distinguished leader in the school of religious education in Boston University, and the author of a number of important books in religious education, confessed with shame and regret before a large assembly of religious leaders that "a naturalistic humanism is sweeping almost unimpeded through educational and religious circles. There is rapidly developing a cult of Christian atheists, persons who say that they accept the ethical program of Christ, but who deny the existence of Christ's God, upon whom that ethical program is based. Our greatest task today is to keep religious education religious. The concept of the existence of a personal God is on the defensive." [128]

Let us begin our brief survey of contemporary atheism by returning to the teachings of the most distinguished philosopher in our country of our day, Dr. John Dewey. Frankly Dewey declares that "God is the work of human nature, imagination and will." [129] This idea that God is only in the imaginations of men we find scattered everywhere in twentieth century books on religion and philosophy. Columbia University's distinguished Professor of History, Dr. James Shotwell, probably the greatest authority on historiography in America, said, thirty years ago, and he has never retracted his statement, "We must be prepared to see anthropology explain the genesis of the very ideas of God." [130] By this Professor Shotwell means that the idea of God arose from the development of early man, and is not to be related to any divine revelation, for there is no divine being to reveal Himself. Probably the greatest philosopher at Columbia University, from the standpoint of pure philosophy, a colleague of Professor Dewey's, is Dr. William Pepperrell Montague, chairman of the Department of Philosophy at Barnard College, and Johnsonian Professor of Philosophy at Columbia University. In 1930, Professor Montague, in Yale lectures on the same foundation as those of Professor Dewey, dared to say, and this at Yale, famous for its Christian activity: "Zeus and his cousin of old Judea never were at all, except as nightmare dreams, in the minds of their worshipers."[131] That Professor Montague has not, in any way at all, altered his atheistic position of 1930 is shown in a recent article of his, "Philosophy in a World at War," in which he says: "There are many who feel that the assumption of any sort of a personal God with a humanlike love for human animals is immeasurably absurd, and explainable only as a relic of primitive ignorance and fear."[132] This is not the place for comment on these remarks, but we cannot refrain right here from saying that we think no man—Professors Montague, Dewey, nor anybody else in the world, can honestly speak of Augustine, Calvin, Erasmus, Galileo, Kepler, Sir Isaac Newton, the older Agassiz, Dana the geologist, Lord Kelvin the physicist, Gladstone the statesman and classical scholar, or Increase Mather, the greatest of all the Puritan fathers, with the wildest stretch of imagination, or even the most careless use of terms, as ignorant. But every one of these men believed in and prayed to God! Professor Montague may talk about philosophy as the search for truth, but he is not speaking the truth when he talks about the idea of God being the result of the fear and ignorance of man. This is a falsehood. Some gods, some goddesses, some hideous monsters, in some religious systems of the world, may be the result of the fear of man, but not the God and Father of our Lord Jesus Christ Himself, who was never the product of the imagination of any man, but the most startling revelation in history of holiness and love, and divine power.

Another famous teacher at Columbia, in the Department of Philosophy, whose books have had greater circulation than probably any other man teaching in Columbia University today, though of course he has not developed a philosophy of his own as has Professor Dewey, nor is he as profound as Professor Montague, is Dr. Will Durant. These are Dr. Durant's words written as late as 1932: "God who was once the

consolation of our brief life and our refuge in bereavement and suffering, has apparently vanished from the scene; no telescope nor microscope
discovers Him. Life has become in that total perspective, which is
philosophy, a fitful pullulation of human insects on the earth, a planetary
eczema that may soon be cured; nothing is certain in it except defeat and
death, a sleep from which it seems there is no awakening." Even Durant
is not afraid to face the consequences of an atheism like this. "The
greatest question of our time is not communism vs. individualism, nor
Europe vs. America, not even the East vs. the West; it is whether men
can bear to live without God."[133] In the same symposium, edited by
Professor Durant from which we have just quoted, *On the Meaning of
Life,* a similar, though even more irreverent expression of atheism is to
be found proceeding from a fertile mind, one of our most brilliant essayists, H. L. Mencken. This is his confession, "As for religion, I am
quite devoid of it. Never in my adult life have I experienced anything
that could be plausibly called a religious impulse. The act of worship,
as carried on by Christians . . . involves grovelling before a Being,
who, if he really exists, deserves to be denounced instead of respected
. . . It seems to me that on the strength of his daily acts he must be
set down as a most stupid, cruel, and villainous fellow."[134] I wonder how many who daily read Mencken's articles, frequently buy his
books, and count him as one of the prophets of our day, realize that
it is this man who said, "The noblest man I think is that one who fights
God and triumphs over him."

While we are discussing such popular writers as Will Durant and
H. L. Mencken, we should mention the confessed atheism of one of
the few great men of literature in our country today, Carl Van Doren.
Some years ago, and I have never seen any retraction of this statement
of faith, Professor Van Doren, in an article, "Why I Am an Unbeliever"
said, "I do not believe in any God that has ever been devised in any
doctrine, that has ever claimed to be revealed, in any scheme of immortality, that has ever been expounded . . . there is no trustworthy
evidence as to a God's absolute existence."[135] Let us return now, if
you will, to the environment of our great universities. Moving away
from Columbia University, we might for a moment look into a new
volume by Dr. Alexander Meiklejohn, with the interesting title,

Education Between Two Worlds. Dr. Meiklejohn was an instructor in philosophy in Brown University for fifteen years and, from 1926 to 1938, Professor of Philosophy in the University of Wisconsin. In this new book, Meiklejohn, who has always been known as a social radical, says: "It is but the authority of that principle that one questions the existence of God . . . and if God does not exist, if the assertions about Him are myths, then the very presence of those myths is a fact of supreme importance for our knowledge of mankind . . . Who wrote the Bible? It seems clear that God did not do so. Nor did He inspire men to do it. But that implies that the aspirations of the Bible were created by men, created by their own unaided efforts."[136]

Dr. Edwin A. Burtt, for a quarter of a century a member of the Department of Philosophy in the University of Chicago, accepting these radical, negative conceptions of God, in discussing the Church—the Church, if you please—of the future, says: "It would go without saying that a Church organized with the principles so far suggested would not require belief in the existence of God as a condition of membership."[137] When we hear of Professor Albert Einstein denying the personality of God, we seem to be shocked, yet how is it that the Christian Church even supports men in its seminaries and universities who with equal definiteness deny God as much as Einstein ever has? We speak of the scientist Einstein as an atheist. We should speak of such men as we have just noted as atheists also. In fact, even President McGiffert, of whom we have previously spoken, though the President of the largest theological seminary in the East, and probably the most influential in the Western world, held that Christian theism has taken so many forms that, as far as he was concerned, there have been some true forms of religion, like Buddhism, without a personal God. He dared to say, president of a seminary that he was, where young men were being trained for the Christian ministry, in regard to the teaching of Jesus concerning God, that "while we may use His teaching to aid us in framing our conception of God, or in determining which of the many gods worshiped by Christians is the true God, to say that the God of Christian history is the God of Jesus does not help so much in our present task."[138]

Dr. Edward Scribner Ames, a member of the Department of Philophy in the University of Chicago for thirty-five years, for five of those years chairman of that department, and since 1927 Dean of the Disciples Divinity House of the University of Chicago, has gone on record in his own writings as saying: "God is neither a Being nor existence of any sort, but rather an order of nature which includes men and all the processes of aspiring social life."[139]

We would refer to one more member of the present faculty of the University of Chicago, in this discussion of contemporary atheism, Dr. A. Eustace Haydon. Dr. Haydon is typical of many so-called leaders of religion in our country, and it would be well to remind ourselves in brief of his career. He was educated at the University of Toronto, taking his A.B. Degree there in 1901, his Bachelor of Theology in 1903, a Bachelor of Divinity Degree at the University of Chicago in 1911, and a Doctor of Philosophy Degree at the same University in 1918. He was ordained into the Christian ministry in 1903, was pastor of various Baptist churches in Canada for the following ten years, and then became general secretary of the Y.M.C.A., in Saskatoon. For six years, from 1918 to 1924, he was minister of the First Unitarian Church in Madison, Wisconsin, and, since 1919, a member of the Department of Comparative Religions in the University of Chicago, and full professor there since 1929. In his book, *The Quest of the Ages,* Dr. Haydon says that "changing gods are no novelty to the student of religions, but it is evident that the change which is taking place in the modern world is different from and more fundamental than that of any previous age. The gods of the past are vanishing . . . The idea of god meant help for man in his quest for the ideal, but it can no longer be affirmed that men of the olden, long-dead days had captured the true nature of that help in the net of their theologies. Instead of asking, 'Does God exist?' meaning one of the well known gods of yesterday; instead of rationalizing the vital conception of an earlier generation, the question is asked direct, 'What support does the universe give to our moral ideals?' Answered frankly, without bias or presupposition, in the light of the best available knowledge, this question should reveal what for modern man may function as did the ancient gods . . . Spiritual values are evolutionary products. Not from any supernal or external source, neither from above nor behind the world do they come! . . . Gods and institutions alike were incidental to the end they served. More fundamental than either, was and is the undeviating thrust of life in the human line for complete fulfillment. . . . What God meant He can no longer mean."[140] For Dr. Haydon, not only are the gods dead, but the only living God is dead also. He is dead, because for Dr. Haydon He never lived.

Some of the most terrible confessions of atheism among leaders of thought in our own country have appeared in print just within the last three or four years. For instance, Dr. Edward Grant Conklin, for years the brilliant Professor of Biology in Princeton University and at present, Professor Emeritus, at one time President of the American Philosophical Society, in his new and highly-praised book (strange to say, praised in many of our religious papers) *Man Real and Ideal,* is found to be a nonbeliever in God and in the supernatural. He says toward the end of his volume, "If this is true (that nature is everything) there is no wonder-working God outside of nature, who suspends the order of nature when it pleases him or in answer to human prayer."[141] Professor Conklin, so prominent in the realm of biology, leads us to think at once of the pronounced emphatic atheism of the present President of the American Society for the Advancement of Science and for a quarter of a century the distinguished Head of the Department of Physiology in the University of Chicago, Professor Antone J. Carlson. In February 1940, four leaders of thought in this country on four successive Saturday nights gave addresses at the University of Michigan Chapel on their own religious beliefs, one a Catholic priest of the Catholic faith, one a Protestant, though a liberal, one a Jewish Rabbi, and one to speak on atheism, Professor Carlson whose address was delivered on February 16, 1940. I have before me the official mimeographed copies of these four addresses together with an account of th questions that were asked and answered at the end of each of these fou sessions. Without comment, let me quote Professor Carlson's ow admission that he does not believe in God, in prayer, or in a life t come: "Now, in my judgment, the evidence from history, but pa ticularly the evidence from physics, astronomy, geology and biolog renders it highly improbable that such attitudes or views are anythin more than emotional, wistful thinking; that there can be any suc thing as the persistence of the individual personality after the deat and disintegration of our body. As a matter of fact, we know perfectly well that our personality changes with time and changes with health. You and I are not exactly the same person or the same personality that we were twenty years ago. We all know perfectly well that unfortunately there are some cases where the genes, the germ plasm that determines the quality or quantity of our brain, may be defective, at the start, so that we are stupid morons. Even too little thyroid hormone will play that tragic trick. In view of that, so far as I am personally concerned, honesty compels me to say that I cannot entertain the theory of a personal immortality, and I have no particular desire for it. I know of the various heavens, the various happy hunting grounds, the valhallas, the nirvanas and what have you, and none of them have any particular appeal to me. . . . A belief in a personal God, and a heaven of peace and rest seems to give many people renewed hope in life, especially under difficult conditions, and life is difficult most of the time. It seems to give some hope or strength, to believe in the benevolent ordering the universe. However, I must say that if I was compelled to ascribe everything that I see about me in the earth, in man, and in the history of the universe as we know it, if I was compelled to ascribe all that to a personal, omnipotent God, I would be very unhappy, far more so than I am today . . . Now if there are no moral elements in the natural forces outside of human consciousness and if there is no personal God in the biblical, or in the Mohammedan, or in the sense of Father Divine, or the Great 'I Am' the curious religion recently developed in California, what is the meaning of prayer and how did this habit originate? Of course, prayer, obviously, presupposes some person who oversees the human scene and then does something about it. Prayer and propitiation are also a childhood form of behavior. Those who are old enough to have had children of their own and who have known those simple childhood beliefs, like Santa Claus and hobgoblins, and particularly the happy side of it, will agree that these develop certain attitudes, certain agreeable emotions, something like the pleasure, after years and years in distant lands, we get back at the old swimming hole, the old cherry tree and the old cottage. To those who are emotionally conditioned to such beliefs, prayer offers something in the way of a happy feeling. To me prayer is impossible. In this connection I am reminded of the story of the old colored deacon. I heard this back in Illinois, from the lips of the late Governor Altgeld. The story runs thus: At the experience meeting the colored deacon said: 'Brothers, I have noted that when I pray the Lord to send me a turkey, I rarely get it, but if I pray the Lord to send me after a turkey, I usually get it.' "[142]

Probably the most violent propaganda for atheism in any university in our land at the present time, is that carried on by Professor M. C. Otto, member of the faculty of the University of Wisconsin since 1910, and Professor of Philosophy in that University since 1921. In his book, *The Human Enterprise,* which is used, among others, as a textbook for the young men and women attending the University of Wisconsin, two of his later chapters are headed the "Two Atheisms" and "Existence of God." The chapter on the Existence of God is devoted to an attempt to prove to his young readers and students not only that there is no God and that he, himself, does not believe in God, but that a much better life can be lived by any man if he lives in a denial of the existence of God. To me his words are dreadful and I think they will be found dreadful by more than those who are evangelical Christians, "Dependence upon human effort more and more replaced dependence upon God . . . In proportion as men have ceased to lean on God, they have opened up undreamed-of resources for the satisfaction of the noblest desires of which they are capable. Whenever men and women have been able to act as if there were no divinity to shape human needs, and have themselves assumed responsibility, they have discovered how to turn their abilities to good account. Not believing in God has worked well. It has worked better than believing did . . . I have for myself arrived at an affirmative faith in the nonexistence of God."[143]

For myself, one of the most surprising confessions of the atheistic position has come from that great scholar and distinguished humanist Dr. W. MacNeile Dixon, regius professor of English Language and Literature in the University of Glasgow, 1904–1935. Dr. MacNeile Dixon had the honor of giving the Gifford Lectures in 1935–1937, publishing them in a large book entitled, *The Human Situation*. This book has been declared by some of the greatest scholars, both in Great Britain and in our own country, one of the few great works of the twentieth century. It is really the mature thought of a true scholar concerning life, its meaning, its hopes, its fundamental principles, its health, its riches, its possibilities, and something of his own convictions. Dr. Dixon lets it clearly be known that in the issue between naturalism and supernaturalism it is his conviction that supernaturalism must be given up, and that even God Himself has no real existence. "The theologians of all ages and races have formed an image of God after their own fancies, and nothing could be more improbable than that He resembles in the least particular their conceptions of Him." "In fact," says the great scholar, "we are wholly in the dark about everything." And then he makes this tragic statement: "The heaven of my choice would, I fear, contain but few saints . . . I am not sure it would contain any . . . My affections have, I suppose, betrayed or undermined my moral principles. Holiness is a strong perfume and a little of it goes a long way in the world."[145] It is not necessary to ask what love Professor Dixon has for the God of holiness, what he believes about the death of Christ who came that He might sanctify us and make us whole. This is what I call intellectual atheism.

Let me close this survey of contemporary atheism in our country by calling attention to a work which has just come from the press, which for many reasons must be considered significant, and expressive of a wide field of thought. I refer to *Science and Criticism: The Humanistic Tradition in Contemporary Thought,* by Dr. Herbert J. Mueller, published at New Haven by the Yale University Press, 1943. Toward the end of the book, under the general heading, "The Implications of Modern Science," he has a chapter on "The Relation to Religion," that is, the relation of scientific humanism to religion, and without any remarks at this place, I would like to bring to the attention of my readers some of the things Professor Mueller has said about God and the Christian faith. "At the very least, God remains the most immense and splendid of all metaphors . . . In short, God must literally be taken on faith. The objection to most arguments for God is that they fail to meet the given terms of this problem . . . The whole official business of worship and service of God . . . the petitions, flatteries, compliances, covenants, indulgences—is frequently condemned as a sordid, contractual machinery by which men bargain for special favors, gratify their somewhat monstrous obsession with an immortal, individual existence . . . At any rate, the religious experience itself is primary. To have it in the name of God may no doubt facilitate, deepen and enrich it; but the experience came first, before the Name" (by this Professor Mueller means that before man knew of the existence of God he had an experience of God, and therefore constructed God out of this experience). "More important it is, not totally different in kind from other experiences, and it need not have a conventionally religious setting. It may be stimulated by a passage from Shakespeare, a moonlit ocean, a heroic or generous deed, or simply comradeship, a fellow feeling. Any experience that comes as an intense, unqualified good, that unifies the self and unites it with the larger impersonal good, and that reinforces our most cherished goods is religious in quality and . . . realizes the function usually attached to the idea of God." (Here Dewey is quoted as we can well believe from our preceding study of his own similar beliefs.) "Finally," Professor Mueller says: "it would at least seem reasonable to explore the possibilities of going along without God, to try to make the best of the conditions of our knowledge and experience."[146] It is not necessary to tell our readers that Professor Mueller finds no place for the Bible, nor the Christ of the Bible, nor the God of Christ. He holds to the word *religion,* and identifies it with personal experience, as Dewey and all the impersonalists likewise do.

I would not even mention this work, did not its publication involve a number of very serious factors. In the first place, Professor Mueller is a teacher of English Literature in Purdue University, and therefore, of course, hundreds of students every year are sitting at his feet This book suggests that we experiment in life to see what we can do without God; in other words, the suggestion that the world carry on a great experiment in atheism is published by the Yale University Press. What can Yale University mean by publishing a large book, a fine piece of publishing in itself, in which God is denied, and in which it is suggested that men experiment in living without God? What has happened in a great university, famous for its Christian work, concerning which, in fact, a noted book could be written a few years ago called *Two Centuries of Christian Activity at Yale University?* Perhaps another book can be written, shortly, with the title, *A Quarter of a Century of Atheistic Propaganda at Yale University.* But this is not all. We notice on the page preceding the title page of this volume of three hundred pages, a declaration that the cost of the publishing of this book was, in part, borne by the Dwight Harrington Terry Foundation, established at Yale University by the late Dwight H. Terry, of Bridgeport, Connecticut, an endowment fund of $100,000, for the delivery of lectures on "Religion in the Light of Science and Philosophy," and for the "Publication and Dissemination of Said Lectures and Other Objects or Literature Originating Outside the Foundation Which Are in Line with the Objects Herein Specified." This means that large sums of money given to Yale University for lectures in religious subjects are now being used for the publication of books that deny God, that dismiss sarcastically, without an examination of evidence, the whole concept of Christian redemption, and of the supremacy of Jesus Christ our Lord. In fact, if one will examine the nine columns of Index in this volume, he will not find even a single incidental reference to Jesus Christ—even as a Man. Finally, the author of this volume says in his acknowledgments: "I also wish to express my deep gratitude to the John Simon Guggenheim Memorial Foundation, whose generosity assisted me in embarking upon this work." So, Professor Mueller, in his writing and teaching, involving the promotion of atheism, is supported by funds from one of America's great foundations; when the work is finished the cost of publishing it is carried by another foundation, established for lectures on religion; this work, financed by two trust funds, comes from the press of Yale University, stamped with its imprimatur, and as this person is undoubtedly declaiming his atheistic convictions in his own classroom, he is supported by a prominent university in the Middle West. This, I think, reveals a tragic situation in our country concerning which we cannot be too keenly aware.

Such an arraignment of the evidence of intellectual atheism in our contemporary Western world needs no additional comment or interpretation. Professor D. C. Macintosh, not an evangelical himself, has not exaggerated the situation when he says that "There is almost nothing upon the destruction of which leading humanists seem so determined as any vital belief in God as a superhuman intelligent Being worthy of human faith and fellowship.[147]

The Atheistic Program to Destroy Religion Becomes the Program of Modern Governments. Karl Marx well said, "Theory becomes a material force as soon as it has gripped the masses." We considered in an earlier part of this chapter the antagonistic attitude of Marxian Socialism and Communism to all religion. We have witnessed, however, since the last World War the incorporation of this antagonism with religion, and particularly to Christianity, in the actual programs of many of the governments of our twentieth century world. We quite fully considered the evidence and atheistic propaganda in Russia in an earlier part of our chapter, so here it will only be necessary to devote a single paragraph to the evidence and place of atheism in the governmental *decrees* of that country. In the circular of January 3, 1922, on "The Teaching of Religion in Churches, etc." the decrees read: "The teaching of religion to children before and during school age assembled in churches and in other ecclesiastical buildings or in houses of private individuals is hereby forbidden."[148] The decree of 1932, dealing with this matter, signed by Stalin, reads in part as follows: "On May 1, 1937, there must not remain on the territory of the U.S.S.R. a single house of prayer to God, and the very conception of 'God' will be banished from the Soviet Union." In the statement known as "Problems and Methods of Anti-Religious Propaganda, adopted by the Party Conference on Anti-Religious Propaganda, and at the Center Committee of the U.S.S.R. Communist Party, April 27–30, 1926," it was declared that "all forms of religion must be fought and destroyed; first, because it was the servant of capital; second, because it is unscientific; thirdly, because it imposes a morality by the ruling class upon the toilers of the nation It is necessary to condemn categorically as the worst type of popery every effort or approachment of Christianity to Communism. Religion must be rejected for good, without reservation and camouflage. At the given moment is this particularly necessary since sectarianism in its effort to hide from the toiling masses its bourgeois essence, is adopting a communistic phraseology."[150]

The provisions of the law of April 8, 1929, supplemented by certain articles in "The Criminal Code" published in 1938, show exactly the laws that are now controlling the religious life of this vast country which is going to be increasingly heard from in the councils of the nations of the world. Here are five of these brief articles:

"Art. 122. The teaching of the religious beliefs to infants or to adolescents in state or public educational institutions and schools, or breaking the rules established therefor, is punishable with correctional work for a period of one year.

"Art. 123. The conducting of deceiving acts with the purpose of arousing superstition in the masses of the population, in order to gain benefit therefrom (is punishable by), correctional work for the period of one year with confiscation of part of the property or fine up to five hundred roubles.

"Art. 124. Forced collections in aid of church or religious groups (is punishable by) correctional work for the period up to six months or fine up to three hundred roubles.

"Art. 125. Assumption by religious or church organizations of administrative, juridical or other public-legal functions and the rights of a juridical person (is punishable by) correctional work for the period up to six months or fine up to three hundred roubles.

"Art. 126. The conducting in state or public institutions or enterprises of religious rites, and also the placing in these institutions or enterprises of any kind of religious images (is punishable by) correctional work for the period of three months or fine up to three hundred roubles" pp. 18, 19.

A most remarkable, unusually authentic and fully documented work has just appeared, *People, Church and State in Modern Russia,* by Dr. Paul B. Anderson—from which by kind permission the following has been taken. The program of the official Soviet Party published in 1932, Article 13, reads as follows:

"With regard to religion, the Communist Party of the Soviet Union does not confine itself to the already decreed separation of church and state and of school and church, i.e., measures advocated in the programs of bourgeois democracy, which the latter has nowhere consistently carried out to the end owing to the diverse and actual ties which bind capital with religious propaganda. The Communist Party of the Soviet Union is guided by the conviction that only conscious and deliberate planning of all the social and economic activities of the masses will cause religious prejudices to die out. The Party strives for the complete dissolution of the ties between the exploiting classes and the organizations of religious propaganda, facilitates the real emancipation of the working masses from religious prejudices and organizes the widest possible scientific educational and anti-religious propaganda. At the same time it is necessary carefully to avoid giving offense to the religious sentiments of believers, which only leads to the strengthening of religious fanaticism."

What really has the Soviet government accomplished in the suppression of religion? Well, in regard to the church, "According to Soviet statistics, in 29 out of 87 provinces, by October 1925 there were sequestered 1,003 Orthodox churches, 29 mosques, 27 Old Ritualist churches, and 29 belonging to other creeds. One hundred fourteen of the Orthodox churches were transformed into schools, 195 into clubs, 280 were used for educational purposes, 79 for dwellings and other exigencies, 298 remained vacant, and 6 were wrecked."

The following comparative figures for the Orthodox Church in 1917 and in 1941 will help one to understand what has happened in Russia.

	1941	*1917*
Religious associations of all kinds	30,000	....
Licensed places of worship	8,338	....
Ministers of cult	52,442	....
Orthodox churches	4,225	46,457
Orthodox priests	5,665	50,960
Orthodox deacons	3,100	15,210
Orthodox bishops	28	130
Orthodox monasteries	38	1,026

All the four great theological academies at Kiev, Moscow, Petrograd and Kazan which trained the teachers and the higher ranks of clergy have been closed, as well as the 58 seminaries for the preparation of village priests.

In the newer cities of Russia no churches are being built. For instance, in the vast industrial city known as Magnitogorsk no church building was built. "Religion was omitted from this new order of power where men were supreme. Consequently there was no enemy for atheism to fight, and anti-religion began to lose its significance, or rather its appeal. Both religion and anti-religion fell into the discard."

It is true that many churches in Russia are open for services. The Russian News Service in London, on August 22, 1941, stated that 8,338 places of worship were open, of which approximately half were orthodox; that is, they belonged to the Orthodox Greek Church. On the other hand thousands of churches have been destroyed. The number of local parish churches in Russia has dropped from about 50,000 in 1917 to less than 10,000 in 1938; that is, in twenty years the church has been reduced 80%, and of course those who go to church for the most part are quite poor. "A friend of the writer, attending Orthodox liturgy in a Soviet village in 1935, noted that the collection consisted of five pieces of black bread, four green apples and one egg. Manifestly the Church could not maintain theological school when the parishes were reduced to such poverty."

"At the meeting of the Executive Bureau of the Society of Militant Godless, June 15–18, 1933, it was reported that 144,161 persons were receiving anti-religious instruction in local groups; 4,135 were enrolled in courses and seminars of the intermediate section, there were 26 Workers' Anti-religious Universities and one for Red Army soldiers, six anti-religious higher educational institutions, and the Anti-religious Correspondence Institute had six departments, giving instruction to 3,799 persons. There is an interesting parallel here, between the 26 'universities' and the 58 orthodox theological seminaries, and between the 6 higher anti-religious institutes and the 4 theological academies, or higher theological schools of the old regime."

"Nearly 50 per cent of all the members of the Militant Godless Society took part in anti-religious study; 13,799 studied in 541 different groups . . . In order to draw into anti-religious work a number of factory workmen, a series of anti-religious subjects was chosen for them to work out in cooperation with the students of the industrial-polytechnical courses and of the workers' technical schools . . . In order to provide leadership for anti-religious work in government schools in the city, the teachers were called together for instruction in the principal anti-religious subjects. Besides introducing anti-religious study into the system of workers' education, and the direct organization of anti-religious workers' groups in the automobile factories and the rubber plant, systematic instruction was organized in an anti-religious seminar of the Communist University, attended by 150 persons . . . The regional staff of the competition in cooperation with the city Department of Public Education helped the schools to elaborate a series of anti-religious topics for groups in which 5,489 took part. Less satisfactory was the progress of anti-religious work in the collective farms, where there were 33 anti-religious groups attended by 732 persons."[151]

Turning to Germany a moment, not to discuss the war, but to consider the fundamental tenets of the German Faith Movement, which counts millions of German youth among its members, Professor Hauer, one of the three outstanding leaders in the new religion now seizing upon Germany, summarizes the ideas of the German Faith Movement in the following words: "We confess the primal religious will of the German people. Through this leadership we believe we can find the road to salvation (Heil) for ourselves and our people.

"For us there is no higher revelation of eternal reality than has sprung from German soil and the German soul.

"We believe in the presence of eternal reality in the universe, in history, and in our soul. We therefore reject the teaching that God is only revealed through certain people or only through one people.

"The world is our home and is nearer to heaven than any paradise.

"It follows that the Near-Eastern-Semitic and the Indo-Germanic beliefs must stand against each other in a mighty struggle. This struggle is the theme of religious world history for the last thousand years, and may perhaps remain so in the future. The struggle between Christianity and the German faith in the German soul is thus an event of unsuspected depth."

Among the objectives of the German Faith Movement officially announced are the following:

"The only accepted standard for our indigenous faith is the German sense of morality.

"Therefore necessarily the German Faith Movement denies Christianity. It rejects Christianity in every shape or form, because its fundamental principles contradict the laws of life of people and race, and are alien to what is intrinsically German.

"It fights for an exclusively German education without any Christian adjuncts; for a remodeling of the foreign-imposed festivals of the seasons and the family till they conform to our German way of life; for the rehabilitation of the religious rites of our pre-Christian ancestors, since their honor is our honor; for a spiritual resurgence based on the strength of our German faith; for true German burial rites and ancestor cult, since cemeteries are sanctuaries of the community and do not belong to the church.

"It fights against the priesthood and their claim on the souls of our fellow Germans; against every abuse of power to enforce religious adherence; against the accusation that non-membership of a Christian church shows a lack of good citizenship.

"The activity of the German Faith Movement is determined by the necessities of the German people and of the Nationalist Socialist State.

"The day will come when it will seem like a bad dream to us, that we Germans ever thought that apart from being German, we would also consider it necessary to call ourselves Christian, when we believed we had not only to fulfill our essentially German destiny, but had to mold it into a form forced upon us by a Jewish-Oriental-Christian philosophy; the day when it will be the accepted and obvious thing to be just German—German also in faith."[152]

This certainly expresses the most violent antagonism to the Christian faith, and a deliberate intention to destroy it. Hitler, himself, expressed, not in *Mein Kampf,* but to Dr. Herman Rauschning, at one time president of the Danzig senate, and a member of the secret party conclaves from 1932–1935, his utter contempt for Christianity in the following words: "The religions are all alike, no matter what they call themselves. They have no future—certainly none for the Germans. Fascism, if it likes, may come to terms with the Church. So shall I. Why not? That will not prevent me from tearing up Christianity root and branch, and annihilating it in Germany. The German is serious in everything he undertakes. He wants to be either a Christian or a heathen. He cannot be both. For our people it is decisive whether they acknowledge the Jewish Christ creed with its effeminate pity ethics, or a strong, heroic belief in God in Nature, God in our own people, in our destiny, in our blood.

"A German Church, a German Christianity, is distortion. One is either a German or a Christian. You cannot be both. You can throw the epileptic Paul out of Christianity—others have done so before us. You can make Christ into a noble human being, and deny his divinity and his role as a Saviour. It's no use, you cannot get rid of the mentality behind it.

"What's to be done, you say? I will tell you! We must prevent the churches from doing anything but what they are doing now, that is, losing ground day by day. Do you really believe the message will ever be Christian again? Nonsense! Never again! That tale is finished. No one will listen to it again. But we can hasten matters. The parsons will be made to dig their own graves. They will betray their God to us. They will betray anything for the sake of their miserable little jobs and incomes." [153]

I do not know whether or not Mussolini, as I heard when in Italy a few years ago, regularly went to mass. Some have tried to make him to be a serious student of religion. He has at times not hesitated to express his own violent antagonism to all religious life. In an interview which he granted December 18, 1934, he boldly declared: "A fight against religion is a fight against the impalpable, against the intangible; it is open warfare against the spirit in its most profound and most significant force, and it is by this time most fully proved that the weapons at the disposal of the State, no matter how sharp they be, are powerless to inflict any mortal blows on the Church . . . which emerges invariably triumphant after engaging in the most bitter conflicts . . . Passive resistance on the part of the priests and of the faithful is sufficient to frustrate the most violent attacks by a State." [154]

I noticed recently an article in one of our better church papers, containing a letter from Bourgas, Bulgaria, in which atheism in this area is most unexpectedly beginning to make itself felt. These are the words of a native Bulgarian minister: "The materialistic philosophy has penetrated deeply into the heart of the Bulgarian people. The national churches as well as the Protestant churches are almost empty. It used to be that people were eagerly arguing whether there is a God or whether there is no such a Being, but at present, most of the people are ignoring God. And that is true of our youth also." [155]

Mr. H. C. Armstrong, in his remarkable book, *Gray Wolf,* says of Kemal Ataturk, certainly the greatest man in Turkey in the twentieth century: "To his friends he had always made it clear that he would root out religion from Turkey. When he talked of religion, he became eloquent and violent. Religion was for him the cold, clogging lava that held down below its crust the flaming soul of the nation. He would tear that crust aside and release the volcanic energy of the people. It was a poison that had rotted the body politic. He would purge the State of the poison. Until religion was gone, he could not make of Turkey a vigorous modern nation.

" 'For five hundred years these rules and theories of an Arab sheik,' he said, 'and the interpretations of generations of lazy, good-for-nothing priests, have decided the civil and criminal law of Turkey.' They had decided the form of the constitution, the details of the lives of each Turk, his food, his hours of rising and sleeping, the shape of his clothes, the routine of the midwife who produced his children, what he learned in the schools, his customs, his sports; even his most intimate habits.

" 'Islam, this theology of an immoral Arab, is a dead thing.' Possibly it may have suited the tribes of nomads in the desert. It was no good for a modern progressive state.

" 'God's revelation!' There was no God. That was one of the chains by which the priests and bad rulers bound the people down.

" 'A ruler who needs religion to help him rule is a weakling. No weakling should rule.'

"And the priests! How he hated them! The lazy, unproductive priests who ate up the sustenance of the people. He would chase them out of their mosques and monasteries to work like men.

"Religion! He would tear religion from Turkey as one might tear the throttling ivy away to save a young tree."[156]

While it does not relate directly to governmental action, we include it in this present discussion because it is an official expression of a determination to combat religion by a well established organization, in such a far away country as India. In February 1931, the Rationalist Society of India expressed its object in these words: "To combat all religious and social beliefs and customs that cannot stand the test of reason and to endeavor to create a scientific and tolerant mentality among the masses of this country." [157]

To take one more illustration, of a country nearer home, we might for a moment consider Mexico, which will be a nation of increasing importance in the economic life of the United States when the war is over. The state of Tobasco has declared its avowed aim to be nothing less than the total destruction of religion. Its governor, Tomas Garrido Canabal, who since his governorship has become secretary of Agriculture in the Federal Company, has himself declared, when he was governor, that it was his determination to accomplish "the emancipation of the Tobascan proletariat from alcoholism and religious prejudices, two tenacles that absorb and mutilate human thought. When we started," he continues, "on the clerical problem, we thought we would turn all churches into schools. That was not enough. Now we are tearing down all churches and erecting new buildings on their sites so that no trace will be left of the institution of religion." [158]

In our own country atheism has crept somewhat nearer to our government than perhaps some of us think. The candidate for president of the United States during the last three presidential campaigns on the socialist ticket was Mr. William Z. Foster, and the following is an official account of his own attitude toward atheism and hope for an atheistic government in our own country, given before the Fish Committee.

"The Chairman: Does your party advocate the abolition and destruction of religious beliefs?

"Mr. Foster: Our party considers religion to be the opium of the people, as Karl Marx has stated, and we carry on propaganda for the liquidation of these prejudices amongst the workers.

"The Chairman: To be a member of the Communist party, do you have to be an atheist?

"Mr. Foster: In order to be—there is no formal requirement to this effect. Many workers join the Communist party who still have some religious scruples, or religious ideas; but a worker who will join the Communist party, who understands the elementary principles of the Communist party, must necessarily be in the process of liquidating his religious beliefs, and, if he still has any lingerings when he joins the party, he will soon get rid of them. But irreligion—that is, atheism—is not laid down as a formal requirement for membership in the Communist party.

"THE CHAIRMAN: Can members of the Communist party in Russia be married in the church and maintain religious beliefs of that nature, and practice them?

"MR. FOSTER: My opinion is that a member of the Communist party of the Soviet Union who would be married in a church would not be of any value to the Communist party.

"THE CHAIRMAN: Could he maintain his membership in the party?

"MR. FOSTER: He would not.

"THE CHAIRMAN: He would be put out of the party?

"MR. FOSTER: Eventually, if not for that specific act.

"THE CHAIRMAN: Would it not be the same in this country?

"MR. FOSTER: As I stated before, workers who would be so imbued with religious superstitions that they would be married in a church would be of no value to the Communist party.

"THE CHAIRMAN: And the same thing would happen to them in this country that happens in Russia?

"MR. FOSTER: Of course."[160]

The Communist candidate for president of the United States in 1936 and in 1940 was Earl R. Browder, at the present time head of the Communistic Political Association of the United States (formerly the Communistic party). The latest authentic biographical sketch of Mr. Browder claims, and no doubt with full justification, that he "has been responsible for the largest number of pamphlets published by any American Communist," as well as for several books. Early in 1944 he became, for the second time, Editor in Chief of *The Daily Worker*. In his book *What is Communism,* which he published in 1936, as the then secretary of the Communistic Party of the United States of America, he says this about religion: "Of course, communists do not consider religion to be a private matter insofar as it concerns members in our revolutionary Party. We stand without any reservations for education that will root out beliefs in the supernatural, that will remove the religious prejudices which stand in the way of organizing the masses for socialism, that will withdraw the special privileges of religious institutions . . . (As for members of the party) we subject their religious beliefs to careful and systematic criticism, and we expect that they will not be able to withstand this educational process. It is our experience that their work in the movement will bring them to see the correctness of our viewpoint on this question."[161]

Monsignor Sheen cannot be said to be unduly alarmed when he says, "We are passing from an age in which religion is tolerated into an age in which religion will not be tolerated, it may very well be that the new age will be an age of barbarianism . . . it will not be barbarianism made by an invasion from without as of old; barbarianism is no longer outside of us, it is beneath us."[165]

The Religion of "The College of the Future" and Some Related Dangers. One of the most serious signs during these last few years in our country in the matter of irreligion is that in almost all the literature which is now being produced relating to the plans and programs of education in the postwar days, naturalism, which is the same as antisupernaturalism, is not only assumed but insisted upon. We call attention here to the statements found in only one of the most authoritative works in this particular field, a large work significantly entitled, *The College of the Future* by Dr. Mowat G. Fraser, Lecturer in Education in the University of Michigan, a volume enhanced by the fact that it was published by the Columbia University Press. Dr. Fraser, when he discusses the subject of teaching religion, boldly says, to begin with, that "The instances of certain very occasional religious events in past history need not be considered nor does 'the first cause' need to be. Our issue concerns only the causes of so-called religious benefits of the present, such as increased insight, mental peace, social helpfulness, and physical regeneration." In other words, in the religious instruction which Professor Fraser hopes will be given in the University of the future, there will be no place afforded for the investigation and explanation of the historical facts concerning the life of Christ, nor of the causes for the vast conquest of early Christianity in the Roman world. He goes on to define what he thinks religion really is, insisting that it is, "The reverence for inclusive aims," and then he adds that all the benefits of religion are to be naturally accounted for: "The full possibilities and requirements for attaining them (these religious benefits) cannot be understood, if natural forces are considered to be uncontrollable and purposeless. They can be deeply appreciated only if one recognizes the tendency in all living things to strive for life and growth, and the power in human beings to strive for life and growth which are ideal." Professor Fraser talks a great deal about indoctrination and then he shows how deeply he objects to any one religious faith being emphatically taught to students, because, he says, this can be done "only at the price of unsound understanding, unfair consideration of minor opinions, inability to meet changing needs or unexpected propaganda, and the not unlikely possibility of extreme reaction of all students when the bias of indoctrinator becomes evident to them . . . to try to indoctrinate the college student with such beliefs amid far different conditions, the so-called scientific spirit, and the prevalent scepticism of today, encouraging him to react not only from those beliefs, as well as to overlook and endure truth and leave historical connotations, but also to react from the teachers and the church which insist upon them."[166] In other words, if Professor Fraser's ideas of education in the future should be carried out no man with Christian convictions, with faith in the God and Father of our Lord Jesus Christ and in Christ as the Son of God, would be permitted to express this faith as truth, nor would he be allowed to teach it to students in the hope that they would accept it, all of which reminds me of some very sane words recently expressed by a distinguished teacher of biology in the University of Aberdeen, Dr. Lancelot Hogben, when he says, "It is plain humbug for a teacher of chemistry to say that he aims at giving his students an open mind about the atomic weights of the elements . . . I cannot think of any form of legitimate instruction in which it is the business of the teacher to give an unbiased view on controversial questions."[167] If men teach chemistry dogmatically and try to steer their pupils from errors which will lead them to disaster, then why cannot we teach Christianity dogmatically and try to steer our young people from the doctrines of contemporary despair, from the hopelessness of humanism, and from the limitations of contemporary paganism which bind down the soul of man to this unsatisfying earth of ours?

The Proposals for Universal Eclectic Religion. By eclecticism, of course, is meant, in religion, a combining of various elements of the principal religions of the world into one so-called universal religion which can appeal to all men everywhere, antagonizing none of them. The most important contemporary advocate of this new religion is none other than Dr. William Ernest Hocking, for the last twenty-five years head of the Department of Philosophy at Harvard University. It was he who was chiefly responsible for the final form of the Christ-denying epochal work *Rethinking Missions.* In his latest book, *Living Religions and the World Faith,* Hocking suggests that in this new world faith everything pertaining to the supernatural in Christianity be given up; the deity of Christ, His virgin birth, His miracles and resurrection, and of course, His atoning work, and he foresees in this desupernaturalized universal cult "a chain of centers set about the world to sustain the continuing enterprise of reconceiving religion through culture, and world culture through religion." One wonders through what world culture of today Christianity is to be reconceived? Would this be Nazi culture, or Fascist culture, or contemporary Russian culture, or the culture of America? e.g., the culture of the City of New York, or the Unitarian culture of Cambridge? In a subtle sentence he says, "It is the law of history that men in groups lose their lives in order to save them,"[168] by which it would seem Professor Hocking means that what is good in Christianity according to his criteria, can only be saved by Christianity giving up its unique doctrines and losing itself in a world cult. This idea is also more brazenly set forth in the new work, *Christian Truth in History,* by Dr. Hugh Miller, of the University of Southern California, who says that in this new world religion, "the vast peace of Buddha, the verve of Mohammed, the iconoclasm of Communism, the wide heaven of the Orient, yes, even the realism of National Idealism, must all have their room in that consummatory of men."

Hope for an eclectic religion seems to be gaining ground everywhere. Professor Edgar Sheffield Brightman, since 1919 Professor of Philosophy at Boston University, a man whose writings have exercised considerable influence in American religion, wrote in his work, *The Future of Christianity,* what he thought of the uniqueness of the Christian faith when he said, "The Christian Church will come to recognize in Buddhism, and Hinduism, Confucianism and Modernism, other roads to God. The Christian will treat representatives of these religions as brothers, not as heathen enemies of the faith . . . The future will see the church moving away from partisanship to a true brotherhood of man."[170] And so this germ of eclecticism, spreading over Christendom, begins to infect even men in high places, in what was once a powerful force in evangelical Christianity. We refer to the Anglican Church in England. In Canon Raven's new book, *Science, Religion, and the Future,* the distinguished churchman's hope and conviction is thus recorded, "That a unifying ideal, that is, a world-wide religion of some kind is essential, would be difficult to dispute."[171]

This idea of a universal religion is that with which Professor Douglas Clyde Macintosh of Yale closes his semiencyclopedic, but quite confusing work, *The Pilgrimage of Faith in the World of Modern Thought* (the italics in the passage we quote are his). "Be it known, then, that *to the building of this modest but firmly founded temple of an empirically scientific theology all religions are invited to bring material, such empirical data of dependably successful and universally valuable religious experience as they may have already acquired or be able hereafter to discover.* What we may expect indeed, is that this temple of a scientifically verified and therefore universally valid theology will be in the future the centre of a truly scientific religious education and a truly scientific evangelism and missionary activity in which different religions will share their values with each other and contribute thus to the spiritual enrichment of all . . . These three, truth, beauty, and goodness, are the generally recognized absolute or eternally and universally valid values. But it is a fair question whether we ought not to recognize one or two other types of universal value. There is the value discovered by the social interest in the narrower and more specific sense of the term 'social,' the value, namely, of true friendship and love, of universal friendliness and ideal social relations in general. Again, while we have said that universal religion must be friendly to all universally valid values, that is, to truth, beauty, morality, and love, the further question arises as to whether the religious value itself ought not also to be recognized as an ultimate end, instead of being regarded as merely instrumental to other spiritual values. This is a question which can be answered in the affirmative with a high degree of assurance, just as soon as we become assured of the existence of a religious Object, or God, of ideal character. Fellowship with such a divine Being would obviously have the social value of love on the one hand and the spiritual values involved in experience of the ideal on the other; but in addition to all this it would seem to have the distinctively religious value which belongs to experience of the 'numinous,' that is, the holy, or divine, as such. From the point of view of even a moderately and sanely mystical development of religion, it becomes very certain, subjectively at least, that this distinctively religious value of fellowship or union with God is of ultimate and absolute validity."[172]

Anyone reading these words will at once acknowledge that in Professor Macintosh's conception of a universal religion, all the unique distinguishing characteristics of Christianity centering in the person of Jesus Christ our Lord are eliminated, and so this professor of theology at Yale is looking for a world religion that will have nothing to do with Christ, the Incarnate Son of God, that eliminates all recognition of His absolute supremacy, of the fact of His vicarious atoning work on the cross, the triumph of His resurrection or His return in glory. The theology of the Pauline epistles will have no place in this universal religion; there will be no place for people to come to God through Jesus Christ our Lord; and, as far as we can judge, there is no place for a hope of eternal life, in a heaven such as the Bible describes, for all the grounds for that hope are eliminated in this conception of a universal religion.

I wonder if I would be pardoned for referring to a personal experience which I had just the other day, that directly relates to this matter of a world religion? Let me move then from professors of religion and canons of the Church of England, to the level on which you and I walk. I was driving on the north side of Chicago one Sunday afternoon, with the son of an evangelical clergyman, a beloved friend of mine, who is preaching the gospel of the Lord Jesus. This son is a deacon in his father's church, and devoted to the services of the church. He is a scientist, well educated, refined, courteous, not trying to air antagonistic views, or proudly refusing to have anything to do with the church—quite otherwise. In the course of the hour we were together, we drove by the Bahai Temple, and, in speaking of the Bahai worship, this young man said, "Well, there is one good thing they have." I was rather astonished to think that a member of an evangelical church could believe that the Bahais had anything for the Christian Church, and so I asked him what he meant. He immediately replied, "They believe in one world religion, and I think that is what we need." So, this subtle enemy of Christianity goes on capturing the hearts of our young men.

Acknowledging the Need for a Return to Religion but Insisting It Must Not Be a Religion of Supernaturalism. In spite of all the evidence which we have presented in this chapter showing the paganism of our day, its antisupernaturalistic and atheistic tendencies and the terrific power of the many forces which are deliberately pounding at the foundations of evangelical Christianity, there are at the same time in our Western civilization some thinkers who are reminding men that what we really need is a return to religion and that unless we do return to some kind of faith we are lost indeed. Now such expressions seem to have in them a good deal of hope, perhaps a revival of religion among our intellectual leaders, and seem to be, as it were, the faint foretoken of a real return to belief in God. When, however, we look more closely into the conception of religion which some of these men hold, we discover that the religion which they would have men return to is not Christianity at all, nor does it have anything to do with the great supernatural factors of the Christian faith. We would mention two of these leaders of our day. One of the most discussed and highly praised books of the last two years is *The Survival of Western Culture* by Ralph Tyler Flewelling, Professor of Philosophy and Director of the School of Philosophy in the University of Southern California. Now probably no recent book dealing with contemporary culture by a non-Christian in our country contains so many sentences expressing the necessity for a return to religious faith as does this one. We continually come upon such phrases again and again as "Spiritual achievements as yet embryonic and most untried." . . . "Unless we can lift it (our sense of destiny) to the higher level of moral and spiritual achievements." . . . "The spiritual and moral readjustments of society." . . . "The mental and spiritual organism of human society." . . . "Broader and deeper pioneering in the spirit."[173] All this sounds very well; in fact, Professor Flewelling has written as strongly against the paganism of our day as any philosopher of the last decade. But what kind of religion does Prefessor Flewelling have in mind, what kind of faith would he have us embrace? The following may perhaps be taken as a characteristic definition of religion by Dr. Flewelling: "Religion is a reverence for a universe and a power within it which is vaster than ourselves, it springs from a desire to seek a mental, moral and spiritual unity with that of which we feel ourselves already a part. There is awe (not fear), there is worship of that which we feel represents a nobler and better part of us." [174] You will note there is nothing here about God, or the confession of sin, or salvation in Christ. While I do not find even the name God in the index to this book, there are a number of references to God in its pages, of a somewhat vague and indefinite nature; yet, when it comes to stating who God is, we find a reappearance of the old conception of the identification of God with man. He says that the mark of God's presence in man may be found in "goodness, love, compassion, charity, uprightness, sincerity, sacrifice, devotion to ideals, these are the heart of true religion, the evidence of the divine spirit of the indwelling of the God and Father of all." [175] And then he adds "once these principles are recognized all else falls. Divinity is evidenced by indubitable testimony, the existence of perfect moral character, the life of perfect love in any religion." We take it, then, that a man of good character is divine, and that he is thereby a religious man. Professor Flewelling goes farther than this, however, for not only is his religion one not centering in a Person, an omnipotent and omniscient Divine Being, but he is insistent that the religion we should have must, at the same time, be stripped of those things which have made Christianity what it is! Listen to these words concerning our Lord, than which nothing could be more inaccurate: "Jesus laid down as the requisites of religion no standards of belief, except in the saving grace of righteousness, love for and devotion to God as the Father of all men, implicit obedience to and love for the Higher Will. This devotion was to be proved by an equal passion for the supreme good of men. The appearance of such service was to be recognized as inspired of Deity, whether it sprang from Jew, Samaritan, or Gentile. He sought to win to His discipleship, without further test, all men of good will and righteousness without respect to theological opinions." [176] Well, anyone who knows the Gospels knows that these statements are false. We would quote only four sentences that fell from the lips of our Lord, to show how wrongly Professor Flewelling has interpreted the Gospels, and we quote them without comment. "He that believeth on the Son hath eternal life; but he that obeyeth not the Son shall not see life, but the wrath of God abideth on him." "He that heareth My word, and believeth Him that sent me, hath eternal life, and cometh not into judgment, but hath passed out of death into life." "This is the will of my Father, that every one that beholdeth the Son, and believeth on Him, should have eternal life; and I will raise him up at the last day." "All authority hath been given unto me in heaven and on earth. Go ye therefore, and make disciples of all the nations, baptizing them into the name of the Father and of the Son and of the Holy Spirit; teaching them to observe all things whatsoever I have commanded you: and lo, I am with you always, even unto the end of the world."[177] The religion Professor Flewelling says we must have, he insists at the same time, must be nontheological and nonsupernatural.

The other writer to whom we would refer is an economist, and at the same time, a communist, even though he is a Professor in Oxford University, Dr. Harold J. Laski, who believes the world will never be right until the whole world has the economic system that Russia now has. Professor Laski, in his *Reflections on the Revolution of our Time,* frankly admits that one of the causes for the lawlessness and utter decay of morality and ethical standards in our contemporary civilization is the loss of confidence in the Christian faith, and he goes so far as to believe, in which most communists do not follow him, that we need to get back to religion; but he insists we must never expect to go back to the religion of our fathers, that is, to a supernatural religion. These are his words: "The decay of the religious spirit is widespread. But if what we seek is a religious revival, we must be careful to define our terms with some precision. If, thereby, we mean a revival of faith in the supernatural, the evidence is clear that especially in any of the historical dogmatic forms, it is unlikely; for their power to offer rational proof of their title to acceptance dwindles with every change in the scientific understanding of the universe . . . The decay of the religious spirit is the natural outcome of historical causes it is now impossible to reverse upon any serious scale."[178] Since the appearance of this volume Professor Laski has published a work in which he deals even more at length with the subject of religion, *Faith, Reason and Civilization*. His chapter,

"The Recovery of Faith," begins with the sentence, "The most important war aim that is before us is the recovery of a faith by which we can all of us stand." But in the same chapter our learned, even though at times dreamy economist repeats the assertion of his earlier volume that we must not expect, cannot think of going back to the great Christian religion, and its supernatural involvements. "There is little reason to suppose that the recovery of a system of values in our civilization would be the outcome of a revival of faith in the supernatural. For, in the first place, there is little reason to suppose that any ecclesiastical organization has now a sufficient hold to act as a means of turning men's effort from force to persuasion. There has been, indeed, historically, a deeper habit of peace in China, where supernatural religion has played but a small part, than in Europe or the rest of Asia, where its hold has been immense. And, in any case, outside the Society of Friends, and a small body of mystic cults, the two thousand years of Christian history suggest that religious creeds are subdued to nationalisms, and even to political opinions, rather than that they possess the power to transcend them. And this is a factor quite apart from the philosophic and historical objections to which all organized forms of the Christian faith give rise. Even if some Christian Church were able to secure acceptance of its principles in Europe and America, it would leave unsolved the problem of the relevance of its dogmas to the other non-Christian world religions. We should then, if we put our trust in the Christian religion as the source of a revival of values, either have to seek its imposition by force upon those who rejected its principles, or find some terms of accommodation between Christianity and its chief alternatives which would drive us, at the end, into something like the civil religion which Rousseau recommended as the unifying cement of state organization." [179]

At the conclusion of such a survey as we have here attempted of the more important forces and agencies engaged in attacking the fundamental truths and principles of the Christian faith, it is impossible to avoid a most solemn question that is bound to arise in the mind of anyone whose sympathies are with the Christian faith: will these attacks become increasingly severe, and powerful, and frequent, or, may we expect their gradual weakening and ultimate disappearance? This question can only be answered as we ask another: are the individual forces which we have in this chapter enumerated moving further and further away from the Christian faith, or are they gradually returning to Christian truth? There is only one answer. Philosophy is more antitheistic in our country today than it has ever been, and, with most of our younger philosophers trained under nontheists, there is no reason for expecting that the next generation will be anything but more atheistic than this has been. Communism, which will always remain uncompromisingly antireligious, rather than decreasing is increasing everywhere in the world—there was a time, even when I was a boy, when a socialist was looked upon with horror, almost shunned as a criminal; today the president of our own United States does not hesitate to appoint openly pronounced communists to high offices. More and more our civilization becomes secularized, with the thoughts of men increasingly centered in inventions, in international politics, in humanistic studies, and in advancing those sciences which pertain exclusively to things seen and heard and felt. Ignorance of the Bible grows deeper and more extensive, until our present generation of young people know infinitely more of the stars of Hollywood than they do of the great characters of the Old and New Testaments. When the Russian revolution brought into power the rule of communists the whole world stood aghast, and western nations said failure would quickly mark the end of such a godless regime. Such predictions have been completely contradicted by the history of the last quarter of a century. Now, instead of the world beholding one government determined to crush out every vestige of religion, we have the same rationalist opposition to religion growing up not only in many Occidental countries, but even in the (now) slowly awakening empires of the East.

Unless some unexpected supernatural force enters our contemporary civilization compelling a change in the course which it is now pursuing, no carefully drawn chart of the intellectual, religious and economic tendencies of the twentieth century will foretell anything else, for the years immediately before us, than that there will be even more frequent and increasingly powerful attacks upon the Christian faith. If the next fifty years should reveal in western civilization an apostasy from the Christian faith, and a weakening of its hold upon thinking people, as great as the last fifty years have witnessed, true believers will then have become hardly more than a persecuted remnant, the church for the most part nothing more than an institution devoted to the welfare of men, and a true knowledge of the Bible rarer than a knowledge of Greek myths. God grant that other forces than those arising from the darkened, self-centered, proud, God-hating hearts of men may soon begin to powerfully manifest themselves in the midst of our increasingly irreligious era, turning men, by the convicting power of the Holy Spirit, from a way that leads to anarchy, death and destruction, to the way which leads to redemption, emancipation, and holiness of life, indeed, to the throne of Grace, and the presence of God.[180]

Chapter II

THE TRAGIC RETREAT OF CONTEMPORARY EVANGELICAL PROTESTANTISM

In our opening chapter we undertook a survey of some of the most powerful and important forces and agencies of our modern Western world which are deliberately antagonistic to evangelical Christianity, and which are purposely working to undermine the foundations of the faith expressed in the great Christian creeds. Now the question will arise in the mind of any reader, "Well, with all of these forces attacking the foundations of the Christian faith, have there been any serious, regrettable consequences, following these attacks? Is not the Church today just as strong, or stronger, than ever; are not these agencies finding their attacks completely unsuccessful, and must not they soon realize the utter futility of contending against the faith?" To these questions some people in our country complacently answer, in an optimistic tone, that nothing can hurt the Christian faith, nothing can disturb the great Church of Christ on earth, and we need not worry concerning any of the ultimate consequences of this great struggle. In this they show themselves the most deluded of men. Optimistic they may be, but factual they are not. Not only must we recognize this great conspiracy of forces attempting to destroy evangelical Christianity, but if we are sincere, and carefully consider the facts that are available, we must recognize that, again and again, in the last one hundred years, *evangelical Christianity has suffered tragic defeat, and is being beaten back in almost every important area which once it occupied*. I am an evangelical, of course; I fully believe that, though the grass withereth and the flower fadeth, the Word of God abideth forever. I believe the Christian faith will never be destroyed. The Church of Christ is the only institution on earth that will have an *eternal* existence. I believe all that. But I am compelled to admit, by the very facts of the case, that evangelical Christianity is growing increasingly ineffective and anemic. I do not mean it is going to die; I do not mean there cannot come a great change for the better. I am talking about the situation *as it now exists.* We who believe the faith ought to awaken from our slumber, and our glib optimism, and face some of these realities. This chapter will prove a very sober and sad one, but I am forced to write it, and do write it, not for unbelievers, but, for the most part, that the great body of evangelicals, of which I am one, might come to recognize the seriousness of the hour at which we have arrived.

General Statements Concerning the Decline of Religion and the Growth of Skepticism. First of all, let me bring together four or five statements by outstanding thinkers and molders of thought of the last fifty years, from different fields of leadership. Let us begin with the one who probably knew more about European thought, and saw more clearly the disappearance of spiritual life in Europe, than any other man at the close of the nineteenth century, Professor Rudolf Eucken. In his profound and important volume, *Main Currents of Modern European Thought,* Eucken did not exaggerate the situation in continental Europe when he said, "The denial of religion is becoming more and more popular among the masses."[1] No man can deny that.

Dr. Edgar Sheffield Brightman in his volume, *The Problem of God,* frankly says, and I do not believe that he can be contradicted, "If we survey the advance of doubt from the Middle Ages when it was practically non-existent, down through the eighteenth, nineteenth, and twentieth centuries, we may be tempted to say that it bids fair to overrun civilization. Theistic belief may be represented by a declining curve which seems rapidly to be approaching a zero value."[2] To come closer to evangelical leaders in the Christian Church, let us take a statement from the man who is probably recognized as the greatest authority in the Christian Church of Europe today, Dr. Adolf Keller. In his latest book, acknowledged to be authoritative, *Christian Europe Today,* Dr. Keller says, "Between the areas of solid ground—the continents of the churches—there is a desert of religious indifference, a religious nihilism—and the area of an amorphic religion of the Christian or pagan type. The vocal manifestations of the churches in their own witness and defense should not leave any illusion about the gradual extension of this religious no man's land, not only among the masses, but in the circles of the higher bourgeoisie and the intellectual elite of our time. The Church cannot ignore the fact she has lost millions who had received her religious education and had heard her message during many generations." [3]

One of the greatest theologians of our day, Dr. Emil Brunner, in one of the best studies we have seen of the present conditions and tasks of the Church in this hour, begins with these challenging sentences, "The shattering events of these present days, and their dark forebodings for the future, oblige the Church to give especial thought to its own condition and to basically review its strengths and deficiencies. We are experiencing in the political-military area the tragic consequences of a certain civic *laissez faire,* an inability to rise to the necessary special exertions, or even to a realistic appraisal of the situation, in the face of a threatening danger. Who would contend that we are not confronted in the Church with something analogous? Who would say that all in the Church is well? We do not desire to paint the devil on the wall; but are we armed against events like those we have seen transpiring during he last two decades in great 'Christian' countries where the functions of the Church have been either destroyed or greatly compromised hrough political revolutions, without the Church as a whole even naking an effort to offer serious resistance? Is it so out of keeping vith the times today to raise the clarion cry, Church, awake; act, as ong as there is day, for the night is coming when no one can act any onger?" [4]

Speaking of Europe as a whole, Brunner, in the article from which ve have previously quoted, says: "When we remind ourselves that in ertain urban communities, both middle class and so-called workers' ections, the population has doubled, tripled, and even quadrupled in he last fifty years, while the Sunday school attendance has only comaratively maintained itself, or that in both urban and rural communiies the number of people attending church is often only 5 per cent of he population, then the language of statistics suddenly acquires sigificance." [5]

The State of Protestantism in Continental Europe. In discussing the onditions of the Christian Church in continental Europe today, I shall omit the largest of all continental areas, that of Russia, for we have already given considerable consideration to the condition of Christianity in Russia in the first chapter of this volume. For the material of this paragraph I am entirely dependent upon what, I believe, is the most important recent survey of the conditions of Protestantism in continental Europe, by Dr. Alexander McLeish, entitled, *Europe in Transition,* recently published by the World Dominion Press, in three parts. Of Germany, Dr. McLeish says that less than one-tenth of the Protestant children are enrolled in its two Sunday school associations, and that, as is to be expected, the attendance has steadily decreased in recent years. "Confessional candidates for the ministry have no hope of appointment to a parish, while no Confessional student can attend any of the four university theological faculties now left. . . . Of non-Confessional students taking up theological study, the number of such in al Germany was recently reported as only thirty-nine. Religious papers Bibles, and hymn books cannot now be printed."[6] In Denmark there is a falling off in Sunday school attendance so marked that only abou one-sixth of the children of Sunday school age are enrolled, and "as i all Scandinavian countries, not one in ten of the church members is communicant."[7] In the Netherlands, "all the churches are facing a de clining membership, and the forces of anti-religion are on the in crease."[8] France, of course, has always been more or less an atheisti country. Dr. McLeish says concerning the situation, that "only abou one-fourth of her population of forty-two millions maintain any con nection with the Roman Church, and some would put it even lowe four million. Out of thirty-six thousand Catholic parishes, nearly twelv thousand were nominally without a priest, so that in every diocese 15 to 200 parishes had no curé."[9] In Czechoslovakia "all theological sem naries, colleges and universities have been closed, including the Carolin University founded in 1348—the first in Central Europe. All the Prote tant youth organizations which were exceptionally vigorous, includin the Christian Student Movement, the YMCA, YWCA, and the Sunda School Union have been suppressed."[10] When this war is over we wi have a Europe to confront more pagan than Europe has been sin perhaps the days of Constantine.

The Tragic Condition of the Church in Great Britain Today.

1935 Dean Inge confessed at a church conference, "I do not believe that more than 20 per cent of the country are in any possible sense of the word Christian." Dr. J. D. Jones, of Bournemouth, when moderator of the Free Church Council in England a few years ago, speaking out of the experience of a distinguished career of half a century, one of England's truly great preachers, said that the "great mass of the people seem to be drifting away from religion; the habit of worship seems to be falling into disuse; the Sabbath is rapidly ceasing to be a day of rest, and 75 per cent of the manhood of the nation is clean outside the Church." The well-informed English journal, *The Guardian,* less than three years ago, remarked "There are few communities where the majority of the worshipers were not born in the last century." [13] J. T. Christie, headmaster of Westminster School, speaking in Durham in September, 1942, said that about 75 per cent of the youth in England seem to care nothing at all for religion, and added, "They do not think about it or talk about it; they never say a prayer or enter a church or have a conscious thought about God from one year's end to the other." [14]

The most amazing report of the religious conditions of England that has recently appeared is in the *Christian Century,* from the pen of one of England's most popular preachers and writers (we are not here discussing his theology), Dr. Leslie Weatherhead. These are his opening words, "I have just returned from a Sunday afternoon spent in Hyde Park. The preacher was brief and to the point. One might give his sermon the title, 'The Centrality of Christ.' He invited questions. Not one questioner mentioned Christ. The hearers wanted to know what the preacher thought of the Beveridge report. Was he a socialist? Didn't he think the Duke of Blank's recent speech was disgraceful? Would the Church in the new age take the workers' side? Why did the Church own slum property? Why did an archbishop get 110,000 a year? And so the questions came. It is the old story. The man in the street thinks of the church mainly as an organization for affecting social reform. Britain is humanist. In Hyde Park the listeners—nearly all workingmen—want the preacher to declare himself a socialist, dress down the capitalist, support all measures for social reform, talk about sex problems, damn the Nazis, and say nothing about the sins of his hearers or of the necessity of God. Britain is—with the exception of the very small minority, mostly within the churches, who have the real Christian outlook and experience—*humanist to the core.* The Church is, in the main, regarded as either irrelevant or as a weapon to be used in its value as a means to that end. The idea of worship, of God as an end, of man as having significance only in so far as he is a means to that end, is as far from the mind of the man in the street as it can be. Such an idea has, in fact, never entered his head. . . . There is no sign anywhere of a religious revival. Wireless services are listened to by large numbers, but most churches are empty, and most Christians disheartened. If peace came tomorrow most people would slip back into the old grooves. Indifference to the very name of God, neglect of His day, and of private prayer and complete ignorance of the Bible, or of the message and relevance of Jesus Christ, would resume their former sway in the lives of the masses. It is probable that even the newly awakened social conscience would go to sleep again. Unless the present situation can be spiritually capitalized before men harden their hearts now softened by the shocks of private and public misfortune—then Britain will be as pagan as she was in 1928."[15]

A recent two-year survey in Great Britain has just been published under the title, *Religion and the People,* which is generally considered to be as authentic as any religious survey of this generation. Among the people interviewed in this extensive survey, 20 per cent said they had no religious belief, and of these, people under forty reported no faith with twice the frequency as those over forty. Of the remaining 80 per cent, only half indicated they were members of a church. Half of those interviewed never pray, about 25 per cent said they attended church. It is reported that in the last twenty-five years the Sunday school attendance in the Free Church has decreased from 1,744,725 to 1,323,406. However true it may be that there has been some deepening of faith in the hearts of some in beloved Britain, generally speaking, it is admitted on every hand that religion is at the lowest ebb in that formerly great Christian country that it has been for many generations.[16]

Some Observations Concerning the Present Status of Religion in Our Own Country. In discussing the condition of the Protestant faith in America, may I speak of it first, statistically, whatever be the value of statistics, and then in a more general manner. Dr. Conrad Henry Moehl man, Professor of the History of Christianity at the Rochester Divinity School, in his new book, *School and Church: The American Way,* has brought to our attention some amazing figures regarding religious life in our country at the present time. I have been granted permission to quote from the first page of his interesting chapter, "Facing the Facts": "One hundred and fifty years later the religious pattern of American life is about this. Catholicism in all its branches, Roman, Greek, and provincial, reported a membership of about 16 per cent of the population; all Protestant groups taken together, about 23 per cent; all the cults, Mormonism, Christian Science, Unity, New Thought, Spiritualism, and many more, less than 1 per cent; Judaism, less than 4 per cent. In other words, the 256 religious bodies in the United States claimed only 43 per cent of the population. But every minister knows that all religious statistics are optimistic. If all the churches report a membership amounting to 43.46 per cent of the population of the United States, then the contributing and active and attending membership may reach 30 per cent of United States population. *Christianity is a minority group in the United States.* In 1936 the five to seventeen-year-old population in the United States was 31,618,000. The total Sunday school enrollment was less than five million. About 57 per cent of the Catholic five to seventeen-year-old children were not in parochial schools. In Protestant parochial schools the total enrollment was only 275,643. Between 1926 and 1936, Sunday school enrollment decreased 40 per cent. In that year the United States Baptists had over three million less Sunday school pupils than church members." [17]

The 1936 Census of Religious Bodies indicates that during the ten-year period beginning with 1926, the Southern Baptists lost 680,000 Sunday school scholars; the Northern Baptists 160,000; the Protestant Episcopal Church 46,000; the Presbyterian Church, U. S. A., 250,000; and the Methodist Episcopal South, 540,000. These are alarming statistics and can probably not be denied. [18] My friend, Mr. J. Elwyn Wright, president of the New England Fellowship, who knows the condition of Protestantism in New England probably as well as any man in our country today, in answer to an inquiry of mine, has communicated the following most amazing information: "A careful survey of thirteen scattered counties in New England, supplemented by other data which has been accumulated, reveals the fact that since the turn of the century, approximately one thousand New England churches have closed their doors. In some instances, these churches are open for one or two Sundays in the summertime, but have no regular pastor. About 20.5 per cent of all the towns in Maine have no church services or Sunday schools of any kind, either Catholic, Jewish, or Protestant. Conditions in Vermont are believed to be even worse although no state-wide survey has been made in that area. Church attendance has dropped to the amazing figure of 5½ to 8 per cent of the population in the various counties where the survey was conducted, several years ago. From the standpoint of getting new members in the churches, it is costing in one county approximately $3,150 for each new member received. The cost in other counties runs from $1,200 up to that figure."[19]

In many of our great cities, it is commonly expected that churches will be closed on Sunday night. I have known friends to start out at seven o'clock on a Sunday evening in a city where they were visiting, walk until 8:30 past twenty-two church structures, and find not one of them having an evening service. There are cities in our country today of from fifty thousand to a hundred thousand population, where not one church is open in the evening where a gospel message can be heard, with the possible exception of the Holiness tabernacles, and as much as we disagree with these people on some principles, I am sure God will honor them for keeping open their chapels and trying to save souls when the great Protestant denominations choose to close and lock their doors. May I mention something out of my own experience. Twenty years ago it was my great privilege to be the pastor of the Lafayette Square Presbyterian Church on the north side of the city of Baltimore. Within a radius of one-half mile of our church were some of the finest, strongest, best attended Protestant churches in that grand city—Grace Methodist Church, the First English Lutheran, the Episcopal Church of the Atonement, Brantley Baptist Church, etc. Colored people came in and all these churches, I think there were twenty in all, had to sell their commodious plants. Even in my time, 1922–1925, these churches had great congregations. Where are they now? Though many of them have rebuilt in the suburbs, the great congregations for the most part are not there. I love Baltimore, but Baltimore today compared with

Baltimore thirty years ago, is a spiritual wilderness as Christian Baltimorians themselves acknowledge with grief. I only speak of that city because I know the change that has come over it. There are many like it. Churches that a quarter of a century ago knew congregations that crowded to the doors, now, and I could name the churches, have congregations so small that in some cases they have forsaken the main sanctuary and are meeting in a room once used for prayer meetings.

I would not dare myself to propose the idea which I am going to speak of in this paragraph, even if I thought it, because I would at once be condemned as being utterly abnormal and erratic. So, without comment of my own, may I bring to your attention some remarks of Dr. Ralph Henry Gabriel, a professor in Yale University since 1915, full professor of history in that distinguished university since 1928, and author of a great many books. In his important volume, *The Course of American Democratic Thought,* which was published in 1940, he frankly admits that the foundation of our democratic faith "was a frank supernaturalism derived from Christianity. . . . The basic postulate of the democratic faith affirmed that God, the creator of man, has also created a moral law for His government, and has endowed him with a conscience with which to apprehend it." In supporting this statement he quotes a verdict of Justice Joseph Story, given in 1828, in which it is declared that "in assenting to the great principles upon which all society rests, it must be admitted that there are some which are of eternal application and arise from our common dependence upon our Creator." [20] Now, granting all this, Professor Gabriel goes on to say, later in his book, that the Supreme Court of the United States has, whether we welcome the fact or not, replaced the Christian Church as a symbol of security. "Churches do not dominate urban America as they once did the countryside and the rural village. As the religious interpretation of the fundamental law declined in prestige, the influence of their interpreters increased. . . . Judicial supremacy is then but another aspect of man's age-old search for security. The Supreme Court has replaced the Church as the American symbol of social stability." [21] He follows this statement with a detailed consideration of what he calls "the cult of Abraham Lincoln." Reminding us of Secretary Hubert Work's remark in 1926, that the Lincoln memorial was holy ground, he adds, "In such temples and with similar inscriptions, the citizens of ancient Greece placed statues of Apollo. By so little is the twentieth century after Christ separated from the fifth before His coming." [22]

Though we have discussed the religious situation in our country here with brevity, we believe that no one can deny the tragic fact that the influence of Christianity is decreasing, and that evangelical Protestantism has been on the retreat for now too many years in our beloved land. Having considered our country as a whole from, we might say a statistical standpoint, let us now turn to the subject of religion in some of our American educational institutions, and then, specifically, in our theological seminaries.

The Drift of American Educational Institutions from the Christian Church. Every textbook in the History of Education confesses, whatever be the faith of the author, that all the great educational institutions of our country that can trace their history back to colonial days, sprang from religious faith, were founded upon the great truths of Christianity, and that within their walls the Word of God was honored and given pre-eminent place, and in their services, through the week and on the Lord's day, the gospel of Jesus Christ could be heard proclaimed. All this has passed, and instead of our educational institutions pouring into our American life, as they once did, streams of spiritual truth and life for the renewal of faith, they now have become, for the most part fountains of skepticism, pouring forth the muddy waters of unbelief and atheism, until our whole land has become contaminated by these foul exudations. I want to be specific in this part of our chapter, so that no one can say I have in any way exaggerated, or have said what evidence fails to support. Of course, we all know that Harvard has been Unitarian, anti-Christian, and anti-biblical, for three quarters of a century, and that its most famous president, at least of the last hundred years, Dr. Charles Eliot, was in every way an enemy of all that pertains to New Testament truth. We pass by Harvard, and come to its neighbor and rival, at one time one of the greatest Christian institutions in America, Yale University. Dr. Cyrus Northrop, in his Introduction to *Two Centuries of Christian Activity in Yale,* which was published at the beginning of our century, proudly and truly wrote: "Yale College was founded by Christian ministers in the interest of education, but especially of religious education, in order that there might be an adequate supply of Christian ministers. The most important part of the college is the religious history. . . . For the first century no less than forty per cent of its graduates became ministers of the gospel. Yale College has fearlessly followed investigation to whatever truth it might lead, and while some old ideas have had to be abandoned as the result of modern scientific and historical investigation, neither the college nor its students have discovered anything which makes God less glorious than He was to the Fathers who founded the college, or Jesus Christ less a manifestation of God to men nor less dear to all humanity than He has been for nineteen hundred years. 'The foundation of God standeth sure; and nothing shall separate us from the love of God which is in Christ Jesus our Lord.' "[23]

Dr. Anson Phelps Stokes, who probably knew Yale better than any other man of our generation, wrote, a few years ago: "A Yale atheist, or a Yale cynic, or a Yale pessimist, is rarely found. . . . The first words of the original charter, obtained in 1701, put this in the foreground, where it has ever remained: 'Whereas several well disposed, and public-spirited persons of their sincere regard to the zeal for upholding the propagating of the Christian religion, etc. . . .' One-third of the biographies given in these volumes are of men who were ordained ministers, or regularly licensed to preach. The overwhelming majority is made of earnest Christians regularly identified with some branch of the Church. There is not a professed atheist among them. . . . This is worthy of remark in view of the unusually large number of nineteenth century scientists included."[24]

And now what do we have at Yale? Well, as we saw in the first chapter of this book, we have the Yale University Press publishing volumes in which the very existence of God is denied. We have men invited to lecture on the Terry Lecture Foundation at Yale who are outstanding atheists, and uncompromising enemies of everything supernatural. It was at Yale University, on the Terry Foundation, that John Dewey gave his lectures *The Common Faith,* to which we have already referred. It was on the same foundation that his colleague, Dr. Montague, gave his lectures, *Belief Unbound.* Going into the very center of Yale's religious life, that is, the famous Divinity School, we state, with sadness, that Dr. Douglas Clyde Macintosh, a member of the faculty of the Divinity School since 1909, and the Dwight professor of Theology in the same institution from 1916–1933, is one who has repudiated all the miracles concerning Christ, and has gone so far as to declare, as we noted before, that "The Jesus of Christian tradition must die that He may live." [25] Elsewhere Professor Macintosh has said that "While the history of Jesus was indispensable to the rise of the Christian religion, and so to the Christian experience and faith of today, a continued belief in that historicity is not indispensable, though very available, to the Christian religion." [26] In other words, the most distinguished of those teaching in the Department of Theology at Yale, since the dawn of our century, rejects the great Christian convictions concerning Christ, and as he elsewhere says, works and hopes for the day when Christianity as a unique religion will be abandoned and we will have a universal religion made up of the things that are good in all the so-called great religions of the world.

Concerning Smith College, it is interesting to recall that the third article of the will of its founder, Sophia Smith, reads as follows: "Sensible of what the Christian religion has done for myself, and believing that all education should be for the glory of God and the good of man, I direct that the Holy Scriptures be daily and systematically read and studied in said college, and that all the discipline shall be pervaded by the spirit of evangelical Christian religion." [27] What a change has come over this famous school for young women in the century that has followed! Let us give just one illustration. For eight years, 1923–1930, Dr. Harry Elmer Barnes held the chair of Historical Sociology, and was allowed to drill into the thousands of students that sat under him, his own hatred for the Christian religion. He has said that he is "unutterably opposed to all vestiges of the old supernaturalism," [28] and he wrote a whole book, not one of great influence, but one of vicious bitterness, significantly called, *The Twilight of Christianity*. Elsewhere this prolific writer, an outstanding historian, has said: "It behooves all honest and informed friends of religion to construct the framework of the new religion on a tenable superstructure. To do so it appears to the writer that they will have to surrender these essential characteristic of the older religion: (1) the reality and deity of the biblical God; (2) the uniqueness and divinity of Jesus and His special relevance for contemporary religion; (3) the belief in immortality." It is a long way from the will of the founder, to such a position of antagonism to the things which she considered fundamental.

Another famous school for young women is Bryn Mawr College. President Rhoads, in his inaugural address, spoke of the founder of Bryn Mawr, Dr. Joseph Wright Taylor, in the following words: "It was his prayer that Bryn Mawr should become in the highest and most blessed sense a school of Christ, in which the student should learn of Him under the training and gracious discipline of His Holy Spirit, the lessons of His truth and love." It was at Bryn Mawr, we remember, that Professor William Lyon Phelps was told that he would not be allowed to express his faith in evangelical Christian truths, if he were a member of the faculty. It was at Bryn Mawr that one of the outstanding antagonists of even theism itself was a member of the faculty for forty-four years, Dr. James Henry Leuba, the psychologist, who, in his book, *God or Man,* devotes an entire chapter to what he calls "The Evils Done by Christianity."[29] We could multiply the unbelief of the members of the faculties of these schools.

Amherst College was once one of the most markedly Christian collegiate institutions in America, but the President of Amherst College from 1912–1924 was Alexander Meiklejohn, who, in his latest book, *Education between Two Worlds,* has come out emphatically as a denier of the existence of God, an atheist, if you will. As far as we know, he had the same convictions during his presidency of this famous college. Of course, if he had those convictions he would express them freely, for Dr. Meiklejohn is not one who has ever been known to be timid in declaring what he believes.

Columbia University began as King's College, in the city of New York. The advertisement in the *New York Gazette* for June 3, 1752, affirmed, "The chief thing that is aimed at in this college is to teach and engage the Children to *know God in Jesus Christ,* and to love and serve him, in all *Sobriety, Godliness,* and *Righteousness* of life, with a *perfect heart, and a willing mind.*"[30] Columbia University today has the greatest concentration of antisupernaturalists on its faculty of any university in our country, including the three famous men of the Department of Philosophy, John Dewey, William P. Montague, and Will Durant, as well as a great host of rationalists scattered in other departments.

For over fifty years Mark Hopkins was a professor of Psychology and Philosophy at Williams College (1830–1887), and published in 1846 his famous *Lectures on the Evidences of Christianity,* one of the most important apologetic works to appear in the nineteenth century. A successor, not his immediate successor, but the one holding the same chair, for over a quarter of a century, since 1905, was Professor James Bissett Pratt. And it is this Professor Pratt who has said, "Men can get on without the Bible."[31]

And what of Princeton University? Its president for twenty years, from 1868 to 1888, was Dr. James McCosh, scholar, theologian, Calvinist, defender of the faith; and for the next four years, to 1892, its president was the distinguished philosopher, Dr. Francis L. Patton, one of the outstanding apologists of the last half century; both of them mighty servants of God, glorying in the pre-eminence and the redemption and the deity of the Lord Jesus Christ. All that has gone in Princeton University. For example, as we have noticed before, the one who for many years was the distinguished head of the important department of Biology, Dr. Edward Grant Conklin, in his last book, just recently published, denies the supernatural, denies the personality of God, and says that "The religion of sciences leaves us to faith in the work and dignity and almost boundless possibilities of man."[32] I have before me as I write a printed copy of the inaugural lecture of Dr. George F. Thomas, professor of Religious Thought on the Harrington Spear Paine Foundation, given in McCosh Hall at Princeton University on Thursday, October 24, 1940. This address was distributed by Princeton University and has an introductory word by President Harold W. Dodds. Dr. Thomas admits that "Today, at least in American culture, the Hebraic and with it the Christian element has been seriously undermined, and in some circles it has almost disappeared."[33] And what does the new professor of Religious Thought in Princeton University propose to offer, in that famous institution of learning, in a day when the Christian tradition, as he confesses, is dying out in our country? After three careful readings of this lecture, I would say that he does not intend to present Jesus Christ as the Son of God, nor the fact that Christ died for sins on the cross, nor that only by faith in Christ may man have eternal life. He does once speak of the doctrine of the incarnation, but he says it means "not only the condescension of the divine to the human, but also the elevation of the human to a higher dignity." I do not find that he speaks of Christ as the Son of God, but he does speak of man as "a son of God."[34] He talks about the love of Jesus in the Gospels, but I do not discover that he says anything about that love leading Christ to the cross to die for us. No atonement, no regeneration, no confession of sin, no indwelling of the Holy Spirit, no justification by faith. The great truths taught, preached, emphasized, defended by Witherspoon, McCosh, and Patton are here forgotten.

Let me turn in conclusion to only one more institution and this, in my opinion, presents us with the most tragic example of the eclipse of the Christian faith that can be found in any one of the older, greater educational institutions of our country. I refer to Dartmouth College.

Dartmouth College was founded by Eleazar Wheelock, an ordained clergyman, who wanted to establish a school where Indians of New England could be trained in the truth of the gospel of the Lord Jesus Christ, and who was the first president of Dartmouth (1769–1779). He was followed by his son, John Wheelock, president for a third of a century (1779–1815). As a later president said, at Dartmouth's centenary celebration, "Dartmouth College was conceived in the fervor of piety; born in the throes of a great missionary zeal, dedicated at birth to Christ; cradled the first year in a revival, and stands wedded to religion—until death."[35] One of its greatest presidents, under whom Dartmouth experienced unusual growth, Nathan Lord (1828–1863), was one who, says the latest historian of Dartmouth, "based the entire philosophy of life upon a belief in the literal accuracy and inerrancy of Holy Writ . . . He was insistent that God should be the main spring of all the activities of man."[36] It was Nathan Lord himself who, in a famous letter to the alumni of Dartmouth College on its anniversary in 1869, said: "For Christ the college was founded and has been administered. To Christ all its influence in all time belongs."[37]

Of the first fifteen classes graduating from Dartmouth, a majority-sometimes as many as five-sixths of the class—entered the ministry. From 1810–1830, one-third of its graduates became clergymen, and from 1830–1868, nearly one-fouth of its graduates continued to enter the ministry. "And," says one of its presidents, "the astonishing thing was that one-fourth of the preachers graduating from twenty-nine consecutive classes at Dartmouth were converted during their college course."[38] Even as late as 1886, the catalogue of Dartmouth College included the following statement regarding its religious life and biblical emphasis: "A biblical exercise systematically arranged is being attended by each class on Monday morning. For the present, the subject in the freshman year is the Historic Origin of the Bible; in the sophomore year, New Testament History; in the junior year, the Development of the Church as Exhibited in the Acts; in the senior year, Old Testament History from the Creation to the Entrance into Palestine, with special references to Inspiration and the Historic and Scientific Relations to the Scriptures."[39]

And what is the condition of Dartmouth today? In the first place, chapel is not compulsory, nor any religious meeting. Furthermore, no course in Bible is compulsory. All of its religious courses are called electives. Eight courses in the latest catalogue of Dartmouth are designated in the Department of Biblical History and Literature, one in Archeology and History, one in Philosophy of Religion, one in the Great World Religions, and one in Ethics. The catalogue would not really indicate that any course is to be found in Dartmouth College strictly devoted to the interpretation of the Word of God. There are more courses offered in Dartmouth College today in the one subject of Biography than in the whole realm of biblical history, religion, and religious literature. These are what we might call only technical matters of curriculum. There is more to be said than that.

In the student periodical published by Dartmouth, and about Dartmouth, *The Dartmouth,* in 1927, the following terrible statement appears: "Dartmouth has always been considered a liberal college. Graduate and undergraduate alike take pride in the freedom of thought that is permitted here. . . . On the religious question it is only to be expected that Dartmouth shows a large percentage of atheists and agnostics. Dartmouth is proud of her disbelievers."[40] This statement arising from the student body has never been publicly repudiated by the faculty or trustees of Dartmouth College, and we take it to be a true statement of the religious conditions prevailing in that school of two thousand students with a faculty of two hundred.

The famous Mexican artist, at that time, we believe, a member of the faculty at Dartmouth, José Clemente Orozco, was asked to paint a series of fourteen panels setting forth an epic of civilization, in the great Baker Library, for which he was given three thousand square feet of wall space. The last of these fourteen panels, photographs of which are reproduced in an elaborate brochure on this particular work published by Dartmouth College, is called, "Modern Negation of the Spirit." Under it, at least in the official description of it, is the following statement: "Here a militant Christ figure is shown, axe in hand, and his cross at his feet, symbolic of an aroused and aggressive spirituality. He stands against a great junk heap in which appear the destroyed symbols of antiquated creeds and of the confessional forms of all religions." The words hardly communicate what the picture so dreadfully sets forth. It is actually a picture of Christ with a hideous, ascetic, glaring, almost satanic gaze, with an axe in His hand, *having chopped down His own cross,* which rests on the ground before Him. In other words, in our modern day we have come to such a place of wisdom and freedom and emancipation that these can only be represented by a picture in which the cross itself is shown as a despised symbol.[41] To the voice that was heard from heaven, saying, "This is my beloved Son, in whom I am well pleased," Dartmouth answers, "This is one who in His holy death we despise and reject." This is what sixty years have done to one college in America.

A perfect illustration of the skeptical and anti-religious influence which Dartmouth officially is determined to exercise is given in a book published by Dartmouth in 1924, *Essays Toward Truth: Studies in Orientation.* These chapters, so the title page tells us, were selected by Kenneth Allen Robinson, William B. Pressey, James Dow McCallum, of the Department of English, Dartmouth College. These essays, we are told in the Preface, "Represent no one point of view, advance no propaganda, and dispose of nothing completely. Their purpose is rather to present many points of view, some of them definitely conflicting. Their purpose is to stimulate the student to develop his own capacity for rational thinking and thereby achieve for himself the beginnings of a social perspective and a social philosophy."[42] When however, one looks at the material in this book and the authors whose essays are here brought together, one realizes that what these professors mean by "rational thinking" is thinking strictly apart from any divine revelation, thinking that leaves out God, and thinking that centers exclusively in man. Among the authors of these essays are James Harvey Robinson, Alexander Meiklejohn, John Dewey, Bertrand Russell, John Haynes Holmes, and James Bissett Pratt. All these men are antisupernaturalists, and some of them are pronounced atheists. The essay by Dr. Holmes is called, "The New Basis of Religion," and the one by Dr. Pratt, "Religion and the Younger Generation." Dr. Pratt's chapter is a reprint of his article appearing in the *Yale Review*, in April 1923, in which appears the statement, which we have previously quoted: "Men can get on without the Bible, etc."[43] Dr. Holmes, whose extreme liberalism is well known throughout the country, says: "Wherever in the past religion has come to the point of organizing itself in the form of temples, priesthoods, sacred books, and holy days central to the whole system of institutions, there has been a preconceived abstraction known as deity." Later he becomes, if the author may use the word, nothing less than blasphemous. It seems to me his words are of the very spirit of Antichrist. Let my readers judge. "It is man first and not God. It is as much of God only as man may seem to suggest or prove! Before all it is God revealed by man and not man by God! Our revelation today is from earth to heaven, from clod to God—not vice versa, as in olden days . . . Man is his own creator. He makes the world to suit his needs. He cries, Let there be God, and there *is* God . . . Man not God is the center of our faith and the object of our hope and love."[44] I take it that essays like this are in the book because these are the views of the members of the faculty of Dartmouth College. And one may only think, with fear and horror, of the influence of reading lessons made up of such pages as these godless, irreligious, humanistic essays, with professors emphasizing these agnostic and atheistic views days by day, year after year, in their classrooms. Such can only produce a generation of men without God and without hope.

To bring to a conclusion this discussion of increasing paganism in American college life, let me quote from two contemporary educators, one the headmaster of what is probably the outstanding Christian evangelical school for boys in our country, Dr. Frank E. Gaebelein, headmaster of the Stony Brook School for Boys, and Dr. Nicholas Murray Butler, of Columbia University, who has been its president for the last forty-three years. Dr. Gaebelein, in his valuable booklet, *From a Headmaster's Study,* tells us, after twenty years of constant devotion to educational problems, that, "Now I know that the modern university today is neither liberal nor fair in its religious policy. No sensible Christian parent would expect a state university or a non-sectarian college to teach Bible Christianity. The most that he could reasonably expect is a neutral attitude that rules out discussions of such matters, or a truly liberal point of view that accords to both Modernism and Fundamentalism, both faith and unbelief, an equal hearing. And that is just what the American university today does *not* do. In thousands of classrooms (and this includes classrooms in many a denominationally supported college) there is being carried on a subtle atheistic propaganda. It is not the professors of religion, for they are few in number, who are most successfully carrying forward this propaganda; it is the cynical professor of English, or the brilliantly ironical lecturer in Philosophy, or the sardonic psychologist who is doing the damage."[45] This is the verdict of President Butler as late as 1934, appearing in the official Bulletin of Information of that university: "The whole force and influence of the tax-supported schools is on the side of one element of the population, namely, that which is pagan and believes in no religion whatever."[46] We have often wondered why President Butler, who certainly has an enormous power in Columbia University, on the one hand frequently speaks of the need of religion in contemporary education, and on the other hand allows to continue in his great university the most distinguished body of atheists that is gathered together in any one educational institution in America.

Unbelief in Some of Our Theological Seminaries. When we come to discuss the condition of our theological seminaries, we approach indeed a delicate matter, but one which needs frank consideration. I shall confine myself here to evidence concerning theological seminaries in our own country for two reasons—in the first place, I know very little, of an *exact* nature, concerning the theological seminaries of Great Britain, at the present time; in the second place, in our English world, so unified in thought at the present time, conditions which exist here may be counted upon as existing in England, not only to an equal degree, but, because Modernism is much older in England than in America, to an even greater degree. Let me give only one quotation from a distinguished theologian of Great Britain of a few years ago, whose influence is still of considerable weight. I refer to Dr. J. F. Bethune-Baker, Lady Margaret's professor of Divinity at Cambridge, a position which in itself would be one exercising great influence. In 1914 Professor Bethune-Baker wrote: "By far the greater danger that threatens the Church at the present time in this respect seems to me to be failure to recognize fully enough the new conditions of intellectual background and outlook under which our younger men are growing up, and the consequent risk of alienation from the Church of men and women who feel they cannot honestly serve as ministers or even worship as members of that Church, because it appears to have bound up its Faith and its Life inextricably with 'proofs' that are no proofs to them, and to declare that belief in the miracle of Christianity—the miracle of the Christian life—depends upon belief in 'miracles' for which no evidence that is really convincing to them, is forthcoming."[47] No comment is necessary to understand what Bethune-Baker recommends the Church to abandon.

That there are some sound evangelical seminaries in our country, where the Word of God is honored, and where professors are devoted to the Lord Jesus Christ, and out of which every year men graduate strong in the faith and sealed to a holy calling forever, we all gladly admit, and for this we daily thank God. They are really the hope of the Church. But they are not typical of the present condition prevailing in theological seminaries in our land. This is a serious matter, and I would like in this section of our chapter only to present evidence of a factual nature, that my readers may not think I am writing this in some spirit of blind antagonism, or that these pages form some blanket accusation, rather than present specific facts. First of all, may I quote from a work appearing during the course of the first World War, from the pen of the outstanding Baptist theologian of our land, the most distinguished president of a Baptist Theological Seminary in all of its history in this country. I refer to Dr. Augustus Hopkins Strong, president, and professor of Systematic Theology in Rochester Theological Seminary for forty years (1872–1912), president of the American Baptist Missionary Union (1892–1895), and the author of one of the greatest works on theology ever produced in this country. In 1918 when he had reached the advanced age of eighty-two, after a brilliant and noble life devoted to educating ministers, in a seldom-seen work, Dr. Strong described the condition of the theological seminaries in the United States at the time of writing, using phrases of greater severity than we ourselves would dare use (though we trust our earnestness would not be less than his). The statement is an extended one, and should be before us at this time when the theological situation in our land is even more serious than it was when Dr. Strong wrote. Remember, these are the words of a man who, at the time he was writing, was the most famous theological seminary president in our country. "Professor Kirsopp Lake, in a recent address before the Harvard Divinity School, deprecated the use of the term 'theology.' 'Theology,' he said, 'presupposes divine revelation, which we do not accept.' He proposed the term 'philosophy,' as expressive of the aim of the Unitarian school. This is honest and plain. What shall we say of those who speak of the 'new emphasis' needed in modern theology, when they really mean that the preaching of the old doctrines of sin and salvation must give place to 'another gospel' of cooperative Christian work? From their neglect to put any further emphasis upon 'the faith once for all delivered to the saints,' we can only infer that, for their structure of doctrine, no other foundation than philosophy is needed, and that they, like the Unitarians, no longer accept the fact of a divine revelation. 'Other foundation can no man lay than that which is laid, which is Jesus Christ,' and to lay greater emphasis upon the fruits of Christianity than upon its roots, is to insult Christ, and ultimately to make Christianity itself only one of many earth-born religions, powerless like them either to save the individual soul or to redeem society. Professor Lake is quite right: If there is no divine revelation, there can be, not only no systematic theology, but no theology at all.

"What is the effect of this method upon our theological seminaries?

It is to deprive the gospel message of all definiteness, and to make professors and students disseminators of doubts. Many a professor has found teaching preferable to preaching, because he lacked the initial Christian experience which gives to preaching its certainty and power. He chooses the line of least resistance, and becomes in the theological seminary a blind leader of the blind. Having no system of truth to teach, he becomes a mere lecturer on the history of doctrine. Having no key in Christ to the unity of Scripture, he becomes a critic of what he is pleased to call its fragments, that is, the dissector of a cadaver. Ask him if he believes in the preexistence, deity, virgin birth, miracles, atoning death, physical resurrection, omnipresence, and omnipotence of Christ, and he denies your right to require of him any statement of his own beliefs. He does not conceive it to be his duty to furnish his students with any fixed conclusions as to doctrine but only to aid them in coming to conclusions for themselves. The apostle Paul was not so reticent. He was not ashamed of the gospel of Christ, but rather gloried in it. He even pronounced his anathema upon any who taught other doctrine. It is no wonder that our modern critics cry, 'Back to Christ,' for this means, 'Away from Paul.' The result of such teaching in our seminaries is that the student, unless he has had a Pauline experience before he came, has all his early conceptions of Scripture and of Christian doctrine weakened, has no longer any positive message to deliver, loses the ardor of his love for Christ, and at his graduation leaves the seminary, now to sow his doubts broadcast, as teacher in some college, as editor of some religious journal, as secretary of some Young Men's Christian Association, or as agent of some mutual life insurance company. This method of interpretation switches off upon some side-track of social service many a young man who otherwise would be a heroic preacher of the everlasting gospel. The theological seminaries of almost all our denominations are becoming so infected with this grievous error, that they are not so much organs of Christ, as they are organs of Antichrist. This accounts for the rise, all over the land, of Bible schools, to take the place of the seminaries. The evil is coming in like a flood, and the Spirit of the Lord will surely raise up a standard against it. But oh, the pity that money given by godly men to provide preachers of the gospel should be devoted to undermining the Christian cause!"[48]

To pass from a general indictment of the unbelief of our seminaries,) a personal confession of religious faith on the part of a man who is ow President of one of our outstanding middle west theological semi-aries, may I call your attention to the nontheistic convictions of Dr. lbert W. Palmer, Professor of Practical Theology in, and President of ie Chicago Theological Seminary (Congregational) since 1930, who ecently was honored by the Protestant churches of the city of Chicago 1 being elected President of the Chicago Federation of churches! In is book *Paths to the Presence of God,* Dr. Palmer says, "The old exter-al semi-materialistic conception of his divinity, which laid emphasis pon his body and upon miracles like the Virgin Birth and the physical esurrection, has passed away for modern men. It just doesn't fit the erms in which we have to think. It belongs to a thought-world where iod was a separate entity—like a man, only more powerful, sitting in nmeasurable grandeur upon a throne away up in a heaven miles above ie earth and demonstrating his existence by coming down and per-orming miracles from time to time. We just can't think that way any iore. Our God is the Soul of the Universe, its inner mysterious direct-ig Power, and creation itself is the supreme miracle, continually nacted before our eyes. The idea of a virgin birth doesn't help us everence Jesus; it only troubles us as something out of the ordinary, ard to accept, difficult to explain."[49]

Concerning the resurrection of Christ, Dr. Palmer says: "And so the esurrection also has meaning for us only on the spiritual level. That ie body of Jesus should be brought back from the tomb, reanimated nd given a brief additional physical existence for a few days among is followers, helps us not at all. Indeed it only troubles us. It raises far iore questions than it satisfies."[50] From his volume *The New Chris-ian Epic,* after telling us that we have just as much religion today as ny of the authors of the Bible ever had, he goes on to say that the vorld will be saved "not by external miracle, not by blind acceptance f some judicial fiction, but by actually achieving salvation, by man-ind's catching the beauty and greatness and utter inevitableness of Christ's ideal and putting it into practice. And such a salvation comes nly by saviours! David Livingstone in the African forest and Watts O. Pye in China, Dr. Grenfell and John Bunyan, Abraham Lincoln and

Arnold Toynbee and all the rest of the saviours of mankind of all races, ages, and countries must do their perfect work; for not apart from human hopes and dreams and sacrifices can salvation come!"[51] Finally, concerning the Bible, Dr. Palmer says: "Similarly the New Testament grew up around the little collection of St. Paul's Epistles, and for hundreds of years it was uncertain just which books would 'make' the New Testament and which would not. Now this process cannot be stopped! The race goes on building a larger Bible. The real Bible of the intelligent Christian today includes devotional books like *Pilgrim's Progress* and the *Imitation of Christ,* great hymns like the *Te Deum* and Jesus, Lover of My Soul, creeds and confessions like the Apostles' Creed, biographies like those of St. Francis or David Livingstone, poems like *In Memoriam* and *Rabbi Ben Ezra,* great documents of freedom like the Magna Charta and the Emancipation Proclamation, epics like *Paradise Lost* and *The Divine Comedy*. These books have far greater religious influence in our lives and are more continuously and appropriately used in our churches than Esther, Chronicles, or Ecclesiastes. The true and larger Bible is never complete!"[52]

In fact, he concludes his discussion of the atoning work of Christ by saying, "The world is not to be saved by Jesus alone, not by his three hours' agony on the cross merely, but by thousands of men and women who themselves become saviours and give themselves unselfishly even as he did . . . And so Christ shall be reduplicated in a myriad of saviours, and the world be reconciled to the God who is a God of love."[53] Dr. Palmer's view of God, then, is pantheistic; the Bible is not supreme, Christ is not the Son of God, He alone is not the only Saviour of men, and salvation can come to men from almost anybody else, as well as from Christ upon the cross. And this author has been a president of a theological seminary now for nearly fifteen years, preaching in many of the Protestant churches in our land, is prominent in ecclesiastical councils, and guides the theological thought of hundreds of young men. Nothing could be more tragic than this for the future of evangelical Christianity in our land. And there are *many* today in seminaries, and teaching courses on "religion" in our colleges, whose convictions are identical with these.[54]

Let us turn our attention now to an institution of a different faith or at least once of a different faith, namely, the Divinity School of the University of Chicago, at one time related to the Baptist church of this country. We might begin with a statement by one who is most definitely neither conservative nor evangelical, probably not even a modernist, but a strict naturalist, Professor G. P. Conger. In his recent volume, *The Ideologies of Religion,* he boldly says: "Religious naturalism seems to have developed more extensively and consistently at the University of Chicago than anywhere else. Its chief proponents in America have been G. B. Smith and H. N. Wieman; three other Chicago teachers, E. S. Ames, Shailer Mathews, and A. E. Haydon, have much in common with them."[55] Perhaps we would do well to take these men in the order named, though I gathered the evidence concerning this particular matter before I saw Conger's statement. Dr. Gerald Birney Smith became an instructor in Theology in the Divinity School of the University of Chicago in 1900, and was the professor of Christian Theology from 1913–1929. (Some of the men we will refer to appear in the catalogue of the University of Chicago as members of the faculty of the university and not always of the Divinity School. But in the fields of religion and theology, there is little difference, for the Divinity School has always used members of the faculty in Religion and Theology of the university as well as their own professors.) In 1925, Professor Smith, in an article, "Is Theism Essential to Religion?" affirms first that men can be good citizens without appealing to God; secondly, that men can be good scientists without affirming theism; and third, most astonishing of all, that men can be sincerely religious without believing in God. His conclusion is that "theism comes to be a matter of taste rather than a fundamental doctrine."[56] One would suppose then that if all the students sitting before Professor Smith for a quarter of a century announced themselves atheists, they would nevertheless be permitted to graduate from the Divinity School (!) and go into the Christian ministry. Professor Wieman has written extensively. His outstanding thesis in theology seems to be that God is not a person. "If observation and reason make it unmistakably evident that God is a personality, it would be another matter. But observation and reason do not so testify. I believe it can be shown that God is not a personality . . . Under no circumstances can God be thought to be a personality. The idea is self-contradictory. Therefore, we conclude that whatever else God is, He is not a personality . . . God is that kind of interaction between things which generates and magnifies personality in all its highest values."[57] Dr. Wieman has been the professor of the Philosophy of Religion in the Divinity School of the University of Chicago since 1927. Therefore, for nearly twenty years, now, he has been telling students that God is not a person. Dr. Edward Scribner Ames has been dean of the Disciples Divinity House in the University of Chicago since 1927, a member of the Department of Philosophy since 1900, and chairman of that department from 1931–1935. His faith is expressed in these words: "At last religion has come to reckon with the fact that its highest quest is not for the supernatural order but just for natural goodness in largest and fullest measure. The idea of worship as mere praise and adulation of the Creator has become almost irreligion. God has come to be regarded in so imminent and dynamic a way that it seems quite inconsistent to conceive Him as honored and gratified by adoration and flattery, such as were formerly given to tyrants and despots . . . In our democracies men do not bow themselves to the ground, nor prostrate themselves before the mightiest individuals."[58] The Modernism of Dr. Shailer Mathews is too well known even to need discussion here. Probably no man at the University of Chicago has spoken so viciously of God as Professor Haydon, even going so far as to say that "God is dead." These are his words: "We may still say, 'God exists,' but we must mean by 'God' and by 'exist' something entirely different from that which the words have meant in the religious philosophy of the past. God in the old sense, is dead . . . The Parent God, guardian of life and giver of immortality, is no more."[59]

That a great many other seminaries we could name teach this kind of theology, or something near to it, cannot be denied. We are not making a *list* here of modernistic seminaries, and all the professors who are nontheistic in their views. Enough has been said to reveal some of the conditions which are prevailing today in many of the larger and more influential institutions in this country where the future generation of ministers is being trained. The largest seminary of all need but one concluding word. We refer to Union Theological Seminary New York. That its famous president for nine years, Dr. Arthur Cush man McGiffert, not only denied the deity of Christ, but came in his latter days to deny the very existence of a personal and sovereign God is well known, and some of the evidence for this tragedy has appeared in the earlier pages of this book.[60] It is in Union Theological Seminary that one of the greatest enemies of evangelical Christianity of the twentieth century has been teaching now for twenty years. I refer to Dr. Harry Emerson Fosdick. In his famous sermon, "The Peril of Worshiping Jesus," which was distributed by hundreds of thousands of copies, Dr. Fosdick said: "To say that God was in Christ seems to me no theological puzzle. I think God was in my mother, the source of the loveliness that blessed us there! And I rise up from that with a profound sense of what I am doing when I confess my faith that God was in Christ." Dr. Fosdick even went so far as to say: "The world has tried in two ways to get rid of Jesus: first by crucifying Him, and second by worshiping Him . . . He did not fear being opposed; He feared being worshiped."[61] Again and again, Dr. Fosdick has shown his bitter antagonism to everything of a supernatural nature and has insisted, in all of his books, in his classes, and in his church, "We moderns have lost faith in miracles." "This endeavor to believe in miracles and to make faith in them significant, when all the time we are thinking of miracles as indissolubly associated with ancient ignorance and as vanishing when intelligence arrives, is not Christian faith at all . . . Biblical miracles will more and more become unreal ghosts lost in antiquity and, gradually becoming dimmer, will disappear into utter incredulity."[62] Dr. Fosdick denies the inspiration of the Scriptures, the virgin birth, the resurrection and the deity of Christ, and, with his brilliant gifts for expression, he has been allowed to teach these things to young men for twenty years in what is probably the most influential theological seminary in the English world today. We have often wondered how a man like Dr. Henry Sloan Coffin, who, in his early days, declared his faith in the Westminster Confession of Faith, and took a vow to defend the truths therein stated, during his long tenure of office as president of Union Seminary, has allowed to remain on the faculty one like Dr. Fosdick, who could not allow an hour to go by in any classroom, nor a page to be composed under his hand, without denying and ridiculing some sacred truth of the Christian faith.

The Implications of Some Recent Denominational Actions. If the question is asked, "Are our denominations in America" (that is, the larger ones for the most part, speaking now from the standpoint of ecclesiastical organization), "in their official expressions, more or less conservative today than they were at the beginning of the twentieth century?" there can be but one answer. The entire drift in Protestant circles in our country, with rare exceptions, has been toward the left, toward liberalism, and, if one may say it, toward a spirit of indifference as regards the great doctrines of the Christian faith. In 1895 the General Assembly of the Presbyterian Church, U.S.A., issued an official warning to the churches found within the boundaries of its juris diction, advising them that it would be unwise and unsafe to call as pastors men who had been graduated from the Union Theologica Seminary of New York.[63] Less than fifty years have gone by, when, in 1943 the same denomination lifted to the highest office to which it is possible for it to elect anyone, the moderatorship of the General Assem bly, the president of Union Theological Seminary, not only a man who has graduated from Union, but a man who had been for some seven teen years president of Union Theological Seminary, during which time it was far more radical than Union dreamed of being in 1895. The Presbyterian Church in 1924 declined to allow Dr. Fosdick to remain as pastor of the First Presbyterian Church in New York, but Dr. Henry Sloan Coffin, a Presbyterian, allowed Dr. Fosdick to remain on the faculty of the seminary all these years while he was president. The Presbyterian Church once warning us against Union, and refusing a church to one of Union's most famous professors, now elects as its Moderator the president of that very institution. And let no one think that Dr. Coffin is a conservative in the midst of liberals. He himself, in his latest expression of belief, in a chapter on "The Scriptures," in the recently published symposium, *Liberal Christianity,* says this concerning the Bible: "Liberalism is opposed to external authority because it obstructs free response to truth; and the liberal Christians have examined carefully the nature of the authority of the Bible . . . The Gospels conclude with the promise of Jesus to be with His Church in His spirit His followers are not under a law prescribed long ago, but under present Leader . . . And the Spirit's contemporary guidance free

Christianity from any shape of things past, and keeps them advancing under his inspiration to create with him the diviner shape of things to come." [64] I take it from this that Dr. Coffin could well believe that a greater religion than that which we have in Christ might be reasonably expected to be given, some time in history; certainly he means to imply that we ought to have in these modern days some literature even more acceptable, if not divinely inspired, than the pages of a volume written centuries ago. The Word of God concerning the atoning work of the Lord Jesus Christ, and the confession of faith of the Presbyterian Church, says that Christ offered Himself as a sacrifice for sins unto God, but Dr. Coffin says: "The revolt from various theories of the atonement has been due to their unchristian views of God. A father who had to be reconciled to His children, whose wrath had to be appeased or whose forgiveness could be purchased, is not the Father of Jesus Christ—the God in whom He believed and whose character He revealed in His teaching and whose nature was embodied in Himself . . . such a God freely forgives. Certain widely used hymns still perpetuate the theory that God pardons sinners because Christ purchased that pardon by His obedience and suffering. But a forgiveness that is paid for is not forgiveness. The God of the prophets and psalmists, the God and Father of Jesus' own teaching, forgives graciously all who turn to Him in penitence" [65] . . . This is the one whom the Presbyterian denomination, with such a noble ancestry as the Westminster Confession of Faith and the Shorter Catechism, lifts to its highest office.

There was a time when the Methodist Church recommended that Dr. Mitchell, a professor in Boston University, be denied a further contract to teach theology in that institution, because of his liberal views. Now Professor Wieman teaches in Boston University, in the Department of Theology; a member of the Methodist Church, who denies the personality of God. There was a time when the Methodist Church carefully watched the views of its theological professors, and, somewhat, the views of its bishops; now the Methodist Church allows to remain in the bishopric, for example, Dr. William McConnell, who denies the deity of the Lord Jesus Christ. There is no need for adding further illustrations.[66]

There was a time when such a one as Dr. Charles A. Briggs, who in many ways was quite conservative, or a man like Dr. David Swing, could be tried before the Presbyterian Church of this country for liberal views, and a verdict could be found against them.[67] Today if a man suggests a trial for heresy, in many of our great denominations he would be considered a freak and a fanatic. Men would rise up and talk about "bondage" and "dogmatism," and suggest that we were instituting an "inquisition," and that men must be free to think as they please, etc. Great conventions of Protestant denominations today can easily create in their meetings a burning enthusiasm for world peace for prohibition, for church union, for a social manifesto, but in how many of these great denominational conferences do we witness any great exaltation of Jesus Christ as a conference theme, any great passion laying hold of our ecclesiastical leaders to exalt the glory of the Lord Jesus Christ? It cannot be denied that, for the most part, our denominational officials are more concerned with maintaining the membership the wealth and the organization of a denomination, than they are with maintaining the truths of the New Testament. I do not believe that the late Dr. J. Gresham Machen, recognized even by his enemies as one of the keenest thinkers and best equipped New Testament scholars in our country, in any way exaggerated the situation when he said, in 193 "It is a fact whether we like it or not, that the larger and olde Protestant faiths have in their corporate capacity, for the most par ceased to witness in any clear-cut way to the gospel of the Lord Jesu Christ."[68]

The Absence of Faith in God Among the Majority of the Intellectu Leaders of the Western World Today. One of the most serious an tragic anti-religious situations in the western world today is the unden able fact that most of the outstanding leaders of thought of our gener tion, and the generation just gone, are men without any religious fait at all, and for the most part, men who continually throw the gre weight of their influence against all that is identified with supernatura ism, and with the idea of a personal, sovereign, loving God. This fa needs careful consideration and specific illustration. The outstandin authority on historiography in the world today is Benedetto Croce. his now rarely seen book, *The Conduct of Life,* he declares his co viction regarding religion in the following terms: "Religion is mytho ogy; and mythology is a conception of reality where universals are personified, and pure ideas are replaced by a body of imagery, to explain the origin, laws, and purposes of the universe . . . Philosophy overthrows such idols, such objects of worship . . . So Reason is cursed in prose and in verse by numerous souls who cannot overcome the destruction of their gods."[69] The outstanding authority in the same field of historiography in our own country is Dr. James T. Shotwell, for many years the distinguished professor of History in Columbia University, and a rationalist. The one who has had more influence on Psychology than any other individual in the last half century, is, of course, Sigmund Freud. His atheism is known to all. One sentence from his pen is sufficient to indicate what he thinks in this field: "Religious doctrines . . . are all illusions, they do not admit of proof, and no one can be compelled to consider them as true or to believe in them."[70]

The man whose writings have had more influence through his famous *Outline of History,* and his vast output in the fields of Sociology, over younger people in the English world of this century, is H. G. Wells. His hatred of Christ and all that pertains to the Christian religion has been considered in a previous part of this book.[71] Julian Huxley, co-writer with Wells in his well-known and quite brilliantly executed *Outline of Life,* frankly says: "The scientific approach . . . renders either futile or illogical all straightforward personification of divinity."[72] One of the most distinguished classical scholars of this century, probably exercising more influence than any other one man in his own field, in Great Britain or in this country, is Gilbert Murray, who is a follower of Comte. His strict Humanism is revealed in this short confession: "What we mean by 'the divine in man' is, I fear, merely the same thing as the human in God; some sublimation of the highest human qualities which we have projected from ourselves on to the image of this intractably anthropomorphic God created by our own man-thinking and wish-thinking. It is our dream returning to us in the guise of an external being."[73]

That Professors Dewey, Montague, Durant, and Randall, of the Department of Philosophy at Columbia University, are atheists, every one recognizes. A colleague of theirs, in a different department, Dr. Carl Van Doren, one of the leaders in the realm of literature in our country today, in an article of some years ago, "Why I Am an Unbeliever," dared to say: "I do not believe in any God that has ever been devised, in any doctrine that has ever claimed to be revealed, in any scheme of immortality that has ever been expounded . . . The unbelievers have, as I read history, done less harm to the world than the believers."[74] When one adds to this list the names of Bertrand Russell and Albert Einstein, who do not believe in a personal God, Professor Edward Grant Conklin, the distinguished biologist of Princeton University, and the long list of educators, from some of whom we have quoted in previous pages, one begins to realize what the young men of our generation are up against, how deep the darkness of contemporary unbelief rests upon our present generation, and threatens to grow even deeper, as a new generation shall produce an even greater proportion of skeptics, unless heaven should graciously bless us with a revival.

Does the New Testament Teach That the Last Days of This Age Will Be Marked by a Falling Away from the Christian Faith? I do not wish in this book to enter into the disputed questions of Eschatology (aside from the great fundamental doctrine of judgment to come, which we will consider in a later chapter), but I cannot in my own thinking regarding the unbelief of our day, divorce myself entirely from what the New Testament has to say about unbelief in the latter days of this age. Some of my readers may not even believe there will be any latter days, or any end of the age, but the New Testament is the New Testament, and in it the Lord Jesus Christ speaks, and (later) the greatest Christian that ever lived has written some books for our admonition from which the Church has derived strength and power and wisdom for more than eighteen hundred years. Whatever be our views in these matters of Eschatology, we cannot utterly ignore the fact, however we interpret it, that the New Testament does speak of growing unbelief in the end of this age which began by the preaching of the gospel. Our omnipotent and omniscient Lord once asked a question when He was on earth, "When the Son of man cometh shall he find faith on the earth?" or, as the margin of the Revised Version reads, "When the Son of man cometh shall he find *the* faith on earth?"[75] Bishop J. C. Ryle in his well known *Notes on the Gospels,* says, "There will be compar tively few believers upon the earth when He comes again. True faith will be found as rare as it was in the days of Noah when only eight persons entered the ark, and in the days of Lot when only four persons left Sodom."[76] One of the greatest of all modern exegetes, H. A. W. Meyer, said: "In connection with the glad promise, to wit, which Jesus has just given in reference to the elect, there comes painfully into His consciousness the thought of a want of faith in Him He would nevertheless meet with at His *parousia*. This He expresses in the sorrowful question. Theophylact well says, 'indicating in the form of a question the fewness of those who will then be found faithful.' The *pistis* is *the faith in Jesus the Messiah*, which many of His confessors not persevering unto the end will have given up, so that they do not belong to the elect, and He will meet them as unbelievers."[77] Charles Spurgeon, in a sermon on this text which is, in itself, more or less optimistic, frankly says, "My brethren, at the winding up of all things, when revelation shall have received its utmost confirmation, even then faith will be such a rarity on the earth that it is a question if the Lord Himself will find it."[78] One of the greatest of all preachers of modern times, grand and noble, learned and powerful, was Alexander Whyte, who says on this same text, "Christ shall surely find faith, but it will not be strong faith; it will not be bold faith; it will not be generous and venturesome faith; it will not be an overcoming and a victorious faith."[79]

No writer that I know of, however, has seen quite so clearly into the meaning of this question of our Lord's, as Dr. John A. Hutton, for these many years the gifted editor of the *British Weekly*, in his very precious volume, *The Fear of Things*, published in 1911. In a sermon on this text, which he very significantly calls, "A Passion Shadow on the Soul of Jesus," Dr. Hutton says: "It is a very disturbing question which our Lord asks here. It is not really a question, for there was nobody present who could give an answer to it. It is rather an ejaculation, something which He muttered to Himself. Occurring where it occurs, it is like a sigh.

"The words are among the most disturbing in the whole Bible. It is truly an awful idea that perhaps the world as such is getting worse, that with all our enlightenment and freedom, there is something vital to man, which he may slowly be losing, until a day arrives when he shall have lost it utterly. That is a very terrible idea to come into our heads. And it is all the more terrible because our heads, for a long time now, have been full of quite other ideas! We have been talking for the last fifty years about nothing else but evolution, development.

"If there is one idea which above all others had taken up its place within our mind, it is that things are improving, and are bound to improve, with the corollary, of course, that this old world of ours is going to conclude its long business with a final outburst of hallelujahs.

"Coming, therefore, fresh from the rhetoric of modern ideas to these words of Jesus Christ, we are conscious of a kind of contradiction and collapse. We are like people who have their peace broken by sudden news."[80]

William E. Gladstone, who knew probably more about the deeper tendencies in the thoughts and desires of the whole Western world especially the English world at the close of the nineteenth century, than any other one man, was a profound classical scholar, the greatest prime minister England had had for many decades, a devoted churchman, a constant student of the Word of God; his words cannot be easily discredited. Writing to Sir Thomas Ackland, December 3, 1893, when he himself was past eighty, Gladstone looked back across the years and beholding the conditions that were then existing and tendencies then beginning in the realm of church life and thought, he said: "I am rather more painfully impressed with the apprehension that the seen world is gaining upon the unseen. The vast expansion of its apparatus seems to have nothing to balance it. The Church which was the appointed instrument of the world's recovery, seems, taking all its branches together, rather unequal to its work . . .

"I am driven back more and more upon the question, 'When the Son of man cometh, shall he find faith upon the earth?' which cannot be frivolous or unmeaning, since it was put by the Saviour."[81]

The greatest Christian that ever lived, the greatest missionary that ever toiled and suffered for Christ, profoundest theologian the Church has ever known, was the Apostle Paul. Now that I have been fair, I trust, in quoting great leaders of thought who are against Christianity I will not be accused of narrowness, if I quote one who thoroughly believed in the Christian faith. The Apostle Paul often reminds us that, in the last days, there *will be* a tragic departure from the faith, and that the spirit of delusion will mysteriously fall upon men. In his second letter to the Thessalonians, he writes: "For the mystery of lawlessness doth already work: only there is one that restraineth now, until he be taken out of the way. And then shall be revealed the lawless one, whom the Lord Jesus shall slay with the breath of His mouth, and bring to nought by the manifestation of His coming; even He, whose coming is according to the working of Satan with all power and signs and lying wonders and with all deceit of unrighteousness for them that perish; because they received not the love of the truth, that they might be saved. And for this cause, God sendeth them a working of error, that they should believe a lie: that they all might be judged who believed not the truth, but had pleasure in unrighteousness."[82] At the end of his life, glorious, victorious, triumphant, joyful, blessed life, approaching the hour of his death, without fear, full of hope, longing to see the face of the Lord, and knowing he soon would, the same great apostle, instead of saying that he believed that it would not be long before the gospel he preached would bring everyone within its embrace, said, by divine inspiration, "The Spirit speaketh expressly that in latter times some shall fall away from the faith, giving heed to seducing spirits and doctrines of demons."[83] In his last epistle, he writes even more emphatically on this particular matter. After describing with some eighteen or twenty different phrases the awful, brutal, wild, godless character of men, as they will be "in the last days," he adds that these also "withstand the truth; men corrupted in mind, reprobates concerning the faith." When he comes to his last charge, he says to Timothy, and to the Church of Christ: "I charge thee in the sight of God, and of Christ Jesus, who shall judge the living and the dead, and by his appearing and his kingdom: preach the word; be urgent in season, out of season; reprove, rebuke, exhort, with all longsuffering and teaching. For the time will come when they will not endure the sound doctrine, but, having itching ears, will heap to themselves teachers after their own lusts; and will turn away their ears from the truth, and turn aside unto fables."[84]

Dr. Geerhardus Vos has rightly said, "The idea of antichrist in general and that of apostasy in particular reminds us that we may not expect an uninterrupted progress of the Christianization of the world until the parousia. As the reign of truth will be extended, so the forces of evil will gather strength, especially toward the end. The universal sway of the kingdom of God cannot be expected from missionary effort alone; it requires the eschatological interposition of God."[85]

And yet, I would not close this chapter with a note of pessimism, rather with a note of encouragement. Out of these verses which we have quoted from the last passage that Paul ever wrote, the saintly late Bishop H. C. G. Moule brings out a wonderful truth concluding with a strong exhortation, and it is this with which I would like to close my chapter: "There is present still around him, in fair measure, a willingness to listen, worship, and obey; he must use it to the uttermost for the message of Christ, the preaching of pardon, and holiness, and heaven. Not very long yet, and he will find his congregations dwindling, and will learn that many of the disciples are following one or another of a band of uncommissioned propagandists whom they have invited in to tell them something newer, something more mysterious, something more alluring to curiosity, than the gospel of the Crucified and the dutiful path of holiness. They will be listening to the 'myths,' nebulous stories and reveries of 'Aeons,' of 'Depths' and of 'Silences,' things pretending to solve the riddle of existence and to emancipate the spirit from its material chain, but not at all tending to make sin hateful, holiness dear, or the Christ of Bethlehem and Calvary glorious. No, *that* message will be neglected, if not actually scouted. It will be put away as a thing belonging to the lower levels of thought; cold, bare, angular; the seekers of a wisdom worthy of elect human spirits must turn another way than this! Yet all the while that other way will be the 'broad way, which leadeth to destruction'; a 'wisdom' which will stifle the conscience and harden the heart through its flattery of the mind.

"Well, Timothy must all the more 'devote himself,' while yet he can find hearers, to the divine, unfashionable, man-humbling, Christ-glorifying 'Word'—remembering God, and Christ, and the Appearing and the Kingdom. Through that message the eternal Spirit can and will yet work miracles in men. Aye, and even when it shall seem as if the whole world has gone after the pseudo-gospel, and the days for winning a hearing may be thought to be over, still let him 'devote himself' to the delivery of his Master's message not only 'in' but 'out of season.' Some will still be listening; more will listen than he knows; and a brighter day will even yet dawn again." [86]

Chapter III

SOME REASONS FOR THE UNBELIEF OF MEN AND THEIR ANTAGONISM TO GOD

No man ever spake with such power, so clearly and convincingly, every word supported by a flawless character, yearning only that men should come out of darkness into light and out of bondage into liberty, as the Lord Jesus Christ, during His three years on earth. Strange that He who was the truth was rejected, that against the light which shone through Him, men turned their backs, that the gift of eternal life which He gave, some spurned, and that the truths which He set forth many refused to believe. So strange a phenomenon was this, that the very truth itself should be rejected of men that our Lord, while teaching in Jerusalem, in mid-October, A.D. 29, some six months before His crucifixion, was compelled to ask His listeners the searching question, "If I say the truth why do ye not believe me?"[1] This is a reasonable chapter in which these words occur, the eighth chapter of John's Gospel. Here in this one discourse our Lord describes Himself as truth, and as proclaiming the truth, "A man who told you the truth." He adds the astonishing statement that He came from the Father, had never done anything to displease the Father, that He actually had proceeded from God in a way in which, of course, no other being ever has proceeded. He then declares Himself to be without sin, and challenges His listeners, who contradicted this assertion. In fact, the sinlessness of His character and the truthfulness of His message are both found in the same verse, in succeeding interrogations: "Which of you convicteth me of sin? If I say the truth, why do ye not believe me?" As Westcott has remarked, "The absence of sin includes necessarily the absence of falsehood."[2] Our Lord answered His own question with a knowledge of the human heart and of the deeper reasons for the unbelief of men beyond anything that the natural man himself would ever be able to discover. "He that is of God heareth the words of God: for this cause ye hear them not, because ye are not of God." Godet's comment here should be carefully pondered. "We must imagine this question as followed by a pause sufficient to give opportunity to whoever should wish to accuse Him to be heard . . . No one opens his mouth. The admission involved in this silence serves as a premise for the following argument. In the face of His innocence which has just been established He leaves them a moment, now to pass judgment on their conduct towards Him. After this silence, He pronounces the sentence. The expression *to be of God* indicates the state of a soul which has placed itself and which now is, under the influence of divine action. It is the opposite of the phrase *no truth,* affirmed with regard to Satan. This state does not exclude, but implies, the predetermination of the man."[3] "'These Jews see and know that what Jesus says is truth, and for that very reason they spurn it. The fault is not in Jesus, that He did not make the truth plain enough as truth, that if He had done better in this regard they would have believed. The reverse is the fact. The more the Jews were made to realize that they were face to face with genuine truth, the more they struggled to rid themselves of it at all hazard. An unreasonable act cannot have a reasonable explanation. When truth is rejected because it is truth all that can be said is that the act is the heart of unreason, is vicious, devilish, and some times self-condemned."[4] It is this question that Jesus asked, "Why do ye not believe?" that we would like to face in this chapter, with some thoroughness.

Some Preliminary Considerations. Before entering upon a more or less exhaustive treatment of this subject, the causes for unbelief (as much as our space permits), a few preliminary considerations should be set forth. In the first place we are not in this chapter attempting to discuss why men disbelieve certain specific truths, as for example, the divine origin of the Bible, the miraculous conception of Christ, or His resurrection. Reasons why men reject these, and other truths, will be discussed in later sections of this volume, but here we want to face, not the rejection of any one particular Christian doctrine, but unbelief as a whole, the state of universal unbelief now developing over the world, which fundamentally and categorically refuses to believe in the supernatural, and denies the reality of a personal God.

There is considerable difference between not believing a certain truth, and fighting against that truth, or the body of doctrines of which it is a part. There are vast multitudes of people in the world today who believe nothing but who, at the same time, are really indifferent to the whole problem involved in their denial. Thus, e.g., there are many people who in their hearts really do not recognize God, but are so indifferent to the subject of whether God is or not, that they are not even interested in spreading their own atheistic convictions. On the other hand, there are some who make the supreme object of life the propagation of skepticism, who attempt to inject the virus of their own unbelief into the veins of all with whom they come in contact, and, when corporately united as in Russia, set out with the intention of destroying every vestige of religion among the people of the earth. Both of these aspects of unbelief and antagonism to God are brought together in this chapter.

It is sometimes difficult to distinguish between *causes* for unbelief, *manifestations* of unbelief, and the *results* proceeding from unbelief. Certainly the darkness of the mind of natural man and a supreme devotion to the material things of life might strictly be called *causes* for unbelief. When, however, we come to such a matter as the influence of the atmosphere of unbelief, the spirit of unbelief which rests upon our modern world, it is difficult to say which is the more true, that unbelief has brought about this unbelieving age, or that our age, characterized fundamentally by skepticism, is the cause for men rejecting the truth of God and all that is involved in such a denial.

The author would be the first to admit that he has not exhausted this subject. In the first place, while the evidence of unbelief is vast, the material for studying the *causes* of unbelief is not so abundant. Men are perfectly willing to boldly declare their own skepticism, but not many of them have been willing to carefully analyze the reason *why* they have come to such skeptical positions. Furthermore, I believe there are deep and mysterious causes for the depth, and vigor, and universality of the unbelief of our modern age, possibly beyond the full comprehension of finite minds. The subject is worthy of ten years of study but I do not have the ten years to give to it. I suppose many scoffers agnostics, unbelievers who may read here and there in this volume and I pray there may be many, will object to one fundamental procedure to which I have frequently resorted in this particular chapter, and that is that I have attempted to examine this whole problem of disbelief in the light of the Word of God. Yet I make no apology for doing so. Philosophers do not hesitate to quote Plato and Aristotle; in fact, they rest many of their conclusions on the assertions of these early sages. Historians writing of the ancient world would never hesitate to quote from Herodotus, Pliny, or Suetonius, as dependable authorities. Now no man ever brought such a blessing to the world as the Lord Jesus; no man ever saw so deeply into the human heart as He; no man ever brought such deliverances to men. It is reasonable to give the words of Jesus just as much weight as the words of any ancient philosopher, or modern psychologist. The Apostle Paul understood more of the human soul, its conflicts, its hopes, its disappointments, its possibilities, than any other man of the first century, apart from our Lord. He accomplished an enormous amount of work. His labors changed the face of the Roman world. He was a man of strong and powerful character, and has exerted an enormous influence over men for nineteen hundred years. I do not hesitate to quote from the Apostle Paul, and to accept what he says concerning causes and manifestations of unbelief, not with as much assurance as I would the statements of the atheist John Dewey, or the philosopher Professor Montague, but even more. The writer of the epistle to the Hebrews in a famous passage says that, "The Word of God is living and acting, and sharper than any two-edged sword, and piercing even to the dividing of soul and spirit, of both joints and marrow, and quick to discern the thoughts and intents of the heart. And there is no creature that is not manifest in his sight: but all things are naked and laid open before the eyes of him with whom we have to do."[5] To discover some of the causes for the cancer of unbelief I am using as a guide the Word of God. Natural man, in his pride, has never cared to devise a surgical knife to expose these dark depths of man's soul.

Man Fallen Away from God Has a Bias Against God. Both the Word of God and the history of the human race testify to this astonishing truth that man, in having fallen away from God, has developed a strange antagonism against God. Someone will at once say, "Oh, but don't you know that in these modern days, when the history of man and his continuous progress are dominated by an evolutionary conception, don't you know that men today cannot be persuaded to believe in any such thing as a falling away from God?" Well, it is not my business, in a volume like this, to consider the fall of man: we have more than enough to occupy our attention without trying to cover the whole gamut of theology. Yet in a work dealing with apologetic matters such as this volume discusses, I cannot pass by this fundamental idea of an early fall of man without bringing to the attention of my readers the verdict of one of the greatest scholars and humanists of the last half century, Sir William Mitchell Ramsay, probably the greatest authority on the life of St. Paul, and the writings of St. Luke, in modern times. Sir William Ramsay held the highest scholastic positions his country could offer him, was honored by degrees from universities throughout Europe and in our own country, and wrote books that changed the whole tendency of Pauline literature. His volumes were consulted by every important New Testament scholar in the Western world. After a lifetime spent in the study of the ancient Greek and Roman world, especially the religions of those times, together with an uninterrupted devotion to the writings of St. Luke, and the historical aspects of the work of St. Paul, this is his verdict concerning the necessity for believing in an original departure of man from the truth which once had been given to him:

"Nowadays we are all devotees of the theory of development. It is no longer a theory. It has become the basis and guiding principle of our thought and mind. We must see development everywhere. But it is necessary to be very sure first of all that we have got hold of the right law of development in history; and we are sometimes too hasty. We can easily arrange religions in a series from the lowest to the highest, and we are wont to assume that this series represents the historical development of religion from the most primitive to the most advanced. The fetish, the totem and the sacred animals, and so up step by step to Jehovah and the Ark of the Covenant. Is that the true line? You observe that the assumptions here are very serious. Is the modern savage really primitive? Paul would have said that he represents the last stage of degeneration, that he is the end and not the beginning, that he has lost almost everything that is really primitive, that he has fallen so completely from the ancient harmony with the order of nature and sympathy with the Divine as to be on the verge of death, and an outrage on the world and on human nature. Who is right, Paul or the moderns? For my own part, I confess that my experience and reading show nothing to confirm the modern assumptions in religious history, and a great deal to confirm Paul. Whatever evidence exists, with the rarest exceptions, the history of religion among men is a history of degeneration; and the development of a few Western nations in invention and in civilization during recent centuries should not blind us to the fact that among the vast majority of the nations the history of manners and civilization is a story of degeneration. Wherever you find a religion that grows purer and loftier, you find the prophet, the thinker, the teacher, who is in sympathy with the Divine, and he tells you that he is speaking the message of God, not his own message. Are these prophets all impostors and deceivers? Or are they speaking the truth? Is it not the fact of human history that man, standing alone, degenerates; and that he progresses only where there is in him so much sympathy with and devotion to the Divine life as to keep the social body pure and sweet and healthy?"[6]

To quote Professor Ramsay from another volume. "We hold that revelation of the divine to the human is a necessary part of the order of nature, and therefore is, in the strictest sense, 'natural'; and also that all revelation of the divine to the human nature must necessarily be 'superhuman.' The nations had one by one rejected that revelation, or, as we might say, in modern phraseology, their history had become a process of degeneration. After the beginning of learning, of comprehension, and of improvement, their will and desire soon became degraded. The result was a steady process of degradation, folly, vice, crime, which St. Paul pens in terrible colors. History justifies this picture of the nations over which St. Paul's view extended. Where we can trace the outlines of their history over a sufficient time, we find that in the earlier stage and up to a certain point, their religious ideas and rites were simpler, higher, and purer. Sometimes we can trace a considerable period of development in advance. But in every case, the development turns to degeneration, and throughout the Graeco-Roman world the belief was general and thoroughly justified, that the state of immorality in the first century was much more degraded than it had been several centuries earlier. In religion the number of gods had been multiplied, but its hold on the belief of men had been weakened, and its worst characteristics had been strengthened, while any good features in it had almost wholly disappeared."[7]

After this digression, let me reaffirm what was said at the beginning of this part of our chapter, that man, having turned from God, developed a hatred for God. In the very chapter which Sir William Ramsay is here discussing, where Paul outlines his own philosophy of history, the first chapter of Romans, the apostle speaks of men as "haters of God."[8] In the same Epistle, in an altogether different context, St. Paul returns to the idea in declaring that, "the mind of the flesh is enmity against God."[9] Writing to the Colossians he concisely declares that "men by their wicked works have become the enemies of God."[10] This animosity is expressed most graphically in the opening of the second Psalm: "Why do the nations rage, and the peoples meditate a vain thing? The kings of the earth set themselves, and the rulers take counsel together, Against Jehovah, and against his anointed, saying, Let us break their bonds asunder, and cast away their cords from us."[11] As the famous German theologian Julius Müller wrote some years ago, in the greatest treatise on the doctrine of sin that has probably ever appeared, "There is no contradiction in maintaining that an awe of God may linger in the soul, in connection with aversion against God and everything Godlike. It is founded in the very exalted nature of man created as in the likeness of God, that when he has once estranged himself from God, especially if at some earlier period he has expressed something of living fellowship with God, that he more easily lapses into a concealed hatred against God, then into dead indifference. He cannot easily, wholly withdraw himself from the silent, knowing consciousness of his essential obligation to God, although he incessantly strives to do so, and feels himself driven to react against the same."[12] Just so men hated Christ because of their own evil hearts, and their refusal to give up sin and embrace the holy Son of God. As Professor Flint said years ago, "There is that in human nature which makes it possible for men to hate religion because of, and in the measure of its purity and excellence."[13] Even in our own day when men are so prone to exalt humanity, decry religion, and try to persuade men that we are actually on the threshold of a new era of human welfare, when we won't need God, or prayer, or church, or a Bible, it is refreshing to hear a word from Oxford University, by one of its finest Christian scholars, Dr. Herbert H. Farmer, which frankly acknowledges with grief that "Many people find belief in God difficult because there is in their mind a bias which predisposes them against it. Needless to say, the bias is not often a conscious one. Biases seldom are. The conclusion to which a bias impels usually seems reasonable enough in itself, and supporting arguments are soon found which make it seem more reasonable still. None the less, the fact remains that the conclusion is come to primarily because of the bias and only secondarily, if at all, because of the arguments. The latter are found afterwards and often appear astonishingly unconvincing to anybody who has not the same bias to assist his convictions."[14] Sinful man is biased against God.

The Darkness of the Mind of Natural Man. The New Testament epistles emphasize continually, in striking sentences, with profound insight, the constitutional darkness of the mind of fallen man. For some strange reason, not only do our theological treatises, for the most part, fail to give to this subject the prominence it receives in the writings of the Apostles, but even works on New Testament psychology here are somewhat silent. In works by outstanding expositors of the Word on the more important passages of the New Testament setting forth the condition of unregenerated man, there seem to be none which bear a direct relation to the subject we are discussing in this chapter, some reasons for the unbelief of men. It is necessary, therefore, to give it some attention in this particular chapter. In St. Paul's remarkable survey of the historic deterioration of mankind from a spiritual and material standpoint, to which we have previously referred, he tells us that men "because that, knowing God, they glorified Him not as God; neither gave thanks; but *became vain in their reasoning and their senseless heart was darkened.*"[15] The words of Godet here deserve the most careful consideration, "Now man could not remain stationary. Not walking forwards in the way of *active religion,* he could only stray into a false path, having neglected to set God before it as the supreme object of its activity, the understanding was reduced to work *in vacuo;* it was in some sort *made futile;* it peopled the universe with fictions and chimeras. The term translated *reasonings* is always taken by the writers of the New Testament in an unfavourable sense; it denotes the unregulated activity of the *understanding,* in the service of a corrupt heart. The corruption of the heart went side by side with the errors of reason, of which it is at once the cause and the effect. The *heart* is, in the New Testament, as in the Old, the central seat of personal life, that inner power which determines at once the activity of the understanding and the direction of the will. Destitute of its true object, through its refusal to be thankful to God as God, the heart of man is filled with inspirations of *darkness;* there are the guilty lusts inspired by the egoistic love of the creature and self."[16] Approaching the conclusions of this sweeping survey of man's tragic history, Paul emphasizes the same truth in the phrase, "without understanding."

The same Apostle in his second letter to the Corinthians, supplements this teaching concerning the darkness of the mind of fallen man by insisting upon its satanic origination, when he says that of those who are perishing, in whom the Gospel is failing, "The God of this world hath blinded the minds of the unbelieving that the light of the Gospel of the glory of Christ—whose is the image of God, should not dawn upon them."[17] The comment of Charles Hodge here is infinitely more important than any I could make myself, "Satan is here said to assert such an influence over those who believe not as to prevent their apprehending the glory of the Gospel. This control of Satan over the human mind, although so effectual, is analogous to the influence of one created intellect over another in other cases, and therefore is perfectly consistent with free agency and responsibility. It should, however, make us feel our danger and need of divine assistance, seeing that we have to contend not only against the influence of the rulers of darkness; the pantocrators of this world . . . The blindness abides in all humanity apart from those who believe and are regenerated, whose minds have been renewed by the Spirit of God."[18] So the Apostle writes to the Ephesians that men are "darkened in their understanding, alienated from the life of God because of the ignorance that is in them, because of the hardening of their hearts." In the same Epistle, he reminds those who were in the Christian church that they "were once darkness."[19] To quote Hodge once again, "Darkness of mind is the cause of ignorance, ignorance and consequent obduracy of heart are the cause of alienation from God. This is both the logical and theological sequence. The soul in its natural state cannot discern the things of God, therefore it does not know them, therefore the heart is hard. The blind cannot see . . . you cannot heal them; by light the eye must first be opened, then comes vision, and then joy, and love. Of the heathen the Apostle says a film is over their eyes and they are alienated from God because of the ignorance. This dreadful fact we ought never to forget, it explains many things that are otherwise utterly inexplicable."[20]

No serious Christian can help but ask himself at times, "Why are so many of the great intellectual leaders of modern times enemies of the Christian faith? Why is it that these things which are so true concerning Christ and His redemption are not immediately accepted as true by the great mass of mankind?" Here is the answer which the Apostle gave to the church at the very threshold of its glorious history—the minds of men are *darkened*. There is in this verse one word which needs particular emphasis, the one here translated *blindness,* which should be more accurately translated *hardness*. The Greek word is *porosis,* from which comes our word *porous,* originally meaning hardening of the skin, and at times used by medical writers in referring to callus formed at the end of fractured bones. "Hence from the insensibility of the parts covered with hard skin, the verb means to make dull or insensible."[21] This idea is picked up again in the very next verse where these same men are said to be "past feeling." "The disease began in the callous heart. It bluntly hardened itself against impression and warning, and left the mind uninformed and indifferent, alienated itself from the life of God, and was at last shrouded in the shadow of death."[22] This certainly describes the condition of vast multitudes of people today.

With this brief consideration of Paul's teaching concerning the darkness of the human mind, we can better understand what he means in the famous passage, near the beginning of his first Epistle to the Corinthians when he says, "The natural man receiveth not the things of the Spirit of God; for they are foolishness unto him; neither indeed can he know them, because they are spiritually discerned."[23] Likewise at the very end of his ministry, although he had seen thousands of people born again, coming out of darkness into light of the Gospel, and although he knew the mind of men in his age probably better than any other man of the first century, his verdict of mankind as a whole, apart from the Gospel, was that they were "corrupted in mind and bereft of truth."[24] It is to this condition of darkness that our Lord Himself refers, in the Sermon on the Mount, "If thine eye be evil, thy whole body shall be full of darkness. If therefore the light that is in thee be darkness, how great is the darkness."[25]

Professor Candlish, in his great volume on the first Epistle of John, from which we never tire of quoting, and to which we hope to direct the attention of men as often as we can, has written with the profoundest understanding concerning this darkness of the human mind, and we believe that in a volume such as ours, though the quotation is somewhat long, it is important to insert it. "Now, without making too much of the figure, let the one thought of darkness being that which hides, dwell in our minds; and by the test of that thought let us try ourselves. Are we living, practically in a moral and spiritual atmosphere, such as may cause distorted or disturbed vision, and so admit of things appearing different from what they really are? Is the room we sit in so shaded that what we care not to look for may escape our observation, and the somewhat coarse or crazy furniture may be skilfully arranged: its blemishes varnished over; its doubtful beauties magnified? . . .

"It is not merely that my walking thus in darkness is so irreconcilable with my having fellowship with him who 'is light and in whom is no darkness at all,' that to claim such fellowship is to lie. That is implied in this statement. But it is not all that is implied in it. The walking in darkness is itself the lie; the acted, not spoken, untruth. Apart from anything I may say, my walking in darkness is in itself practical lying. I do not the truth. I am not acting truly. I am not willing to have all that I do and all that I am brought fairly out and placed fully in the broad clear light of truth. I would wish it to be excused, or explained, or somehow obscured or coloured; huddled up or hurried over. I am not for having it exposed in the glaring sunshine. There is something in or about it that to some extent needs and courts the shade.

Therefore I lie and do not the truth. And I cannot have fellowship with God. For to have fellowship with Him who is light is to walk in darkness no more. It is to be altogether open, upright, sincere."[26]

After being cursed with a disease that robs them of power to behold spiritual truth, without divine aid, the Apostle in the last letter which he ever wrote, describes the same men, not only as constitutionally ignorant of the truth, but as deliberately contending against the truth, "So do these *withstand* the truth, men corrupted in mind, reprobates concerning the Faith."[27] These words accurately describe many of those whose hatred of the Christian faith we have considered in previous passages of this volume.

Such a darkened mind possessed by man makes him so easily the subject and dupe of error. That giant among all the Puritans, John Owen, in his (now so seldom read) profound work, *Nature and Causes of Apostasy from the Gospel,* brings this out as no other writer with whom we are acquainted, "Error once received under the notion of truth takes firm root in the carnal mind of men, then truth doth or can not whilst their minds are so carnal, and the reason of it is because all error is some way suited unto the mind as thus depraved and there is nothing in it that is enmity thereto."[28]

The Pride of Man. When our Lord said "How can ye believe who receive glory one of another, and the glory that cometh from the only God ye seek not?"[29] he gave one of the major reasons why men have been unwilling to recognize a holy, sovereign God. When man says he believes in a Supreme Being, and especially in Jesus Christ His Son, he at the same time, if he is honest, confesses that God is holy, and he, himself, unholy, that God is independent and can do according to His own will, while man is dependent. All this is humiliating; it takes away any cause for pride, for if there is one thing that man has always liked to feel it is that he is sufficient for all things, that he is going to bring about a better world by his own ingenuity, that he is the greatest and highest and most important phenomenon in the world, and that beyond him there is nothing worth considering. The world through its own wisdom has rejected God. Let us take one or two statements of contemporary leaders of thought, as confirmation not only of man's pride but of his confessed and arrogant pride. Take, for example, the late Dr. Henry Fairfield Osborn, until his death an internationally recognized anthropologist, director for many years of the American Museum of Natural History. In one of his later books he compresses into a single sentence this very fact we have been discussing. "In truth from the period of the early ages of Greek thought, man has been eager to discover some natural cause of evolution and to abandon the idea of supernatural invention in the order of nature."[30] Clearly Dr. Osborn means men have made every attempt to get rid of even the idea of God, which he calls an "invention." At the conclusion of the third Annual Conference on Science and Philosophy and Religion in Their Relation to the Democratic Way of Life, held in New York City in the summer of 1942, in a formal statement given out as the final thought of the conference, is this amazing declaration: "A world which has gained a unique sense of power through its inventive ability and its scientific knowledge, which has been trained to think in concrete terms and their immediate ends, and which enjoys the thrill of a continually changing panorama of obtainable knowledge is peculiarly resistant to the teachings of religion with its emphasis on ultimate objectives, and absolute truths."[31] This was written in the midst of a war that was showing man to be a beast, with civilization going down in awful ruin, and man retreating into the darkness of the Middle Ages, yet these scholars unite in saying that contemporary knowledge is so wonderful that it must resist the teachings of religion. Well, this is exactly what Brunner means when, speaking of the world-wide antagonism to Christianity, he says: "Behind it, as its real source, lies the emancipation of reason, the self-sufficiency of the natural man."[32] This whole idea of the increasing pride of modern man finds an interesting confirmation in a nontheological work, a recently published survey of European civilization, by a well-known contemporary historian, in a chapter significantly called "The Intellectual Revolution," in which we are told, "The new learning offered man a more vain-glorious picture of himself, and rooted itself in his pride; whereas his religious beliefs had been the fruit of his humility."[33] No word of Calvinistic theology could better express what we are attempting here to state than this single sentence from a secular work, "The Christian religion begets humanity, modern civilization creating sins. As pride increases humility decreases and as man finds himself self-sufficient he will discard his religious convictions, or having none, he will fight those of others."

To quote once again from the work by the Puritan Owen, in summarizing this particular truth, "The innate *pride and vanity of the minds of men* is another means whereby they are disposed and inclined unto an apostasy from the profession of evangelical truth. With respect hereunto the design and work of the gospel is, to 'cast down imaginations, and every high thing exalteth itself against the knowledge of God,' taught therein, 'bringing into captivity every thought to the obedience of Christ.' The mind of man is naturally lifted up with high thoughts in itself.

"In all things the mind of man would be its own measure, guide, and rule, continually teeming with these two evils:

"It exalts *imaginations* of its own, which it loves, applauds, dotes on, and adheres unto. This is the original of heresy, this hath given birth, growth, and progress, to error; for 'God hath made man upright, but they have sought out many inventions.' Seeking out and exalting inventions of our own, in things spiritual and religious, is the principal and most pernicious consequent of our fall from that state of uprightness wherein of God we were created.

"It makes *itself* the sole and *absolute judge* of what is divinely proposed unto it, whether it be true or false, good or evil, to be received or rejected, without desire or expectation of any supernatural guidance or assistance; and whatever is unsuited unto its own prejudicate imaginations, it is ready to scorn and despise.

"That, therefore, which we are now to demonstrate is, that where this pride and principle are predominant, where the one is not mortified by grace nor the other eradicated by spiritual light, there men can never receive the truths of the gospel in a due manner, and are ready to renounce them when they have by any means been brought unto the profession of them for a season."[34]

The Determination to Live without God. The ancient Psalmist, who knew the human heart so well, and who knew God, wrote thousands of lines that have brought comfort, strength and cleansing to human hearts through nearly thirty centuries, beyond all the comfort and strength that have ever been derived from the pages of

Homer and Plato, Aristotle, Cicero, and Seneca together, was not sarcastic or bitter, or one fraction of a centimeter away from the truth, when he wrote, "The fool hath said in his heart, there is no God." Literally this should read, "The fool hath said in his heart—no God,"[35] i.e., he is determined not to have God. It is the verdict of his heart that for him there will be no God. As one of the greatest expositors of modern times once said, with truest insight, "The fool's saying in his heart *there is no God,* implies his seeking out arguments to persuade himself that there is none. Where the heart is concerned, it will quickly employ the head; and reason shall be put to the drudgery of humoring a depraved mind, by providing it with a suitable hypothesis. The invention must be set a-work to hammer out something that may sit easy upon an atheistical disposition . . . For the fool to say in his heart *there is no God,* implies not only a seeking for reasons and arguments, but also a marvelous readiness to acquiesce in any seeming probability or appearance of reason that may make for his opinion."[36]

The late Professor David Smith, scholar, historian, and preacher (and the author of this book makes no apology at all for quoting from some of the great preachers of the Western world—no apology at all, for he is convinced that a minister, as well educated as any professor, spending his life with the Word of God, and dealing with the souls of men, constantly in prayer, living for others, listened to by thousands, writing books that bring the greatest blessing, he believes that such men have as much right to be heard, and have as keen an understanding of truth, as any unbelieving professor, be he philosopher, sociologist, or psychologist, sitting in any university chair in the world) —David Smith has a very fine paragraph on this verse. He reminds us first that the Hebrew word for "fool" means literally *withered,* being the word which occurs in the First Psalm, where it is said of the godly man that he is "like a tree planted by the streams of water, that bringeth forth its fruit in its season, whose leaf does not *wither.*" "And so the fool here is one whose soul is withered, shrivelled, and atrophied, and if you glance over the Psalm, you will see what it is that has wrought the mischief. It is not intellectual aberration but moral depravity—the blight of uncleanness, the canker of corruption. 'They are corrupt, they have done abominable works; there is none that doeth good. They are all gone aside; they are together become filthy; there is none that doeth good, no, not one.' It is this that withers the soul; and it is the man whose heart has thus been eaten out of him that says and thinks that 'there is no God.'"[37]

What the Psalmist of the old covenant declared, the great Apostle of the Christian faith reaffirmed, when speaking of mankind as a whole, after reviewing a tragic decline and deterioration from its original state. In his Roman Epistle he affirms that men had given themselves to idolatry and to unspeakable wickedness because, "they refused to have God in their knowledge."[38] The verb translated *refused* means literally "to put to the test, to examine, to approve," and, when followed by the infinitive, means "to think it not worth the trouble to retain the knowledge of God. They considered religion as useless, and supposed they could live without God." If ever there was a time when humanity as a whole seems to be determined to live without recognizing God, individually, socially, governmentally, and in the affairs of world parliaments, that time is now. Our current fiction would never indicate to a visitor to this world that men were recognizing God, but rather ignoring Him. When men are determined not to let God rule in their lives, or, worse, when they are determined, as far as they are able, in no way to recognize God, then, when in one way or another, the fact of God, the commandments of God, the holiness of God, and the Word of God, are presented to them, or in some way come to their attention, they are compelled, if they are going to persist in their godlessness, to create reasons for their unbelief. In our day it is not so much that men cannot believe in God because the facts of life contradict Him, or deny His existence, but *men are determined not to believe in God,* because the way they want to live requires a freedom from all divine restraint.

Early Manifestations of Hatred to God. Why I do not know, but it cannot be denied that autobiographical records clearly indicate that some who in their maturity become noted advocates of atheism, or skeptics, have experiences, even in childhood, in which they actually hate God. Thus for instance such a person as H. G. Wells could say of his early boyhood, "I was so set against God . . . He and His hell were the nightmares of my childhood; I hated Him while I still believed in Him, and who could help but hate? I thought of Him as a fantastic monster perpetually spying, perpetually listening, perpetually waiting to condemn me . . . when I was still only a child of thirteen, by the grace of the true God in me I flung this Light out of my mind and for many years, until I came to see that God Himself had done this thing for me, the name of God meant nothing to me but the hideous scar in my heart where a fearful demon had been."[39] It is not only with our advanced atheists, but with some of our teachers of theology that such a hatred of divine truth in the days of youth has been experienced. Dr. Walter Marshall Horton, in an autobiographical passage of a few years ago wrote, "I still remember the curdling nausea which overwhelmed me when I was first taken to Sunday school; my father stopped to speak to a friend outside the chapel door, while inside arose the alarming sound of a hymn loudly chanted by young and old together—'At the cross where I first saw the light . . .' until my father felt me tugging in terror at his hand and took me home."[40]

Why such men as Wesley and Spurgeon could know exalted experiences of love for God, when children, and other men know an actual hatred for God when in their early years, I do not attempt to explain. I would only call attention to a sad phrase in Mark's account of the demon-possessed lad, whom the Lord delivered immediately after his Transfiguration. When Jesus asked the boy's father, "How long time is it since this hath come unto him?" the father replied, "From a child."[41] Whatever explanation we may give, at least the account indicates definitely that this boy had been beset by an evil spirit from early childhood.

Educational Influences That by Their Character Must Create an Attitude of Skepticism. It cannot be doubted that a vast number of men today, between the ages of twenty-five and fifty, are confirmed unbelievers, living apart from any recognition of God, with no reverence for the Word of God, and no knowledge of it, because of the skeptical influences that surrounded and profoundly influenced them during their collegiate and graduate academic life. As Professor W. Macneile Dixon well said, in his Gifford Lectures of a few years ago, "All reasoning is in a manner biased, and the bias is to the nature, surrounding and education of the thinker."[42] Personally, I believe that this particular cause for contemporary unbelief has been too continually ignored. Many men today do not believe, not because the processes of logical thought have led them to a denial of God, but because while at school they had injected into their minds the spirit of unbelief and skepticism of which their older professors were proudly boasting. Let us take an example from the earlier training of one whom we have just mentioned, Dr. Horton of Oberlin, who took his M.A. and Ph.D. degrees at Columbia University. "It was generally understood that there was but one true philosophy, and Dewey was its prophet." We should remember, however, that Dewey is an atheist, a confirmed antisupernaturalist, and that when these young men accepted Dewey's philosophy, they rejected God, and everything that was uniquely identified with the Christian religion. In fact, Professor Horton admits this: "In the discussion among students majoring in philosophy, it was generally taken for granted that religion was no more than an interesting survival of an early period in mental evolution. It was commonly supposed that philosophy had now disposed for good of those questions concerning the ultimate nature of things and the ultimate meaning of life with which religion used to be concerned . . . All were practically unanimous in admitting the fact of her decease."[43] I cannot see how there is much difference between Nietzsche's constant cry "God is dead, God is dead," and the environment at Columbia University in which religion was thought to have died. In the same chapter Dr. Horton says, "Among those who gave me most *food* for thought and compelled me willy-nilly, to re-think my position, I would name A. C. McGiffert, Henry Ward, and George Albert Coe."[44] These three men were teaching at one time in Union Theological Seminary, all of them rejected Christ as the Son of God, the authority of the Bible, and as far as I am able to determine, all of them at one time or another denied the personality of God, making man to be his own God. What can you expect from a professor of theology who has spent his youth, when all his habits of thought were being formed, in an atmosphere like that?

A contemporary of Dr. Horton is Professor Henry Nelson Wieman, who has been Professor of Philosophy in the Divinity School of the University of Chicago since 1927. These are Professor Wieman's own words: "Since leaving Harvard, an appreciation of the thought and work of John Dewey has been growing on me . . . Evil forms of religion and disastrous uses of the idea of God have stirred him to valiant combat until now he shies away from any mention of these matters. But surely the towering greatness of the man must be plain to anyone with eyes to see. And most of the criticism directed against him by religious people is, I think, mistaken."[45] Ignoring the criticism of Wieman concerning those who object to Dewey's philosophy, whatever be one's faith, there can be no denial of the fact that Dewey is an atheist, and that he believes humanity will not come into its full rights until everything identified with supernaturalism is given up. Is it not strange that a professor in a theological seminary would defend an atheist, confess the influence this man has had over his thinking, and criticize Christians for finding fault with Dewey's naturalistic philosophy? When a man takes Dewey for his philosophic guide, he can never be expected to be led by the Spirit of God, nor to listen very carefully or respectfully to the Word of God.

This subject of influence is so important that we tarry for one further illustration. Dr. Edgar Sheffield Brightman, for the last quarter of a century Professor of Philosophy in the graduate school of Boston University, tells us that in his undergraduate days in Boston University (1906), his philosophy heroes were Plato, whom he read in the original; Marcus Aurelius, Epictetus, Berkeley, and Nietzsche, and then continues, "As I began to think more, Kant and Schopenhauer influenced me profoundly . . . Following the tendency of the then Dean Alexander Meiklejohn, I long rejected the freedom of the will and for some years was a rigid determinist . . . Leuba has my unqualified respect as a student of religion."[46] Aside from the ancient philosophers one will recognize at once that those who most influenced Professor Brightman while in his formative years at college were the great haters of Christ, Nietzsche, Kant, who denied the significance of the historical facts of Christianity, the pessimist Schopenhauer, and Leuba. What influences to recognize as dominant for a professor of philosophy and a writer on religion! In the same chapter he says, "Nothing abides, all things flow. Individuals, nations, ideas, faiths, institutions are born, flourish, grow old and die. May not Christianity some day be as dead as Mithraism is now?"[47] Why some men do not believe in God and in the Christian faith today is not difficult to understand, when one really begins to inquire concerning the dominating influences of their student days. The great tragedy in education in this country, since the beginning of the twentieth century, is that our students in our great universities and colleges have burned the midnight oil poring over the pages of the great philosophers, have fallen in love with Plato, who could never lead any man to God, have had held before them the works of men who themselves long ago gave up God, have sat under professors who seized every conceivable opportunity to declare their own irreligiousness, but were never allowed to balance these skeptical tendencies with an equally serious study of the Word of God, and have no professor anywhere near them who could interpret, with love, power, and learning, the literature of Apostolic Christianity. (I happen to know that only last year a student in the Divinity School of Harvard University said to a fellow student rooming in the same building, "They are assigning work in the Bible, and I guess I'd better go out and buy one. I never owned one.") If this is what has happened to men who are now holding many of the great chairs of philosophy and religion in our country, what depths of unbelief we may expect to face in the second generation of such godlessness. I do not care to speak definitely of certain individuals whom I myself have come upon in my own experience, but I must say, if I am allowed one sentence out of my own life, that I have known people who taught Sunday school classes up through high school, and went on to the university, to come back within three months telling their friends in the same city that they had now come to realize that God did not exist, and that they never intended to be a fool again. Many fathers and mothers have I seen broken-hearted because, having sacrificed to send their children up to the university, they discovered, when they came back within a year or two, that they did not even care to walk with them to the house of God on the Lord's Day. I believe that more than any other one thing, the atheism of our educational institutions is the greatest cause of the deep and dark unbelief of our own day. This is a terribly serious matter, and something that should deeply concern us. It is a very unwholesome sign when Christian people, hearing of young men by the thousands losing their faith and giving up any conviction concerning God, shrug their shoulders and say, "Oh, it will come out all right, this is only a temporary mood of youth." But it doesn't come out all right, and the mood of skepticism in youth grows deeper, until we behold not only a scoffing at religion, a ridiculing of holy things, but a willingness to cooperate with others to actually destroy the religious foundations of our land.

The Increasing Supremacy of the Material Means the Subordination of the Spiritual. We are living in one of the most wonderful ages of the world, if looked at from a materialistic standpoint. Even since the writer of this book was a boy have there come into modern life the automobile, the radio, and the aeroplane. What an enormous difference just these three inventions have made in the life of man! Our occupation with war itself, both the First World War and the Second World War, is an occupation with material things—inevitable, but nevertheless materialistic. Men turning to scientific pursuits must handle those things that pertain exclusively to matter, to the things that can be seen and heard, touched and tasted. Our movies make for absorption with *things*. The result of such preoccupations is the snuffing out, as it were, of spiritual thoughts, or, a turning away from spiritual values. Material contentment often makes for spiritual indifference. At the beginning of our century one of Europe's outstanding philosophers, who always insisted upon the importance of the spiritual and grieved because of its decline in modern European life, Rudolf Eucken, clearly saw that "the center of gravity of life shifts toward the objective, and life finds its meaning in work occupied with and conditioned by external things. This work completely emancipates itself from the mere individual; it develops an independent and very extensive network of relationships, and swells in volume so unceasingly that man becomes more and more a mere servant and tool. This tendency was first illustrated in the case of factory work, and then it spread rapidly into other spheres of life. The more human thought and effort were concentrated upon joint tasks of an outward and visible character, the more unimportant became all that took place in the soul of the individual, the more his condition became a matter of indifference, the more the subject came to be considered a mere cog in the vast machinery of the whole, a quantity to be set aside with impunity."[48] As Dr. Herbert H. Farmer of Cambridge has just said, in his new book, *Towards Belief in God,* "Basic to all life, in all its stages, is the necessity to sustain itself by food and to protect itself from physical injury and destruction. The 'primary' real is the 'physical' real—that which can be touched, manipulated, repelled or absorbed, by the physical organism. This is as true of man as of any other creature. Even though we grant fully that man shall not live, indeed in a sense cannot live without ceasing to be distinctively human, by bread alone, the way in which we state the truth reveals our sense that, none the less, bread is the first need, and that without it there could be no living at all. And the need for bread, warmth, shelter, etc., is certainly of a much more immediate and stinging kind than any other. To be deprived of food is to have within a few hours a massive organic discomfort and weakness which prohibits the pursuit of any other interest whatsoever, even the most exalted. The injurious effects of other deprivations are much more subtle and slow-working, and provided one is fed, can be endured for a much longer period. All this is obvious enough; but what is not so obvious, and what it is well not infrequently to call to mind, is the effect of this primacy of the physical upon our mental habits."[49]

Dr. Edward Watkin, in a work we have already noticed, very suggestively speaks of this same fault of modern society. "Man today is fixing his attention wholly upon a horizontal plane to the exclusion of the vertical." Speaking of atheistic Soviet Russia he says: "As this movement of exclusive outlook, this naturalism, and religious humanism has grown in power and self-confidence, it has produced an increasing blindness to religious truth. Those whose minds it has formed, and they are the majority of civilized mankind today, have their attention fixed so exclusively upon the phenomena visible along the horizontal line of vision that they can no longer see the spiritual realities visible only in the depths by a vertical direction of the spirit."[50]

To introduce the testimony of one more witness, regarding the effect of our increasing materialism upon the Christian faith, the following words of one of England's most careful theological scholars of today are worth considering: "The true enemy of religion in the modern world is not philosophy or science; it is the purely secular habit of mind engendered in the hurrying life of great cities, where the heavens are veiled from view by the blaze of electric light, and a display of many-coloured signs intended to advertise all manner of commercial enterprises is substituted for the solemn spectacle which Kant placed side by side with the moral law as an object of reverent awe; where the news of all the world is continually proclaimed by night and day and emphasized in proportion, not to its true importance, but to its journalistic effectiveness; and whence there is rapidly spread all over the globe, through the improvement of the means of communication, an external similarity of life among people of utterly different traditions, who are thus torn from their spiritual roots in the religious experience of their forefathers." But Professor Webb continues, and rightly for our encouragement, "To this secular habit of mind it is probable that Christianity alone of the historical religions can hope to offer an effectual resistance."[51]

This crowding out of the spiritual by the secular is exactly that to which our Lord referred, in His parable of the sower and the seed. "Now the parable is this: The seed is the word of God. Those by the wayside are they who hear; then cometh the devil, and taketh away the word out of their hearts, lest they should believe and be saved. Those on the rock are they who, when they hear, receive the word with joy; and these have no root, who for a while believe, and in time of temptation fall away. And that which fell among thorns are they, who, when they have heard, go forth, and are choked with cares and riches and pleasures of this life, and bring no fruit to perfection."[52] What our Lord referred to as taking place, primarily in individuals, now seems to be occurring on a universal scale.

The Exaltation of Science. Closely related to the prevalence of the power of secularism in our world today, is the absorption of men with the themes of science, natural science, if you will. It is to be expected that men shall be fascinated with the exploration of the wonders of nature, and ever be allured to elicit from her, if possible, some of the great secrets of life, the laws of our universe. The very word "laboratory" has in it the connotation of certainty, of wonder, of the discovery of secrets. Millions of people are living today because of the development of medicine, and thank God for that! Many are able to walk the streets today because of insulin, who, otherwise, would long ago have been in their graves. One discovery drives men on to another. The eliciting of one secret is only the opening of the door into another realm of mystery and delight. There is a positiveness, definiteness, and promise about mathematical equations, physical laws, and chemical formulae, which make men feel that here their feet are on solid rock, that their minds are grappling with realities. But science is no synonym for spirituality, and the life of men is made up of more things than can be measured with test tubes and balances. Yet, man is so absorbed in the pursuit of nature's secrets that he is increasingly ignorant of his inner spiritual life, and this is one of the tragedies of our day. Men engaged in science are themselves partly to blame for this. They devote days and nights, months, sometimes years, to the discovery of some one scientific fact, but they will not give twenty minutes a day to pondering the Word of God, nor five minutes a day to the exercise of their soul in prayer to God.

While in this chapter it is our purpose only to set forth causes of unbelief, and not in any way to develop long answers to these matters, yet I think that when we are speaking of science, as it is being almost worshiped as a god today by our young people, we should never forget the indictments which are brought against science by those who have spent their lives in pursuing its fascinating paths of discovery and exploration. Sir James Jeans, e.g., in his volume *The Stars in Their Courses,* makes the very significant confession that, "Science knows of no change except the change of growing older and of no progress except progress to the grave." [53] If we need truth which will lead us into eternal life, and into an abiding hope, we will not find it in science. Unquestionably the outstanding authority on the history of science of modern times is Dr. George Sarton, of Harvard, and of the Carnegie Institution. In his *History of Science and the New Humanism,* which was published in 1937, Sarton says a very wholesome thing about the folly of expecting anything from science, that in itself will lift and transform the human soul. "As long as science is looked at only from the technical and utilitarian angle, there is hardly any cultural value in it. For example, I cannot help smiling when I hear young enthusiasts exult because our universe is constantly increasing. Now it tickles our imagination to hear that the depth of the universe extends to so many millions of light-years, but there is nothing especially cultural or 'uplifting' in that. The quality of our souls is independent of the size of the universe; we do not find ourselves better or worse, happier or more unfortunate because the universe is shown to be so much larger than we had fancied." [54]

"Ye Shall Be as Gods." Far back in the beginning of history the devil himself, the father of lies, with many devices to lead man away from the will of God, used one of particular power when he promised our first parents that if they would obey him they should become as gods.[55] Whatever was the power of that promise then, such an idea has ever held an amazing influence over fallen mankind. The whole tendency to deification of man roots in his desire to be God. Brunner sums it up in one sentence when he says, "The origin of sin is the deification (by man), the grasping after the divine right, the disputing of the divine authority." [56] Probably most of the gods of antiquity were originally only deified forms of great human heroes. This tendency reappeared with force and authority when the Caesars of Rome were set up as gods, and the populace forced to recognize them as divine. The whole system of Japanese religion for centuries has rested upon the deification of the emperor. Although we may not see in our own English world a resurgence of pagan idolatry as such, yet this tendency to deify men we now find everywhere evident in our humanist philosophies, which, in the absence of great contemporary heroes likely to be worshiped by men, mankind itself is put up as the god to worship, as we have seen in a preceding chapter. Of course if men are going to lift such a miserable thing as humanity to a pedestal, then a holy and invisible God must be not only ignored, but despisingly rejected and hated, which is why many of our intellectual leaders today who look upon humanity as divine, must irritatingly and scornfully declare their conviction that a transcendent, omnipotent, sovereign and eternal Being can, for them, have no meaning. At the time of the French Revolution it was humanity that this wild, bloodthirsty, law-hating, reason-exalting, immoral mob lifted up to a pedestal for worship. It may be that the next revolution, which everyone regretfully believes will be

universal, and not confined to a small area like France, will see many such spectacles as this, and our present day atheistic philosophers, ignorant of the Word of God, rejecting the Christ of God, deniers of the sovereignty of God, are preparing mankind for a passionate participation in such a diabolic program.[57]

The Relation of Sin to Unbelief. One of the most important questions that can ever be proposed in discussing the complicated problem of unbelief and opposition to the Christian faith is this: is there any direct relationship between a man's determination to live contrary to the law of God and his rejection of the Word of God? To put it more bluntly, does a man's moral life, or, rather, immoral life, account, in part at least, for his persistent rejection of Christ as his Saviour, and of a belief in a sovereign, holy God? The answer through all the ages has been overwhelmingly in the affirmative. This is a very serious subject, and we approach it prayerfully and, we trust, sanely. Let us first of all consider what the Scriptures say about the relation of sin to unbelief, and then we may harken to the confirming testimony of some of our leading thinkers. The Apostle Paul, in the opening chapter of his epistle to the Romans, which we have previously drawn upon in this chapter, definitely declares that men in general, men who reject the gospel, men in every age, and men of every type, "hinder the truth in unrighteousness," or as it is otherwise translated, "hold down the truth in unrighteousness."[58] As Chalmers says on this passage, "Men have the truth—they are in possession of it. But they keep it down. They chain it, as it were, in the prisonhold of their own corruptions. They throw the troublesome adviser into a dungeon—just like a man who has a conscience to inform him of what is right, but who stifles its voice and brings it under bondage to the domineering ascendancy of passion and selfishness and all the lawless appetites of his nature. Thus it is with men who restrain the truth, or suppress the truth in unrighteousness."[59] Our blessed Lord, when He was on earth said that, "Everyone that doeth evil hateth the light."[60] Here is a direct connecting-link between a life of evil and a determination to reject the light. The generation which rejected the Lord Jesus Christ did so because it was, our Lord said, "an evil and adulterous generation."[61] Writing to the Thessalonians, Paul spoke of men who "believed not the truth, but had pleasure in unrighteousness"; writing to the Colossians, he said that men are enemies of God in their mind by wicked works.[62] The writer to the Hebrews refers to the unbelief of men as "an evil heart of unbelief."[63] On this, then, the Scriptures are clear, that one of the greatest causes, perhaps the most important of all causes for unbelief is the determination of men to continue in sin. In a reflex way this continuance in sin brings about an ever deepening darkness of mind, and an increasing hardness of heart. Some years ago the distinguished Baptist theologian, Dr. Augustus Hopkins Strong dwelt on this matter of the relation of evil to unbelief in a sermon on "Unrighteousness of Sin," which perhaps many of my readers have not had the opportunity of seeing, and I would like to quote from it here as the verdict of one of the best theologians that America has produced:

"Sin itself has a blinding influence upon the mind. Evil seldom presents itself to us in its own hideous nature; when it seeks to tempt us, it comes as an angel of light; it always furnishes us with abundant excuses for admitting it to our hearts; otherwise it could have no power to lead us captive. To be 'blinded by passion' has passed into a proverbial phrase. One evil habit will often completely destroy one's power of sober judgment with regard to all things relating to the cherished sin. The opium eater will persist in believing that his life is bound up with the use of the bitter drug, when everybody else sees clearly that the only chance of life for that wasted and shattered form is in the total abandonment of the destroying habit at any cost of pain and suffering. The man intent on murder is never more thoroughly foolish than when contriving ways to conceal his crime. His sin so blinds him that in covering his bloody tracks he weaves the very web of his own detection. And the reason is that the set purpose of the heart controls the attention. Passion will not permit the calm consideration of the difficulties and dangers that lie in its way. Sin will never look into the mirror of God's law to discover its own deformity. It does not think of God's nature and requirements, the certainty of His promises of wrath, the futility of all earthly judgments when they contradict His judgments. The sinner will not look at the numberless transgressions of his life, his unlikeness to God, his rejection of Christ but he persists in fixing his thoughts on the seemingly good things in his character. Like Eve in the garden, he chooses to forget God's Word; 'In the day thou eatest thereof, thou shalt surely die,' and to listen instead to Satan's whisper: 'Thou shalt *not* surely die.' By controlling his attention, sin leads the man to believe the enemy of his soul and to make God a liar.

"This unbelief becomes a fixed habit of mind; but this is not all. Every new sin adds to the inveteracy and strength of the habit. While his sins increase at an alarming rate, his blindness and unconcern increase in exact ratio with his sins. You can see this in the callousness of hardened criminals. The boy who once shuddered at obscenity learns to indulge in it without a qualm of conscience, and even to make merry over the days of his innocence. The soul loses its sensitiveness just in proportion as it is sunk in sin. There are wretches confined in our state prisons whose souls are stained with every lust and crime upon the catalogue, but who have no apparent sense that they are sinners; aye, the most hoary-headed villain of them all may have knelt once by a mother's knee, and felt her hot tears falling upon his face as she brought the case of her little wayward son before her God in prayer. Those tears and sobs went to his heart once, and answering ears flowed freely from his eyes; but that day is long past; the tears vill not flow now; he has broken away from every influence human and divine; and now he cannot feel—cannot even see his sin in breaking that mother's heart. Oh, how dreadful is this fact of human naure, that while the true Christian feels God's truth with regard to his own sins more and more, the unbeliever feels it less and less, until the ime comes at last that the soul is 'past feeling.'"[64]

It is now necessary for me to enter upon a subject which I would ever approach except that to ignore it, in the matter we are here iscussing, would be to only partially treat this problem of the relationship of evil to unbelief. I refer to the problem of vice and sensulity, sins of the flesh, in relation to this whole question of free thought, nd what we call infidelity. Is it not significant, to begin with, that the vord *infidel,* which means in itself *unfaithful, unbelieving,* meant, first f all "one who does not believe in the true religion," and then an "adherent of a religion opposed to Christian, as for example a Mohammedan?" and then, "a disbeliever of religion of divine power, professed unbeliever," came later to mean unfaithfulness or disloyalty to a person, especially, in modern use, to a husband or wife, called, more fully, "conjugal infidelity."[65] Professor William G. Shedd, in his volume *Orthodoxy and Heterodoxy* has a brief chapter on "The Connection between Infidelity and Sensuality" which he begins with a quotation from Robert Baxter: "'I observed, easily, in myself, that if at any time Satan did more than at other times weaken my belief of Scripture and the life to come, my zeal in religious duty abated with it, and I grew more indifferent in religion than before.' This good man found that infidelity is favorable to sin, and that in proportion as doubt concerning God and the Bible rises, religion declines. But if this is true of the renewed man, it is still more so of the unrenewed.'" Shedd then concludes his chapter with the statement that men who refuse to believe in God and a divine revelation, "thereby remove a positive restraint upon their appetites and passions and promote sensuality, either refined or gross."[66] This is true as the history of radical unbelief testifies, but the point we are making here is not so much that unbelief leads to sensuality as that sensual sins will confirm one in his determination not to believe. James Denney, and how we need such men a Denney in our generation, in his remarkable work on Paul's Epistle t the Thessalonians, has some words that need to be pondered these days as we grapple with this terrible problem of unbelief: "The holy law o God, wrought into the very constitution of our bodies, takes care tha we do not violate it without paying the penalty. If it is not at the mo ment, it is in the future, and with interest,—in premature old age; i the torpor which succeeds all spendthrift feats, excesses of man's prime in the sudden break-down under any strain put on either physical c moral courage. They are avenged in the soul. Sensual indulgence ex tinguishes the capacity for feeling: the profligate man would love, bu cannot; all that is inspiring, elevating, redeeming in the passions lost to him; all that remains is the dull sense of that incalculable los Were there ever sadder lines written than those in which Burns, wit his life ruined by this very thing, writes to a young friend and warr him against it?

"'I wave the quantum o' the sin,
The hazard o' concealing;
But Och! it hardens a' within,
And petrifies the feeling.'"

Some of my readers by this time will be saying, "You are only quoting theologians, you are only quoting men who really believe in the Christian Faith, who are bringing false indictments against those who differ with them." It is not only our theologians and Christian thinkers who bear testimony to this matter of the relation of sensuality to unbelief, it is the communist and free-thinkers themselves who present us with the most powerful evidence. Thus for instance, the Manifesto of the Communist Party in 1847 made this declaration, as everyone knows who is acquainted with the history of socialism, "There are besides eternal truths, such as Freedom, Justice, etc., that are common to all states of society. Communism abolishes eternal truths, it abolishes all religion, *and all morality,* instead of constituting them on a new basis; it therefore acts in contradiction to all past historical experience." Notice the phrase, "all morality,"—that is what they want to get rid of, and what in most cases they have got rid of. The late Karl Pearson, in his *Ethic of Free Thought,* in its concluding essay, "Socialism and Sex," advocates freedom in all sexual relations.[68] So do most of the free-thinkers of our day, especially such men as Bertrand Russell. In fact, some of our free thinkers go so far as to rejoice in the dissolution of the marriage relationship. I was astonished recently to come upon a statement in a work by a former professor at Northwestern University, *The New Universe,* wherein, speaking of the ratio of divorces to marriage as being 7.2 per cent, he adds, "It is a situation far more wholesome than of courts where divorce is hard to get"; and then he goes on to say: "Marriage and morality and the press upon conventions of our lives are, after all, but rules made to confound what man has found worth-while, and when rules like these become the ends of life they lose their moral value. They distort the human purpose, and become in an accurate way, dogmatic immorality."[69] Imagine young people sitting under such a professor as this, hearing him continually calling the standards of Christendom, "immoralities."

I will be criticized for what I am about to say, by those who have deliberately rejected our holy Faith, but the whole history of free-thought supports me in the statement, namely that socialism, free-thinking, communism, skepticism, have generally been accompanied by what is definitely known today as infidelity or immorality. All one has to do is to carefully read any good history of free thought which is fully documented and frank, such as the recent one by Dr. Robert Post, *Popular Free Thought in America,* to obtain all the evidence one needs to support such an accusation.[69a] Then let us remind ourselves of the lives of some of these greatest free thinkers of whom our modern age seems to be so proud. The word Voltaire is a synonym for impurity of thought, uncleanness of life, and dishonesty in business; Thomas Paine was exactly what Theodore Roosevelt said he was, "a dirty atheist," mentally dirty, and physically dirty, and that he was dismissed again and again from his jobs in England because of dishonesty, no one can deny. The immoral principles of Bertrand Russell are so noteworthy that he has actually been forbidden to teach in some of our tax-supported schools. The point I am making is this: one of the reasons why men refuse to accept the Christian Faith is because the very principles of their lives are in every way contradictory to the ethical principles of the Bible, and, determined to remain in the lawlessness of their own sensuality, they could not possibly embrace a holy religion nor walk with a holy God, nor look for salvation to His holy Son, nor have any love for His holy Word. I do not mean by this that all professors in our country who are notable atheists, who are fighting Christianity, who are attempting to destroy the faith of young people are all immoral. Of course not; many of them are living what we call moral lives. I am speaking here generally, and emphasizing a principle to which of course there are exceptions, that one of the deepest, profoundest, most powerful causes for unbelief, holding men back from Christ is a life of sin. No matter how bitterly the world resents it and how much we are criticized for it, Jesus said it, the Apostles said it and the church must say it, courageously. When cancer is discovered in a body some perfumed ointment is not recommended by a doctor for remedy, but a knife, and excision; and in this day of despair and unbelief we need surgical operations. Canon Liddon, in a noteworthy sermon "Truth Unwelcome to the Evil" on the words of the king of Israel, "There is yet one man, Micaiah, the son of Imlah, by whom we may inquire of the Lord; but I hate him, and he doth not prophesy good concerning me but evil," says: "Many an objector to Christianity in our day, if he said what he really thinks, would say, 'I hate Christianity, because, if it is true, it does not prophesy good concerning me, but evil. It makes such serious demands: it proposes so high a standard: it implies that so much of what I think, say, and do is a great mistake, that I must away with it. I cannot do and be what it enjoins without doing great violence to my inclinations, my passions, my fixed habits of life and thought.' Augustine tells us in his Confessions how completely he was enchained by his passions, and how, after he had become intellectually satisfied of the truth of the Creed of the Church of Christ, he was held back from conversion by the fear that he would have to give up so much to which he was attached. In the end we know he broke his chains, the chains which held Ahab captive.—In such cases lasting self-deceit is easy. Men treat what is really a warp in the will as if it were a difficulty of the understanding; but the real agent—ought I not to say, the real culprit?—is the will. The will sees Revelation advancing to claim the allegiance of the soul; it sees that to admit this claim will oblige it to forego much and to do much that is unwelcome to flesh and blood, and so it makes an effort to clog or hinder the action of the understanding. Its public language is, 'I cannot accept this religion, because it makes this or that assertion which, to my mind, is open to historical, or philosophical, or moral objections of a decisive character.' But if it saw deeper into itself, it would say, 'I hate this Creed, for it doth not prophesy good concerning me, but evil, if I continue to live as I do.' "[70]

Ignorance of the Word of God and of True Christianity a Major Cause of Unbelief. The subject referred to in the heading is one to which we could well devote an entire volume, but here we have space for only the briefest mention. One of the three greatest causes for men not accepting Jesus Christ as their Saviour is that they do not know who Christ is, what He said, what He has done; they know nothing of His glory and love, His grace, and power, and Godhead. If they do not know they cannot believe. The Apostle Paul in his greatest defense of the Word of God, said that the Holy Scriptures, inspired of God, were first of all profitable for *teaching,* that is, for teaching the truth, and if one does not know the truth *how can* one believe? [71] "Faith cometh by hearing and hearing by the Word of God," and if the Word of God is not heard how can people believe, and if they do not believe, they are unbelievers. In thousands and thousands of Protestant churches today (we are not criticizing but simply stating a fact, which everyone recognizes) the Word of God concerning Christ and salvation is not expounded, unfolded, and explained, from one year's end to another. There are congregations of a thousand and fifteen hundred people today who, from the first Sunday of January to the last Sunday of December, hear nothing about the divine plan for saving men, through the grace of God in Jesus Christ. We are substituting international peace, a new world order, a love for humanity, the wonders of science, the various popular phases of philosophy, attacks upon capital, cooperation with labor unions, economic problems, social problems, prohibition, psychology, the history of religion, the holidays of the year, why men should go to church, the beauty of worship, the errors of some cult, etc. etc. But all these together could never save a soul, and do not help men to understand *the Word of God.* If the Bible is mentioned, in many places it is with a tone of apology, with additional clauses warning men not to put too much confidence in what it has to say. Our young people today are just ignorant of the Bible; they know philosophy, they know science, they know a little bit of history, they know a good deal about mechanics, they know much psychology, but they hear nothing about the Bible, either in school, or in church, or in their homes. They are growing up in a pagan atmosphere, and if all they know about the Bible is what somebody has critically said about it, they will never open its pages and read for themselves. What can one expect but a deep midnight of darkness, resulting from such ignorance? One could multiply illustrations by the hundred. Let me just give two that have come to my attention. Some years ago the distinguished Professor Kittredge of Harvard was hearing a class in Macbeth and during the class a student reading aloud came upon the word Golgotha. The Professor asked this student what Golgotha meant, to which he replied, "I don't know, in fact I never heard the word before." "Do you know what Ca vary means?" "I have never heard the word." As may easily be believed, by those who knew Kittredge, the learned and frequently sarcastic Professor simply bowed his head, and said, "The class is dismissed." [72]

To come out of academic institutions, this came to my attention the other day. A certain individual went to a post office in the city where I am writing, to mail a small package to a soldier, and the one weighing the package asked what was in the package. She replied, "A New Testament." "What is that?" he asked. "It is a part of the Bible." To this the clerk replied, "Do they call it the *New* Testament because someone just wrote it?" This man is thirty-five years old, and intelligent enough to pass a Civil Service examination. I would call him above the average—a typical American citizen, yet he never had heard of the New Testament. There are millions like him in our own land, and there are millions more in Europe. It is not amazing that unbelief today is so general. It is impossible for it to be anything else, for if people do not know the truth they cannot believe, and seeing and hearing perverted truth only makes them hate the Truth about which they truly know nothing.

Unbelief Begets Unbelief. Unbelief unless checked, only engenders more unbelief; it is like a contagious disease. Unless it is restrained it grows in intensity, and will infect an increasingly large number of people. It is difficult to determine whether this is an age of unbelief because so many men do not believe, or many men do not believe because it is an age of unbelief. I suppose that some would say you cannot have an age of unbelief unless it is caused by the unbelief of men. Well, I am not so sure. There are certain intellectual and moral characteristics that mark each age of human history, and it would seem that the outstanding mark of our particular age is Unbelief. This is recognized by most of our leaders of thought. Everyone knows the significant confession of Mr. Walter Lippmann at the beginning of his epochal work, *A Preface to Morals,* but it is still true, and most pertinent for our chapter. "This is the first age, I think, in the history of mankind when the circumstances of life have conspired with the intellectual habits of the time to render any fixed and authoritative belief incredible to large masses of men. The irreligion of the modern world is radical to a degree for which there is, I think, no counterpart. . . . I do not mean that modern men have ceased to believe in God. I do not mean that they no longer believe in Him simply and literally. I mean they have defined and refined their ideas of Him until they can no longer honestly say He exists, as they would say their neighbor exists. Search the writings of liberal church men, and when you come to the crucial passages which are intended to express their belief in God, you will find, I think, that at just this point their uncertainty is most evident." [73] Supplementing Mr. Lippmann's words are those uttered by President Angell in his Baccalaureate sermon preached in Yale University in June 1930: "The period in which we are living may well come to be known in religious history as 'the age of unbelief'; the latest of any, for the lineage runs direct and substantially uninterrupted from the Greek philosophers of the fourth century B.C., with occasional later high points such as the British skepticism of the eighteenth century and the radical movement of the French revolution . . . I doubt whether any vital element in Christianity, to say nothing of other religions, has wholly escaped this assault." [74]

Great thinkers, leaders of thought, men of achievement, men with great gifts of expression, inevitably must influence vast multitudes of people who look up to them as their leaders, as their guide, and when the outstanding men of the great segments of thought in our generation are atheistic, and antagonistic to the Christian Faith, what can one expect the younger generation to be, willingly following in their steps?

The Will Not to Believe. We do not know whether or not, logically, what we would now discuss deserves a separate treatment, for it is difficult sometimes to keep wholly separate one from the other by definite lines of discrimination the causes of unbelief which we are here attempting to consider. One of the reasons why men do not believe in Christ, and in the Word of God, is that *they are determined not to believe.* This is the deliberate, predetermined attitude of their mind. No matter what arguments are presented to them, no matter how accurate they find the Word of God to be, how incontrovertible the evidence for the resurrection of Christ is shown to be, they do not intend to believe. Someone will say, "No one can possibly be as stubborn as that." Yes, it is not only possible, it is continually manifested. Thus for example, the outstanding church historian of the nineteenth century, speaking of the Lord's miracle of quieting the waves in a storm on the Sea of Galilee, frankly said regarding a storm being quieted by a word, "We do not believe and we shall never again believe."[75] Harnack does not mean that the evidence is not sufficient for belief, he means that whatever the evidence is, he is not going to believe. Goethe took exactly the same attitude concerning the resurrection, "A voice from heaven would not convince me . . . that a woman gives birth without knowing man, and that a dead man rises from the grave. I rather regard this as blasphemy against the great God and His revelation in nature."[76] I have a letter from a Professor in a theological seminary in this country regarding the resurrection of Christ (the writer's name cannot be divulged because of a promise made in regard to this correspondence), who frankly told me that he would not judge the miracle of the resurrection by historical evidence, for, from a scientific and psychological point of view, he was *prejudiced against it,* and no evidence would ever change his mind. William James of Harvard wrote a remarkable book once which he aptly called *The Will to Believe:* a new book could be written today, even from the same University, with an equally true title, *The Will Not to Believe.*

Demonic Influences. Behind the age-long enigma of unbelief, according to the clear teaching of the Word of God, there is the power of Satan and of those hosts who do his work, known in the New Testament as demons. The very first sentence of which we have record proceeding from the heart of Satan, the enemy of God, and the enemy of man, was the question which he asked of our first parents, "Yea, hath God said?"[77] It is Satan's eternal, never-forgotten, everlasting, self-appointed task to destroy the faith of men in the Word of God, because in this way he will destroy faith in God, and ensnare men in the delusions and deceptions of his own evil nature. Our Lord reminds us that it is Satan's work to remove the Word of God out of the hearts of men.[78] Among the many words which Jesus Himself spoke revealing to men the character and work of this enemy of God and of all that pertains to God, there is an outstanding passage spoken toward the end of His ministry which we ought frequently to have before us: "Ye are of your father the devil, and the lusts of your father it is your will to do. He was a murderer from the beginning, and standeth not in the truth, because there is no truth in him. When he speaketh a lie, he speaketh of his own: for he is a liar, and the father thereof."[79] This is significantly preceded by the clause "Ye cannot hear my word." Every lie concerning the Bible, every attempt to destroy man's faith in the Bible, every denial of God, every scheme for turning man from God, every force that minimizes the preeminence of Christ, the personality of God, the truthfulness of the Holy Scriptures, the need for salvation, the reality of a judgment to come, all these, ultimately proceed from the heart of the evil one himself. It is his business to deceive men, to deceive nations, to deceive the world. He is a liar, and the result of following him is to believe a lie. For accomplishing his purposes he has created a vast number of clever, deceiving, subtle schemes, referred to once by the Apostle Paul as "the wiles of the devil."[80] As Professor Eadie once said, "The great enemy of man, a veteran fierce and malignant, has a method of warfare peculiar to himself, for it consists of 'wiles.' His battles are the rush of a sudden ambuscade. He fights not on a pitched field, but by sudden assault and secret and cunning onslaught."[81] When the Apostle Paul came to the end of his life, after a quarter of a century of knowing Christ, and the animosity of men and the hatred of the devil, and the power of the world, that were set against the gospel, he said that we believers were wrestling not with flesh and blood but "with principalities, with powers, with the world rulers of this darkness, with wicked spirits in the heavenly places."[82] Notice how the idea of *power* under lies all these characterizing phrases. We are led to believe from the Word of God that the one who is mastering, controlling, and directing these evil beings, who desires to duplicate their own darkness, in darkening the minds of men, is nothing less than the evil one himself. This is what Paul means when, in his First Epistle to Timothy, he says that in the last days men will give heed to *seducing spirits, to doctrines of demons.*[83]

Now, I do not want to be radical, and I do not want to go to any extreme in the interpretation of the Word of God, but personally I am becoming more and more convinced that many of the awful and blasphemous teachings that are now found in the literature of our day, indeed, in some of the most widely-circulated and highly-praised book of our generation, have been prompted, though their authors do not know it, and would scoffingly deny it, by evil spirits. The very sober words of that great theologian, Dr. James Denney, in his magnificent commentary on Paul's Second Epistle to the Corinthians, should be carefully considered here by every student of this problem of contemporary unbelief. "It does not seem an extravagance to the apostle to describe Satan as the god of the present aeon; and if it seems extravagant to us we may remind ourselves that our Saviour also twice speaks of him as the *prince* of this world. Who but Christ Himself, or a soul like St. Paul, in complete sympathy with the mind and work of Christ, is capable of seeing and feeling the incalculable mass of the forces which are at work in the world to defeat the gospel? What sleepy conscience, what moral mediocrity, itself purblind, only dimly conscious of the height of the Christian calling, and vexed by no aspirations toward it, has any right to say that it is too much to call Satan 'the god of this world'? Such sleepy consciences have no idea of the omnipresence, the steady persistent pressure, the sleepless malignity, of the evil forces which beset man's life. They have no idea of the extent to which these forces frustrate the love of God in the gospel, and rob men of their inheritance in Christ. What St. Paul saw, and what becomes apparent to everyone in proportion as his interest in evangelizing becomes intense, is that evil has a power and dominion in the world, which are betrayed, by their counteracting of the gospel, to be purely malignant—in other words, Satanic—and the dimensions of which no description can exaggerate. Call such powers Satan, or what you please, but do not imagine they are inconsiderable. During this age they *reign;* they have virtually taken what should be God's place in the world." [84]

Perhaps many of my readers will be saying, "Well, that may be in your Bible, but you cannot *believe* in Satanic and demonic power today." Such a statement is definitely contrary to a great mass of evidence; not only *can* we believe in demonic powers today, but many of our best thinkers *are* believing in such. One certainly would not accuse Dr. John A. Hutton, for many years the brilliant editor of the *British Weekly,* of a radical fundamentalism, or of holding spiritual fantasies, but Dr. Hutton gives it as his own opinion that, "The dark flood sweeping at the souls of men would seem to be under a malignant control. It is so unified, so contributory in all its parts to one planned result, and one issue, that it must be the work of one Mind. Since that one mind cannot be the mind of God, we are left with no alternative except to say, 'it is the devil.' "[85]

When a man produces the greatest Greek grammar of modern times, showing an amazing mastery of all that has been done in modern research in New Testament Greek, writing at least forty volumes, and teaching thousands of young men the glories and profundities of the New Testament, one cannot accuse him of having a mind which cannot be trusted, or of being ignorant. It is such a person as this, the late Professor A. T. Robertson, of the Baptist Theological Seminary at Louisville, who wrote, "One wonders today if the degenerates and confirmed criminals so common now are not under the power of demons."[86]

This recognition of demon forces has even appeared, amazing as it may seem, in such a liberal, Unitarian, scholarly periodical as the *Hibbert Journal*. The outstanding authority on the subject of demons, angels, and evil spirits in the English world today is the Rev. Edward Langton, whose scholarly treatises on these subjects will, for years, remain the authoritative works in this field. In an article on "The Reality of Demonic Powers Further Considered," he begins by saying that, "The time has come when the Church's attitude to the belief in the reality of the demonic powers should be fearlessly re-examined in the light of all the evidence available to the modern student. At the present time the Church's attitude to this important aspect of Christian doctrine must be held to be far from satisfactory. Having recently had occasion to review the evidence for the belief in demons, historically and critically, from the Middle Ages until the present time, we have been forced to the conclusion that there is far more evidence for the belief in the reality of evil spiritual powers than has been recognized in recent years by Christian theologians." He then continues:

"No theory so far proposed as a substitute for the traditional doctrine of evil spirits or demons has proved itself capable of explaining *all* the facts so well as the traditional theory does. We share to the full the desire to explain the facts of nature, however mysterious they may be by means of naturalistic interpretations, when that is possible. But no theory will be finally satisfying to the truth-loving mind which leaves certain important phenomena unexplained. And before we relinquish our hold upon the traditional belief in demons we need to make reasonably sure that there are good grounds for so doing."[87]

Dr. Edwyn Bevan, of New College, Oxford, formerly lecturer in Hellenistic literature and history in King's College, London University, in a book from which we have already quoted, *The Kingdom of God and History,* frankly and boldly acknowledges the power of the kingdom of evil in our world today. "In any case, what we see when we speak of 'history,' is this continuous process of human lives, directed partly by circumstances outside man's control, but very largely by human acts of choice: and of these acts of choice a very large proportion, we recognize, are made in opposition to God, or in disregard of Him. This gives us the Kingdom of Evil. For the wrong volitions are not simply isolated acts of the persons willing, but they form a concatenation, each wrong volition disposing the person who makes it to further wrong volitions, and having effects in his social environment, disposing other persons to similar wrong volitions. Such wrong volitions in the mass may form customs, institutions, social atmospheres of evil character, which will surround everyone born into the society from his earliest movements; enslave him to standards of conduct and value completely discordant with the divine—a Kingdom of Evil from which it may be difficult for any individual, even with the best will, wholly to emancipate himself. 'The whole world lieth in the Evil One.' It may be questioned whether the evangelist when he represents Satan as saying to the Lord, after he had set before him the kingdoms of the world, 'all this power is delivered unto me: and to whomsoever I will, I give it,' supposed the Evil One, in that statement at any rate, to have spoken in his character of liar."[88]

We consider one more contemporary statement—that of Dr. Paul Tillich, formerly professor honorarium of Leipzig, and professor ordinarius of philosophy at the University of Frankfurt am Main, now for some years the associate professor of philosophical theology at Union Theological Seminary. While he probably does not believe in a *personal* demonic power, yet he cannot explain the contemporary opposition to the kingdom of God without speaking continuously of history being "a battle field of the divine and the demonic." He goes on to say that the loss of this idea "in modern times is connected with the rise of the idea of progress and the destruction of the original Christian interpretation of history. It is understandable that the breakdown of the idea of progress amid the historical catastrophies of the present and recent past has given a new significance to this category."

Professor Tillich applies this recognition of the power of the demonic to the present rise of political and military dictatorships. "Unrestricted exercise of power is a demonic temptation which none who possess it can resist. The early church expressed this in its condemnation of the Roman Empire. Henceforward tyranny has always evoked the opposition of Christian historical thought. Tyranny is presumption towards God and oppression of man. Hence it falls under the condemnation of that combination of love and power represented by the idea of the Kingdom of God.

"This is the case, in the first place, when dictatorship is surrounded by a halo of an almost religious kind, or when it proceeds to attack the church. The deification of the dictator, whether as the representative of the ruling power or as an individual, the interference of the state, with its totalitarian claims, with the sphere of religion, the quasi-religious character of its decrees imposed like taboos, the enforced conformity of the church to the state, or its destruction, and creation of martyrs in the narrower sense of the word—these are the anti-Christian implications of the exercise of absolute power. They force the churches into a campaign of direct resistance, and they provoke those who hold the Christian and prophetic view of history to make a vigorous protest against this 'demonic' exercise of power."[89]

One of the most penetrating, scholarly, authentic works on Christian missionary activity among pagan people is the famous volume by Johann Warneck, who, for some years, was a successful missionary among the animistic heathen of the Archipelago. His language is so concise, his loyalty to Christ so unswerving, and his own experiences so wide and revealing that we take the liberty of quoting one extensive passage on the power of Satan among the heathen of the other side of the world. His concluding sentences are sufficient to justify the inclusion of this remarkable statement.

"One of the main evidences of the truth and power of Christianity was the casting out of devils in the name of Jesus, which the Christian apologists turned to account as a convincing proof of the truth of their faith. It was believed then, as it is believed in heathendom today, that wherever Christians make their appearance the strength of the Satanic powers is broken. We shall speak of this further on. Here it is sufficient to say that the Christians of the first days, like the heathen Christians in the mission fields of today, though they knew that they themselves were free from those influences, nay were able to mock and challenge the devil, took a very serious view of idolatry. They knew its sinister power was something real. They did not believe that heathenism could be considered merely a lower stage of the knowledge of God which only needed to be further developed. On the contrary they viewed it as opposition and enmity to God, a bondage to devilish powers endowed with a power of misguidance, lying, and seduction. The testimony of those who have renounced heathenism, and who know its power from experience, deserves, at least, as much attention as the theories of philosophies of religion.

"Man cannot be isolated. It seems that he is never destined to stand alone. Rival powers are contending for the mastery of his soul. On the one hand is the 'express' and personal guidance of the Holy Spirit of God. On the other hand are the malign and mischievous influences of 'seducing spirits' and 'demons' determined on man's ruin. The Spirit of truth and the spirits of error are in deadly conflict for man's soul. It is well he should know it and know also the peril of parleying with the foe." [90] We are not surprised at this passage, when we mark the language of the whole New Testament and of the early Church in the first three centuries. The spiritual hosts of wickedness in the heavenly places are represented by both as striving with man. Every system, whether of idolatry, philosophy, or necromancy, which held man's minds in thraldom and fear was solemnly regarded as an influence from Satan personal in character, calling for a solemn exorcism.

"We cannot understand the Christianity of that first age at all unless we realize it as engaged in a stern conflict with demons in the name and power of an incarnate, crucified, and exalted Saviour. The possession might take the form of ordinary sickness. It might reveal itself in paroxysms of madness. It might enshrine itself in a mere idol of wood or stone. It might express itself, as here (I Tim. 4), in some false philosophy of life. It might win its adherents by magical arts (as e.g., II Tim. 3:13, where 'seducers' is really 'magicians,' 'imposters'). Always behind these manifestations there was a personal source of the evil which had to be exorcised, and the great mission of the Church and the disciples lay in that exorcism. Much that we attribute today, with but poor grounds for doing so, entirely to natural causes, was then regarded as the direct work of Satanic influence. And at least we must own that, while the Church held that belief, she was able to deal with such evil far more effectively than when she began to lose that more spiritual view of evil, and exchanged it for our more materialistic view. The reaction, indeed, from such materialism is once again beginning to be manifest in our midst. It may take some strange and exaggerated forms, but it is essentially a return to primitive Christianity. The view that the world then 'lay in the Evil One' and his followers was 'not a mere theory. It was a most vital conception of existence.' We shall never battle with evil in any form successfully unless we track it to its personal cause, and then, in the light of that knowledge, hurl against it the whole might of prevailing prayer. When we come to see in error, in sickness, in heresy, in madness, the victorious activity of the Evil One, we shall begin to realize that the power to exorcise evil which thwarts the will of God is given us still as Christians, and must be used. 'In default of it, evil streams in and prevails. But prayer that is one with God's will smites and conquers evil, till God's will is perfectly done, whose will is perfect love.' "[91]

Some years ago Professor Eucken said, "We feel that we are face to face with forces which we dare not allow to overpower us; yet at the same time we do not seem to be able to successfully confront them."[92] These forces, which Eucken does not identify, are those which the Apostle Paul speaks of, the principalities, and powers, and rulers of darkness. Toward the end of his famous book, *The Impregnable Rock of Holy Scripture*, William E. Gladstone summed up all we have been saying in one simple sentence, "It is the great world-power within us and around us which at the present time gives to skepticism the chief part of its breadth and its impetus."[93] This "great world power" is exactly what Paul referred to when he said we wrestle with the rulers of this darkness. It is not our purpose here to discuss how we may have victory over these powerful Satanic energized beings, but only to point out that they have a great deal to do with the unbelief that is increasingly revealed in modern humanity.

I would like to bring this long chapter concerning unbelief to a close by quoting a passage from the one book in the Bible devoted to the early history of the Christian church, the Book of Acts, which, though it would seem to be a passage of great importance, has been for some strange reason almost wholly ignored in works dealing with Pauline theology, and indeed the exposition of the Book of Acts. I refer to Paul's verdict which he gave while in his own private house, a prisoner of Rome, when he saw that as a result of his preaching, morning till evening, concerning the Kingdom of God, and persuading men of Christ, "some believed the things which were spoken and some disbelieved." We then read that Paul "spoke one word"; this is what he said: "Well spake the Holy Spirit through Isaiah the prophet unto your fathers, saying, Go thou unto this people, and say, by hearing ye shall hear, and shall in no wise understand; and seeing ye shall see and shall in no wise perceive: For this people's heart is waxed gross, and their ears are dull of hearing, and their eyes they have closed; lest haply they should perceive with their eyes, and hear with their ears, and understand with their heart, and should turn again, and I should heal them."[94] Paul's words are quoted from the sixth chapter of Isaiah, words that were spoken from heaven to the prophet immediately after the convulsive experience which he records in the earlier part of this autobiographical passage. We must remember that the man who uttered these words was no pessimist, rather, an optimist, filled with the hope of God; he was not discouraged because of a fruitless life, or because of repeated failures in his labors throughout the Roman world, quite otherwise, for no man ever had such success as the Apostle Paul. He saw men accepting Christ by the thousands; he saw churches springing up, as it were, right under his feet; he saw souls converted by his preaching, and priests becoming afraid that their temples would be soon forsaken; he was brought before kings and governors because of the power of his preaching; he had friends all over the Roman world; his words were listened to as the words of no other man that ever lived except the Lord Jesus. He is not speaking then because of the bitterness of failure. These words were uttered because of thirty years of mingling among men, faithfully preaching the Lord Jesus, continually expounding the Word of God, and yet seeing men turn away in a stubborn refusal to believe. This is the Apostle's verdict at the end of life concerning the hearts of many men, then and now. Whether we be Calvinists or not, whatever part of unbelief we ascribe to the sovereign work of God, throughout this passage there at the same time moves the theme of human responsibility, as Rackham says in his superb work on the Book of Acts: "Where there is the power of choice, there the presentation of new light and truth, if it is rejected, becomes a judgment. Before the coming of the light and truth, the darkness is not felt, the sin is dormant; when the light and truth come and are rejected then the sin becomes alive, the darkness conscious. Accordingly, the effect of the preaching of the Gospel is to harden the hearts of those who will not receive it: and this hardening is not to be thought of as a faith predestined for certain individuals but as a judgment allowed by, and in fact but the expression of the divine law. Thus St. Paul's preaching was for life or death; wherever he went, he divided the Jews into two: they had either to believe or disbelieve." [95]

Summary. Probably at no time since the beginning of the Christian church could we discover so many powerful forces working together for the creation and deepening of religious skepticism and unbelief as in the last quarter of a century. There was a time when so-called Christian nations shuddered at the blatant atheism, say of France in the time of Voltaire. Even when I was a boy at the dawn of this century, we, here in a God-fearing nation at that time, looked with horror upon the long faith-destroying period of rationalism in German theology and philosophy. There was a time when the great majority of people thought of Thomas Paine as a true child of the devil, and Robert Ingersoll as a man who, in defying God, was walking straight into the mouth of the bottomless pit. That time has gone. Voltaire never denied the existence of God, and we are told, would even tip his hat when an uplifted crucifix in a procession passed where he was standing. Today we have men in our theological seminaries denying the existence of

God, and using every subtle artifice at their command to make ridiculous and unbelievable the vicarious work our blessed Lord accomplished on the cross. Unbelief has laid hold of the two extremes of our social order, the intelligentsia and the workingman. The bootblack will now tell you he doubts if there is a heaven, and workingmen by the thousands passionately loyal to communism or labor organizations, are utterly indifferent to the claims of the Son of God and rather hate the church.

If this is a true analysis of today, what of tomorrow, with the increase of fascinating, labor-saving, stimulating inventions, with ever deepening ignorance of the Word of God, with sensuality laying an ever firmer hand upon the youth of the western world through literature, the movies, a false psychology, and the very coarseness of life as it now is, with millions accustomed to shooting and the sight of blood and the slaughter of war, to the sound of aeroplane motors, to the handling of innumerable instruments of death, to risking their lives every hour, day and night, some of them for years? What of the future?

As far as I can see, humanly speaking, the forces which have created the unbelief of today are going to grow more powerful rather than less powerful. What is going to stop them? We certainly are not going back to the days of our forefathers, and in many ways we do not want to. What force is going to bring about a knowledge of the Word of God in place of the ignorance of our day, what power is going to deliver us from the ever deadening influence of materialism, what force in the world is able to cope with the demonic influences that have been released in our century? There is only one power that can ever break the spell of all these earthly and superearthly powers combined, and that is the power of an omnipotent God manifested through the Holy Spirit, as He works through yielded servants of God, that with great boldness and increasing power they might proclaim the only gospel which is able to deliver men from the present wicked world, from the grip of sin and the power of evil, and translate them into the kingdom of the Son of God. Unbelief as it now is, is blighting the very life of the church; unbelief as it is going to be will work even worse havoc unless —unless we who believe give ourselves to prayer and the Word of God, and boldly stand up in a skeptical yet ignorant world to give a reason for the hope that is within us, setting ourselves for the defense and the confirmation of the gospel.

No fundamental element of unbelief, no primary cause, its relation to supernatural powers of evil was hidden from St. Paul. He not only analyzed the causes and manifestations of unbelief more exhaustively than any other writer of the New Testament, but he was allowed to see that in the future a great apostasy would set in, and many would turn away from the truth. Yet St. Paul knew the secret for the victory of Christian believers in the great struggle with these hosts of wickedness. The moment he concludes his enumeration of our spiritual enemies, he exhorts all who are on the side of Christ—"Wherefore take up the whole armour of God, that ye may be able to withstand in the evil day, and having done all, to stand. STAND, THEREFORE." [96]

Chapter IV

THE PESSIMISM OF OUR MODERN SKEPTICS

WHETHER man was made for joy or not is, it seems, a much disputed question in philosophical literature, but there is no genuine argument about the question in the human heart, whatever philosophers may say. Any normal man, at any time, prefers joy to despair, prefers happiness to gloom, hope to pessimism. It is not that we are to be hedonists, and justify the experiences of life by the pleasures they bring, but a life which has come to certain convictions that inevitably lead to a hopeless pessimism, is a life that at least seems frustrated, incomplete, and, as the most radical pessimists admit, not worth living. This question of whether a man ought to have joy or not, was long ago settled in the affirmative by our Lord, Himself. At the very end of His ministry, indeed on the very last day before His crucifixion, when everything would seem to have been dark indeed, overcast with a shadow of imminent death, to His own disciples, in the midst of these Thursday discourses, Jesus said, "These things have I spoken unto you that my joy may be in you and that your joy may be made full" . . . "Hitherto have ye asked nothing in my name: ask and ye shall receive that your joy may be made full." In His high priestly prayer of the same day He said to the Father, "These things I speak in the world that they may have my joy made full in themselves."[1] Certainly we must admit that the New Testament, while sternly facing the realities of life, is a book vibrating with joy. The early church was filled with joy. The Lord Jesus, though possessed with a deeper knowledge of the awfulness of sin than anyone who ever lived on this earth, was yet a joyous man. The Epistles of Paul, even those written as he was chained to a soldier in the prison, are radiant with joy, and from his dark and dismal prison cell he could write to his friends throughout the Roman world that in everything they were to rejoice. The glorious light, the unquenchable hope, the undiminishing energy and vigor, the tenderness and compassion, the infinite love, manifested by the redeemed who move across the pages of the New Testament, all speak of a life of joy. I think there can be hardly any argument that it is joy that men long to have. Many look for it in the wrong way, in sensual pleasure, and the acquisition of money, in the exercise of power, in the tasks of creative arts, in solitude and meditation; nevertheless, fundamentally, men want joy. What I want to do in this chapter is to bring into court for personal confession some of the outstanding skeptics, and enemies of Christianity, of modern times, and ask them if in their skepticism, their rejection of the Bible, and denial of God, they have found joy. The replies may vary, but they will be unanimous in declaring this, that unbelief leads straight to pessimism. The two go together. Our young men today should at least be forewarned that if they are going to be disciples of these lords of naturalism, they must expect never to come into the experience of joy for which their very hearts were created. This will be a dark chapter, but darkness is a state of the human soul which neither the New Testament ignores nor can we in our so-called age of psychological investigation refuse to recognize.

The Despair of Europe's Greatest Cynic. There is no doubt that the man who did more to destroy the faith of men in the Bible and in Christ, at the beginning of what we might call our modern age, than any one writer in Europe was Voltaire. With the immoralities and deceptions and the dirt of Voltaire's life we are not concerned here, not even with the blasphemous things which he uttered against our holy Faith. What we want to know is did all this iconoclasm, this unrestrained liberty which he took, to curse the holiest things in the world, did all this wallowing in his own sensualities, together with more fame than any other one literary man of his century, with disciples bowing down before him not only in continental Europe, but in Great Britain, and, sad but true, on our own colonial shores—did this man, with the worship of the world, doing as he pleased, with brilliant gifts, stand up and tell the world when his life was coming to a close that he at least had found joy? Listen to these words: "Strike out a few sages, and the crowd of human beings is nothing but a horrible assemblage of unfortunate criminals, and the globe contains nothing but corpses. I tremble to have to complain once more of the Being of beings, in casting an attentive eye over this terrible picture. I wish I had never been born . . . The box of Pandora is the most beautiful fable of antiquity. Hope was at the bottom." Thus as Professor Cairns well says, "The last utterance of Voltaire is a groan."[2]

Between Voltaire and Our Generation. It will be acknowledged by all, conservatives and liberals, that the man whose writings did more to destroy confidence in the validity and dependability of the four Gospels, and the supernatural aspects of the incarnation, was David Strauss, at the time when his first work on the life of Christ was published, a professor of theology. What did Strauss find at the end of this road (as he claimed) of following the truth wherever it might lead? This is his verdict: "In the enormous machine of the universe, amid wheel and hiss of its jagged iron wheels, amid the deafening clash of its stamps and hammers, in the midst of this whole terrific commotion, man finds himself placed with no security for a moment, that a wheel might not seize and render him, or a hammer crash him to pieces."[3]

Buried away in Leonard Huxley's *Life and Letters of Sir J. D. Hooker,* is a letter from the father, William Hooker, to his son, speaking of Robert Brown (1773–1858), Curator of the British Museum Herbarium, and called by Humboldt, *"Facile Botanicorum princeps, Britanniae gloria et ornamentum."* The father said to the son of this noble scientist, "He has, unfortunately, skeptical notions on religion, which often make life itself a burden to him: and which bring him no comfort in the prospect of eternity."[4] So even men who never think of attacking the Christian faith, who give their lives unselfishly to the pursuit of scientific knowledge, know likewise the same overshadowing mood of despair.

There was a time in the last half of the nineteenth century when everyone was reading Professor Seeley's anonymously published *Ecce Homo.* In his later book, *Natural Religion,* Professor Seeley makes the following pitiful confession of what denial of the supernatural had done for his own soul: "When the supernatural does not come in to overwhelm the natural, and turn life upside down, when it is admitted that religion deals in the first instance with the known and natural, then we may well begin to doubt whether the known and the natural can suffice for human life. No sooner do we try to think so than Pessimism raises its head. The more our thoughts widen and deepen, as the universe grows upon us, and we become accustomed to boundless space and time, the more petrifying is the contrast of our own insignificance, the more contemptible become the pettiness, shortness, and fragility of the individual life. A moral paralysis creeps over us. For a while we comfort ourselves with the notion of self-sacrifice; we say, 'What matter if I pass, let me think of others!' But the *other* has become contemptible no less than the self; all human griefs alike seem little worth assuaging, human happiness too paltry at the best to be worth increasing . . . The affections die away in a world where everything great and enduring is cold; they die of their own conscious feebleness and bootlessness."[5]

The Pessimism of Four Leaders of Thought Whose Deaths Have Occurred within the Last Generation. Before we speak of the pessimism of the anti-supernaturalists and rationalists of our own day, may I call your attention to the note of despair which is to be found in the lives and writings of four distinguished unbelievers whose death has occurred within the last twenty years, men who, therefore, have lived somewhat into our own day. First of all, let us take these concluding reflections of the man who has been called, "The saint of rationalism," John Morley, at the very close of the second volume of his *Recollections.* A friend of most of the great men and women of the late nineteenth and early twentieth centuries, Morley makes the following if not despairing, at least hopeless, confession: "Has not your school—the Darwins, Spencers, Renans, and the rest—held the civilised world, both old and new alike, European and transatlantic, in the hollow of their hand for two long generations past? Is it quite clear that their influence has been so much more potent than the gospel of the various churches? *Circumspice.* Is not diplomacy, unkindly called by Voltaire the field of lies, as able as it ever was to dupe governments, and govern by grand abstract catchwords veiling obscure and inexplicable purposes, and turn the whole world over with blood and tears to a strange Witches' Sabbath? These were queries of pith and moment indeed, but for something better weighed and more deliberative than an autumn reverie.

"Now and then I paused as I sauntered slow over the fading heather. My little humble friend squat on her haunches, looking wistfully up, eager to resume her endless hunt after she knows not what, just like the chartered metaphysician. So to my home in the falling daylight."[6]

Another famous rationalist, who however could never be called a saint, rather indeed, was definitely a sensualist, whose writings no clean-minded person would often care to read, the most brilliant literary genius of modern France, was Anatole France. His own secretary, Jean Jacques Brousson, two decades ago allowed us to see into the soul of this man, in an authentic and intimate record of the convictions and inner experiences of the famous novelist and critic. Without comment, this is the confession which his secretary frankly records:

"'In all the world the unhappiest creature is man. It is said: "Man is the lord of creation." Man is the lord of suffering, my friend. There is no clearer proof of the non-existence of God than life.'

"'But you are among the envied of this world. Every one envies your genius, your health, your youth.'

"'Enough, enough! Ah, if you could read in my soul, you would be terrified.'

"He takes my hands in his, and his are trembling and feverish. He looks me in the eyes. His are full of tears. His face is haggard. He sighs: 'There is not in all the universe a creature more unhappy than I. People think me happy. I have never been happy for one day, not for a single hour.'"[7]

Let us tarry a moment longer in this ever brilliant, cultured, atheistic and now saddened France, to consider the verdict of the greatest woman to adorn the history of modern science, probably the most famous woman of France since the French Revolution, indeed the most worthily famous woman of France since Joan of Arc. I refer to Madame Curie. No more fascinating biography has appeared in our generation than the life of Madame Curie by her brilliant daughter, Eve Curie. That we might not unjustly judge of the true mood of Madame Curie's soul, and her deepest attitude toward life, let me turn to this volume, then, at three different periods of her life. In 1904, when pregnant with her second child, her daughter says, "It seemed that she no longer loved anything: neither science nor life, and not even the child which was about to be born. She cried out, 'Why am I bringing this creature into the world? existence is too hard, too barren. We ought not to inflict it on innocent ones.'" On April 19, 1906, her equally brilliant husband, Professor Pierre Curie, co-discoverer with her of radium, was run over by a carriage, and instantly killed. The chapter describing Madame Curie's awful grief is one of the most tragic narratives in contemporary literature, telling us how she kissed his face, clung to the bloody garments as his body was being dressed, and actually had his brains put in a glass jar, and set upon the mantle. For weeks, she wrote to him every day, in her diary. Here is one of the entries: "Your coffin was closed and I could see you no more . . . they came to get you, a sad company . . . We saw you go down into the deep, big hole. Then the dreadful procession of people that wanted to take you away. Jacques and I resisted, we wanted to see everything to the end. They filled the grave and put flowers on it, everything is over. Pierre is sleeping in his last sleep beneath the earth; it is the end of everything, everything, everything." Madame Curie had no religious faith, as anyone can see in reading this volume, neither did those who came near her, as the famous mathematician, Jules Henri Poincare, who in extolling the memory of his distinguished friend, uttered these terrible words: "It matters little what God one believes in; it is the faith and not the God that makes miracles."[8] How tragic to have to go through such a sorrow as Madame Curie experienced, and though having around her some of the most brilliant minds in all Europe, find none who seemingly could say a word of comfort, so godless has our modern civilization become.

But the most terrible revelation of the wretchedness, the despair of life, when one has no hope for a life to come, is to be found in the last chapter of this biography, "The End of the Mission." When they knew their mother was dying, the children took her away to a sanatorium, near Saint Gervais. When her fever rose to about 104 degrees, a fact that could not be hidden from the dying woman, who, herself, always insisted on reading the thermometer, the daughter says, "She hardly spoke, but her pale eyes reflected a great fear . . . Then began the harrowing struggle which goes by the name of 'an easy death.' Eve at her mother's side was engaged in another struggle; in the brain of

Madame Curie, still very lucid, the great idea of death had not penetrated. This miracle must be preserved to save Marie from immense pain that could not be appeased by resignation . . . No family reunion called at that bedside of a dying woman. Seeing her would be suddenly to strike at the heart by an atrocious certainty. The two doctors alternated in Marie's room, they supported and solaced her, they also took care of Eve, helped her to struggle and to tell lies, and even without her asking them, they promised to lull Marie's suffering by injections. On the morning just three days before the end, for the last time Madame Curie could read the thermometer held in her shaking hand, and distinguish the fall of fever which always precedes the end. She smiled with joy, and as Eve assured her that this was the sign of her cure, and that she was going to be well now, she said, looking at the open window, turning hopefully toward the sun and the motionless mountain: 'It wasn't the medicines that made me better, it was the pure air and the altitude.'"[9] And so the woman who made so many great discoveries in the realm of nature, at the end of her life had to be lied to, about the great and final truth, that death had come. What is the use of a life devoted to the pursuit of truth in physics and chemistry, when the truths that concern the soul we never take time to consider or to confirm?

The last of this group of four, is an American, the famous essayist and biographer, Gamaliel Bradford. What fullness of joy one would normally think would be the lot of so gifted a man, who could read o many languages, write so brilliantly, be so sensitive to music and the ine arts. Consider for a moment such a schedule as this, which Bradord inserts in his diary for September 11, 1916 (and sometimes this henomenal schedule was enlarged), yet Bradford had no God, no aith, no hope, and said himself he dared not open and read the New Testament, for fear that it might change his long-held views! "In he morning, then, I write till half-past ten or thereabouts. After that, begin my morning reading with fifteen minutes of poetry, this according to a system which I have followed for years by successive months, irst two days of Dante or Milton, then a Greek or Latin play or Homer, hen a French or Spanish play, then from the twentieth to the twentyifth of the month either English or Latin poetry, then French poetry in alternate months and in the others German, Italian, or Spanish. The remainder of the morning I spend on the American work which prepares for my portraits. In the afternoon, after playing on the piano and doing such accounts or correspondence as may be necessary, if I am at home I read Latin if I have any time before going to work out-of-doors, then, after working and going down for the paper, I read Greek till supper. In the evening I begin first with a few pages of Shakespeare or some Elizabethan play, these all according to a system; then some pages of what I call the gossip of history—letters and diaries—all according to an elaborately prearranged system, which has become part of my life; then a few pages of the great critics, according to a system again. Then some reading in different languages for different portions of the month, then a half-hour of novel or play reading." With all this, Bradford was miserable: "Here I am, old, decrepit, and decayed, with the oil of life utterly spent in me, and yet I long as passionately to live as I did forty years ago. How? What do I mean by living? I do not know. Loving? Yes, loving. Succeeding, getting glory, notoriety, prosperity and money? They all seem pretty enough in themselves. I do not know what life is. But I want it, oh, I want it. For what is the world's life except an infinity of such lack of living as mine?" [10]

The Pessimism of Three of Our Most Distinguished Contemporary Intellectuals. Whatever be our repudiation of the radical views on sex and marriage of Bertrand Russell, we must recognize that he is considered in scientific circles as one of the outstanding mathematicians of the twentieth century, and we are bound to admit that his writings are exercising an enormous influence, or at least have exercised a great influence, over the thought of our generation. Bertrand Russell was born in 1872, and educated in Trinity College at Cambridge, where later he became a Fellow. In 1915 he received the Butler gold medal awarded once in five years. His first book appeared in 1896, so that we may say he has been writing for almost half a century. Some of his books have gone into a number of successive editions, and his own rationalistic views have been studied, adopted, and presented by multitudes on both sides of the Atlantic. Now a man like Bertrand Russell (who is an absolute atheist, who has no use at all for any of the fundamental truths of the Christian faith), who has had the advantages of full and rich education, has had the joy of producing some widely read books, understands much of modern science, which in itself must be fascinating indeed and somewhat satisfying; without financial worries whatever, with invitations extended to him for lectures in some of the most famous centers of learning in the English world, such a life, from a worldly standpoint, would be called successful. One would think a person with these assets and achievements would have a heart overflowing with joy. Instead Bertrand Russell's is probably the darkest and most dismal pessimism of our contemporary age. In his famous essay, *A Free Man's Worship,* which has been reprinted in a score or more of anthologies, and quoted in all types of literature, Bertrand Russell gives this as his own bitter, gloomy, hopeless attitude toward the deeper meanings of life: "That Man is the product of causes which had no prevision of the end they were achieving; that his origin, his growth, his hopes and fears, his loves and his beliefs are but the outcome of accidental collocations of atoms; that no fire, no heroism, no intensity of thought and feeling, can preserve an individual life beyond the grave; that all the labors of the ages, all the devotion, all the inspiration, all the noon-day brightness of human genius, are destined to extinction in the vast death of the solar system, and that the whole temple of Man's achievement must inevitably be buried beneath the debris of a universe in ruins—all these things, if not quite beyond dispute, are yet so nearly certain, that no philosophy which rejects them can hope to stand. Only within the scaffolding of these truths, only on the firm foundation of unyielding despair, can the soul's habitation henceforth be safely built.

"Brief and powerless is man's life; on him and on his race the slow sure doom falls pitiless and dark. Blind to good and evil, reckless of destruction, omnipotent matter rolls on its relentless way; for man condemned today to lose his dearest, tomorrow himself to pass through the gate of darkness, it remains only to cherish, ere the blow falls, the lofty thoughts that ennoble his little days—proudly defiant of the irresistible forces that tolerate for a moment his knowledge and his condemnation, to sustain alone a weary but unyielding Atlas, the world that his own ideals have fashioned despite the trampling march of unconscious power." His verdict on human life is summarized thus: "The life of Man is a long march through the night, surrounded by invisible foes, tortured by weariness and pain, towards a goal that few can hope to reach, and where none may tarry long."[11]

As the last of our witnesses in this subject of pessimism, as a dominating temper of our contemporary skeptics, we will call the chief apostle of modernity himself to the stand, Mr. H. G. Wells. Mr. Wells, born in 1866, began publishing pamphlets and magazine articles before the nineteenth century had closed. From a wordly standpoint, using the word in its best connotation, one would think that Mr. Wells had everything which would make life supremely happy, and abundantly satisfying. He must have an enormous amount of vigor and energy, in spite of his diabetes, or he could not have produced such a great amount of work. He has a fertile mind, and that should be a delight to any man. His writings have been enormously influential, and phenomenally profitable; his one book *Outline of History,* published in 1921, has sold something over two million copies, and has been translated into almost every literary language, except the Italian, in both the East and the West—probably enjoying the greatest circulation of any nonfiction book of modern times. Mr. Wells has had the delightful good fortune of seeing many of his predictions come true, which makes him, for many people, a sort of prophet of these last days. I am sure that Mr. Wells is very well off, and has nothing to worry about from a financial standpoint for the rest of his life, which is one great problem out of the way With all this, original genius, and abounding energy, keen foresigh and genuine insight, with such phenomenal success in the field o writing, and followers and disciples all over the world, one would think that Mr. Wells would find life exceptionally satisfying, and his hear without any deep unsatisfied desires, with the single exception, of course that he will not live to see come to pass the socialistic utopia which ha always been in his dreams, from the time he was a young man. Wha he has found in such an abundant life, Mr. Wells tells us, himself, i his amazingly frank *Experiment in Autobiography,* a volume of some thing over three hundred thousand words, which he published in 193 when approaching seventy years of age. He confesses that he is "intol erably hampered by irrelevant necessitics." At the very close of his con fession we find him still longing for "an escape from individual vexa tions and frustrations from the petty overwhelming pains recriminative of the too ego-centered life." The great longing of Mr. Wells' heart, which somehow he has never been able to satisfy, is peace, "The time has come," he says, "to reorganize my peace," and then, conscious of his own inability to find what he so much wants, what he wants more than anything else in the world, he cries out, "I cannot adjust my life to secure any fruitful peace . . . Here I am at sixty-five still seeking for peace . . . That dignified peace . . . is just a hopeless dream." A confession of frustration now and then breaks out in the labor-filled life of our author, concerning which we need quote only one expression. "A spirit of great restlessness came upon me in 1923 to 1924, I was doing what I felt to be good work of making a modern knowledge of ideas available for the general reader but this did not fully engage my imagination; I made speeches and when I read the reports of them I could not believe I had said so little. I gave interviews and was overwhelmed by a sense of incumbrance. Surroundings and time run to seed." [12] With all the fullness of life which Mr. Wells has known, and all his achievements, financial security, world-wide fame, and a place in the encyclopedias of the western world, as long probably as civilization shall stand—the thing that Mr. Wells most wants in his inner self, at the end of life, he neither has found, nor does he now expect to find.

It would seem that Mr. Wells' pessimism grows deeper as he grows older. In a later volume which actually carries a pessimistic title, *The Fate of Man,* which he published in 1939, we come upon these desperate expressions: "There is no creed, no way of life left in the world at all, that really meets the need of the time . . . There is no reason whatever to believe that the order of nature has any greater bias in favor of man than it had in the favor of the ichthyosaur or the pterodactyl. In spite of all my desperation to a brave looking optimism, I perceive that now the universe is bored with him, is turning a hard face to him, and I see him being carried less and less intelligently and more and more rapidly, suffering as every ill-adapted creature must suffer in gross and detail, along the stream of fate, to degradation, suffering and death." [13]

Probably the most bitterly expressed despair of life of our generation is one that comes from a more or less unexpected source, the philosopher, and unusually successful, popular historian of philosophy, Professor Will Durant, of Columbia University. In the summer of 1931 he sent a now famous letter to a number of famous contemporaries, asking them, among other things, "What is the meaning or worth of life?" The replies received he put together in a volume now seemingly quite scarce, *On the Meaning of Life*. Chapter I is significantly entitled, "An Anthology of Doubt," and in it he reveals the utter hopelessness of his own heart. "God, who was once the consolation of our brief life, and our refuge in bereavement and suffering, has apparently vanished from the scene; no telescope, no microscope discovers him. Life has become in that total perspective which is philosophy, a fitful pullulation of human insects on the earth, a planetary eczema that may soon be cured; nothing is certain in it except defeat and death—a sleep from which, it seems, there is no awakening . . . Faith and hope disappear; doubt and despair are the order of the day . . . It seems impossible any longer to believe in the permanent greatness of man, or to give life a meaning that cannot be annulled by death. We move into an age of spiritual exhaustion and desponding like that which hungered for the birth of Christ."[14]

The Mood of Despair Is the Result of Unbelief or the Abandonment of a Formerly Held Faith. While we do not say that there are not exceptions to the law, we still believe that a careful study of the pessimism of our modern skeptics will show that it is the direct result of their abandoning all faith in a living God, in the supernatural, and in the soul's eternal existence. In some cases the fact that the despair is the product of unbelief, is confessed, or at least recognized. The late Mr. Alec Wilson was, before his death, the greatest living authority on Thomas Carlyle, and his many-volumed life of Carlyle, which he did not live to complete, will forever remain the greatest storehouse of material for all future students of the famous Scotch essayist and historian. Mr. Wilson, himself an agnostic, with more regard for Hindu faith than for Christianity, as any reader of these fascinating pages quickly discovers, often goes out of his way to point out the early skepticism of Mr. Carlyle, without ever hinting that Carlyle in his last days came back to a genuine faith in God, yet, though he re joices in Carlyle's skepticism, he is honorable enough to admit that *"the loss of the old creed made Carlyle wretched."*[15]

The confession of the scientist, George Romanes (who, as everyone knows came back to a real faith in Jesus Christ as his Saviour, before he died), concerning the loss of his faith in divine truth at the age of twenty-four, is worth repeating here: "It is with the utmost sorrow that I find myself compelled to accept the conclusions here worked out. I am not ashamed to confess that with this virtual negation of God the universe has lost its soul of loveliness . . . The nature of man without God is thoroughly miserable."[16] This is the very sum of what we are saying, that for men who cut adrift from God and from Christ "the universe has lost its soul of loveliness." Radicalism and skepticism and humanism have never been able to create another "soul of loveliness" for this universe, to take the place of that which their unbelief destroys.

"When the idea of God, which is equivalent to the idea of a reason at the foundation of things, is surrendered—whether in *Agnosticism*, or in some form of dogmatic denial, makes little difference—it becomes a wholly unwarranted assumption that things must certainly go on from better to better. The opposite may quite as well be the case, and progress, now that a given height is reached, may rather be from better to worse. The analogy of nature shows that this is the law in regard to natural life. The plant blooms, reaches its acme, and dies. So, it may be plausibly argued, it will be with humanity. The fact that some progress has been made in the past does not guarantee that this progress will go on indefinitely; rather, the spurs to this progress consisted in what we are now told are illusions, and when these are exploded the motives to progress are gone. A more highly evolved society may lead to an increase of misery rather than of happiness; the growth of enlightenment, instead of adding to men's enjoyments, may result in stripping them successively of the illusions that remain, and may leave them at last sad, weary, disappointed, with an intolerable consciousness of the burden and wretchedness of existence."[17]

In spite of our increased knowledge of the universe, our rising literacy, the marvels of invention which have given us such wonderful devices for the enjoyment of life, as the automobile and the radio, in spite of all these things, the spirit of pessimism is not lifting, rather it is deepening. The words of the famous Italian historian, written a few years ago, would apply to our whole western world: "We see then in Rome, as today in France, wealth, power, culture, glory, draw in their train—grim but inseparable comradeship—a pessimism that times poorer, cruder, more troubled, had not known."[18] In a sermon never published in book form, and perhaps forgotten by our generation, on this very subject of Pessimism, that profound thinker, Principal P. T. Forsyth, more than a half century ago, well said, "Pessimism is the vengeance of God on an age that is prone to do right more for the pleasure than for the goodness of it. It is not only the fruit of an over-driven age but of an age that idealizes mere culture and picks daintily amongst all the resources of taste till it comes to patronize a religion whose deity is the pink of all exquisiteness in shade, movement and thrill. Pessimism is the Nemesis of a society whose grand and fundamental distinction is not right and wrong, false and true, but simply pleasure and pain. It is a Sybarite religion and a finicking philosophy, with a blunder for its first principle and annihilation for its forlorn hope.' And then with his customary ability to see deeply into a problem, Principal Forsyth adds, "Pessimism is the form assumed by the skepticism of an age unprecedently sensitive to pain, it is a revolt more from pain than from evil. If it engaged the larger foe it might find a strength it did not expect to be with it in the night, for it is in conflict with good and evil that we find the means of dealing with pleasure and pain."[1

Is There Any Hope for a Pessimistic Age Like Ours? If skepticism is going to increase, will our pessimism keep step and grow deeper and deeper? I hope there is some truth in the idea of Professor James Orr, in believing that when a man strikes bottom in a life of pessimism, "he can only do one thing and that is to grope after Christ for a deliverance from such despair."[20] There have been intimations of this. John Stuart Mill angered his agnostic friends when he came back to some faith in his last days, as he tells us in his famous Autobiography. There have been others. God grant the number may be multiplied. But we see few signs of it among the deep-dyed skeptics of this, shall we say, third generation of modern agnosticism? "Sooner or later," once said Canon Liddon, "the sadness with which a non-Christian age contemplates pain and death will lead men to turn their eyes to a faith which makes these inevitable facts of human life not merely endurable but welcome."[21] We hope this will prove true. Anyway, the unbelief and the accompanying pessimism of our day, are much deeper and more universally prevalent, than in the bright and happy days of the Victorian age in which Liddon lived.

There are some things Satan has the power to do; there are some things, thank God, neither he nor all his evil hosts can ever do. Satan can never make a man permanently happy in known sin; he can never make a heart sing with joy, with all his wisdom and subtilty; he has never been able to endow his skeptical dupes with a desire to create a hymnal, or a book of songs, with which unbelieving men can express to the world their undisturbable peace, and their unchangeable joy. There is another thing that Satan cannot do, and that is he can never, never bestow anything that would be recognized by man himself, as peace of heart, a peace which Christians know to be so wonderful as to pass all understanding, a peace which the world has never known, but which the world is never able to take away, the very peace of God. If man is determined to live without God, man must also accept the fatal consequence that he is going to live without peace. Well said the Scotch philosopher, Robert Flint, "The heart can find no secure rest except on an infinite God. If less than omnipotent He may be unable to help us in the hour of sorest need; if less than omniscient He may overlook us; if less than perfectly just we cannot unreservedly trust Him; if less than perfectly benevolent we cannot fully love Him. The whole soul can only be devoted to One who is believed to be absolutely good."[22]

In discussing this matter of pessimism, and admitting without strain of reason that skepticism leads directly to a dark mood, to an ugly condition of man's inner life, we can hear someone say, "Well, it is better to know the truth, and be pessimists, if that is what we must be, than to be deceived by some ancient fable, or to find encouragement in some dream or hope, that rests on no foundation." Yes, we would agree with that; let us know the truth, whatever the price be. What book in all the world speaks so sincerely and so constantly of the supreme necessity for truth as our New Testament? Jesus called Himself the truth. He said He came as the *true* Bread and the *true* Life. He asked men frankly the question, if He spoke the truth why did they not believe Him?[23] It was the paganism that prevailed in the world into which Christ came that was a lie. The world was a world of darkness, which would have never known the light of truth had not the Light of the world, Christ Himself, appeared in it. Let us never minimize the importance of truth, but at the same time, let us not allow these leaders of skepticism, these enemies of supernaturalism to say that we, who have found our rest in Christ, our hope in God, and truth in His Holy Word, that we are not as eager for truth as they are. With the truth we have there is the gift of peace, a resultant hope, a divine joy, and the religion which gives truth, hope, peace, and joy must be the one alone which was ever made to satisfy the deepest needs of the human heart, and to give to life the dignity and the glory which God intended for man, created in His image. Let us always prefer truth to myth. Of course, we prefer joy to despair. When *truth* in Christ results in unfading and indestructible joy, and philosophies and cults arise to attempt to allure away our souls from the Son of God, then we can answer instantly, with the disciples of old, and millions of the redeemed since, "To whom shall we go, Thou hast the words of eternal life."[24] Two short phrases found in Paul's writings contain everything we have here tried to say. One is "having no hope, and without God in the world."[25] If we are without God, then we are going to be without hope, whatever we do, and whatever else we have. This age of ours, more atheistic than any age since men laughed at the gods on the streets of Rome, is at the same time an age that confesses it has no hope, outside of the dream of a man-made utopia, in some far-off day, and the more we devise schemes for attaining that utopia the more awful and bloody and chaotic our own world becomes. The other phrase is, "all joy and peace in believing."[26] Just as truly as a man, determined to put God out of life, is at the same time bidding farewell to hope, so contrariwise, a man who will believe in God as revealed in Jesus Christ, is a man who will know a peace and joy that will grow richer, and deeper, more satisfying and more sure, up to the hour of death, when he will enter upon an even greater experience of both these precious things, in the presence of Christ Himself. This latter theme will be more fully considered in the next to the concluding chapter of this book.

CHAPTER V

THE CIVILIZATION OF ANCIENT ATHENS: ITS ACHIEVEMENTS AND ITS IMPOTENCIES

As was said in the preface, there are three primary subjects brought under consideration in this volume: first, the present attack upon evangelical Christianity, and its consequent retreat, with a supplementary study of the causes for unbelief in our modern life; secondly, the powerful, comprehensive apologetic address of the Apostle Paul to the Athenian philosophers with its three-fold theme; and, finally, some suggestions for an immediate vigorous offensive in the defense of the Christian faith. Our first subject has now been as thoroughly discussed as space will permit. We are now to undertake a consideration of the Athenian address of the great Apostle. Before, however, investigating with some exhaustiveness its three fundamental truths, I have felt led to devote one full chapter to a discussion of the civilization of the ancient Athenians, as a background for our study of Paul's address in that most famous of all ancient centers of intellectual activity. This chapter is inserted in this book for two reasons: in the first place, we ought, it seems, to know something of the intellectual history, the convictions, and the religious life of ancient Athens, previous to the first century of our era, for a better understanding of the appropriateness of Paul's message, and that we might more accurately apprehend the utter contrast between the truths which he so clearly, and, may we use the word, dogmatically, affirmed, with the confusion and vagueness and contradictions that were then prevailing in Athens. Secondly, this chapter is written that we may see briefly to what great heights of achievement man can ascend, and still be without a knowledge of the true God, and without a divine revelation, and that we might see the tragic failure of this civilization in its utter inabilty to discover final truth, to arrive at a satisfactory knowledge of God, to deliver itself from its own sins, and to create a hope that nothing could take away. It is doubtful if we may expect to ever see again such genius as was revealed among the Greeks, especially during the fifth century B.C. One thing is certain—if we are going to depend upon our intellect, our own genius, however great, our own scientific researches, and humanly-developed philosophies, there is no ground whatever for expecting that we can discover for ourselves any more than did the Greeks of old, of those things which the human heart most needs, a knowledge of God, an abiding hope, victory over sin, and final truth. What they did do may well be an inspiration for all, but what, even with their genius, they never could achieve, should likewise prove a warning to all. Inasmuch as Greek philosophy, Greek literature, and the whole fascinating field of Greek civilization, is a world in which I have not *lived* all these years, though I have often visited it (I trust not too often), I will, throughout this chapter, be compelled to present matters that are here considered in the words of some of the great modern authorities on ancient Greek life and activity, together with a few important statements by the Greeks themselves, from the inexhaustible pages of their own eternal masterpieces. I have felt it *necessary* to deal with Greek achievements with some thoroughness, that we may the better appreciate what the Christian faith could contribute to Athens and to our day.

In Praise of the Ancient Greeks. "Europe has nearly four million square miles; Lancashire has seventeen hundred; Attica has seven hundred." So does R. W. Livingstone of Corpus Christi College, Oxford, begin his important volume, *The Greek Genius and Its Meaning to Us.* "It has given us the staple of our vocabulary in every domain of thought and knowledge. Political tyranny, democracy, anarchism, philosophy, physiology, geology, history, these are all Greek words. It has seized hold, up to the present, of our higher education."[1] Lord Macaulay, in middle life, declared, "I have gone back to Greek literature with a passion quite astonishing to myself . . . I felt as if I had never known before what intellectual enjoyment was. Oh, that wonderful people! there is not one art, not one science about which we may not use the same expression which Lucretius has employed about the victory over superstitions 'Primum Graius homo.' I think myself very fortunate in having been able to return to these great masters while still in the full vigor of life and when my taste and judgment are at maturity."[2] It may be an exaggeration, but Henry Moore was a man of great learning and balanced judgment, and he could say in his famous *Rede* Lecture, "Except the blind forces of nature, nothing moves in this world which is not Greek in origin."[3] As Rome's system of government and her legal codes have stamped themselves upon Western civilization forever, so Greek culture, art, philosophy and science, literature, ethics, and political theory, have given to Europe its ideals in these realms, its vocabulary, and its greatest masterpieces. In almost every major department of life, and certainly of the inner life, with the single exception of religion, Greece has given us the noblest achievements of the race. Ancient Greek culture is that which has forever been looked up to as almost perfect, and, at the same time, almost incapable of being repeated, except in inferior copies. Of the entire period of Greek history, it was the age of Pericles in which the greatest concentration of human genius ever appeared, in one locality, at one time. The Periclean age, we may identify generally as the fifth century B.C. Pericles himself was born in 495, and flourished from 461–429. Let us just recall some of the names of this period: Herodotus the historian (484–424), Empedocles (490–430), the dramatist Aeschylus (525–456), Sophocles (496–406), and Euripedes (485–406); among the philosophers, two of the three greatest, Socrates (469–399), and Plato (428–347), and then, a little later their greatest disciple, Aristotle (384–322). Born the same year was the greatest of all orators, Demosthenes (384–322). In a lecture on this period which Sir Richard Jebb gave in 1889, he said, "Within those thirty years (460–430) the political power of Athens consummated; within those thirty years created works of art in literature, in architecture and in sculpture which the world has ever since regarded as unapproachable masterpieces . . . Pericles, during his period of political struggle . . . realized the essential idea of the Greek city more fully than it had ever been realized before, or was ever realized after; and he did this by enabling every citizen, poor no less than rich, to feel that he was a citizen, indeed, taking his part in the work of the city without undue sacrifice of his private interest, and sharing in the noblest enjoyment which the city had to offer."[4] "The period which intervened between the birth of Pericles and the death of Aristotle," says Shelley, "is undoubtedly, whether considered in itself or with reference to the effects which it has produced upon the subsequent destinies of civilized man, the most memorable in the history of the world . . . The wrecks and fragments of these subtle and profound minds, like the ruins of a fine statue, obscurely suggest to us the grandeur and perfection of the whole. Their very language . . . in variety, in simplicity, in flexibility, and in copiousness, excels every other language of the western world."[5]

The Pre-eminence of Athens. If the Greek genius was the most unique from a human standpoint (we are not, of course, comparing it with the divine inspiration which came upon the Hebrew prophets) that the world has ever seen, and if in its history the age of Pericles was that of the greatest achievement, so in that age it was in the city of Athens that the greater part of its glorious accomplishments were brought forth. It is significant in itself that the great *Cambridge Ancient History* has for the title of its fifth volume, simply this, *Athens, 478–401 B.C.,* as though everything important that happened in Europe in those eight decades must be identified with the city of Athens. Thucydides called Athens "The School of Greece." Hippias, in the *Protagoras* of Plato, appeals to the Athenians with the stirring words, "How great would be the disgrace then if we who know the nature of things and are the wisest of the Hellenes and are such as get together in this city, which is the metropolis of wisdom, and in the greatest and most glorious house of this city, should have nothing to show worthily of this height of dignity but should only quarrel with one another like the meanest of mankind."[6]

The Corinthian allies of Sparta said to the Laodiceans, "You have never considered what manner of men are these Athenians with whom you will have to fight, and how utterly unlike yourselves. They are revolutionary, equally quick in the conception and in the execution of every new plan; while you are conservative—careful only to keep what you have, originating nothing, and not acting even when action is most necessary. They are bold beyond their strength; they run risks which prudence would condemn; and in the midst of misfortunes they are full of hope. Whereas it is your nature, though strong, to act feebly; when your plans are most prudent, to distrust them; and when calamities come upon you, to think that you will never be delivered from them. They are impetuous, and you are dilatory; they are always abroad, and you are always at home. For they hope to gain something by leaving their homes; but you are afraid that any new enterprise may imperil what you have already. When conquerors, they pursue their victory to the utmost; when defeated, they fall back the least. Their bodies they devote to their country as though they belonged to other men; their true self is their mind, which is most truly their own when employed in her service. When they do not carry out an intention which they have formed, they seem to have sustained a personal bereavement; when an enterprise succeeds, they have gained a mere instalment of what is to come; but if they fail, they at once conceive new hopes and so fill up the void. With them alone to hope is to have, for they lose not a moment in the execution of an idea. This is the lifelong task, full of danger and toil, which they are always imposing upon themselves. None enjoy their good things less, because they are always seeking for more. To do their duty is their only holiday, and they deem the quiet of inaction to be as disagreeable as the most tiresome business. If a man should say of them, in a word, that they were born neither to have peace themselves nor to allow peace to other men, he would simply speak the truth."[7]

The well-known classical scholar, Mr. G. Lowes Dickinson, in his remarkable work, *The Greek View of Life,* sums up years of study of Greek intellectual life with these words: "All the beauty, all the grace, all the joy of Greece; all that chains the desire of mankind, with a yearning that is never stilled, to that one golden moment in the past, whose fair and balanced interplay of perfect flesh and soul no later gains of thought can compensate, centres about that bright and stately city of romance, the home of Pericles and all the arts, whence from generation to generation has streamed upon ages less illustrious an influence at once the sanest and the most inspired of all that have shaped the secular history of the world."[8]

Ancient Greek Literature. It is hard to say in what one realm the Greeks most amazingly proved themselves superior to all the other peoples of ancient Europe, and, we might say, of the whole ancient world, whether in literature, or art, or science, or oratory, or the theory of government. I know of no way in arranging these inexhaustible subjects in any logical order, and the order in which they appear here has itself no particular significance. All students of world literature are unanimous in acknowledging that the literature of ancient Greece is, for many reasons, superior to the literature of any other people that have ever lived on this earth, at least up until the Reformation, and the birth of what we might call modern German, French and English literature. As it is impossible to even list the great literary creators of ancient Greece in a brief review like this, let me say just a word about three or four of the most outstanding masters. At the head of Greek literature stands Homer, writing, perhaps, about 800 B.C. Professor Couch, in his brilliantly written new work, *Classical Civilization: Greece,* begins his chapter on this subject with the simple affirmation, "The greatest heritage of all European literature is the poetry of Homer."[9] One of the greatest of all modern historians, Professor J. B. Bury, in his famous *History of Greece,* says that the Iliad was "the first and greatest epic poem of the world."[10] The late Dr. Paul Shorey declared, what all who have made a study of European literature must acknowledge, that "there is a sense in which all Greek literature and civilization, not to say all European civilization, flow from this fountain."[11] Harvard's greatly beloved Professor Barrett Wendell begins his large volume on *The Traditions of European Literature* with an extended discussion of Homer in which, among other things, he says, "Each time you thus recur on them (the lines of Homer) you will find in them a quality which will impress you the more the better you know them. No matter how familiar they may become, it is hardly possible to read them without a sense that they are almost as new as if you had never read them before. Age cannot wither, nor custom stale them."[12]

I must say that the pages of Homer have always presented a mystery to me, not a mystery as regards the meaning of his lines (though occasionally they are difficult), but a mystery in regard to how any one man, at the very threshold of a new, great literature, could present his subjects, his story, if you will, with such variety, such beauty, such simplicity, such economy of words, and with such a vast and rich vocabulary. I know that in the last two generations we have had some discussion about pre-Homeric literature, and the civilization of Crete, etc., but there is no real *literature* in Greece before Homer. With him Greek literature is born full-grown. I think few Christians today realize that in these pages first occur hundreds of the great words which fill the pages of our precious New Testament. Where did Homer get these words—for priest, for prophet, for hades, for altar, for sacrifice, and all the rest? I have often wondered. I continue to wonder. I have never seen an explanation of it. Here is a genius such, seemingly, as the world sees but once. And then, as Herodotus tells us, it was Homer together with his successor, Hesiod, who gave to Greece her vast pantheon of Olympian deities.[13] With Homer, then, is born not only Greek literature, but also Greek religion, at least here appear in all their unforgettable majesty the great gods and goddesses of Greek religion, whatever may have been their previous place in earlier Mycenaean civilization.

Passing by some centuries we come to the great tragedians of Greece, Aeschylus and his successors. Speaking of the work of Aeschylus, and the tragedies of the fifth century B.C., Professor Rostovetzeff, with some detail, says: "In the dialogue between the chorus and the narrator he introduced a second narrator, and this apparently trifling change in the mechanism of the drama, this introduction of a second actor, made it possible to convert the ritual acting at the festival of Dionysus into real drama and real tragedy, the same, in its essential features, as the tragedy of our own stage. The dialogue between the actors, divided up by songs from the chorus, enabled Aeschylus to thrill the spectator with pictures of the intense passions that fill the heart of man, while he supplemented these in the choric songs with his own feelings and reflections. The plots of his plays were almost all taken from mythology and not from actual life. But mythology offered such an endless variety of vivid stories in the lives of gods and heroes, that it was not difficult to get from these stores material for human drama. His plays, and those of his successors, were arranged in trilogies: that is, he produced three plays together on one subject, and also a satyr-play, a parody of tragedy, to end up with; but each of the three had to be complete in itself, while the connexion between them was maintained by the identity of the dramatis personae. Aeschylus wrote a great number of tragedies, perhaps as many as ninety. Seven have been preserved, and they include one trilogy, the *Oresteia*—the tremendous story of a son's vengeance on his mother for the murder of his father, and of the son's tortured conscience and final purification. The *Persians* is an exception to the rule: the subject was taken from recent history—from the Persian war, in which Aeschylus himself had taken an active part and fought in the ranks at Marathon. In the general opinion of antiquity, with which modern criticism entirely agrees, Aeschylus, from the artistic point of view, not merely created the tragic drama but also wrote tragedies whose perfection has never been surpassed either in ancient or in modern times."[14]

Turning from tragedy to historical writing, it is agreed that Herodotus (484–424) was the father of history, and Thucydides (471–400) the greatest master of historical writing. In fact, says the author of the chapter devoted to these writers in the *Cambridge Ancient History,* "Herodotus and Thucydides appear to stand, together and alone, an elder and a younger contemporary as earth-born colossi, to guard the portal of Greek history, that is to say, of Greek literature."[15] To consider Thucydides in detail for a moment, let us listen to the verdict of the one who, more than any other writer in our language in the last two generations, became the master of Greek historical literature, Professor J. B. Bury of Cambridge. In his *Ancient Greek Historians,* he writes as follows of the second of these two great names: "The work of Thucydides has limitations which we must beware of underrating; but it marks the longest and most decisive step that has ever been taken by a single man towards making history what it is today. Out of the twilight in which Herodotus still moved wondering, he burst into the sunlight where facts are hard, not to wonder but to understand. With the Greeks historical study never acquired the scientific character which it was reserved for the nineteenth century to impress upon it. But within the limits of the task he attempted Thucydides was a master in the craft of investigating contemporary events, and it may be doubted whether within those limits the nineteenth century would have much to teach him. If he had admitted his readers into the secrets of his workshop, if he had more clearly displayed his raw material and shown how he arrived at his conclusion, if he had argued and discussed, he might have exercised a greater influence than he did on the *methods* of subsequent Greek historians."[16] One of the greatest authorities on Greek literature of our generation, if not perhaps the greatest, has summed up the glory of the inexhaustible writings of ancient Greece in this tribute: "The literature of Greece is the only one in the civilized world that developed wholly of itself, which brought forth in profusion not only perfect work of art but rigorously exclusive artistic types and styles, through which it became the basis and model of the European and of various extra-European literature. Greek literature is the vessel that contains, or has contained, the fundamental work of all science; for it was the Greeks and no others that brought science as such into the world."[17]

The Art of Ancient Greece. In speaking of Greek art, I must write warily, for though I have spent hours, I am glad to say, on the Acropolis and in the museums of Athens, and have tried to do some reading in this subject, I am not a student of art nor an art critic. Nevertheless we must all recognize the important part that art plays in the history and thought of every people, and especially with the Greeks, and when it comes to speaking of their genius and greatness, I cannot pass by this particular field of activity and expression of thought. With the preliminary characteristics of Greek art which together made it so beautiful and perfect, such as simplicity, naturalism, balance in measure and ideality, I cannot write with any fullness: this is not a volume on aesthetics. Let us turn our attention to just one great product of the age of Pericles, in the realm of creative art, namely the Parthenon, built 447–432, and consider only, and that briefly, the perfectness of the curves which give it its beauty, and something of the power and vividness of some of its carvings. The words of Plutarch concerning this greatest of all masterpieces of architecture are famous: "And it is true that deftness and speed in working do not impart to the work an abiding weight of influence nor an exactness of beauty; whereas the time which is put out to loan in laboriously creating, pays a large and generous interest in the preservation of the creation. For this reason are the works of Pericles all the more to be wondered at; they were created in a short time for all time. Each one of them, in its beauty, was even then and at once antique; but in the freshness of its vigour it is, even to the present day, recent and newly wrought. Such is the bloom of perpetual newness, as it were, upon these works of his, which makes them ever to look untouched by time, as though the unfaltering breath of an ageless spirit had been infused into them."[18] One can say that the Parthenon is the most perfect building ever built by man and let it go at that, or, one can begin to carefully examine the structure, and discover some of the reasons for its absolute perfectness. Even though the sentences are technical, I have chosen the latter course here, that those of my readers who are not students of art may have some conception of what this exquisite structure means in the history of architecture: "The 'refinements' of the Parthenon consist, for the most part, in the substitution of curves for straight lines, and in the tilting inwards or outwards of vertical members. The surface of the stylobate is not flat; it rather resembles the edges of a mat nailed at its four corners and raised from the floor by the wind. This rise amounts to about 4 inches on the long sides, which measure nearly 230 feet, and to about 2¾ inches on the short sides, which measure just over 100 feet. The execution here is not perfect, for the corners are not all on the same level, and the lines are not true curves. This horizontal curvature is repeated in the entablature. The columns all lean slightly inwards, those at the angles having a double inclination, which incidentally eases the problem of the angle triglyph: the entablature has the same tilt; the antae beside the porches lean forward. The columns not only taper upwards, as Greek columns almost always did, but do so with a subtle curve, called the 'entasis': the angle columns are a little stouter than the rest. . . . The various refinements may well have been invented for different purposes, curvature of the stylobate for drainage, tilting and thickening of the columns for strength, entasis for beauty: and though the illusion theory may well be as old as the fifth century, it is likely that architects at that date were in truth chiefly influenced by an instinctive dislike of mechanical straightness." The greatest sculptor of all ages, Phidias, was in charge of the adornment of this temple and while its sculptures were conceived and designed by him, "it is unfortunately quite impossible to determine just which pieces were carved by him and which by his associates." The amount of the work is too great to have been achieved by any one man in a lifetime. There were sculptured metopes of the Doric frieze, some fifty colossi figures in the pediment and more than 520 feet of continuous Ionic frieze. Let us consider for a moment just one segment of the carving on these pediments, the cherilean of Athena on the west side of the temple. One has said, "The horses are made with such great art that the sculptor seems to have outdone himself by giving them more than seeming life; such a vigor is expressed in each posture of their prancing and stamping natural to generous horses." Because of mutilation and accidents and attempted theft these horses for the most part have been destroyed but the heads remain of the horses of the team of Sun and Moon in the eastern pediment and, says a well-known authority, "the horses of the sun god, as they rise from the sea, throw up their heads with nostrils dilated to inhale the breath of the morning; in the other end of the pediment the horse of the Moon goddesses, the only one of the team which is preserved—though tired as he approaches the end of his course, still shows his mettle; indeed this horse is equal in mastery of handling to any piece of work in the Parthenon. There is a wonderfully sensitive treatment of the skin of muscle which seems almost to quiver and to contrast with the smooth surface of the cheek showing the bone beneath."[19]

The Origin of Science. Whole volumes have been written to show how all our modern science derives its principles, and a great part of its elementary truths, from this small group of thinkers gathered together in the city of Athens (and occasionally in some other Greek city), during two centuries of such amazing intellectual activity. Here we can only hurriedly mention a few of its more important achievements. To begin with mathematics: "Mathematics is a Greek science. So far as true astronomy is concerned, the mathematician's technical equipment is almost wholly Greek. The Greeks laid down the principles, fixed the terminology and invented the methods *ab initio;* moreover they did this with such certainty that in the centuries which have elapsed there has been no need to reconstruct, still less to reject as unsound any essential part of their doctrines."[20] It was Pythagoras (582–507 B.C.) who first held that the earth was spherical in shape "and he was aware that the sun, moon, and planets have independent movements of their own in a sense opposite to that of the daily rotation."[21] Aristarchus so carefully studied the heavenly bodies that he was able to determine that: "1. The diameter of the sun is between eighteen and twenty times the diameter of the moon; 2. that the diameter of the moon is between two forty-fifths and one-thirtieth of the distance of the center of the moon from our eye; 3. that the diameter of the sun is between nineteen-thirds and forty-three sixths of the diameter of the earth."[22] It was Archimedes who invented the whole science of hydrostatics. Eratosthenes was able to measure the earth so accurately that he concluded that its circumference was 252,000 stadia, that is, 7,850 miles, only fifty miles less than the true polar diameter! Within a period of 350 years the Greeks, "starting from the very beginning, brought geometry to the point of performing operations to the integral calculus."[23]

When we turn to Aristotle and his vast encyclopedic researches in natural science we are utterly astonished at the amount of accurate knowledge that he was able to accumulate in his century. Darwin once said, "Linnaeus and Cuvier have been my two gods, though in very different ways, but they were mere school boys to old Aristotle." The outstanding authority of our generation on Greek science sums up Aristotle's pre-eminence in these words: "So it comes to pass that for two thousand years and throughout all lands men have come to Aristotle, and found in him information and instruction—that which they desired. Arab and Moor and Syrian and Jew treasured his books while the western world sat in darkness; the great centuries of Scholasticism hung upon his words; the oldest of our Universities, Bologna, Paris, Oxford, were based upon his teaching, yea, all but established for his study. Where he has been, there, seen or unseen, his influence remains; even the Moor and the Arab find in him, to this day, a teacher after their own hearts: a teacher of eternal verities, telling of sleep and dreams, of youth and age, of life and death, of generation and corruption, of growth and of decay: a guide to the book of Nature, revealer of the Spirit, a prophet of the works of God."[24]

In regard to medicine, the Greeks discovered the pulse as early as 400 B.C. and they had developed a conception of human physiology with the arteries arising from the heart and veins from the liver, which lasted for two thousand years, until the time of Harvey. "It is the distinction of the Greeks alone among the nations of antiquity that they practised a system of medicine based not on theory but on observation accumulated systematically as time went on. The claim can be made for the Greeks that some at least among them were deflected by no theory, were deceived by no theurgy, were hampered by no tradition in their search for the facts of disease and in their attempts at interpreting its phenomena. Only the Greeks among the ancients could look on their healers as *physicians* (=naturalists, *phusis*-nature), and that word itself stands as a lasting reminder of their achievement."[25] Of course as everyone knows the Hippocratic oath for physicians remains the ideal of the whole medical profession among Arabs, Jews, and Christians alike, found in almost every important work on medicine even in our modern times. We have only begun to sketch the brilliant achievements of the ancient Greeks in science, but this will be enough to make us realize, probably with amazement, what those men were able to achieve within so short a period of time, and without the vast apparatus which we now so expertly use in our laboratories.

The Founding of True Philosophy. When we come to the study of Greek philosophy, we might just frankly acknowledge at once that no one, for two thousand years, has been able even to begin a study of philosophy without going back to the foundations of this science laid by the Greeks. "Rational science," says one of our greatest modern students of Greek thought, "is the creation of the Greeks, and we know when it began. We do not count as philosophy anything anterior to that."[26] Says the same author, in another work, "The word philosophy is Greek and so is the thing it denotes. Unless we are to use the term in so wide a sense as to empty it of all special meaning, there is no evidence that philosophy has ever come into existence anywhere except under Greek influences."[27] In fact, Professor R. W. Livingstone goes so far as to say that, "The only *thinking* civilization in the world before our own is that of Greece."[28] The Greek philosophy began, we may say, with a great group of philosophers in the sixth century: Thales, Anaximander, Anaximenes, and Heracleitus, all of Milesia, and the Eleatic philosophers, Zenophanes who believed in one God, Paramenides and Zeno, and the greatest of all of that period, Pythagoras the mathematician. Early Greek philosophy, most significantly, was what we would call cosmological, that is, truly devoted not to a study of man, or the soul, or the mind, but the nature of the world. "Since man begins by looking outwards upon the external world, and not inwards upon his own self, this is the character of the first period of Greek philosophy. It concerns itself solely with nature, with the external quality, and only with man as a part of nature . . . It is not until the time of the Sophists that the Greek spirit turns inwards upon itself and begins to consider the problems of man, of life, of human destiny, of ethics."[29] I have always thought, although I have not seen this referred to in any volume, as far as I can remember, that it is rather significant that where Greek philosophy begins, is exactly where the Bible begins, of course, with a great deal more truth, simplicity, and spiritual meaning. When we say that Greek philosophy begins with the problems of the world, of nature, we can also say that that is exactly where the Word of God begins, with the creation of the world. If it was reasonable that the Greeks' profoundest of all thinkers should begin their philosophical speculations with a consideration of the world of nature, is it not according to every law of reason that the Bible should there begin its marvelous record of redeeming work?

Thousands of books, of course, have been written concerning Greek philosophy, and no history of philosophy can possibly begin at any other place than with the ancient Greeks. It is not our purpose in this book to set forth even a summary of what the Greeks thought. We are speaking in this chapter generally of the vast abiding achievement of the Greeks, which have exercised such an enormous influence upon western civilization for the last two thousand years. Yet it seems hardly adequate to say simply that Plato and Aristotle have dominated the forms of thought for all of western Europe since Europe knew any civilization. Instead of attempting to reduce the vast system of Plato's philosophy to a sentence or two, or to summarize in my own inadequate words the significance of Aristotle in the thinking of the western world, I am taking the liberty of first quoting some words concerning the great primary conception in Plato's philosophy, the matter of Ideas, as expressed by Professor Clement C. J. Webb in his very valuable though brief *History of Philosophy:* "As, in order to *think* that this or that act is just, we must *know* what justice is; so, also, in order to *think* that the line A B is straight or that the lines A B and C D are equal, we must *know* what straightness or what equality is. Here, too, there is a permanent nature, apprehended by the understanding, not by the senses, which does not become, even while we speak of it, something else than what we are saying that it is. These permanent natures, discovered by Socrates in his efforts to find an abiding object for our moral judgments, which should not be at the mercy of custom and circumstance, became the corner-stone of Plato's philosophy, and are called by him Forms or, to use the Greek word, Ideas. This word Idea is familiar to us; but in modern English it usually means something very different from what it meant to Plato. With us, it means something in our minds which may or may not correspond to an independent reality outside of them. With him, it meant the form—not the mere outward shape, but the inner essential structure or nature of anything, which made it the kind of thing it was. Even when it was what we call a corporeal or material thing, it was not the senses (which have only to do with superficial appearances) that could take account of this inner essential nature. The Form or Idea is, therefore, the proper object, not of the senses, but of the understanding. Yet we must be careful to remember that this does not mean that it is what we call a 'notion' or 'concept,' something which has its being only in the mind; it is that of which we have a notion or concept, but which does not by any means depend for its existence upon our thinking of it. . . . The Ideas of Plato are the eternal natures, whatever they be, which constitute the inner reality of the universe, and which alone can be objects of true knowledge. They are not perceptible by the senses; they can be apprehended by the understanding only. But, just as we commonly take the things which the senses perceive to have an existence quite independent of our perception of them, so the Platonic Ideas are no product of the mental activity by means whereof we apprehend them; they are rather its presupposition."[30] Of Aristotle a distinguished American scholar has said that he "strove, as no man before or since has striven, to comprehend this world in which we live, its physical base, its cosmic order but no less the culture and institutions of our mankind. No single intellect with so universal and so enduring approbation of men (as his) ever directed itself to solve and understand almost the whole sphere of human interests."[30a]

The mind of Aristotle swept over practically every important subject known to men, even in the brilliant civilization of Greece in which he lived, and of which he was so shining an adornment. It is impossible to give even a paragraph to each of the subjects Aristotle touched upon; let me then quote a few sentences concerning the most important things, probably, about Aristotle, from the very fine chapter on this philosopher, in one of the most interesting and satisfying volumes on philosophy I have seen, *The Critical History of Greek Philosophy* by W. T. Stace, "In the first place, Aristotle loved facts. What he wanted was always definite scientific knowledge. Plato, on the other hand, had no love of facts and no gift for physical enquiries. And what disgusted Aristotle about the system of Plato was the contempt which it poured upon the world of sense. To depreciate objects of sense, and to proclaim the knowledge of them valueless, was a fundamental characteristic of all Plato's thinking. But the world of sense is the world of facts, and Aristotle was deeply interested in facts. No matter in what branch of knowledge, any fact was received by Aristotle with enthusiasm. To Plato it appeared of no interest what the habits of some obscure animal might be. That alone which should be pursued is the knowledge of the Idea. And he went so far as to deny that knowledge of the sense-world could properly be described as knowledge at all. But the habits of animals appeared to Aristotle a matter worthy of investigation for its own sake . . . What his style loses in beauty it gains in clearness of conception. For every thought or shade of thought which it is desired to express there is an accurate term. If no term in common use will express the thought, Aristotle coins one. Hence he is one of the greatest terminologists that ever lived. He adapted or invented an enormous number of terms. He may be not unjustly regarded as the founder of philosophical language, as the inventor of a vocabulary of technical terms. Many of the terms used to this day to express man's most abstract thoughts were invented or introduced by Aristotle. It must not be supposed that Aristotle wrote in a rigidly scientific style because he had no aesthetic sense. The very contrary is the case. His treatise on art shows him by far the best critic of the ancient world, and in his appreciation and estimation of the beautiful he far excels Plato. . . . What we now know as 'formal logic,' what is to this day contained in all text-books, taught in all schools and universities, is, in all its essentials, nothing more than the logic of Aristotle. His writings upon the subject include the treatment of the well-known laws of thought, the doctrine of the ten categories, the five predicables, the doctrines of terms, of propositions, of syllogisms, and of the reduction of the other figures to the first figure of the syllogism. And these heads might well form the list of contents of a modern work on formal logic. In only two respects has any advance been made upon Aristotle by subsequent logicians." Perhaps one more word might be added concerning Aristotle's psychology: "Within human consciousness there are lower and higher grades, and Aristotle has taken great pains to trace these from the bottom to the top. These stages of consciousness are what are ordinarily called 'faculties.' But Aristotle notes that it is nonsense to talk, as Plato did, of the 'parts' of the soul. The soul, being a single indivisible being, has no parts. They are different aspects of the activity of one and the same being; different stages of its development. They can no more be separated than the convex and concave aspects of a curve. The lowest faculty, if we must use that word, is sense-perception. Now what we perceive in a thing is its qualities. Perception tells us that a piece of gold is heavy, yellow, etc. The underlying substratum which supports the qualities cannot be perceived. This means that the matter is unknowable, the form knowable, for the qualities are part of the form. Sense-perception, therefore, takes place when the object stamps its form upon the soul. This is important for what it implies rather than what it states. It shows the thoroughly idealistic trend of Aristotle's thought. Next in the scale above the senses comes the common sense. This has nothing to do with what we understand by that phrase in every-day language. It means the central sensation-ganglion in which isolated sensations meet, are combined, and form a unity of experience. . . . Above the common sense is the faculty of imagination. By this Aristotle means, not the creative imagination of the artist, but the power, which everyone possesses, of forming mental images and pictures. This is due to the excitation in the sense-organ continuing after the object has ceased to affect it. The next faculty is memory. This is the same as imagination, except that there is combined with the image a recognition of it as a copy of a past sense-impression. Recollection, again, is higher than memory. Memory-images drift purposelessly through the mind. Recollection is the deliberate evoking of memory-images. From recollection we pass to the specifically human faculty of reason. But reason itself has two grades. The lower is called passive reason, the higher active reason. The mind has the power of thought before it actually thinks. This latent capacity is passive reason. The mind is here like a smooth piece of wax which has the power to receive writing, but has not received it. The positive activity of thought itself is active reason. The comparison with wax must not mislead us into supposing that the soul only receives its impressions from sensation. It is pure thought which writes upon the wax."[31]

The Ethical Principles of Aristotle. I do not wish to discuss here the moral life of the Greeks, but rather, to confine myself to those ethical principles set forth in the greatest work on ethics, apart from the doctrines of revealed religion, that has ever been composed in the history of the human race, I mean of course the *Nicomachean Ethics* of Aristotle. The *Ethics* begins with these famous words: "Every art and every scientific inquiry, and similarly every action and purpose, may be said to aim at some good. Hence the good has been well defined as that at which all things aim. But it is clear that there is a difference in the ends; for the ends are sometimes activities, and sometimes result beyond the mere activities. Also, where there are certain ends beyond the actions, the results are naturally superior to the activities. . . . Does it not follow then that the knowledge of this supreme good is of great importance for the conduct of life, and that, *if we know it,* we shall be like archers who have a mark at which to aim, we shall have a better chance of attaining what we want? But, if this is the case, we must endeavour to comprehend, at least in outline, its nature, and the science or faculty to which it belongs."[32]

As we turn the pages of this most remarkable work we come upon discussions concerning what is good, the nature of happiness, the function of the good man, the truth that the end of human life will be some good of the soul, that happiness is determined by virtue and activity. The second book of the *Ethics* begins with a discussion of the intellectual and moral virtue of *excellence,* with a profound consideration of the question of the relation between virtue and pleasure and pain. In chapter seven occurs a most elaborate discussion of particular virtues, arranged in three columns, those which are said to be in excess; then a mean state, that is, a medium state; then those which express deficiency. Thus, e.g., as excess is licentious, the mean or desired state is temper, while the state of deficiency would be insensible; if the state of excess is vanity, the mean state is high-mindedness, and the state of deficiency is little-mindedness; if the state of excess is boastfulness, the mean state is truthfulness, and the state of deficiency is self-depreciation. Here some of the most important ethical words, even in the Pauline vocabulary of Christian virtues, are worked out with amazing fullness, richness and accuracy. Recognizing of course the infinite superiority of the New Testament over Aristotle, or any other ancient writer, it must be acknowledged that many of the words which appear without definition in the New Testament epistle are here unfolded in all the fullness of their meaning. Take e.g., the word *gentleness* (*praotes*) which appears in Paul's epistles nine times. Aristotle devotes a whole chapter to it. There is nothing finer, probably in all this work than Aristotle's chapter on high-mindedness, of which he says the principal characteristics are these: shrinking from encountering small dangers but ready to encounter great dangers; to be fond of conferring benefits, but ashamed of receiving them; to try to return benefits with interest; to be unwilling to ask favors; to bear one's self with dignity toward the great, but with moderation toward the middle class; to be free from assertions; to avoid fussiness or hurrying; to act seldom but effectively; to be open in one's hatreds and friendships; to care more for reality than for reputation, therefore to be truthful; to eschew servitude; to be more given to admiration, not to bear grudges; to avoid gossip or evil speaking; not to whine over the inevitable, or what is insignificant; to prefer nobleness to profit. No treatment of such a subject could ever surpass this, coming from the pen of a man who knew nothing of the inspiration of the Holy Spirit, and did not have the advantage of inspired writings before him. What Aristotle did in this work, no other man has even approached, apart from the light of the Word of God.

Political Theory. I was going to say a word about oratory, but it is not necessary here. Let me speak of just one more general subject, the theory of government. In speaking of the Greek conception of politics, I am not here discussing the qualities, the virtues, and the deficiencies of the Greek state, as it actually existed, for the simple reason that I am not a student of political economy, and I haven't the slightest capacity for comparatively appraising the various systems of governments that have existed in the Western world. I know that many dogmatically say that the Greeks had about the finest form of government that man has ever known, but for myself, I cannot think that a state which produced the tyrants which Greece allowed, cultivated slavery, and rested solidly upon aristocracy, never upon equality, could be said to be a perfect type of government. If I know anything of how the Greeks lived, politically speaking, even in the days of their glory, I would not exchange it for a few years here in our own country. I am only speaking here of the *theory* of government. "The first valuable contribution the Greeks made to political study was that they invented it. It is not too much to say that, before fifth-century Greece, politics did not exist. There were powers and principalities, governments and subjects, but politics no more existed than chemistry existed in the age of alchemy. An imitation of an idea, as Plato has taught us, is not the same as an idea; nor is the imitation of a science the same as a science. Rameses and Nebuchadnezzar, Croesus the Lydian and Cyrus the Persian, ruled over great empires; but within their dominions there were no politics because there were no public affairs. There were only the private affairs of the sovereign and his ruling class. Government and all that pertained to it, from military service and taxation to the supply of women for the royal harem, was simply the expression of the power and desire of the ruler. The great advance made by Greece was to have recognized that public or common interests exist and to have provided, first for their management, and secondly for their study. In other words, the Greeks were the first to rescue the body politic from charlatans and to hand it over to physicians.

"How great an achievement this was we can best recognize when we consider how large a place the true study of politics, and the terms and ideas to which it has given rise, fills in the life of the modern man—especially of the modern Englishman. Justice and liberty, law and democracy, parliament and public opinion—all these and many more we owe to the peasants and craftsmen of the small Greek republics who, having felt the need for a better management of their humble concerns, set to work to provide it, with the same inventiveness, the same adaptation of means to end, which led them, in other fields, to the invention of the classic temple or of the drama. If it is going too far to say that every modern politician owes his stock-in-trade of general ideas to the Greeks, there are certainly few who do not owe them their perorations."[33]

Aristotle begins his epochal work *Politics* with this famous affirmation; "Every state is a community of some kind, and every community is established with a view to some good; and mankind always acts in order to obtain that which it thinks good. But if all communities aim at some good, the state or political community, which is the highest of all, and which embraces all the rest, aims at good in a greater degree than any other and at the highest good."[34] We do not have time to consider all the various theories, proposals, and principles, concerning education and government which Aristotle here lays down, but one quotation will suffice to show how rich and full and really up-to-date his treatise is: "Thus it is manifest that the best political community is formed by citizens of the middle class, and that those states are likely to be well administered, in which the middle class is large, and stronger if possible than both the other classes, or at any rate than either singly; for the addition of the middle class turns the scale, and prevents either of the extremes from being dominant. Great then is the good fortune of a state in which the citizens have a moderate and sufficient property; for where some possess much, and he others nothing, there may arise an extreme democracy, or a pure oligarchy; or a tyranny may grow out of either extreme—either out of he most rampant democracy, or out of an oligarchy; but it is not so ikely to arise out of the middle constitutions and those akin to them. The mean condition of states is clearly best, for no other is free rom faction; and where the middle class is large, there are least ikely to be factions and dissensions. For a similar reason large tates are less liable to faction than small ones, because in them the middle class is large; whereas in small states it is easy to divide all the citizens into two classes who are either rich or poor, and to leave nothing in the middle. And democracies are safer and more permanent than oligarchies, because they have a middle class which is more numerous and has a greater share in the government; for when there is no middle class, and the poor greatly exceed in number, troubles arise, and the state soon comes to an end."[35] Just as Aristotle's *Ethics* was the greatest work of its kind ever produced, apart from those who have written from the inspiration of the New Testament, so his *Politics* is recognized on every hand as at least the profoundest work in this difficult field of thought down to modern times.

The Verdict of Thucydides. The greatest extended praise of the Athenians that was offered by the Greeks themselves is the famous passage in Thucydides, a portion of which may appropriately conclude this part of our discussion of Greek civilization. "Before I praise the dead, I should like to point out by what principles of action we rose to power, and under what institutions and through what manner of life our empire became great. For I conceive that such thoughts are not unsuited to the occasion, and that this numerous assembly of citizens and strangers may profitably listen to them.

"Our form of government does not enter into rivalry with the institutions of others. We do not copy our neighbours, but are an example to them. It is true that we are called a democracy, for the administration is in the hands of the many and not of the few. But while the law secures equal justice to all alike in their private disputes the claim of excellence is also recognized; and when a citizen is in any way distinguished, he is preferred to the public service, not as a matte of privilege, but as a reward of merit. Neither is poverty a bar, but a man may benefit his country whatever be the obscurity of his condition. There is no exclusiveness in our public life, and in our privat intercourse we are not suspicious of one another, nor angry with ou neighbour if he does what he likes; we do not put on sour looks a him which, though harmless, are not pleasant. While we are thus ur constrained in our private intercourse, a spirit of reverence pervade our public acts; we are prevented from doing wrong by respect fc authority and for the laws, having an especial regard to those whic are ordained for the protection of the injured as well as to those unwritten laws which bring upon the reprobation of the general sentiment.

"And we have not forgotten to provide for our weary spirits many relaxations from toil; we have regular games and sacrifices throughout the year; at home the style of our life is refined; and the delight which we daily feel in all these things helps to banish melancholy. Because of the greatness of our city the fruits of the whole earth flow in upon us; so that we enjoy the goods of other countries as freely as of our own.

"Then, again, our military training is in many respects superior to that of our adversaries. Our city is thrown open to the world, and we never expel a foreigner or prevent him from seeing or learning anything of which the secret if revealed to an enemy might profit him. We rely not upon management or trickery, but upon our own hearts and hands. And in the matter of education, whereas they from early youth are always undergoing laborious exercises which are to make them brave, we live at ease, and yet are equally ready to face the perils which they face.

"If then we prefer to meet danger with a light heart but without laborious training, and with a courage which is gained by habit and not enforced by law, are we not greatly the gainers? Since we do not anticipate the pain, although, when the hour comes, we can be as brave as those who never allow themselves to rest; and thus too our city is equally admirable in peace and in war.

"For we are lovers of the beautiful, yet with economy, and we cultivate the mind without loss of manliness. Wealth we employ, not for talk and ostentation, but when there is a real use for it. To avow poverty with us is no disgrace; the true disgrace is in doing nothing to avoid it. An Athenian citizen does not neglect the state because he takes care of his own household; and even those of us who are engaged in business have a very fair idea of politics. We alone regard a man who takes no interest in public affairs, not as a harmless, but as a useless character; and if few of us are originators, we are all sound judges of a policy. The great impediment to action is, in our opinion, not discussion, but the want of that knowledge which is gained by discussion preparatory to action. For we have a peculiar power of thinking before we act and of acting too, whereas other men are courageous from ignorance but hesitate upon reflection. And they are surely to be esteemed the bravest spirits who, having the clearest sense both of the pains and pleasures of life, do not on that account shrink from danger.

"To sum up: I say that Athens is the school of Hellas, and that the individual Athenian in his own person seems to have the power of adapting himself to the most varied forms of action with the utmost versatility and grace. This is no passing and idle word, but truth and fact; and the assertion is verified by the position to which these qualities have raised the state. For in the hour of trial Athens alone among her contemporaries is superior to the report of her. No enemy who comes against her is indignant at the reverses which he sustains at the hands of such a city; no subject complains that his masters are unworthy of him. And we shall assuredly not be without witnesses; there are mighty monuments of our power which will make us the wonder of this and of succeeding ages; we shall not need the praises of Homer or of any other panegyrist whose poetry may please for the moment, although his representation of the facts will not bear the light of day. For we have compelled every land and every sea to open a path for our valour, and have everywhere planted eternal memorials of our friendship and of our enmity. Such is the city for whose sake these men nobly fought and died; they could not bear the thought that she might be taken from them; and every one of us who survive should gladly toil on her behalf."[36]

The Threefold Passion of Greek Genius. To discover what were actually the final determining factors that together gave to the Greeks their unsurpassed genius has been a problem to baffle all students of ancient civilization for centuries. We are not attempting here some new solution. Some scholars emphasize youthfulness, some excellence, some justice, others freedom, beauty, truth, compassion, naturalness, directness, etc. I think, however, we will not be far wrong if we say that the three outstanding characteristics of Greek genius were, a love of knowledge or the truth, a love of beauty, and a love of freedom. Plato, in the midst of the glory of Greek civilization, emphasized the fact that for the Greeks a love of knowledge was as marked a characteristic as the love of money was of the Phoenicians. The late Professor Butcher of

Harvard truly says that, "The love of knowledge worked on the Greeks with a potent spell which came to them as did the siren's voice to Odysseus, alluring him with the promise that he should know all things—the things that have been and those that are to be." [37] Related to this love of knowledge was, of course, a passion for truthfulness. This does not mean "that the Greeks told fewer lies than other races but that they had the desire and power to see the world as it is. . . . To the Greeks truthfulness is spontaneous, natural and effortless—the negative quality of artistic, who sees and forgets himself in the vision. . . . The objectivity of the Greeks is a quality of mind. They have the power of standing aloof from matters in which they are not personally interested, and surveying them from the outside like impartial spectators with the keenest interest but without bias." [38] With this love of knowledge and truth there was an equally passionate love of beauty. The two are not necessarily correlative. Many of our novels may be said to be true, at least realistic, but their scenes are ugly, coarse, crude. With the Greeks that which they attempted to express must appear in the form of the most perfect beauty conceivable. This is the vital principle which guides the hands of its sculptors, to give us the most remarkable portrayals of human life in marble that the world has ever seen. The whole body of their literature seems to have resting upon it the very halo of elegance of form. As they attempted to give beauty to their creations in art and literature, so also they passionately devoted themselves to the development of the beauty of the body, especially the masculine body, with their vast system of Olympic contests, etc., ever striving for excellency in the realm of physical prowess. Finally, the Greeks seem to have been born with a driving zest for freedom, with a hatred of tyrannical despotism. Liberty was their chiefest good, and they paid a terrific price in blood and tribute both, as they fought, frequently winning, but at last losing, in this eternal conflict for the right to live unhindered by the galling yoke of external authority. We must not think, however, when we speak of the ancient Greeks as possessed by this threefold love, that *all* Greeks loved and strove for knowledge and beauty and freedom. There was notable illiteracy, even in the midst of the glory of its culture; many who toiled on the farm, then as now, must have had no taste whatever for philosophy, or scientific research, or the wonders of astronomical discovery; all the Greeks were not Aristotles, just as we may say all Englishmen have not the intellectual power of a Lord Bryce, nor all Americans the genius of a Benjamin Franklin. There must have been many ugly things in Greek life, as well as so much that was the expression of every aspect of the beautiful. Human nature does not undergo any *absolute* change, and ancient Athens must have had some of the dirt and filth and hovels that modern Athens has. All the Greeks did not love liberty: there were some traitors. Still these three—a love of truth, a love of beauty, and a love of liberty, may be said to have stamped themselves indelibly on every major achievement of these ancient people.

Concerning Greek Religion. I have purposely separated the subject of Greek religion from what we call the "achievements of Greek Civilization," because I do not consider Greek religion an *achievement,* whatever else it was. We will have more to say about some of the more important aspects of this sphere of Greek life in the subsequent part of this chapter, but we feel that we must at this point give some brief attention to that which played so important a part in the life of this searching race of men. What Greek religion *was,* and what it meant to the people, it is difficult to say, even though hundreds of books, and thousands of pages, have been written on this subject. Hardly any man of his generation, and no man in France, worshiped the pagan world more than Renan, but he himself confessed that, "The ancient Greeks had no well determined rule of faith, and their religion, charming when taken as poetry, is, when viewed according to our theological ideas, a mere mass of contradictory fables, the true meaning of which it is very hard to unravel."[38a]

When we begin to discuss the religion of ancient Greece we are at once faced with a number of problems. First of all, the religion of Greece was of different types, at different times, in Greek history. There is what we call the religion of Homer and Hesiod with their vast pantheon of Olympian deities; later we have the cult of Dionysos and then the Orphic and Eleusinian mysteries; and later still we have that kind of religion that depended upon miraculous utterances, primarily that which centered around the oracles at Delphi. There was no unity in all these different forms of religion, nor did all the Greek state ever come to unite in the worship of any one God. These religions were never subjected to any political centralization, nor did any theological-minded priesthood systematize them. Of course there were ideas latent in Greek religion that we find in almost all the important religions of the world, but there is nothing here that might be called *distinctive*. As Professor George Foot Moore reminds us, "Sacrifice and offering, hymn and prayer, expiation and purification, propitiation of the kindly gods and thanksgiving for their bounty, placation of the dreaded powers of the nether world, riddance of demons and ghosts—these are the components of the cultus, as among other peoples on the same plane of civilization all over the world."[39] No doubt there were some beautiful things, humanly speaking, about Greek religion, the festivals of the seasons, beautiful statues, magnificent processions, and, at times, some attempt at attaining an external purity. But there were other darker aspects of the whole religious life of ancient Greece which were inevitable, when one considers the acknowledged immorality of their gods, the absence of any true salvation from sin in all their cults, and the actual violation of the sanctity of life in many of their religious practices. To quote once again from one of the outstanding authorities on the history of religion of modern times: "It is a serious error to imagine, as many do, that the Greek religions were all sunny and beautiful because this is the side of them that is turned out. There was a great deal in them—and not the least sacred part either—that was ugly, obscene, and barbarous, and it is wholly unwarranted to stamp these features as foreign. Nothing is more genuinely and persistently Greek than some of the grossest of the performances."[40]

The cult of Dionysos was savage in the extreme. "As men enacted the savage myth, rushing breathlessly through the mysterious solitude of the mountains in the light of flaring torches, or rending the victim limb from limb, and tearing its palpating flesh with their teeth, the divine frenzy overcame them, the god himself possessed them." This cult had even grosser aspects, as for instance, its phallic processions and songs, which need not be described in these pages. The state of immorality which this particular cult emphasized seemed to reach its climax in a continuous debauch of drunkenness, so that even Plato had to define it as thinking that "an immorality of drunkenness is the highest reward of virtue." [41] In fact, the very passions and shame of men were actually deified in the religion of these Greeks, which some in our modern time try to tell us was the most beautiful religion that the earth has ever seen, " 'Each man's fearful passion becomes his god.' Yes, and not passions only, but every impulse, every aspiration, every humour, every virtue, every whim. In each of his activities the Greek found something wonderful, and called it God: the hearth at which he warmed himself and cooked his food, the street in which his house stood, the horse he rode, the cattle he pastured, the wife he married, the child that was born to him, the plague of which he died or from which he recovered, each suggested a deity, and he made one to preside over each. So, too, with qualities and powers more abstract. Violence, Fear, Revolution, Sport, Drunkenness, Democracy, Madness, Envy, Revelling, Persuasion, Sleep, Hunger, are personified and in some cases worshipped. Everything has its worship, even 'the Unknown God.' (That is why, viewing his religion, it is possible to represent the Greek as a miracle of vice or of virtue.) A Greek wished to be drunk, Dionysus was his patron; to be vicious, and he turned to Aphrodite Pandemos. He was a thief, and could rely on the help of Hermes; he had a passion for purity, and there was the worship of Artemis." [42]

Above everything else in considering ancient Greek religion, we must remember, and this none can deny, that no matter how much we try to idealize the life of these ancient people, Greek religion was emphatically mythical, not historical, its gods had no real existence, they were the creations of men, and of finite sinful men, without divine inspiration of any kind. Our entire religion, even the roots of it in Judaism, rests solidly upon historical fact, a revelation to historic personalities, as well as a clear revelation in historic movements. Zeus never lived: Abraham did. No gods ever spoke from Mt. Olympus, but Jehovah did speak to Moses on Mt. Sinai, and he came down from that mountain with laws and principles, precepts, judgments and commandments, which no man in all the world could have ever humanly conceived, by his own ingenuity. The Greeks told stories about the gods coming down to earth, but our faith does not rest in a story told in some king's palace, but upon an historic Person, Jesus of Nazareth, born at a certain time, not arising in the vague obscurity of a dim pre historic mythology, but born in Bethlehem, of a mother of flesh and blood, walking the roads of Palestine, visiting its citizens, calling Galileans to be His disciples, quieting the waves on the sea of Galilee, breaking bread to feed five thousand on its shores, delivering from blindness at Jericho, raising the dead at Bethany, standing before Caiaphas and Herod and Pontius Pilate in Jerusalem, dead, buried, and risen again—not a myth, but a historic reality—so real as to change the whole face of the world, so real as to slay every other contemporary religion but one, Judaism, which even then began to die. The gods of Greece were myths, and this is what doomed Greek religion. If myths are humanly created, then other men could create other myths, and what kind of stories could men produce but those which simply exaggerated their own love and vices both? Myths must die, as far as their effectiveness is concerned, as far as faith in their personages is concerned, when knowledge increases, and science is pursued, and philosophy becomes the passion of the hearts of men. "The entire fabric of mythology was ill fitted to bear an examination. It must betray its weakness the moment it is exposed to the light of rational inquiry. The expansion of the Greek mind brought with it the spirit of investigation. Natural philosophy had another explanation to give their physical phenomenon than that of the insistent interference of a crowd of personal divinities. Historical study dissolved many a sacred legend, taught many to know proofs where no proofs could be forthcoming, intended to inspire a general temper of distrust in regard to the popular creed. As civilization advanced and men in large numbers were trained to use their reason in the complex affairs of peace and war, the weak places in the traditional faith must become more and more exposed to view." [43]

The Impotencies of the World's Most Brilliant Civilization. Though all those who despise creeds, and think dogmas are a bondage, the enemy of intellectual freedom, consider it to be an advantage with the ancient Greeks (as in modernism), nevertheless, it must be put down as a fundamental failure in this ancient, brilliant civilization, that its great thinkers so completely failed to arrive at any positive, final, assured truth in religious matters pertaining to God, the future, salvation, atonement, sin, and all those great matters with which we are acquainted in our rich Christian inheritance. The Greeks never framed a system of doctrine, they never produced what might be called a creed, nor even a single volume that attempted to sum up the fundamental elements of ancient Greek religion. Of course all know that sometimes the Iliad and the Odyssey, and especially the Iliad, are referred to as "The Bible of the Greeks," but the Greeks really had no Bible, and these two masterpieces are not even primarily religious, though their great personages are, it is true, Olympian gods and goddesses. It may be that Greek religion, as Herodotus says, arose from Homer's myths, but anyone who compares that work with the inspired literature of the ancient Hebrew people, and the New Testament, will admit that whatever else the writings of Homer may be, they are not a *Bible*. I must admit that it was some years after I began to read in Greek literature, as much as time would permit me, that it dawned upon me there really were no religious doctrines ever formulated among these people. I think the truth was most powerfully brought to my attention by the opening paragraph in Mr. Dickinson's excellent volume, *The Greek View of Life,* and I take the liberty of quoting this paragraph: "In approaching the subject of the religion of the Greeks it is necessary to dismiss at the outset many of the associations which we are naturally inclined to connect with tha word. What we commonly have in our mind when we speak of re ligion is a definite set of doctrines, of a more or less metaphysical char acter, formulated in a creed and supported by an organisation distinc from the state. And the first thing we have to learn about the religio of the Greeks is that it included nothing of the kind. There was n church, there was no creed, there were no articles; there was n doctrine even, unless we are so to call a chaos of legends orally hande down and in continual process of transformation by the poets. Priest there were, but they were merely public officials, appointed to perfor certain religious rites. The distinction between cleric and layman, a we know it, did not exist; the distinction between poetry and dogm did not exist; and whatever the religion of the Greeks may have bee one thing at any rate is clear, that it was something very different fro all that we are in the habit of associating with the word." [44]

Without some definite doctrinal formulation the Greeks were le to really believe anything they chose, and to interpret the life ar character and acts of their mythical deities as they felt inclined. Greek religion became a matter of rite, involving initiatory ceremonies, secret instruction, rituals of purification, sacrifices and festivals, but not faith, belief, truth, deep convictions, the solution of life's problems, the certainty of hope based upon a divine revelation. For this reason, while oratory rose to probably its greatest heights among the ancient Greeks, and again with the orators of the time of Cicero, yet though these ancient peoples could declaim powerfully and movingly concerning personalities, politics, principles, there was no such thing in the ancient world as *preaching*. "The Graeco-Roman oratory at its best estate was lacking in one great essential to the highest eloquence. It had no religious content, and but incidentally a moral one. The accepted division of oratory into its kinds was threefold: deliberative, or political; forensic, or judicial; and epideictic, or declamatory. The first two are easily enough understood, the last is not so clear. At first it was meant to embrace funeral or memorial orations, or panegyrical discourses upon living persons, or patriotic speeches, or, as Aristotle defines it, was concerned chiefly with praise and blame. But in this classification of orations there is notable omission of the didactic element. There was nothing in ancient oratory corresponding to our lecture platform or pulpit."[45] When the Christian faith burst upon the Graeco-Roman world, with its historical content, its great affirmations, its divinely-bestowed revelation of truth, its illumination of the dark places of the human mind and heart, its clear offering of a saving gospel, its exaltation of the very Son of God, any religion without a creed, without dogmatic truth, without the bulwark of revelation, was doomed, and back to that ancient mythical religion no one today can possibly think of going, for comfort, for help, for truth, or hope.

Greek Religion Unrelated to Moral Conduct. The greatest single blight on Greek religion, apart from the fact that it never led its followers into the presence of God is this:—on the one hand, it was derived from myths which made the gods themselves shamefully gross and evil, and on the other hand, it failed to exert any permanent, genuine influence upon the moral life of those who claimed to be its followers. This is not a modern verdict rendered by Christians alone, but was a tragedy to which the Greeks themselves confessed. In the earliest days of the Greek thought, Xenophanes acknowledged, "Homer and Hesiod have ascribed to the gods all things that are a shame and a disgrace among mortals, stealing and adulteries and deceiving of one another."[46] Plato, in his *Republic* insisted that many of the stories of gods must not be told to the young.

"There was that greatest of all lies in high places, which the poet told about Uranus, and which was a bad lie too,—I mean what Hesiod says that Uranus did, and what Cronus did to him. The doings of Cronus, and the sufferings which in turn his son inflicted upon him, even if they were true, ought certainly not to be lightly told to young and simple persons; if possible, they had better be buried in silence. But if there is an absolute necessity for their mention, a chosen few might hear them in a mystery, and in order to reduce the number of hearers they should sacrifice not a common (Eleusinian) pig, but some huge and unprocurable victim.

"Why, yes, said he, those stories are certainly objectionable.

"Yes, Adeimantus, they are stories not to be narrated in our State; the young man should not be told that in committing the worst of crimes he is far from doing anything outrageous; and that if he chastises his father when he does wrong, in any manner that he likes, he will only be following the example of the first and greatest among the gods.

"I quite agree with you, he said; in my opinion those stories are not fit to be repeated.

"Neither, if we mean our future guardians to regard the habit of quarrelling as dishonourable, should anything be said of the wars in heaven, and of the plots and fightings of the gods against one another, which are quite untrue."[47]

Euripides in his famous tragedy *Ion,* renders a fearful indictment against the Greek gods when he says,—and we must remember that the tragedies of Euripides were written for public performances, and won the unanimous approval of the Greeks—"Yet I must admonish Phoebus. What ails him? He ravishes maidens and forsakes them, begets children by stealth and cares not, though they die. O, do not so. Since thou art powerful, follow after goodness! When a man has an evil nature, the gods punish him. How is it right that you gods should prescribe the law for man, and then be guilty of lawlessness yourselves? If—it cannot be, yet I will put it so—if you were to pay to men the fine for lustful violence, thou, and Poseidon, and Zeus the lord of heaven, would beggar your temples of their treasure in paying for your vrongs. For wrong it is, to seek your pleasures with no regard to onsequence.

"No more can men justly be called wicked, if we only imitate what he gods call good. Wicked rather are those who so instruct us!"[48]

Inasmuch as the Greek gods were themselves guilty of almost every onceivable crime, it is to be wondered at that the Greeks even deired to have an *external* purification, but this longing continued, someıow, to manifest itself in the hearts of some of these ancient people, vandering about in the darkness of human speculations. There is robably no greater authority in the English world, in the last half entury, in the field of Greek religion, than Professor L. R. Farnell, vho devoted all his life to a sympathetic study of this subject. His erdict is that, "Purification in the Apolline and other Hellenic cults nust be understood in a ritualistic sense. The process of purification imed at washing away certain stains from a man's person that endered him ritualistically unclean, that is, unable to approach the ltars and temples of the gods, or to mix with his fellows without preading a deadly miasma around him, such stains to be contracted y harmless, physical acts, but especially by contact with blood."[49] Now we know that there is much of this ritualistic purification in the Old Testament, but what we are insisting upon is that this is all these Greeks knew of religious rites, whereas ritualistic purification, with ie ancient Hebrews, led, necessarily, and by divine intent, to a corespondingly inner purification.

With the gods of Greece of such a nature as we have seen, of course, iere could be no real conception of sin among these people. As Sir William Ramsay has told us, "There could not be a real conception of n, for it is of the essence of Hellenism to be perfectly content with ie human nature, to rejoice in it, to find in it the divine perfection."[50] Even with men like Socrates and Plato" says one of our best Greek cholars, R. W. Livingstone, "it may be questioned how far moral riving was the center of their souls. Their whole moral atmosphere as different from that of a man like St. Paul. The Greeks had no eal sense of sin. They regarded their offenses as shortcomings and alled them 'bad faults.' Such things were bound to happen and when iey happened were best forgotten. It is useless to spend thought and remorse on bad faults: it is best to go forward and improve the aim for next time."[51] One of the most distinguished of all classical scholars in our country, who at the same time was a devout Christian, after giving his life to the study and teaching of ancient Greek and Latin literature, Dr. Ernest G. Sihler, wrote, a few years ago: "Neither Purity nor Humanity nor Mercy has a seat at the Olympian board. Often had Zeus fallen a victim to Aphrodite. So in reprisal (*Homeric Hymn to Aphrodite*) he fills her with a passion for the comely mortal youth Anchises. In all these epics the avowal of concupiscence is made with absolute frankness, as by the suitors of Penelope, or as between Odysseus, Kirke, Kalypso."[52]

Throughout this chapter we have confined ourselves exclusively to the civilization of Greece, antedating the advent of Christ, but we trust that our readers will not consider us unfair if we introduce in this particular discussion, the words of Clement of Alexandria, of the second century, A.D., in his remarkable *Exhortation to the Heathen:* "Besides, the nuptials of the deities, their begetting and bringing forth of children that are recounted, their adulteries celebrated in song, their carousals represented in comedy, and bursts of laughter over their cups, which your authors introduce, urge me to cry out, though I would fain be silent. Oh the godlessness! You have turned heaven into a stage, the Divine has become a drama; and what is sacred you have acted in comedies under the masks of demons, travestying true religion by your demon-worship (superstition). 'But he, striking the lyre, began to sing beautifully.' Sing to us, Homer, that beautiful song

> " 'About the amours of Ares and Venus with the
> beautiful crown:
> How first they slept together in the palace of
> Helpaestus
> Secretly; and he gave many gifts, and dishonoured
> the bed and chamber of king Hephaestus.'

"Stop, O Homer, the song! It is not beautiful; it teaches adultery, and we are prohibited from polluting our ears with hearing about adultery for we are they who bear about with us, in this living and moving image of our human nature, the likeness of God,—a likeness which dwells with us, takes counsel with us, associates with us, is a guest with us, feels with us, feels for us. We have become a consecrated offering to God for Christ's sake: we are the chosen generation, the royal priesthood, the holy nation, the peculiar people, who once were not a people, but are now the people of God; who, according to John, are not of those who are beneath, but have learned all from Him who came from above; who have come to understand the dispensation of God; who have learned to walk in newness of life. But these are not the sentiments of the many; but, casting off shame and fear, they depict in their houses the unnatural passions of the demons . . . O ye that have done violence to man, and have devoted to shame what is divine in this handiwork of God, you disbelieve everything that you may indulge your passions, and that ye may believe in idols, because you have a craving after their licentiousness, but disbelieve God, because you cannot bear a life of self-restraint. You have hated what was better, and valued what was worse, having been spectators indeed of virtue, but actors of vice."[53]

The Inability of Men to Discover an Adequate Ethical Power. "Greek religion demanded holiness; it did not provide means of attaining," is the verdict of one of our best modern scholars, and he is only repeating what all Christian scholars have been compelled to confess.[54] Sir William Ramsay, classicist and Christian both, has well said that "The Greek *Sophia* was entirely devoid of power over the will and heart of mankind. It remained purely theoretical and abstract: it could do nothing for men, it was the property of a few, and had no effect, or a miserably inadequate effect on the life and character of those few. Where it did to some degree touch the heart and affect the life of some rare individual, it produced a philosophic and affected prig rather than a true man; and in the case of some of its most elegant exponents, such as Seneca, there was a woeful contrast in spirit between their words and their life."[55] Mr. G. Lowes Dickinson, from whom we have frequently quoted before, although he nowhere expresses himself in favor of the Christian religion, frankly says that, "It was a distinguishing characteristic of the Greek religion that it did not concern itself with the conscience at all . . . To the Puritan the inward relation of the soul to God is everything; to the average Greek one may say, broadly, it was nothing."[56]

The achievements of Pericles were so brilliant, and his accomplishments for Athens in almost every sphere of life were so unique, even in that day of glorious deeds, that that period of Greek history has forever since been known as the age of Pericles. Yet, if one but reads Plutarch's famous *Essay on Pericles,* he will come upon things so sordid and common, that, were they recognized of a statesman prominent either in British or American life today, he would be put out of office. I do not know how others react to certain pages in Greek literature, but I must confess that nothing but loathing comes over my soul, an absolute disgust, when I find such a *man* as Socrates, whom some dare to favorably compare with Jesus, saying, at a banquet table, concerning the young man Charmides, "Oh rare! I caught a sight of the inwards of his garment, and took the flame, then I could no longer contain myself. I thought how well Cydias understood the nature of love, when, in speaking of a fair youth, he woos someone 'not to bring the fawn in the sight of the lion to be devoured by him,' and I felt that I had been overcome by a sort of wild-beast appetite. But I controlled myself, and when he asked me if I knew the cure of the headache, I answered but with an effort, that I did know."[57] This very impotency of Greek culture, with its love of knowledge and passion for science, finally led to total despair concerning any real ethical satisfaction. "Since there was nowhere to be found a power comparative to the gigantic task of a moral removal of the ancient world, this power must come from another source, from above. When to those who were sometimes foolish, disobedient, deceived, serving divers lusts and pleasures, living in maliciousness and hatred, hating one another, the kindness and love toward man of God our Saviour appeared, then was first opened the fountain from which a new and healthful life flowed forth for diseased humanity; then the Gospel gathered communion, the opposite of that which the heathen world had become,—modest, chaste, diligent, their affections set upon things above, the salt of the earth, the light of the world. We *were* sometimes foolish, disobedient, deceived; we were, but are no more."[58]

The Failure to Attain Final Truth. All people, ancient and modern

Greek, Roman, occidental and oriental, believer and unbeliever, would probably unanimously agree, unless hopelessly sunk in sin and despair, that the one thing man most longs for is *truth,* and not just to know about geology, or the heavenly orbs, or muscles, nerves and veins in the human body, or chronological and geographical data in historical events, but the *truth,* ultimate truth, final truth, satisfying truth, truth on which we can depend, that never changes, truth that lifts, truth in which we can rest, truth that satisfies. The New Testament is filled with statements that recognize such yearnings in the human heart. Our Lord said He was *the* Truth. He said that men, if they believed in Him would come to know the truth, and that truth would set them free. He prayed to the Father "sanctify them with the truth; Thy Word is truth."[59] The Apostle Paul pled with men to think on those things that were *true.*[60] Now the Greeks sought this truth, but with all their seeking, with all their discoveries, with their vast accumulations of facts, with their profound exploration of the human soul, and the analysis of the processes of the human mind, the Greeks failed to find the truth, and they knew it. To me, one of the most remarkable sentences in all of Plato, is his confession in the *Phaedo*—"I dare say that you, Socrates, feel as I do, how very hard or almost impossible is the attainment of any certainty about questions such as these in the present life. And yet I should deem him a coward who would not prove what is said about them to the uttermost, or whose heart failed him before he had examined them on every side. And he should persevere until he has achieved one of two things: either he should discover, or be taught the truth about them, or, if this is impossible, we would have him take the best and most irrefragable of human theories, and let this be the raft upon which he sails through life—not without risk, as I admit, *if he cannot find some word of God which will more surely and safely carry him.*"[61] No one ever heard any of the apostles say that they were going to trust themselves to the "raft" of human wisdom, hoping that some day a more sure word of God would come. The Word of God had come to them: and they were trusting their souls to a divine and perfect, a final and satisfying revelation—the truth of God as it is in Jesus Christ.[62] Pindar in one of his odes, with more despair than Plato said:

"But o'er men's hearts unnumbered errors hang;
Nor can dim Reason's glimmering show
The flowery path untrod by woe,
Or find the day's delight, that brings no sorrow's pangs." [63]

Cicero asked concerning the soul, "'What is truth?'" and then answers, "Which of these, for instance, may be true a god may know, which may be only probable is a difficult question." [64] Later an equally distinguished Roman philosopher cried out, "Ah! if one might only have a guide to truth." One of our modern philosophers expressed the whole thing in one simple sentence, "Philosophy found out *many truths* but not *the truth.*" [65]

"The World by Wisdom Knew Not God." One would not want to deny that there are occasional flashes of truth in ancient Greek literature, revealing some fragmentary idea concerning one supreme God, especially in Xenophanes, who taught consistently that there is one real Being, one supreme God:

"One god, greatest among gods and men, not like mortals in form, nor yet in mind.

"He sees all over, thinks all over, and hears all over.

"Without any trouble he sways all things by the thought of his mind.

"He remains always in the same place, not moving at all; it does not befit him to move about hither and thither." [66]

But even Xenophanes conceived of his supreme God as one only among a number of other deities, so that while we would like to call him a monotheist, his own writings clearly indicate he was, after all, a polytheist. Plato, in his famous passage in the *Timaeus,* confesses, "To find out the Father and Maker of all this universe is a hard task, and when we have found Him, to speak of Him to all men is impossible." [67] There is a great deal of difference among Platonic authorities as to whether or not Plato actually believed in a personal God; sometimes he seems to confuse the idea of the Good with the conception of God, and many claim that Plato did not believe in one personal, sovereign, independent, loving, holy Being. The very fact that there is disagreement here indicates that Plato's writings are not clear on this point.[68] Aristotle, seemingly, had less of a god than Plato, and at least confesses that the god he knows cannot be loved. "Love to God does not exist; it is absurd to talk of such a thing; for God is an unknowable being."[69] Professor Sihler, from whom we have quoted above, speaking of Aristotle's God says, "One cannot quite rid oneself of the impression or inference that the Aristotelian god is to some degree an abstraction from, or a creature of, the great thinker and scientist's personal ideals, and activities. It would be folly to pray to, or to seek any relation with such a god. It is an academic and cosmic god, but singularly and utterly severed from human beings by his essence."[70] Whatever fragment of truth Greek philosophy may at times have possessed regarding one God, it is undeniable that it never came to know the God and Father of the patriarchs in His perfect attributes, revealed to us in the Holy Scriptures, never a God of absolute holiness, or love that would redeem, of an unswerving righteousness, an eternal, omnipotent, omniscient, and all-seeing God, beside whom there is no other. The only God men can really worship is the true God, who is living forever. The gods of Greece were corrupt and evil, our God is without sin, holy, and infinite. And so, after eight hundred years of the development of mythology, and five hundred years of philosophical speculation, Greek civilization led to an altar on which was the inscription "To the unknown God." Those people who were wise beyond any that have ever lived in the wisdom of this world, knew not God.[71]

The Deepening Despair of the Ancient World. The Apostle Paul, writing to the church at Ephesus where many of its members were Greeks and proud of it, looking across the Graeco-Roman world, and knowing Greek and Hebrew and Roman civilization, their culture and literature, said that mankind, apart from those who knew God, was without hope.[72] In saying this he was only echoing, if we may use the word, the verdict of all Greek thinkers from the dawn of Greek civilization. Homer puts in the mouth of Achilles these words, "Don't recommend death to me; I would prefer in the fields to be a day-labourer for another, with a man who has no land lot of his own, who has not much of a living, rather than rule over all the dead."[73] The chorus in the *Oedipus Tyrannus* thus exclaims:

"Ah last of mortal men
How as a thing of naught
I count ye though ye live;
For yourself and of men
That man of blessing knows
Just a little while
To seem to prosper well
And having seen to fall." [74]

In the Theognis we find the lamentation, "It is best of all things for the children of men not to be born, nor to see the rays of keen sunlight; but if born to pass as soon as may be the gates of Hades, and to lie beneath a vesture of much earth." [75]

Euripides once wrote, "It were better that we should call our friends together to lament over the newly-born, that he has come to such a world of sorrows.

"And when a man is dead and has found rest from trouble, we should rejoice and carry him from the house with songs of gladness." [76]

Pindar echoes the same pessimism when he says, "Daughter of Zeus the Deliverer, O Saviour Fortune, keep watch, I pray, over wide-ruling Himera. Thy power is upon sea and land; by thee swift ships are piloted; and thou guidest men in the assemblies of peace and in the counsels of sudden war. To and fro toss the hopes of man, cleaving the waste foam-drift of a perfidious sea. No man upon earth has found a sure token from heaven of how it shall fare with him. Warnings of what will come are wrapt in blind darkness." [77] Cicero, who had every reason to be happy, humanly speaking, says in one of his famous essays, "If these miseries are to be permanent, I only wish, my dearest, to see you as soon as possible and to die in your arms, since neither gods, whom you have worshipped with such pure devotion, nor men, whom I have always served, have made us any return." [78] Pliny's despair is famous. Though he knew more of natural history than any other man of his age, yet concerning life itself he could only say: "There is nothing certain save that nothing is certain, and there is no more wretched and yet arrogant being than man. The best thing which has been given to man amid the many torments of this life is, that he can take his own life." [79] The words of Professor Butcher, whom we have previously quoted, sums up the whole dark mood of that long-ago time, so brilliant and yet so incapable of bestowing on man the peace and hope for which he so painfully longed, "In the Greek Anthology, Hope and Fortune are two companion goddesses who make a sport of human life. The future indeed hung like a heavy cloud over the ancient world, charged with catastrophes, reversals of fortune, the wreck of states, the breaking up of homes, exile and death. In the face of these uncertainties the virtue of the Greeks was Resignation rather than Hope, a cheerful acceptance of the gods' will, without any joyful or assured anticipations." [80]

"In the Fullness of Time"—God Sent Forth His Son. The time of our Lord's advent was the hour of greatest need for a Divine Saviour that the world has ever known, a time when every attempt on the part of man to create a satisfying religion, an adequate redemption, an unfading hope, and a sufficient power for high ethical life had totally failed. Although the world had seen upon its stage the greatest men of genius that ever adorned human history, religion was mocked, unbelief was growing deeper, philosophy had proved itself incapable of discovering final truth, and the whole Mediterranean world was sinking deeper and deeper into an indescribable sensuality, all of which together inevitably resulted in an unbroken spirit of despair, a dark hopelessness through which no shafts of light were now penetrating. In every conceivable way it was *the fullness of time* [81] for God to send forth His Son, and to provide the world with that for which many were hungering and thirsting.

The late Professor Clifford Herschel Moore of Harvard, at the end of his *Pagan Ideas of Immortality During the Early Roman Empire,* gives such a verdict as this: "The last centuries before the birth of Jesus and the opening centuries of our era were marked by an increasing religious longing and unrest, first among the Greeks and then among the Romans. There was a weariness and a dissatisfaction with the inherited forms of religious expression; and many felt a sense of separation from God, of a gulf between the human and the divine, which they hoped might be bridged by a direct revelation, by a vision, which would grant immediate knowledge of God. These eager desires led in part to an increase in superstition and credulity, over which we need not now pause; in part to the resort to the oriental mysteries of which I have just spoken; and in part to a revival of Pythagorean mysticism and of mystic Platonism among the intellectuals, who no longer felt that the reason and the will gave them the assurance which they required."[82]

It would seem that the ancient world itself was, in a very mysterious way, conscious that its religions were decaying, and its gods forever disappearing. Plutarch, in his *Obsolescence of Oracles,* refers to a very remarkable incident, occurring in the reign of Tiberius, which has always fascinated students of the ancient world, and which I cannot refrain from quoting, as we bring this chapter to a close. What deeper meaning there may be to this paragraph, I am not saying: I prefer to let it speak for itself, as coming from one of the greatest writers of all antiquity. "As for death among such beings, I have heard the words of a man who was not a fool nor an imposter. The father of Aemilianus the orator, to whom some of you have listened, was Epitherses, who lived in our town and was my teacher in grammar. He said that once upon a time in making a voyage to Italy he embarked on a ship carrying freight and many passengers. It was already evening when, near the Echinades Islands, the wind dropped, and the ship drifted near Paxi. Almost everybody was awake, and a good many had not finished their after-dinner wine. Suddenly from the island of Paxi was heard the voice of someone loudly calling Thamus, so that all were amazed. Thamus was an Egyptian pilot, not known by name even to many on board. Twice he was called and made no reply, but the third time he answered; and the caller, raising his voice, said, 'When you come opposite to Palodes, announce that Great Pan is dead.' On hearing this, all, said Epitherses, were astounded and reasoned among themselves whether it were better to carry out the order or to refuse to meddle and let the matter go. Under the circumstances Thamus made up his mind that if there should be a breeze, he would sail past and keep quiet, but with no wind and a smooth sea about the place he would announce what he had heard. So, when he came opposite Palodes, and there was neither wind nor wave, Thamus from the stern, looking toward the land, said the words as he had heard them: 'Great Pan is dead.' Even before he had finished there was a great cry of lamentation, not of one person, but of many, mingled with exclamations of amazement. As many persons were on the vessel, the story was soon spread abroad in Rome, and Thamus was sent for by Tiberius Caesar. Tiberius became so convinced of the truth of the story that he caused an inquiry and investigation to be made about Pan; and the scholars, who were numerous at his court, conjectured that he was the son born of Hermes and Penelope." [83]

Well could Justin Martyr, in his *Discourse to the Greeks,* plead with men to give up the foolishness of their myths, and to abandon their impotent gods for the Divine Word, and the receiving of a glorious salvation through Jesus Christ: "Henceforth, ye Greeks, come and partake of incomparable wisdom, and be instructed by the Divine Word, and acquaint yourselves with the King immortal; and do not recognize those men as heroes who slaughter whole nations. For our own Ruler, the Divine Word, who even now constantly aids us, does not desire strength of body and beauty of feature, nor yet the high spirit of earth's nobility, but a pure soul, fortified by holiness, and the watchwords of our King, holy actions, for through the Word power passes into the soul. O trumpet of peace to the soul that is at war! O weapon that puttest to flight terrible passions! O instruction that quenches the innate fire of the soul! The Word exercises an influence which does not make poets: it does not equip philosophers nor skilled orators, but by its instruction it makes mortals immortal, mortals gods; and from the earth transports them to the realms above Olympus. Come, be taught; become as I am, for I, too, was as ye are. These have conquered me—the divinity of the instruction, and the power of the Word: for as a skilled serpent-charmer lures the terrible reptile from his den and causes it to flee, so the Word drives the fearful passions of our sensual nature from the very recesses of the soul; first driving forth lust, through which every ill is begotten—hatreds, strife, envy, emulations, anger, and such like. Lust being once banished, the soul becomes calm and serene. And being set free from the ills in which it was sunk up to the neck, it returns to Him who made it. For it is fit that it be restored to that state whence it departed, whence every soul was or is." [84]

Chapter VI

ST. PAUL'S ADDRESS TO THE ATHENIAN PHILOSOPHERS

Into the university city of the world some time in August, A.D. 51, there came a man walking on foot, about fifty years of age, a Jew, who had probably never been heard of in this center of intellectual preeminence, by the name of Paul. What a vast difference there can be between men, what multitudes of comparatively insignificant men and women the world *has* known, easily led, ready to listen, blown hither and thither by every kind of doctrine, walking according to this world. Now and then there breaks from the shell of this mediocrity a man of genius, of profound insight and unswerving convictions, who early in his youth passes from a condition of being led to that of leading, until it seems that the whole world is molded by this man's thinking. Such were Plato in philosophy, Aristotle in science, Sir Isaac Newton in physics, Martin Luther in religious belief, Darwin with his doctrine of evolution. Such a one was this man Paul.

Sir William Ramsay, himself a brilliant scholar, a master of classical learning, intimately acquainted with the work of most of the great men of genius of the ancient Greek and Roman civilization, after thirty years spent in studying the life and writings of the Apostle Paul, accompanied by many extended examinations of the country of Asia Minor in which Paul extensively labored, concluded, "Of all the men of the first century, incomparably the most influential was the Apostle Paul. No one man exercised anything like so much power as he did in molding the future of the Empire. Among the imperial ministers of the period there appeared none that had any claim to the name of statesman except Seneca, and Seneca fell as far short of Paul in practical influence and intellectual insight as he did in moral character. Had it not been for Paul—if one may guess at what might have been—

no man would now remember Greek and Roman civilization." (This is a remarkable statement, when one recognizes that it is the conclusion of one of the greatest Greek scholars of modern times.) "Barbarism proved too powerful for the Graeco-Roman civilization unaided by the new religious bond; and every channel through which that civilization was preserved, or interest in it maintained, either is now or has been in some essential part of its course Christian after the Pauline form." [1]

The apostle Paul travelled much greater distances than from Chicago to New York, not in the ease of a train, an automobile, or a plane, but for the most part on foot, and that not on level roads such as we know, but through sandy deserts, along fever-ridden coastal plains, swimming icy rivers, set upon by robbers, beaten by his own countrymen, thrown into prison, sometimes left as one dead. Look at a map of the Roman world that shows you Paul's journeys, and then confess that our travels are insignificant compared to his. But there was more than mere travel with this man, Paul. Our day is a travel age, vast multitudes move from the city to the country, and from the small town to the great city, in innumerable excursions, for a change of scenery, rest and entertainment, without accomplishing anything except having a good time. Paul did not travel for travel's sake; he traveled to preach—to stir up men, to bring conviction to human hearts, to assault the strongholds of paganism, to do everything in his power, by the grace of God, for the deliverance of men from the bondage of darkness and serving dead idols, to beholding the light of the glory of God in the face of Jesus Christ. Frankly, my fellow believers and fellow preachers, even when we do travel to preach, what happens in the great cities we visit? Nothing! a morning audience of people already Christians, a delicious dinner, a few kind words, a generous check, and we go on our way. What does the city know of our coming? Nothing! What does the city care? Nothing! What are our results? So meager as not to be reckoned. But this man Paul, when he went into a city, turned it upside down, riots broke out, men left the temples; the sale of images immediately showed a decrease; he was seized by the populace; he was brought before kings. Through this man paganism was dealt a death blow. Look at that map—Colosse, Ephesus, Corinth, Thessalonica, Philippi, Lystra, Derbe, everywhere great and flourishing churches, with bishops, before the end of the century!

And then open your New Testament and see what he did in the way of writing, such epistles that nineteen hundred years of study have not exhausted them. There has never been any man as great since the death of our Lord, as this man. This is that servant of Christ, the mighty Apostle, who is entering on foot this summer day, the city of Socrates, of Plato, of Aristotle, of Demosthenes, Pericles, and Solon, where almost everyone in philosophy worthy the name had been born and grown to maturity, where art had reached its greatest glory, and oratory had been heard in its greatest power, where a knowledge of everything then worth knowing, of the skies above, the earth on which we live, and much that is under the earth, had been brought together, in a passion for truth. What could this man Paul do, what would he want to do, in this city of Athens?

"The City Full of Idols." A man's character, a man's interest, the purposes of a man's life, will determine what he sees, wherever he goes. Paul's interest, if one may use the word rightly, was religion, one religion, a redeeming religion. He was interested in the redemption of men, which he knew could only be brought about through the declaration of the Gospel of Christ Jesus, the Son of God. Paul was a Jew, a member of a race that once had sunk into the abyss of pagan idolatry, and its accompanying sensuality—but had been cleansed, at least of the former foulness, by the divine chastisement of exile. As a Jew, Paul had a loathing of images. But he was more than a Jew, he was a Christian. He had seen the Lord in all His glory, he knew the Son of God. Christ was his friend. He had an unquenchable passion to know Him better, to enter into the fellowship of His suffering, and the power of His Resurrection. Christ lived in him; he was walking in the liberty of a child of God, delivered from the power of the darkness of Roman paganism, and from the vain entanglements and dissatisfactions of Greek speculation. As he walked into this city the first thing that smote his heart was the fact that here in the world's center of learning was the most foolish thing that men could ever create, a vast multitude of them—dead gods, that, having eyes never saw, and having mouths never spoke, and having ears never heard a prayer. The city was so

filled with idols that Pausanias tells us it was easier to meet a god or a goddess on the main street of Athens, than to meet a man. Probably no one of the last century, at least in the English world, came to the study of Paul's life with a richer knowledge of the archeological and topographical details of the city into which Paul was now entering than Mr. Thomas Lewin, whose *Life and Epistles of Paul* was published at the same time that the more famous work, carrying the same name, by Conybeare and Howson, was published. It is from Lewin's book that we take the following lines: "Taking our stand then at the end of the street which descends from the Piraic gate, we find ourselves in the heart of the city where the principal ways meet. Behind us is the street of the Piraic gate, by which we entered. On the right runs off the Royal Portico, and in front of us is a triumphal gateway, opening upon the road which passes in front of the Painted Portico, or Porch of the Stoics. Here also is the statue of Hermes Agoraeus, or Mercury of the Market, and this is regarded as the very centre of the Agora.

"The Royal Porch, the colonnade on our right, as we stand at the end of the Piraic Street, is so called because here the king archon sits for the trial of causes, and upon the summit are mounted the statues of Theseus throwing Sciron into the sea and of Aurora carrying away Cephalus, and before the cloister stand the statues of Conon and of his little less celebrated son Timotheus. The colonnade in front of us as we stand at the end of the Piraic Street, the colonnade which lines the west side of the street which continues the Piraic Street, is the celebrated Painted Porch, so called from the numerous paintings with which it is decorated. Here Zeno, the Stoic, founded his school of philosophy, and here his followers, the philosophers of the Porch, may still be seen in their loose-flowing gowns, with venerable beards and pale faces and thoughtful brows, either seated in deep study and pondering over some abstruse problem, or perambulating up and down discussing the subtlest questions of morals and metaphysics.

"Passing the Painted Porch, we now turn to the left and walk up the Ceramicus, the street leading to the Dipylum Gate, which opens upon the Sacred Way, the road to Eleusis. This street is remarkable for the stone pillars called the 'Mercuries,' square blocks of about a man's height, and surmounted with the head of Mercury. They are inscribed with moral sentences for the edification of the wayfarer, and some are as old as Hipparchus, the brother of Hippias the tyrant, for on one of them we read, 'The gift of Hipparchus: Go and think no ill'; and on another, 'The gift of Hipparchus: Never betray thy friend.' The Mercuries serve also as direction posts; for when a single road, as Vesta Street, branches off from the Ceramicus, there stands at the corner a three-faced Janus, with the three routes underwritten; and where a street crosses so that four ways meet, we find a fourfaced Mercury as a guide to the embarrassed traveller. About halfway up the street is an open space, called specially 'the Mercuries,' from the number of Mercuries here congregated to indicate the various routes. A little to the right is one of the oldest and at the same time one of the grandest works in all Athens, viz., the Theseum, or Temple of Theseus, erected in the fifth century before the Christian era, and still standing. The temples and statues and public buildings that are crowded into the area of the Agora between the Areopagus and Acropolis on the north, the Pnyx on the west, and the Museum on the south, are countless. There is the Temple of Apollo, called the Patroum, and the Temple of the Mother of the Gods, or the Metroum, and the circular Tholus, where the prytanes take their meals and offer their sacrifices, the council house, where the six hundred meet, the famous altar of the Twelve Gods, the statues of the heroes from whom the wards or quarters of Athens take their names, called the Eponymi, the statues of Eirene, Amphiaraus, Lycurgus, Demosthenes, Harmodius and Aristogeiton, Hercules, Apollo, and Pindar, the Temple of Ares, or Mars, at the foot of the Areopagus, the Temples of Aphrodite, Pandemus, and Vulcan, the Odeum, the Eurysaceum, etc., and near the western limit of the Agora is the statue of the Cretan poet Epimenides, whose testimony to the lying rascality of his countrymen is cited by St. Paul in the Epistle to Titus; and in another part may be seen the statue of a Jew in pontifical robes, the High Priest Hyrcanus, whose friendship for the Athenians had called forth this testimony of their regard. The traveller may gaze also on the statue of a Jewish Princess, viz., the beautiful Berenice, the sister of Agrippa II., that very Berenice before whom Paul was some years after this to plead the cause of Christianity." [2]

The Unknown God. In addition to statues and images of the old pantheon of Greek deities, representing every conceivable function and aspect of human life, as well as the heavenly bodies above, and the underworld beneath, the seasons of the year, the vices and virtues of men, there was in this city an altar of an Unknown God. What a strange thing, in the city of Athens! The word *unknown* which Paul saw on this particular altar is the word *agnostos,* which for all the eight hundred years of Greek literature up to Paul's time, that is from the days of Homer, meant just one thing, *unknown.* It derives of course from the word *Gnosis,* meaning knowledge, and preceded by what is known as the "a privative," and means *without knowledge.* Everyone will recognize it as the word from which is derived the modern term *agnosticism.* This is the only time that this particular word is found in the New Testament. But how strange that it should be found in Athens! The Athenians were supposed to know everything—they did almost; but God they did not know. Moreover they knew they did not know *the* God, and so they put this title on this altar to the Unknown God. It was not placed there by Paul: it was engraven on that stone by the Greeks who were so proud of their superior wisdom.

Just what the Greeks meant by "an unknown God," scholars are not quite agreed. Professor Hackett, in his well-known commentary on the Acts of the Apostles, excellently summarizes the various views that have been held: "One is that they (these altars to unknown gods) were very ancient and that it was at length forgotten to whom they had been originally built, and that the words in question were placed on them at a later period, to apprise the people that it was unknown to what gods they belonged. If that was their character, it is not easy to see what proper point of connection the apostle could have found for his remark with such a relic of sheer idolatry. Another is that in some time or times of public calamity the Athenians, not knowing what god they had offended—whether Minerva or Jupiter or Mars—erected these altars so as to be sure of propitiating the right one. The same objection may be made as before, since their ignorance in this case relates merely to the identity of the god whom they should conciliate, and involves no recognition of any power additional to their heathen deities. The most rational explanation is unquestionably that of those who suppose these altars to have had their origin in the feeling of uncertainty, inherent, after all, in the minds of the heathen, whether their acknowledgment of the superior powers was sufficiently full and comprehensive; in their distinct consciousness of the limitation and imperfection of their religious views, and their consequent desire to avoid the anger of any still unacknowledged god who might be unknown to them. That no deity might punish them for neglecting his worship or remain uninvoked in asking for blessings, they not only erected altars to all the gods named or known among them, but distrustful still lest they might not comprehend fully the extent of their subjection and dependence, they erected them also to any other god or power that might exist, although as yet unrevealed to them."[3]

The words on this altar were, says one of the greatest Greek scholars of the nineteenth century, "the confession at once of a bastard philosophy and of a bastard religion. The restless fear of unseen powers which was characteristic of all idolatry, in its decay reached its highest point in this superfluity of irrational awe."[4] Probably few today consult the great series of commentaries on most of the books of the Bible by that peer of all exegetes, John Calvin (and it may be for many of us that we have Calvin's works upon our shelves rarely consulted), and for this reason I trust my readers will allow me to place before them, for their own quickening of heart and mind, this superlative, keen, passionate analysis of the great reformer. In my own judgment I feel it is one of the most remarkable passages on the religious conditions of Athens that has ever been written. "The city, which was the mansion-house of wisdom, the fountain of all arts, the mother of humanity, did exceed all others in blindness and madness. We know with what commendations witty and learned men did set forth the same, and she had conceived so great good liking of herself that she counted those rude whom she had not polished. But the Holy Ghost condemning the whole world of ignorance and blockishness, saith that those masters of liberal sciences were bewitched with an unwonted madness. Whence we gather what man's wit can do in matters which concern God. Neither need we doubt of this, but that the Lord suffered the men of Athens to fall into extreme madness, that all the world might learn by them, and that they might teach all ages that the foresight and wit of man's mind being holpen with learning and instruction doth altogether dote, and is mere foolishness when it cometh to the kingdom of God. They had undoubtedly their cloaks and colours, wherewith they did excuse their worshippings, how preposterous and corrupt soever they were. And yet, notwithstanding, it is certain that they did not only deceive men with childish and frivolous toys, but that they themselves were deluded shamefully with gross and filthy jugglings, as if they were deprived of common sense, and were altogether blockish and brutish. And as we learn what manner (of) religion proceedeth from man's understanding, and that man's wisdom is nothing else but a shop of all errors, so we may know that the men of Athens, being drunk with their own pride, did err more filthily than the rest. The antiquity and pleasantness and beauty of the city, did puff them up, so that they did boast that the gods came thence. Therefore, forasmuch as they did pull down God from heaven, that they might make him an inhabitant of their city, it was meet that they should be thrust down into the nethermost hell. Howsoever it be, the vanity of man's wisdom is here marked with eternal infamy by the Spirit of God; because, where it was principally resident, there was the darkness more thick. Idolatry did reign most of all there; and Satan carried men's minds to and fro more freely by his mocks and juggling." [5]

The Paroxysm of the Apostle Paul. St. Luke tells us that when Paul beheld a city of such learning polluted by this mass of dead superstition, he was *provoked,* really, provoked to anger. The Greek word here is *parozuno,* which means to stimulate, to urge on, and then, to irritate, to provoke, to arouse to anger. In the Septuagint we find that in almost every case in which this word is used the reference is to the anger of God (Deut. 32:41; Psalm 106:29; Isaiah 65:3; Jer. 32:37; Hosea 8:5; Zech. 10:3). As God is provoked to anger with the sins of His people, for rebellion and idolatry, so Paul, possessed by the Spirit of Christ, was provoked to anger with these awful monuments proclaiming the victory of Satan, the power of darkness, and dooming men to an ignorance of God, to a degrading superstition, to a perpetual darkness, and to an unending despair. Only in one other place is this particular word found in the New Testament, and that is in Paul's beautiful hymn of love (I Cor. 13:5), where he says that love is not easily provoked—but though not easily provoked, it can be provoked, and when it is aroused it becomes wrath. Would to God every Christian could have an experience like this, even if only once in a lifetime, as he beholds if not the visible idols of men, then at least the false cults that draw the souls of men away from Christ—books written for the express purpose of destroying the faith of young men in God, universities into which precious lives have come with all the hope and glow of youth only to be bowed out, with a sheepskin in their hands and their hearts filled even with a hatred for everything religious, and a loathing for Jesus Christ. It is time we were *moved* by some of these things. Calvin was right when he said, "Those who are not touched when they see and hear God blasphemed and do not only wink thereat but also carelessly brush over it are not worthy to be counted the children of God, who at least do not give Him so much honor as they do an earthly father." [6]

Stoics and Epicureans. In addition to what Paul saw, Luke's account of this visit, which he probably had from the apostle himself, tells us that he came in contact immediately with representatives of the two great Greek schools of Philosophy, Stoics and Epicureans. It is impossible, and unwise, in a work of this kind, in a book such as we are attempting here on apologetics, to dwell with great detail upon these two schools, and yet what Paul is about to say to these Greek philosophers will deal with some of the fundamental principles of both of these systems, and though we have read extensively in works devoted exclusively to a discussion of the Stoics and Epicureans, we would quote not from a volume of philosophy but from what we believe is the very best brief summary there is of these two groups, namely, that given by Dr. R. J. Knowling in what is in some ways the greatest commentary on Acts of our day. He reminds us that, "The Epicureans were so called from their founder Epicurus (342–270 B.C.). His disciples were known also as the School of the Garden, from the garden in Athens where the master instructed them, in distinction from the disciples of the Porch or the Academy. We must be careful to remember that as in numberless other cases, so the system of the founder suffered at the hands of his successors and that the life of Epicurus himself was far removed from that of a mere sensualist, or 'Epicure' in its later sense. But it was evident that a life which made pleasure and happiness the be-all and end-all of existence, however safeguarded by the conditions imposed at the outset by Epicurus, was liable to degenerate to a mere series of prudential calculations, or a mere indulgence of the senses and appetites. In his determination to rid men of the superstitious fears which were the chief cause of the miseries of humanity, Epicurus opposed the popular Polytheism, and regarded the gods as living a life of passionless calm far removed from Mundane strifes and sorrows, 'careless of mankind.'" The beliefs of the Epicureans deserves one additional paragraph of description from a different viewpoint: "In regard to religion, the Epicureans believed in the gods; but to satisfy their own conception of blessedness, the gods were banished to a distant celestial sphere of bliss altogether removed from the disturbances of this life and the cares of providence. So this world was left to itself; and their view of it was very much that of modern materialism. In fact they held the atomic theory of modern science, although of course in a crude form. Their theory carried with it the denial of life after death. Like everything else, the human soul was composed of material atoms which, in themselves indestructible, were dissipated at death, so that personal existence came to an end. But neither theories of the universe nor physical science were in themselves attractive to the Epicureans. They only studied these subjects as weapons of criticism for the sake of deliverance from popular superstitions and the fear of death."[7]

The Stoics "were so-called from the *Stoa Poecile* at Athens where Zeno of Citium, the founder of the school (340–260 B.C.), met his pupils. Their creed was essentially Pantheistic, though the verses of Cleanthes' Hymn seemed to breathe the accents of a higher and nobler belief. But no devotional phrases could disguise a Pantheism which regarded the world as the body of God and God as the soul of the world, which held that apart from exterior nature the supreme God had no existence which identified Him with fate and necessity, while the history of the universe was an unfolding of the providence of God, but a providence which was but another name for the chain of causation and consequently, inviolable, eternal. The leading maxims of the ethical system of the Stoics was the injunction to live according to nature, although the expression of the rule varied in the earlier and later schools. But as this life was best realized in conformity to the law of the universe, in conformity with reason as the highest element in man, the Stoic ideals, in spite of its recognition of virtue, became not merely stern and intellectual, but impassive and austere; in aiming at *apathy* the Stoic lost *sympathy* with the most ennobling and energetic emotions, and thus wrapped up in the cloak of his own virtue he justified, at least from an ethical point of view, the description which classed him as the Pharisee of Greek philosophy. In addressing an audience composed of representatives of these two great philosophic schools, it may be said that St. Paul was not unmindful of his own former training in the early home of Stoicism. And so in speaking of creation and providence, of the unity of nations in the recognition of all that was true even of Pantheism, St. Paul has been described as taking the Stoic side against the Epicureans, or at least we may say that he in his speech asserts against some of the cardinal errors of the Epicureans the creative and superintending power of God. But to the Stoic and Epicurean alike the Christian Creed would proclaim that *All's Love, yet All's Law;* to the Stoic and Epicurean alike, the Pharisee and Sadducee of the world philosophy, the bidding came to repent and obey the gospel, no less than to the crowd whom sages and philosophers despised." The greatest saint of them all was Seneca, and while he has often, though unfairly, been compared to the Apostle Paul, it is true that in some of his sayings he seemed to come close to some New Testament truths; yet his philosophy was strictly pantheistic, and a personal, loving God to whom one could pray was really unknown to this, in some ways, great man.[8]

The Appropriateness and Magnificence of Paul's Address. It was into such a city that Paul had now come, a city proud of its intellectual achievements, basking in the glory of its great men, though all were now long dead, a city adorned with greater works of art than any other city in all the ancient world, where philosophy was the subject of any ordinary day's conversation, where an orator would be recognized at once and appreciated, yet a city that had lost its faith in its once adored deities who crowded its highways with altars, and idols that had no influence whatever on the moral life of those who passed by, a city that dared not look ahead, that had no hope that it could offer to mankind. There was a feverish, restless longing for many things. Here in art and literature were incarnated the beliefs of paganism, revealing what man could do by his own intellectual ingenuity, and revealing at the same time the fearful inabilities of the same intellects to discover and explore those truths which alone can bring peace and joy to the human soul. In such an environment as this, the Apostle Paul stood up to speak. The words of Dr. J. S. Howson, in what is probably the greatest life of Paul ever written, must be repeated in this place, for no one has quite described this scene as he did so vividly: "There is no point in the annals of the first planting of Christianity which seizes so powerfully on the imagination of those who are familiar with the history of the ancient world. Whether we contrast the intense earnestness of the man who spoke, with the frivolous character of those who surrounded him—or compare the certain truth and awful meaning of the gospel he revealed, with the worthless polytheism which had made Athens a proverb in the earth,—or even think of the mere words uttered that day in the clear atmosphere, on the summit of Mars' Hill, in connection with the objects of art, temples, statues, and altars, which stood round on every side,—we feel that the moment was, and was intended to be, full of the most impressive teaching for every age of the world. Close to the spot where he stood was the Temple of Mars. The sanctuary of the Eumenides was immediately below him; the Parthenon of Minerva facing him above. Their presence seemed to challenge the assertion in which he declared here, that *in temples made with hands the Deity does not dwell*. . . . Wherever his eye was turned, it saw a succession of such statues and buildings in every variety of form and situation. On the rocky ledges on the south side of the Acropolis, and in the midst of the hum of the Agora, were the 'objects of devotion' already described. And in the northern parts of the city, which are equally visible from the Areopagites on the seats near him, he would have been in almost as great danger as Socrates before him. Yet he not only avoids the snare, but uses the very difficulty of his position to make a road to the convictions of those who heard him. He becomes a Heathen to the Heathen. He does not say that he is introducing new divinities. He rather implies the contrary, and gently draws his hearers away from polytheism by telling them that he was making known the God whom they themselves were ignorantly endeavoring to worship. And if the speech is characterized by St. Paul's prudence, it is marked by that wisdom of his Divine Master, which is the pattern of all Christian teaching. As our Blessed Lord used the tribute-money for the instruction of His disciples, and drew living lessons from the water in the well of Samaria, so the Apostle of the Gentiles employed the familiar objects of Athenian life to tell them of what was close to them, and yet they knew not. He had carefully observed the outward appearance of the city. He had seen an altar with an expressive, though humiliating, inscription. And, using this inscription as a text, he spoke to them, as follows, the Words of Eternal Wisdom."[9]

In his famous Boyle Lectures for 1864 on the *Conversion of the Roman Empire,* Charles Merivale, at the very beginning of his volume, states, I believe, for all time the apologetic value of this magnificent address of Paul's. This address, he says, seems to reveal "more directly the fundamental question between God's revelation and human speculation than any of the simple apologies or explanatory defenses of Christianity set forth by the revelation of our faith in the century next ensuing. Augustine and Lactantius, witnesses of the triumph of the new religion, expose to scorn the vain pretenses of the priests of Jupiter and Apollo; but the preaching of St. Paul, in the short fragment before us, goes in one word to the root of the matter, and sets before us the question of questions, which all generations must ask and do of themselves—in private, in their own hearts, if not in public debate and controversy—namely, whether God has given us the assurance of His being, of His providence, and of His righteousness, by the sure and certain promise of a future existence."[10]

Our young men are being taught from the pages of Plato and Aristotle, are led to adore the works of Pericles, to consider almost as having once lived the gods and goddesses of this ancient state, but how few ever know that the greatest hour in Athens' history was this hour, in which all it had longed for, it now hears proclaimed, and the God whom it groped after now being truly revealed by the lips of this inspired messenger of God. So, rightly says Professor Schaff, "On the consecrated ground of classic antiquity and of the religion of the beautiful in the birthplace of the most splendid forms which reason and imagination, in the dim twilight of the Logos, could of themselves produce, appears a man of feeble, uncomely person, but of the noblest mind and heart, and the most disinterested zeal, nay, filled with the Spirit of God Himself, proclaiming the religion of the True and of eternal life. Before the philosophers of Greece and amidst the renounced temples and statues of all conceivable idols, a despised Jew preaches that foolishness of God which confounds the wisdom of the Grecian schools and appeals more eloquently to the guilt-stricken heart than ever Demosthenes or Aeschines to the sovereign people;—the doctrine of the crucified Nazarene, who revealed the only true God; whose beauty, veiled in the form of a servant, far outshines that of the statues of Phidias and the temple of Minerva on the Acropolis; takes its bold flight beyond the ideals of Plato; no longer, like the myths of Prometheus and Hercules and the tragedies of Aeschylus and Sophocles, leaving men to grope wishfully after the blissful harmony of existence, the reconciliation of God and man; but actually giving it, and giving all that the most earnest and profound heathens could ask or think."

In this one sermon preached in Athens on the only visit that Paul ever made to this now decaying city, "In preaching the true God he pronounced the death doom of polytheism and the sentence is without appeal." I firmly believe Stier is right when he says, "In that hour it was given to the apostle what he should speak."[11]

Did Paul Fail in Athens? It has often been said, and frequently by those of a conservative viewpoint that Paul made a great mistake in delivering this particular address, and that his results were exceedingly meager. With this viewpoint the author has no sympathy whatever. I believe that the Apostle Paul was as definitely led of the Holy Spirit to utter this particular discourse on Mars' Hill as he was to give his apologies before Festus or Agrippa, or to preach any of the sermons that ever proceeded from his lips throughout his thirty years of powerful presentation of the Gospel. We must recognize in the first place that the results of this address were not, even then, altogether nil; some were saved that day, which would be a dual miracle, considering the audience he had to speak to. There were a few even of the *notable* people of the city who believed, as a result of Paul's address. Would to God that on every occasion that you and I had ever spoken it could be said that some believed, noble or ignoble! Nevertheless it is true that there was no great church in Athens until at least three centuries had gone by. The words of Harnack are not exaggerated, "Corinth and Thessalonica had flourishing churches. But the major part of the peninsula cannot have had more than scanty population of Christians up to 325. . . . From the outset the church at Athens was small and small it remained, for in this city of philosophers Christianity could find little room."[12] With the few notable Christians who were identified with the Athenian church during the first four or five centuries we need not concern ourselves in these pages.

The question now must be faced: why were the results of Paul's powerful, magnificent address on Mars' Hill so meager? The reason was not in the nature of the presentation of this particular message that Paul delivered; the reason is not in Paul, but in the Athenians. It should be remembered that even our Lord did not always have results. We seem to forget such statements which we find in the Gospels as "He could not do many mighty works there because of their unbelief."[13] We would not say the cause here was in the *impotency* of Christ, but the hardness and unbelief of his listeners. Most unexpectedly I came upon some words confirming this point, from one from whom we have previously quoted, and inasmuch as he knew pagan Greece so intimately and lived practically all his life, when he was not traveling, in the atmosphere of a modern university, his words should come with double force. I refer to Sir William Mitchell Ramsay "It was not among the 'wise after the flesh,' the professors and lecturers of the University, that the new teaching could find a ready audience: and the history of the world ever since has proved, time after time century after century, that the established teachers of the Universities are, with rare exceptions, the slowest to move and the last to accept any new ideas, while their young pupils as a rule are the quickest to respond to every new movement in thought. . . . The Athenian University was the home of dilettantism and of the cool, cultivated, critical intellect, which had tried all things and found all wanting; and in it there were few hearers and no open door for the new teaching."[14]

The famous French historian, the Abbè Constant Fouard, approaching this matter of the apparent smallness of the results of Paul'

Athenian ministry, well reminds us that while the ancient Greeks had an extremely rare appreciation for the beauties of nature, for the marvels, for statuary, and paintings, for the development of the human body, for conversation, and speculation, they had lost any mood of seriousness in their pursuit of life. "The habit of looking at everything as food for clever argument had had its fatal result in the loss of all good faith and sincerity; it was no longer a question of convincing them, but of tickling their ears with bright talk. No difficulty of the mind could be more repugnant to a man of Paul's firm character than this want of seriousness in the intellectual world. Such fickleness of soul paves the way to a state of frivolity, thoughtlessness, and in practical affairs, degenerates into double dealing and duplicity. The upright and honest hearts which the Gospel was addressing were but few and far between in this race, so noble in appearance but in reality so crafty, hard, selfish and vain."[15] As it was in Athens in the days of Paul, so it is now in our own university centers. In the great city of Cambridge, Massachusetts, in the halls of Harvard University, let anyone who loves the Gospel stand up and tell how pitifully feeble would be the immediate consequences of the proclamation of a crucified and risen Saviour within the hearing of that student body. What hearing does the *Gospel* have today in New Haven? What grip does the Gospel of Jesus Christ the Son of God today have upon the great student body of Princeton University? Let anyone who has been to Hanover, New Hampshire, confess the sorrow of seeing less than seven per cent of the great student body of Dartmouth College, and probably less than five per cent of the faculty within the walls of its two churches on the Lord's Day. I do not mean that there are not some rue believers within the environments of these cities—there were some in Athens, but oh! how few and for the most part how hard to each those living in these citadels of intellectualism. The university is necessary, but from the standpoint of the Gospel today we are paying a dreadful price for our education.

The Athenian Mood of the First Century and the Temper of Our Contemporary Civilization. I do not wish in any way to distort or force he matter that we are now about to consider, and I want to be exeedingly careful not to exaggerate any of the aspects of our contemporary civilization which we will briefly consider in this concluding part of our chapter, for the sake of making a point. After long consideration of the subject, however, I feel convinced that at no time in the history of the modern world, with the possible exception of the days of the Renaissance, have we had an attitude toward life, a conception of the deeper problems of life, so similar to those prevailing in Athens in the days of Paul. Let me speak of a few. In the first place, we are living in a time of supreme intellectualism. The percentage of literacy has risen in the twentieth century to the highest point ever reached in modern European civilization, perhaps we should say in any period of civilization. We can be grateful for this. This intellectualism has been produced by certain powerful causes and, in turn, results in certain definite inescapable consequences. Never in all the world's history has there been so much printed matter in circulation, never have books multiplied as they have in the last half century; newspapers and magazines are available at every street corner; adult education grows rapidly; more of our youth attend universities and colleges than ever before; doctorate degrees are conferred by the thousands in our land every spring. I do not dare say it on my own information but one of our best equipped modern scholars has made the statement in a book which Yale University has chosen to publish that, "Any sixteen-year-old boy in any one of our schools knows more today about the physical structure of the world than Aristotle or Plato ever did; he can give rational explanation of phenomena which once appeared to the greatest minds as puzzling mysteries. The universe of *qua* science existly consists of that part of the total universe from which, owing to human reason, mysteries have been removed."[16] Intellectualism such as characterized the single city of Athens in antiquity now rests upon our entire western world.

The Athenians were said to be always looking for something new especially after such great men as Socrates, Plato, and Aristotle had disappeared, never to return again in men of similar gigantic stature. Trench says this word new means "something not only new but sufficiently diverse from what had gone before to stimulate a jaded and languid curiosity."[17] "It is," says the distinguished philologist Cremer "that *blasé* state in which men need ever fresh impressions and sensa tions, without being able to be permanently affected." [18] Such a passion for newness is acknowledged to be dominant today by all students of our contemporary civilization. The well-known European philosopher, Rudolf Eucken, soon after the beginning of our century, wrote, "We have a continual eager pursuit of the new, the dazzling, the exciting; seeking after sensations, a pandering to the whims and condition of the crowd, the low average of humanity." [19] This passion for the new accounts for many of the symptoms of our present age, for example, seeing some new movie two or three times a week, a disease that has laid hold of our children with as powerful a grip as it has our adult minds; the ability of some new novel to sweep the country with a previously unheard of sale because, in finding little satisfaction in the masterpieces of earlier literature, we must be stimulated by the less important just because it is new. This manifests itself in the whole underlying tendency to demand something new in all realms of life, a new deal, a cult of new thought, a program of "modern education," the talk about the necessity for "a new outlook of life," as though no one during the last six thousand years ever had a correct outlook of life, until two terrible world wars fell upon us. We, like the Athenians, unless we have new life from God through Christ, and know His grace and blessing for us new every day, and have the confidence of a new heaven and a new earth, we of this generation are vitally afflicted with the same disease.

As Athens of Paul's day was compelled to worship at the altar of a god they correctly called *Agnostos, The Unknown,* so in the same mysterious way do we seem today not only to confess how much is unknown, but really to pride ourselves on the vast realms of the unknowable, and to worship at the altar of The Unknown. First of all, as we saw in an earlier chapter, the great body of contemporary philosophers, and many of our theologians, if they do not actually deny the very existence of God, at least say God cannot be known, and boast of it. Even so distinguished a philosopher, of a preceding age, as Sir William Hamilton, wrote, "To think that God is, as we can think Him to be, is blasphemy. The last and highest concentration of all true religion, must be an altar Agnostos Theo, 'To the unknown and unknowable God.'" This idolizing of the unknown, using such a word to describe all that should be God, was the first fundamental postulate of the whole vast philosophical system of Herbert Spencer.

"The man of science realizes with a special vividness the utter incomprehensibleness of the simplest fact considered in itself. . . . The deepest, widest and most certain of all facts (is) that the Power which the universe manifests to us is utterly inscrutable. . . . (It is) alike our highest wisdom and our highest duty to regard that through which all things exist as the Unknowable." It was Spencer's contemporary, Thomas J. Huxley, who gave to our English vocabulary the word *agnosticism*. His own insistence that the Unknown must be recognized as an inescapable reality, may be seen, e.g., in these words—"The theology of the present has become more scientific than that of the past, because it has not only renounced idols of wood and idols of stone, but begins to see the necessity of breaking in pieces the idols built up of books and traditions and fine-spun ecclesiastical cobwebs, and of cherishing the noblest and most human of man's emotions, by worship, 'for the most part of the silent sort,' at the altar of the Unknown and the Unknowable."[20] It has been set forth by a number of our philosophers as, for instance, George Santayana, in his Herbert Spencer Lecture, "The Unknowable," in which he concludes, "The existence of this world is certain, or at least it is unquestionably to be assumed. Experience may explore the adventurous and science may describe it with precision; but after you have wandered up and down it for many years and have gathered all you could of its ways by report, this same world, because it exists substantially and is not invented, remains a foreign thing and a marve to the spirit; unknowable as a drop of water is unknowable, or unknowable like a person loved."[21]

Our Lord came that we might know God. The Gospel of John wa written that we might know that Christ was the Son of God. Th Apostle Paul spoke again and again of the things we *know* as believer —we know God, we know the peace of God, we know the love c Christ, the grace of our Lord Jesus, the power of His Resurrectio that the trying of our faith worketh patience, that God is righteou that we are of the truth, that God hears us, and that we are love of God. One of the greatest tragedies of this anaemic and almo cowardly attempt to escape from frankly facing the facts of the Christian religion, and giving some genuine thought to its precepts and evidences, is that now on every hand in our contemporary Christological literature we are reading that we cannot even know Christ, and that the New Testament fails to reveal to us any real historical personage, but, rather, a fleeting phantasy, of whom we cannot ever expect to be sure of much. Thus Schweitzer at the end of his work, *The Quest of the Historical Jesus,* concludes, "He comes *as one unknown,* without a name, as of old, by the lakeside, he came to those men who knew him not."[22] So likewise, Dr. Robert Henry Lightfoot, Professor of Exegesis of Oxford, in his Gifford Lectures for 1934, *History and Interpretation in the Gospels,* tells us in his concluding paragraph that it seems that "the form of the earthly, no less than the heavenly Christ is for the most part hidden from us and all the inestimable value of the Gospels are little more than a whisper of His voice. We trace in time just the outskirts of His ways. Only when we see Him in His fullness shall we know Him as He was on earth. And perhaps the more we ponder the matter the more clearly we shall understand the reason for it and, therefore, shall not wish to otherwise, for probably we are at present as little prepared for the one as for the other."[23] Here you have not only a confession that, at least for this scholar, Christ is unknown and unknowable, but a strange declaration that we are better off not knowing—how pitiful, how misleading, how contrary to every purpose for which Christ came into the world. And yet we call this "modern scholarship."

Athens knew about everything that was knowable, except the most important things: she did not know God, she did not know what to do with her sins, she did not know where to find a life of peace and joy and victory, she had no hope, and she knew nothing of a life to come. That is exactly where men are today who have excluded God from their thinking, who deny the Bible to be a divine revelation, and who are stumbling and groping about in the twilight, or even deeper darkness, of the mind of fallen nature.

The recrudescence of paganism. There is no more tragic, though powerful underlying tendency of our century, which is carrying our whole western world back into a state which, should the tendency continue and increase, will result in a condition more rotten and more dreadful than any which the Roman world knew at the coming of the time of Christ, than a return to paganism. Let me approach this subject first through the minds of two of the most distinguished thinkers of this present generation, one a historian and the other a theologian. Probably the outstanding authority in the world on the history of the Near and Middle East at the present time is Dr. Arnold Toynbee, Director of Education at the Royal Institute of International Affairs, and Professor of International History at the University of London. In 1937, in a well-known periodical in this country, Professor Toynbee gave us a penetrating study of what he called, "The Menace of the New Paganism," in which he defined the idolatry of our paganism, for the most part displayed by Fascism and Communism, as, "a religion which either does not know or else refuses to recognize that there is no God but God and which, therefore, worships the creature instead of worshiping the Creator. This post-Christian paganism has succeeded in capturing for its own trivial and narrow ends some of that wholehearted Christian devotion which ought to be given to God alone and if this has really happened, it should be taken deeply to heart by Christians, because it shows up the lukewarmness and indecisiveness in so much of the Christianity of the modern age; for if the church had remained true to herself, she would not have seen her children transferring their allegiance elsewhere and laying their Christian spirit of devotion at the feet of false gods. And then again, there is nothing so dangerous and so destructive as a wholehearted devotion that has been diverted from the service of God to the service of some lower object." [24] Mentioning first the tribal worship of Sparta and the other cities of Ancient Greece, Professor Toynbee goes on to say that upon their ruins was established that Roman Empire which became an object of idolatrous worship in its turn, an idol which stood for the whole of mankind. The idolatrous worship of organized human power is the fatal error which, due in part to two great wars, is becoming almost universal. The triumph of this paganism can spell nothing but disaster for mankind.

I do not know of anyone among those whose voice is often heard in our country, who has so clearly seen the nature and threat of the paganism of our day as Monsignor Fulton J. Sheen, of the Catholic

University of America. In the concluding chapter of his *Old Errors and New Labels* Dr. Sheen says, rightly, that "In our day the religion of Christ is facing a crisis such as it has not faced, probably, since the days of Constantine. By that I mean that up to this time the Church has been engaged in a kind of civil war, in which a Christian idea has battled with a misunderstanding of a Christian idea or in which sect has fought with sect. None of the great heresies of the first sixteen hundred years of the Christian era denied the existence of God, but they had misconceived the notion of the Trinity, the nature of Christ, the nature of Divine Grace, and the mission of the Church. In the last four centuries the conflict was not so much of idea and idea as the conflict of sect and sect. To-day we are faced with something entirely novel. We are engaged now not so much in what might be called a civil war, but we are confronted with what Mr. Belloc has called 'an invasion,' that is, a force of ideas that is as strange to traditional Christianity as Christianity was strange to Paganism. This new invading force is New Paganism. New Paganism may be defined as an outlook on life that holds to the sufficiency of human science without faith, and the sufficiency of human power without grace. In other words, its two tenets are: Scientism, which is a deification of the experimental method, and Humanism, which is a glorification of a man who makes God to his own image and likeness." Continuing, Professor Sheen makes a very fine point, in saying that the New Paganism differs from the old in this, that whereas in ancient Greek Paganism the spiritual and the material were confused; in the New Paganism they are divorced, God from the cosmos, and after the divorcement has been accomplished the New Paganism "immediately throws away the better half and lives worse with the other half. That is why today there is religion without God, Christianity without Christ, and psychology without a soul. From this point of view, the old Paganism was preferable to the New, for at least it acknowledged the necessity of some power above man, even though it was only a household God." This brilliant orator makes one final comparison, when he says that the old Paganism put out the light of the candle of reason by refusing to come to a knowledge of the invisible from the visible things of the world, but that the new Paganism puts out the light of the sun of Faith.[25] We do not agree with Monsignor Sheen's exaltation of the Roman Catholic church in this book, his refusal to believe there is any other church in the world worth considering but his, but he rightly sees this terrible thing of Paganism, and I am afraid the tragedy is that the Roman Church is talking about it much more than our anaemic Protestantism.

In discussing ancient paganism and modern paganism, I suppose that some will immediately say, "Well there is one thing you have to admit, we do not have the old idols and the many gods that Greece had in Paul's day." One should not speak too quickly in this matter. In the literature of the modern German Faith Movement, Wotan, the old Germanic god, is said to incarnate the divine principle that dwells in all true Germans. One of the leaders of this movement, Wilhelm Feudt, in rewriting the 87th Psalm, makes the Nazi version to read, in part, "But on Osning (part of the Teutoburger Forest) the Lord shall count those sprung from blood of the sons of Mannus: Ingo, Istu and Ermin (ancient Germanic gods)."[26]

This present exaltation of German gods is the fruit of that glorification of the Greeks, and ancient paganism, which culminated in Lessing, Goethe, and Heine. Heine went so far as to say that he preferred the deities of Olympus to the grey mist of Christians. "Goethe, a universal genius, but in character at this time Euripidean, transformed his 'Ephigenie' from prose to an exquisitely simple and stately verse, in which the antique marble blushes, one might say, with a faint rose color."[27]

I suppose some of my readers will say, "Well this happened in Germany, but of course this could never happen in our own country." I am not so sure. The other day I happened to be turning the pages of a book by a former Associate Professor of the University of Pittsburgh, Dr. O. L. Reiser, a volume published in 1935, with the title, *Philosophy and the Conception of Modern Science,* and in the midst of this book I was astonished to find a chapter on "The Religion of Light," in which this Professor boldly said, "The God whom we here propose to substitute for the God of traditional theology may seem a strange God to many, i.e., the God of light, and yet this God alone makes possible the only light we know of; this God is the source of all energy on earth, it sustains man and his institutions. In brief I wish to argue that God is light." Later he has a whole section, "The Chemistry of Sun Worship," and at the end of his volume appear the words, "Freed from supernaturalism, fostering such ideals as love and the brotherhood of man, religion could be an effective instrument in the development of the proper subjective attitudes in conduct." [28]

I remember when a boy, a wild looking elderly man walking down Clark Street in Chicago with a great mass of hair covering his head, a face yellow like parchment, and learned by his talk that the man was a sun worshiper. Well, it was always in my mind that such people are rare and need not even be considered, but when sun-worship is taught by our own professors, it becomes more than a freakish fancy of some foolish man.

A far more influential man than the professor to whom we have just referred is Julian Huxley, who goes so far as to actually commend polytheism (and no doubt many support him in this): "One of the obvious attractions of Greek Paganism was the variety of human activities and aspirations which it could accommodate within its boundaries. Freed from the necessity of propitiating or imitating a unitary being, a modern religion could revert to that rich variety." [29] That Paganism is coming back upon us no one can deny, but let us not forget that if it comes in greater and greater force it will introduce the most awful age this wicked world of ours has ever known. As Hilare Belloc, in an essay on this very subject said a few years ago, "Men do not live long without gods; but when the gods of the New Paganism come they will not be merely insufficient as were the gods of Greece, nor merely false; they will be evil . . . The New Paganism foolishly expecting satisfaction will fall, before it knows where it is, into Satanism." [30]

The message Paul gave to the Athenians is a message which the church needs to powerfully proclaim, before our whole western world is engulfed in the diabolical reappearance of that which we used to think had long ago received its mortal blow.

The Apologetic Value of Paul's Address to the Athenians. The great truths which St. Paul set forth in this address are: the nature and character of God, the creation of the world by God, the resurrection of

Christ, a judgment to come, and, because of these truths, the need for men to repent. It is a source of great gratification to the author to be able to close this chapter with a testimony from a most unexpected source, to the truth we have here been trying to emphasize, that the apologetic of Paul on Mars' Hill is the apologetic which is needed today in our crumbling and bewildered civilization. In 1941 there was held in the City of Philadelphia, the University of Pennsylvania, a famous bicentennial conference at which a number of distinguished thinkers of our day spoke. Among these was Dr. Joseph L. Hromadka, who for some years was the Professor of Systematic Theology at the University of Prague, but at the time at which he spoke, he was the Professor of Philosophy and Christian Ethics of Princeton Theological Seminary. The subject of Dr. Hromadka's address was "The Modern Trend in European Protestant Theology." In the sentences which we are about to quote it will be noticed that this European scholar says nothing about Paul's address to the Athenians (I doubt if he had it in mind), which makes his testimony all the more remarkable because the very terms which he here declares should be the fundamental truths presented in our contemporary apologetic are exactly the truths which the Apostle Paul proclaimed to the Athenians that day on Mars' Hill. We close this chapter, then, with this extended quotation from Professor Hromadka:

"The modern theology has realized the fact that our civilization is at stake, and that all the essential heritage of the Christian history is in a great peril. And it recognized its own tremendous responsibility for this situation. The theology cannot evade and escape the question as to what ought to be the foundation of our life outside the Church. Very likely the civilization is breaking down because we theologians have not done what was our mission and obligation. Apparently we have distorted the very essence of the divine truth, thus depriving civilization of its living and sustaining power.

"The post-war theology begins to establish a new philosophy of history and civilization, a philosophy rooted in the fundamental message of the gospel. As over against the pre-war theology, the new theology points to the central pillars of faith as being central pillars of our civilization.

"The faith in creation as a barrier against pessimistic nihilism and rude naturalism.

"The faith in the incarnation as a barrier against modern relativism and the mood of spectatorship.

"The faith in the resurrection of Christ as a challenge to the skeptical mentality of indifference and carelessness.

"The faith in the ultimate Judgment as a basis of creative earnestness and moral vigor—a continuous protest against any kind of monism obscuring and obliterating the definite line between good and evil, truth and falsehood, right and wrong, holiness and wickedness.

"The faith in Christ, the supreme Lord, as barrier against any kind of totalitarianism.

"The post-war theology has chosen a new (and still old) gallery of teachers and leaders. Whereas the old theology tried to adjust itself to the philosophical thinkers, the new theology goes in another direction. It does not minimize the greatness of Kant and Comte, Hegel and William James; however, it is oriented essentially towards the men of faith: St. Augustine and St. Anselm, St. Thomas and Erasmus, Luther and Calvin. The old struggle is going on: Who is the best or the most reliable interpreter of the Christian revelation? But it is a struggle with weapons which are far more appropriate than were the weapons of philosophical systems.

"We are living in a terrific crisis. However, this crisis is a great challenge for us. If we theologians are faithful to the divine truth, we might be once credited with bringing good news and remedy to unhappy humanity."[31]

Chapter VII

THE CREATION OF THE WORLD BY GOD THE APOLOGETIC FOR THIS ERA OF SCIENTIFIC EMPHASIS

The Apostle Paul began his address to the Athenian philosophers with a declaration concerning that problem which, sooner or later, must confront every serious-minded man who attempts to understand some of the elementary things of the universe in which he lives, that subject with which the Bible begins, because it concerns the beginning; which, if we rightly understand it, can bring infinite peace and joy and strength to the human heart, and which if left as an insoluble enigma of agnosticism makes it impossible for the mind of any man to come to rest. We refer, of course, to the work of the creation of this universe by God. These are Paul's opening words to the Athenians, after his unique and appropriate introduction, "The God that made the world and all things therein, he, being Lord of heaven and earth, dwelleth not in temples made with hands; neither is he served by men's hands, as though he needed anything, seeing he himself giveth to all life, and breath, and all things; and he made of one every nation of men to dwell on the face of the earth, having determined their appointed seasons, and the bounds of their habitation; that they should seek God, if haply they might feel after him and find him, though he is not far from each one of us: for in him we live, and move, and have our being; as certain even of your own poets have said."

The Origin of the Universe an Inescapable Problem. That we live in a universe made up of a vast number of innumerable bodies, dominated by inexorable laws of what we call nature, a universe that can be seen and handled, studied, and in part understood, embracing both inorganic matter and organic objects, which we call living, is of course at the very foundation of anything called sane thinking. With the intricate, fantastic, irrational theories concerning the *non-reality* of this great universe, and of life itself, we have no time in a work like this, nor, for that matter, do we think any time is ever necessary. Let us, as realists, discuss the things which all our senses, and the very laws of logic, compel us to believe, and avoid those speculations which the common man will never understand, and upon which philosophers will never agree. Acknowledging the present existence of this universe, we cannot escape, in mature life, coming face to face with an inevitable question: How did this universe come into existence? This is the problem of *cause,* a problem that has baffled men since the beginning of philosophic contemplation, with the cosmologists of early Greece, and continues to be a problem from which modern man can never reasonably and honestly escape. As Professor McCosh said, years ago, "There is the intuition which leads us, when we discover an effect to look for a cause . . . This is the most active and potent of all mental principles, in compelling us to the scrutiny of nature. We are not satisfied with the immediate present, we are sure that it has proceeded from the past; and we go back from the nearer to the more remote past and we are not content until we reach a sufficient cause which is not itself an effect."[1] When Julian Huxley says, "A scientifically based philosophy enables us in the first place to cease tormenting ourselves with questions that ought not to be asked, because they cannot be answered—such as questions about the Cause or Creation or Ultimate or Reality,"[2] he, in the stubborn agnostic attitude of all his writings, is simply attempting to dismiss one of those vast and fundamental problems which will lead to God, if properly solved, and which if not thoroughly searched out, will leave man suspended in the air.

Science Acknowledges It Does Not Know and Is Incapable of Discovering the Origin of the Universe and of Life. Before we even discuss the Biblical doctrine of the creation of the world, we should fully realize that modern science itself unanimously confesses that it can tell us *nothing* about the *origin* of the world in which we live, or of that ever interesting thing, called life. This is so significant, in this day when science so completely dominates the thinking and conceptions of our Western civilization, that I believe it is important to bring to the attention of my readers the testimony of a number of scientists of the last century supporting the statement that heads this section of our chapter.

The most illustrious botanist in the history of American science, Dr. Asa Gray, for many years the Professor of Botany at Harvard University, and author of the most important Flora that was ever written for any one country, up to the middle of the last half of the nineteenth century, in his volume *Natural Science and Religion*, said, "A beginning is wholly beyond the ken and scope of science, which is concerned with questions about how things go on, and has nothing to say as to how they absolutely begin."[3]

Toward the end of his life, T. H. Huxley acknowledged, "It appears to me that the scientific investigator is wholly incompetent to say anything at all about the first origin of the material universe. The whole power of his organon vanishes when he has to step beyond the chain of natural causes and effects. No form of nebular hypothesis that I know of is necessarily connected with any view of the origination of the nebular substance."[4] Ernst Haeckel, a contemporary agnostic of Huxley, in his *The History of Creation* confessed the same thing, "The process of creation as the coming into existence of matter is completely beyond human comprehension and can therefore never become a subject of scientific inquiry."[5]

Dr. L. L. Woodruff, Professor of Biology in Yale College, in one of the most noteworthy works on science written in our day, summarizes in one sentence all that modern science can say about this great question of origins, "Biologists are at the present time absolutely unable, and probably will be for all time unable to obtain empirical evidence of any of the crucial questions relating to the origin of life on the earth." And so says the outstanding authority on the history of science in the world today, Dr. George Sarton of Harvard: "Science can explain everything except the essential mysteries of life."[6]

Sir Oliver Lodge in his famous book *Man and the Universe*, remarked near the beginning of this century, "It (science) has not yet witnessed the origin of the smallest trace of life from dead matter; all life, so far as has been watched, proceeds from antecedent life. Given the life of a single cell, science would esteem itself competent ultimately to trace its evolution into all the myriad existences of plant, and animal, and man, but the origin of protoplasmic activity itself as yet eludes it . . . The law of evolution not only studies change and progress, it seeks to trace sequences back to antecedents; it strains after the origin of all things. But ultimate origins are inscrutable. Let us admit as scientific men, that of real origin, even of the simplest thing, we know nothing, not even of a pebble."[7] Sir Arthur Keith somewhat later likewise confessed, "Biologists do not know as yet when or how life began; they have no explanation to offer of its inner significance and ultimate meaning. Therein lies the weakness of their case, for the human mind craves for a solution of the great mystery and is restless until it is satisfied as to its place in the great scheme of the universe."[8] One of the great biologists of the twentieth century, Professor J. Arthur Thomson, in his *Science and Religion,* after years of brilliant study in the deeper problems of biology, remarked, "It is quite legitimate for the biologists to say: I take initial primitive organisms as given. Perhaps this is at present the wisest thing to do, for biology does not do more than hint at the way in which even the simplest living creatures may have come into being. Science is very vague in regard to most beginnings. And yet it is usually the first step that counts."[9] The same author in his famous widely distributed *Outline of Science* makes the same confession, even with an inclusion of words from the very chapter we are studying, "If we say, as was said long ago, 'in the beginning was Mind' we may be expressing or trying to express a great truth, but we have gone BEYOND SCIENCE."[10]

Looking back over these confessions, notice particularly the phrase of Sir Keith, "The human mind craves for a solution of the great mystery," and the statement by Sir Oliver Lodge that evolution "strains after the origin of all things." In other words, what science cannot discover, scientists long to know; what the human mind must ever seek after, a first cause, modern man, with all his brilliant achievements in the investigation of nature, has not been able to discover. As the knowledge of facts increases and the knowledge of first cause continues to escape the infinite toils of the scientist exploring in the earth and in the heavens and in his laboratory, man is left, unless he has some other source of knowledge, a restless being indeed. As Pasteur, himself a believer, once said, "Believe me in the face of these great problems, these eternal subjects of man's solitary meditation, there are only two attitudes of mind: one created by faith, the belief in a solution given by Divine revelation; and that of tormenting the soul by the pursuit of impossible explanations."[11]

The Biblical Doctrine of Creation. As we approach the subject of what the Bible says about the creation of the universe we find ourselves in exactly the mood of which Calvin speaks, as he begins his Argument at the beginning of his commentary on the Book of Genesis. "Since the infinite wisdom of God is displayed in the admirable structure of heaven and earth, it is absolutely impossible to unfold THE HISTORY OF THE CREATION OF THE WORLD in terms equal to its dignity. For while the measure of our capacity is too contracted to comprehend things of such magnitude, our tongue is equally incapable of giving a full and substantial account of them."[12]

The Prominence Given to the Doctrine of Creation in the Bible. The whole system of Christian doctrine, all of its fundamental truths, are derived from one book, the Bible, which contains, among many other things, the only dependable record of the words and deeds, the life and death and resurrection of Jesus Christ our Lord that has ever been composed. The New Testament, however, rests upon the Old, frequently points back to the older records, and claims that the historical events and the Person around whom it is written are the fulfillment of Old Testament prophecy. Together the Old and New Testaments are considered as the Word of God. Now the beginning of this volume we call the Bible is the book of Genesis, appropriately so designated, for two reasons: it stands at the beginning of our Bible, and it records the beginning of our universe. All subsequent revelation presupposes a knowledge of the origin of the universe, of life, and man, such as is here recorded. As someone has said, "The first note struck on the lyre of revelation with which all other strings are in harmony which sounds throughout the whole anthem," is this truth that the world has been made by God. Again and again throughout the Old Testament God is appealed to as the Creator of the heavens and of the earth; and it is as such that He is worshiped as a Creator. Men pray to Him with the full confidence that He is able to answer their prayers. The creation may be called one of the three great truths of the Psalter.

It is a truth frequently upon the lips of the prophets as they rebuke Israel for her gross idolatry and her superstitious worship of the heavenly bodies.[14] In the New Testament the profoundest and most theological of the four Gospels begins with the reaffirmation of this creative work of God; the Apostle Paul opens his magnificent epistle to the Romans by showing men that their ignorance of God is inexcusable, because the created universe which surrounds them should have sufficed as a revelation to them of the invisible things of the Godhead.[15] Again and again in his other epistles Paul exalts Christ as the one by whom the worlds were framed, a truth that the author of the epistle to the Hebrews likewise places at the very beginning of his massive Christological document.[16] It is to a faithful Creator that the Apostle Paul points as one to whom we can trustfully commit our souls. Of the life of the redeemed in heaven, the book of The Revelation reveals that the multitudes of all the hosts of angels and redeemed creatures join in singing praises to Him who has made the heavens and the earth.[17] Destroy faith in the Genesis account of creation, and the great structure of doctrinal truth built up through the ages, in the Word of God, is without foundation. For these reasons we make no apology for an extended treatment of this subject. It has been of pre-eminent importance in the great battles that have been waged around the question of the truthfulness of the Word of God, and it will probably be increasingly important in the present conflict of the faith, a fortress which must be held against all our enemies. It can only be held if we are persuaded that what it says is true and believable.

A Summary of the Biblical Doctrine of Creation. Before we begin to discuss some of the more important aspects of this inexhaustible subject, we ought to attempt a concise summary of what the Christian church holds in regard to the universe being created by God. The following definition, from the most outstanding work on theology published in our country since the beginning of this century, is as good as any. "Creation in the strict sense of the word may be defined as that free act of God whereby He, according to His sovereign will and for His own glory in the beginning brought forth the whole visible and invisible universe, without the use of pre-existent material, and thus giving it an existence, distinct from His own and yet always dependent on Him."[18] Most of what will be said in the pages that now follow will be in support of and an elaboration of these brief compact phrases, although we have not written this part of our chapter with any idea of expounding this sentence.

The Meaning of the Hebrew Word Used to Express the Act of Creating. No data of the biblical account of creation should probably be considered until we have investigated the meaning of the Hebrew word which is used in this passage, indicating the act of creation. While there are three words variously used in these verses, the one which contains most definitely the idea of creation by miracle or divine fiat is the word *bara.* Its original meaning is *to split, to cut, to divide;* but in addition to this it also means *to fashion, to create,* and, in a more derivative sense, *to produce, to generate, to regenerate.* The word itself does not convey the idea of bringing forth something out of nothing, for it is even used in works of providence (Is. 45:7; Jer. 31:22; Amos 4:13), yet it has a distinctive character: "it is always used of divine, and never of human production; and it never has an accusative of material, and for that very reason serves to stress the greatness of the work of God."[19] It should be emphasized, and therefore we repeat in the words of another, that this word and its Greek equivalent, "are used in Scripture only where God is the agent, and are never employed when the act of man is to be described."

The Universe Was Created Ex Nihilo. The only doctrine regarding the divine creation of the world that can reasonably be held, that has won almost unanimous acceptance in the Christian church in every age, that is implied in all the creeds of the church, is that God created the world *ex nihilo,* by which of course we mean that He created the world *out of nothing.* The universe was not created by God out of matter that previously existed. Anything else but a creation *ex nihilo* demands that matter is as eternal as God, and if that is ever assumed, no one could be really sure that God was greater than the matter which was co-eternal with Him; in fact, if matter and God are the two great eternal coexisting realities, then as masses of matter can and often have destroyed men, we could not be wholly assured that a collision of enormous heavenly bodies might not some time destroy God. If, however, all matter has been created by God, as well as all creatures in the universe, then God must have created all these things from nothing. At once it will be said that there is no such phrase in the Bible indicating that God created everything out of nothing. It is true, the exact phrase is not there, but its equivalents are there, e.g., in Romans Paul wrote, "God calleth those things which be not as though they were," and in Hebrews it is said, "Things which are seen were not made of things that do appear." [20] Paul, writing to the Colossians, in one of the profoundest passages of all the Bible, says that all things visible and invisible "were created by Christ the first begotten," and certainly in such a phrase all matter that has ever existed must be included—there was nothing in the world before God began to create the world, no matter of any kind.[21] Of course this raises and provokes questions which we cannot answer, but it is not unreasonable, and to deny a creation *ex nihilo* involves even greater problems, and destroys the idea of the absolute eternity and creative work of God. "That the Scriptures do teach this great doctrine of a creation *ex nihilo* is plain from the fact that no mention is ever made of any pre-existing substance out of which the world was made. The original creation is represented as a molding of matter into form and imbuing it with life." [22] Dr. Charles Hodge at the end of his very rich discourse on this subject of divine creation remarks: "The doctrine of creation flows from the infinite perfection of God. There can be but one infinite being. If anything exists independent of his will, God is thereby limited. The idea of the absolute dependence of all things on God pervades the Scripture, and is involved in our religious consciousness. The God of the Bible is an extramundane God, existing out of, and before the world, absolutely independent of it, its creator, preserver, and governor. So that the doctrine of creation is a necessary consequence of Theism. If we deny that the world owes its existence to the will of God, then Atheism, Hylozoism, or Pantheism would seem to be the logical consequence. Hence, on the one hand, the Scriptures make that doctrine so prominent, presenting it on the first page of the Bible as the foundation of all subsequent revelations concerning the nature of God and his relation to the world, and appointing from the beginning one day in seven to be a perpetual commemoration of the fact that God created the heaven and earth."[23]

Creation Was Voluntary and Not of Necessity. We will discuss in a subsequent part of this chapter, in considering non-biblical theories of creation, a theory called "creation by necessity," but here we would simply affirm the fundamental truth, that, according to the Scriptures, God brought the universe into existence by His own determination and volition. "He freely willed the existence of creatures, being equally free not to will it had He pleased; or to will the existence of creatures other than those actually created had that been His choice. This is the only legitimate inference from the infinitude of the divine perfection. Had God been compelled by necessity to create, He must have been so compelled because His infinitely perfect intellect represented to His infinitely perfect will that creation was a necessity required to supply some deficiency, otherwise discernible in His Being, but creation could not have this effect. To infinite perfectness nothing further in the way of perfection can be added, and again, to view the same truth in a different light created perfection is derived perfection . . . Creation adds nothing to the divine excellency which it did not already possess. Although creation is seen to be an act which does not increase the divine perfection, it is also seen to be an act good in itself and therefore, though not necessary, still worthy of election should God so please."[24]

The World Is Separate from Its Creator. The original account of creation as given us in the opening chapters of Genesis, and all that is said about the universe in its relation to God throughout the rest of the Scriptures, clearly insist that the Creator is always to be recognized as distinct from that which He has created. Pantheism affirms that the world and God are one, and in our day it is increasingly important to insist upon the distinction between the two, because there is an alarmingly strong pantheistic tendency, not only in much of our philosophy but in no little of our theology. In Genesis 1:1 heaven and earth are clearly distinguished from God, as of an altogether different substance. "God and the universe are not one substance, but two substances; one primary and the other secondary, one necessary and the other contingent. God and the universe do not constitute one system of being, but two distinct and different systems; for a system implies that all the parts are one nature and unequal in dignity and duration. The three Trinitarian persons, for example, constitute one system of divine Being. The universe is not infinite but finite and therefore cannot belong to the system of the infinite. The universe is capable of increase and diminution, the infinite is not, space, time and matter are unlimited; they can be added to, subtracted from and divided. God is infinite and incapable of addition, of subtraction, or of division."[25]

Creation Was "By the Word of God." In spite of all that we have thus far said about the divine creation of our universe, many will long before this have begun to ask the question, "Well, granted that God did make the world, and that it is not eternal, and that He did make it out of nothing, *how* did God create the world?" All that the Scriptures tell us, in regard to this profound subject, is that the world was made *by the Word of God*. The Genesis account of creation itself tells us that the various parts of our universe came into existence by the mere fiat of God: God said "Let there be light and there was light." "By the Word of Jehovah were the heavens made; and all the hosts of them by the breath of His mouth," says the Psalmist. Speaking of the heavens, another Psalmist says "He commanded and they were created." It is by faith, says the writer to the Hebrews, that "we understand that the worlds were framed by the Word of God."[26] The Apostle Peter speaks of those who "are willingly ignorant of this that by the Word of God the heavens were of old."[27] The Apostle John begins his Gospel by declaring that by the Word of God (who is the Lord Jesus Christ) "all things were made."[28]

The Ultimate Meaning of Creation as an Act of God Is Inexplicable. The ultimate *manner* of creation we, with our finite minds, cannot fathom. The Word of God does not suggest that we should, and the whole history of human thinking testifies that for man it is impossible. No one has set this forth in stronger, or more acceptable language, than Dr. Tennant in his wonderfully rich work, *Philosophical Theology:* "Theism must frankly confess that the kernel of positing meaning in the notion of creation, viz., position, is inexplicable. Indeed if it were explicable it would not be creation. The various analogies that have been employed for its elucidation, such as man's 'creative' art, throw no light on the ultimate mystery. Just as the gradations between the infinite One and the finite many, devised by Philo, Plotinus, Spinoza, etc., conduct nearer to the abyss but do not bridge it, so these comparisons break down at the crucial point—origination of something out of no pre-existent material such as is forthcoming and utilised in the case of causation within the course of Nature, and in all 'creative' imagination or ideation within the minds of men of genius. The *modus operandi* of divine creativity is wholly unimaginable and inconceivable. And this inexplicability is inevitable. For explanation, in all its forms, establishes some connexion, similarity, or continuity, with what is experienced or lies within Experience; whereas creation is the activity through which experients and what is experienced by them come to be. The notion of creation, consequently, is not derivable from experience, and analogies valid within experience cannot reach beyond its bounds. But while the theist must confess that a conception which is fundamental in his philosophy is inexplicable, he may do so without shame and without reproach. Some ultimates, analysable and unassimilable, there must be. Theism needs but to allow that creation is one of them. And in invoking it theism sets up no new mystery where there was none before, as seems often to be tacitly presumed by those who regard the notion with disfavour. The ultimate mystery of the origination of the world confronts all theories alike, and to think it does not exist for any one kind of non-theistic world-view is but to hush it up. In giving articulate expression and particular form to the mystery theism is not uniquely burdening itself with a superfluous load. And however much a philosopher may be inclined to disparage the notion of creation on the score of its obscurity, there is certainly no more intelligible a notion which he can substitute for it."[29]

The Reasonableness of the Idea of a First Cause.—1. The Denial of a First Cause in Contemporary Philosophy and Science. A century ago Comte, whose system of positivism predicted the ultimate elimination of any faith in God in the future of a progressing humanity, was driven by his own refusal to recognize God as the Creator of the universe to declare, "The word cause must be banished from the vocabulary of true philosophy."[30] While it has *not* been banished, it certainly is a truth which an increasing number of modern thinkers are denying. Thus, Karl Pearson, in his *Grammar of Science,* in a long discussion of "Cause and Effect," gave as his opinion, "We can no longer infer even the possibility of the existence of first causes, for there is nothing like them in our experience, and we cannot by the second canon of logic inference pass from the known to something utterly unlike it in the unknown. Science knows nothing of first causes that cannot be inferred from any branch of scientific investigation . . . It is more honest to say 'here for the present our ignorance begins' than, 'here is a first cause.' "[31] Likewise, Professor G. Watts Cunningham, of Cornell University, in his well-known text, *Problems of Philosophy,* dogmatically says, "If by a First Cause is to be understood a cause which is first in time, there seems to be no very convincing reason to assume that there is such a First Cause. As we have already argued, the only reason for assuming any causal connection at all among existents lies in the consideration that such a connection seems necessary to account for their meaningful reference to each other; unless there were such a causal connection among them, it is not easy to understand how they could be meaningfully related as they are. This, of course, is simply saying over again what we have already said, namely, that causal connection among existents is assumed as an integral constituent of existential meaning-situation. But in this assumption there appears to be no warrant for concluding that there must be some cause which is the beginning of a causal series; the most that is warranted is the conclusion that there must be a causal connection among existents within a given existential meaning-situation. To show that a First Cause must be assumed as the beginning of a series of causes, one would have to show that a series of existential meaning-situations is inherently such as to demand a beginning; and this, it appears, could hardly be shown, since what the judging of existential meaning-situations calls for is nothing more than a causal relation among the existents involved in the situations within which judging functions. . . . It appears either that causal connection must be admitted only among existents without any reference to a temporally first, or that the distinction between causal connection and implication connection must be softened if, indeed, not dissolved utterly."[32]

It is just here where young men will simply have to take their stand. If there is such a thing as cause and effect and, thus, there is such a thing as cause, as all will agree, and if it seems reasonable from causes for all things that we seek to ascend to a First Cause, as the originator of this universe, then the creation account in Genesis is not only reasonable, and acceptable, but it sets forth a truth to which logic inevitably leads us. If, on the other hand, one is determined to say that there is no cause, to dogmatically affirm, without scientific proof, that real causes can never be discovered, and a first cause can never be assumed, then one will have to find some other theory, illogical as it may be, to account for the universe in which we live. Here is where young men will have to make a decision for themselves. Philosophers and some scientists, it is true, are rejecting the whole idea of causation, and especially the idea of a first cause, but they are doing this primarily, not because anything in modern science leads them to such a conclusion, but because they are proceeding on the assumption that there must not be any rational argument for God, nor any ground for postulating a First Cause, and, therefore, they must get rid of the whole idea that underlies this truth. One of our brilliant philosophers, Etienne Gilson, in his new work *God and Philosophy,* has not made too severe an indictment against such men, when he says, "They prefer to say anything rather than to ascribe existence to God on the ground that a purpose exists in the universe. For centuries final causes have been mistaken for scientific explanations by so many generations of philosophers that today many scientists still consider the fear of final causes as the beginning of scientific wisdom."[33]

2. *The Law of Cause and Effect.* "Every science except the purely mathematical sciences," says Professor Stace in his excellent work, *A Critical History of Greek Philosophy,* "affirms the truth of the law of causation. Every student of logic knows that this is the ultimate canon of the sciences, the foundation of them all. If we did not believe in the truth of causation, namely, everything which has a beginning has a cause, and that in the same circumstances the same things invariably happen, all the sciences would at once crumble to dust. In every scientific investigation this truth is assumed. . . . How do we know that water always freezes at zero degree centigrade

(neglecting questions of pressure, etc.)? How do we know it is true that there are regions of the earth where no one has ever been to see? Only because we believe that in the same circumstances the same thing always happens, that like causes always produce like effects. But how do we know the truth of this law of causation itself? Science does not question the cause, it stresses its assertions back to this law, but goes no further. Its fundamental canon it takes for granted."[34] We should remember this passage from Professor Stace and frequently refer to it when we come upon contemporary denials of the whole fundamental law of cause and effect.

Aristotle's Four Categories of Cause. No discussion of the problem of causation, however brief, should avoid at least a reference to the most famous discussion of causes in all ancient philosophy, namely, the two treatments of this subject by Aristotle, in his *Physics,* and, later, in his *Metaphysics.* It is not my purpose in this volume to discuss the intricacies of Aristotelian philosophy, but I feel it necessary at least to place before my readers the more important sections of Aristotle's discussion of the four categories of causes, without any interpretation. Difficult as it is to comprehend them, I think it is better for us to have the text of Aristotle before us rather than some later attempted interpretation of these passages. In the second book of his *Physics,* the third chapter begins with these words: "Now that we have established these distinctions, we must proceed to consider causes, their character and number. Knowledge is the object of our inquiry, and men do not think they know a thing till they have grasped the 'why' of it (which is to grasp its primary cause). So clearly we too must do this as regards both coming to be and passing away and every kind of physical change, in order that, knowing their principles, we may try to refer to these principles each of our problems.

"In one sense, then, (1) that out of which a thing comes to be and which persists, is called 'cause,' e.g., the bronze of the statue, the silver of the bowl, and the genera of which the bronze and the silver are species.

"In another sense (2) the form or the archetype, i.e., the statement of the essence, and its genera, are called 'causes' (e.g., of the octave the relation of 2:1, and generally number), and the parts in the definition.

"Again (3) the primary source of the change or coming to rest; e.g., the man who gave advice is a cause, the father is cause of the child, and generally what makes of what is made and what causes change of what is changed.

"Again (4) in the sense of end or 'that for the sake of which' a thing is done, e.g., health is the cause of walking about. ('Why is he walking about?' we say. 'To be healthy,' and, having said that, we think we have assigned the cause.) The same is true also of all the intermediate steps which are brought about through the action of something else as means towards the end, e.g., reduction of flesh, purging, drugs, or surgical instruments are means towards health. All these things are 'for the sake of' the end, though they differ from one another in that some are activities, others instruments.

"This then perhaps exhausts the number of ways in which the term 'cause' is used . . .

"All the causes now mentioned fall into four familiar divisions. The letters are the causes of syllables, the material of artificial products, fire, &c., of bodies, the parts of the whole, and the premises of the conclusion, in the sense of 'that from which.' Of these pairs the one set are causes in the sense of substratum, e.g., the parts, the other set in the sense of essence—the whole and the combination and the form. But the seed and the doctor and the adviser, and generally the maker, are all sources whence the change or stationariness originates, while the others are causes in the sense of the end or the good of the rest; for 'that for the sake of which' means what is best and the end of the things that lead up to it. (Whether we say the 'good itself' or the 'apparent good' makes no difference.)"[35]

In the first book of his *Metaphysics,* Aristotle returns to the subject of causes. In the last eight chapters of book I, he enlarges upon the earlier discussion of this problem. The second book, composed of three short chapters, has more to say about that which immediately concerns us in our discussion, that is the necessity for postulating a *first* cause. These are Aristotle's words: "But evidently there *is* a first principle, and the causes of things are neither an infinite series nor infinitely various in kind. For (1) neither can one thing proceed from another, as from matter, *ad infinitum* (e.g., flesh from earth, earth from air, air from fire, and so on without stopping), nor can the sources of movement form an endless series (man for instance being acted on by air, air by the sun, the sun by Strife, and so on without limit). Similarly the final causes cannot go on *ad infinitum*—walking being for the sake of health, this for the sake of happiness, happiness for the sake of something else, and so always one thing for the sake of another. And the case of the essence is similar. For in the case of intermediates, which have a last term and a term prior to them, the prior must be the cause of the later terms. For if we had to say which of the three is the cause, we should say the first; surely not the last, for the final term is the cause of none; nor even the intermediate, for it is the cause only of one. (It makes no difference whether there is one intermediate or more, nor whether they are infinite or finite in number.) But of series which are infinite in this way, and of the infinite in general, all the parts down to that now present are alike intermediates; so that if there is no first there is no cause at all . . .

"At the same time it is impossible that the first cause, being eternal, should be destroyed; for since the process of becoming is not infinite in the upward direction, that which is the first thing by whose destruction something came to be must be non-eternal.

"Further, the *final cause* is an end, and that sort of end which is not for the sake of something else, but for whose sake everything else is; so that if there is to be a last term of this sort, the process will not be infinite; but if there is no such term, there will be no final cause, but those who maintain the infinite series eliminate the Good without knowing it (yet no one would try to do anything if he were not going to come to a limit); nor would there be reason in the world; the reasonable man, at least, always acts for a purpose, and this is a limit; for the end is a limit."[36]

Although Aristotle insisted upon a first cause, one does not have to read long in his treatment of the subject without recognizing that he fails to identify the first cause with God, or that he even finds any purpose in this ultimate cause of the universe. "Aristotle never construes the process of nature" says Professor Stocks, "as the purpose of God. Purpose for him is foreign to the Being of God, and proper only to imperfect beings."[37]

The Necessity for Believing in a First Cause. This conception of the necessity for recognizing a first cause is tremendously important, and must be firmly laid hold of by all Christians today who expect to meet the deniers of causation in contemporary philosophy. The following statement by Professor Robert Flint, in his famous work *Theism,* will suffice for our consideration of the fundamental conception of a first cause: "To say that the idea of cause can never demand belief in an uncaused cause, sounds as self-evident; to say that the idea of cause can find no satisfaction save in the belief of an uncaused cause, sounds as a paradox; but let a man meditate for a little with real thoughtfulness on the meaning of these two statements, and he cannot fail to perceive that the former is an undeniable falsehood, and the latter an undeniable truth. An uncaused cause, a first cause, alone answers truly to the idea of a cause. A secondary cause, in so far as secondary, in so far as caused, is not a cause. I witness some event—some change. I am compelled as a rational being to seek its cause. I reach it only to find that this cause was due to a prior cause. What has happened? The cause from which I have had to go back has ceased to be a cause; the cause to which I have had to go back has become the cause of two effects, but it will remain so only if I am not reasonably bound to seek a cause for *it*. If I am, its causality must pass over to its explanatory antecedent. We may go back a hundred, a thousand, a million times, but if the last cause reached be not truly a first cause, an uncaused cause, the idea of cause in our mind will be as unsatisfied at the end of our search as at the beginning, and the whole process of investigation will be aimless and meaningless. A true cause is one to which the reason not only moves but in which it rests, and except in a first cause the mind cannot rest. A first cause, however, is certainly not one which has been itself caused."[38] This subject is so important that I am taking the liberty of quoting one more contemporary theologian on the necessity for assuming a First Cause:

"We observe in the world around us subordinated causality. We see things acting. They are dependent on other agents for their existence and causal activity. It is impossible that a series of causes, each of which depends for its existence on the cause above it, should be infinite. We are forced to the conclusion that there exists a First

Cause, itself uncaused. If it is denied that there is a First Cause, that there is an Uncaused Being, one is confronted by a dilemma. Either all beings are effects, or they form an endless series. The first alternative denies the principle of causality. The second is an attempt to get rid of the difficulty by an infinite multiplication of it. Even if it were possible that acorns and oak-trees had succeeded one another throughout infinite time, it would be altogether impossible that an infinite number of eternal cog-wheels should eternally rotate apart from something which set them in motion. An infinity of subordinate agents can no more initiate action than can one alone. It is no solution of the difficulty to say that wheel A is moved by wheel B, wheel B by wheel C, and so on to infinity. Either the wheels are not moving at all, or they have been set going by some originating principle of activity. An effect cannot contain any perfection which does not belong to its cause. A cause is that which makes a thing to be what it is. Unless it possesses a certain perfection it cannot confer it. Nothing can confer on another what it does not itself possess. To deny this would be to assert that nonentity would produce being. Every perfection found in the effect must exist in the cause. But among the effects produced by the First Cause are persons endowed with intelligence and free-will. Hence the First Cause must be a personal Being, intelligent and free."[39]

The First Cause Can Only Be a Mind. Granted that a First Cause, in considering the origin of the universe, must be postulated, unless we remain suspended in the chaos and contradictions that result from a denial of such a truth, we can go one step further and say that the first cause from which such a universe as ours has proceeded can only be a Mind. "The most rapid glance at the universe powerfully confirms the conclusion that its first cause can only be a Mind, a Reason. The universe is a universe; that is to say, it is a whole, a unity, a system. The First Cause of it, therefore, in creating and sustaining it, must comprehend, act on, and guide it as a systematic whole; must have created all things with reference to each other; and must continually direct them towards a preconceived goal. The complex and harmonious constitution of the universe is the expression of a Divine Idea, of a Creative Reason. This thought brings me to my next argument and next lecture."[40] It is probable, though in a less convincing way, that it is this same idea to which Sir James Jeans points when he speaks of the architect of our universe being first of all a mathematician. "From the intrinsic evidence of his creation, the Great Architect of the Universe now begins to appear as a Great Mathematician . . . The universe can best be pictured . . . as consisting of pure thought, the thought of what, for want of a better word, we must describe as a mathematical thinker."[41]

The Cosmological Argument. In all studies of the doctrine of God, when the subject of the proofs for God's existence are considered, one of the major lines of argument developed is what is known as the cosmological argument, that is, the argument based upon the nature and order of the world in which we find ourselves living. I have left the statement of the cosmological argument to the last. It has been discussed elaborately by almost every theologian of the Christian church. The single paragraph of consideration which is given to it in this place, I have taken from the excellent work by Professor G. D. Hicks, in his Hibbert Lectures for 1937, *The Philosophical Bases of Theism*. The paragraph is not easy reading but if we are to reach rock bottom in this very important problem of the creation of the universe, we must be ready to do some hard thinking. "This argument may, in a concise fashion, be stated thus. Starting from an undeniable deliverance of experience,—namely, that there are such entities as existing things and events,—it is noted that these existing things and events reveal themselves, even on the most cursory inspection, to be contingent in character,—that is to say, as not being there in virtue of any intrinsic necessity of their own. Such necessity as appertains to them is relative and hypothetical. We can say that if the event C be given the event D necessarily follows. The occurrence of the event D is, in other words only conditionally necessary—necessary in the sense that it is constrained. In virtue of its own character merely, and apart from the existence of the event C, this event D would not exist. And similarly, of course, in regard to the event C; its existence is only conditionally necessary on the occurrence of an event B; and again the existence of the event B is only conditionally necessary on the occurrence of an event A, and so on *ad infinitum*. Throughout nature we find, accordingly, only this conditional necessity; nothing happens there except as a consequence of something else happening. And, if this be true of all that nature contains, it must likewise be true of nature in its entirety. In the long run, therefore, the existence of nature must depend upon a Being whose existence is intrinsically or unconditionally necessary,—a Being, that is to say, that is not dependent for its existence upon the prior existence of something else. Or, to bring out the contention in another way, just as in the realm of knowledge we cannot go on indefinitely giving reasons for propositions that we hold to be true, but must come in the end to propositions that are self-evident, or contain within themselves their own justification, so in the realm of existence, we cannot be condemned forever to the mere treadmill exercise of an indefinite regress; but must, presuming, of course, that our intellectual powers are adequate to the task, come ultimately upon a reality that is there, so to speak, in its own right, the conception of which does not need the conception of something else upon which it is dependent."[42] When the Bible declares that "In the beginning God created the heavens and the earth," it clearly intends us to conclude that the first cause for this universe is God and God alone. All the laws of logic when free from the twisting influences of atheistic prejudice lead to the same affirmation, which even without a Bible were our minds not so dark and our hearts not so antagonistic to God, we would be compelled to acknowledge. I think that it is right here that young men will have to take their stand and insist they believe what science so emphatically insists upon, that for every effect there is a cause, and from that to go on and say that for this universe there must be a correspondingly adequate cause and that cause can only be the first cause, God Himself.

Ancient Greek Cosmogonies Contrasted with the Doctrine of Creation Set Forth by St. Paul in His Address to the Athenians. One may say without fear of contradiction, that the three great problems which any philosophy must face, if it is to be comprehensive and satisfying, are the problems that relate to the nature of the origin of the universe, the problem of God, and the problem of man, the latter of which includes psychology, epistemology, and sociology (as well as other sciences). It has always interested me, when reading early Greek philosophy, to note that the first great problem which the Greeks tried to frankly face and solve, was not a theological problem, one concerning the Being of God, nor the problem of man's soul and the nature of knowledge, but the problem of the universe, its nature or being, and, finally, its origin. One must admit that the ancient Greeks had a lot of good things to say, profound, and often true, concerning the problem which we are discussing in this chapter, namely the creation of the universe. The first to approach it in any philosophical manner was Hesiod, writing, probably, in the middle of the eighth century. In his famous work *Theogony,* after some considerations of foolish fables concerning the origin of some of the gods, Hesiod approaches the question of the creation of the earth. "Verily at the first Chaos came to be, but next wide-bosomed Earth, the ever-sure foundation of all the deathless ones who hold the peaks of snowy Olympus, and dim Tartarus in the depth of the wide-pathed Earth, and Eros (Love), fairest among the deathless gods, who unnerves the limbs and overcomes the mind and wise counsels of all gods and all men within them. From Chaos came forth Erebus and black Night; but of Night were born Aether and Day, whom she conceived and bare from union in love with Erebus. And Earth first bare starry Heaven, equal to herself, to cover her on every side, and to be an ever-sure abiding-place for the blessed gods. And she brought forth long Hills, graceful haunts of the goddess-Nymphs who dwell amongst the glens of the hills. She bare also the fruitless deep with his raging swell, Pontus, without sweet union of love. But afterwards she lay with Heaven and bare deep-swirling Oceanus, Coeus and Crius and Hyperion and Iapetus, Theia and Rhea, Themis and Mnemosyne and gold-crowned Phoebe and lovely Tethys. After them was born Cronos the wily, youngest and most terrible of her children, and he hated his lusty sire."[43] I am not myself squeamish about frankness in literature, but in a work of this kind, I trust I will be pardoned for omitting three or four phrases of Hesiod that to a Christian appear coarse. Granted that some of these phrases in this particular chapter seem to parallel the Genesis account, some of them are so crude and polytheistic, that they are utterly contrary to our biblical record of creation. When we come to a later passage in the *Theogony* we will see even more vividly how utterly fantastic and unbelievable and nonsensical are Hesiod's lines, read in our modern day, "And Night bare hateful Doom and black Fate and Death, and she bare Sleep and the tribe of Dreams. And again the goddess murky Night, though she lay with none, bare Blame and painful Woe, and the Hesperides who guard the rich, golden apples and the trees bearing fruit beyond glorious Ocean. Also she bare the Destinies and ruthless avenging Fates, Clotho and Lachesis and Atropos, who give men at their birth both evil and good to have, and they pursue the transgressions of men and of gods: and these goddesses never cease from their dread anger until they punish the sinner with a sore penalty. Also deadly Night bare Nemesis (Indignation) to afflict mortal men, and after her, Deceit and Friendship and hateful Age and hard-hearted Strife.

"But abhorred Strife bare painful Toil and Forgetfulness and Famine and tearful Sorrows, Fightings also, Battles, Murders, Manslaughters, Quarrels, Lying Words, Disputes, Lawlessness and Ruin, all of one nature, and Oath who most troubles men upon earth when anyone wilfully swears a false oath.

"And Sea begat Nereus, the eldest of his children, who is true and lies not: and men call him the Old Man because he is trusty and gentle and does not forget the laws of righteousness, but thinks just and kindly thoughts. And yet again he got great Thaumas and proud Phorcys, being mated with Earth, and fair-cheeked Ceto and Eurybia who has a heart of flint within her." One more passage concerning Atlas will suffice for our purpose. Clymene bore to Iapetus, "A stout-hearted son, Atlas: also she bare very glorious Menoetius and clever Prometheus, full of various wiles, and scatter-brained Epimetheus who from the first was a mischief to men who eat bread; for it was he who first took of Zeus the woman, the maiden whom he had formed. But Menoetius was outrageous, and farseeing Zeus struck him with a lurid thunderbolt and sent him down to Erebus because of his mad presumption and exceeding pride. And Atlas through hard constraint upholds the wide heaven with unwearying head and arms, standing at the borders of the earth before the clear-voiced Hesperides; for this lot wise Zeus assigned to him. And ready-witted Prometheus he bound with inextricable bonds, cruel chains, and drove a shaft through his middle, and set on him a long-winged eagle, which used to eat his immortal liver; but by night the liver grew as much again everyway as the long-winged bird devoured in the whole day. That bird Heracles, the valiant son of shapely-ankled Alcmene, slew; and delivered the son of Iapetus from the cruel plague, and released him from his affliction—not without the will of Olympian Zeus who reigns on high, that the glory of Heracles the Theban-born might be yet greater than it was before ever the plenteous earth."[44]

No one today discusses the relation of the *Theogony* of Hesiod to modern science, for the simple reason that it is so definitely mythological and fantastic that it has no likeness at all with conclusions of modern science, such as Genesis has.

One of the outstanding historians of science in our country of this generation, Professor Louis T. More, calls attention to the vast difference between these early Greek speculations, and the Hebrew conception of creation when he says, "One cannot but be amazed at the difference between the two. The Greeks were still in the period of pure mythological animalism, but in the mind of the prophet of Judah (More dates these early literature of the Hebrew people as late as 700 B.C. but the date of their composition is not something for discussion here, and does not affect Professor More's argument) the world is the act of a single creative spirit. Inorganic phenomena are not personified, and living forms are brought into existence according to a preordained classification in species . . . There is a quite remarkable sequence in the order of creation of the various types of forms which by a guess or by an acute perception of relationship of form, agrees with the succession according to modern evolutionists."[45]

We come somewhat nearer to one particular subject of the first chapter of Genesis, in the writings of Anaxagoras, who flourished in the middle of the fifth century B.C., whose death occurred, it is thought one year before the birth of Plato (429 B.C.). The distinguished German Philosopher, Professor Windleband in his famous *History of Philosophy,* says that Anaxagoras "describes how the beginning of the world was preceded by a chaotic primitive condition, in which the elements were intermingled without order and without motion. Then came the *nous,* the 'Reason-stuff,' and set it into ordered motion . . .

The teleological motive of the doctrine of Anaxagoras is due essentially to his admiration of the order in the *stellar world*. . . . There is no ground for assuming that this teleological cosmology directed attention to the adaptation to ends in living beings, or even to the connected system of Nature as beneficent to man; its gaze was fixed on the beauty of the starry heavens."[46]

The most famous and profound discussion of creation in all the ancient world, in fact, in any literature of any people, exclusive of the Hebrew account in Genesis, is of course the exhaustive discussion of this matter in the *Timaeus* of Plato (428–347 B.C.), aptly called "the Bible of Hellenistic cosmogony." Professor Jowett, who has given us the most famous of all the translations of Plato in our own language, in his Introduction to the Timaeus, expresses what a great many Christians have themselves concluded (although I am not discussing it here, ither pro or con), that the genius of this work "seems by a divine ower in many instances to have anticipated the truth." I think it will e best for our purpose to have the actual language of Plato before s: "Let me tell you then why the creator created and made the uni-erse. He was good, and no goodness can ever have any jealousy of any-hing. And being free from jealousy, he desired that all things should e as like himself as possible. This is the true beginning of creation nd of the world, as we shall do well in believing on the testimony of vise men: God desired that all things should be good and nothing ad in so far as this could be accomplished. Wherefore also finding the vhole visible sphere not at rest, but moving in an irregular and dis-rderly manner, out of disorder he brought order, considering that this vas far better than the other. Now the deeds of him who is the best an never be or have been other than the fairest; and the creator re-ecting upon the visible work of nature, found that no unintelligent reature taken as a whole was fairer than the intelligent taken as a hole; and that intelligence could not exist in anything which was de oid of soul. For these reasons he put intelligence in soul, and soul in ody, and framed the universe to be the best and fairest work in the rder of nature. And therefore using the language of probability, we ay say that the world became a living soul and truly rational through e providence of God.

"Now that which is created is of necessity corporeal, and also visible and tangible. And nothing is visible where there is no fire, or tangible which is not solid, and nothing is solid without earth. Wherefore also, God in the beginning of creation made the body of the universe to consist of fire and earth. But two things cannot be held together without a third; they must have some bond of union. God placed water and air in the mean between fire and earth, and made them to have the same proportion so far as was possible (as fire is to air so is air to water, and as air is to water so is water to earth), and thus he bound and put together a visible and palpable heaven. And for these reasons, and out of such elements which are in number four, the body of the world was created in harmony and proportion, and therefore having the spirit of friendship; and being at unity with itself, was indissoluble by the hand of any other than the framer."[47]

Of the many different aspects of creation which Plato considers, let us consider briefly what he has to say about the creation of bones: "The bone was composed by him in the following manner. Having sifted pure and smooth earth he kneaded it and wetted it with marrow, and after that he put it into the fire and then into the water, and once more into the fire and again into the water—in this way by fre quent transfers from one to the other he made it insoluble by either With this bone he fashioned, as in lathe, a globe made of bone, whicl he placed around the brain, and in the globe he left a narrow opening and around the marrow of the neck and back he formed the vertebra like hinges, beginning at the head and extending through the whol of the trunk. Thus he preserved the entire seed, which he enclosed i a case like stone, inserting joints, and using in the formation of then the power of the diverse as an intermediate nature, in order to obtai motion and flexion. Then again, considering that the bone would b too brittle and inflexible, and when heated and again cooled woul soon mortify and destroy the seed within—having this in view, he con trived the sinews and the flesh, that so binding all the members tc gether by the sinews, which admitted of being stretched and relaxe about the vertebrae, he might thus make the body capable of flexio and extension, while the flesh would serve as a protection against th summer heat and against the winter cold, and also against falls, lik articles made of felt, softly and easily yielding to external bodies, and containing in itself a war moisture which in summer exudes in the form of dew, and imparts to the body a natural coolness; and again in winter by the help of its own fire would form a very tolerable defence against external and surrounding cold. The great moulder and creator considering this, mingled earth with fire and water and put them together, making a ferment of acid and salt which he mingled with them and formed a soft and pulpy flesh; and as for the sinews, he made them of an unfermented mixture of bone and flesh, attempered so as to be in a mean, and gave them a yellow colour, and hence the sinews have a firmer and more glutinous nature than flesh, but a softer and moister nature than the bones."[48]

In this day of revival of the study of Plato's writings, when many philosophers are insisting that we should return to the Platonic conceptions of the universe, and of man, let us never forget that there are innumerable ideas in Plato that no modern educated man can ever again accept. Granted that he was one of the three greatest philosophers that ever lived, we ought to thank God every day for such a book in our hands as the Bible, which has delivered us from much of the nonsense of these ancient thinkers. Rather than summarize Plato's development of the study of creation in my own words, I would like to quote a penetrating summary, from one of the most distinguished philosophical theologians of our generation, Dean W. R. Matthews: "From the Christian standpoint, the Platonic idea of creation suffered from two defects. It fell short of the assertion of an absolutely creative God. The agent in creation is not, it would appear, for Platonism, the Supreme Being; for the Demiurge, contemplating the ideas and their harmonious unity in relation with the idea of the good, reproduces this heavenly pattern, as far as is possible, in time and space. The highest value is not the Creator. There is also doubt in the Platonic teaching concerning the dependence of all the elements of the created world upon the Creator, for in the *Republic* (379 c) we are told that God cannot be the cause of all things or indeed of many things, since He is the cause of only the good. It seems to be an essential part of the Platonic view of creation that the creative act is limited by 'necessity' or by matter."[49]

In another work, Dean Matthews, Professor of the Philosophy of

Religion in Kings College, London, has excellently set forth the difference between the whole ancient Greek conception of creation, and that which we find in the Bible, so fundamental to Christian thought, a verdict to which he has, after years of careful and sympathetic study of Greek philosophy, reached: "The idea of absolute creation which is implicit in the highest teaching of the Hebrew Prophets, is entirely absent from the philosophical reflection of the Greeks. We have to observe that the explicit affirmation of a creation *ex nihilo* appears to have been a peculiarity of Christian thought. It is only in Christian theology that we find the clear renunciation of dualism, together with the belief that all things proceed from God by an act of will."[50]

The Testimony of Famous Scientists to the Belief That the Universe Was Created by God. Now that we have, with as much thoroughness as our space allows, considered what the Bible says about the creation of the universe, and the inevitable problem of a first cause, I think before proceeding to other matters which must still be discussed in this vast and important subject of creation, it might be well to recall the fact that most of the great scientists of modern times have been firm believers in a divine creation of the universe, and have again and again declared their firm belief that the universe, to the study of the secrets of which they have given their life, was brought into existence by God Himself. I would like to arrange these testimonies to faith in a divine creation in an approximate chronological order, with one single exception, with the greatest scientist of all times, Sir Isaac Newton. The first authority in the English world in the history of science, Dr. George Sarton of Harvard, says that Newton's *Principia* "was really the foundation stone of modern thought. Our conception of the world was utterly changed by it; that is the world itself was changed."[51] All one needs to do is to open the pages of Newton's *Philosophical Principles of Natural Mathematics* to understand something of the gigantic intellect of this man of genius and of the vast advance which he made in the world of the laws of the natural world over all those who preceded him. This is the testimony of Sir Isaac Newton to the truth we are here considering: "This Being governs all things, not as the soul of the world, but as Lord over all; and on account of his dominion he is wont to be called *Lord God pantocrator,* or *Universal Ruler;* for God is a relative word, and has a respect to servants; and *Deity* is the dominion of God not over his own body, as those imagine who fancy God to be the soul of the world, but over servants. The Supreme God is a Being eternal, infinite, absolutely perfect; but a being, however perfect, without dominion, cannot be said to be Lord God; for we say, my God, your God, the God of Israel, the God of Gods, and Lord of Lords; but we do not say, my Eternal, your Eternal, exists necessarily; and by the same necessity he exists *always* and *every where.* Whence also he is all similar, all eye, all ear, all brain, all arm, all power to perceive, to understand, and to act; but in a manner not at all human, in a manner not at all corporeal, in a manner utterly unknown to us. As a blind man has no idea of colours, so have we no idea of the manner by which the all-wise God perceives and understands all things. He is utterly void of all body and bodily figure, and can therefore neither be seen, nor heard, nor touched; nor ought he to be worshipped under the representation of any corporeal thing. We have ideas of his attributes, but what the real substance of anything is we know not. In bodies, we see only their figures and colours, we hear only the sounds, we touch only their outward surfaces, we smell only the smells, and taste the savours; but their inward substances are not to be known either by our senses, or by any reflex act of our minds: much less, then, have we any idea of the substance of God. We know him only by his most wise and excellent contrivances of things, and final causes; we admire him for his perfections; but we reverence and adore him on account of his dominion: for we adore him as his servants; and a god without dominion, providence, and final causes, is nothing else but Fate and Nature. Blind metaphysical necessity, which is certainly the same always and every where, could produce no variety of things. All that diversity of natural things which we find saited to different times and places could arise from nothing but the ideas and will of a Being necessarily existing. But, by way of allegory, God is said to see, to speak, to laugh, to love, to fight, to frame, to work, to build; for all our notions of God are taken from the ways of mankind by a certain similitude, which, though not perfect, has some likeness, however. And thus much concerning God; to discourse of whom from the appearances of things does certainly belong to Natural Philosophy."[52]

One of the greatest pioneers in modern astronomy was Johannes Kepler (1571–1630), a true Christian and a real genius, who placed the science of astronomy on a new, secure base of mathematical precision. At the end of one of his astronomical works, he concludes with this marvelous paragraph, really a prayer:

"It remains only that I should lift up to heaven my eyes and hands from the table of my pursuits, and humbly and devoutly supplicate the Father of lights. O Thou who by the light of nature dost enkindle in us a desire after the light of grace, that by this thou mayest translate us into the light of glory; I give Thee thanks, O Lord and Creator, that thou hast gladdened me by thy creation when I was enraptured by the work of thy hands. Behold, I have here completed a work of my calling with as much of intellectual strength as thou hast granted me. I have declared the praise of thy works to the men who will read the evidences of it so far as my finite opportunity could comprehend them in their infinity. My mind endeavored to its utmost to reach the truth by philosophy; but if anything unworthy of thee has been taught by me—a worm born and nourished in sin—do Thou teach me that I may correct it. Have I been seduced into presumption by the admirable beauty of thy works, or have I sought my own glory among men in the construction of a work designed for thine honor? O then graciously and mercifully forgive me; and finally grant me this favor that this work may never be injurious but may conduce to thy glory and the good of souls."[53]

The next scientist of our series is one not nearly so well known as Newton or Kepler, or those whose names will follow, but who is nevertheless, acknowledged by historians of science to be one of the great botanists of modern times. I refer to John Ray (1627–1705). Perhaps a word about Ray should be mentioned here, that we might understand somewhat his place in the development of modern science. Ray took his B.A. degree at Trinity College, Cambridge, in 1647; was lecturer on Greek in 1651, mathematical lecturer in 1653, humanit reader in 1655, Junior Dean in 1658, and college Steward in 1659–166

When only thirty-three years of age, in 1660, he published a duodecimo volume of 285 pages, enumerating 626 species, which has been called "the first local catalogue of the plants of a district which has been issued in England." [54] Twenty-two years later, after two decades of enormous labor, he issued his *Methodus Plantarum Nova,* in which, "by basing his system mainly upon the fruit and also in part upon the flower, the leaf and other characteristics, . . . he made practically the first decided step towards a natural system of classification." In 1690 he published his *Synopsis Methodica Stirpium Britannicorium,* which has been called "the first systematic English flora, for more than seventy years the pocket companion of every British botanist." Pulteney calls Ray "without the patronage of an Alexander, the Aristotle of England and the Linnaeus of his age." He is often spoken of as "the father of natural history" in Great Britain. Of his *Synopsis Methodica Animalium* which he published in 1693, Hallam says, "This work marks an epoch in zoology . . . as the first classification of animals that can be reckoned both general and grounded in nature." In Ray we have one of the greatest scientists of the seventeenth century, and really the founder of British botany. The article in the *Dictionary of National Biography* lists twenty-five different titles by Ray. I would like to quote here from just one of them, a work which he wrote when at college, though he did not publish it, for some reason, until 1691. It carries the title, *The Wisdom of God Manifested in the Works of the Creation.* The edition from which I am quoting is that of Edinburgh, 1798. These are the opening words of the preface to this remarkable book:

"I shall now add a word or two concerning the usefulness of the argument, or matter of this discourse, and the reason I had to make choice of it, besides which I have already offered. First, The belief of a Deity being the foundation of all religion (religion being nothing but a devout worshipping of God, or an inclination of mind to serve and worship him) 'for he that cometh to God, must believe that he is God,' it is a matter of the highest concernment to be firmly settled and established in a full persuasion of this main point; now this must be demonstrated by arguments drawn from the light of nature, and works of the creation; for, as all other sciences, so divinity proves not, but supposes its subjects, taking it for granted, that by natural light, men are sufficiently convinced of the being of a Deity. There are indeed supernatural demonstrations of this fundamental truth, but not common to all persons or times, and so liable to cavil and exception by atheistical persons, as inward illuminations of mind, a spirit of prophesy, and foretelling future contingents, illustrious miracles, and the like; but these proofs, taken from effects and operations, exposed to every man's view, not to be denied or questioned by any, are most effectual to convince all that deny or doubt of it; neither are they only convictive of the greatest and subtlest adversaries, but intelligible also to the meanest capacities; for you may hear illiterate persons, of the lowest rank of the commonalty, affirming, that they need no proof of the being of a God; for that every pile of grass, or ear of corn, sufficiently proves that; for, say they, all the men of the world cannot make such a thing as one of these; and if they cannot do it, who can or did make it but God: To tell them, that it made itself, or sprung up by chance, would be as ridiculous as to tell the greatest philosopher so.

"Secondly, The particulars of this discourse serve not only to demonstrate the being of a Deity, but also to illustrate some of his principal attributes; as, namely, his infinite power and wisdom; the vast multitude of creatures, and those not only small, but immensely great, the sun and the moon, and all the heavenly host, are effects and proofs of his almighty power." [55]

The name of Michael Faraday (1791–1867) was a synonym for science throughout the world during his lifetime. No one would question the vast influence his discoveries exercised in the realm of physics and chemistry. He was the Fullerian Professor of Chemistry in the Royal Institution for over a generation, a fellow of the Royal Society, the recipient of the doctorate of canon law from Oxford. Faraday was an outstanding Christian and was a member of a very small, obscure group known as the Sandemanians, in London. He preached from 1839–1842 every alternate Sunday at the Sandemanian Church in London when he was in the city. His biographer tells us that in preaching "his object seemed to be to make the most use of the words of Scripture and to make as little of his own words as he could. Hence a stranger was struck first by the number and rapidity of his references of texts in the old and new testaments; and secondly by the devoutness of his manner." [56] It is in his famous lecture on mental education, delivered in 1854, when he was sixty-three years of age, that Faraday's belief in the creating power of God finds perhaps its fullest expression. These are his words, "High as man is placed above the creatures around him, there is a higher and far more exalted position within his view; and the ways are infinite in which he occupies his thoughts about the fears or hopes or expectations of a future life. I believe that the truth of that future cannot be brought to his knowledge by any exertion of his mental powers, however exalted they may be; that it is made known to him by other teaching than his own, and is received through simple belief of the testimony given. Let no one suppose for a moment that the self-education I am about to commend, in respect of the things of this life, extends to any considerations of the hopes set before us, as if man by reasoning could find out God. It would be improper here to enter upon this subject further than to claim an absolute distinction between religious and ordinary belief. I shall be reproached with the weakness of refusing to apply those mental operations which I think good in respect of high things to the very highest. I am content to bear the reproach; yet even in earthly matters I believe that the invisible things of Him from the creation of the world are clearly seen, being understood by the things that are made, even His eternal power and Godhead; and I have never seen anything incompatible between those things of man which are within him, and those higher things concerning his future which he cannot know by that spirit." [57]

The outstanding scientist of the middle of the nineteenth century in our own country, one of Europe's most distinguished authorities on fishes and fossils when he was only twenty-five, organizer of the great geological museum at Harvard, and recognized as one of the master teachers of modern times, was the Swiss geologist Louis J. R. Agassiz (1807–1873). Agassiz was not only a pronounced believer, he was even, to the disgust of many of his friends, a strong, constant opponent of Darwinian evolution. By his travels, by his determination to know the facts of the fields in which he was working, by his ability to bring perfect order out of a vast collection of details, and to construct great systems in the field of geology, and especially paleontology, Agassiz did more to advance the cause of geology in this country than any other one man. In the first volume of his famous, *Contributions to the Natural History of the United States,* a work which was never finished, in his "Essay on Classification," Agassiz makes this fine confession of his own faith in God the Creator,—"Though I know those who hold it to be very unscientific to believe that thinking is not something inherent in matter, and that there is an essential difference between inorganic and living and thinking beings, I shall not be prevented by any such pretentions of a false philosophy from expressing my conviction that as long as it cannot be shown that matter or physical forces do actually reason, I shall consider any manifestation of physical thought as an evidence of the existence of a thinking being as the author of such thought, and shall look upon an intelligent and intelligible connection between the facts of nature as direct proof of a thinking God . . . All these facts in their natural connection proclaim aloud the one God whom man may know, adore and love, and natural history must in good time become the analysis of the thoughts of the Creator of the universe as manifested in the animal and vegetable kingdoms."[58]

Here we might consider the words of Professor James Dwight Dana, one of the most distinguished scientists in the entire brilliant history of American achievement (1813–1895), who, at the early age of twenty-seven became Editor of the *American Journal of Science,* and at the age of thirty-six succeeded Silliman as Professor of Natural History at Yale University (later known as Professor of Geology and Mineralogy), a chair he held for over forty years. In 1862 he published his famous *Manual of Geology* which went through edition after edition, and for many years was the standard text book in our country. A recent biographer of his has said that "Dana's industry and productivity were without counterpart in American Geological History. Throughout the entire active period he stood head and shoulders above his contemporaries." Professor Dana's own confession of faith in God as the Creator of the world is as follows: "Within the soul, as part of its nature or of this Divine image, there are certain principles which are a bases of all reasoning above nature: as that, leading to a recognition of a higher Power above, the infinite God, the Cause of causes; that, leading to a recognition of the relation of cause and effect in consecutive events;

that, leading to a recognition of the truthfulness of the God of nature, demanding faith in return from his creatures; of the unity of nature, its oneness in plan as in Author, and thence the harmony of all laws, systems, or events in nature. . . . Nature is an intelligible minister appointed to lead us up to God, being a revelation of him in one range of his attributes, his power and wisdom, brought down to our comprehension, as the Spirit, and the manifestation of the Divinity in Christ, are our means of rising to a knowledge of God in his holiness and love, and of man in his duty and destiny. Even nature, also, is radiant with God's love; for the earth's history evinces that man's welfare was regarded in the whole program of creation; but Christ is the only expression of the infinite fulness of that love. In these two ways we gather strength, from the earth about us and God above, for the progress of the human soul."

One more distinguished American scientist, more or less unknown to the present generation, ought to be added to this list—in this case, an astronomer. I refer to Professor Charles Augustus Young, who spent most of his active life as the Professor of Astronomy in Princeton University. His grandfather, on his mother's side, was Ebenezer Adams, Professor of Mathematics and Philosophy at Dartmouth College from 1810–33. His father was Dr. Ira Young, holding the same chair at Dartmouth College, from 1833–58. Charles Augustus graduated from Dartmouth in 1853, at the age of 18, as head of his class. After teaching some years at Western Reserve University, he, like his father and grandfather before him, was made Professor of Natural Philosophy and Astronomy at Dartmouth, from 1866–77. From then until his retirement, twenty-eight years later, he was the Professor of Astronomy at Princeton University, one of the most distinguished professors of this science in any American university during the nineteenth century. His famous book, *The Sun,* went into numerous editions, and was translated into several languages. His later *Textbook of General Astronomy for Colleges and Scientific Schools* (1888) and his *Manual of Astronomy* (1902) were so widely used and so far ahead of any other similar texts for this study, that a recent biographer of Young is led to affirm that "There would be almost unanimous agreement that Young's books were among the best textbooks in astronomy ever written; his pupils as nearly unanimously considered him the best of teachers."[59]

Professor Young published many years ago a sermon, which he often delivered, "God's Glory in the Heavens," which has now become very scarce. I would like to quote more extensively from Professor Young's testimony to faith in a creator than I have from any preceding scientist we have considered, because Professor Young's sermon is exceedingly scarce and will probably not be accessible to one-tenth of one per cent of my readers, and I trust that some of them would like to have permanently before them this strong witness of one of our greatest astronomers to a faith in the Creator, especially for such a day as the one in which we are living when so many of our scientists do not even care to name the name of God. "It is still as true as when the Psalmist wrote it first, that 'the heavens declare the glory of God and the firmament showeth His handiwork. Day unto day uttereth speech, and night unto night showeth knowledge.' In some ways it is even truer now than then, because today the words have a more impressive and a grander significance than they could have had to David. To him the heavens were not so very vast, nor so very far away; for him they, and the sun and moon, were mere appendages of the earth, of no importance or significance except as beautiful and useful servants of mankind. Now we know an immeasurable universe, compared with which our great world itself is the merest speck—a drop in the ocean, a mote in the sunbeam.

"I think it is unquestionable that, as men have come to know more of the material universe, they have had continually revealed to them something more of the glory and majesty of its Creator. Here, and for the present, we see, of course, only 'through a glass darkly': but as time goes on, we catch more frequent glimpses of the ineffable brightness and the majestic outlines: we recognize more and more distinctly the presence and the power of the Omnipotent; lying still beyond our vision and our touch indeed, but intimated, and to some extent manifested, in all the phenomena which we can apprehend.

"Let us for a moment emphasize one other thought that has recurred continually to my mind, as I presume it has to yours, while we have been considering the great universe of matter, law and energy, which the eye and the telescope reveals to us:—this, namely that after all the human mind and soul is greater and more wonderful, higher and nobler than even the stars of heaven. We are made in the image of God, an expression the fullness of whose meaning I imagine we shall better understand hereafter: we share His nature,—I speak it reverently,—and His eternal life. Strange as it sometimes seems, when we measure our weakness and littleness against the immensities of the heavens, still it is true that God '*is* mindful of man, and visits the Son of man,' in whom is the breath of the Most High." [60]

James Clerk-Maxwell (1831–1879) was one of the outstanding physicists of the nineteenth century, who advanced our knowledge of the laws of nature as few men have done in modern times. At a meeting of the British Association, in Bradford, in 1873, he brought to a conclusion a very difficult address, "On Molecules," with the following words: Atoms, "the true foundation stones of the material universe continue this day as they were created, perfect in number and measure and weight, and from the ineffaceable characters impressed on them we may learn that those aspirations after accuracy, measurement, truth in statement, and justice in action, which we reckon among our noblest attributes as men, are ours because they are essential constituents of the image of Him who in the beginning created not only the heaven and the earth, but the materials of which heaven and earth consist." [61]

Some have said that Lord Kelvin (1824–1907) was probably, all things considered, the greatest scientist since Newton. He was a master of the fields of Dynamics, Sound, Light, Heat, Magnetism, Electricity, and advanced the knowledge of man in all these fields in a most phenomenal way. A week after he had given an address at the University College May 5, 1903, in answer to a letter from Mr. James Knowles, Kelvin made this clear statement concerning his own faith in God as Creator: "I cannot admit that, with regard to the origin of life, science neither affirms nor denies Creative Power. Science positively affirms Creative Power. It is not in dead matter that we live and move and have our being, but in the creating and directing Power which science compels us to accept as an article of belief . . . There is nothing between absolute scientific belief in a Creative Power, and the acceptance of the theory of a fortuitous concourse of atoms . . . Forty years ago I asked Liebig, walking somewhere in the country, if he believed that the grass and flowers that we saw around us grew by mere chemical forces. He answered, 'No, no more than I could believe that a book of botany describing them could grow by mere chemical forces' . . . Do not be afraid of being free thinkers! If you think strongly enough you will be forced by science to the belief in God, which is the foundation of all religion. You will find science not antagonistic but helpful to religion."[62]

Let us consider the faith of just one more outstanding man of science, Dr. Arthur H. Compton (1892–). Dr. Compton received the Nobel prize for Physics in 1923 at the age of thirty-five, was appointed four years before this, when hardly past thirty, Professor of Physics in the University of Chicago, and since 1940 has been the Dean of the Division of the Physical Sciences in the same University. He is probably the outstanding authority in the world today on cosmic rays. In 1936 in an article in a Chicago daily paper, Dr. Compton said, "For myself, faith begins with a realization that a supreme intelligence brought the universe into being and created man. It is not difficult for me to have this faith, for it is incontrovertible that where there is a plan there is intelligence—an orderly, unfolding universe testifies to the truth of the most majestic statement ever uttered—'In the beginning God.'"[63]

The Scientific Accuracy of the First Chapter of Genesis. Approaching the subject of the value of the first chapter of Genesis in the light of the conclusions and convictions of modern science, we are face to face with one of the most serious problems that can confront any believer in the Word of God, or anyone who is seriously attempting to ascertain for himself whether this book we hold in our hand is indeed an inspired record which can be fully trusted whenever and wherever it is consulted. Before considering the various issues which this problem presents it is well to read again the two opening paragraphs of Martin Luther's famous commentary on the book of Genesis, which show it was not only at the close of the nineteenth century that the opening chapter of Genesis presented real problems to man, nor that confusion regarding its purpose and value is but a recent phenomenon in the Christian church: "This first chapter of our Holy Bible is written in the simplest and plainest language, and yet it contains the greatest and at the same time the most difficult themes. Therefore the Jews, as Jerome testifies, were forbidden to read it or hear it read before they were thirty years of age. The Jews required that all the other Scriptures be well known by every one before they were permitted to approach this chapter. Their Rabbins however accomplished little good by this, for even many of the Rabbins themselves, whose years were more than twice thirty, give in their commentaries and Talmuds the most childish and foolish explanations of these, the greatest of all subjects.

"Nor has any one yet in the church to the present day explained all these momentous things correctly and satisfactorily in every respect. For interpreters have confused and entangled every thing with such a variety, diversity and infinity of questions that it is very clear that God reserved to himself the majesty of this wisdom, and the correct understanding of this chapter, leaving to us only the general ideas that the world had a beginning and was created by God out of nothing. This general knowledge may clearly be taken from the text. But with respect to the particulars, there is so much that one cannot be clear about and hence innumerable questions have continually been raised in commentaries."[64]

The Purpose of This Particular Record. As we approach the complicated details of this famous and inspiring record of Creation with which our Bible begins, we ought to ask ourselves the question: "After all what was the purpose of presenting this record to mankind?" or if we believe in inspiration, let us put it this way, "What was the purpose in the mind of God when He gave this record to men?" However that communication was accomplished is not our problem here. Of course the *primary* purpose here was not to instruct men in the sequences of geological history but to reveal to mankind something concerning the vast and ever present question "Whence came this universe?" The first chapter of Genesis is placed at the beginning of our Bible, (1) to show mankind that the world in which he lives originally proceeded from the creative activity of God; (2) that God alone, the one true God, is the creator of the world; (3) that in creating the world He reveals Himself to be the eternal God, of omnipotence, omniscience, and infinite goodness; and (4) finally to inform man of the noble origin of the human species, and of the exalted dignity which must ever attach to the human race, because of the fact that man was originally made in the image of God. Probably all conservatives, and liberals who retain any appreciation of the value of the Bible in the cultivation of the spiritual life, would agree to what has been said thus far.

But now we must ask, "Is there any *other* purpose in this chapter, than that we might know spiritual truths?" Marcus Dods in the introduction of his *The Book of Genesis,* says that the object of the first chapter of Genesis was not to teach physical sciences, and anticipate the investigations for which natural human faculty is sufficient: "its object is the higher one of determining the connection of nature with God. We do not need an inspired narrative to tell us that the sun is set to rule the day and the moon to rule the night—at no period of the world's history would men need this information; but at every period of the world's history, when science was unborn and in our own day when it is full grown do we need to know that which this narrative was written to assure us of, that, it was God who created and appointed the sun and all natural forces. We do not need this chapter that we may learn in what order animals and plants appeared upon the earth but we do need to be assured that whatever was the order of succession in which they appeared that order was determined by the intelligent will of God . . . It seems to me therefore that a mistaken and dangerous attempt, which is often made to reconcile the account of physical facts given here with that given in nature herself . . . in interpreting the Bible or any book we must always have regard to what is to be understood by those for whom it was written. It was written not for scientific and learned men but for common people; and as among ourselves, common people . . . It was not meant to be a revelation of nature but a revelation of God and the ideas regarding God which it conveys are just and weighty."[65] Now we agree that this narrative was given to men fundamentally to teach spiritual truths, and that mankind could discover and has discovered many of the great facts of the geological ages before the advent of man himself apart from any divine record. In fact we would go further and say that we do not believe it is the purpose of the Word of God in any place to instruct man concerning those great branches of knowledge, geology, biology, astronomy, anthropology, ancient history, chemistry, geography, etc., etc., a knowledge of which man himself can acquire by his own patient researches and continuous exploration of facts in these respective fields. But this is the problem which faces us and from which we cannot reasonably escape: granted that the first chapter of Genesis was not primarily given to teach us scientific facts but to tell us about God in his relation to the world of nature and man, is it possible for this record to be found false in its reference to those things which science has discovered to be true, and yet be dependable and accurate in what it says about a far greater and most mysterious subject, the nature and character of God? We have many today who say that if this record is proved to be inaccurate scientifically it can, nevertheless, be depended upon theologically. Thus for instance, Canon Driver in his famous commentary on Genesis says what almost all modernists believe, and I am afraid many conservatives, "The value of the first chapter of Genesis lies not on its *scientific* side but on its theological side. Upon the false science of antiquity its author grafted a true and dignified representation of the relation of the world to God."[66] I must say that for myself, and I believe here I am speaking for many other Christians, a contradiction like this makes the creation story of Genesis something that we may admire but not something that we can trust. If this record is wrong about the sun, moon, and stars, about water and earth, about plants and animals, mundane matters, which we see with our eyes and handle with our hands, how can the author at the same time, ignorant of these things, rightfully claim a true knowledge of the omnipotent and eternal God, whom he has never seen? Personally if this opening chapter of Genesis must now be recognized as only one of the many ancient mythical attempts to account for the universe about us, and, with these other contemporary accounts, must be abandoned in our modern day, whatever else the Bible has to say about God and His creating work, I can have no faith in a chapter so full of errors, if errors they be. That is why I have felt it so necessary to give large space to the consideration of the scientific value of this opening chapter of what we call the Word of God.

The Order of Creative Acts in Genesis I, and the Sequences of Geology. We have now come to that subject the study of which is considered by unbelievers, and many Old Testament scholars to be the death blow of any faith in a literal interpretation of the first chapter of Genesis. The majority of books, either in science or theology, which make reference to the first chapter of Genesis, begin by saying that modern research has forever destroyed any hope Christians may have of counting this record to be of scientific value. We would like to deal with this subject with thoroughness, and we shall introduce into our discussion only authors who are either in the first rank of Hebraic scholars, or are recognized as outstanding geologists of modern times. This is not the place to quote contemporary clergymen, or pseudo-scientists, who take pleasure in producing a pamphlet literature that is neither theologically profound nor scientifically accurate.

First of all, we must dismiss from our mind any conception of a definite period of time, either for creation itself, or for the length of the so-called six creative days. The Bible does not tell us when the world was created. The first chapter of Genesis could take us back to periods millions of years antedating the appearance of man. Whether the Old Testament itself definitely identifies the exact year of Adam's appearance we are not here discussing. That man, as we know him today, this race of men to which we belong, the only race of which we have any *historic* records, appeared in recent times, history, geology, and the Word of God, all agree.

When those who wish to ridicule the Word of God begin by saying something like this, "We have long ago been compelled to abandon the idea that the world was created six thousand years ago," they are only repeating medieval affirmations, which had no biblical foundation in the first place, and which do not express the correct interpretation of the first chapter of Genesis, however great the names were that dogmatically promoted such ideas. In the second place, we must disabuse ourselves of the idea that these six periods of creation corresponded to our "day" of twenty-four hours. Some still hold this view, but it certainly is not necessary, and the fact that the word *day* in the Old Testament, even in the first three chapters of Genesis, carries many meanings other than that of a period of twenty-four hours, gives us perfect freedom in considering it here as an unlimited, though definite period, set off from those preceding and following.

The Initial Creative Work of Verse 1. Creation's story begins with this magnificent, simple, well known sentence: "In the beginning God created the heavens and the earth." There are two views concerning this verse, one of which we think is definitely wrong, and the other in every way correct, exegetically and scientifically. Some hold that this first verse is a mere heading and summary, as it were, of the entire creative activity of these six periods. The more reasonable way to consider this statement is to count it as describing the initial creative work of God, and not a mere heading. This, says Professor James G. Murphy, of Belfast, in his magnificent commentary on Genesis, is abundantly evident from the following reasons: "(1) It is the form of a narrative, not of a superscription; (2) the conjunctive particle connects the second verse with it; which could not be if it were a mere heading; (3) the very next sentence speaks of the earth as already in existence, and therefore its creation must be recorded in the first verse; (4) in the first verse the heavens take precedence of the earth; but in the following verses all things, even the sun, moon, and stars, seem to be but appendages to the earth; (5) if the first verse belong to the narrative order pervades the whole recital; whereas if it be a heading the most hopeless confusion enters . . . It is manifest that the heavens here denote the heavenly orbits themselves for the following cogent reasons: (1) Creation implies something created and not mere space which is nothing and cannot be said to be created. (2) As the earth here obviously means the substance of the planet we inhabit, so the heavens must mean the substance of the celestial luminaries. (3) The heavens are placed before the earth, and therefore must mean that reality which is greater than the earth; for if they meant space and nothing real, they ought not to be before the earth. (4) The heavens are actually *mentioned* in the verse, and therefore must mean a real thing; for if they meant nothing at all, they ought not to be mentioned. (5) The heavens must denote the heavenly realities because this imparts a rational order to the whole chapter . . . These heavens mean the fixed and planetary orbits of space . . . This is the absolute and aboriginal creation of the heavens and all that in them is and of the earth in its primeval state."[67] We know of nothing better in the English language on the meaning of this verse, apart from its theological significance, than these sentences, and we trust our readers will keep them in mind.

The Chaos of Verse 2. A vast literature has arisen concerning the real meaning of the second verse, or, we might more accurately say, a vast literature has arisen attempting to explain what happened, if anything, between the original creation of verse 1, and this condition of chaos to which we are immediately afterward introduced. There are two primary interpretations. We must say we have never been able to come to any final decision, in our own mind, concerning this very difficult matter, and, after all, though the questions involved are important, whichever solution we prefer does not affect the remaining argument of our discussion. Some say that this condition, described by the famous Hebrew phrase, *tohu vabohu,* is a condition of chaos, of desolateness, and must express "the condition in which the new created earth was, not innumerable ages but very shortly after it was summoned into existence. It was formless and lifeless; a huge, shapeless, objectless, tenantless mass of matter. The gases and solid elements co-mingled, in which neither organized structure nor unmated form, nor even distinctly traced outline of any kind appear."[68] With Mr. Whitelaw's interpretation many agree, including the geologist Guyot, who says this second verse refers to "the primitive state of matter when first created."[69] Opposed to this are those who believe in what is called the theory of catastrophe, which has had many different constructions, and a great host of defenders during the last century, some of them carrying great weight. This interpretation insists that between the first and second verses of Genesis some great and dreadful catastrophe came upon the created universe, bringing it into this condition of *waste and void*. Thus Professor Murphy, from whom we have just quoted, says: "The verb here translated *be* has here the meaning *become;* and the import of the sentence is this: 'And the land had become waste and void.' This affords the presumption that the part at least of the surface of our globe which fell within the cognizance of primeval man, and first received the name of land, may not have been always a scene of desolation or a scene of turbid waters, but may have met with some catastrophe by which its order and fruitfulness had been marred or prevented. This sentence, therefore, does not necessarily describe the state of the land when first created, but merely intimates a change that may have taken place since it was called into existence. What its previous condition was or what interval of time elapsed between the absolute creation and the present state of things is not revealed. How many transformations it may have undergone, and what purpose it may have heretofore served, are questions that do not essentially concern the moral well-being of men, and are therefore to be asked of some other interpreter of nature than the Written Word . . . It is further to be noted that the darkness is described to be on the face of the deep. Nothing is said about any other region throughout the bounds of existing things. The presumption is, so far as this clause determines, that it is a local darkness confined to the face of the deep."[70] This theory of catastrophe has been adopted, among others, by Bush, and that greatest of all Hebraists, Delitzsch. If one will examine the other verses of the Bible in which these Hebrew words translated *waste and void* occur (Job 12:24; 26:7; Isa. 34:11; Jer. 4:23), one, I think, will be inclined to believe that such a condition as verse 2 describes seems to imply some judgment of God, at least a condition in nature which is neither beautiful nor desirable.

The Primacy of Water. We now begin to get a little nearer to events concerning which the geological and astronomical sciences have something to say. Carefully notice that among all the elements of the universe the first mentioned here is *water*. There is an interesting confirmatory phrase in the New Testament, in the Second Epistle of Peter which speaks about our earth being "formed of water and by water."[71] Here geology comes immediately to the support of this description of the earliest condition of our earth, namely, that it was covered with deep waters. Thus, for instance, Professor Joseph Barrell, of Yale, in a famous chapter on "The Origin of the Earth," says: "At such a comparatively low temperature, and even at somewhat higher temperatures, there would be little disassociation of water into its component gases, and the earth would be capable of holding to itself, even in its molten stage, an envelope of water in the form of a deep and heavy atmosphere of water gas."[72] So likewise, another Yale professor, writing a little later than Professor Barrell, Dr. Charles Schuchert, who in his *Outlines of Historical Geology,* says: "Once the temperature had fallen 374° another profound change followed rapidly, for at that temperature the water vapor could condense, and rain fell in torrents beyond human conception, covering the earth with seas, and initiating the geologic processes of erosion and gradation. This marked the beginning of geologic as distinct from cosmic history."[73] If one will look at this sentence carefully, one will discover that this geologist is saying exactly what the Word of God says, as to the beginning of the geologic history of our earth. All agree that without the action of water we would never have had an earth capable of producing its flora and fauna, for, as the most important textbook in geology at the beginning of our century says: "Of all geologic agencies, water is the most obvious and apparently the greatest."[74]

Light Penetrates to the Earth (*vv. 3–5*). When we come to the subject of the creation of light, and light carriers, we are face to face with what is thought by some to be the greatest stumbling block in accepting the first chapter of Genesis as a record possessing any scientific value. Everything will depend here upon what we think happened in this first day, regarding the creation of light. Hundreds of pages have been written concerning the various ways in which light in this early period could possibly reach the earth, and concerning the sources of light extraneous to the heavenly bodies, etc., etc. For ourselves, we believe that the simplest interpretation here is that which is adopted by most of the great conservative exegetes of the Church (though not all of them). Whitelaw sums it all up in one single sentence: "The exigencies of the text, as well as the ascertained facts of physical science, required the first day's work to be the original production of light throughout the universe, and in part, throughout our planetary system."[75] With this Professor Murphy agrees, when he says: "The interference of supernatural power to cause the presence of light in this region, intimates that the powers of nature were inadequate to this effect. But it does not determine whether or not light had already existed elsewhere, and had even at one time penetrated into this now darkened region and was still prevailing in the other realms of space beyond the face of the deep. Nor does it determine whether by a change of the polar axis, by a rarefaction of the gaseous medium above, or by whatever other means light was made to visit this region of the globe with its agreeable and quickening influence. We only read that it did not then illumine the deep of waters, and that by the potent Word of God it was then summoned into being. The act of omnipotence here recorded is not at variance with the existence of light among the elements of that universe of nature, the absolute creation of which is framed in the first verse."[76]

The Dividing of the Waters (*vv.* 6–8). The second day is occupied with only one great event, preparing for the appearing of plants and animals on the earth, namely the dividing of the waters, which we found prevailing in the first day. The fundamental meaning of this passage simply is that this vast body of water was separated so that between the mass that was lifted up and that which was left upon the earth, that which we call the atmosphere, the air, was interjected, so that as a result of the activity of this second day, we have water upon the earth and water above the earth. If one thinks this is an incidental matter, one should remember that the amount of aqueous vapor continually suspended in the air above the earth is estimated to be 54,460,000,000,000 tons. When one remembers that water is 773 times the weight of air, one also begins to have some conception of the power required for separating these bodies of water. Of course, the water above is that from which rain continually falls upon the earth. It is estimated that the annual amount of rain and snow falling upon this earth is equivalent to 186,000 cubic miles, enough to cover the earth with a depth of three feet. The constant supply of water above the earth is maintained by what we call evaporation, the lifting of the water from the earth into what we call the sky, by the power of sunlight. "The state of things before this creative movement may be called one of disturbance and disorder, in comparison with the present condition of the atmosphere. This disturbance in the relations of air and water was so great that it could not be reduced to the present order without a supernatural cause. Whether this disorder was temporary or of long standing, and whether the change was effected by altering the axis of the earth's rotation and thereby the climate of the land of primeval man, or by a less extensive movement, are questions on which we receive no instruction because the solution does not concern our well-being." [77] The activity expressed in this second day of creation is exactly that which geologists refer to as occurring in the geologic periods of the earth before the appearance of grass and water animals. Professor Brigham, of Colgate, for example, sums up what is here assigned to the work of the second day in this sentence: "Cooling, condensation, the formation of seas, atmosphere and early lands, are the features of the pre-Paleozoic era." [78] This is exactly what the Bible says in non-scientific but, nevertheless, accurate language.

Before we go into the more or less difficult problems of these next four days of creation, we must give brief attention to what is called the periods of geologic time. If this seems dull and complicated to some of my readers, they may pass over it, but we can never pretend to have any satisfying conviction concerning the scientific accuracy of the first chapter of Genesis, unless we know some of the conclusions of science itself relating to the very important matters about which God has chosen to give us a revelation in this early record. We may not like the long technical terms, but we must understand something of what is being said in contemporary geological literature. According to one of the most important textbooks of historical geology of our day, now in its third edition, by Professors Charles Schuchert and Carl O. Dunbar, of Yale University, geological periods are broken up into four main eras. The first, by which we mean the earliest, is called the Cryptozoic; the second the Paleozoic; the third the Mesozoic; and the last the Cenozoic. With the first we are not concerned in our particular study, for no life appeared in that period, and we have already considered what geologists say about the early condition of chaos, and the later prevalence of water upon our globe, all of which testimony accords with the scriptural record. The Paleozoic era begins with what is called the Cambrian period, where we have for the first time fossils, and ends with what is called the Permian period. It is interesting to note that concerning the pre-Cambrian period these two distinguished geologists admit that, "For these early eras we have only the fragments of a record that we can recover from the ruin time has wrought. Enormous groups of ancient rocks lying in tangled confusion below the Paleozoic strata form an impressive record of these early times, but there are no fossils to date them . . . In this respect, the beginning of the Cambrian period is a notable period in geologic history, for the abundant fossils in younger strata serve, like the pagination of a manuscript, to date the record and marshal the sequences of events." [79]

The Appearance of the Earth (*vv. 9, 10*). The first event recorded of the third day of creation is the appearance of the earth above the waters. This is simple, inevitable, logical. The word here translated earth, *aretz,* means a breaking in pieces, crumbling, and probably is related to a Sanskrit word, *ahara,* meaning to grind. In the Greek the word is *xthon,* to bind to itself, and in the Latin the word, as we all know, is *terra,* from the verb *terro,* to wear away. After all, that is about what the earth is—it is rock ground to pieces, and most of this grinding is done by water, in the process we call erosion. Whether the earth had risen from submergence before any geologic convulsions, the text does not say. If geology insists upon it, there is nothing in the Bible that prevents this having taken place. What is now about to be revealed is the clothing of the earth with grass and herbs, and the appearing of animals, preceding the advent of man.

The Creation of Grass and Herbs (*vv. 11–13*). That plant life preceded animal life has been generally understood by all students of the geologic and biological history of our earth. Professor Rowlin T. Chamberlain, of the University of Chicago, in a well known chapter on "The Origin and Early Stages of the Earth," says, "When the earth reached the stage where water was abundant on its surface, and the temperature was favorable it became suitable for the abode of life." [80] There are three different Hebrew words here for plant life. The word translated grass is *deshe;* the word translated herb is *eseb;* and the word translated fruit trees is *peri.* Murphy has a very fine statement here when he says of these three groups: "In the first the seed is not noticed, is not obvious to the eye; in the second the seed is the striking characteristic; in the third the fruit 'in which is its seed,' in which the seed is enclosed, forms the distinguishing mark. This division is simple and natural. It proceeds upon two concurrent marks—the structure and the seed. In the first the green leaf or blade is prominent; in the second the stalk; in the third the woody texture. This division corresponds with certain classes in our present system of Botany. But it is much less complex than any of them, and is founded upon obvious characteristics." [81]

Now we must go back for a moment to our technical geological classification. Professors Schuchert and Dunbar, in their chart of geologic time, say that in this early Cambrian period, when fossils are first found, the only plants of which the rocks leave us any record are lime-secreting *algae,* and that not until the Devonian era, in the middle of the Paleozoic era, do we find the more important genera of plants. "The first adequate record of land plants is found in the Devonian rocks. Sea weeds are abundantly indicated as far back as the pre-Cambrian, and low types of plant life such as moss and lichens were probably widespread on the lands before the Cambrian. But the development of plants having woody fibers for the circulation of fluids apparently took place in the Devonian since fossil wood is unknown in the older rocks, and is abundant in those of all later ages."[82] In other words, these two geologists claim that there was animal life in the ocean before there was plant life on the earth, whereas our text does not mention any animal life, even water animals, until the fifth day of creation, whereas plants occur in the third. Two things I think ought to be said here: first, the words of these two Yale geologists testify to the fact that the evidence which they have is very meager, and they willingly admit this. But I think the real solution here is that the grass and herbs, mentioned as being created on the third day, belong to the land and not to the water, and that our Bible does not even tell us when such primitive animal life as *algae* appear. The first chapter of Genesis was not written to teach a scientific classification, but was written to tell men how the great objects of natural history which were before them, and around them, and above them, had come into existence. We want to repeat what we have said frequently before. This chapter was given to reveal God as the Creator, not to teach science, but at the same time nothing in this chapter may be said to be scientifically inaccurate. It does not give us the origin and sequence of *all* that nature has revealed, but the order and sequence of that which is recorded is according to the conclusions of modern science.

The Setting of the Lights (*vv. 14–19*). We now come to what is probably the most disputed and the most debated subject of this whole opening passage of the Word of God, namely, the appearance of lights. If our readers have carefully noted what we have said up to this point, they already are aware that we believe that the heavenly bodies are already in their places in the stellar universe and in other universes. We have read hundreds of pages explaining how plants could grow without sunlight, proposing various sources for light on earth. We believe that some plants can grow without sunlight, but anyone knows that there is not much light, apart from the sun, and the moon, and the stars. This section here needs careful consideration, and we are taking the liberty of quoting extensively once again from the inimitable pages of Professor Murphy: "The work of the fourth day has much in common with that of the first, which, indeed it continues and completes. Both deal with light, and with dividing between light and darkness, or day and night. *Let there be*. They agree also in choosing the word *be,* to express the nature of the operation which is here performed. But the fourth day advances on the first. It brings into view the luminaries, the light radiators, the source, while the first only indicated the stream. It contemplates the far expanse, while the first regards only the near . . . The first day spreads the shaded gleam of light over the face of the deep. The fourth day unfolds to the eye the lamps of heaven, hanging in the expanse of the skies, and assigns to them the office of 'shining upon the earth.' A threefold function is thus attributed to the celestial orbs—to divide day from night, to define time and place, and to shine on the earth. The word of command is here very full, running over two verses, with the exception of the little clause, 'and it was so,' stating the result . . . Now let it be remembered that the *heavens* were created at the absolute beginning of things recorded in the first verse, and that they included all other things except the earth. Hence, according to this document, the sun, moon, and stars were in existence simultaneously with our planet. This gives simplicity and order to the whole narrative. *Light* comes before us on the first and on the fourth day. Now, as two distinct causes of a common effect would be unphilosophical and unnecessary, we must hold the one cause to have been in existence on these two days. But we have seen that the one cause of the day and of the year is a fixed source of radiating light in the sky, combined with the diurnal and annual motions of the earth. Thus the recorded pre-existence of the celestial orbs is consonant with the presumptions of reason. The 'making' or reconstitution of the atmosphere admits their light so far that the alternations of day and night can be discerned. The *making* of the lights of heaven, or the display of them in a serene sky by the withdrawal of that opaque canopy of clouds that still enveloped the dome above, is then the work of the fourth day. All is now plain and intelligible. The heavenly bodies become the lights of the earth, and the distinguishers not only of day and night, but of seasons and years, of times and places. They shed forth their unveiled glories and salutary potencies on the budding, waiting land. How the higher grade of transparency in the aerial regions was effected, we cannot tell; and, therefore, we are not prepared to explain why it is accomplished on the fourth day, and not sooner. But from its very position in time, we are led to conclude that the constitution of the expanse, the elevation of a portion of the waters of the deep in the form of vapor, the collection of the subaerial water into seas, and the creation of plants out of the reeking soil, must all have had an essential part, both in retarding till the fourth day, and in then bringing about the dispersion of the clouds and the clearing of the atmosphere. Whatever remained of hindrance to the outshining of the sun, moon, and stars on the land in all their native splendor, was on this day removed by the word of divine power." [83]

With the statement of Professor Murphy agrees the following concise summary of Mr. Whitelaw: "The reference in these verses is not to the original creation of the matter of the heavenly bodies which was performed in the beginning, nor to the first production of light, which was the specific work of day, but to the permanent appointment of the former to be the place or center of radiation for the latter. The purpose for which this arrangement was designed, so far at least as the earth was concerned, was threefold: first, to divide the day from the night; second, to let them be for signs and seasons and days and years; and third, that they might give light upon the earth—not to introduce light for the first time to this lower world, but to serve as a new and permanent arrangement for the radiation of the light already called into existence." [84]

The Creation of Water Animals and Birds (*vv.* 20–23). In the creative work of the fifth day it is interesting to note that the first animals referred to here are water animals, called *great sea monsters.* The Hebrew word is *tanninim,* which is sometimes used in reference to serpents (Exod. 7:9; Deut. 32:33), or crocodiles (Ezek. 29:3; 32:2). We must now go back for a moment to our geologic outline. We are still in what may be called the end of the Paleozoic era. It is interesting to note that our geological authorities agree that the first animal life ever appearing on this globe was that which lived in waters. "Animals had not yet learned to breathe air and did not appear on the land until nearly three long geologic periods had passed. The seas, however, teemed with inverte brate animals of many kinds, finding both food and shelter among the varied and abundant sea weeds." [85] On this day also, birds were created. One should recall how closely related birds and fishes are, in structural matters. Both are egg-shaped, with gradually tapering bodies for swift movement. As a rule, their main means of locomotion are not feet, but fins and wings. Both are covered with shingle-like fins or feathers; both have hollow, light bones, both are egg laying, in both the blood corpuscles are oval, not round, and both possess a migratory instinct.

The Appearance of the Cattle and Beasts (*vv.* 24, 25). Here again, as with plants so with animals, we have a threefold classification—*cattle, creeping things,* and *beasts of the earth.* The Hebrew word translated cattle is *bhemah,* from a word meaning to be dumb or dull, or heavy, and here as elsewhere is "the name of four-footed domestic animals," as Delitzsch says, or, according to Driver, "large quadrupeds." The word translated creeping things is *remes,* from a word meaning to move, to swarm, and Driver says it refers to animals "which move along the ground either without feet or with imperceptible feet." [86] The last word *chaiyah* is a Hebrew word meaning wild animals. We are now in what is called the end of the Mesozoic period and the beginning of the Cenozoic era. Professor Brigham says of the earlier part of the Cenozoic period that "it is the vertebrates which form the great feature of this era." This is the age of mammals, and says Professor Brigham, they appear "in a manner which geologically is sudden." [87] Professor Schuchert says that it is in the second, or Eocene epoch, that "modern orders of mammals appear and evolve rapidly." [88] And so we have another confirmation from science of the accuracy of the order of Genesis, for concerning animals both agree it was first those of the water, then those of the land, rising to mammals, the highest type of animal life on earth before the appearance of man. Between this mammalian era and the advent of man neither science nor the Bible interject any other era. The next thing we read of, on the very same sixth day of creation, is the appearance of man himself who, according to one of the geologists we have been following, Professor Brigham, is "the consummate of the series of living forms, and about to become the master of the organic and inorganic world." [89] It is worth noting, as Principal Dawson said some years ago, that while different species of plants and animals are referred to, "the Bible knows but one species of man. It is not said that men were created after their species, as we read of the groups of animals. Man was made male and female, and in the fuller details afterwards given in the second chapter, but one primitive pair is introduced to our notice. We scarcely need the detailed doubles of affiliation afterward given, or the declaration of the apostle who preached at Athens that 'God has made of one blood all nations,' to assure us of the scriptural unity of man."[90] The Genesis record terminates with the creation of man; in fact, it says that God finished His work. And that is where science ends its history of life upon earth, and knows that nothing further need be expected. The late Professor J. Arthur Thomson succinctly expressed this in one short sentence when he said, "No startling new departure in general bodily structure is likely to be exhibited."[91]

Now that we have with some fulness surveyed the subject of the order of creative acts of the first chapter of Genesis and find them most remarkably confirmed by modern geologists and the writings of contemporary scientists, may we bring this particular examination of evidence to a close by quoting two distinguished scientists regarding this very fact of accuracy of sequence in the various records, one from a former day and one from our own. Cuvier, one of the great naturalists of Europe, once wrote: "Brought up in all the wisdom of the Egyptians but in advance of his age, Moses has left us a cosmogony of which the accuracy verifies itself every day in a marvelous manner. Recent geologic researches are in perfect agreement with the book of Genesis as to the order in which organized beings were successively created."[91a]

If some of our readers object to Cuvier's statement because of the subsequent advances in geological science, then let me mention one of just a few years ago, by one of the outstanding authorities in the history of science in America, probably the first authority on the life and work of Sir Isaac Newton of our generation, Professor Louis T. Moore, who, in a series of lectures a few years ago at Princeton University, remarked concerning this first chapter of Genesis: "Inorganic phenomenon are not personified, and living forms are brought into existence according to pre-ordained classification in species . . . There is a quite remarkabl sequence in the order of creation of the various types of forms which, by a guess or by an acute perception of relationship of form, agrees with the succession according to modern evolutionists." [91b]

The Origin of the Genesis Account of Creation. Professor Moore's statement brings us immediately to the question of from whence did the author of this chapter derive his information? Well, he either received it from contemporary Babylonian records, as some hold, or it was the product of his own meditation and reasoning, or, he received it by divine revelation. That he did not write this from contemporary Babylonian records is clear, because the Babylonian records did not have the scientific accuracy of this chapter, and were filled with myths and grotesque ideas which are wholly absent here. No man could have *guessed* the order of creation and written about events that happened vast eras before he was born, in that ancient time before geologic and biological sciences had even begun. There is but one origin for this chapter, and the longer I study it and the more I read about it, and read in literature which denies its importance, the more I am absolutely convinced of the accuracy of Professor Guyot's words at the end of his book, *Creation,* when he says: "The same divine hand which lifted for Daniel and Isaiah the veil which covered the tableaux of the time to come, unveiled to the eyes of the author of Genesis by a series of graphic visions and pictures the earliest ages of the creation. Thus Moses was the prophet of the past as Daniel and Isaiah and many others were the prophets of the future." [91c]

The Fixity of Species. Three verses in the Genesis account of creation certainly lead us to believe that species as such were fixed at creation. Now inasmuch as scientists all over the world more or less fail to agree on an absolute definition of species, rather than attempt one myself, I am simply going to place before my readers statements by leading scientists regarding this subject of the fixity of species in which it is assumed that the reader has a general idea of what species may be. The famous French botanist Buffon said, "The type of each species is founded in a mold of which the principal features have been cut in characters, which are ineffaceable and eternally permanent, but all the traits vary; no one individual is the exact facsimile of any other and no species exist without a large number of variations." [92] Darwin himself, in a letter to the famous botanist Bentham, confesses that "The belief in natural selection must at present be grounded entirely on general causes . . . when we descend to details we can prove that no one species has changed; nor can we prove that the supposed changes are beneficial which is the ground work of the theory"[93]—a most amazing statement from Darwin. Darwin's contemporary, T. H. Huxley, in his famous *Lay Sermons,* felt compelled to say that "It is our clear conviction that as the evidence stands it is not absolutely proven that a group of animals having all the characteristics as exhibited by species in nature has ever been originated by selection, to the natural or artificial."[94]

Professor Vernon Kellogg, one of the outstanding Darwinians of our generation, in his *Darwinism of Today* admitted that "Speaking by and large we only tell the general truth when we declare that no indubitable cases of species, forming or transforming, that is, of descent, have been observed. For my part it seems better to go back to the old and safe ignoramus standpoint."[95] Professor J. Arthur Thomson, one of the most gifted biologists in Great Britain during the early part of our century, asked, "Have we any concrete evidence to warrant us believing that definite modifications are ever, as such, or in any representative degree transmitted? It appears to us we have not."[96] Dr. D. H. Scott in his address before the British Association for the Advancement of Science, meeting in Edinburgh, September 1921, made this statement for the biologists of his generation, "Variation itself the foundation on which the Darwin theory seemed to rest so securely, is now in question. The small variations on which the natural selectionist relied so much have proved for the most part to be merely fluctuations, oscillating about a mean and therefore incapable of giving rise to permanent, new types . . . At present all speculation on the nature of past changes is in the air; and variation itself is only a hypothesis."[97] We believe, much evolution literature to the contrary, that the Bible statement that species were fixed at the time of their first appearance is confirmed by the statements of those who are the greatest authorities in this very field.

The Cessation of Creative Activity. At the close of the entire series of creative accounts we read, "God finished His work which He had made." This clearly indicates that creative activity ended when man was brought into the world. Now we hear a great deal in philosophical literature of what is now called "continuous creation" but there are two facts which science seems to be increasingly convinced of, which support the Biblical statement that with man creative activity terminated. Let me bring to your attention two statements concerning this truth, Professor James Weir in his *The Energy System of the Universe,* says "The finger of Nature ever points to closed energy circuits, to the earth as a complete and conservative system in which energy, mutable to the highest degree with respect to its plurality of form, attains to the perfection of permanence in its essential character and amounts."[98]

A later examination of the same truth may be found in the latest edition of Sir James Jeans' famous work, *The Mysterious Universe,* "The three major conservation laws, those of the conservation of mass, matter and energy reduced to one. One simple fundamental entity which may indicate many forms of matter and radiation in particular is conceived through all changes; the sum total of this entity forms the whole activity of the universe; which does not change its total quantity."[99]

Some have from time to time suggested that a new species of superman will some day appear on earth; at the present time we seem to be beholding an outburst of what might be called "subman," almost beastly man. Although the fact that man climaxes the entire series of organic life and no one would ever raise his voice against this particular aspect of the biblical account of creation, many readers may be interested in considering for a moment a most remarkable presentation of this truth by no less a scientist than Alfred Russell Wallace, in an article, "Man's Place in the Universe," which he wrote when eighty years of age after a long, brilliant career: "During the last quarter of the past century, the rapidly increasing body of facts and observations, leading to a more detailed and accurate knowledge of stars and stellar systems, have thrown a new and somewhat unexpected light on this very interesting problem of our relation to the universe of which we form a part; and although these discoveries have of course no bearing upon the special theological dogmas of the Christian, or of any other religion, they do tend to show that our portion in the material universe is special and probably unique, and that it is such as to lend support to the view, held by many great thinkers and writers today, that the supreme end and purpose of this vast universe was the production and development of the living soul in the perishable body of man." Professor Wallace supports this remarkable statement by a number of facts which, of course, we cannot give in detail here. He says that man's place in the universe is proven by the distance of the earth from the sun, so as to keep up the temperature of the soil to the exact required amount; that the earth has an atmosphere of sufficient extent and density to serve as an equalizer of sun heat to allow of the needed circulation of aqueous vapor, all of which is largely dependent upon the mass of the planet which alone renders Mars quite unsuitable. A very large proportion of the earth is covered by deep oceans, which, by their tides and currents keep up a more continuous circulation and are thus the chief agents in the essential equalization of temperatures. The enormous average depth of these oceans is such that the bulk of water they contain is about thirteen times that of the land which rises above their level. This indicates that they are permanent features of the earth's surface, thus ensuring the maintenance of continuous land areas and of uniform temperatures during the whole period of the development of life upon the earth. The uninterrupted supply of atmospheric dust, which is now known to be necessary for the production of rain clouds and which gives some indication of the utility of deserts and volcanoes, is extensively considered. "All the evidence," he concludes, "goes to assure us that our earth alone in the Solar System has been from its very origin adapted to be the theatre for the development of organized and intelligent life. Our portion within that system is, therefore, as central and unique as that of our sun in the whole stellar universe . . . Those thinkers may be right who hold that the universe is a manifestation of Mind and that the orderly development of Living Souls supplies an adequate reason why such an universe should have been called into existence."[100] We often read in our modernistic theological works that the Genesis account of creation is geocentric, centered in the earth, and that it fails to show the sun to be the center of the universe. Well, we are more interested in the earth than in the sun at any time, and this statement of Professor Wallace is a remarkable justification of the Genesis record giving pre-eminent place to the earth on which we live.

Genesis Is the Only Book of Antiquity Which Is Ever Considered

When Discussing the Scientific Accuracy of Ancient Literature on the Creation of the World. When Darwin's *Origin of Species* appeared in 1859, Huxley immediately called it "Anti-Genesis." Why did he think that it was the *book of Genesis* which Darwin's theory of natural selection confuted? Why did he not say anti-Hesiod, or anti-Timaeus, or anti-Metamorphosis in reference to Ovid's account of the creation? In the very fact that Huxley spoke of Darwin's work as anti-Genesis he confessed that the book of all ancient literature that contained an account of the creation of the world worthy of being discussed in our modern scientific age as of any scientific value at all was the book of Genesis. A vast number of books, and hundreds of articles, during the past one hundred years have been written, maintaining or denying the scientific accuracy of the first chapter of the book of Genesis, but where are you going to find any books and articles even discussing *the scientific accuracy* of other ancient accounts of the creation of the world? Whenever you hear anyone speaking disrespectfully of the book of Genesis, in its relation to modern science, remember that this first book of our Bible is the only piece of literature of all the ancient nations which anyone even thinks worthy of discussing, even if condemning in the same breath, with the phrase "modern science." It is of great significance that for two thousand years men have felt it necessary to consider this ancient Hebrew record when discussing the subject of creation. The Babylonian, the Greek, and the Roman accounts of the same beginning of our universe are, for the most part, counted mythological, and utterly incapable of being reconciled with the conclusions of modern science.

The Superiority of the Biblical Account of the Origin of the World Over the Babylonian Creation Records. In discussing the subject of other ancient accounts of the origin of the world, antedating the cosmogonies of the early Greeks, which we have already considered, we will confine ourselves to the most famous of all these records, namely, the so-called Babylonian account of creation. That there are a number of lines and ideas in the various Babylonian creation records that have been discovered somewhat similar to lines appearing in the first chapter of Genesis, no one would deny. At the same time all students of Babylonian literature admit frankly that there are many grotesque, coarse, and fanciful mythological elements in these records of which not a vestige appears in the Hebrew account. Let us read for ourselves a few segments of this Babylonian record and then consider what some of the most famous students of this early literature have said about the relation of these accounts to the record we have at the beginning of our Bible. The Babylonian text begins as follows:

"When above the heaven was not named,
And beneath the earth bore no name,
And the primeval Apsu, who begat them
And Mummu and Tiamat, the mother of them all,—
Their waters were mingled together,
And no field was formed, no marsh seen,
When no one of the gods had been called into being,
And none bore a name, and no destinies (were fixed)
Then were created the gods in the midst of (heaven),
Lakhumu and Lakhamu were called into being . . .
Ages increased . . ."

The second tablet begins as follows:

"Tiamat made strong her handiwork,
Evil she devised among the gods her children.
(To avenge) Apsu, Tiamat planned evil
As she had collected her (army, against) Ea she marshalled them.
Ea (listened) to this word and
He was (sadly) afflicted and sat in sorrow.
The days went by, and his anger was appeased,
And to *the place* of Anshar, his father, he made way.
He went before Anshar, the father who begat him,
All that Tiamat had planned, he announced to him:
Tiamat our mother has conceived a hatred against us,
An assembly has she made, she rages in anger.
All the gods have turned to her,
Even those whom ye have created march to her side."

Then we have lines such as these:

"Among the gods, who were her first born, who formed her troop
She exalted Kingu; among them she made him great.
To march before the troops, to lead the throng,
To seize the weapons, to advance, to begin the attack.
The primacy in the combat, the control of the fight

She entrusted to him, in costly raiment she made him sit, *saying*,
'I have uttered the spell, in the assembly of the gods I have made thee Lord,
The lordship over all the gods, I have entrusted to thee.
Be thou exalted, thou mine only spouse,
May the Annun*aki* exalt thy name over all.' "

The fifth tablet begins as follows:

"He made the stations for the great gods;
The stars, their images, as the stars of the Zodiac he fixed.
He ordained the year, he marked off its sections,
For the twelve months he fixed three stars for each.
After he had fashioned images for the days of the year,
He founded the station of Nibir, to determine their bounds;
That none might err or go astray
He set the station of Bel and Ea by his side.
He opened gates on both sides,
He made strong the bolt on the left and on the right.
In the midst thereof he fixed the zenith;
The Moon-god he caused to shine forth, to him confided the night." [101]

The latest scholarly treatment of this subject is by Dr. Alexander Heidel, Research Assistant on the Assyrian Dictionary Project of the Oriental Institute, The University of Chicago. In his recently published *The Babylonian Genesis. The Story of Creation,* he pays a remarkable tribute to the definite superiority of the Hebrew record of creation over the Babylonian accounts, "A comparison of the Babylonian creation story with the first chapter of Genesis makes the sublime character of the latter stand out in even bolder relief. *Enuma elish* refers to a multitude of divinities emanating from the elementary world-matter; the universe has its origin in the generation of numerous gods and goddesses personifying cosmic spaces of forces in nature, and in the orderly and purposeful *arrangement* of pre-existent matter; the world is not *created* in the biblical sense of the term but *fashioned* after the manner of human craftsmen; as for man, he is created with the blood of a deity that might well be called a devil among the gods, and the sphere of activity assigned to man is the service of the gods. In Genesis 1:1–2:3, on the other hand, there stands at the very beginning *one* God, who is not counited and coexistent with an eternal world-matter and who does not first develop Himself into a series of separate deities but who creates matter and remains *one* God to the end. Here the world is created by the sovereign *word* of the Lord, without recourse to all sorts of external means. The Lord speaks, and it is done; he commands, and it stands fast. Add to this the doctrine that man was created in the image of a holy and righteous God, to be the lord of the earth, the air, and the sea, and we have a number of differences between *Enuma elish* and Gen. 1:1–2:3 that make all similarities shrink into utter insignificance. These exalted conceptions in the biblical account of creation give it a depth and dignity unparalleled in any cosmogony known to us from Babylonia and Assyria."[102]

From a literary standpoint, another weighty testimony to the fact that we are here setting forth has appeared from the pen of Dr. Samuel A. B. Mercer of the University of Trinity College in which he says that not only is the Hebrew account of creation of the earth "preeminent among all ancient oriental accounts of creation . . . but what is of more importance it is the only ancient account of creation which can morally and religiously satisfy a modern mind."[103]

Some Tributes to the Superlative Value of the First Chapter of Genesis. In an earlier section of this chapter we brought together a number of statements from famous scientists confessing their faith in God as the Creator of the universe; here we would like to bring together a number of statements not alone of scientists but also of philosophers, of men of literature, and theologians regarding the great value, importance, and beauty of this entire first chapter of Genesis, apart from the conception of God as the Creator of our universe.

One of the best known geologists of the nineteenth century was Arnold Guyot, for thirty years Professor of Physical Geography and Geology at Princeton University, whose series of textbooks published betwen 1866 and 1875, "were the first definite attempt at a scientific presentation of geography in American schools, and were in a large measure the models for textbooks in geography during many succeeding years.[106] At the very beginning of his famous volume, *Creation and the Biblical Cosmogony in the Light of Modern Science,* Guyot pays this tribute to the first page of our Bible: "The Bible narrative by its simplicity, its chaste, positive, historical character, is in perfect contrast with the fanciful, allegorical, intricate cosmogonies of all heathen religions . . . By its sublime grandeur, by its symmetrical plan, by the profoundly philosophical disposition of its parts, and, perhaps, quite as much by its wonderful caution in the statement of facts, which leaves room for all scientific discoveries, it betrays the supreme guidance which directed the pen of the writer, and kept it throughout within the limits of truth." [107]

In 1924, Professor William Cecil Dampier-Whetham, author of the finest one-volume history of science in our language, published through the Cambridge University Press a most interesting work, of nearly 300 pages, bearing the title, *Cambridge Readings in the Literature of Science.* Of course, the man who is among the most distinguished historians of science in our generation is certainly qualified to publish such a work as this. He says in the preface that "We have picked out as threads on which to string our anthology of science the ideas of mankind on three problems of transcending importance: (1) the structure of the universe—cosmogony; (2) the nature of matter—atomic theories; (3) the development of life—evolution. Along these three lines we try to trace the thoughts of man from the inspired poetry of the book of Genesis to the latest revelations of the telescope and laboratory." [108] The first of the three sections of the book occupies sixty-eight pages. Here we have quotations from Aristotle's *On the Heavens; The Sizes and Distances of the Sun and Moon,* by Aristarchus; extended quotations from Archimedes, Copernicus, Galileo, Newton's *The Mathematical Principles of Natural Philosophy;* and the *System of the World,* by Laplace. *The first page* of this text, under the heading of Cosmogony is, without comment, *the first chapter of the book of Genesis*—standing with Aristotle, Archimedes, Galileo and Newton. Remembering that this is a volume entitled *Cambridge Readings in the Literature of Science,* I take it that this distinguished scholar looks upon the first chapter of Genesis as a part of the great literature of science of the ages.

Quoting one more scientist, though in places we admit that this author does make some sharp criticisms of the Hebrew account of creation, we call attention to the tribute made by the late Professor L. T. More, the Professor of Physics in the University of Cincinnati, in his famous *The Dogma of Evolution.* "In spite of the speculations of centuries, we have not advanced a step beyond the noble and dignified description of the creation as imagined by the Hebrew prophet in the book of Genesis."[109]

Among philosophers, let me quote from one only, Professor Francis Bowen, for over thirty years the Alvord Professor of Natural Religion, Moral Philosophy, and Civil Polity in Harvard University. In a small volume *A Layman's Study of the English Bible,* published when the author was nearly seventy years of age, he gives this remarkable testimony: "I have faithfully studied most of what the philosophy of these modern times, and the science of our own day, assume to teach, and the result is, that I am now more firmly convinced than ever, that what has been justly called the 'dirt philosophy' of materialism and fatalism is baseless and false. I accept with unhesitating conviction and belief the doctrine of the being of one personal God, the Creator and Governor of the world, and of one Lord Jesus Christ, in whom dwelleth all the fulness of the Godhead bodily; and I have found nothing whatever in the literature of modern infidelity, which, to my mind, casts even the slightest doubt upon that belief."[110]

In turning to distinguished men of literature, let me confine myself to two statements, both of which, however, I believe are unusually significant, one principally because of the great truth it emphasizes, and the other because of the fame of the one making the statement. Probably the most gifted of all professors of English Literature in the South, Dr. C. Alphonso Smith, for many years Head of the department of English Literature in The University of Virginia, and, during the last ten years of his life, Professor of English Literature in the United States Naval Academy at Annapolis, in 1919 published a book which should have received greater attention than it did, a volume which, I fear, is almost unknown to our own generation. I refer to his *Keynote Studies in Keynote Books of the Bible*. The opening chapter in Professor Smith's volume deals with Genesis, and I think in many ways what he says about the first chapter of the Bible is the most striking statement on the subject from the pen of any distinguished professor of literature in any period of our American life. The quotation is quite extended but I do not apologize for it, for we are here discussing and considering some of the greatest themes that can ever occupy the mind of man:

"No single chapter in the Old Testament so impresses me with its inherent greatness as the first chapter of Genesis. In its blend of beauty and power, in the recurrent beat of its planetary rhythms, in the consciousness of a great truth adequately embodied at last, in a certain proud disdain of all embellishment except that which attends unsolicited upon great thought greatly expressed, the first chapter of Genesis seems to me alone and unapproached.

"This chapter abolished mythology throughout the civilised world. There were doubtless mythological germs among the Hebrews themselves but this chapter sterilized them. Latin, Greek, Norse, and Oriental mythology lived on for a while but the warrant of dispossession had been served and gods and goddesses, demigods and demigoddesses, naiads, dryads, and hamadryads, all had to go. Some of them found refuge in poetry and romance; some in the ornament and complement of oratory; some in the metaphors and similes of rhetoric. But in exact proportion as the first great thought of the Bible had free circulation among races and nations, the big gods and the little gods were doomed. Mythology became a mere toy of the mind. The preface to the Bible had throned one God as maker and preserver of all. It served as a sort of cosmic Monroe Doctrine, announcing to the old deities that any attempt on their part to extend their system to any portion of the universe would henceforth be considered dangerous to the well-being of mankind. It had its effect. The dignity and the authoritativeness of the announcement, the splendour of the vision that it unfolded, and the instant appeal made to what we now call intuitional probability marked the inauguration of a new era in human thought.

"There is in fact nothing finer in the Old Testament than the way in which the author of the first chapter of Genesis takes the elemental timbers of the world and cleans them of all the incrustations that had gathered upon them. Earth, water, night, sun, moon, stars,—read what Greek and Roman intellects had done with these, how buried they were beneath the sediment of bizarre fancy and grotesque history. There is not a verse of this chapter that does not by its mere omissions register an altitude of spirit immeasurably beyond all that had gone before.

"The poets have sometimes attributed the passing of mythology to the revelations of science. It was not modern science, however, that sent mythology to the discard. It was the first chapter of Genesis. Mythology did not live long enough to give modern science a chance to get at it. And the death of mythology, so far from injuring nature poetry, helped it. These countless myths of creation not only kept men from a knowledge of nature but made a genuine love of nature impossible. They substituted for the laws and charms of nature the capricious doings of gods and godesses.

"But the greatest achievement of the first chapter of Genesis is that it announced unity, order, and progression in nature. Compare this chapter with any preceding account of the creation of the world and it will be found unique not only in dispossessing gods and goddesses of their former holdings but in staging the hitherto unrecognized qualities of unity, order, and progression. The claim is sometimes made that other and older accounts of creation have been exhumed that anticipate many of the details of the Hebrew record. If this were true it would not invalidate our thesis, for the Hebrew antiquated at one stroke all preceding accounts and became alone the torchbearer of the new view. But the claim made for other accounts is not true. Of course many of the created things mentioned in Genesis may be found in other accounts, but there is no unity, no order, no progression."[111]

The other statement is from Yale's most beloved professor and, certainly, the most influential professor of English Literature in our country during the last forty years, Professor William Lyon Phelps, Lamson Professor of English Literature of Yale, Orator of Yale University, Director of the Hall of Fame, author of many well-known studies of English Literature, the man who could crowd the largest classrooms in Yale with lectures on Browning and Wordsworth. In his volume, *Human Nature in the Bible,* Dr. Phelps pays this glowing tribute to the opening pages of our Bible:

"The early chapters of Genesis are a kind of Outline of History, like that by H. G. Wells, only better written. They are even more condensed than his, and like his book, they attempt to account for the things we see: light, the sun, moon, stars, land, water, animals and man. No one knows how any of these came into existence, but the Bible account is sublime in its simple dignity, and begins in a reasonable and orderly manner by putting the First Cause first. I have read accounts of the origin of the world in the bibles of other religions, and they all, while containing some fine and interesting remarks, seem to have much that is trivial and silly. There is nothing childish or silly in our Bible. The narrative opens like a great symphony:

'In the beginning God created the heaven and the earth. And the earth was without form and void; and darkness was upon the face of the deep. And the Spirit of God moved upon the face of the waters. And God said, Let there be light; and there was light.'

"Lotze said that the Mosaic cosmogony was more sublime than any other, and he was right. It represents physical changes coming from the Divine Will, coming easily and immediately. The control of mind over matter seems to me more natural and reasonable than the other way round, in spite of the fact that some reasonable men are materialists. In the last analysis the idea that the human mind developed out of matter seems to me as curious as the idea that an automobile should make a man, rather than a man make an automobile. I wonder if those who believe that thought, imagination, poetry and music were made by matter do not fall into a vicious circle by somehow thinking that the creative matter had mind in it. . . .

"As a representation of continuous masterpieces in art, such as an artist throws off in his happiest moods, the first chapter in the Bible has a magnificence all its own."[112]

In considering some of the great tributes to the supreme value of the first chapter of Genesis, now that we have heard from scientists, philosophers, and men of literature, I trust I will not be condemned if I conclude with a few words from distinguished theologians who, more than any of the others, spent all their lives in biblical literature, and most of them being also acquainted with the classics of the ancient world, and somewhat familiar with the literature of modern science, should be able to give us, I would think, statements carrying even more weight than those which proceed from men who only occasionally turn to the holy Scriptures for study and inspiration. I have always felt that in many ways the greatest commentary on the book of Genesis, appearing in England, is the one by Dr. James G. Murphy, Professor of Hebrew in the Presbyterian College at Belfast from 1847–1896.

His opening words are so forceful and comprehensive, so much more profound than much of the superficial stuff that frequently appears today concerning the subject we are discussing, that I do not hesitate to quote the entire passage in its fullness:

"This great introductory sentence of the book of God is equal in weight to the whole of its subsequent communications concerning the kingdom of nature. It assumes the existence of God; for it is he who in the beginning creates. It assumes his eternity; for he is before all things; and as nothing comes from nothing, he himself must have always been. It implies his omnipotence; for he creates the universe of things. It implies his absolute freedom; for he begins a new course of action. It implies his infinite wisdom; for a kosmos, an order of matter and mind, can only come from a being of absolute intelligence. It implies his essential goodness; for the Sole, Eternal, Almighty, All-wise, and All-sufficient Being has no reason, no motive, and no capacity for evil. It presumes him to be beyond all limit of time and place; as he is before all time and place. . . .

"It bears on the very face of it the indication that it was written by man, and for man; for it divides all things into the heavens and the earth. Such a division evidently suits those only who are inhabitants of the earth. Accordingly, this sentence is the foundation-stone of the history, not of the universe at large, of the sun, of any other planet, but of the earth, and of man its rational inhabitant. The primeval event which it records may be far distant, in point of time, from the next event in such a history; as the earth may have existed myriads of ages and undergone many vicissitudes in its conditions, before it became the home of the human race. And, for ought we know, the history of other planets, even of the solar system, may yet be unwritten, because there has been as yet no rational inhabitant to compose or peruse the record. We have no intimation of the interval of time that elapsed between the beginning of things narrated in this prefatory sentence, and that state of things which is announced in the following verse.

"With no less clearness, however, does it show that it was dictated by superhuman knowledge. For it records the beginning of things of which natural science can take no cognizance. And not only this sen tence but the main part of this and the following chapter communicates events that occurred before man made his appearance on the stage of things; and therefore before he could either witness or record them. And in harmony with all this, the whole volume is proved by the topics chosen, the revelations made, the views entertained, the ends contemplated, and the means of information possessed, to be derived from a higher source than man."[113]

A contemporary of Professor Murphy, Dr. W. Lindsay Alexander, Professor of Theology for a quarter of a century, and Principal of the Congregational Theological College of Edinburgh 1877–81, in his well-known *Biblical Theology,* briefly sums up the significance of just the opening verse of this first chapter of Genesis in two sentences that might well be memorized: "In this short sentence (Gen. 1:1), the Bible places itself in antagonism to a whole phalanx of opinions taught in ancient schools of philosophy or incorporated with ancient systems of religion. This sentence is a denial of the Greek doctrine of the eternity of matter, of the Epicurean doctrine of a fortuitous concourse of atoms, as that out of which the Kosmos arose, of the Stoic doctrine of an all-compelling fate, of the Pantheistic doctrine of the identity of God with the universe, of the Polytheistic doctrine of a good and a bad principle dividing the formation and the rule of the world between them."[114]

Some of the volumes from which we have been quoting in these passages are probably more or less unfamiliar to, and for the most part inaccessible to, many Christians of this generation, but let me conclude with two paragraphs from that magnificent volume on the book of Genesis, in many ways the greatest ever written, by the distinguished German theologian, Professor Lange, on the shelves of almost every serious student of the Scriptures. This is his grand and sweeping verdict, born of one of the most fertile and well equipped theological minds of the nineteenth century:

"It is no imitation. Copies may have been made from it, more or less deformed, but this is an original painting. The evidence is found in its simplicity, unity, and perfect consistency; whilst in all others the marks of the traditional derivation are to be detected. Overloaded additions, incongruous mixtures, inharmonious touches, all prove that the execution and the original design, the outline and the deformed or crowded filling up, are from different and very dissimilar sources. Take the scriptural representation of the original formlessness, the primeval darkness, the brooding spirit, the going forth of the light, or the first morning, the uprising of the firmament, the emerging of the land from the waters, and compare it with the Greek fables derived from the Egyptian, and which Hesiod has given as the traditional cosmogony. How is all this sublime imagery transformed and deformed in the mythical genealogy that tells us how from Chaos (the yawning abyss) were born Night and Erebus, and how from them arose the Aether and the Day, and how afterwards Earth was born, from whom, and 'like to itself on all sides surrounding,' came 'starry Ouranos!' There is enough to show that the Greek or Egyptian cosmogony had its origin in this ante-historical, ante-mythical account, but no less clear is it that the pure, the holy, the consistent, the sublimely monotheistic narrative was the most ancient, and that these deformities grew out of the nature-worship, whether pantheistic or polytheistic, which, in the course of human depravity, succeeded the earlier, more grandly simple, and less assumingly philosophic idea of the world and its one creator.

"It is greatly in favor of the Bible account that it has no philosophy, and no appearance of any philosophy, either in the abstract form, or in that earlier poetical form which the first philosophy assumed. Its statements of grand facts have no appearance of bias in favor of any class of ideas. Its great antiquity is beyond dispute; it is older, certainly, than history or philosophy. It was before the dawning of anything called science, as is shown by the fact that everything is denoted by its simplest phenomenal or optical name. There is no assigning of nonapparent causations, except the continual going forth of the mighty Word. It is impossible to discover any connection between it and any mythical poetry. The holy sublimity that pervades it is at war with the idea of direct and conscious forgery, designed to impose on others, and the thought of it as a mere work of genius, having its interest in a display of inventive descriptive talent, is inconsistent with every notion we can form of the thinking and aims of the early youth of the human race. It was not the age then, nor till long after, of literary forgeries or fancy-tales. We are shut up to the conclusion of its subjective truthfulness, and its subjective authenticity."[115]

Theories Which Are Opposed to the Biblical Conception of the Origin of the Universe. We cannot close this chapter without giving brief consideration to some of the conceptions of modern philosophy which are in themselves contradictory to the biblical conception of the origin of the world.

As far back as the days of Origen, and in recent times by Martensen, Dorner, Rothe, and Pfleiderer, it has been affirmed that this created world must be considered as having existed from eternity, as never having nonexistence. Now as Professor Orr has well pointed out, the doctrine of evolution which is generally advocated in the world of science today, annihilates this very idea of an eternal universe, for "if the universe were a stable system—that is if it were in a condition of constant development and change—it might with some plausibility be argued that it had existed from all eternity. But our knowledge of the past history of the world shows us that this is not its character; that on the contrary, it is progressive and developing. Now it lies in the very thought of a developing universe that if we trace it back we come at last to a beginning—to some point at which the evolutionist started. Science can give no proof of an eternal succession but so far as it has any voice on the subject, points in an opposite direction by showing that when the universe has parted with its energy as it is in constant process of doing, it has no means of restoring it again."[116] One of the greatest physicists of the nineteenth century, Clerk-Maxwell, in an address which he delivered before the Mathematical and Physical section of the British Association in 1870, reminded his audience, and no scientist has any knowledge today with which he can contradict this statement, that "this idea of a beginning is one which the physical researches of recent times have brought home to us more than any observer of the course of scientific thought in former times would have had reason to expect."[117]

Not only does modern science deny an eternal creation but any theologian speaking from the biblical data must most emphatically reject the whole conception of a world existing from eternity for many reasons. One here will suffice: "Creation from eternity is inconsistent with the divine individuals and personality. Since God's power and love are infinite, a creation that satisfied them must be infinite in extent as well as eternal in past duration—in other words, a creation equal to God. But a God thus dependent upon external creation is neither free nor sovereign. A God existing in necessary relations to the universe, if different in substance from the universe, must be the God of dualism; if of the same substance with the universe, must be a God of pantheism."[118]

The Theory of Logical Derivation. Another theory proposed by some and accepted by a few of the more radical philosophers of our time, is that the world is self-caused, that is, it has evolved from itself by what is technically known as "logical derivation." This theory insists that it was of absolute *necessity* that the universe should come into existence; there was nothing else possible. For a concise reply to this theory, I would like to turn once more to the invaluable pages of Professor James Orr, who summarizes the reasons which makes this view impossible of acceptance in the following words: "This doctrine of a necessary derivation involves an amazing assumption. The assumption is that this universe which exhibits so much evidence of wise arrangement and of the fresh selection of means to attain ends is the only universe possible and could not by any supposition be other than it is. Such a theory may be the only one open to those who hold the ground of the universe to be impersonal; but it is not one which a true theism can sanction, and it is unprovable. Why should infinite wisdom not choose its ends and also choose the means by which they are to be accomplished? Which is the higher view—that which regards the divine being as bound down to a single system, one, too, which wisdom, love and freedom have no share in producing, but which flows from the nature of its cause with the same necessity with which the properties of a triangle flow from a triangle; or that which supposes the universe to have originated in a free, intelligent act, based on the counsels of an infinite wisdom and goodness? Secondly, as in this theory no place is left for freedom in God so logically it leaves no place for freedom in man. Freedom implies initiative, control, a choice between possible alternatives. But on this theory we are considering freedom can never be more than a semblance. Whether the individual recognizes it or not, all that he sees around him and all that takes place within him is but the working out of an eminent, logical necessity. Things are what they are by a necessity as stringent as that which obtains in mathematics and as little room is left for human initiative as on the most thoroughgoing, mechanical or materialistic hypothesis. The consciousness of freedom, however, is a fact too deeply rooted in our personality; too many interests depend on it to admit what is being thus put aside at the bidding of any theory, metaphysical or other; and so long as human freedom stands this view of the origin of the universe can never gain general acceptance."[119]

The Identification of the World with God—Pantheism. The outstanding theory found today in works of philosophy in which the truth of the creation of the world by God is denied is what we call pantheism. One of the saddest tendencies in some circles in theological discussion today is the strange acceptance of this soul-destroying philosophy. We even find it in the recent *Gifford Lectures* by Professor Laird.[120] Perhaps we ought to define pantheism to begin with, and I use here an excellent brief paragraph by a distinguished theologian on the meaning of pantheism: "Pantheism derives its name from the motto, i.e., One and All, which was first brought into vogue by the Greek philosopher Xenophanes. According to his view, God is the universe itself; *beyond* and *outside* the world He does not exist, but only *in* the world, and all nature is His body. In reality, God is everything, and beside him there is nothing. Thus, making God the Soul of the world, Pantheism is distinguished, on the one hand from Materialism, according to which God and nature are immediately identical; and, on the other hand, from Theism, that is, from the belief in a self-conscious, personal God, who created the world and guides even its most minute details. For the main point of pantheistic belief is that this Soul of the world is *not a personal, self-conscious* Being, who appears in his *totality* in any one phenomenon or at any one moment, so as to comprehend himself or become comprehensible for us, but that it is only the One ever same Essence which, filling everything and shaping everything, lives and moves in all existing things, and is revealed in all that is visible, yet is Itself never seen."[121]

Rather than discuss the antichristian, anti-biblical aspects of pantheism myself, I am going to take the liberty of bringing this matter before my readers in the words of one of the finest apologetic scholars of our generation, Dr. Charles Harris, who, it seems to me, has set forth the inadequacy of pantheism better than any other writer in the last quarter of a century. His words, in summary, are as follows: "(1) If the First Cause is identical with the universe, then the First Cause is liable to change. The universe, if not as a whole, at least in its parts, is subject to evolution or development. The First Cause, therefore, must evolve or develop, and be sometimes more perfect and sometimes less perfect. This is fully admitted by many Pantheists.

"But the First Cause must, as has been already shown, be absolutely complete and perfect in all respects. If it changes, it must thereby become either more complete or less complete. If more complete, it was not complete before it changed; if less complete, it ceases, after the change to be the First Cause. Therefore it cannot change at all.

"(2) If God is identical with the universe, contradictions and absurdities must be affirmed of Him. He must be conscious and unconscious, rational and irrational, material and immaterial, hot and cold, round and square, moving and at rest. He must be identical with the Theist who believes in a God distinct from the world, with the Pantheist who believes that the universe is God, and with the Atheist who denies that there is a God at all. Moreover, since the universe consists of parts and is extended, God must consist of parts and be extended.

"(3) But this is not the worst. If God is identical with the actual world, moral distinctions disappear altogether. Since evil exists as well as good, God must be sinful as well as holy, cruel as well as merciful, unjust as well as just. He must be the coward as well as the hero, the murderer as well as his victim, the criminal as well as his judge. The more thorough-going Pantheists admit this. Hegel for example says: 'What kind of an absolute being is that which does not contain in itself all that is actual, even evil included?' And an Indian Pantheist only develops the moral consequences of his creed when he says: 'Though the soul plunge itself in sin, like a sword in water, it shall in no wise cling to it.'

"But a creed which denies the distinction between right and wrong, a distinction grounded on the direct testimony of consciousness, must be false."[122]

"Where Was God before He Created the World?" While in this particular portion of our chapter we are discussing the anti-biblical theories of creation, it seems that right here we should say a word about the question which a great many men so easily and superficially and almost sneeringly ask, "Where was God before He created the world?" Now there are some things regarding the nature and being and work and attributes of God which simply are beyond the human mind. Eternity itself is something that we cannot adequately comprehend. While we do not deny that one might ask oneself now and then exactly this question, we will not be able to fully answer it because we are so ignorant; all we know is what God has chosen to reveal to us. In this matter I think the words of Charles Hodge should be carefully considered, and accepted as all that can be reasonably said on this question. Our inability to answer this particular question ought not in any way to lead to doubts concerning the creation of the world. Science has ten mysteries regarding this matter to one in the Christian faith. Hodge says that questions like this are "drawn from a region which is entirely beyond our comprehension: They assume that we can understand the Almighty unto perfection and search out all His ways; whereas it is obvious that with regard to a Being who is eternal and not subject to the limitations of time, we are using words without meaning when we speak of successive duration in reference to Him. If with God there is no past or future, it is vain to ask what He was doing before creation. It was stated, when treating of the attributes of God, that there are two methods of determining our conceptions of the divine nature and operations. The one is to start with the idea of the Absolute and Infinite and make that idea the touchstone; affirming or denying what is assumed to be consistent or inconsistent therewith. Those who adopt this method, refuse to submit to the teachings of their moral nature or the revelations of the Word of God, and make Him either an absolutely unknown cause, or deny to Him all the attributes of a person. The other method is to start with the revelation which God has made of Himself in the constitution of our own nature and in His holy Word. This method leads to the conclusion that God can think and act, that in Him essence and attributes are not identical, that power and wisdom, will and working in Him, are not one and the same, and that

the distinction between *potentia* (inherent power) and act applies to Him as well as to us. In other words, that God is infinitely more than pure activity, and consequently that it is not inconsistent with His nature that He should do at one time what He does not do at another.

"A second remark to be made on these objections is that they prove too much. If valid against a creation in time, they are valid against all exercise of God's power in time. Then there is no such thing as providential government, or gracious operations of the Spirit, or answering prayer. If whatever God does He does from eternity, then, so far as we are concerned, He does nothing. If we exalt the speculative ideas of the understanding above our moral and religious nature, and above the authority of the Scriptures, we give up all ground both of faith and knowledge, and have nothing before us but absolute skepticism or atheism. These objections, therefore, are simply of our own making. We form an idea of the Absolute Being out of our own heads, and then reject whatever does not agree with it. They have, consequently, no force except for the man who makes them." [123]

The Nature of God as Revealed in His Creation of the World. The very word which we use as a synonym for the world itself declares that the world is one. That word, of course, is *universe,* the root of which is, as one can see, the root of the word unity. The God who made this universe must be one God. Here monotheism rises infinitely above polytheism. No group of gods with their contradictions and jealousies and various assignments to different functions in the world could have brought this universe into being. Unity dominates the laws of nature: what is a law of nature in one part of the universe is considered to be equally effective, all things being equal, in some other part of the universe, and all the laws of the universe together "form a system so harmonious and mutually coherent that a single Cause is strongly suggested, if not actually necessitated . . . The Laws of Reason, and the World of Knowledge based upon Eternal and Necessary Truth, form a system so absolutely coherent, that it is necessary to assume that the Eternal Mind, in and for which these Laws and Truths are true, is *one* . . . The Moral Law is universal in its scope, and binds with an absolute obligation all rational natures." [124] This strongly suggests that Ultimate Reality is *one.*

If it was in the beginning that God created the heavens and the earth, then God was before the beginning. In other words God is eternal. God must be before time began, and He and He alone may be considered as from everlasting to everlasting. Charnock, in one of the greatest works on the attributes of God ever written, has some words that in our materialistic age of superficial thinking, we do well to carefully ponder: "Time began with the foundation of the world; but God being before time, could have no beginning in time. Before the beginning of the creation, and the beginning of time, there could be nothing but eternity; nothing but what was uncreated, that is, nothing but what was without beginning. To be *in* time is to have a beginning, to be *before* all time is never to have a beginning; . . . If He has a beginning, he must have it from another, or from Himself; if from another, that from whom He received His being would be better than He, so more a god than He. He cannot be God that is not supreme; He cannot be supreme that owes His being to the power of another. . . . If He had given beginning to Himself, then He was once nothing; there was a time when He was not; if He was not, how could He be the cause of Himself? It is impossible for any to give a beginning and being to itself; if it acts it must exist, and so existed before it existed. A thing would exist as a cause before it existed as an effect. He that is not cannot be the cause that He is: if, therefore, God doth exist, and hath not His being from another, He must exist from eternity. Whatsoever number of millions of millions of years we can imagine before the creation of the world, yet God was infinitely before those. If there be any existence of things it is necessary that that which was the 'first cause' should 'exist from eternity.' Whatsoever was the immediate cause of the world, yet the first and chief cause wherein we must rest, must have nothing before it; if it had anything before it, it were not the first; he therefore that is the first cause must be without beginning; nothing must be before Him; if he had a beginning from some other; he would not be the first principle and author of all things; if the first cause of all things, he must give himself a beginning, or be from eternity: he could not give himself a beginning; whatsoever begins in time was nothing before, and when it was nothing, it could do nothing; it could not give itself anything, for then it gave what it had not, and did what it could not . . . If we deny some eternal being, we must deny all being; our own being, the being of everything about us; unconceivable absurdities will arise. So, then, if God were the cause of all things, He did exist before all things and that from eternity."[125]

One cannot even once read through seriously the first chapter of Genesis without being aware that the God who brought such a universe as this into existence by the power of His Word must be nothing less than omnipotent, or as the Hebrew Prophet said, "Almighty God." Professor Flint, in discussing the necessary power of the First Cause well says, "All the power which is distributed and distinguished in secondary causes must be combined and united in the first cause. Now, think what an enormous power there is displayed even in this world. In every half-ounce of coal there is stored up power enough, if properly used, to draw two tons a mile. How vast, then, the power which God has deposited in the coal-beds of the world alone! The inhabitants of this little island, by availing themselves of the natural forces which Providence has placed at their disposal, annually accomplish more work than could by any possibility be effected by the inhabitants of the whole earth, if they exerted merely the power which is in their own bodies, the power of human bones and muscles. And yet there can be little doubt that, even in this country, we make no use at all of many natural agents, and only a wasteful use of any of them. 'Weigh the earth on which we dwell,' says an astronomer; 'count the millions of its inhabitants that have come and gone for the last six thousand years; unite their strength into one arm; and test its power in an effort to move the earth. It could not stir it a single foot in a thousand years; and yet, under the omnipotent hand of God, not a minute passes that it does not fly far more than a thousand miles.' The earth, however, is but a mere atom in the universe. Through the vast abysses of space there are scattered countless systems, at enormous distances, yet all related; glorious galaxies of suns, planets, satellites, comets, all sweeping onwards in their appointed courses. How mighty the arm which impels and guides the whole! God can do all that, for He continually does it. How much more He could do than He does, we cannot know. The power of no true cause, of no free cause, is to be measured by what it does. It must be adequate to produce its actual effects, but it may be able to produce countless merely possible effects. It has power over its powers, and is not necessitated to do all that it is capable of doing."[126]

Of course the God who made the universe must be a God of infinite wisdom. Somewhere recently I read that a Swedish physiologist, after long research, had finally enumerated seventeen hundred different nerves centered in or near the spinal column of man. It has taken over twenty-five hundred years of study of human anatomy just to know that. To know what each nerve is for, and how it functions, is something that medicine even today does not claim to know. Man has still vast mysteries to explore concerning the very body in which he lives, which means that the body of a man demanded more wisdom for its creation than man himself now possesses, or else he would know all there is to know about his body. So likewise with the heavenly bodies: every time you pass an observatory, or hear of some man devoting his life to the science of astronomy, or read some new work on the stars, or the sun, remember that man is only now beginning to discover those laws which God Himself, in infinite wisdom, put in the universe which He created. A few months ago I happened to be the guest of a friend of mine who has been working at the Mellon Institute, in Pittsburgh, where a great group of brilliant young men are laboring in their separate laboratories, on some of the outstanding problems that relate to chemistry, physics, etc. My friend was working on the subject of flour, for a flour corporation in Minnesota. He was not the only one working on flour; I believe there were three other scientists in the same building, working at different problems connected with this fine stuff that we get from wheat kernels. When I asked him if men did not yet know all there is to know about flour, it seems such a simple thing, he took me over to a bookcase of his, and showed me entire volumes devoted to this one subject, some of them just bibliographies of articles and books about flour! Then he said, "We have only begun to explore the secrets of this substance." The God who made flour, the God who made the rest of this universe, the God who made man with all his infinite mysteries, He is a God of infinite wisdom.

It seems that no one attribute of God is more purposely emphasized in the first chapter of Genesis, and for that matter in the second chapter, than His goodness. At the end of the very first period of creation we read that "God saw the light that it was good"; on the third day, after separating the earth from the water, and bringing forth grass and herbs, "God saw that it was good." This is repeated for His activity on the fourth day, and on the fifth, and the early part of the sixth day, and then at the end of the chapter we read, "And God saw everything that He had made, and behold it is very good." "The judgment is merely another branch of the apprehensive or conitive faculty, by which we know the physical and ethical relations and distinctions of things. It comes immediately into power on observing the object now called into existence. God saw 'that it was good,' that is, good in general which fulfills the end of its being. The relation of good and evil has a place and an application in the physical world, but it ascends through all the claims of the intellectual and the moral. That form of the judgment which takes cognizance of moral distinctions is of so much importance as to have received a distinct name—the conscience, or moral sense.

"Here the normal rectitude of God is vindicated, inasmuch as the work of his power is manifestly good. This refutes the doctrine of two persons, the one good and the other evil, which the Persian sages have devised in order to account for the presence of moral and physical evil along with the good in the present condition of our world."[127] In no one place in the Old Testament is the goodness of God so revealed, it would seem, as in the second chapter of Genesis, in regard to the particular creation and enduement of man. God gave to Adam, at the time of his creation, a perfect body, free from all ailments, disease and imperfections; an intellect, revealed in two definite ways, first in Adam being immediately able to take care of the garden of Eden and to till it (and some of us who have been in school all our lives, would have a little difficulty taking care of a garden), and in being able to give names to the animals as they came before him (many of us would not even be able to *recall* the names of most of the animals of the earth, even after their names were long ago assigned); in giving to man a perfect and beautiful environment, not a desert, nor the brick walls of a city, but a garden, with rivers, undoubtedly the most beautiful place that the earth has ever known; a wife to love, certainly, created by God, the most beautiful woman who ever lived, with whom Adam, the moment he saw her, immediately fell in love, and burst forth into song; the capacity for communication with God, as the entire chapter, and the following chapter, reveals; guidance from God concerning what is right and wrong, accompanied with a warning that Adam might be kept from doing what God forbade him to do. In everything that God did He manifested His infinite goodness.

Some Consequences of Believing in God the Creator. Professor Robert Flint, from whose philosophical writings we have often quoted in this work, published, toward the close of the last century, a volume not so well-known as his works on Theism, and Agnosticism, but in which it is recognized some of the greatest things that Flint ever wrote or said are to be found. I refer to his *Sermons and Addresses.* In these moving and lifting pages Flint, after forty years of thinking profoundly on the problems and truths relating to the Being of God, gave expression to the significance of a faith in God as Creator in these words: how true they are, and how we need to lay hold of them and what they express:

"Whatever man or nation has learned to know that the heavens and the earth are the creatures and subjects of God, is thereby necessarily delivered from all the errors of polytheism, from bondage to false gods, from the debasing worship of idols, from the intellectual and moral darkness of heathendom. On that man and nation a great light has arisen, a terrible night, filled with hideous spectres and haunting fears, has passed away, and a serene day shines. They can walk with the freedom, the safety, the joyousness, of those who are in the light.They see that in nature there is nothing to deify, and yet that nature is full of Divine life and energy, of Divine beauty and goodness. They are strong in the Lord the true God, and so tremble not nor grovel before any other gods or lords.

"It is also only through realizing the truth affirmed in our texts that the chief and most dangerous forms of false speculations are deprived of their power to seduce, ensnare, and destroy. He who believes in God as the Creator and ruler of the universe can be neither atheist, materialist, or pantheist. His faith is directly antagonistic to that of those who suppose that there is no God; that matter explains itself, and that there is nothing else; or that some indeterminate substance or impersonal force has originated all that exists. The only sure protection against any error is possession of the truth which contradicts it; the only sure preservative against the power of those imposing systems of error to which I refer, and from the consequences which they involve, and which must be so inevitably ruinous to the moral life alike of individuals and of societies, is a firm, well-grounded, carefully tested faith in the truth which is so plainly laid down in the first verse of our Bibles.

"Then, this faith in God as the Creator is the necessary basis of all higher spiritual faith. It is only in virtue of so believing in God that we can also believe in Him as a Heavenly Father, as one who reveals Himself in the soul of man, in the history of the world, in the experiences of the pious. He cannot be a Christian who is not a Theist. The Christian faith,—faith in the love and mercy, salvation and kingdom of God, as revealed through the teaching and work of Christ,—could have been built on no other foundation than on that knowledge of God as the Creator and Lord of the Universe into which ancient Israel was divinely guided and educated to the benefit and blessing of all the nations of the earth."[128]

The life of a man who recognizes God as his Creator, and the Creator of the universe, is always infinitely richer, deeper, more satisfying, happier, and stronger, than the life of an unbeliever who denies the creating work of God could ever be. First of all, of course, man is led to worship God, when he recognizes Him as the one from whom all things come. This is exactly what Paul is referring to in his Athenian address, when he rebukes these philosophers for their idolatries, and the various temples in which they offered sacrifices, and sometimes prayer, without even knowing the God who made the world: "The God that made the world and all things therein, he, being Lord of heaven and earth, dwelleth not in temples made with hands: neither is he served by men's hands, as though he needed anything, seeing he himself giveth to all life, and breath, and all things; and he made of one every nation of men to dwell on all the face of the earth, having determined their appointed seasons, and the bounds of their habitation; that they should seek God, if haply they might feel after him and find him, though he is not far from each one of us." Again and again throughout the Psalms the heart of man is lifted up in adoration of Him whom the Psalmist recognizes as the Creator of the heavens above, of the earth on which he walks, and of man himself. When we turn to the last passages of our Bible and are allowed to look into heaven itself, we find that those who are before the throne of God cast down their crowns before Him, saying, "Worthy art thou, our Lord and our God, to receive the glory and the honor and the power: for thou didst create all things, and because of thy will they were, and were created."[129]

We Confidently Pray to Such a God. The relation of the doctrine of creation to fervor and confidence in prayer is, I must confess, a subject which I had failed to notice in reading the Word of God until about two years ago. Since then I have wondered why no one (as far as I know) has given us a study of this most important aspect of our prayer life. Take, for instance, the prayer of Hezekiah, who, when taunted by the Assyrians as they threatened to destroy the city of Jerusalem, begins with this adoration: "And Hezekiah prayed before Jehovah, and said, O Jehovah, the God of Israel, that sittest above the cherubim, thou art the God, even thou alone, of all the kingdoms of the earth; thou hast made heaven and earth. Incline thine ear, O Jehovah, and hear; open thine eyes, O Jehovah, and see; and hear the words of Sennacherib, wherewith he hath sent him to defy the living God." Jeremiah, in confessing the disobedience of Israel, cried out, "Ah Lord Jehovah! behold, thou has made the heavens and the earth by thy great power and by thine outstretched arm; there is nothing too hard for thee." Later, Ezra, in that wonderful prayer of confession which is almost, it seems, never read today or at least never spoken of, Ezra begins with these words: "Thou art Jehovah, even thou alone; thou hast made heaven, the heaven of heavens, with all their host, the earth and all things that are therein, and seas and all that is in them, and thou preservest them all; and the host of heaven worshippeth thee."[130] Early in the history of the church, in the first persecutions, when Peter and John had been released from prison, forbidden to teach and preach in the name of Christ, we read that the Christians, assembled together in Jerusalem, began their prayer with these words: "O Lord, thou that didst make the heaven and the earth, and the sea, and all that in them is."[131]

The Foundation of Hope. If God has created the world, and, in so doing, reveals Himself to be omnipotent, omniscient, and infinitely good, then the realization of such truth should beget in our hearts an unquenchable hope. In one of the darkest periods of Israel's history, God encourages his despondent people by reminding them that He *is* the Creator, and, being such, will never forget them or His covenant with them: "To whom then will ye liken me, that I should be equal to him? saith the Holy One. Lift up your eyes on high, and see who hath created these, that bringeth out their host by number; he calleth them all by name; by the greatness of his might, and for that he is strong in power, not one is lacking. Why sayest thou, O Jacob, and speakest, O Israel, My way is hid from Jehovah, and the justice due to me is passed away from my God? Hast thou not known? hast thou not heard? The everlasting God, Jehovah, the Creator of the ends of the earth, fainteth not, neither is weary; there is no searching of his understanding. He giveth power to the faint; and to him that hath no might he increaseth strength. Even the youths shall faint and be weary, and the young men shall utterly fall: but they that wait for Jehovah shall renew their strength; they shall mount up with wings as eagles; they shall run, and not be weary; they shall walk, and not faint."[132] Later in the same prophecy we read, "Thus saith Jehovah, the Holy One of Israel, and his Maker: Ask me of the things that are to come; concerning my sons, and concerning the work of my hands, command ye me. I have made the earth, and created man upon it: I, even my hands, have stretched out the heavens; and all their host have I commanded . . . For thus saith Jehovah that created the heavens, the God that formed the earth and made it, that established it and created it not a waste, that formed it to be inhabited: I am Jehovah; and there is none else . . . Look unto me, and be ye saved, all the ends of the earth; for I am God, and there is none else. By myself have I sworn, the word is gone forth from my mouth in righteousness, and shall not return, that unto me every knee shall bow, every tongue shall swear."[133] The Psalmist, meditating upon the creative work of God, confesses, "Happy is he that hath the God of Jacob for his help, whose hope is in Jehovah his God: who made the heaven and earth, the sea, and all that in them is; who keepeth truth for ever."[134]

Learned John Pearson, in his great work on the Apostles' Creed, from which we have previously quoted, well says, in reference to the happiness begotten in the human heart when contemplating God's creative work, "By virtue of the first production He hath a perpetual right unto and power to dispose of all things: and He who can order and dispose of all must necessarily be esteemed able to secure and satisfy any creation . . . This happiness consisteth partly in a comfortable assurance arising from this meditation, of the will of God to protect and succour us, of His desire to preserve and bless us . . . 'Behold,' says He, 'I have created the smith that bloweth the coals in the fire, and that bringeth forth an instrument for his work. No weapon that is formed against thee shall prosper. This is the heritage of the servants of the Lord!"[135]

The Creation of a Sense of Humility. In this same work by Pearson, there is a great paragraph on a theme which somehow has almost totally disappeared from our contemporary thinking, in this age of supposed self-sufficiency, namely that the doctrine of creation begets in the heart of man a sense of humility: "As there is nothing more destructive to humanity than pride, and yet not anything to which we are more prone than that; so nothing can be more properly applied to abate the swelling of our proud conceptions, than a due consideration of the other works of God, with a sober reflection upon our original. 'When I consider the heavens the work of Thy fingers, the moon and the stars which Thou hast ordained' (Ps. viii. 3); when I view those glorious apparent bodies with my eye, and by the advantage of a glass find greater numbers, before beyond the power of my sight, and from thence judge there may be many millions more which neither eye nor instrument can reach; when I contemplate those far more glorious spirits, the inhabitants of the heavens, and attendants on Thy throne; I cannot but break forth into that admiration of the prophet, 'What is man that Thou art mindful of him?' What is that offspring of the earth, that dust and ashes? 'What is that son of man that Thou visitest him?' What is there in the progeny of an ejected and condemned father, that Thou shouldest look down from heaven the place of Thy dwelling, and take care of notice of him. But if our origin ought so far to humble us, how should our fall abase us? That of all the creatures which God made, we should comply with him who first opposed his Maker, and would be equal unto Him from whom he now received his being . . . How should a serious apprehension of our own corruption mingled with the thoughts of our creation, humble us in the sight of Him, whom we alone of all the creatures by our unrepented sins drew unto repentance? How can we look without confusion of face upon that monument of our infamy, recorded by Moses, who first penned the origin of humanity, 'It repented the Lord that He had made man on the earth, and it grieved Him at His heart'?"[136]

"By Faith We Understand That the Worlds Have Been Framed by

the Word of God." We often hear of series of sermons being preached on the characters appearing in that wonderful roll-call of Heroes of Faith in the eleventh chapter of Hebrews, but how easily we forget that the chapter *begins,* not with an illustration of faith in the life of some great Old Testament character, but with a statement referring to creation. It is affirmed that it is by faith that men come to believe that the worlds were made by the Word of God. Delitzsch, in his profound way has well said, "Scripture starts with a fact which only faith can recognize: the divine origin of the universe is a noumenon of faith—of such faith as patriarchs and prophets and other saints continue to exhibit throughout the time of the times of the Old Testament . . . It is not meant, of course, that faith unaided by divine revelation could have discovered the fact that the world was made in just six days (neither more nor less), and by means of ten creative words, but that faith could and did discern in creation the working out of a divine purpose and uttered will, in a fixed order, and according to a certain predetermined plan." [137]

In the beginning of his rich, brilliantly conceived, series of discourses on the book of Genesis, Professor S. Candlish has a whole chapter on "Creation Viewed as a Matter of Faith," which, it may be, most of my readers have not seen, and many do not have access to. I am taking the liberty of placing before them here an extended quotation from what is probably the most remarkable exposition of this particular verse in the Bible that has ever appeared in our language: "The fact of the creation is regarded in the Bible as a fact revealed; and as such, it is commended to our faith. Thus the scriptural method of this subject is exactly the reverse of what is called the natural. It is not to ascend from nature up to nature's God, but to descend, if we may so speak, from God to God's nature, or his works of nature; not to hear the creation speaking of the Creator, but to hear the Creator speaking of the creation. We have not in the Bible an examination and enumeration of the wonders to be observed among the works of nature, and an argument founded upon these that there must be a God, and that he must be of a certain character, and must have had certain views in making what he has made. God himself appears, and tells us authoritatively who he is, and what he has done, and why he did it. . . .

"We believe on his testimony. We believe what he says, and because he says it. In thus simply receiving a fact declared by another, and that other fully credible and trustworthy, the mind is in a very different attitude and posture from that which it assumes when it reasons out the fact, as it were, by its own resources. There is far more of dependence and submission in the one case than in the other,—a more cordial and implicit recognition of a Being higher than we are, a more unreserved surrender of ourselves. The one, in truth, is the act of a man, the other of a child. Now, in the kingdom of God—his kingdom of nature as well as his kingdom of grace,—we must be as little children. When I draw inferences for myself concerning the Author of creation,—when I reason out from his works the fact of his existence, and the chief attributes of his character,—I am conscious of a certain feeling of superiority. The Deity becomes almost, in a certain sense, my creature,—the product of my own elaborated process of thought. I am occupied more with my own reasonings than with the transcendent excellencies of Him of whom I reason. The whole is very much an exercise of intellect, attended, certainly, with those emotions of beauty and sublimity which the exercise of the intellect on matters of taste calls forth;—but with scarcely anything more of the real apprehension of an unseen Being, in my conclusions respecting the author of nature, than in my premises respecting nature itself.

"But now, God speaks, and I am dumb. He opens his mouth, and I hold my peace. I bid my busy, speculative soul be quiet. I am still, and know that it is God. I now at once recognize a real and living Person, beyond and above myself. I take my station humbly, submissively at his feet. I learn of him. And what he tells me now, in the way of direct personal communication from himself to me, has a weight and vivid reality infinitely surpassing all that any mere deductions from the closest reasoning could ever have. Now in very truth my 'faith' does become the substance of things hoped for, the evidence of things not seen.' Now at last I am brought into real personal contact with the Invisible One. And he speaks as one having authority. He whom now I personally know and see tells me of the things which he has made; and so tells me of them, that now they start forth before my eyes in a new light. The idea of their being not only his workmanship, but of his explaining them to me as his workmanship, assumes a distinctness—a prominence and power—which cannot fail to exercise a strong influence and exert a sovereign command over me, as a communication directly from him to me."[138]

Conclusion: Let Us Then Entrust Our Souls to a Faithful Creator. The Apostle Peter, toward the end of his First Epistle, in speaking to Christians who were suffering for the sake of Christ, who were being reproached and persecuted and ostracised, cried out "Wherefore let them also commit their souls in well-doing unto a faithful Creator." "In God being our *Creator,*" Alford well reminds us, "without whom not a hair falls to the ground, we have an assurance that we are not overlooked by Him; in His being a *faithful* Creator, whose covenant truth is pledged to us, it is implied that we are within that covenant, suffering according to His will and as His children."[139]

Though thousands of years separate our day from the time the Genesis record was composed, and though the earlier record was written in simple language and not with a technical terminology, we find that the laws of logic and the testimony of our physical universe confirm the testimony of the Scriptures, and enable us still to say with fullest confidence, *"I believe in God the Father, maker of heaven and earth."*

Chapter Eight

THE RESURRECTION OF CHRIST FROM THE DEAD: THE APOLOGETIC FOR AN AGE DEMANDING HISTORICAL CERTAINTY

Of the three great themes of Paul's Athenian address—the creation of the world by God, a righteous judgment to come, and the resurrection of Christ from the dead, only one may be designated as strictly belonging to the realm of *history*. While the creation of the world by God is an actual event, man was not then on earth and what is strictly called history had not yet begun; the judgment to come, though it will some day be a matter of history, is now to be assigned to the realm of prophecy. We are living in a day when, as never before, the value of historical certainty is dogmatically insisted upon, with the corollary dogma that nothing in all the past history of man is to be accepted unless it comes certified with indisputable historical evidence.

In an age like ours, insisting upon historical certainty, the origins of the Christian faith and the person of Jesus Christ are given, if one may use the term, added confirmation. One thing is sure, and that is that *Jesus of Nazareth belongs to the realm of history*. We know when he lived, between 5 and 6 B.C., and 30 to 32 A.D. We know where he was born, in Bethlehem, a real town, not some mythological cloud; we know where he spent most of the years of his life, in Nazareth, far north in Galilee, where he worked as a carpenter. We know many of the characters of this day from literature apart from the New Testament, for the names of Herod the Great, his son, Herod Agrippa, Pontius Pilate, Tiberias Caesar, Felix, Festus, etc., are found in many of the secular writings of the first century. Every history of the ancient world, embracing the first century of our era, is compelled to say something about Christ Jesus; every encyclopedia published in the western world must record the fact that Jesus lived. Though H. G. Wells has an utter con-

tempt for Christ, in fact, a hatred of Him, and for all the articles of th
Christian faith, he is, nevertheless, compelled to give scores of lines t
Jesus of Nazareth in his *Outline of History*. The very dates we use
designated by the letters A.D. and B.C., bear testimony to the fact tha
one Jesus Christ once appeared on this earth. You cannot today nam
any event of ancient Babylonia, or Greece, or Rome, and try to tell me
when it happened, without bearing testimony to the fact that Chris
lived. Every newspaper, every court document, every letter, ever
monument that carries a date, say of 1945, all add their testimony t
the reality of an historic Christ.

Not only did this person, Jesus of Nazareth, live here on earth, amon
men, at a definite time, in a definite place, among historic character
speaking as man to man, and going about doing good, but this man
Jesus, also died. We will have occasion to consider once again th
reality of His death when we come to the theory of Christ swooning a
an explanation of the empty tomb, but here let it simply be said tha
we know more about the details of the hours immediately before an
the actual death of Jesus, in and near Jerusalem, than we know abou
the death of any other one man in all the ancient world. In fact, w
know more about what happened and what was said during the la
week of His life on earth than we know about any other enti
year of His life previous to Passion Week. We know what He sai
to His disciples throughout Thursday of that week—the institutic
of the Lord's Supper that night, the agony of suffering in Gethsen
ane, the nature of the crowd that came out to arrest Him in Gethsan
ane, and how He was betrayed with a kiss. We know of the fiv
trials which Jesus underwent within the last eight hours: two befo
the Jewish authorities, two before Pilate, and one before Herod. W
know what men said to Christ, what they said against Him, and wh
He said to them. We know how the soldiers despitefully used Him; ho
the Sanhedrin bribed witnesses to condemn Him. We know even th
name of an obscure person who carried His cross to Golgotha. We kno
of the two men who were crucified on either side of Him, the wor
that came from His holy lips, while He hung upon the cross, and th
insults that were thrown up to Him during those hours. We know wh
the soldiers did at the foot of the cross, what the women felt, looki

upon Him as He hung there; what the repentant thief said to Him; how darkness enveloped Him; how the veil of the temple was rent, and an earthquake shook the city. Nothing here is what we might call mythical, or even "theological": it is all solid, definite, historical fact.[1]

Something happened to the body of Jesus when it was taken down from the cross. The New Testament testifies that it was placed in a tomb of Joseph of Arimathaea, a fact we will consider in detail shortly. On Sunday morning, for one reason or another, that tomb was empty, as everyone admits—Christian, unbeliever, disciple, scoffer, Jew and Gentile, conservative, and modernist. We are here in the realm of history. The reality of the Resurrection of Christ is something we may judge as we do any other historical event. The criteria for determining what Caesar did at Gaul, or how the Goths sacked Rome, or what happened at Waterloo, are the criteria by which we determine what happened on this first Easter Sunday.

Young people especially who are being swept off their feet with all kinds of skeptical speculation, and unjustified accusations concerning the "mythical" aspect of the Christian faith, should be careful to note that *in this one realm concerning the greatest of all miracles, we are face to face with definite, historical data.* This is one of the reasons that makes our own faith superior to all other faiths of history. The distinguished classical scholar, Dr. Clifford Herbert Moore of Harvard University, in a famous work *The Religious Thought of the Greeks,* has well said, "Christianity knew its Saviour and Redeemer not as some god whose history was contained in a mythical faith, with rude, primitive, and even offensive elements, as were the stories of Attis or Osiris, and to a degree of Dionysus. Such myths required violent interpretation to make them acceptable to enlightened minds. On the contrary, the Christian Saviour had lived and associated with men whose minds and senses had apprehended his person, acts, and character. These witnesses had transmitted their knowledge directly, and they had testified to the life of Jesus Christ and his teaching. Jesus was then a historical, not a mythical being. No remote or foul myth obtruded itself on the Christian believer; his faith was founded on positive, historical and acceptable facts."[2]

Dr. Warfield expressed some years ago, in an article that seems to have been forgotten by our generation, a fact we need often to remember. "The Incarnation of an Eternal God is Necessarily a Dogma; no human eye could witness his stooping to man's estate, no human tongue could bear witness to it as a fact and yet, if it be not a fact, our faith is vain, we are yet in our sins. On the other hand the Resurrection of Christ is a fact, an external occurrence within the cognizance of man, to be established by other testimonies and yet which is the cardinal doctrine of our system: on it all other doctrines hang."[3]

The Meaning of "Resurrection" Determines the Meaning of "The Resurrection of Christ." The word *resurrection* in itself means a rising from the dead, a coming forth from the dead, a return from the dead, and assumes that death has been experienced. There can be no such a thing as a *resurrection* until something has died. Whether we are trichotomists or dichotomists, whether we believe that men have a body, soul, and spirit, or simply a body and soul, we will all agree that the soul of man, itself, never dies. The soul of Jesus did not die. He said, "Father, into thy hands I commend my spirit."[4] The *spirit* of your loved one and mine, your mother and mine, has not died; your mother and my mother are consciously alive, but their bodies having suffered death, were laid away in a grave. When we speak of the resurrection of anyone who has died, we can only mean the resurrection of that person's body. There never will be and never can be the "resurrection" of a spirit, for the simple reason that a spirit has never, and can never, suffer death. Modernists today say they believe in the Resurrection of Christ, but when you examine their faith you find that they do not believe at all in the Resurrection of Christ's body, but simply that Christ is still living. We will consider this further when we come to examine Harnack's famous phrase, "The Easter Faith." If death affects the body and the body is not raised, death is the conqueror; if Christ can be said to have conquered death then His own body must have been delivered from death's power. In no other way can we account for the empty tomb, and for the appearance of Christ after His Resurrection, and in no other way can we say that Christ conquered death, unless His body was raised on Easter day. As Professor James Denney said some years ago in his epochal work, *Jesus and the Gospel,* "If we cannot speak of the bodily resurrection we should not speak of resurrection at all."[5] Gnosticism which worked such havoc in the early centuries of the Christian church, emphatically and continuously denied that Christ rose from the dead in His own body, denying the resurrection of the flesh, on the ground that "the flesh is ignoble and unclean substance," but Gnosticism was a heresy, and condemned by the entire church. Today Gnostic teachings are to be found in a great number of books dealing with Christian doctrine, by many of our teachers of theology, by whom the church expects to be led into truth, but who, rather, are destroying the Christian faith by their departure from the truth. Before one begins to discuss any such a great subject as the Resurrection of Christ, one should be careful to recognize that resurrection means bodily resurrection. Any other use of the term is a misuse of the word. Modernists may say that this is *their* interpretation of the Resurrection of Christ, but it was never so understood in the New Testament, nor by those who formulated the great creeds of the Christian church. At least let us be accurate in our use of terms, whatever we may conclude about the evidence for the ideas of which they speak.

The late Professor Thoburn has summed up the whole faith of the church in the relation of resurrection to the body of Christ in these words, "The body of Jesus, if merely revivified could hardly be termed 'glorified'; even such a word could convey only an indefinite meaning to our minds. If the statements of the narratives are to be received we must understand that the resurrection was no mere revivification of the former body which was like ours; but some inauguration to a different life of the former body which had undergone a complete transmutation of some kind without, however, destroying its identity and resemblance."[6]

Jesus Staked the Future of the Gospel and His Church upon the Fulfillment of His Prediction Regarding His Own Resurrection. One of the most amazing things that ever came from the lips of Jesus, as the apostles and His disciples listened to Him, was His frequent assertion, not only that He was going up to Jerusalem to die, at the hands of the religious leaders of Israel, but that on the third day after His death He would rise again. Let us consider the prophecies first, and then their significance. Early in His ministry, immediately after the cleansing of the temple, our Lord said to the Jews of Jerusalem, "Destroy this temple, and in three days, I will raise it up . . . He spoke of the temple of His body." During the second period of His Galilean ministry, after the healing of the demoniac, He declared, "As Jonah was three days and three nights in the belly of the whale, so shall the Son of Man be three day and three nights in the heart of the earth." Immediately following Peter's great confession, we read that "Jesus began to show unto His disciples how that . . . the third day He must be raised up." This prophecy was repeated immediately after the Transfiguration. Just before Passion Week, our Lord emphatically once again predicted that, on "the third day" He would be raised up. Once during Passion Week, following the Lord's supper, He revealed His unwavering faith in His stupendous miracle, speaking of events to take place, "after I am raised up."[7]

If you or I should say to any group of friends that we expected to die, either by violence or naturally, at a certain time, but that, three days after death, we would rise again, we would be quietly taken away by friends, and confined to an institution, until our minds became clear and sound again. This would be right, for only a foolish man would go around talking about rising from the dead on the third day, only a foolish man, *unless* he knew that this was going to take place, and no one in the world has ever known that about himself except One Christ, the Son of God. Mr. R. M'Cheyne Edgar, in his remarkable but exceptionally scarce work, *The Gospel of a Risen Saviour,* has set this forth more vividly than any other writer with which I am acquainted, "Here is a teacher of religion and he calmly professes to stake his entire claims upon his ability, after having been done to death, to rise again from the grave. We may safely assume that there never was, before or since, such a proposal made. To talk of this extraordinary test being *invented* by mystic students of the prophecies, and inserted in the way it has been into the gospel narratives, is to lay too great a burden on our credulity. He who was ready to stake everything on his ability to come back from the tomb stands before us as the most original of all teachers, one who shines in his own self-evidencing life!"[8]

The Primacy of Christ's Resurrection in the Preaching of the Apostles. All the preaching of the apostles in the early church emphasized more than any other known fact relating to Christ, His miraculous resurrection. The first sermon of the divinely established church, the one delivered by St. Peter on the day of Pentecost, is "wholly and entirely founded on the Resurrection. Not merely is the Resurrection its principal theme, but if that doctrine were removed there would be no doctrine left. For the Resurrection is propounded as being (1) the explanation of Jesus' death; (2) prophetically anticipated as the Messianic experience; (3) apostolically witnessed; (4) the cause of the outpouring of the Spirit, and thus accounting for religious phenomena otherwise inexplicable; and (5) certifying the Messianic and Kingly position of Jesus of Nazareth. Thus the whole series of arguments and conclusions depends for stability entirely upon the Resurrection. Without the Resurrection the Messianic and Kingly position of Jesus could not be convincingly established. Without it the new outpouring of the Spirit would continue a mystery unexplained. Without it the substance of the apostolic witness would have disappeared. All that would be left of this instruction would be the Messianic exposition of Psalm xvi.; and that, only as a future experience of a Messiah who had not yet appeared. The Divine Approval of Jesus as certified by His works would also remain: but apparently as an approval extended only to His life; a life ending like that of any other prophet whom the nation refused to tolerate any longer. Thus the first Christian sermon is founded on the position of Jesus as determined by His Resurrection." [9]

If we study the great sermons recorded in the Acts, those of Simon Peter and those of the Apostle Paul, we will discover that "so far from being a mere accessory or appendage to the apostolic message, a detached event added on to the life and teaching of Jesus to assure the disciples of his survival of death and the truth of his claim, in this lay, germinally and as in a kernel, the whole gospel they had to preach; so that the preaching of Christ is for the apostles the preaching of his resurrection, and their primary function is to be witnesses of the fact." [10] Well could Paul say, "If Christ hath not been raised, then is our preaching vain." [11] If one carefully investigates the subject of witness-bearing in the New Testament he will realize that in almost every case where the word *witness* occurs in relation to what Christians are to say concerning the Lord Jesus, it will be found it has to do with their testimony to His resurrection. Thus, in its first occurrence, in the great commission as given by St. Luke, we read, "Thus it is written and thus it behooved Christ to suffer and to rise from the dead the third day: and that remission of sins should be preached in his name among all nations, beginning at Jerusalem and ye are *witnesses* of these things." [12] In the first chapter of the Book of Acts, when the early Christians were gathered together for the purpose of choosing a successor of Judas Iscariot, it is recorded that the apostles agreed that they should only choose one from among their number who had companioned with them and knew the Lord Jesus; "beginning from the baptism of John unto that same day that he was taken up from among us, must one be ordained to be a *witness* with us of his resurrection." In his Pentecostal sermon, Simon Peter declared, "This Jesus hath God raised up whereof we are all *witnesses*." In Peter's second sermon delivered in Jerusalem after the miracle of the healing of the lame man, he cried out to his Jewish brethren, "But ye denied the Holy One and the Just, and desired a murderer to be granted unto you; and killed the Prince of life, whom God hath raised from the dead; whereof we are *witnesses*." After the second persecution, the apostles confessed to the Sanhedrin that they were witnesses of the crucifixion and the exaltation of Christ. In his sermon in the house of Cornelius, Peter again states that he, with the other apostles, were witnesses "of all things which he did both in the land of the Jews and in Jerusalem, whom they slew and hanged on a tree; whom God raised up the third day, and showed him openly; not to all the people but unto *witnesses* chosen before of God, even to us who did eat and drink with him after he rose from the dead." In the very first sermon of the greatest of all missionaries, St. Paul, on his first missionary journey, in the Synagogue of Antioch in Pisidia, after vividly describing the death of the Lord and His burial, he added "but God raised him from the dead and he was seen many days of them who came up with him from Galilee to Jerusalem, who are his *witnesses* unto the people." St. Paul, later, in speaking of his convulsive experience on the Damascus Road, said that the Lord has commanded him to be a *witness* unto all men of the things which he had seen and heard.[13]

Once in the Book of Acts, in a remarkable passage which seems for some strange reason to be overlooked today, is the witnessing of the apostles described as having been *with great power,* and this when they witness to the resurrection. "And with great power gave the apostles witness of the resurrection of the Lord Jesus: and great grace was upon them all."[14] All the apostles, Paul most of all, set forth the resurrection of Christ as one of the two great fundamental themes of the gospel. Writing to the Thessalonians, in his first letter of which we have record, he declared, "For if we believe that Jesus died and rose again, even so them also which sleep in Jesus will God bring with him." Writing later to the church at Corinth, he elaborated the same truth, "For I delivered unto you first of all that which I also received, how that Christ died for our sins according to the scriptures; and that he was buried, and that he rose again the third day according to the scriptures." And is not that a remarkable statement which Paul makes in the midst of his Roman epistle: "If thou shalt confess with thy mouth the Lord Jesus, and shalt believe in thine heart that God hath raised him from the dead, thou shalt be saved." Later, again to the Corinthians, he could write: "For the love of Christ constraineth us; because we thus judge, that if one died for all, then were all dead: and that he died for all, that they which live should not henceforth live unto themselves, but unto him which died for them, and rose again."[15]

Not only was the resurrection of Christ one of the two great foundation stones of the gospel, but on the fact of Christ's resurrection almost every great Christian theme seems to rest. Paul says that it was by His resurrection that Christ was declared to be the Son of God; it was for our justification that He was raised. We are assured of a judgment to come by the fact that God raised Christ from the dead. Our one great assurance of being raised ourselves from the dead is in the conviction that Christ is the first fruits of them who sleep, and that if God raised Him, He will also raise us from the dead.[16] If Christ has *not* been raised from the dead our preaching is vain, our faith is vain, we are yet in our sins, and those that have fallen asleep have perished.

Faith in the Resurrection of Christ Acknowledged to Be the Primary Cause of the Phenomenal Growth and Power of the Early Church. That it was faith in the Resurrection of Christ, and the preaching of this stupendous truth, that gave the early church its power to win thousands and then millions of idolatrous citizens of the great Roman Empire for Christ, though vast multitudes of them in confessing their faith knew they were dooming themselves to torture and social ostracism, is recognized among all who have given any careful consideration to the intricate, difficult problems of the establishment of the Christian church in the Roman world. The rationalist, Dr. Guignebert, in his volume *Jesus,* in the famous History of Civilization Series, who undertakes to deny everything of a supernatural nature in the life of our Lord, including, of course, his resurrection, is forced to make the following confession, "There would have been no Christianity if the belief in the resurrection had not been founded and systematized . . . The whole of the soteriology and the essential teaching of Christianity rests on the belief of the Resurrection, and on the first page of any account of Christian dogma must be written as a motto, Paul's declaration: 'And if Christ be not risen, then is our preaching vain, and your faith is also vain.' From the strictly historical point of view, the importance of the belief in the Resurrection is scarcely less . . . By means of that belief, faith in Jesus and in His mission became the fundamental element of a new religion which, after separating from, became the opponent of Judaism and set out to conquer the world."[17]

To quote a scholar of our own race, himself a modernist, Dr. H. D. A. Major, Principal of Ripon Hall, Oxford, editor of *The Modern Churchman,* "Had the crucifixion of Jesus ended His disciples' experience of Him, it is hard to see how the Christian church could have come into existence. That church was founded on faith in the Messiahship of Jesus. A crucified messiah was no messiah at all. He was one rejected by Judaism and accursed of God. It was the Resurrection of Jesus, as St. Paul declares in Romans 1:4, which proclaimed him to be the Son of God with power."[18]

One of the most pitiful attempts to explain the establishment of Christianity, and its phenomenal power in its earliest days, without recognizing the enormous fact of faith in the Resurrection, is to be found in that historical work, *The Cambridge Ancient History.* In the second volume the late Canon Streeter, considered one of the finest scholars of the English church of our generation, writes the chapter "The Rise of Christianity," which is, it seems to me, one of the most mysteriously chaotic and inadequate accounts of the early church written by any English or American scholar in the last half century. He utterly ignores the influence of the whole conception of the resurrection of Christ in the faith and preaching of the early church. The greater tragedy is that many men, not students of the literature of church history, will take their conceptions of the origin of Christianity from this strange and misleading chapter. More recently, Canon Charles E. Raven, recognized as one of the leading scholars of the church of England, and a prolific writer, also ignoring the resurrection, makes this utterly ridiculous statement: "It was the precise combination of Hebrew religion and Greek science which gave to early Christianity its compelling power and won Europe for the faith."[19] We deny this. We believe that the whole history of the Christian church repudiates such an idea. The great mass of testimonies of reputable church historians refute this. The statement is deliberately false, unsupported and insupportable, by a scrap of evidence. The power of the early church, and this is what Canon Raven is talking about—"its compelling power"—is certainly revealed first of all in the Book of Acts, and if anyone can find in this record any power of "Greek science and Hebrew religion," he is reading a different text than that with which I am acquainted. There is no Greek science here at all, and as far as the Jewish religion giving the apostles any power in their preaching, except as they allowed the prophecies of the ancient Scriptures to testify to the Messiahship of Jesus, we will find that Judaism, from the day it crucified Christ, to the very end of Paul's life, was bitterly, viciously, hatefully opposed to the spread of the Christian faith. How can a scholar write such a sentence as that, when all the evidence which anyone can assemble utterly contradicts it?

Christ's Resurrection Always an Inseparable Part of the Faith of the Church. From the first day of its divinely bestowed life, the Christian church has unitedly borne testimony to its faith in the Resurrection of Christ. It is what we may call one of the great fundamental doctrines and convictions of the church, and so penetrates the literature of the New Testament, that if you lifted out every passage in which a reference is made to the Resurrection, you would have a collection of writings so mutilated that what remained could not be understood. The Resurrection entered intimately into the life of the earliest Christians; the fact of it appears on their tombs, and in the drawings found on the walls of the catacombs; it entered deeply into Christian hymnology; it became one of the most vital themes of the great apologetic writings of the first four centuries; it was the theme constantly dwelt upon in the preaching of the ante-Nicene and post-Nicene period. It entered at once into the creedal formulae of the church; it is in our Apostles' Creed; it is in all the great creeds that followed. In one of the most commendable books on Christian doctrine that has appeared for a long time, by a contemporary scholar, namely, *Christian Doctrines* by Dr. J. S. Whale, is as stirring a statement of this truth as I have seen for a long time, and, by permission of the publishers, I take the opportunity of quoting it to my readers: "To say that God revealed himself in Jesus, or that God was in Christ reconciling the world unto himself, is to say nothing of real meaning unless we take our stand with the New Testament at one decisive point. That point is where God manifests Jesus as the Son of God with power, by the Resurrection from the dead.

"All evidence of the New Testament goes to show that the burden of the good news or gospel was not 'Follow this Teacher and do your best,' but, 'Jesus and the Resurrection.' You cannot take that away from Christianity without radically altering its character and destroying its very identity. It is the presupposition, explicit and implicit, of every chapter in the New Testament. At the Cross, the Christian Church sees not merely a striking illustration of the Sublime, but the Sublime in omnipotent action. If the Passion had ended with the Cry of Dereliction in the darkness; if the immemorial problem of evil and pain is only intensified by the Cross; if he came, not to the rescue like a second Adam, but only to the old hopeless fight against sin and death, why should mortals worship this fellow-mortal as their victorious Saviour? If, after all is said, he is one more unfortunate gone to his death, the pathos of man's mortality is increased rather than lessened, and the dark riddle of human existence is darker, for ever. So far from unravelling the knot of human death, this death ties it tight once and for all; and the Christian faith, so far from lightening the burden and the mystery of all this unintelligible world, is its supreme and most pathetic illustration."[20]

The Evidence Affirming That the Body of Jesus Was Interred in the Tomb of Joseph of Arimathaea. We know more about the burial of the Lord Jesus than we know of the burial of any single character in all of ancient history. We know infinitely more about His burial than we do the burial of any Old Testament character, of any king of Babylon, Pharaoh of Egypt, any philosopher of Greece, or triumphant Caesar. We know who took His body from the cross; we know something of the wrapping of the body in spices, and burial clothes; we know the very tomb in which this body was placed, the name of the man who owned it, Joseph, of a town known as Arimathaea. We know even where this tomb was located, in a garden nigh to the place where He was crucified, outside the city walls. We know minute details concerning events immediately subsequent to our Lord's entombment, that a stone was rolled against the tomb, that this stone was sealed, and that, by the wish of the Jews, Roman guards were set before the tomb to prevent the body being stolen. We have four records of this burial of our Lord, all of them in amazing agreement, the record of Matthew, a disciple of Christ who was there when Jesus was crucified; the record of Mark, which some say was written within ten years of our Lord's ascension; the record of Luke, a companion of the apostle Paul, and a great historian; and the record of John, who was the last to leave the cross, and, with Peter, the first of the Twelve on Easter to behold the empty tomb.[21] Now, we have many historical records of events occurring in the Near East in the first half of the first century of our era, which records have many things to say concerning such characters as Herod the Great, and his son, Herod Agrippa, Pontius Pilate, and Caiaphas, etc., facts that are not found in the Word of God, some of these records being in Roman histories, and many of them found in the pages of Josephus. But we do not have one single sentence about the burial of Jesus, outside of the Gospel records, anywhere in Greek, Roman, or Jewish literature in the first three centuries of our era. In other words, all we know about the burial of Jesus we know from our New Testament. We cannot know anything additional, or contrary to these records, because there is no other contemporary statement concerning this particular event. If we believe the Gospels are valid as historical documents, we receive this evidence as true. If, of course, we do not believe the Gospels are valid historical documents, and thus place ourselves outside of the whole tendency of contemporary historical scholarship, we cannot say anything about the burial of Jesus, because we know nothing about it.

Professor Guignebert, to whom we have referred above, in his work *Jesus,* makes the following utterly unfounded statement: "The truth is that we do not know, and in all probability the disciples knew no better, where the body of Jesus had been thrown after it had been removed from the cross, probably by the executioners. It is more likely to have been cast into the *pit* for the executed than laid in a new *tomb.*"[22] What are the references for the support of such a statement as this? None whatever! Guignebert makes no reference here to any literature of the first three centuries. He presents no historical evidence for this statement. He denies the fact which the four Gospels clearly set forth, that the body of Jesus was placed in the tomb of Joseph of Arimathaea. Denying this he presents no evidence to contradict it, but makes a statement which proceeds out of his own imagination. In fact, one would say his statement about the body of Jesus proceeds not alone from his imagination, but from his preconceived determination to refuse to believe in the Resurrection of Christ. Professor Guignebert is forced to admit, as every modern scholar is, that the tomb of Joseph of Arimathaea on Sunday morning was empty. To avoid the significance of this empty tomb, and to propose some theory to account for its being empty, refusing at the same time to believe in the Resurrection of Christ, Professor Guignebert creates a theory of his own, by which the body of Jesus was never placed in the tomb of Joseph of Arimathaea. Now, whether we are Christians or not, whether we believe Christ was the Son of God, or not, our very processes of reasoning, our insistence upon evidence, if we insist on it (and if we do not, there is no need of discussing any of these things), condemn the theory of the French professor, and we dismiss it, as being utterly without historical foundation, and for this reason not deserving further consideration, in studying the four *historical* documents we have in front of us, known as the Gospels.

This question of the burial of our Lord in the tomb of Joseph of Arimathaea has received frequent, careful consideration, but Dr. W. J. Sparrow-Simpson in his wonderfully rich and too little known volume, *The Resurrection and Modern Thought,* from which we take the liberty of quoting the following, has, we feel, dealt with the matter most satisfactorily: "The Roman practice was to leave the victim of crucifixion hanging on the cross to become the prey of birds and beasts. But who would dream of saying that there were no exceptions to this rule? Josephus induced the Emperor Titus to take down from the cross three crucified persons while still alive. Would any one argue that this cannot be historic because the rule was otherwise? The Jewish practice, no doubt, was the burial of the condemned. This was the Jewish law. But Josephus assures us that even the Jews themselves broke the law of burial at times. In the 'Wars of the Jews,' he writes: 'They proceeded to that degree of impiety as to cast away their dead bodies without burial, although the Jews used to take so much care of the burial of men, that they took down those that were condemned and crucified, and buried them before the going down of the sun.'

"Loisy thinks that relatives might obtain permission for burial of one condemned. No relative, however, obtained it for Jesus' body: nor any of the Twelve. The three crucified men whom Josephus induced the imperial authority to take down from the cross were not relatives; they were only friends. He 'remembered them as his former acquaintances.' A strong case might be made out against the likelihood of Josephus' request, still more of its being granted. No one, however, appears to doubt the facts. They are constantly quoted as if they were true. Why should not Joseph of Arimathaea make a similar request to Pilate?" [23]

The Testimony of the Empty Tomb. The two primary testimonies, and there are many secondary ones, to the fact of Christ's Resurrection, have always been recognized as resting upon two facts, concerning which the New Testament is most emphatically insistent, and we believe transparently clear: the fact that the tomb in which Jesus was buried was, on Sunday morning of the same week, found to be *empty,* and the fact that Christ Jesus, in His own risen body, *appeared* to His own disciples. We will consider these two lines of evidence, with considerable detail, in this order.

No man has ever written, pro or con, on the subject of Christ's Resurrection, without finding himself compelled to face this problem of Joseph's empty tomb. That the tomb was empty on Sunday morning, is recognized by everyone, no matter how radical a critic he may be; however anti-supernatural in all his personal convictions, he never dares to say that the body was still resting in that tomb, however he might attempt to explain the fact that the tomb must have been empty. Professor Denney, years ago, emphasized the importance of this particular fact, when he said that, "the empty grave is not the product of a naive apologetic spirit, a spirit not content with the evidence for the Resurrection contained in the fact that the Lord had appeared to His own and had quickened them unto new victorious life; it is not the first stage in a process which aims unconsciously as much as voluntarily at making the evidence palpable, and independent, as far as may be, of the moral qualifications to which we have already adverted; it is an original, independent and unmotived part of the apostolic testimony. The whole mysteriousness of the Resurrection is in it; in combination with the appearances of Jesus, and with all that flowed from them, it brings us to a point at which the resources of science are exhausted, the point at which the transcendent world revealed in the Resurrection touches this world, at once enlarging the mind and bringing it to a stand."[24]

The Witnesses to the Fact That the Tomb Had Become Empty. The evidence pertaining to the fact that the tomb of Joseph of Arimathaea, in which the body of Jesus was placed on Friday, was empty of that body on Sunday morning, is more abundant than one would think upon the first reading of the Gospels. First of all, the women who had carefully watched from a distance the burial of Jesus in this very tomb, coming back to it within a period of seventy-two hours found, to their utter astonishment, that the stone was rolled away and the body was gone.[25] We will consider some theories about the testimony of these women a little later: we allow the narrative to stand as it reads for the time being. They rushed back to Jerusalem, and reported this to the apostles, two of whom, Peter and John, not mystics from a cloistered cell, but hard-fisted fishermen of the sea of Galilee, hurried away from Jerusalem to see if what the women told was true, they not believing the story. *They found the tomb empty*. Moreover, the women found two angels sitting before the tomb, who frankly said to them, "He is not here. He is risen, come see the place where the Lord lay." Furthermore, the guards who were appointed to watch that tomb came into the city Sunday morning, and reported the tomb was empty. Finally, the Sanhedrin itself bears witness to the fact that the tomb was empty, because they concocted a story which they commanded the soldiers to thereafter repeat to explain how the tomb became empty, namely, that the body was stolen by the disciples. There is, then, a fivefold testimony to the fact itself. Whatever theories have been proposed to explain the Resurrection of Christ, they will all acknowledge the fact of an empty tomb. In the most rationalistic Christological literature of our day there is not even the suggestion that these witnesses were falsifying a report.

The First Attempt to Escape the Testimony of an Empty Tomb. Let us now face the question which every intelligent student of this problem, rationalist and believer, must consider: how did the tomb of Joseph of Arimathaea become empty? It will probably surprise a great many Christian people, whatever be their professed love for the Word of God, to be told that the first theory ever proposed to rationalistically explain away the phenomena of this empty tomb on Easter morning is found in the Bible itself—a most remarkable passage which somehow rarely ever receives careful consideration from New Testament students. We refer to St. Matthew's account of the report of the soldiers, who had been assigned to watch the tomb by the Jewish authorities. Let us first read the passage carefully and then give it some detailed consideration. "Now while they were going, behold, some of the guard came into the city, and told unto the chief priests all the things that were come to pass. And when they were assembled with the elders, and had taken counsel, they gave much money unto the soldiers, saying, Say ye, His disciples came by night, and stole him away while we slept. And if this come to the governor's ears, we will persuade him, and rid you of care. So they took the money, and did as they were taught: and this saying was spread abroad among the Jews, and continueth until this day."[26]

It should be noticed first of all that the Jewish authorities never questioned the report of the guards. They did not themselves go out to see if the tomb was empty, because they knew it was empty. The guards would never have come back with such a story as this on their lips, unless they were reporting actual, indisputable occurrences, as far as they were able to apprehend them. The story which the Jewish authorities told the soldiers to repeat was a story to explain how the tomb became *empty*. The next thing to be noticed here is that these soldiers were bribed to tell a story, they were paid to report a lie, a lie concocted by the same men who earlier had sought false witnesses by whose testimony they might condemn Jesus to death.[27] What a large part money played in the wicked condemnation of our Lord, and in this first attempt to deny the fact of His Resurrection: Judas Iscariot betrayed Him for money; now soldiers are bribed to tell a lie about what happened at the tomb. The ordinary instincts of any honorable man for honesty and fairness will make him revolt in disgust from believing such a story as these soldiers were paid to tell—this is bribery, and, according to the laws of any state, bribery is a crime, it is a mark of corruption, it is always related to an attempt to suppress the truth. That, in itself, destroys the value of the subsequent story of these soldiers. If, however, you look carefully at the words which they were paid to report, you will notice a strange inconsistency. In a simple sentence they were told to say that *while they were asleep* the disciples came and stole the body of Jesus. Whatever might happen late some night in front of your home or in front of my home, leading, let us say, to murder, would be something which city authorities would be compelled to investigate, that they might apprehend the criminal. But if you were asleep when this murder occurred, and continued to sleep through the night, hearing nothing, your testimony in court the next day, whatever be your reputation or your character, would be absolutely worthless, for, being asleep you would not know what had gone on about you. These guards were the ones who did not know what happened to the body of Jesus, if they were asleep, as they said they were, when it was stolen.

Furthermore, the very idea that the disciples of Jesus came and stole the body away is unbelievable, for at least three reasons. In the first place, these disciples were in no mood to go out and face Roman soldiers, subdue the entire guard, and snatch that body out of the tomb. I think, myself, if they had attempted it, they would have been killed, but they certainly were in no mood even to try it. On Thursday night of that week Peter had proved himself such a coward, when a maid twitted him in the lower hall of the palace of the high priest, accusing him of belonging to the condemned Nazarene, that, to save his own skin, he denied his Lord, and cursed and swore.[28] What could have happened to Peter within those few hours to change him from such a coward to a man rushing out to fight Roman soldiers? In the second place, the disciples had absolutely no reason for taking away the body, which had been honorably buried. They could do no more for the body of their Lord than had been done. Joseph of Arimathaea never told them to remove the body from its first burial place; it was not suggested by anyone else; and therefore, if they *had* undertaken such a task, it would only be, not for the honor of the Lord, or for their own preservation, but for the purpose of deceiving others; in other words, to foist a lie concerning Jesus upon the people of Palestine. Now whatever else these disciples were, who had followed the Lord for three years, they were not liars, with the exception of Judas, who was already dead. They were not mean men given to deceit. It is inconceivable that the eleven, after having companioned with the Holy Son of God who, Himself, condemned falsehood and ever exalted the truth, after hearing Him preach a gospel of more exalted righteousness than had ever been heard anywhere in the world before, it is inconceivable that these eleven disciples should all suddenly agree to enter into such a vile conspiracy as this. Most of all, however, the subsequent history of these disciples utterly contradicts, indeed utterly destroys the very possibility of such a diabolical act on their part. It is these disciples who are soon to move out into the world preaching one great truth—that Christ was raised from the dead, by the power of God, and was thus declared to be the Son of God. This truth had already transformed them from cowards, who always were attempting to persuade Jesus not to go up to be crucified, to men of such courage and conviction that they now boldly stood before thousands and frankly accused them of crucifying the Son of God, for which they were soon in prison, frequently beaten, and ultimately put to death. The power of God so came down upon Peter on the day of Pentecost that on that one day, in a sermon occupied, for the most part, with the truth of the Resurrection of Christ, three thousand souls were won to the Lord. One thing is true—*Peter was at least preaching what he believed:* that God had raised Christ from the dead. You cannot conscientiously preach lies with power like this. The disciples went on preaching the Resurrection, until the whole world was turned upside down by faith in this glorious truth. No, the disciples did not and could not have stolen the body of our Lord.

This theory proposed by the Sanhedrin apparently had a wide vogue among the Jews of succeeding generations, for in Justin's *Dialogue Against Trypho,* the Jew speaks of "one Jesus, a Galilean deceiver whom we crucified; but his disciples stole him by night from the tomb, where he was laid when unfastened from the cross, and now deceive men by asserting that he has arisen from the dead and ascended unto heaven."[29] Tertullian likewise, in his famous *Apology* says, "The grave was found empty of all but the clothes of the buried one, but nevertheless the leaders of the Jews whom it nearly concerned both to spread abroad a lie and keep back a people tributary and submissive to them from the faith, gave it out that the body of Christ had been stolen by his disciples."[30] This whole fabricated story about the body being stolen by the disciples "represents, in fact, the bankruptcy of all attempts on the part of the Jews to suggest any other explanation."[31] It is a theory found in no work attacking the validity of the Resurrection narratives today. Something better than this fantastic theory must be proposed even for our modern sceptical mood.

The Theory That the Body Was Removed by Joseph of Arimathaea. From time to time, other theories have been proposed to explain how the tomb became empty, but they (with the single exception we are about to discuss) are insignificant and not of great influence in contemporary Christological discussion. We confine ourselves then to the theory, which if the author may so say, is the only one he has ever heard of that appears to have any reasonableness in it at all, and even then cannot possibly be accepted, if we carefully examine the evidence that is available. This theory has been occasionally suggested by scholars of former generations, but we bring it to the attention of our readers as it is presented by the professor of Hebrew Literature in the great National University in Palestine, Dr. Joseph Klausner, recognized as one of the foremost authorities on Hebrew Literature and history in the world, and the writer of some of the most outstanding works on Hebrew History in our generation. A few years ago, Professor Klausner published a volume which dropped upon theologians in Europe like a bomb, *Jesus of Nazareth,* originally published in Hebrew, then translated into the German, French, and English languages. In this work, Klausner, definitely an orthodox Jew, writes line after line of glorious tributes of the nobility of Jesus. But Klausner, as a scholar, is faced with the problem of the empty tomb, and he has to do something about it. It is his suggestion that the tomb was found empty on Easter morning because the only one who had a right to take out that body, the owner of the tomb, had removed it during the night or early morning.[32] Let us consider this carefully.

First of all, we should clearly recognize that there is absolutely *no evidence* that this was done, nor does Professor Klausner attempt to give one single reference to any literature dealing with the problem. There is not the slightest hint anywhere in the Gospel records that this was what happened. When a theory has absolutely no evidence to support it, it is not something that we can quickly or with confidence embrace. In the second place, there was *no reason* for Joseph removing the body of the Lord, who was his Lord, for he too, as the Scriptures say, was a disciple of Jesus.[33] On the day of our Lord's crucifixion, the city of Jerusalem was seething with hatred for Christ, and when Joseph went to Pilate and begged that he might have the privilege of taking the body of Jesus from the cross, and lay it in his own tomb, he was practically taking his life in his hands. As a member of the Sanhedrin, a counsellor, in revealing his love for the Lord, he would have immediately earned the hatred of these Jews, who were in a good mood to put to death any of the followers of the Nazarene. If Joseph then desired to place the body of his Lord in his own new tomb, even though it might endanger his life, what could possibly have come over him during the next twenty-four or thirty-six hours to so totally change his heart in this matter, that he would be led to dishonor this same body by removing it from its worthy resting place, and hide it in some obscure and dishonorable plot of burial? There is not a single line in the New Testament that would even hint at any reason for Joseph suddenly changing his mind in this matter.

Even if Joseph had wanted to remove the body, and there is nothing to indicate that he did, the problem of the Roman soldiers still faces us. When they were paid to watch that tomb, they were not told to make an exception of Joseph. The Jewish authorities did not say that they were to watch that the disciples only might take away the body, but they were told to watch that the body should not be removed by any one, lest the report get around that Jesus was raised from the dead. They would no more have allowed Joseph to take out that body than they would have allowed one of the disciples to do so. And, if it had been Joseph who had removed the body, then what a really good, believable story the soldiers would have had to tell to the Jewish authorities on Easter morning. That would have been enough, and the Sanhedrin would have been saved the trouble and expense of creating a foolish story, and bribing the soldiers to repeat it.

Finally, we must consider what such an act on the part of Joseph would have meant in the later history of the apostles. It is significant how many adjectives are used to describe the character of this man Joseph. In Mark, we read that he was "an honorable counselor," and in Luke that he was "a good man and a just."[34] Now, an honorable man, a good man, a just man, is a man who tells the truth and who would not purposely, deliberately deceive others. It is inevitable that Joseph, a disciple of Jesus, would be in frequent touch while they were in Jerusalem with the other disciples of Christ, bound together as they were by one great love and loyalty. Sooner or later, Peter and John, and the other disciples, would be meeting Joseph of Arimathaea. The apostles, having seen the empty tomb, and being convinced of the Resurrection of Christ, would joyfully witness to this glorious fact when they first saw Joseph, after Easter morning, whenever that might be.

Now, if the apostles were glad because, having seen the empty tomb, they believed Jesus was raised from the dead, and Joseph had himself removed the body of Jesus, creating an empty tomb, what would he, as an honorable man, have been compelled to say to those rejoicing disciples? He, by the sheer force of his own honesty and goodness, would have felt himself solemnly obligated, however much pain he caused, to tell those disciples that the tomb was empty because he had removed the body of Jesus. But, he never told the disciples that, for had he done so they would not have gone out preaching the resurrection of Christ. It would have been the end of their confidence in such a miracle. It would have meant the collapse of their faith in a risen Lord. The theory of Professor Klausner has nothing really to support it, and everything to oppose it.

The Theory That the Women Went to the Wrong Tomb. Recently two scholars have proposed the theory that the women who found a tomb empty on Easter morning, for one reason or another failed to get to the tomb of Joseph of Arimathaea, but stopped in front of another tomb in which no body had been recently placed. This is not the theory of some erratic or demented person, as one might imagine upon first hearing of such an idea, but of two outstanding New Testament scholars of our day, Professor Kirsopp Lake, and Dr. Gardiner-Smith.[35] They believe that the reason the women missed the tomb was that they were convulsed with sorrow, their eyes blinded with tears, and hardly knowing where they were going. Let us consider this for a moment. In the first place we believe that it was utterly impossible for these women to make such a mistake on that particular day. If we have to travel to a distant city for the burial of a loved one, it is reasonable to expect that, if the cemetery was previously unknown to us, coming back to the place ten years later, we would have to ask someone to guide us to the plot of ground where the body of our loved one was resting. But the circumstances of this case are altogether different. These women had carefully watched where this body of Jesus had been interred, less than seventy-two hours before their visit which revealed to them the astonishing fact that the tomb was empty. Do you think that you or I, or these women, or any other rational person, would forget in seventy-two hours, the place where we had laid to rest our dearest loved one? Furthermore, we read that when these women ran back to the city and reported what they had experienced to the disciples, Peter and John, hurrying back to the burying place, also found the tomb empty. Is it to be argued that not only these tear-blinded women, but Peter and John also went to the wrong tomb? I doubt if their eyes were blinded with tears. Furthermore, an angel, sitting here on a stone said, "Come see the place where the Lord lay." Did the angel make a mistake too? Someone has suggested, in trying to force this theory of a mistaken tomb, that the angel's words really meant, "You are in the wrong place, come over here to see where the Lord's body was placed." Well, in nineteen hundred years of the study of the New Testament, it took our modern, sophisticated age to find *that* in the Gospel records, and no trustworthy commentary on any of the Gospels entertains such a foolish interpretation as that. There is something else here also to consider, and that is that this was not a public cemetery but a private burying ground, and there was no other tomb there which would allow them to make such a mistake. The whole idea is so utterly fantastic that Professor A. E. J. Rawlinson, no conservative, in his epochal commentary on St. Mark's Gospel, felt compelled to say of Lake's suggestion "that the women went by mistake to the wrong tomb, and that the attempt of a bystander to direct them to the right one was misunderstood, is a rationalization which is utterly foreign to the spirit of the narrative."[36]

No doubt you will ask yourself as I have often asked myself, why do these men propose such foolish theories, without a shred of evidence? Well, I have my own idea which may be exactly what your idea is; if I expressed it in my own words, a liberal picking up this book would say I was unfair with those who disagree, and that I had made an unjust accusation concerning the search for truth on the part of the rationalists. So, instead of using my own words, let me place before you a verdict given some time ago by a noted English scholar, in what every one recognizes to be the most notable theological liberal quarterly of our century, *The Hibbert Journal,* edited by a Unitarian who himself, denies the bodily Resurrection of Christ. This is the verdict of Professor Morse, which the editor of *The Hibbert Journal* allowed to be published: "Their theory that the women were approaching the wrong tomb arises, not from any evidence, but from disbelief in the possibility of the supernatural emptying of our Lord's tomb." That is exactly my opinion. Of course, as everyone knows, Professor Lake has become more and more radical, and extremely rationalistic, so that, even years ago he denied the very value of prayer. Dr. Gardiner-Smith, in a later work, while still at a loss how to explain what happened on Easter morning, does not even hold to the theory which some years before he had proposed, that the women went to the wrong tomb, which I take to be a confession that his own former theory no longer satisfies him.[38]

The Swoon Theory. All theories which have been proposed to explain the apostolic faith in the Resurrection of Christ, and in the disappearance of Christ's body, admit that our Lord actually died, i.e., all theories but one. Some have dared to propose that our Lord never did die on the cross, but that He only *swooned* away, and, though placed in the tomb of Joseph of Arimathaea, He was not dead. Those who hold this theory are more or less compelled to supplement it by saying that Christ came out of the tomb by His own strength, after recovering from this swoon state. Even Strauss, however, who did not at all believe in the Resurrection of Christ, repudiated such a fanciful idea as this with scorn. His words are famous, and worth repeating: "It is impossible that one who had just come forth from the grave half dead, who crept about weak and ill, who stood in need of medical treatment, of bandaging, strengthening, and tender care, and who at last succumbed to suffering, could ever have given to the disciples that impression that He was a conqueror over death and the grave,—that He was the Prince of Life,—which lay at the bottom of their future ministry. Such a resuscitation could only have weakened the impression which He had made upon them in life and in death,—or at the most could have given it an elegiac voice,—but could by no possibility have changed their sorrow into enthusiasm, or elevated their reverence into worship." [39]

There are many other objections to the theory, the main one being, if Christ did not die at this time, then when did He die, and under what circumstances? Furthermore, as Professor Milligan has well said, "When the first fears of the disciples were dispelled, it was one of joy, of boldness, and of enthusiasm; we see none of those feelings of pity, of sympathy with suffering, of desire to render help, that must have been called forth by the appearance of a person who had swooned away through weariness and agony, who had continued in unconsciousness from Friday afternoon to Sunday morning, and who was now only in the first moments of recovery." [40]

An Illustration of How Modern Scholars Are Driven to Impossible Extremes When They Are Determined to Deny the Resurrection of Christ but Are Faced with the Fact of the Empty Tomb. The author trusts he will be allowed at this point to introduce a paragraph on this subject of the empty tomb out of his own experience and correspondence. Five years ago I took the liberty of writing some twenty outstanding authorities in New Testament literature in this country, asking them how they accounted for the tomb of Joseph of Arimathaea being found empty on Easter morning. Most of these men, I knew as I wrote, were of a liberal turn of mind. In my correspondence I said I would not divulge their names, in any public way, if they chose to frankly reply to my letter. I have never broken this promise, and no one today knows to whom I am about to refer; moreover, the person whose reply I would now consider has since died. There was no promise not to generally discuss the replies and I think I am not in any way violating the original agreement in what I am about to say. To begin with, I should like to state that the answer to which I am now referring was a very, very gracious one indeed, not sarcastic, or bitter, or a vindictive communication at all, in fact, a real outreach for friendship. It was written by one who had been teaching then for some forty years, in one of our largest theological seminaries, a member of a conservative body of believers (though not teaching in a seminary belonging to his own denomination), one who had received a Ph.D. degree in Germany toward the end of the last century, and was the author of perhaps ten or twelve books in the field of New Testament criticism. In his letter he admitted that once he had believed in the Resurrection of Christ but that he could no longer do so because, he said, his students who had been trained in science would not accept such a doctrine! But coming to the matter of the empty tomb, he said he could no more explain how the tomb of Joseph of Arimathaea had become empty on Easter morning than he could explain how Santa Claus comes down the chimney at Christmas time! Now, of those who may be reading this volume, let us never forget that there is one vast difference between the problem of Santa Claus coming down the chimney at Christmas time, and the problem of the empty tomb of Joseph of Arimathaea—just one vast difference, and that is this: there never was a Santa Claus, and therefore he never came down a chimney, but there was a Jesus, and He was buried, and on Sunday morning the tomb in which His body was placed was found to be empty. Santa Claus coming down a chimney at Christmas time is no historical problem—we abandon such myths when we are six or seven, but the disappearance of the body of Jesus from the tomb of Joseph presents a problem which the greatest scholars of every age have considered, and about which a thousand times a thousand pages have been written. I do not know how you feel, but my heart is heavy when I find a New Testament scholar, past the age of seventy, having to resort to the kindergarten fable of Santa Claus in trying to escape the evidence for the empty tomb of our Lord.[41]

Of Only the Founder of the Christian Faith Is an Empty Tomb Claimed. Of the four great religions of the world resting directly upon personalities, rather than upon some philosophical system, the Christian religion is the only one that even talks about an empty tomb in relation to its founder. Abraham, the father of Judaism, died somewhere about 1900 B.C., but no resurrection has ever been claimed for Abraham. In fact, his tomb has been most carefully preserved for almost four millennia, in Hebron, in southern Palestine, now covered with a Mohammedan mosque, recognized by almost all authorities on biblical history as being the genuine burial place of the great patriarch. The original accounts of Buddha never ascribe to him any such thing as a resurrection; in fact, in the earliest accounts of his death, namely, the *Mahaparinibbana Sutta,* we read that when the Buddha died it was "with that utter passing away in which nothing whatever remains behind." One of the outstanding modern authorities on Buddhism, Professor Childers, says, "There is no trace in the *Pali* scriptures or commentaries (or so far as I know in any Pali book) of Sakya Muni having existed after his death or appearing to his disciples."[42] Mohammed died June 8, 632 A.D., at the age of sixty-one, at Medina, where his tomb is annually visited by thousands of devout Mohammedans. All the millions and millions of Jews, Buddhists, and Mohammedans agree that their founders have never come up out of the dust of the earth in resurrection.

To go aside from these great oriental religions to consider for a moment our much less significant and far less reasonable modern cults, let us remember that the one who, herself, said that death was something unreal, in fact, that there was no death, is held in the chains of death in a burial plot outside of Boston, where her grave is visited by many of her deceived followers each year. I refer to Mrs. Mary Baker Eddy.

A Final Word Concerning the Importance of the Evidence for the

Empty Tomb. The evidence for the reality of the disappearance of th body of Jesus from the tomb of Joseph of Arimathea is so overwhelm ing that we find scholars on every hand who, in their own minds, hav already rejected the miraculous Resurrection of Christ continuall baffled as how to explain this phenomenon. One of the strangest state ments any scholar has made is the following of Dr. Kirsopp Lake, "Th empty tomb must be thought out on doctrinal, not on historical or criti cal grounds."[43] The only reason why Professor Lake does not want t think out this problem on historical grounds is because the historica evidence is so definite, and abundant, that a man who sets out to resis it has a conviction that he cannot succeed, and that his case will no win. The *meaning* of the resurrection is a theological matter, but th fact of the resurrection is a historical matter; the nature of the resur rection body of Jesus may be a mystery, but the fact that the bod disappeared from the tomb is a matter to be decided upon by historica evidence. The place is of geographical definiteness, the man who owne the tomb was a man living in the first half of the first century; tha tomb was made out of rock in a hillside near Jerusalem, and was no composed of some mythological gossamer, or cloud-dust, but is some thing which has geographical significance. The guards put before tha tomb were not aerial beings from Mt. Olympus; the Sanhedrin was body of men meeting frequently in Jerusalem. As a vast mass of litera ture tells us, this person, Jesus, was a living person, a man among me whatever else He was, and the disciples who went out to preach th risen Lord were men among men, men who ate, drank, slept, suffere worked, died. What is there "doctrinal" about this? This is a historica problem. It is time our young people stood on their feet and told u believing teachers that they are going to consider this from the stan point of history. It is time that our younger generation, talking so muc about freedom, assert itself, and at least exercise its right to consider narrative like this apart from the blinding and antagonistic prejudi of anti-supernaturalistic teachers. As the great Canon Liddon once sai preaching in St. Paul's, London, "It is the central sanctuary of ou Christian faith. No other spot on earth says so much to Christian fait as does the tomb of our Lord. Observe, it is 'the place where our Lor *lay.*' He lies there no longer. He was not lying there when the ang addressed Mary Magdalene. With most tombs the interest consists in the fact that all that is mortal of the saint or hero or the near relative rests beneath the stone or the sod on which we gaze."[44]

The Testimony of Christ's Post-Resurrection Appearances—The Appearances Enumerated. We come now to the second great body of evidence proving, we believe, the resurrection of Jesus Christ from the dead, i.e., His appearances to the believers between the morning of His resurrection, and His ascension forty days later. It is generally believed, whatever one may think of these so-called post-resurrection appearances of our Lord, that we have in the New Testament ten different occasions on which the Lord is said to have appeared to His followers in addition to His appearances to the Apostle Paul. It will be best, we think, to enumerate these here before we proceed to discuss the meaning of these appearances.

(1) To certain women as they returned from the sepulchre, after having seen the angel who told them Christ had arisen (Matt. 28:1–10).
(2) To Mary Magdalene at the sepulchre, probably upon her second visit to it that morning (John 20:11–18; Mark 16:9–11).
(3) To the Apostle Peter, before the evening of the day of the Resurrection, but under circumstances of which we have no details (Luke 24:34; I Cor. 15:5).
(4) To the two disciples, Cleopas and another, on the way to Emmaus, on the afternoon of Easter (Mark 16:12, 13; Luke 24:13–35).
(5) To the ten apostles, Thomas being absent, together with others whose names are not given, assembled together on the evening of Easter day at their evening meal (Mark 16:14–18; Luke 24:36–40; John 20:19–23; I Cor. 15:5).
(6) One week later, to all the eleven apostles, probably in the same place as the preceding appearance (John 20:26–28).
(7) To several of the disciples at the sea of Galilee, while they were fishing, the exact time undesignated (John 21:1–23).
(8) To the apostles, and above five hundred brethren, at once, on an appointed mountain in Galilee (Matt. 28:16–20; I Cor. 15:6).

(9) To James, under circumstances of which we have no informatio (I Cor. 15:7).

(10) To the apostles at Jerusalem, immediately before the ascensio on the Mount of Olives (Mark 16:19; Luke 24:50–52; Acts 1:3–8

General Characteristics of These Appearances. We should remin ourselves in studying this evidence that these appearances were of gre variety. Two of them were to single individuals, one on Easter mornin to the apostle Peter, and one, we do not know where or when, to Jame Others were to the ten apostles, or to the eleven, and one to five hur dred brethren, gathered together in one place. Some of the appearanc were to men, and some to women; contrary to all custom at that tim the first appearance of our Lord after His resurrection was to a woma The appearances occurred in different places, some in the garden ne His own tomb, some in the Upper Room, where previously the Lord Supper had been instituted; some on the highway from Jerusalem t Emmaus; and others far north in Galilee. On each occasion, both th acts and the words of our Lord show great variety—His words are n framed in a single mold, as the new theories related to form-criticis insist. Indeed, we have no words at all for some of His appearance e.g., to Peter, and James, which is the strangest thing in the world these appearances were later produced by the imagination of the apostle Of Mary Magdalene He could ask, "Woman, why weepest thou?" T some He granted permission to clasp His feet. To her, for sufficie reason, He said, "Touch me not; for I am not yet ascended to m Father." To the assembled disciples He gave a message of peace an assurance, persuading them He was not a spirit; to the disciples on th Emmaus road He opened the Scriptures, showing that Christ mu needs suffer and rise again from the dead; to certain disciples at th sea of Galilee, He gave a commission regarding the feeding of H sheep, asking Peter, and only Peter, if he loved Him—the whole narr tive incapable of being produced out of imagination. To the di ciples, near to the time of the ascension, He gave the Great Commissio The words of Jesus spoken after His resurrection are natural, and y they are remarkable, and in one way quite amazing. The things H spoke about of a natural character would be the last things that an lisciple, in a far subsequent age could have imagined: think of our ord going down to the sea of Galilee where some of His disciples were ishing, and saying, first of all, not "let us praise God," not "let us pray," ıot "Hallelujah, I am risen!" but, "Have ye anything to eat?" On the ther hand, the words bear the mark of triumph, of victory, of the urden of a world mission, and the foreknowledge that some of His lisciples must suffer for Him. They are the words of a risen Redeemer, he words of command, the words of a universal Saviour, the words of he Son of God. There is nothing else in all literature like this.

Another thing we should remember regarding these appearances of ur Lord is that they were wholly unexpected. One of the most interestng passages in the Bible, one which many Christians seem not to know, f my own experience at Bible conferences has any weight, is the statenent in Mark 16:10, that when Mary Magdalene went and told the lisciples on Easter morning that the tomb was empty, she found them nourning and weeping. The disciples were so far from expecting their ord to rise from the dead, even though He had said again and again, He would, that they would not believe the women when they reported he tomb was empty. They were utterly astonished and frightened vhen He appeared to them in the Upper Room, on Easter night, and hought it was a spirit. These appearances could not have been prouced, as we shall see shortly, by the feverish imagination created by rooding over the hope that they would soon see the risen Lord, for hey had no such hope. They were disappointed and downcast, knowng He had died, and believing they would never see Him again on arth.

The Empirical Nature of This Evidence. About a year ago, after udying over a long period of time, this entire problem of our Lord's esurrection, and having written some hundreds of pages upon it at ifferent times, I was suddenly arrested by the thought that the very ind of evidence which modern science, and even psychologists, are so nsistent upon for determining the reality of any object under considration is the kind of evidence that we have presented to us in the ospels regarding the Resurrection of the Lord Jesus, namely, the hings that are seen with the human eye, touched with the human and, and heard by the human ear. This is what we call empirical evidence. It would almost seem as if parts of the Gospel records of th Resurrection were actually written for such a day as ours when empiri cism so dominates our thinking. I had intended writing a page or tw on this aspect of the evidence of Christ's Resurrection in this presen volume when, belatedly, I read a volume which I wish had been in m hands many years ago, namely, that monumental work, *The Resurrec tion and Modern Thought,* by Canon W. J. Sparrow-Simpson, in whic I noticed that this particular subject was developed with great detai I would like to bring the results of his own personal investigation t the attention of my readers, by the kind permission of the publisher who have allowed me to use these extended extracts. In relation to th sense of sight, Canon Sparrow-Simpson says: "This is naturally first, a the initial form of gaining their attention. It is described in the Gospe by various expressions: 'Jesus met them.' 'They saw Him,' but this see ing included those who doubted. 'They knew Him.' 'They . . . sup posed that they beheld a spirit.' 'See (*eideo*) My hands and My fee that it is I Myself; handle Me and see, for a spirit hath not flesh an bones as ye behold (*theoreo*) Me having. And when He had said th He shewed unto them (*deiknuo*) His hands and His feet.' Similar also in the fourth Evangelist: 'I have seen the Lord.' 'He shewed unt them His hands and His side.' 'They saw the Lord.' 'Except I shall se in His hands the print of the nails.' 'Because thou hast seen Me.' 'An none of His disciples durst inquire of Him, Who art Thou? knowin that it was the Lord.' 'Appearing unto them by the space of forty days

"Appeal is made by the Risen Lord in these Appearances to th marks of the wounds inflicted in the Passion. St. Luke speaks of th hands and the feet. St. Matt. mentions neither. St. John mentions 'H hands and His side.' "[45]

In relation to the sense of touch, we turn again to the fine sum mary of our learned author: "By far the most emphatic words in th respect are those in St. Luke: 'Handle Me and see; for a spirit hat not flesh and bones, as ye behold Me having.' Here it is that moder thought chiefly recoils. Flesh and bones! Here we have the Resurrectio in its most realistic gross and earthly form. And this is not all. For th passage continues that He asked for food. 'And they gave Him a pie of a broiled fish. And He took it, and did eat before them.'

"But this is a confusion of thought. For all the human senses are variations of the sense of touch. That is the primitive form out of which ll the human senses originated. And every appeal to the senses is an ppeal through the medium of material processes. Nothing but that which is material is verifiable by human organs of sight. The appeal to ight is, essentially, as material as the appeal to touch. If the person of he Risen Christ was verifiable by human sight, the form of its appearance was just as truly materialized as any solid body can be. The idea hat what appeals to sight is less material than what appeals to touch s a popular confusion of the ethereal with the spiritual. It is popular, ut it is wholly unphilosophical."[46]

Now in regard to the words which the disciples heard, and which hey have recorded for us in these precious Gospel narratives, a careful ummary of Canon Sparrow-Simpson's deserves the weightiest consideration: "But more than this, the sayings of the forty days are marked y the same qualities of *identity* and *difference* which has been already oticed in the Appearances themselves. They show identity of mind and urpose with the utterances of the Jesus of the ministry. There is the ame searching, penetrating knowledge of the human heart, the same everity mixed with tender compassion, as in words spoken before He ied. There is the same assumption of authority, only more lofty and nearthly than before. There is also a concentration into special comnands of thoughts and teachings found in the previous period of the isciples' training. There is the conferring of new powers which nothing but the Resurrection can explain. The notion that these utterances vere really spoken during the ministry, and were transferred to the nterval after the death, is singularly refuted by their contents and by heir implications. They belong to the period where the Evangelists ave set them: to that period, and neither before it nor after it.

"But together with this quality of identity, there is, equally conspicuus, the quality of *difference* in the whole bearing of the Risen Lord owards His disciples. There is an indescribable remoteness in the apparently simple but yet profound saying, 'These are my words which spake unto you, *while yet I was with you.*' While I was yet with you: simple is the phrase, we might easily miss its force. Was He not 'with hem' at the very moment when He uttered the phrase? He was no

longer 'with them' in the former terrestrial way. It is an express re
minder that He has not returned to the old conditions. The earlier stat
of existence will never again be resumed. And, significantly, this wa
spoken at the very time of His most materialistic self-revealing; even
while He disclaimed a purely immaterial existence, and took food, and
ate it before them. Hence also His words to Mary Magdalene, while
gently disentangling Himself from her desire to detain Him: 'touch
Me not for I am not yet ascended . . . I ascend.' *There* is the dominan
note of difference.

"Now while every appeal to the human senses is an appeal to the
mind and spirit, there is a higher appeal in words, because they are the
more direct revelation of self. In His words the Risen Lord offers the
highest proof of His identity. The recognition of a person is partly based
on physical identity, but ultimately on spiritual identity. The testimony
of the apostolic age is that they knew Him again not merely by sight
and touch, but by the deeper evidence of personality." [47]

Renan's Mythological Reconstruction. More than a century ago th
French rationalist Renan, in his feeble and long ago repudiated attemp
to explain how the early church came to believe in the Resurrection o
Christ, with no evidence whatever to support his theory, in his usua
brilliant style, in referring to the visit of Mary Magdalene to the tomb
declared, "We must follow her step by step for during one hour of tha
day she carried within her all the workings of the Christian consciou
ness. Her testimony decided the faith of the future . . . At such dec
sive hours a breath of air, a rattling window, a chance murmur ma
decide the belief of nations for centuries." [48] Hardly any serious studen
of this century has dared reaffirm Renan's ridiculous hypotheses, an
for that reason we were the more amazed to discover that Professo
Joseph Klausner, in his book *From Jesus to Paul,* begins his chapte
"Jesus of Nazareth in the Conception of His Disciples," with a quota
tion from this passage of Renan's rationalizing of the life of Christ, giv
ing it his own approval, adding, "His memory was preserved from th
beginning by three women among them Mary Magdalene from whom
seven demons had gone out; that is to say, a woman hysterical to th
point of madness." Then Klausner makes this concession, though o
course he most emphatically repudiates the Resurrection of Christ, "Th

memory of Jesus was not blotted out as was the memory of the other false messiahs because of the story of His Resurrection." He then asks how it was that Jesus and not some other false messiah made such a strong impression upon His disciples that they believed He had been raised from the dead. Among the ten things fixed and preserved in the minds of the disciples, which kept alive the memory of Jesus, the last one, according to Professor Klausner, is "that Jesus after He was crucified rose from the dead and ascended to heaven, having been seen in a vision by Mary Magdalene and her companions and afterwards by Simon Peter and his companions." Later in the same work, he says that upon the death of Jesus the disciples were delivered from such disillusionment by "belief in the resurrection of the dead. By means of the resurrection it was proved to them that God had exalted His Messiah, as the latter had been degraded by the crucifixion."[49] Klausner admits that faith in Christ was kept alive by faith in His Resurrection, but how this faith was ever established so that these men spent their lives preaching this truth with such power that the whole Roman world was convulsed, and how this matter of the Resurrection became a corner stone of Christian doctrine, Klausner does not pretend to tell us.

When it comes to this foolish idea of Renan which Klausner accepts, that a little blowing of the wind or the rattling of a window decided the belief of multitudes for centuries, I very much like the deservedly biting reply of Christlieb, "Windy hypotheses in good sooth," "Did ever unbelief give a more flagrant proof of its inability to afford a natural explanation of divine facts than this? Woe be to us if a breath of air may at any time chain us and our posterity for centuries to a momentous error from which there is no escape, especially if we happen to be in an excited frame of mind! How thoroughly must one who can thus speak, have given up all belief, even in the *moral* harmony of the world, to say nothing of a holy providence! Unbelief delivers mankind of its choicest treasures, all its moral religious convictions, to the mercy of the merest chance, and here we see in glaring colors *how deeply, in consequence of this, it degrades man, and how shamefully it defiles his moral dignity.*"[50]

The Vision Hypothesis. Probably the most accepted theory among rationalists today who, on the one hand, are determined not to believe that Christ rose from the dead, but, on the other hand, are face to face with a considerable body of evidence in historically accredited narratives, such as appear in the Gospels, is the so-called vision theory. In fact, a great many men who are not, in themselves, skeptical, are also found holding such a theory as this, and it deserves our most careful consideration. First of all, the theory, itself, as set forth by one who holds it should be before us for consideration, and I take the liberty here of quoting from Professor Klausner's work, *Jesus of Nazareth,* in which he devotes an entire chapter to the subject of Christ's Resurrection. These are Klausner's words: "Here again, it is impossible to suppose that there was any conscious deception: the nineteen hundred years' faith of millions is not founded on deception. There can be no question but that some of the ardent Galileans saw their Lord and Messiah in a vision. That the vision was spiritual and not material is evident from the way Paul compares his own vision with those seen by Peter and James and the other Apostles. As to his own vision we know from the description in the Acts of the Apostles and from his own account that what he saw was no vision of flesh and blood but a vision 'born of the light,' 'a heavenly vision, in which God had revealed in me His Son.' Consequently, the vision seen by the disciples, a vision which Paul deliberately compares with His own, was a spiritual vision and no more. This vision became the basis of Christianity: it was treated as faithful proof of the Resurrection of Jesus, of His Messiahship, and of the near approach of the kingdom of heaven. But for this vision the memory of Jesus might have been wholly forgotten or preserved only in a collection of lofty ethical precepts and miracle stories. Could the bulk of the Jewish nation found its belief on such a cornerstone?" [51]

A vision is generally received by one person at a time. There is no such thing as a vision appearing to a crowd. We could believe that the women at the tomb, somewhat excited and bewildered, would be subject to such an experience, but what about hard-headed Peter, and doubting Thomas, and then what about the five hundred brethren to whom Jesus appeared at one time? This is not the way visions are experienced by people in any age. Moreover, as Professor LaTouche has well said, "The principal conditions of vision-seeing are time for the visions to arise, and a state of mind, ecstatic and unbalanced, which is favorable to the adoption of convictions without critical examination. Neither of these conditions existed in the case of the disciples. The resurrection took place on the third day after the crucifixion, and all the appearances, with one exception, were completed within forty days. The disciples were depressed and despairing, never dreaming that they would again see those sacred features, or hear those well beloved tones on this side of the grave; and finally, when a great number of them were gathered together, they saw the Lord. Nothing is more remarkable in the whole history of Christianity than the dull perception of the disciples; they persisted in their unspiritual and material conceptions of the kingdom of God even after the resurrection was an accomplished fact; and they were sufficiently unexpectant, after they had heard of four distinct appearances of the risen Lord, to be terrified when He appeared to them on that first Easter evening, and attempted at first to account for the phenomena by this very theory of visions, or hallucination, for they cried out, thinking that He was a spirit! This fact, that the ghost theory occurred to them, and that they tried to explain some of their earlier experiences by it, is a valuable testimony to the normal state of their minds when they saw the Lord, and ought to commend their witness to those who are still attempting to account for the appearances by this theory." [52]

But this is not all there is to say about this widely-accepted theory. The questions raised by Dr. John McNaugher are definitely to the point, and clearly indicate how unfounded, after all, the theory is seen to be when carefully considered. "If the post-mortem appearances of Jesus were just visions, why did they end so suddenly, all lying within six weeks? What cured these visionaries of their hallucinations so speedily and cured them simultaneously? How did flurried fanaticism yield so quickly to sobriety? Self-generated visions tend to become exuberant, tend to multiply. Phantasmal appearances ought to have intensified the emotional excitement from which they sprang, and thus ought to have continued as long as the distempered, diseased minds of the disciples could have furnished soil for such a crop of illusions. But within forty days the appearances ceased abruptly and permanently. The vision theory provides no explanation of this fact." [53]

Though many conservative scholars have revealed the insufficiency and the irrationality of this vision theory, probably no one has spoken of it more incisively than Theodore Christlieb, in his epochal work, *Modern Doubt and Christian Unbelief,* from which I should like to quote in part, the conclusion of his discussion of this particular aspect of our Lord's resurrection. He says that those who propose the vision theory "are compelled to suppose that the passionate imagination of the disciples stretched out its feelers after their indispensable Master. Instead of this, we see that on each occasion He appears to His followers *quite unexpectedly;* so much so that at first they will not believe and He must rebuke their unbelief. It is clear that they were not prepared for the immediate reappearance of Jesus. *Here the psychological precondition of visions is wanting. The deep dejection on account of their Master's shameful death could scarcely give wings to a new and joyous faith.* We see the poor, shepherdless sheep in fear of the Jews, in doubts and conflicts respecting their Messianic hopes, in perplexity as to the future. These are not the frames of mind from which ecstatic visions might be expected to proceed, but rather the contrary." And then speaking of the fact that these appearances were often to many people at once, Christlieb says: "We do not deny that science can tell us of cases in which visions were seen by whole assemblies at once; but where this is the case, it has always been accompanied by a *morbid excitement of the mental life,* as well as by a morbid bodily condition, especially by nervous affections. Now, even if one or several of the disciples had been in this morbid state, we should by no means be justified in concluding that all were so. They were surely men of most varied temperament and constitution. And yet, one after another is supposed to have fallen into this morbid condition; not only the excited women, but even Peter, that strong and hardy fisherman who was assuredly as far from nervousness as any one, James, the two on their way to Emmaus, and so on down to the sober, doubting Thomas, aye, and all eleven at once, and even *more than five hundred brethren together.* All of these are supposed to have fallen suddenly into some self-deception, and that, be it noticed, at the most different times and places, and during the most varied occupations (in the morning by the grave; in conversation by the wayside; in the confidential circle of friends at work on the lake); in which their frames of mind most assuredly have been very varied and their internal tendency to visions most uneven. And could they, all of them, have agreed to announce these visions to the world as bodily appearances of the risen Christ? Or had they done so, could it have been pure self-deception and not intentional deceit? Surely, some one or other of them must afterwards seriously have asked himself whether the image he had seen was a reality. Schleiermacher says most truly, 'Whoever supposes that the disciples deceived themselves and mistook the internal for the external, accuses them of such mental weakness as must invalidate their entire testimony concerning Christ and make it appear as though Christ Himself, when He chose such witnesses, did not know what was in man. Or, if He Himself had willed and ordained that they should mistake inward appearances for outward perceptions, He would have been the author of error, and all moral ideas would be confounded if this were compatible with His high dignity.' "[54]

The concluding sentences of Professor Milligan, one of the great scholars of the last generation, after a long discussion of this vision theory, can be profitably quoted as we, too, bring our discussion of this particular theory to a conclusion. "Of these objections, the vision theory is undoubtedly the most formidable; but it, as well as the others that have been mentioned, fails to satisfy the indispensable conditions of inquiry. It also, therefore, must be rejected and we have no legitimate resource but to acknowledge the fact. We may be thankful that it should be so. We may believe that the Church of Christ has not grounded her life and hope for eighteen centuries upon a delusion; and, in the fact of either denial or scorn, we may assert that our words are those of truth and soberness, when we proclaim that He who died upon the cross rose on the third morning from the grave."[55]

The So-called Telegram Theory. We have one more theory to consider, and this one of the strangest that has ever been devised, that which has been called the "Telegram" theory, the latest advocate of which is no less a scholar than the late Canon Streeter, recognized as probably the outstanding British authority of our generation on the critical problems of the Gospels. This theory assumes that the ascended Lord, i.e., ascended in His Spirit, not (in such a theory) of course in His body, *telegraphed* back (if we may use the phrase) pictures of Himself to the minds of the Apostles, in such a vivid way that they actually were led to believe they had seen the risen Lord in their midst.[56] Just how any true scholar can ever consider such a fantastic theory as this, we do not quite know. For one thing, it is more of a manifestation of supernatural activity than even the Resurrection itself would be. And then, such telegraphed visions, or messages, or pictures, if they were real, would not have remained in the minds of the Apostles for hours: you cannot conceive of a telegraphic message so real that it developed from moment to moment like a moving picture in the minds, say, of the two disciples, as they walked the Emmaus road. But the most important and truly fatal objection to the whole theory is this, that Christ, had He undertaken to communicate such pictures to the minds of the Apostles, would have actually participated in deluding the disciples, for they would then be led by something that Christ Himself did to believe Christ had appeared to them in His actual bodily presence, whereas no such appearance had taken place, and He, instead of being near them, was in reality, unknown to them, in the glory above. This is not the way our Lord brings about conviction in the hearts of men!

The Relation of the Appearances of Christ to the Fact of the Empty Tomb. It should be carefully noted that the two facts, that the tomb of Joseph of Arimathaea was empty on Easter morning and that Christ definitely, visibly, purposely appeared on certain occasions during the days immediately following His Resurrection to His own disciples, are corollaries. Even if we did not have the evidence for the empty tomb, we do have the testimony of the disciples to Christ's post-resurrection appearances; and vice versa. On the other hand, we could not have a tomb with a body, and any real bodily resurrection appearances. One involves the other. We can only have true appearances of Christ in His own body after the resurrection if the tomb of Joseph of Arimathaea is empty, and that it was empty allows for the appearances, and the appearances explain the empty tomb. Had anyone carried away the body of Christ, the post-resurrection appearances of the Saviour would have been impossible. Together the testimonies for these two stupendous facts form, indeed, a mass of evidence that can never be destroyed with any of the laws of literary criticism, or of logic, known to men. They have, consequently, stood the fiercest opposition, investigation, and criticism, of at least eighteen successive centuries.

The Purpose of Christ's Appearances. In considering the various detailed empirical evidences of sight, hearing, and touch for our Lord's Resurrection, we must always beware of the subtle danger of forgetting the spiritual aspects of this, the greatest of all miracles. Not only did our Lord truly appear to His disciples, but He in so appearing had a definite spiritual purpose in mind. Professor William P. Armstrong of Princeton has done well to emphasize this for us in his article of some years ago, "The Resurrection of Jesus," and his words deserve repeating in this study:

"If Jesus sought to quicken faith in His message and in Himself before His death, it is but natural that His activity subsequent to His death and resurrection should have been directed toward the same end. The purpose, therefore, of the appearances to those who had faith in Him must be understood in the light both of Jesus' work of implanting a true faith and of the relation of the resurrection to such a faith. This faith, both before and after Jesus' death, had for its essential content Jesus the Messiah. Of this content, however, Jesus' own self-consciousness and perfect knowledge of His work were the standard, into conformity with which, in its measure, it was necessary that faith in Him should be brought. In other words, the work of informing faith was, equally with that of quickening faith, an essential part of Jesus' work. The Gospel records of the earthly ministry of Jesus reveal how much He did to give to faith an adequate content. This work He continued after His resurrection both by personal intercourse with His disciples and after His ascension through the agency of the Holy Spirit. Since the resurrection stood in closest relation to Jesus Himself, and to the content of faith, which before His death He had sought to perfect, it was but natural that the self-revelation of Jesus after His resurrection should have been made to those of faith. The Gospel records reveal plainly the fact that the appearances of Jesus had a very direct relation to faith. They were intended,—and hence their recurrence and the words of instruction which accompany them,—to inform the faith of the disciples in regard to Jesus Himself and His work. This informing of faith consisted primarily in the self-revelation of Jesus in such a manner as to convince the disciples not only of His resurrection, but also of His entrance into a life in which His Messianic power and authority were henceforth to be exercised, without restriction of time and space, in the interest of His Messianic kingdom."[57]

The Historic Certainty of the Resurrection of Our Lord. Having now placed before our readers the evidence for the two principal lines of testimony to the reality of our Lord's having been raised from the dead, we might, perhaps, at this point close the entire discussion of this aspect of the truth we are considering by listening for a moment to what some of the historical scholars of our day have themselves said about the final verdict, which reason leads us to render. First of all we should remember the words of a great scholar of many centuries ago, a world traveler, a master of the Greek language who has written what has often been called "the most beautiful book in the world." I refer to St. Luke, a man accustomed to scientifically considering any subject which he is studying. Luke says at the beginning of his second book, the Acts of the Apostles, that our Lord showed Himself alive after His Passion "by many infallible proofs," or more literally, "in many proofs."[58] The word here translated proofs is from a Greek word *tekmairomai* which means to fix by a mark, to appoint, to preserve some certain signs, and then, to conclude. The verb comes from a root *tekmar,* meaning a fixed mark or boundary, and then, a sure token. Now of all the writers in the New Testament, Luke was the one who knew better than any of them, from his own medical experience, that it was utterly impossible for a dead body to come to life again by its own power. He was also a man who would have no faith in such a great doctrine as the Resurrection of Christ, were it based upon a vision, a hallucination, a mental excitement, or the blowing of the wind, or the rattling of a window. It is a conviction of this scientist and scholar, true Grecian, and true Christian, that the Lord manifested himself to His disciples "in many proofs."

Professor Edwin Gordon Selwyn in his able apologetic work of a few years ago, *The Approach to Christianity,* did not use one phrase of extravagance when he said, "The fact that Christ rose from the dead on the third day in full continuity of body and soul, and passed into a mode of new relationships with those who knew him on earth—that fact seems as secure as historical evidence could make it."[59]

Later in this chapter we will consider the convictions of some of the great characters of history regarding the truth of Christ's Resurrection, but here we are only using expressions which relate to the validity and sufficiency of the evidence itself. With one added testimony we close this particular part of our discussion. Probably the most distinguished authority in our country in the field of the ancient history of the near east, especially Assyria and Babylonia, is Dr. A. T. Olmstead, the Professor of Oriental History in the University of Chicago, and author of a number of monumental works in the field of ancient history. In 1942 Professor Olmstead published his work, *Jesus in the Light of History,* which aroused a great deal of discussion on both sides of the Atlantic. We are not here taking up some of the many vigorous disputed assertions in this work of Professor Olmstead's, but are interested only in what this historian has to say about the Resurrection of Christ. These are his words, "Such is the outline of the Resurrection appearances . . . Our picture may not be quite exact, but it cannot be far wrong. These stories must have originated within a few days after the discovery of the empty tomb, and have been written down within the first few years after the organization of the primitive church (note this carefully, a most overwhelming contradiction of all those theories concerning the Resurrection which demand a long lapse of time between the death of Jesus and the Resurrection story) . . . The appearances cannot be reckoned as mere literary devices. Not only do they betray their primitive character, they do not hesitate to relate to their discredit, the doubts of their church leaders, written down and circulated while those leaders were yet living and able if they wished to refute them."[60] So, St. Peter, certainly the outstanding figure throughout the earliest days of the church, until the advent of the great Apostle Paul, some thirty years at least after the Resurrection, with thirty-five years of experience with Jesus, and in preaching Christ, could write to fellow Christians and unbelieving Jews throughout the world that all who believed with him "had not followed cunningly devised fables when we made known unto you the power and coming of the Lord Jesus Christ."

The So-called Contradictions in the Resurrection Narratives. One of the inexcusably weak and logically unjustified ways that modern rationalists have of getting rid of the whole problem of the Resurrection of our Lord, and the evidence supporting it, is to slurringly speak of what they call the "contradictions" in these narratives, as though just the use of the word "contradiction" is enough to destroy the whole great massive structure built up by the evidence of the Gospels. This is the way Dr. Harry Emerson Fosdick deals with the subject, in his widely-used and strangely overrated work, *A Guide to Understanding the Bible,* "Certainly if the idea of Jesus' risen life started with any factual elements associated with an empty tomb, that element was never clearly visualized, even in the imagination of the first disciples, and is now confused for us in narratives that contradict each other in every important detail." [61] Now these narratives do not contradict each other "in every important detail." The truth is that in every *important* detail they are in total agreement and when, in spite of this, Dr. Fosdick dares to make the statement we have just quoted, he is saying something that is not true, and because Dr. Fosdick has really been reading and studying the Bible for many years,—well, I leave the sentence unfinished.

If the four Gospel narratives of the events connected with our Lord's Resurrection are placed in parallel columns, a number of differences will at once be discovered. But this seems ultimately to strengthen one's conviction in the validity of these records, rather than weaken it. No one of the Gospels gives all the details of the events, even of Easter Sunday. Only Luke gives a detailed account of the walk to Emmaus; only Matthew gives a record of the first appearance to the women; Matthew and Luke never mention the appearance to Mary Magdalene; only St. John tells us of the second appearance to the eleven Apostles, with Thomas present; he also is the only one who gives the beautiful picture of the later appearance on the sea of Galilee. Only Matthew records the appearance to a great multitude of brethren. None of the four evangelists gives us any details regarding the private appearance to James, and only Luke, among the four, even refers to Christ's private appearance to Peter on the day of the Resurrection. Furthermore, we must remember that "no two men see the same thing exactly in the same way, or receive from it precisely similar impressions. If they are faithful to themselves, they must differ from one another, and it is the province of the impartial judge to disentangle different statements, and to determine whether the fact as a whole or how much of it, is true . . . Statements directly and positively contradictory as to the main point at issue would, undoubtedly, justify our rejecting it; but where the main point is admitted by every witness, slighter divisions are not only perfectly consistent with its truth, but are of the utmost importance for establishing it." [62]

In the great fundamental facts of our Lord's Resurrection, all the narratives are in absolute agreement, namely, that Christ's body was placed in a tomb of Joseph of Arimathaea on Friday afternoon; that this tomb was sealed with a great stone, and that before it guards were set to keep it from violation; that on Easter morning, when women came to the tomb, they found the stone rolled away and the body gone; that on Easter morning these early visitors were told by an angel that the Lord had risen indeed; that during the day our Lord appeared at least on five different occasions; that in all cases of Christ's appearances during these forty days, He showed Himself only to believers; that He showed Himself in a true body, His person identical with the person of the Lord with whom these disciples had walked for three years; that during these days He gave to His disciples the great commission to evangelize the world; that all these experiences abruptly terminated forty days after the Resurrection, when our Lord was taken up from their midst, as they beheld Him, and received into heaven. In these fundamental truths, there are absolutely no contradictions. The so-called variations in the narratives are only the details which were most vividly impressed on one mind or another of the witnesses of our Lord's Resurrection, or on the mind of the writers of these four respective Gospels. The closest, most critical, examination of these narratives throughout the ages never has destroyed and can never destroy their powerful testimony to the truth that Christ did rise from the dead on the third day, and was seen of many.

As to the minor differences which we all admit are present, Bishop Headlam, in a recent work of his, *Christian Theology. The Doctrine of God,* has some sensible things to say: "Take for example the battle of Waterloo. If you read the many narratives of persons who were present at the battle you will find remarkable discrepancies between them. To take an instance. Not long ago there was a discussion in the papers on which of the days before Waterloo it was that the famous ball took place. Yet no one doubts the reality of the ball. Or take an event nearer our own time. Most of us have talked to those who were in the battle of Jutland, yet how difficult it is to get a coherent and satisfactory account of that battle. It appears to become more difficult the larger the number of eye witnesses it is possible to consult. Each person present has seen just one particular part and formed his own conception of the whole. Yet no one doubts that the battle of Jutland was really fought . . . The necessity of harmonizing independent accounts does not take away from the truth of the event. In fact, it is a condition of truth. Supposing that all the narratives of the Resurrection in the four Gospels and in St. Paul's exactly harmonized, it would be apparent that they all came from one source and they would have no independent value. It is because there are different stories and accounts of events after the Resurrection, clearly independent of one another, but witnessing to the same fundamental conditions, but from different points of view, that we have grounds for a strong conviction of the truth that underlies all the narratives."[63]

If our readers who have thus far followed our discussion of this important subject are at all acquainted with even a fragment of that portion of contemporary Christological literature in which the miraculous aspects of Christ's life on earth are denied, or at least diminished to almost a vanishing point, they will, we believe, be in full accord with the assertion which the present author makes in this paragraph, that a great many carelessly written, historically inaccurate, and logically unfair sentences have been written by men producing learned works on the life and work of Christ, which deceive the ordinary Christian into believing that in our sophisticated day, an intelligent man can no longer afford to believe in the Resurrection of Christ and that those who did so believe in the early church were either ignorant, superstitious, or extremely gullible. I know of nothing in contemporary religious literature that reveals the deliberate determination of many so-called authorities in New Testament criticism to wreck the faith of men in the miraculous aspects of Christ's incarnate life than their wicked, unfair statements categorically casting aside the evidence which we have found to be more than sufficient for convincing a normally intelligent and unprejudiced person of this supreme, divine manifestation. The most exhaustive work on the Acts of the Apostles in the twentieth century is the five-volume work carrying the title *The Beginnings of Christianity,* by Dr. F. J. Foakes Jackson and Professor Kirsopp Lake. In the first volume of this, in many ways, scholarly work, we find this sentence, "It is particularly necessary to remember that the New Testament does not present the intellectual accuracy of a theological autopsy, but the confused language of men whose religion was too much for their powers of expression."[64] This sounds very clever, and has no doubt deceived many. Let us look at it for a moment. It means that such men as the Apostle John, and St. Luke, and the Apostle Paul, two of them brilliant men, with the finest kind of education, did not have the intelligence to examine accurately this problem of the Resurrection, such intelligence as, for example, Professor Jackson and Professor Lake have. They will not believe in the Resurrection; the early Christians we know did; and so, the early Christians must be put down as intellectually incapable of passing upon the validity of historical evidence, even if it was of that century. More than that, the writers of the New Testament who have discussed the Resurrection are said to have expressed their ideas in a "confused language." Well, I would like just here to quote the verdict of one of the greatest classical scholars of our century, the outstanding authority on Homer of all American scholars, Dr. John A. Scott, Professor of Greek in Northwestern University for the last forty years, at one time President of the American Philosophical Association, and at one time President of the Classical Association of the Midwest and South. Writing at the age of seventy, certainly at a time of mature and ripened convictions, in his too-little-known work, *We Would See Jesus,* Professor Scott says this of the author of the third Gospel and the Book of Acts, "Luke was not only a Doctor and historian, but he was one of the world's greatest men of letters. He wrote the clearest and the best Greek written in that century."[65] Young people want to be careful these days that they do not allow grossly erroneous statements concerning the writers of the New Testament, from the pens of rationalists, to be lodged in their minds as something worth believing.

The Implication Forced upon Us by the Multiplicity of Theories Proposed to Rationalistically Explain Away This Miracle. No doubt what we are about to say in this brief paragraph has already come into the minds of all my readers. If so many different theories have been proposed to rationalistically account for the faith of the early church in the Resurrection of our Lord, e.g., that it is all a fraud, that the body was stolen either by the disciples or by Joseph, or by somebody else, that after all the Lord was never in this tomb, or that He never died, or that the women went to the wrong tomb, the vision hypothesis, the telegram theory, and all the others proposed at different periods during the last nineteen centuries, by minds of different capacities, and different temperaments, winning followers for a time, and then being laid up on the shelf of the museum of Christological speculation, does not all this really show that no theory has ever been proposed that has been able to win the consent and approval of the great body of men who have predetermined in their own minds that there could not be such an event as the bodily Resurrection of Christ? If after 1900 years of such theories and hypotheses, beginning with a lie the Sanhedrin concocted that first Easter morning, right down to the present, not one is accepted today as *the* conception generally held by those who deny the miraculous aspects of Christianity, are we not forced to conclude that no really satisfactory theory is going to be found, even with centuries more of denial, scheming, criticizing, and theorizing? The reason why no theory has ever been proposed, which meets the needs of an unprejudiced, rational person, is because the Lord did rise from the dead, and the evidence for His Resurrection is so overwhelming that by no honorable intellectual device can the evidence be set aside. I do not want to be sarcastic, or mention anything of a fantastical nature, but after looking at this problem myself for about thirty years, I have about come to believe that theories which attempt to explain away the faith of the early church in the bodily Resurrection of Christ are about as foolish as the theory held by a few strange persons in this world that the earth is flat. I do not know how you feel in the matter, but the author, now in middle life, with perhaps not more than a quarter of a century yet to live, cannot afford to take time to read a book attempting to set forth the foolish idea that the earth is flat, and does not see why any of us, after years of study, are under moral obligation to continue to read and study and ponder every new work that comes from a rationalist's brain that refuses to give honest, full, deserved consideration to this stupendous miracle which has moved the world, established the church, destroyed paganism, quickened the lives of millions, and proved a light that no wind of infidelity has ever been able to extinguish.

The Nature of the Body of the Risen Christ. Whether or not the New

Testament told us anything definite about the risen body of our Lord, or left us without any light on this particular problem, the evidence for the reality for this miracle of Resurrection stands. The fact of Christ's Resurrection in no way depends for belief upon what we think of the *nature* of our Lord's risen body. Certainly it is somewhat of a serious problem, and inevitably the question will arise in the minds of everyone studying the subject of our Lord's Resurrection, with what kind of a body did He rise from the grave? I do not think the question should be put aside as one which we should not at least think about. The best brief summary I have ever seen is that by Van Oosterzee, in his commentary on Luke's Gospel, which reads as follows: "It is palpable, not only as a whole, but also in its different parts; able in a much shorter time than we to transport itself from one locality to another; gifted with the capability, in subjection to a mightier will, of being sometimes visible, sometimes invisible. It bears the unmistakable traces of its former condition, but is at the same time raised above the confining limitations of this. It is, in a word, a spiritual body, no longer subject to the flesh, but filled, guided, borne by the spirit; yet not less a body. It can eat, but it no longer needs to eat; it can reveal itself in one place, but is not bound to this one place; it can show itself within the sphere of this world, but is not limited to this sphere."[66]

Bishop Gore, in his well-known lectures on the *Body of Christ,* gives his own opinion of this reverent subject in the following words: "The risen body of Christ was spiritual . . . not because it was less than before material, but because in it matter was wholly and finally subjugated to spirit, and not to the exigencies of physical life. It had become the pure and transparent vehicle of spiritual purpose."[67] Theodore Christlieb, years ago in his epochal work, *Modern Doubt and Christian Belief,* gives an extended discussion on this matter from which we would quote the following: "In this resurrection body the Lord stands during those forty days, as it were, on the boundary line of both worlds; He bears the impress of this as well as a future state of existence. It is therefore no contradiction—as Strauss would have it—that this body sometimes manifested the force of repulsion (when touched), and at other times not (when penetrating through closed doors); for it could do so or not, according to the will of the spirit. Doors could not keep out that which is in a *spiritual* state of existence. Since all matter, too, is well known to be porous, it can form no absolute barrier for the spirit. We cannot wonder, moreover, that this body, being formed from the same essential elements as the former earthly one, should be capable of eating food, though not needing it, especially as the same thing is mentioned in the case of angels (Gen. xviii. 8). *The terrestrial body as such is destined to be spiritualized;* but if this is its destiny, it must also possess the *capability*. This shows us at the same time the reason why the sinless body of Christ could be immediately transmuted. Its purity was the possibility of its transformation."[68]

"The Easter Faith" without the Easter Fact. Some years ago the greatest authority on the early history of Christianity of the 19th century, in continental Europe, Adolf Harnack, gave a series of lectures in the University of Berlin during the winter term of 1899–1900, which, in their English form, were published in a volume carrying the title *What is Christianity?* In this volume Harnack, who was a rationalist, as everyone knows, and denied the miraculous aspects of our Lord's incarnate life, and of course His deity, introduced into contemporary Christian thinking the idea of an "Easter faith," as he called it, without the Easter fact. These are his own words: "The Easter *faith* is the conviction that the crucified one gained a victory over death; that God is just and powerful; that He who is the firstborn among many brethren still lives. Paul based his Easter faith upon the certainty that 'the second Adam' was from heaven, and upon his experience, on the way to Damascus, of God revealing His Son to him as still alive. . . . Certain it is that what he and the disciples regarded as all-important was not the state in which the grave was found, but Christ's appearances . . . Whatever may have happened at the grave and in the matter of appearances, one thing is certain: *this grave was the birthplace of the indestructible belief that death is vanquished, and there is a life eternal* . . . It is not by any speculative ideas of philosophy but by the vision of Jesus' life and death and by the feeling of His imperishable union with God that mankind, so far as it believes in these things, has attained to that certainty of eternal life for which it was meant, and which it dimly discerns—eternal life in time and beyond time. Of every attempt to demonstrate the certainty of immortality by logical process, we may say in the words of the poet:

Believe and venture: as for pledges,
The gods give none."[69]

We regret that this idea of Harnack has been accepted by thousands and thousands of men who minister the Word of God in the pulpits of our day, and is found scattered everywhere in contemporary religious literature. Somehow, men seem to think that they are expressing something exceedingly spiritual, when they talk about the Resurrection of Christ not having to do with any such a thing as His body. They seem to have an abhorrence for anything physical, as it relates to Christ, and go back to the old Greek conception, which is philosophical but not according to divine revelation, that the body is only a curse, and the quicker we get rid of it the better. Let us remember this, that death's victory first begins in separating the soul from the body, and carrying that body down into a grave and into a condition of dissolution. If that body forever remains separated from the soul, then death has won a permanent victory. If, as Dr. Harry Emerson Fosdick and many others affirm, the dust of the body of Jesus is still in the ground of Palestine, then death defeated Christ. To say that Christ is "alive" is not in any way to say that Christ is risen from the dead. I believe St. Peter is alive, and St. Paul is alive, and your mother and my mother in heaven, are alive, but they are certainly not raised from the dead. The God of Abraham, Isaac, and Jacob is not the God of the dead, which means that even Abraham, Isaac, and Jacob are alive. To say merely that Christ is "alive" is not to distinguish Him in any way from any other great believer in God, who has died in the past ages. If the body of Christ is in the ground of Palestine, Christ was defeated by death. What is the use of talking about Easter *faith* unless we have an Easter *fact?*

This past Easter (1944) an article appeared in *The Christian Century,* of five columns in length, entitled, "The Resurrection Fact." I had read some rather amazing confessions of the editor of this weekly in the last few years, in which he acknowledged the failure of modernistic theology and gave evidence of moving toward a full belief in the Christianity of the New Testament. Our heart leaped with joy as we saw before us so long an editorial emphasizing the Resurrection *fact.* But when we got into it, what did we discover but that the "fact" which is implied in the Resurrection was here really repudiated. The writer admits that without the post-Resurrection faith of the early Christians, history would know no such thing as Christianity, and then he goes on to talk about the impossibility of harmonizing the "numerous difficulties and inconsistencies" of these New Testament records, adding that they are "artificially enforced. They are convincing only to those whose liberalism treats the Scriptures as a sort of jigsaw puzzle enabling them to connect this clause or statement with another clause or statement in a manner that will produce the result which their fixation on the letter of the Scripture requires." So, in the midst of this editorial on "The Resurrection Faith" the dependability of the Scriptures is repudiated. Frankly, and a little emphatically, I think that men, great giants of intellect, men whose works have been consulted by the scholars of many generations, men like Bengel, Schaff, Bishop Lightfoot, Bishop Westcott, Bishop Ellicott, Dr. A. T. Robertson, Professor James Orr, would justly resent as an insult the fact that they, in finding proof of the bodily Resurrection in the New Testament, were only like a lot of children fitting together "a jigsaw puzzle." Thus in an editorial on the Resurrection, men are really condemned for trying to find the facts. The editor goes on to say that the writers of the Gospels were none of them "eyewitnesses of the things about which they wrote. They set down the tradition which had been in circulation many years after the church was founded." (This is the worst kind of scholarship for, as everyone knows, Matthew and John were eyewitnesses of a risen Lord.) Then, in a sort of smart way, we read that the Resurrection faith does not rest wholly upon scholarship, that the "fact of the Resurrection of Jesus is one thing, the mode of His Resurrection is quite another." Finally the editor tells us what he thinks of the Resurrection fact: "To claim that Christianity rests upon a sensuous experience so obscure and perplexing as the reappearance of the physical body of Jesus is to introduce an utterly incongruous element into the Christian gospel . . . Whatever these occurrences were, and however described, the important fact for us as for them is that He is indeed alive forevermore. . . . The Christian church is the living embodiment in history of the memory of Jesus Christ. . . . Our faith in the Resurrection is therefore not derived primarily from the New Testament writings . . . We must not yield to the illusion which identifies the events with the record of them . . . The *primary* evidence is not in the written record but in the living memory and faith of the Christian church."[70] This is Harnack all over again, the rationalist Harnack. If the writers of the New Testament cannot be trusted in their recording of things they heard, and things they saw, and the things men felt, we wonder how it is we trust their memory so implicitly in what they have told us, not simply that Christ was alive but that they had seen Him, heard Him, handled Him, that He said He was not a spirit, that He showed them His wounds, that He had come out of a tomb—that the tomb was empty and that He, Himself, was appearing in His own glorious and risen body. That is what they *remembered;* and, if this is not our foundation for belief in the actual Resurrection of Christ, we have no foundation, unless we prefer some imaginary experience of our own, or some philosophical reconstruction of a mysterious, psychological experience of these untrustworthy men. The shame, the tragedy, the destructiveness, the deceptiveness, of setting before men today an appeal to exalt the Resurrection *fact* which, upon reading, is discovered to be an argument for denying all the facts which really give us the Resurrection hope.

The Testimony of the Apostle Paul. More is said in the New Testament about the last of all the post-appearances of Christ, namely, the one to the Apostle Paul some years after the Ascension of Christ, than is said about any other of the ten appearances of the forty days between the death and Ascension of our Lord. First of all, we have the original account of appearance of the risen Christ to Saul of Tarsus from the pen of the historian Luke. The event here described is so important that it will be well for us to have the text, itself, before us: "But Saul, yet breathing threatening and slaughter against the disciples of the Lord, went unto the high priest, and asked of him letters to Damascus unto the synagogues, that if he found any that were of the Way, whether men or women, he might bring them bound to Jerusalem. And as he journeyed, it came to pass that he drew nigh unto Damascus: and suddenly there shone round about him a light out of heaven: and he fell upon the earth, and heard a voice saying unto him, Saul, Saul, why persecutest thou me? And he said, Who art thou, Lord? And he said, I am Jesus whom thou persecutest: but rise, and enter into the city, and it shall be told thee what thou must do. And the men that journeyed with him stood speechless, hearing the voice, but beholding no man. And Saul arose from the earth; and when his eyes were opened, he saw nothing; and they led him by the hand, and brought him into Damascus. And he was three days without sight, and did neither eat nor drink." [71] As the first account of Paul's vision of the risen Lord is from the hand of Luke, the other two accounts in the Book of Acts are from the lips of the Apostle Paul, himself, first, before the multitude in Jerusalem which had seized him with the hope of putting him to death. After giving an account of his earlier persecutions of the Christian church, he boldly testified to the convulsive experience that had overwhelmed him on the way to Damascus. "And it came to pass, that, as I made my journey, and drew nigh unto Damascus, about noon, suddenly there shone from heaven a great light round about me. And I fell unto the ground, and heard a voice saying unto me, Saul, Saul, why persecutest thou me? And I answered, Who art thou, Lord? And he said unto me, I am Jesus of Nazareth, whom thou persecutest. And they that were with me beheld indeed the light, but they heard not the voice of him that spake to me. And I said, What shall I do, Lord? And the Lord said unto me, Arise, and go into Damascus; and there it shall be told thee of all things which are appointed for thee to do. And when I could not see for the glory of that light, being led by the hand of them that were with me I came into Damascus." Once again, in his magnificent defense before King Agrippa, with even greater fullness Paul clearly recounted the story of that hour that had changed his life.[72]

It is to this appearance that the Apostle Paul refers in his famous and exceedingly important list of appearances of Christ occurring after His Resurrection, which he places at the beginning of his marvelous chapter on the whole subject of the Resurrection of Christ and all believers. "And that he appeared to Cephas; then to the twelve; then he appeared to above five hundred brethren at once, of whom the greater part remained until now, but some are fallen asleep; then he appeared to James; then to all the apostles; and last of all, as to the child untimely born, he appeared to me also." [73]

The late Professor Doremus A. Hayes, in a volume which is

exceptionally helpful, *The Resurrection Fact,* well reminds us of a number of important details concerning the actuality of this appearance: "It was a veritable appearance of the Resurrected One, but it was different in one respect at least from all which had preceded it. Those appearances had been to believers, disciples, and friends only. This appearance was to the most active enemy the Christian church had. Stephen saw the Risen One when he was filled with the Spirit. Saul had been filled with nothing but hate for this impostor and His cause. He was in no psychological condition for apocalyptical revelation. He was at the farthest remove from the possibility of an ecstatic vision. Nothing but a sudden, unexpected, objective, irresistible revelation of the Resurrected One Himself in the majesty of His divine power could convince and convert a man like Saul. It was such an appearance which was given him.

"It was as real as any of the other appearances had been. At least Paul so considered it. In First Corinthians 15:5–8 he mentions the appearance to Cephas and the appearance to James and other appearances and then adds, 'Last of all, as to one born out of due time, he appeared to me also.' He uses exactly the same verb in all of these cases. He evidently regards the appearance to him as of the same character as all the other resurrection appearances and therefore worthy to be numbered with them. That phrase, 'last of all,' shows that Paul classed this appearance of Jesus with the other resurrection appearances, and at the same time he sharply distinguished it from all the later visions of the Risen Savior which were granted him. He had many visions and revelations from the Lord after this: but they were of a different nature." [74]

No one should question the fact that there are difficulties in the reconciliation of these various accounts of Paul's conversion, but when the text is carefully examined most of the problems disappear. To condense the exhaustive study of Dr. Thorburn, we have the following. In regard to the light, Paul and his companions saw the light but they saw no one, while Paul saw Jesus; the Apostle Paul heard the sound-of-a-voice (*phones*) which means uttering certain words, while those who stood by heard only the *sound;* in the third place, in regard to falling to the earth, Paul admits that he fell down but whether or not they did, in the first account, is not stated, but in the second record Paul says he fell down but his companions "stood speechless." Here, says Dr. Thorburn, the intransitive tenses are often merely a stronger form of the verb "to be" and, therefore, it might at least with equal objective, be translated *they remained there* (i.e., on the ground). Such letters, the falling down, being obviously implied in the letters, they are all said to have fallen down. Dr. Thorburn closes his chapter on this subject with these words, "The objective reality of St. Paul's experience near Damascus is vouched for by a strong line of firsthand evidence corroborated in all essential particulars by the secondary testimony of Luke. The whole tenor of St. Paul's subsequent life and character is explainable only upon the presumption that he both *saw* a vision of the risen Lord, and *heard* from His own lips the commission to be 'a minister and a witness both of the things which he had seen and of those things in which He did appear unto him.' We have been told by a liberal German theologian, Steinmeyer, that even such a radical, Baur, at the close of his life's work, and to the annoyance of many, expressed the opinion that no analysis, either psychological or dialectical, explains the conversion of Paul and that the enigma does not admit of a solution, unless we acknowledge a miracle." [75]

In discussing the appearance of the risen Lord to the Apostle Paul, we must not let this single problem in any way unconsciously result in our forgetting the entire massive continuous testimony which the Apostle Paul bears, in all his preaching, and all his epistles, to the stupendous miracle of Christ's Resurrection, even apart from his experience on the Damascus road. Bishop Headlam has well said in regard to this testimony that here "we are dealing with the beliefs of a power and character whose whole life had been changed by his acceptance of Christianity. He had not accepted that belief lightly, and he had taken trouble to investigate the evidence for himself. He is claiming to tell us (in the fifteenth chapter of I Corinthians) not merely what he preached himself but what the Church taught. The fact that he mentions that most of the five hundred brethren were still alive, plainly implies that he is appealing to living people who can give firsthand evidence." [76] As someone has said, if there was ever a man in the first century who knew all the arguments against the Resurrection of Christ which the Sanhedrin could ever draw up, that man was the Apostle Paul, and yet, in spite of all this, he believed Christ had been raised from the dead by the power of God, and believing this, he preached it everywhere until death took him from the earth.

The Resurrection of Christ the Climax of the Incarnation. A statement in a volume of the late Professor Machen, which, since I first came upon it in those pages I have seen in other writings, has always impressed me as one of significance, something that should constantly be emphasized as we think of the Resurrection of Christ, and especially as we present the evidence for it to the young people of our generation. "You say, my friend, that you have never seen a man who rose from the dead after he had been laid really dead in the tomb? Quite right. Neither have I. You and I have never seen a man who rose from the dead. That is true. But what of it? You and I have never seen a man who rose from the dead; but then you and I have never seen a man like Jesus. Do you not see, my friends? What we are trying to establish is not the resurrection of any ordinary man nor the resurrection of a man who is to us a mere X or Y, nor the resurrection of a man about whom we know nothing, but the Resurrection of Jesus. There is a tremendous presumption against the resurrection of any ordinary man, but when we come really to know Jesus as He is pictured to us in the Gospels, you will say that whereas it is unlikely that any ordinary man should rise from the dead, in His case the presumption is exactly reversed. It is unlikely that any ordinary man should rise; but it is unlikely that *this* man should not rise; it may be said of this man that it was impossible that He should be holden of death."[77]

Possibly Professor Machen took this idea from an earlier volume by one of Britain's finest theologians, a volume which had an enormous influence at the beginning of our century, *Jesus and the Gospel,* by Professor James Denney. His words are so fair, and so forceful, that I would like to take the liberty of bringing them before my readers. We cannot have too much evidence for this stupendous fact of the Resurrection of our Lord, and in the days to come we will need to be more and more intimate with every argument for this supreme miracle. Emphasizing the fact that in the first place this Resurrection of which we are speaking is the Resurrection of Jesus, Professor Denney says: "If the witnesses had asserted about Herod, or about any ordinary person, what they did about Jesus, the presumption would have been all against them. The moral incongruity would have discredited their testimony from the first. But the resurrection was that of one in whom His friends had recognized, while He lived, a power and goodness beyond the common measure of humanity, and they were sensible when it took place that it was in keeping with all they had known, hoped, and believed of Him. When Peter is reported to have said that God loosed the pangs of death because it was not possible that He should be holden of it (Acts 2:24), it is not too much to infer that this was the truth present to his mind. Is it too much to infer that sometimes, when the Resurrection of Jesus is rejected, the rejecter forgets that it is this resurrection which is in question? He thinks of resurrection in general, the resurrection of any one; possibly he thinks of it really as the re-animation of a corpse; and he judges quite confidently, and if this be all that is in his mind quite rightly, that it is not worth-while weighing anything so light against a well-founded conception of reality in general. But if he realized what 'Jesus' means—if he had present to his mind and conscience, in His incomparable moral value, the Person whose resurrection is declared—the problem would be quite different."[78]

The Resurrection of the Body Contrary to Graeco-Roman Conceptions of the After Life. Neither the Greeks, with all their speculations concerning Hades, and their philosophical arguments for the immortality of the soul, nor the Romans, who derived most of their eschatology from the Greeks, ever had the faintest idea that men after being carried off from this earth by death would again possess true bodies. The idea of the resurrection of the body was about as far from the minds of the Greeks as any New Testament truth could possibly be. They not only did not believe in a resurrection of the body, but the principles of Stoic and Epicurean philosophy were unutterably and profoundly opposed to the very idea of a resurrection. Now it is true that the idea of resurrection in relation to some of the gods does occur in Greek literature, and it is also true that certain religious rites were lavishly practiced in the spring of the year by the more devout Greeks, expressing the *idea* of resurrection as it relates to nature; but two things are to be carefully noted here. In the first place, this idea of the resurrection of some of the gods who died is strictly mythical, never historical—no *historical* character in all Greek or Roman history was ever said to have experienced a true resurrection from the dead; the myths were the productions of early Greek thinkers, myths concerning the gods especially derived from Homer and Hesiod. While we grant that the Greeks in their mythology found it imperative that a god who died should come back to life again, and frequently come back to life, every year, they never carry this over, from the experience of fabulous deities on Mt. Olympus to any historical resurrection of a man, following death here upon earth. They could discuss ideas in the realms of the dead, the possibilities of a soul being immortal, and, occasionally, get glimpses of rewards and punishments in another life, but a resurrection for man would have been considered ridiculous to the Greeks, and the Romans. If the Greek did not transfer resurrection myths relating to the gods to the historical experience of men, neither did he relate the spring festivals and religious rites of the return life and vigor of nature to some future experience of the human race. As one who has written exhaustively on the subject has well said: "The idea of a resurrection of the body is contrary to Platonic principles. The entire scheme is to get rid of the body and all of its functions, not to save it. 'The soul is divine, immortal, intelligible, uniform, indissoluble, unchangeable,' but 'the body is mortal' (*Phaedo* 80); the body is the source of endless trouble, and it hinders the soul from the acquisition of knowledge (66); purity is attained only by the separation of the soul from the body (67); the body is an impediment, a hindrance, and the prison of the soul; heaven is reached only in a bodiless condition, in which the soul is free from every taint of the body. The doctrine of immortality had reached its highest point in Plato, and all subsequent writers who dealt with the future life followed in his footsteps. There is one variation, however, and it is utilized by the Fathers, viz., the conception of the Stoics, who taught that the soul is corporeal and that it survives until the world's periodic conflagration. They taught that the entire universe is in a continuous flux, that periodically everything is reabsorbed into Deity, and that the soul subsists until the next reabsorption and conflagration." [79]

In the Athenian address, as we have previously noticed, two great schools of philosophy are particularly noted, the Stoic and the Epicurean. Now the Stoics were fatalists, and also pantheists; they believed that all the troubles in life came from the body, and that the chief end of life was to subdue every bodily appetite and desire, to live as reason ably and sanely as possible, until the hour of death should arrive, when the troubles of this life would be over, because the body had been left behind. Some of the Stoics even went so far as to recommend suicide, so that the soul might escape the body. The Epicureans, on the other hand, "with their thorough-going atomistic materialism would not allow that the soul had any existence apart from the body; on the contrary, they held that the soul came into being at the moment of conception, grew with the body, and at the body's death was once more dissolved into the atoms from which it first was formed." [80]

All the best thought of the Greeks and Romans then, agreed in this, that a resurrection of the body was never to be expected and not to be desired. Recognizing then that the resurrection of men would be ridiculous, illogical, and unbelievable to the Greeks of Athens, one might well ask, "Why then should Paul refer to it as he addressed these philosophers concerning the Lord Jesus Christ?" I think that Canon Sparrow-Simpson has given the one true, acceptable answer: "The introduction of such a doctrine into circumstances eminently unfavourable, might seem to be a failure of that insight and versatility with which we know the apostle was usually endowed to a most exceptional degree. His deliberate selection in this instance of a theme unfavourable to his design surely illustrates remarkably his sense of its fundamental character. It could not, consistently with faithfulness to his message, be possibly left out. Bearing in mind what he said about the Resurrection of Christ in I Cor. xv., we can well understand why he taught it even in Athens. The fact was that S. Paul had no message without it. He had nothing else to teach. He founded Christianity upon it." [81]

The Testimony of Christ's Resurrection to the Truthfulness of His Previous Utterances. One cannot speak to many audiences concerning the Resurrection of Christ without realizing that, before the message is finished, some will be asking, "Well, if it is true that Christ rose from the dead, what is the practical result of that historical event for us today?" I think there are at least four things which we should always remember that the Resurrection guarantees to us. The first is one which is rarely discussed in works dealing with this subject, namely the truthfulness, the dependability of all of Christ's utterances. If our Lord said, frequently, with great definiteness and detail, that after He went up to Jerusalem He would be put to death, but on the third day He would rise again from the grave, and this prediction came to pass, then it has always seemed to me that everything else that our Lord ever said must also be true. If the words concerning His Resurrection were true, then when He said that His precious blood was to be shed for the remission of sins, that is true also. When He said that He came down from the Father above, that the words He spoke the Father had given Him, that He and the Father were one, that He was indeed the Son of God, He was speaking the truth. When our Lord said that whoever would believe on Him would have everlasting life, and whoever refused to believe on Him would be eternally condemned, He spoke the truth. That empty tomb, and the fact of the risen Lord, should assure us forever that when the Lord said He was going to prepare a place for us, that He would come again and receive us to Himself, and also that when the dead heard the voice of the Son of God, they would come forth from their graves, and that He will, Himself, be the Judge of all mankind, He was speaking the truth. There are many difficult things in the New Testament, there are many difficult and profound things in the Gospels, but whether we fully understand every phrase in the Gospels or not, and I am frank to say that I do not, I at least believe that what Christ said was true. We can never accept the Resurrection of Christ, and have any doubt about the truthfulness of any utterance that ever proceeded from His lips.

The Testimony of Christ's Resurrection to the Fact of His Deity. The Apostle Paul, at the very beginning of his epistle to the Romans, in one of the profoundest passages in the New Testament and one of great importance, clearly sets forth the dual nature of our Blessed Lord, in which he affirms that, according to the flesh, Christ is of the seed of David, but that He is declared to be the Son of God *by the Resurrection from the dead.* "He was Son of God throughout; but the reality of His Sonship was concealed by His human infirmities. For to be a Son of God in weakness appears a contradiction of terms. At least it so appeared to the age in which Christ lived. The inferences which men were constrained to draw from His moral uniqueness were compromised, disordered, frustrated, by His apparent failure. If it be said that men ought to have seen through this; the ideal may be granted, yet the fact remains. They did not see the divinity of weakness. Consequently some revelation of the Son of God in power was necessary to contradict the misleading impression of His overthrow. This S. Paul asserts to have been done in Resurrection."[82]

The Relation of the Resurrection to Our Justification. The Apostle Paul in a classic passage tells us that, while Christ died for our sins, He was raised for our justification.[83] Here he certainly implies that that great divine act by which sinners, because of the death of Christ, are justified by a holy and righteous God, is sealed and declared by the Resurrection of the One who died for us. It is, as Mr. Edgar points out, "the positive proof of the sufficiency of the atonement. It is the Father's 'signed manual' that He is satisfied with our Substitute, Sacrifice, our Priest, victim, and that nothing now stands between sinners and forgiveness. All that is needful has been accomplished since Jesus has come back from the dead! Christ embodies reconciliation. He is indeed the Reconciler. In His person we see the Father's righteous demands satisfied, and peace proclaimed between earth and heaven. Pardon, justification, reconciliation are all secured to us in and through our risen Saviour. Easter brought the message of reconciliation unto man."[84]

The Testimony to the Certainty of Our Own Future Resurrection. When our Lord was on earth, He frequently spoke of the resurrection at the last day, and supplemented this truth by the corollary that it was when the dead heard the voice of the Son of Man that they would come forth from the grave.[85] The Apostle Paul carries this truth even further, by the inspiration of the Holy Spirit, when he speaks of Christ as being the first fruits from among the dead, and that we, in that, have the guarantee that the day will come when our bodies would be raised as His. In fact, he tells us elsewhere that we would have in the resurrection a body like unto the glorious body of the now risen Christ.[86] As our Lord was raised from the dead, even will we also walk in newness of life. Where the head is there will the body be also. Our Lord did more than speak of our resurrection. He absolutely guarantees it by His own resurrection. The historic fact of His own rising from the dead is the foundation of our faith that we also shall be raised. No one has dwelt on the profound implications of this particular aspect of Christ's Resurrection more than Canon Barry in the Boyle Lectures which he gave some years ago, in which, in part, he says: "Thus was the certainty of a future resurrection brought out of speculation and hope to the plain light of day. The minds of ordinary men could hardly introduce the subtle reasons of philosophy nor be wholly content with mere promise. They found it hard to dispel, either by mere probability or mere hope, the doctrines which hung over the grave and into which men went down and made no sign. But they could very well understand such declarations as this—'Christ has risen first; as He rose, you who are His shall rise: for such Resurrection is the privilege of the redeemed humanity. Christ is ascended into heaven; He is gone to prepare a place for you, that where He is ye may be forever.' They could understand it, and they showed that they did understand it. What had been at best, the speculation of the wise, or the dream of the saintly became the treasure of all, fixed as one of the great convictions of humanity. How by the knowledge of men, have actually conquered the flesh, defied death, living in the glorious future of heaven, all history tells us." And then Canon Barry goes on in a wonderfully rich way to show how the fact of Christ's Resurrection illuminates the whole subject of the sanctity of the human body. "The identity of the body, even in this ife, depends not on the mere material particles, which are being lissolved and renewed at every moment, but on the impress of ndividuality, which these changes do not impair, and which gives to he body a distinctive character in each one of the countless millions of uman kind. It cannot be incredible that this process of decay and reonstruction—slow and gradual in our earthly life, though strangely udden and complete in lower organisms—should culminate in the ecay of death and the newness of resurrection. St. Paul's argument is rresistible, when he dwells on the mysterious power which from the eed or the first simple cell assimilates, under some hidden law of the nternal structure, the simple physical elements, so as to develop out of common material the distinctions of species and race, even of family nd individual, till the perfect human being stands out, 'fearfully and vonderfully made,' and urges that the same power is surely adequate o work out the change—be it what it may—which shall clothe us in the body of the future, the same, yet not the same, as the body which was mouldered to dust."[87]

Some Confessions of Famous Men in Relation to Their Faith in Christ's Resurrection. There will never be a time when great thinkers will not have the following of great multitudes of people. There never should be a time when certain men in certain fields will not be recognized as authorities, to be followed in what they have to say because of their own genius, their long years of research, their mastery of their subject, their ability to present it clearly, and the later confirmations of their declarations. Even today, men high in our philosophic and theological worlds are tremendously influencing the minds of our young people, and will continue to do so. A young person will say, "Well, there is professor so and so. He is well educated. He has read everything on this or that subject. He seems to love the truth. His mind is open. *He* says he cannot believe in the Resurrection of Christ. I am not as great a scholar as he, and never will be, but I believe in him, and so I will take his verdict for mine." Many people will not care to weigh the evidence for the resurrection for themselves. Some men think they are incapable of doing so, though we believe the Gospels of the New Testament were written for this purpose, and for the common man, as well as the intel lectual. For this reason we have thought it would be worth-while here to bring together, as a body of testimony, the verdicts of some acknowl edged leaders of thought of previous generations, and our own, men whose works have advanced human knowledge, whose names appear in every biographical encyclopedia, and who will have permanent place in the history of human thought, who have confessed their firm convic tion in the Resurrection of Christ.

First of all, and this may surprise many, as it surprised the author o this book when one day he suddenly came upon the statement, there i the remarkable testimony of the philosopher, John Locke, probably th greatest philosopher of his century in Great Britain, and possibly on who will have to be classed as a Unitarian in some of his views. We ar not discussing his theology, but recognizing his place in philosophy We find him making this clear confession of his conviction that Chris rose from the dead. "There are some particulars in the history of ou Saviour, allowed to be so peculiarly appropriated to the Messiah, suc innumerable marks of Him, that to believe them of Jesus of Nazareth was in effect the same, as to believe Him to be the Messiah, and so are put to express it. The principal of these is His Resurrection from the dead; which being the great and demonstrative proof of His being the Messiah, it is not at all strange that the believing His Resurrection should be put forth for believing Him to be the Messiah; since the declaring His Resurrection was declaring Him to be the Messiah. For thus St. Paul argues: 'And we declare unto you glad tidings, how that the promise which was made unto the fathers, God hath fulfilled the same unto us their children, in that he hath raised up Jesus again; as it is also written in the second psalm, Thou art my Son, this day have I begotten thee' (Acts 13:32,33). The force of which argument lies in this, that, if Jesus was raised from the dead, then He was certainly the Messiah: and thus the promise that He was certainly the Messiah was fulfilled, in raising Jesus from the dead . . . Our Saviour's resurrection . . . is truly of great importance in Christianity; so great that His being or not being the Messiah stands or falls with it: so that these two important articles are inseparable and in effect make one. For since that time, believe one and you believe both; deny one of them, and you can believe neither."[88]

We next turn to an American, not a philosopher but an authority in jurisprudence. I refer to Simon Greenleaf (1783–1853), who became the famous Royall Professor of Law at Harvard University, and succeeded Justice Joseph Story as the Dane Professor of Law in the same university, upon Story's death in 1846. It is recognized that "To the efforts of Story and Greenleaf is to be ascribed the rise of the Harvard Law School to its eminent position among the legal schools of the United States."[89] Greenleaf's famous work, *A Treatise on the Law of Evidence,* the first volume of which appeared in 1842, was "regarded as the foremost American authority," passing through edition after edition, is still considered the greatest single authority on evidence in the entire literature of legal procedure. Greenleaf, trained in weighing evidence, while still professor of Law at Harvard, wrote in 1846, a volume that immediately took its place as one of the most significant works on the truthfulness of the Christian religion of his day: *An Examination of the Testimony of the Four Evangelists by the Rules of Evidence Administered in*

Courts of Justice. The author devotes a number of pages to the consic eration of the value of the testimony of the Apostles to the Resurrectio of Christ and I trust that because the one who wrote these lines wa the one who, by his legal works, was quoted thousands of times in th great court battles of our country, for three-quarters of a century, m readers will not be wearied if my quotation from his remarkable discu sion of this evidence is extended to considerable length.

"The great truths which the apostles declared, were, that Christ ha risen from the dead, and that only through repentance from sin, an faith in Him, could men hope for salvation. This doctrine they asserte with one voice, everywhere, not only under the greatest discourag ments, but in the face of the most appalling terrors that can be pr sented to the mind of man. Their master had recently perished as malefactor, by the sentence of a public tribunal. His religion sought t overthrow the religions of the whole world. The laws of every countr were against the teachings of His disciples. The interests and passior of all the rulers and great men in the world were against them. Th fashion of the world was against them. Propagating this new faith, eve in the most inoffensive and peaceful manner, they could expect nothin but contempt, opposition, revilings, bitter persecutions, stripes, imprisor ments, torments, and cruel deaths. Yet this faith they zealously di propagate; and all these miseries they endured undismayed, nay, r joicing. As one after another was put to a miserable death, the survivo only prosecuted their work with increased vigor and resolution. Th annals of military warfare afford scarcely an example of the like hero constancy, patience, and unblenching courage. They had every possib motive to review carefully the grounds of their faith, and the evidenc of the great facts and truths which they asserted; and these motiv were pressed upon their attention with the most melancholy and terrif frequency. It was therefore impossible that they could have persisted i affirming the truths they have narrated, had not Jesus actually rise from the dead, and had they not known this fact as certainly as the knew any other fact. If it were morally possible for them to have bee deceived in this matter, every human motive operated to lead them t discover and avow their error. To have persisted in so gross a falsehoo after it was known to them, was not only to encounter, for life, all th evils which man could inflict, from without, but to endure also the pangs of inward and conscious guilt; with no hope of future peace, no testimony of a good conscience, no expectation of honor or esteem among men, no hope of happiness in this life, or in the world to come.

"Such conduct in the apostles would moreover have been utterly irreconcilable with the fact, that they possessed the ordinary constitution of our common nature. Yet their lives do show them to have been men like all others of our race; swayed by the same motives, animated by the same hopes, affected by the same joys, subdued by the same sorrows, agitated by the same fears, and subject to the same passions, temptations, and infirmities, as ourselves. And their writings show them to have been men of vigorous understandings. If then their testimony was not true, there was no possible motive for its fabrication." [90]

At the time Greenleaf did his most important work, another great legal authority, in Great Britain, was also expressing, though not as fully, his faith in the resurrection of Christ. We refer to John Singleton Copley, better known as Lord Lyndhurst (1772–1863), recognized as one of the greatest legal minds in British history, the Solicitor-General of the British government in 1819, attorney-general of Great Britain in 1824, three times High Chancellor of England, and elected in 1846, High Steward of the University of Cambridge, thus holding in one lifetime the highest offices which a judge in Great Britain could ever have conferred upon him. When Chancellor Lyndhurst died, a document was found in his desk, among his private papers, giving an extended account of his own Christian faith, and in this precious, previously-unknown record, he wrote: "I know pretty well what evidence is; and, I tell you, such evidence as that for the Resurrection has never broken down yet." [91]

Thomas Arnold, for fourteen years the famous Headmaster of Rugby, author of a famous three-volume *History of Rome,* appointed to the chair of Modern History at Oxford, in one of his famous sermons in Rugby Chapel, gave the following testimony to his own persuasion of the historic trustworthiness of the resurrection narrative:

"The evidence for our Lord's life and death and resurrection may be, and often has been, shown to be satisfactory; it is good according to the common rules for distinguishing good evidence from bad. Thousands and tens of thousands of persons have gone through it piece by piece, as carefully as every judge summing up on a most important cause. I have myself done it many times over, not to persuade others but to satisfy myself. I have been used for many years to study the histories of other times, and to examine and weigh the evidence of those who have written about them, and I know of no one fact in the history of mankind which is proved by better and fuller evidence of every sort, to the understanding of a fair inquirer, than the great sign which God hath given us that Christ died and rose again from the dead."[92]

No one can long discuss the history of New Testament criticism, and especially discuss the present test of the Greek New Testament, without mentioning Professor Westcott and Professor Hort, whose edition of the Greek New Testament remains a standard throughout the western world after over half a century. Westcott's writings on the Gospel and the Epistles of John are in many ways the most remarkable volumes on these profound portions of the New Testament which have ever been written. In 1870, Westcott was elected to the Regius professorship of Divinity at Cambridge, a position he held for nearly thirty years. When fifty-four years of age, in the full maturity of a life of study and brilliant interpretation, he wrote his famous work, *The Gospel of the Resurrection,* which probably exerted a greater influence on the thinking of English people regarding the resurrection of Christ than any other work of the last century. This is the verdict of Canon Westcott, scholar, theologian, commentator, preacher, ecclesiastical statesman, man of God:

"Indeed, taking all the evidence together, it is not too much to say that there is no single historic incident better or more variously supported than the resurrection of Christ. Nothing but the antecedent assumption that it must be false could have suggested the idea of deficiency in the proof of it. And it has been shown that when it is considered in its relation to the whole revelation of which it is a part, and to the conditions of the divine action, which we have assumed, this miraculous event requires a proof in no way differing in essence from that on which the other facts with which it is associated are received as true. In a word, the circumstances under which God is said to have given a revelation to men in the resurrection of the Lord Jesus were such as to make the special manifestation of power likely or even natural; and the evidence by which the special revelation is supported is such as would in any ordinary matter of life be amply sufficient to determine our action and belief."[93]

Professor Ambrose Fleming, emeritus professor of Electrical Engineering in the University of London, honorary fellow of St. John's College, Cambridge, receiver of the Faraday medal in 1928, who is given extended notice in the fourteenth edition of the *Encyclopedia Britannica* because of his remarkable researches in physics, is recognized not only as one of England's outstanding scientists, but as a man who has through the years borne strong and faithful testimony to his faith in Jesus Christ. A few years ago, he published a small pamphlet with the title, *Miracles and Science—The Resurrection of Christ,* from which we would like to quote just these paragraphs.

"The only books in which this great event is described in detail are the four Gospels of the New Testament. The original writings are all lost, or at least have never been found. The oldest transcript, dating back to the beginning of the fourth century, is probably in the Vatican Library, Rome. Investigations by learned scholars during the last one hundred years have, however, satisfied them that the Gospel of St. Mark, acknowledged to be the oldest of the four, substantially as we have it now, was in existence, known, and read before the destruction of Jerusalem by the Roman armies, in A.D. 70, and probably some decade or more earlier.

"We must take this evidence of experts as to the age and authenticity of this writing, just as we take the facts of astronomy on the evidence of astronomers who do not contradict each other. This being so, we can ask ourselves whether it is probable that such book, describing events that occurred about thirty or forty years previously, could have been accepted and cherished if the stories of abnormal events in it were false or mythical. It is impossible, because the memory of all elderly persons regarding events of thirty or forty years before, is perfectly clear.

"No one could now issue a biography of Queen Victoria, who died thirty-one years ago, full of anecdotes which were quite untrue. They would be contradicted at once. They would certainly not be generally accepted and passed on as true. Hence, there is a great improbability that the account of the resurrection given by Mark, which agrees substantially with that given in the other Gospels, is a pure invention. This mythical theory has had to be abandoned because it will not bear close scrutiny. . . .

"St. Paul tells us in his letter to the Romans (1:4) that the resurrection proved Christ to be the Son of God, this is divine. But if so, His teaching and authority were not those of a mere man, but were perfect and absolute. If, then, we are willing to accept and follow that teaching and submit to that loving authority, it will have the effect of producing in us a strong conviction of the actuality of these unique and abnormal events which are recorded of Him, which accompanied that teaching, and were a necessary evidence of His divine nature.

"Let me then, in conclusion, invite you to study at your leisure the records in the four Gospels of these events, and you will see that nothing in the certainly ascertained facts or principles of science forbids belief in those miracles. If that study is pursued with what eminent lawyers have called a willing mind, it will engender a deep assurance that the Christian Church is not founded on fictions, or nourished on delusions, or, as St. Peter calls them, 'cunningly devised fables,' but on historical and actual events, which, however strange they may be, are indeed the greatest events which have ever happened in the history of the world." [94]

We come back again to our own country, to the testimony of one who has recently passed from our midst, whose friendship the author of this volume counts as one of the greatest privileges of his life. I refer to Dr. Howard A. Kelly, for thirty years professor of Gynecology in Johns Hopkins University, chief surgeon and radiologist in the Howard A. Kelly Hospital in Baltimore, for nearly half a century, recognized as one of the four men, with Osler, Halstead, and Welch, who made Johns Hopkins the greatest medical school in America, fellow of the Royal College of Surgeons, of Edinburgh, author of standard textbooks in the subject of Gynecology and Radiology, lover of the Word of God, friend of the poor, and daily a witness to the grace of God in Jesus Christ. I should like to quote the following words from his volume, *A Scientific Man and the Bible,* which Dr. Kelly wrote when sixty-seven years of age:

"Thus in the culmination of the ages was the King's Highway opened up by a Man in His corporeal though transformed body, going before us to the realms of glory and to the very throne of God. He first passed over this great royal road and left His footprints to guide all who would follow Him in the way.

"Clear evidences of the resurrection are:

"The fact that it was utterly unexpected by the disciples and that their astonishment was great (Luke 24:4).

"It is constantly certified by the disciples who saw and companied with our Lord after His resurrection (Acts).

"By the evidences of His power over death (during His earthly life).

"By the transformation wrought in His disciples once assured of it and receiving the gift of the Holy Spirit.

"By His eating and drinking with them after rising from the dead (Luke 24:41; John 21:13; Acts 10:41).

"By all the blessed results flowing out over the world through the following centuries.

"As we turn from the last chapters of the Gospels to Acts and the Epistles, we become conscious of a new and mighty unknown force released and at work in the world. So evident is this that even the unbelieving world has testified to its presence ever since Christ's departure, while at the same time there has been one continuous futile series of efforts of that unbelieving world to discover a substitute for it . . .

"What then does the resurrection mean to me?

"A clear hope vested in my risen Saviour which I could not have, had Christ never risen from the dead.

"My justification before the bar of eternal justice so that I shall not come into judgment, through Christ's victory over death.

"My inclusion from henceforth among the witnesses of His resurrection.

"My burial with Christ, my resurrection with Him, and my life's interests henceforth in seeking those things that are above where Christ is seated at the right hand of God." [95]

A final expression of deep conviction of the truthfulness of the resurrection of Christ may appropriately be that of the one who has so recently been taken from the midst of American academic life, the greatly beloved Dr. William Lyon Phelps. For more than forty years, he was Yale's distinguished professor of English literature, author of some twenty volumes of literary studies, public orator of Yale, who probably has said more worthwhile things about the Word of God and given a more definite confession of his faith in Jesus Christ as the Son of God during the last quarter of a century, than any other one famous professor of our generation not in some theological seminary. "In the whole story of Jesus Christ, the most important event is the resurrection. Christian faith depends on this. It is encouraging to know that it is explicitly given by all four evangelists and told also by Paul. The names of those who saw Him after His triumph over death are recorded; and it may be said that the historical evidence for the resurrection is stronger than for any other miracle anywhere narrated . . . Our faith in God, in Christ, in life itself, is based on the resurrection; for as Paul said, if Christ be not risen from the dead then is our preaching vain, and your faith is also vain." [96]

Young men who are hearing in classrooms, or from friends, or reading in contemporary literature, statements which are intended to destroy faith in the Resurrection, or to deny its importance, or to turn the reality of it into some vague spiritual experience, in reading these testimonies of some of our great thinkers, should remember that these are not rare expressions of faith in the Resurrection. On the contrary some of the outstanding thinkers of every age have boldly confessed the same faith. The greatest man in the first century of the Christian era is the one who went everywhere throughout the Roman Empire testifying to the truth of a resurrection, the Apostle Paul. The greatest man of the fourth century was St. Augustine, and he never wearied of referring to the bodily Resurrection of the Lord. The man who is recognized as probably the greatest intellect of modern times, Sir Isaac Newton, believed in the Resurrection of Christ. Those men who laid the foundations of our famous American colleges and universities all believed strongly in the Resurrection of Christ, as can easily be seen by even the most superficial reading of their writings, as for instance, Increase Mather, President of Harvard; Timothy Dwight, President of Yale; Nathan Lord, President of Dartmouth; Edward Hitchcock, President of Amherst; Mark Hopkins, President of Williams College; John

Witherspoon, President of Princeton. No man has to be ashamed of being found in the company of such men.

Illustrations of the Influence of Faith in Christ in the Critical Hours of Men's Lives. Earlier in this volume we saw that many contemporary skeptical writers are falsely saying that men without any religious life at all are not only as well off, and as happy and strong to meet the crises of life, as men who have religious faith, but that, as for example Professor Otto says, men are better off without God than with God.

At the close of this long chapter on the Resurrection we are not going to give details concerning the despair of men who faced life's crises with no hope in the Resurrection, but some testimonies of those who have been able to meet the tragedies of life triumphantly because of such a faith. These could be multiplied by the hundreds, but we confine ourselves here to three.

The leading physician in Scotland in the middle of the nineteenth century was Sir James Young Simpson, the first to use chloroform as an anesthetic, a physician with the mind of a genius, and a vast capacity for hard work. So greatly beloved by his entire nation was this famous Scotch surgeon that at the time of his funeral, 1700 people marched in the processional line, and 80,000 citizens lined the street, as the funeral cortege moved out to the cemetery. When Simpson came to die, he said to his dear friend, the Reverend Mr. Duns, "He (the Lord Jesus) will care for my poor body now and when taken down He will raise it at the resurrection." [97]

Leaping over to our own day, may I call your attention to a remarkable illustration of the influence of faith in the Resurrection of Christ in the awful crisis that some of God's most beloved saints have been forced to meet in the present holocaust of Europe. Pastor Martin Niemoeller in his powerful sermon preached Easter morning, March 28, 1937, used the Resurrection of Christ for encouraging the hearts of his saddened people, as courageously as anyone has used this truth since the days of another Martin, by the name of Luther.

"Dear brethren, today we feel something of the harshness and inevitability of this 'either—or,' which has been in the world since Easter. The hostility against the preaching of the crucified and risen Saviour has blazed up along the world line, and on every side people try to persuade us that the old world is really wondrous beautiful, that the old world is on the best road to becoming the new world by its own efforts, and that the message of Jesus Christ has, therefore, as far as it deals with the forgiveness of sins, now become superfluous; and a convulsive effort is being made to reclaim Jesus for this side of the old world, and to do away with the uniqueness of His life and death, the mystery of His cross and His resurrection, as a meaningless piece of nonsense.

"We may well feel frightened with regard to this newly wakened enmity of a whole world; and people do not forget to tell us how few visible guarantees we have for our belief that God will create the new world—or how few visible guarantees we have for the truth of our faith: a cross and an empty sepulchre, behind which lie nineteen hundred years—what use is that? Is it any wonder that many men and women are beginning to doubt and to lose courage? Does the Easter message of the new world, of the approaching kingdom of God, does this Bible message still hold good, they wonder? Is it not more honest, is it not more fitting to make peace with the old world, the pre-Easter world, which is after all showing itself to be very much stronger and more enduring than we thought or suspected?

"Dear Easter congregation, we can here hold nobody back who wants to go his own ways. We live in a time of decisions, and it is becoming a time of partings. But it is better for us not to trust what our eyes see, for that will pass away! And He tells us, 'Blessed are they that have not seen, and yet have believed.'

"Throughout the centuries, the risen Christ has gone before His community, and today too He goes before us. His victory will be our victory also. And just as our fathers in the faith believed in Him with that assurance which the risen Christ gave to His first disciples, so we too are sure and will continue to proclaim, as a believing and professing community, what makes us glad deep down in our hearts, in the ups and downs amid which we live, in the great world which carries us along with it. I think what makes us glad with a great joy is this: 'The Lord is risen; He is really and truly risen!'

Satan, the World, Death, Sin, and Hell
Are quelled for evermore.

Their rage and power are brought to nought
By Christ whom we adore."[98]

Pastor Sverre Norborg, rector of the cathedral in Oslo, Norway, in his volume written just before the war, *What Is Christianity?* gives an experience out of his own life, at the close of a chapter on faith in the resurrection, concerning one Christopher, whom he does not further identify. These are Norborg's words:

"He occupied a ward together with eight other tuberculosis patients. It was his last springtime. He never saw the dogwood blossom. It was one of those early spring days when the gentle south wind wafts in upon the land the breath of new life. I came into the ward of these young men. Christopher beckoned to me to come over: 'We too are going to have a real Easter this year. Our superintendent says a radio is being brought in; that will make it possible for us also to be along in the services.' His pale face shone in anticipation.

"Good Friday came and the blessed radio waves carried the invisible Word. It reached Christopher. In the afternoon I came through the corridor. Again he beckoned me, more radiant than ever: 'It is Easter today.' 'Indeed,' I answered, 'it is Good Friday and . . .' He became very quiet. In a moment, 'I guess you do not understand. It is Easter today.' With his emaciated white hands, he pointed to his heart. He had laid hold on the words which had created Easter! 'He was wounded for our transgressions, He was bruised for our iniquities, the chastisement of our peace was upon Him.' It was long before we parted. There in a hospital ward we worshiped together that Good Friday afternoon.

"At three o'clock the next morning, the pastor was hurriedly summoned to the hospital. Christopher had had a hemorrhage. He had reached his journey's end. He lay in a heavy sleep on the very threshold of death. Just once toward the end he roused himself, and his last word was a greeting. His voice was almost gone, as he turned on the very threshold of eternity and whispered that last greeting: 'It is Easter today.' There he died unto eternal life. Is there Easter in your life?"[99]

The Place Which the Resurrection of Christ Should Be Given in the Christian Apologetic of Our Day. At the time of the first persecution which came to the Christian Church, after the disciples were released, and "went to their own company and reported all that the chief priests and elders had said unto them," and had united in offering prayer to God, with the result that the place where they were was shaken, they began speaking the Word of God with such boldness, being filled with the Holy Ghost, that "with great power gave the apostles witness of the Resurrection of the Lord Jesus."[100] Is it not significant that power is said to have rested upon these apostles, especially when they preached the Resurrection of Christ? Is it not true that here is our great apologetic, in this day of unbelief? In a time when men, as never before, trained in the science of historical research, demand adequate evidence for believing, is not this the time, above all, when the historical evidence for the resurrection of Christ should be carefully presented, when our young people should be persuaded to examine these narratives without prejudice, and with as open a mind as they would study the historical records of Tacitus or Pliny? In this day when the empirical aspect of philosophy is emphasized, when men demand evidence that science can corroborate, is not this the time to speak of the things which these apostles saw and heard and touched—empirical evidence indeed? In this hour when so many books are pouring from the presses, giving forth a mist by which the minds of men become clouded, resulting in people being lost in the absurdities of speculation, following first one new theory and then another, is not this the time for setting forth before bewildered people, the great, simple, supernatural but incontrovertible fact, that Jesus of Nazareth is revealed to be the Son of God by His resurrection from the dead? As Professor Macgregor said some years ago: "The existence of the belief itself of the resurrection of Christ in the heart of the primeval Christianity, from the instant of the first beginning of this religion in the germ, is historically unquestioned and unquestionable. Unquestionably, as a fact of history, resurrection was the first cry of this religion when it was born into the world; resurrection was the light which dawned upon its earliest morning of life. And so down to this day, wherever there is Christendom, resurrection is an article of primary belief, underlying all the detailed articulations of Christian thought and feeling and action. Even though the individual should not be personally a believer, he is under the influence of the belief, as of a new light of tender gladness, that has come into the world."[101]

No greater threat to the Christian faith has arisen in Great Britain, down to the present dominance of rationalism and materialism, than we find in what was called *deism* in the seventeenth century, when it seemed at one time that almost all of the most influential and best educated people of Britain would be persuaded to forsake the Gospel of Jesus Christ. What stemmed the tide of deism, or, to change the figure, ultimately destroyed its influence? I do not believe Mr. Edgar has in any way exaggerated facts of the case when he says, "It was given to Waterland to vindicate our Lord's divinity, and to Sherlock, Gilbert West, Humphrey Ditton, and Chandler to overhaul the evidence for His Resurrection and place it so far as the assaults were concerned, in a satisfactory position; for that by the middle of the century the risen Saviour was in such evidence that deism had no alternative but to die."[102] Personally, I believe that there is no other single truth in the New Testament supported by such a mass of evidence for those who are looking for historical certainty, so capable of silencing the metaphysical speculations of contemporary non-theistic philosophies and unbelieving theologians, as the great and glorious truth that Jesus Christ is indeed risen from the dead. It rests on the solid rock of historical reality; it relates directly to the person and work of the most remarkable individual that ever walked on this earth; it contains within itself the promise of the hope of a life to come, that satisfies the deepest longings of any human heart. To believe it is to be found in the company of many of the world's greatest thinkers, the truest saints, and the most triumphant contenders in the great spiritual battles from which no man is exempt. If this truth of Christ's Resurrection were sanely and clearly presented to the young people of our age, while still in their teens, if, for instance, they could be taught as much about the Resurrection of Christ as they are taught about the stabbing of Julius Caesar, the escapades of Cleopatra, the iniquities of Nero, and the coming of the Normans to the shores of Britain, we believe there would soon result a turning of the tide in this battle for the Christian faith, and great multitudes would be forever delivered from the ravages of later skepticism, and the destructive consequences of agnosticism and atheistic teachings, which so many of our young people will have to face in their collegiate life.

Be Not Faithless But Believing. When our Lord granted Thomas' request to thrust his hand into His side, to actually behold the wounds of His hands, and Thomas immediately cried out, "My Lord, and my God," the risen Saviour added a word of warning. Grateful as He was for Thomas' confession, He nevertheless felt it necessary that Thomas should be aware of the danger of continuing in the mood in which he had lived since he had heard, but refused to believe, that Christ had risen from the dead: "Be not faithless but believing," which may be more literally translated, "become not unbelieving but believing."[103] "Belief and unbelief" as Bishop Westcott reminds us, "both grow. Thomas was not, but he 'was on the way to being' faithless. The tense of the verb marks the process as we continue going on."[104] This is what is so serious with the skeptical mood of the younger generation of today, they not only, for one reason or another, are not believing this truth, and that truth, they are growing in their unbelief, until they come to the tragic place where they neither believe in Christ nor man, neither in the Christian religion nor any religion, neither in God nor moral authority, and their hearts become kingdoms of anarchy. Godet has a fine comment on this warning of our Lord's. "Jesus makes Thomas feel in what a critical position he actually is, at this point where the two routes separate: that of decided unbelief and that of perfect faith. A single point of truth, a single fact of the story of salvation, which one obstinate person refuses to accept, may become the starting point for complete unbelief, as also the victory gained over unbelief, with regard to this single point may lead to perfect faith."[105] A voice was heard from heaven saying, "This is my beloved Son in whom I am well pleased, hear ye Him." This is a profound and serious matter, whether we believe in or do not believe in the Lord Jesus Christ, and no man can truly believe in Christ unless he believes in Christ's Resurrection. Likewise, no man can believe in the Resurrection of Christ without at the same time believing in Jesus Christ as the Son of God. If St. Paul could say, "If thou shalt confess with thy mouth Jesus is Lord and shalt believe in thy heart that God raised Him from the dead, thou shalt be saved," then, with such faith God is able to save us and without that faith we are lost.[106] It is not only something regrettable, something sad, something unfortunate, not to believe, it is indeed the tragedy of tragedies, the greatest disaster that can ever come to a human life, for it involves everything now, and everything to come, what we are in ourselves, what we are toward others, and our relationship to God. Theodosus Harnack, the Lutheran pastor, wrote to his brilliant son, Adolf Harnack, "Where you stand with regard to the fact of the Resurrection is in my eyes no longer Christian theology. To me Christianity stands or falls with the Resurrection." [107] But Harnack went on growing in his unbelief, and Germany, more and more rejecting Christ and accepting anti-Christ, now finds itself sliding into the abyss of the greatest national catastrophe and ruin known in modern times. It is a serious matter, rejecting or accepting the Lord Jesus, and there is no virtue in the land of the free nor any particular quality in the blood of the veins of us here in America, that should ever be thought sufficient to save us from the same eclipse, if we persist in the way of unbelief. To reject the Resurrection is to go against every law of logic which man has discovered; to reject the Resurrection is to put out the one great light that can illuminate our future; to reject the Resurrection is to involve ourselves, for the rest of life, in all kinds of efforts to explain the principles and teaching and work and influence of Jesus Christ; to deny the Resurrection of Christ is to forfeit any right to preach in a Christian pulpit, to talk to others about the blessing of following Jesus, or to kneel down at the bedside of a dying man or woman and expect to bring them any comfort. To accept Christ's Resurrection is to have in our hearts the key to the Incarnation, it is to know the reason for the phenomenal power and growth of the early church, it is to have peace in our souls, because we are justified before God, and it is to know a joy that nothing can ever take away from us, because our hope is not in the circumstances of the things about us, but in the risen Saviour, confident that we have an inheritance incorruptible and undefiled, reserved in heaven for us, who are being kept here on earth by the same power of God that raised our Lord from the dead.

Chapter IX

A RIGHTEOUS JUDGMENT TO COME: THE APOLOGETIC FOR THIS TIME OF DISAPPEARING ETHICAL STANDARDS

When the Apostle Paul announced to the Athenians that God had "appointed a day in which He will judge the world in righteousness," he declared a truth which in such comprehensiveness was utterly new in the thought of the Greek and Roman world. That souls would experience some form of a judgment after death was the assertion of most ancient religions, but that there would be one great day, or one definite future period, in the history of mankind, when all the souls of men would come before a divine tribunal for final judgment, and the determination of their eternal destiny, was a truth utterly foreign to the religion of ancient Greece. In fact, the earliest documents of Greek religious literature, the writings of Homer, were most indefinite concerning the life of man after his death here on earth. "For Homer's men there was no hope for a future life in which action and personality were continued with values derived and transplanted from the world of sunlight and sense." [1] With the appearance of Orphism and the cult of Dionysus, some elements more or less relating to a future judgment are to be found, but these are altogether different from the conception of judgment as set forth in the writings of the New Testament. Of those who had been guilty of the most grievous sins Empedocles says, "There is an oracle Necessity, an ancient, eternal decree of the gods sealed with strong oaths: when one in sin stains his hand with murder, or when another joining in strife swears falsely, they become the spirits who have long lives as their souls, who are doomed to wander thrice ten thousand seasons far from the blessed, being born in the course of time into all forms of mortal creatures, shifting along life's hard paths. For the matter of the air drives them to the sea, spews them on the ground, the land bares them to the rays of the bright sun and the sun throws them in whirls of ether. One receives them from another, but all hate them. Even I now am an exile from God, a wanderer, for I put my trust in mad strife."[2] Concerning these after-death experiences of men, who had grievously sinned, Professor Clifford Herschell Moore of Harvard University, remarks, "The number of reincarnations was not fixed so far as we know, though apparently ten thousand years was thought to be the limit of process for the ordinary soul, probably it was believed that there was no end of rebirths for the wicked, but that they were condemned to their repeated fate forever; or that they were doomed to endless punishments without rebirth."[3]

In their later development of religious speculation, the task of the judgment of soul was assigned to three gods of Hades, Minos, Aeacus, and Rhadamanthus, the executioners of their judgment being the Erinyes or the Furies.[4] The whole subject of judgment in Greek religion was generally left unconsidered, contrary to the elaborate treatments of judgment in Egyptian religion.[5] The Egyptian religion, however, had flourished long centuries before the advent of Christianity, but had almost no influence over the thinking of the Graeco-Roman world at the time of our Lord's advent. The conception of *a day of judgment* found throughout the New Testament as declared by St. Paul to the Athenians was an idea never previously set forth in Greek religious literature.

Before considering *the* judgment to come, of which St. Paul speaks, we believe it will be advantageous to go somewhat deeply into this whole subject of judgment, as a primary basis for a study of the final judgment. For some strange reason the doctrine of a day of judgment does not find adequate consideration in the great reformed theologies. There are elaborate discussions of hell, of the scriptural doctrine of eternal punishment, and many separate treatises on heaven, but judgment itself is a New Testament doctrine which most theologians seem to treat with unjustified brevity. For this reason we are giving it an extended consideration. If it is necessary to return to the preaching of judgment in this day of disappearing ethical values, the truth involved in such a doctrine should, in our minds, rest upon solid foundations.

Definitions of Judgment. Whatever one may think of the truth or falsehood of a final, universal, righteous judgment by God, no one can possibly deny the fact that judgment itself is an inescapable, daily experience, individually and corporately, for all mankind. Men exercise judgment in innumerable ways, in the ordinary experiences of life. The very stability of governments is maintained day by day by the judgments rendered in courts of law. As an indication of how many profoundly important factors of life are embraced in this idea of judgment, one only need to look at the fifteen columns of the *Oxford English Dictionary* to discover the range of words relating to the actions of this life involved in this matter of judgment, e.g., judge, judicative, judicatory, judicial, judiciary, judicious, justice, just. Fundamentally, the Greek word to judge (*krino*) means, "to divide, to separate, to make a distinction," and thus, "to come to a decision."[6] To illustrate this in a very simple way: if one has a number of silver coins before one for determining which are of great value, and which are of small value, in separating the rare from the common, one would be making a distinction, which is reached by passing *judgment* upon each separate coin. Advancing from the act of personal discrimination and judgment to deliberate decisions of a court of justice, we get a definition for judgment as "a judicial decision or order in court." Every case brought up before any court in a civilized country concludes with a judgment of one kind or another apart, of course, from those trials in which juries fail to reach an agreement.

The matter of judgment in the realm of logic deserves a further word of consideration. Thus, e.g., Dr. James Edwin Creighton, one-time Sage Professor of Logic and Metaphysics in Cornell University, in his work, *An Introductory Logic,* has this to say about judgment as an intellectual act: "Judgment is both the elementary and universal form of knowing. It includes perception and conception and uses them as a means to its own ends of attaining truth. It may perhaps be best described as the interpreted activity of the mind. It is thus the form of the general intellectual activity. To know anything is to express in terms of ideas, to qualify it in our thought as this or that, as belonging to a certain class of things, or perhaps as differing in some respect from another class of things. But it must not be supposed that judgment is concerned only with *our own ideas*. Judgment is the interpreting idealizing response of the mind to the real world, with which it is always in relation."[7] If one keeps in mind this definition of judgment in the realm of logic, when considering the judgment of a man by a court one will see that the latter is only a final expression of the former. In a court of law, the judge, and often the jury, must, from the evidence presented, determine whether one on trial is to be classified among the innocent or the guilty. This is the fundamental conception of judgment, and as such it is a part of life which can never be escaped, whatever one may think of a future, final, divine judgment, such as Paul was speaking of to the Athenians.

Persons to Whom Is Assigned the Right of Passing Judgment upon Others. Since the establishment of a social order among men on earth, it has been recognized, and necessarily so, that only certain men have the right to render official judgments involving the release or punishment of fellowmen. Those who are recognized as possessing this right do not (or at least, should not) possess it because of their wealth, personality, or physical power, but because of a certain position which they hold in a social group, a position which they may have come into either by birth or by the free choice of people. First of all, and fundamentally, there are what we call *judges,* of which the Old Testament names many. Far back in the days of the forming of Israel's early legislation the Lord told Moses that there should be appointed in Israel judges who "shall judge the people with righteous judgment."[8] This type of authority predominated in that period of Israel's history which derives its name from this very divine order, namely, the period of the Judges. Of course there were judges in Israel before this period, and there were many after it. The second group of men to have the right of judgment were kings. It is of kings as judges that Solomon writes when he speaks of "A king that sitteth on the throne of judgment scattereth away all evil with his eye."[9] Consequently, when Pilate sat to consider the guilt or innocence of Christ, it is said that he pronounced his sentence from a "judgment seat." St. Paul once was brought before the judgment seat of Gallio, and later demanded the right to be brought before "Caesar's judgment seat."[10] It is to this entire process of human judgment that the remarkable verse in the ancient code of Deuteronomy refers, "If there be a controversy between men, and they come unto judgment, and the judges judge them; then they shall justify the righteous and condemn the wicked."[11]

God the Supreme Judge of All Mankind. To no *man* could there ever justly be committed the staggering task of judging the entire human race. No man has such omnipotent power that he could compel every man in the universe to appear before him for judgment; no man ever could have a true and complete knowledge of the thoughts and intents of another individual, e.g., of another's hatred, bitterness, avarice, envy, uncleanness of thought, etc. Moreover, men live for only a brief period, and if there were a universal judge today, he would not be here to exercise such a function in another century. If all sin is ever to be judged, only God can be the Judge. And so the Scriptures declare, "for Jehovah is our judge, Jehovah is our king."[12] Even in the days of the patriarchs, Abraham could plead in his prayer for Sodom that "the Judge of all the earth" would do right.[13] So the Apostle Paul, in the terrible indictment he brings against all mankind, in the beginning of his epistle to the Romans, speaks of that day "when *God* shall judge the secrets of men."[14] The great additional truth that at the final judgment of mankind, it is God the Son who has been appointed as the supreme judge we will consider shortly.

Some Divine Judgments of History. While generally we speak of "*the day* of judgment," or, "*the* judgment to come," and think of God's judgment as some single future event, we must remember that the earth has already suffered from a number of different judgments, proceeding from the wrath of God. All the plagues which God sent upon Egypt, before the exodus of the Israelites, are designated as divine judgments. Jerusalem itself, because of its iniquity, its refusal to hear the prophets whom God had sent, its rejection of the Word of God, suffered direct judgment at the hand of God, who had designated this very place as His Holy City.[15] Sometimes the servants of God must endure God's judgment in this life, with, of course, the idea that in so being chastened they would become repentant, and turn back to God. War itself is often looked upon in the Word of God as an act of divine judgment, e.g., in a very remarkable passage in the ancient book of Job: "Be ye afraid of the sword: For wrath bringeth the punishments of the sword, that ye may know there is a judgment."[16] The same truth is echoed toward the end of the divine record when Christ, Himself, appears on a white horse, to "judge and make war."[17] The book of Ezekiel is filled with statements concerning various judgments, e.g., the judgment of God upon Moab, upon nations that despise Israel, and upon the house of Israel itself. There are two judgments of this kind to which the Chroniclers and Psalmist refer when they say, "His judgments are in all the earth."[18] The thrice repeated assertion, "He cometh to judge the earth,"[19] refers not only to a great general judgment to come, but to judgments which have already fallen upon disobedient mankind.

Future Judgments and "The Judgment." In many conservative theological groups of our day it is considered almost a heresy to speak of *a great day of judgment* to come, because of certain dispensational preconceptions. I am, of course, a believer in dispensations, but I believe it has been a great mistake to refuse to speak to the men of our generations of *the judgment* to come. I do not deny that there are a number of judgments to occur in the future; e.g., that great judgment of the living nations on earth when our Lord returns, recorded with great detail in the Olivet discourse; a future judgment of angels and the important judgment of the believers' works, which has to do exclusively with those who have accepted Christ as their Saviour (a judgment that has no relation to the final destiny of man, i.e., a judgment determining his eternal destiny, for that has already been determined when he has accepted the Lord Jesus Christ),[20] yet the Scriptures do definitely speak of one great single event of judgment to come, and we have sinned in almost robbing the preaching of our day of this terrible but divinely-revealed truth. While on the one hand, most theologians have failed to discriminate between the judgment of living nations, the judgments of believers' works, and the judgment of the wicked dead, many of us, on the other hand, have been afraid to stand up and use scriptural language concerning *the day of judgment.* Our blessed Lord uses the phrase "the day of judgment" again and again.[21] The Apostle Paul speaks of "the day."[22] The Apostle Peter talks about "the day of judgment," and "the day of judgment and destruction of ungodly men."[23] The Apostle John speaks of "the day of judgment," and "the time of the dead to be judged."[24] That believers will not be included in this day of judgment will be considered later in this chapter, but we believe it is important to use scriptural language, and to emphasize a dreadful *final day of judgment* for mankind.

Christ the Appointed Judge of the Final Judgment. We are now ready to return to the words of St. Paul in his Athenian address, "He (i.e., God) hath appointed a day in which He will judge the world in righteousness by the man whom He hath ordained." Of course, "the man" refers to the Lord Jesus Christ. Christ, Himself, declares that He will be the one at that time executing judgment upon mankind. "Neither doth the Father judge any man, but He hath given all judgment unto the Son; that all may honour the Son even as they honour the Father . . . For the Father gave Him authority to execute judgment because He is a Son of man."[25] The Apostle Peter, preaching to the Gentiles in the house of Cornelius, declared that God had charged the apostles that they were to "preach unto the people and to testify that this is He who is ordained of God to be the judge of the living and the dead."[26] The Apostle Paul, early in his ministry, wrote to the Romans that "God would judge the secrets of men by Jesus Christ"; and at the end of his ministry reaffirmed this truth in speaking of Jesus as the one "who shall judge the living and the dead."[27]

Probably no one has set forth the significance of Christ as the final Judge of all mankind with such fullness and insight as the late Professor William Milligan, in his remarkable volume, *The Ascension and Heavenly Priesthood of Our Lord,* from which we would make the following quotation:

"Because He has been in the same position, has fought the same battles, and endured the same trials as those standing at His bar; because He entirely knows them, and they by the instinct of a common nature know that He knows them, His judgment finds an echo in their hearts as no simply divine judgment would. Is it a sentence of condemnation? They are speechless, and judgment, by awakening the conscience, becomes judgment, instead of a mere verdict of irresistible power against which we can rebel. Or is it a sentence of pardon? Then that that pardon should be pronounced by One who, in human love and pity, has followed every false winding of their hearts and yet forgives, fills them, even in their forgiven state, with remorse and shame and humility and tender longing to draw still nearer Him."[28]

Long ago the greatest of all American theologians, Jonathan Edwards, set forth this truth (in pages that few men today take time to consult), and, though Edwards does bring together without distinction the judgment of believers and the judgment of the ungodly, yet his words nevertheless do reveal both of these aspects of the judgments: "It was proper that he who is appointed King of the church should rule till he should have put all his enemies under his feet; in order to which, he must be the judge of his enemies, as well as of his people. One of the offices of Christ, as Redeemer, is that of a King; he is appointed King of the church, and head over all things to the church; and in order that his kingdom be complete, and the design of his reign be accomplished, he must *conquer* all his enemies, and then he will deliver up the kingdom to the Father. *Then cometh the end, when he shall have delivered up the kingdom to God, even the Father; when he shall have put down all rule, and all authority and power. For he must reign till he hath put all enemies under his feet.* Now, when Christ shall have brought his enemies, who had denied, opposed, and rebelled against him, to his judgment-seat, and shall have passed and executed sentence upon them, this will be a final and complete *victory* over them, a victory which shall put an end to the war. And it is proper that he who at present reigns, and is carrying on the war against those who are of the opposite kingdom, should have the honor of obtaining the victory, and finishing the war.

"That Christ is appointed to be the judge of the world, will be for the more abundant *conviction of the ungodly.* It will be for their conviction, that they are judged and condemned by that very person whom they have rejected, by whom they might have been saved, who shed his blood to give them an *opportunity* to be saved, who was wont to offer his righteousness to them, when they were in their state of trial, and who many a time called and invited them to come to him, that they might be saved. How justly will they be condemned by him whose salvation they have rejected, whose blood they have despised, whose many calls they have refused, and whom they have pierced by their sins!" [29]

To pass from these days of our colonial quietude to the stormy age in which we now live, concerning the same subject of Christ our Judge, these are the words of Karl Barth: "He in whom the compassion of God as conquering human nature, he divides in that he decides, he sets the sheep on the right hand and the goats on the left, he rewards the doers of good works and punishes the doers of evil works. He leads into eternal joy and hurls into eternal torment."[30]

The Criteria by Which Men Will Be Judged. The final judgment of the human race is as naturally, as rightly, a part of the preëminence and deity of Christ, as His victory over death in Resurrection. The conception of Christ as Judge "seals Christianity as the absolute religion. If Christ were only a finger-post to God along with others who would likewise lead men to the goal of their destiny, or if He were only the beginner and not also the finisher of the kingdom of God, beyond whom there can be no development, then, indeed, the very idea of His office as Judge of the world would be a fanatical presumption. But if the Father has delivered all things to Him, and His whole revelation of salvation then is Christ also the born Judge of the World."[31]

There are two fundamentally different criteria for the final judgment of men, recorded in the Word of God (and of course, apart from the Word of God we know absolutely nothing about a future judgment). The first we may call the criteria of *works.* Even in the pessimistic book of Ecclesiastes, the wise man knows that "God will bring every work into judgment, with every hidden thing, whether it be good or whether it be evil."[32] This is exactly the declaration of the Apostle John, as there is granted to him a vision of the awful judgment of the Great White Throne: "And I saw the dead, the great and the small, standing before the throne; and books were opened: and another book was opened, which is the book of life: and the dead were judged out of the things which were written in the books, according to their works. And the sea gave up the dead that were in it; and death and Hades gave up the dead that were in them: and they were judged every man according to their works."[33] The writer of the Epistle to the Hebrews specifies the sins of fornication and adultery as especially marked for this final judgment.[34] It should be noticed here, as Professor Manson has pointed out, that this final judgment is an *ethical* one. It has to do with goodness, with righteousness, with evil and iniquity. "How else could a righteous judge execute judgment upon men except by the laws concerning righteous conduct? These works of men will embrace not only the external acts which they have committed while on earth, but the very 'secrets' of men, or as Jeremiah puts it, 'the things that were found in the heart and the mind.'"[35]

As supreme among all the criteria of judgment in this last day, both the Lord Jesus and the Apostle Paul emphasize the attitude of men toward Jesus Christ. Early in our Lord's ministry He laid down this fundamental, profound and eternal law; "He that believeth on Him is not judged: he that believeth not hath been judged already, because he hath not believed on the name of the only begotten Son of God."[36] Later in His ministry He emphasized this truth again, "He that rejecteth me, and receiveth not my sayings hath one that judgeth him: the word that I spake, the same shall judge him in the last day."[37] The Apostle Paul, in one of his earliest epistles, speaks of those upon whom God will send a spirit of error "that they all might be judged who believed not the truth, but had pleasure in unrighteousness."[38] Here we find belief and conduct linked together in one clause: those who "believe not the truth" which, of course, refers to Jesus Christ and His gospel, were at the same time living unrighteous lives. Charles Hodge unites these two criteria of judgment in words well worth serious consideration: "Christ is God manifest in the flesh; He came into the world to save sinners; all who receive him as their God and Saviour are saved; all who refuse to recognize and trust him perish."[39] "He that believeth on the Son hath everlasting life; he that believeth not the Son shall not see life."[40] "If any man love not the Lord Jesus Christ," the Apostle says, "let him be Anathema Maran-atha."[41] The special ground of condemnation, therefore, under the gospel, is unbelief—the refusal to receive Christ in the character in which He is presented for our acceptance. It is a very strange thing, yet something no one can deny, that it is only when a man recognizes he has no righteous works of his own, and throws himself upon the mercy of God for forgiveness, that he really begins to manifest some real righteousness. In the midst of this war, with all the dreadful things of which we read, both across the waters and in our own unscarred country, the verdict on the whole human race, apart from those in Christ, is certainly that all men stand condemned before the bar of a righteous God. This matter of accepting or rejecting Christ, this business of believing in Jesus or not, of carefully considering His claims or indifferently brushing them aside, will result in destinies which seem to be almost hidden from the mind of modern man.

The Righteousness of Divine Judgment. There is one word which Paul attaches to the judgment of which he speaks in the Athenian address which, for some reason, though constantly identified with judgment in both the Old and New Testaments, has been almost wholly ignored in modern theological works. That word is *righteousness.* I must confess that when I began to look into this matter I was astonished to find that judgment is hardly ever spoken of in the Word of God unless at the same time it is characterized as *righteous* judgment. Far back in the patriarchal days, in a verse which we have previously considered, we find Abraham asking, "shall not the judge of all the earth do right?" and of course we immediately recognize that the word *right* here is at the base of our word *righteous.* Again and again the Psalmist declares his faith that God "will judge the world in righteousness."[42] In fact when he came to write the 119th Psalm he devotes one entire section of it to the righteousness of God in judgment. It begins as follows: "Righteous art thou, O Jehovah, And upright are thy judgments. Thou hast commanded thy testimonies in righteousness and very faithfulness. My zeal hath consumed me, Because mine adversaries have forgotten thy words. Thy word is very pure; Therefore thy servant loveth it. I am small and despised; Yet do I not forget thy precepts. Thy righteousness is an everlasting righteousness, And thy law is truth."[43] So the prophets frequently declare that it is "Jehovah of hosts who judgeth righteously, who trieth the heart and the mind."[44] The Apostle Paul speaks of the Lord as "the righteous judge," and, consequently, he is able to confess that "we know that the judgment of God is true."[45] Likewise, the Apostle Peter speaks of "Him that judgeth righteously."[46] The same idea appears in the book of Revelation with considerable frequency. "True and righteous are thy judgments," the earth and the hosts of heaven unite in declaring.[47] One of the last great visions therein given of the Lord Jesus is the one in which John saw the heaven open, "and behold a white horse and he that sat thereon called faithful and true; and in *righteousness* he doth judge and make war."[48]

The question now forces itself upon us, what do we mean by righteousness? This is a problem to which an entire volume might well be devoted, but to which here we can only give the briefest space. I think, first of all, the definition of the great lexicographer Cremer should introduce us to the meaning of the word. "Righteousness is first of all what is right, conformable to right, pertaining to right, from a root meaning manner, direction, and hence, a state or condition conformable to order." From this fundamental meaning Cremer proceeds to the larger biblical conception of righteousness, which he defines as "a condition of righteousness, *the standard of which is God,* which is estimated according to the divine standard, which shows itself in behavior conformable to God, and has to do above all things with its relation to God, and with the walk before Him . . . Throughout the New Testament righteousness designates that person or thing which corresponds with the divine norm, whether the reference be to the person's conduct before or towards God, or to his relation to the claims and judgment of God." [49] There is a revealing sentence from the lips of our Lord which in itself might almost be considered as a definition of righteousness, "My judgment is righteous; because I seek not mine own will, but the will of him that sent me." [50] A righteous man is one who lives according to the will of God, whose character reflects the character of God, who is walking in conformity to the law of God, which, of course, embraces holiness, justice, purity, truth, and everything that can be called right.

The reason why the Greeks could never conceive of a final judgment of all men before the throne of any one of their deities, based upon *righteousness,* is because their own gods were notoriously unrighteous. Consider this awful indictment of Euripides, which he puts on the lips of Ion, son of Creusa, daughter of the king of Athens by Apollo. "Yet I must admonish Phoebus. What ails him? He ravishes maidens and forsakes them, begets children by stealth and cares not, though they die. O, do not so! Since thou are powerful, follow after goodness! When a man has an evil nature, the gods punish him. How is it right that you gods should prescribe the law for man, and then be guilty of lawlessness yourselves? If—it cannot be, yet I will put it so—if you were to pay to men the fine for lustful violence, thou, and Poseidon, and Zeus the Lord of heaven would beggar our temples of their treasure in paying for your wrongs. For wrong it is, to seek your pleasures with no regard to consequence. No more can men justly be called wicked, if we only imitate what the gods call good. Wicked rather are those who so instruct us!" [51] In fact, it was commonly admitted by the Greeks that they must live better than the gods lived, or they would be condemned as moral reprobates.

This business of living right is a dreadfully serious business. Men may revolt against the moral law, in a day like ours, and laugh at what they call the restraints of religion, and the narrowness of our Puritan fathers (what would they do without the liberty of mocking our Puritan forefathers!); they may talk about the repressive, and suppressive, influences of the church, total freedom from all restrictions; they may urge revolutions not only in the state but in the realm of morals, that will throw off every binding influence; but righteousness is still the norm of life in the sight of God! It is an unchanging and eternal attribute of God Himself. He has ever been righteous toward men, because He is righteous in Himself, and He demands that men be righteous in every relation of life, in His all-comprehending knowledge of the thoughts and actions of men. It is past time for men to wake out of the stupefying influence of our contemporary passion for lawlessness, license, unrestraint, this eagerness for smashing all previously accepted precepts, this inexpressibly foolish determination to build a new moral foundation for life, made out of materials which have already proved to be treacherous sands. It is time to come face to face with the fact that God is righteous, that God's laws are righteous, that God demands righteousness, that God has sent His righteous Son to save us, and that an hour is coming when men are going to stand before this righteous Judge, and unless they have repented and believed, be condemned for their own deliberately unrighteous life.

If Christ has been appointed by God as the judge of all mankind, and this judgment, as all divine judgments, must proceed according to righteousness, how harmoniously perfect is the revelation of Christ in the New Testament as "Jesus Christ the righteous," or, in the words of the Apostle Paul, "the righteous Judge." He came "to fulfill all righteousness." [52] "He is made unto us the very righteousness of God," [53] and in His holy death He is the display for all eternity of the righteousness of God. In the midst of the bold judgments of the book of Revela ion, John says he heard the angel of the waters saying, "Righteous art hou, who art and who wast, thou Holy One, because thou didst thus udge." [54]

The Testimony of Man's Heart to a Judgment to Come. Learned John Pearson, in the semi-quaint language of his day, reminding us of St. Paul's words in Romans 2:15, 16, truly says: "If we do but reflect upon the frame and temper of our own spirits, we cannot but collect and conclude from thence, that we are to give an account of our actions, and that a judgment hereafter is to pass upon us. There is in the soul of every man a conscience, and wheresoever it is, it giveth testimony to his truth. The antecedent or directive conscience tells us what we are o do, and the subsequent or reflexive conscience warns us what we are o receive. Looking back upon the actions we have done, it either approves or condemns them; and if it did no more, it would only prove hat there is a judgment in this life, and every man his own judge. But being it doth not only allow and approve our good actions, but also doth create a complacency, apology, and confidence in us; being t doth not only disprove and condemn our evil actions, but doth also constantly accuse us, and breed a fearful expectation and terror in us; and all this prescinding from all relation to anything either to be enjoyed or suffered in this life: it followeth, that this conscience is not so much a udge as a witness, bound over to give testimony, for or against us, at some judgment after this life to pass upon us." [55]

The writer of the Epistle to the Hebrews in using the phrase "a cerain expectation of judgment," [56] gives expression to the undeniable fact hat the human heart has, when it truthfully recognizes its deepest conviction, been aware that there must be and will be a final judgment or responsible human beings. "It is impossible to overlook the fact that udgment goes on now in what we call the natural order of things. Men are visited with the consequences of their right and wrong doing, not immediately, but for the most part before they taste of death; and nations, after enjoying long impunity, and even prospering outwardly n their evil courses, are invariably visited with the wrathful justice which they have outraged, and sentenced to the condemnation of suffering humiliation and extinction for their iniquities and immoralities. And from these facts the inference is always drawn that there will be a larger, a more complete, and more decisive judgment at some time beyond. For in the present order of things the judgment is not always manifest. It is rarely prompt, it comes with slowly lingering feet, and to some men it comes not at all; so far as the outward eye can observe, they appear to escape it. The facts are enough to prove that strict and righteous judgment is the rule, but there are sufficient exceptions to suggest and almost force the conviction of a future judgment which will deal with these exceptions, which will be all comprehending, which will make equal, straight, and just all the inequalities and injustices of the earthly lot, rendering to every man according to his doings. This doctrine has been the common property of all civilized and uncivilized people, ancient and modern, Eastern and Western, Greek, Roman, Asiatic, wherever there has been any sort of belief in a future life. Indeed, the belief in a future life has been largely suggested and strengthened by the longing and the conscientious demand for that infallible retribution and complete justice which so often fail in the transitory mortal course."[57]

The frank autobiography of one of the most distinguished publicists of our time, an avowed enemy of Christianity and the whole gamut of Christian truth, since he began to write now some forty years ago, is itself a remarkable testimony to this truth, that the fear of a judgment to come has been implanted in every human breast. I refer to H. G. Wells' *Experiment in Autobiography* which he published (1934) when sixty-eight years of age. It is a strange thing that in less than 250 pages of this book, Wells brings up the subject of hell fifteen times. He says that when a boy he feared hell dreadfully for some time. "Hell was indeed good enough to scare me and prevent me from calling either of my brothers fools until I was eleven or twelve, but one night I had a dream of hell so preposterous that it blasted that undesirable resort out of my mind forever . . . That dream pursued me into the daytime. Never had I hated God so intensely and then, suddenly, the light broke through to me and I knew this God was a lie." If this truth came to Mr. Wells at the age of twelve, and he has held it now for over fifty years, I wonder why he so continually brings up the subject again and again in his autobiography? Well, he, himself, in an undated letter concluding the very chapter in which he says that death no longer has any fear or terror for him, speaks of his evenings as having been passed "in the marking of examination papers and correspondence and his nights in uneasy meditations on Death and the Future Life and Hope and the Indeterminate Equations." In fact, in the chapter that follows this discussion, in a much later period of life, he frankly says, "I will confess that I found life too short for many things I would like to do. I do not think I am afraid of death but I wish it had not to come so soon."[58] So, after fifty years of sneering at hell, and at God, and at Christ, Mr. Wells wishes he didn't have to die.

The Finality of the Last Judgment. The ancient Greeks believed in what is called a series of reincarnations, that man after this life passed, according to his deeds, into another state, generally that of an animal, or suffered punishment for a thousand years in Hades, and then came forth to live again, to suffer again, and so on, endlessly. This, as is well known, is also the doctrine of some of the ancient philosophical systems of India. It has, in a superficial and commercial way, been recently revived in the utterly ridiculous and deceiving cult known as the "I Am" movement. Throughout the Word of God, however, there is one unified testimony to the truth that the judgment of the souls of men at the throne of Christ is *final.* It is determined by what a man does on this earth. All the Scriptures testify that for each man there will be only one period of trial, the length of this life. Judgment does not occur when a man dies; all the wicked are awaiting judgment; and in spite of the unscriptural and monstrously-false doctrine of purgatory, nothing one generation can do will result in any alteration in the condition of the souls of any of the deceased of any preceding generation. From the throne of judgment souls are not sent out to experience a second period of opportunity; the decisions made in this life by men and women involve eternal destiny. "It is given unto men *once* to die, and after this the judgment"[59]—one life, one death, one judgment! The very fact that the Scriptures speak of one final judgment day is in itself sufficient proof that there will not be a second period of probation for the human race, but that all mankind will, when judged, be judged finally. Did we find in the Word of God that every thousand years, for example, a new judgment day would be announced; then finality could not be assigned as a characteristic of the judgment which awaits men. After the judgment of Revelation 20, we have only a vision of the Holy City and a brief glimpse of eternity. The earth's probation is closed, and the destiny of every son of Adam is forever settled, as the earth and the sea give up their dead, and the books are opened for that dreadful day.

Final Judgment in Relation to the Resurrection of Christ. It is significant that final judgment in the teaching and preaching of the Apostle Paul is almost invariably related, as here in the Athenian address, to the resurrection of Christ. Dr. C. H. Dodd, calling attention to the sequence of these two ideas, in such passages as Romans 14:9, 10; 2:16; II Cor. 5:10, has well said, "The fact of judgment to come is appealed to as a datum of faith. It is not something *for* which Paul argues, but something *from* which he argues; something, therefore which we may legitimately assume to have been a part of his fundamental preaching. Judgment is for Paul a function of the universal Lordship of Christ which was attained through death and resurrection and Christ's second advent as Judge is a part of this preaching—as Judge, but also as Saviour."[60] Paul sums up the effect of his preaching at Thessalonica in these words: "For they themselves saw of us what manner of entering in we had unto you, and how ye turned to God from idols to serve the living and true God; And to wait for his Son from heaven, whom he raised from the dead, even Jesus, which delivered us from the wrath to come."

Canon Liddon, years ago, in relating the truth of Christ's ultimate judgment of men to the fact of His resurrection from the dead well argued: "If the reason is convinced, first, of the possibility of miracles—and this possibility cannot be denied by a serious believer in a living and moral God—and, secondly, of the truth of the historical fact that Jesus Christ did really rise again from the dead—and St. Paul will tell him that while the fact was in his lifetime a matter of widespread notoriety, it could not be denied without breaking altogether with anything that could be called Christianity—if, I say, a man be thus convinced that such a miracle as the Resurrection of Christ is historically true, he ought to have no serious difficulty, on the score of reason in believing the Last Judgment. He has already admitted the truth of the supernatural in an instance of capital importance; he has already admitted, upon adequate evidence, that the Lord Jesus, while upon earth, was not uniformly subject to those laws of life and death which govern us within the range of our present experience. If this fact warrants, as in reason it does warrant, confidence in the Words of Jesus Christ, and confidence in His Power, it obliges us to believe that He will come to judge us. For that He uttered the words of the text is beyond question. The most destructive criticism of the day sees in them, what it condescends to term, one of the really historical elements of the first Gospel. That He had a right to utter them, is proved by the fact of His Resurrection; it set the seal upon His Words. Unless, then, reason takes exception either to the possibility of miracles and so rejects any serious theism, or to the truth of Christ's resurrection, and so denies the truth of Christianity, reason must perforce admit that the last judgment is not a difficulty—at least for itself." [61]

The Moral Necessity for a Final Judgment of Men. It is not necessary to rationalize, to find a reason for every truth contained in the Word of God, but the Lord invites men to reason with Him; He urges men to think on the things that are revealed; we are told to gird up the loins of our minds, to give a reason for the hope that is within us, and we believe that it is wholesome, even in the consideration of this solemn and divine revelation of judgment, to consider some of the deeper aspects of the logical *necessity* for such an event in the program of God's redemptive purpose.

Judgment is not only a scriptural doctrine. It is the inevitable, inescapable end of history, if there is anywhere ruling in this world a righteous God. It is not only that God has appointed a day of judgment, but also that the injustices of history, the unjudged cases of all sin, the inequalities of life, the unpunished blasphemies of men, the silence of God throughout most of the centuries—a holy and righteous God—*demand* a day of judgment. As Professor Robert Flint said years ago, "From no mere word, whether law or any other, but from that consciousness of moral dependence which no moral creature can shake off, which conscience implies in every exercise, which reveals itself in a thousand ways in the hearts and lives of men, do we conclude that there is One on whom we morally depend, that we have a holy Creator and Judge to deal with." [62]

I am holding in my hand as I write this page a clipping from a newspaper of one of our largest cities—Chicago—dated July 24, 1943, which carries this heading, "Half of 5,133 Murders in City Since '25 Unsolved." The article goes on to say that between January 1, 1925, and December 31, 1942, a period of eighteen years, of the 5,133 murders committed in the city of Chicago less than fifty per cent of them have been solved, which means that now most of them never will be solved here on earth.[63] Will these murders never be judged? Will there be no punishment, in all the ages to come, for these and all other criminals who have for the time escaped? Will a righteous God go on forever allowing men to raise their fist in His face, to break His laws, and to blaspheme His name? Not if God is righteous and omnipotent. Sin must be judged. This is the truth that runs from the murder of Abel down to the very death of our blessed Lord. "There can exist no law or authoritative rule of conduct for voluntary and morally accountable agents to which a penal sanction is not attached; and the reason of the penalty is just as intrinsic and immutable as the reason of the precept. As the chief end of the precept is the glory of God, that is, the manifestation of His excellence through the exercise of His attributes as they are concerned in commanding, so the chief end of the penalty is His glory through the exercise of His attributes as they are concerned in punishing. As the moral principle involved in every precept cannot be compromised, so the divine judgment of the ill desert of sin involved in all penalty cannot be relaxed. The precept and the penalty alike express the infallible judgment of the Divine Intelligence, on a question of moral obligation founded on the Divine Nature."[64]

The second World War is now producing a whole literature in which judgment plays a prominent part, in which the necessity for a prejudgment of those guilty of awful atrocities among the Axis powers, is insisted upon by the very titles of books now coming from the press bearing witness to the fact that, deep in the heart of man, is irrevocably this idea that crime must be judged. A London publisher recently published a book by Alec R. Vidler, *God's Judgment on Europe*. Another London publisher issued a book by Lt. Col. Allison Ind, with the title *Bataan: The Judgment Seat*. The final chapter in George Creel's just published *War Criminals and Punishment* carries the single word title "Judgment."[65] President Roosevelt, in a press statement of August 21

1942, said, "It seems only fair that they (the Axis invaders) should have this warning that the time will come when they shall have to stand in the courts of law . . . and answer for their acts." Mr. Herbert Hoover and Mr. Hugh Gibson, men of balanced judgment and humanitarian views, in a recent article which they wrote together, "History's Greatest Murder Trial," they tell us that, "We should devote attention now to reaching international understanding as to the distinction to be made between the old idea of a political refugee whose greatest fault was disagreement with those in power, and the Hitlers and Tojos! A muddled conception of international law and humanity must not be used as a shield to protect people from punishment and their crimes . . . We expect them all (the neutrals) to cooperate in making the Axis gangsters available for trial on the same basis as unofficial people committing the same crimes." If all the courts in every civilized country exist because of the necessity for the judgment of personal crimes, if this war has convinced men that international crimes must also be judged and punished, then no one can raise a reasonable objection, say from the laws of logic or the demands of the human heart against a final and universal judgment of God upon men who persist in breaking His laws, in blaspheming His name, and in rejecting His only begotten Son.

Professor James Denney, in his *Studies in Theology,* with his usual brilliance, firmness, and insight, sets forth the absolute necessity of a final judgment in words which deserve to be quoted in this chapter:

"Those who take a materialistic or naturalistic view of the world do not need to raise any questions about its end; it is an essentially meaningless affair for them, and it does not matter whether or how it ends. But if we take an ethical view of the world and of history, we must have an eschatology: we must have the moral order exhibited, vindicated, brought out in perfect clearness as what it is. It is because the Bible is so intensely ethical in spirit that it is so rich in eschatological elements—in visions of the final and universal triumph of God, of the final and universal defeat of evil. It is not ethical to suppose that the moral condition of the world is that of endless suspense, in which the good and the evil permanently balance each other, and contest with each other the right to inherit the earth. Such a dualistic conception is virtually atheistic, and the whole Bible could be read as protest against it. Neither is it ethical to suppose that the moral history of the world consists of cycles in which the good and the evil are alternately victorious. There are, indeed, times when that is the impression which history makes upon us, but these are times when the senses are too strong for the spirit; and as the moral consciousness recovers its vigour, we see how inconsistent such a view is with its postulate, that the good alone has the right to reign. The Christian doctrine of a final judgment is not the putting of an arbitrary term to the course of history; it is a doctrine without which history ceases to be capable of moral construction. Neither does it signify that there is no judgment here and now, or that we have to wait till the end before we can declare the moral significance, the moral worth or worthlessness, of characters or actions; on the contrary, in the light of that great coming event the moral significance of things stands out even now, and when it does come, it is not to determine, but only to declare, what they are. It would be impossible, I think, to overestimate the power of this final judgment, as a motive, in the primitive church. On almost every page of St. Paul, for instance, we see that he lives in the presence of it; he lets the awe of it descend upon his heart to keep his conscience quick; he carries on all his work in the light of it; 'before our Lord Jesus, at His coming'—that is the judgment by which he is to be judged, that is the searching light in which his life is to be reviewed. And it needs no lesser faith than this to keep character and conduct at that height of purity and faithfulness which we see in him."[66]

The subject of a final judgment is so important, and so rarely presented from the pulpit in our day, that we offer no apology for introducing here an extended statement by the late Professor William Caven, in a work now seldom seen, *Christ's Teaching Concerning the Last Things,* which may perfectly close this discussion of the absolute necessity of final judgment: "If the doom of each individual is really fixed at death—fixed by Him who knows the history of every life, as He knows all things—why, it may be asked, should there be a day of judgment afterwards? What further end is to be accomplished thereby? This final, public act of judgment is the complete vindication of God's justice both to those who are judged and to the moral universe. The absolute righteousness of God in all His dealings through life, and in the destiny awarded, is now brought home to those who are judged as never before. Those who are condemned feel in their inmost being that the sentence passed upon them is according to their desert; and, though salvation is entirely of grace, those who are adjudged righteous would see that the reward bestowed upon them is, in every case, according to their works.

"But what presents itself first to the mind when we think of the ends served by the final judgment is the public vindication of Divine justice—the vindication of God's righteousness in the sight of men and angels, of all moral beings. This certainly is a very high end. The manifestation of His own glory—i.e., of the excellency of His own perfection —is an end than which none can be higher. In the whole of His works and in the whole history of His administration God is revealing Himself, and to learn of Him as His perfections are thus manifested is the highest blessedness of the creature. To know Him is the constant aim of all holy beings, and of all who are seeking to be holy. To make known, by the Church, the manifold wisdom of God, to the principalities and powers in heavenly places, enters into the eternal purpose which God has purposed in Christ Jesus.

"The righteousness of God's administration and His justice in recompensing both the righteous and the wicked have at no time and in no place been without attestation. But looking broadly over the field of human history, no one would say that complete proof of God's equity in His dealing with individual men has been presented to the eyes of His creatures. The confidence of faith can ever say: 'That be far from Thee to do after this manner, to slay the righteous with the wicked: and that the righteous should be as the wicked, that be far from Thee: shall not the Judge of all the earth do right?' But how often in thinking of God's providence while His work was unfinished have the best men in all ages longed to see the good man freed from oppression and the proud oppressor rewarded according to his wickedness—to see the aspersions cast upon God's faithful servants removed and the hypocrite unmasked. It is not in the spirit of revenge that saints of earth have joined with the souls under the altar in crying to God that He would avenge the blood of His martyrs. But patience must have its perfect work. No shadow of iniquity will finally rest on the Divine administration. The whole creation will see that God is just in all His ways, and holy in all His works."[67]

The Return of Contemporary Theology to a Reassertion of the Truth of Judgment to Come. There are evils in Barthian theology, but among other things it has done of a commendable and wholesome nature is that it has brought into sharp focus once again in the theological thinking of the western world this inevitableness of final judgment. No one has more strongly reaffirmed this than Dr. Reinhold Niebuhr in his now famous *Gifford Lectures,* given at Glasgow two years ago. These are his words: "There is no achievement or partial relaxation in history, no fulfillment of meaning or achievement of virtue by which man can escape the final judgment. The idea of a 'last' judgment (at the 'end' of history) expresses Christianity's refutation of all conceptions of history, according to which it is its own Redeemer, and is able by its process of growth and development, to emancipate man from the guilt and sin of his existence, and to free him from judgment. Nothing expresses the insecurity and anxiety of human experience more profoundly than the fact that the fear of extinction and the fear of judgment are compounded in the fear of death. It is prudent to accept the testimony of the heart, which affirms the fear of judgment. The freedom of man . . . makes the fear of a judgment beyond all historical judgments inevitable."[67a]

Similarly, Dr. Deissman at the Lausanne Conference, said, "For the last thirty years or so the discernment of the Eschatological character of the Gospel of Jesus has more and more come to the front in international Christian theology. I regard this as one of the greatest steps forward that theological inquiry has ever achieved. We today must lay the strongest possible stress upon the eschatological character of the Gospel which it is the practical business of the church to proclaim: now, that we must daily focus our minds upon the fact that the kingdom of God is near, that God with His unconditioned sovereignty comes through judgment and redemption, and that we have to prepare ourselves inwardly for the *maranatha*—the Lord cometh."

The Need for a New Affirmation of the Truth of a Coming Divine Judgment. It is recognized on every hand that this present hour is one of a complete breakdown in moral and ethical standards throughout the western world. There is no need in a work of this kind, of piling up statistics, or a vast number of quotations to substantiate any such assertion. Our courts are more crowded with criminal cases today than ever, and especially is this true with our juvenile courts. We are compelled to build our penitentiaries larger and larger every year. The justification in totalitarian countries of every conceivable crime and sin, if done in the name of and for the sake of the state, the deliberate denial of such a fact as fundamental moral law, the abandonment of what, for nearly two thousand years has been, as we would say, the very ethical foundation of the western world, all confirm the present crisis in morals. Professor Reinhard Hohn, Deputy Chairman of the Academy of German Law, has given the following order, since the beginning of World War II.—"The police must not be hampered by the law, and the enemies of the State must be identified by their character and ideas rather than by their acts. Consequently the basic enemies are Jews, Communists, Freemasons and Church Officials who meddle in politics. Against these the police must take the offensive, regardless of whether or not they have actually broken the law."[68] The Chief Justice of Germany, Thierack, has been appointed with power "to act independently of all law." Before the American Bar Association, men are now delivering addresses not alone on lawlessness, but on *international* lawlessness.[69] There seems to be an actual *revolt* on the part of mankind everywhere, a determination to ignore what once was felt to be binding upon the human heart. It is not only that we are living in a day of mounting crime, of universal immorality, but, more tragic than this, we are living at a time when our philosophers and many of our leading thinkers are justifying these things, claiming this immoral way is the one for modern man to adopt. As previously pointed out in this volume, we have professors who tell their students that they will be better off without God than with God, and then they add the corollary, that the moral sanctions of preceding generations must in no way bind them down, in this hour of liberty and increased knowledge. A former President of the American Sociological Society, who has been a professor of Sociology in two of our greatest universities for the past quarter of a century, frankly suggests that "in a society undergoing great change there is little guidance to be gained from the past"[70] (!), and, consequently, that the "commandments" once generally followed, are to be abandoned.

If this tendency to crime, to lawlessness, to immorality, continues with the increasing acceleration which it has shown since the First World War, we are indeed fast approaching an abyss. What is there to be done about it? The increased study of psychology, the multiplication of playgrounds, the teaching of hygiene in our public schools, the free discussion among children of the most sacred things in life, the abandonment of all reticence in conversation between men and women, the lifting of prohibition, increased freedom on every hand, with the multiplied wonders of modern science, the radio, the automobile, the airplane, and all the opportunities for increased travel, higher wages, and deliverance from poverty—all these things together are not saving us from moral disintegration. We need to come back to sounding, loudly, convincingly, with the authority of the Word of God, and in the power of the Holy Spirit, with the sanction of Christ Jesus Himself, the great doctrine identified with a righteous and Holy God, declaring a judgment wrath upon men who are in rebellion against His holy laws. This need is exactly what is recognized among some of the outstanding leaders of thought of our day. The greatest of all the newspapers of the western world, the *London Times,* in the issue of May 22, 1943, frankly said, "Among the causes of the drifting away from church going and of the relaxation of moral standards which have come about within living memory, there can be little doubt that one of the chief causes has been the disappearance of the belief in eternal punishment. Rightly or wrongly, men are not afraid of God as they used to be, and have cast off the restraints which fear imposed." I do not think that Dean Inge can be called a conservative, by any means, but long ago, in trying to re-emphasize the necessity for keeping ever before us the biblical doctrine of sin, he frankly admitted, "The disappearance of warning from the pulpit is a remarkable phenomenon, however we may account for it, and whether we approve it or not, pick up any book of sermons by a celebrated preacher who is thoroughly in touch with the younger generation today and you will see that the fear of God's judgment is hardly appealed to."[71] Only recently has this truth been frankly acknowledged by one of the bishops of the church of England, Bishop Chelmsford. "The Christian Faith seems to be dying out. In the days of our grandparents there was a gravity, a solemnity about religion which has completely vanished. This was due to the emphasis laid upon the sterner side of Christian teaching: the fear of God, the guilt of sin, the judgment of man by God, and the consequent punishment or reward in the public mind—these facts are completely discarded. God has become a tolerant, easygoing deity who is certainly not 'extreme to mark what is amiss' but can always be relied upon to let everybody off in the long run, and if there is a heaven—of course there is no truth whatever in hell!—we shall all muddle into it somewhere."[72]

No one ever appeared on earth with such words of tenderness, of love, and compassion, as did the Lord Jesus, and yet, again and again, in fact, more frequently than any one of the apostles, our Lord saw fit to warn men of a judgment to come. "Woe unto thee, Chorazin! woe unto thee, Bethsaida! for if the mighty works had been done in Tyre and Sidon which were done in you, they would have repented long ago in sackcloth and ashes. But I say unto you, it shall be more tolerable for Tyre and Sidon in the day of judgment, than for you."[73] When the Apostle Paul preached to the Athenians he told them they should repent because *God had appointed a day in which He would judge the world,* and it seems from the Word that one of the most powerful forces to persuade men to repent of their sins and turn to God is a fear of a judgment to come. Let us have done with this smart, satanically-conceived idea that a judgment to come and hell are myths, and that in the twentieth century we are too clever, and too well-informed to any longer hold to such superstitions. Well, if they are myths, let us cast them from us; if they are humanly-created superstitions, let us be delivered from them. But if these are the words of the Lord Jesus, if this is the message given by the Holy Spirit, then we do well to return to them, and proclaim this truth again with power. How strange it is that in our sophisticated age we rush after astrological nonsense, thousands cling to the intellectual chaos and fantastically unreal doctrines of Christian Science, others follow this cult, and others that, men and women in crowds almost crushing one another that they may find themselves among the elect of some India-born outworn philosophy, or more modern delusions,—yet we lightly set aside a truth declared by the very Son of God!

When the great Apostle Paul, who turned the world upside down, stood before wicked Felix, we read that he "reasoned of righteousness and self-control and of judgment to come," and—Felix *trembled*.[74] That is an experience which needs to be reintroduced into our unbelieving, God-forgetting, sin-indulging age. Men need to tremble in fear before God. When this happens they will seek a Saviour who is able to save them from the wrath to come. What Paul preached to those learned Athenians is what must be declared to the sophisticated but far less brilliant citizens of our own generation.

In the greatest exposition of the Apostles' Creed that has probably ever been written, the one by that saint and scholar John Pearson, belief in judgment as an experience leading to repentance is well set forth: "Such is the sweetness of our sins, such the connaturalness of our corruptions, so great our confidence of impunity here, that except we looked for an account hereafter, it were unreasonable to expect that any man should forsake his delights, renounce his complacencies, and by a severe repentance create a bitterness to his own soul. But being once persuaded of a judgment, and withal possessed with a sense of our sins, who will not tremble with Felix? Who will not 'flee from the wrath to come'? What must the 'hardness' be of that 'impenitent heart' which 'treasureth up unto itself wrath against the day of wrath and revelation of the righteous judgment of God'? We are naturally inclined to follow the bent of our own wills, and the inclination of our own hearts: all external rules and prescriptions are burthensome to us; and did we not look to give an account, we had no reason to satisfy any other desires than our own: especially the dictates of the word of God are so pressing and exact, that were there nothing but a commanding power, there could be no expectation of obedience. It is necessary then that we should believe that an account must be given of all our actions; and not only so, but that this account will be exacted according to the rule of God's revealed will, that 'God shall judge the secrets of men by Jesus Christ, according to the Gospel.' There is in every man not only a power to reflect, but a necessary reflection upon his actions;

not only a voluntary remembrance, but also an irresistible judgment of his own conversation. Now if there were no other judge besides our own souls, we should be regardless of our own sentence, and wholly unconcerned in our own condemnations. But if we were persuaded that these reflections of conscience are to be so many witnesses before the tribunal of heaven, and that we are to carry in our own hearts a testimony either to absolve or condemn us, we must infallibly watch over that unquiet inmate, and endeavor above all things for a good conscience." [75]

Augustine, addressing a friend on the fall of Rome, speaking of the reaction of the citizens of Rome to the approach of the Goths as an illustration of how men ought to look upon a coming judgment well said: "It is but a little ago since you witnessed how, when at the shrill trumpet-peal, and the clamour of the Goths, the City of Rome, the mistress of the world, oppressed with sadness and terror, trembled. Where then was the rank of nobility? Where definite and distinct grades of dignity of any king? All things were mingled and confused through terror, wailing in every house, equal fear pervading all. Slave and noble were as one; to all the same image of death was present, save only as those to whom life had been most joyous feared death the most. If, then, men so fear their foes and a human hand, what shall we do when the trumpet shall have begun with appalling clangour to sound from heaven, and the whole world shall re-echo the voice of the archangel louder than any trumpet's peal? When we shall see brandished over us not arms made with hands, but the very powers of heaven moved? What fear shall then seize us, what gloom, what darkness, if, often warned, that day should yet find us unprepared!" [76]

Dr. John Hutton in a brilliant paragraph on the rich fool of our Lord's parable, says, "When last we see him he is rubbing his hands together and tasting life at every pool, but our Lord, who ever used such extreme language calls him a fool, and why? for thinking that the play in which he figured was ended! This present world is not the end of anything. The drama of life which is played out here is finished on another stage. This life only sees us so far as the fourth act. Thereupon the curtain falls and when it rises again the scene is—somewhere in the presence of God. And so it happened: just as this poor fool was rubbing his hands and wondering what sensations he would next treat himself to, the bell rang and there was a call for the man's soul to come upon the stage and speak his part." [77]

Men need to be warned that there is another life; to be told there is a Holy God, and to hear through the voice of a prophet, that it is given unto all men once to die, and after this the Judgment. God grant that the economic and life-destroying judgment of this dreadful war may be used as a force with which to break in to the minds of men, to convince them of this eternal truth, that there is an even greater judgment, by God Himself, for all men, even concerning the secrets of our hearts.

"This mention of a future judgment," says Stier, "was induced by the fact that Paul stood as one that had to give account at the ancient and celebrated tribunal in Athens. He thus stands up in his sacred dignity as the ambassador of his God, who is the God of all the world, and entirely reverses the position of things by announcing an impending judgment to those very men who might pass judgment on him." [78] Thus St. Paul, among the philosophers at Athens, as in all places where he proclaimed the Gospel, illustrated, in his life, his admonition to the Corinthians—"Knowing therefore the terror of the Lord, we persuade men." [79]

Chapter Ten

"PEACE AND JOY IN BELIEVING"

Carlyle begins the second part of his *Life of Friedrich Schiller* with this confession, in which every great man of every age would unite: "If to know wisdom were to practice it; if fame brought true dignity and peace of mind; or happiness consisted in nourishing the intellect with its appropriate food, and surrounding the imagination with ideal beauty, a literary life would be the most enviable which the lot of this world affords. But the truth is far otherwise. The Man of Letters has no immutable, all-conquering volition, more than other men. His fame rarely exerts a favorable influence on his dignity of character, and never on his peace of mind: its glitter is external, for the eyes of others; within, it is but the ailment of unrest, the oil cast upon the ever-gnawing fire of ambition, quickening into fresh vehemence the blaze which it stills for a moment. The most finished efforts of the mind give it little pleasure, frequently they give it pain; for men's aims are ever far beyond their strength. And the outward recompense of these undertakings, the distinction they confer, is of still smaller value: the desire for it is insatiable even when successful; and when baffled, it issues in jealousy and envy, and every pitiful and painful feeling."[1] This from one of the greatest literary men of all times, brilliant, gifted, scholarly, upright in morals, with great fame and all that would seem to make life worth living. Such a confession could be multiplied by as large a number as there are famous men in history.

Standing out and above all these confessions of restlessness, unhappiness and disquietude born of unsatisfied longings and only momentary joy, are the promises of Holy Scripture and their undeniable fulfillments in the lives of those who have placed their trust in Almighty God. One of the greatest men who ever lived, also gifted, brilliant, profound in his writings, with a vast number of friends throughout the Mediterranean world, incessant in labor, suffering all things, powerful of speech, master of himself, St. Paul, could write in what is possibly the most amazingly inexhaustible document of all literature, the Epistle to the Romans, that it is the will of God that men should have "peace and joy in believing."[2] Already in this volume we have noticed how that man, unassisted by divine revelation, no matter how brilliant his mind, how great his achievements, or how profound his knowledge, has never been able to attain, in throwing off faith in God, and abandoning belief in the Word of God, anything that could be called either peace or joy. The literature of rationalism, the biographies of unbelievers, the recorded experiences of those who have abandoned faith, whatever else they may be, all reveal this truth, that neither peace nor joy is to be found in their pages.

Now that we have surveyed the evidence for three great truths of the Holy Scripture, the creation of the world by God, the historical resurrection of Christ, and the certainty of judgment to come, we might add one more testimony to the reasonableness of believing the Bible, in this undeniable fact that belief in the truths of the Christian faith has resulted in, and continues to create in the human heart, abiding peace and genuine joy. If this is true, and one cannot doubt it, it is in itself a testimony to the fact that the Word of God does contain that which satisfies the deepest needs of human personality, and in doing so, testifies to the abiding truthfulness of that Word.

Let us turn first of all to the matter of joy. The first time we have any record of singing in the Bible is immediately after the deliverance of the Hebrew people from the pursuing army of Pharaoh, when Moses and the children of Israel sang the song of praise recorded in the fifteenth chapter of Exodus. For three hundred years in Israel's history, i.e., since the days of David, we find but one reference to *singing,* among the people of God, until the revival that occurred under Hezekiah: "When the burnt offering began, the song of the Lord began also." Indeed, "they sang praises with gladness," and, "Hezekiah rejoiced and all the people." The joy was so abundant, its sources so deep, that the children of Israel "kept the feast of unleavened bread seven days with great gladness, and the whole assembly took counsel to keep other seven days: and they kept other seven days with gladness." During the days of Ahaz, when false gods were worshiped, the streets of Jerusalem filled with idolatrous abominations, captives being led off by thousands, all the people trembling for fear of what the next day might bring forth, the gates of the Temple closed, the services of Jehovah no longer conducted, how could Jerusalem know any joy? But now, with all these abominations swept away, and the Lord dwelling again in the midst of His people, "there was great joy in Jerusalem, for, since the time of Solomon, son of David, king of Israel, there was not the like in Jerusalem." [3]

Here was, indeed, on a vast scale, that which David sang out of his own personal experience: "I waited patiently for Jehovah, and he inclined unto me, and heard my cry. He brought me up also out of a horrible pit, out of the miry clay; and he set my feet upon a rock, and established my goings. And he hath put a new song into my mouth, even praise unto our God: many shall see it and fear, and shall trust in Jehovah." [4] The joy constantly referred to in this revival was, says Alexander Smellie: "The joy of God's pardon after our rebellion, the joy of his fellowship, of which we have deprived ourselves to our own undoing, the joy of worshiping him in lowliest reverence and adoration, the joy of knowing, through time and eternity, he is ours and we are his. Then, not for seven days, or for fourteen out of the three hundred sixty-five, but for every day—the commonest, the most exacting, the most trying—our life will be transfigured into a Passover Festival."

The great English Congregational preacher, Dr. R. W. Dale, in speaking of the effect produced by the Moody and Sankey meetings, at the close of their first mission in Birmingham, said:

"What struck me in the gallery of Bingley Hall was the fact that this instant transition took place with nearly every person I talked. They had come up into the gallery anxious, restless, feeling after God in the darkness, . . . they went away, their faces filled with light, and they left me not only at peace with God but filled with joy." [5]

The New Testament opens (chronologically speaking, not in Matthew, but in Luke) with a dual announcement from heaven that what is now about to take place will be the cause for both peace and joy among men. Zacharias filled with the Holy Ghost prophesied even before the birth of Christ that now the Dayspring from on high who was about to visit them would "guide their feet into the way of peace." The angelic host announcing the birth of the Saviour to the shepherds sang "glory to God in the highest and on earth peace to men of good will."[6] The angel of the Lord declared to the shepherds, "Fear not: for, behold, I bring you good tidings of great joy, which shall be to all people."[7] The age of what we call Christianity, the advent of our Lord at least was introduced by heaven declaring that peace and joy were now about to be available to men as never before in human history.

When we come to the public ministry of the last days of our Lord we are face to face with a most astonishing fact, namely that it was in the last twenty-four hours of Jesus' life on earth, that He spoke more frequently both of peace and joy than He did in all the rest of His three years of preaching and teaching combined, as far as the records inform us. It was on this last night that Jesus Himself was betrayed by Judas, He was denied by Peter, He was hated by the world, He was rejected by His own brethren, He was mistreated by the soldiers, He was about to suffer every indignity physical and mental. He knew within twenty-four hours He would be nailed to a cross, He was Himself in such agony that He shed as it were drops of blood and cried out that His own soul was exceeding sorrowful even unto death. And yet it was in this very twenty-four hour period, which in many ways may be called the darkest night in human history, that Jesus spoke exclusively of *His own joy*. I do not find Him speaking of *His own joy* in any other passage in the New Testament. Let us recall his words: "These things have I spoken unto you, that my joy may be in you, and that your joy may be made full." "And ye therefore now have sorrow: but I will see you again, and your heart shall rejoice, and your joy no one taketh away from you . . . Hitherto have ye asked nothing in my name: ask, and ye shall receive, that your joy may be made full." "But now I come to thee; and these things I speak in the world, that they may have my joy made full in themselves."[8] At the same time our Lord continually referred to His own peace: "Peace I leave with you; my peace I give unto you: not as the world giveth, give I unto you. Let not your heart be troubled, neither let it be fearful." "These things have I spoken unto you, that in me ye may have peace. In the world ye have tribulation: but be of good cheer; I have overcome the world."[9] After He was raised from the dead it was this peace that He so desired His disciples to possess. "When therefore it was evening, on that day, the first day of the week, and when the doors were shut where the disciples were, for fear of the Jews, Jesus came and stood in the midst, and saith unto them, Peace be unto you. And when he had said this, he showed unto them his hands and his side. The disciples therefore were glad, when they saw the Lord. Jesus therefore said to them again, Peace be unto you: as the Father hath sent me, even so send I you . . . And after eight days again his disciples were within, and Thomas with them. Jesus cometh, the doors being shut, and stood in the midst, and said, Peace be unto you."[10] What gave our Lord this peace and joy? I think the same thing that gives us peace and joy. Paul says we have these two precious things in believing. Christ as a Man had them likewise in believing, in the things He knew, in the things He was sure of, in His knowledge of His father, of Himself, His work and of the future.

The Apostle in his eternally true epistles speaks first of a God of peace who is able to comfort us and to abide with us. This God of peace is the one who bestows peace upon us. Again and again the Apostle opens his epistles, to the Christians in Rome, Ephesus, Colossae, and Philippi, great pagan cities of idolatry, intellectual power, commercial activity, and sensuality, with the prayer that they might enjoy peace from God.[11] When the Apostle has finished his great argument in the Epistle to the Romans, showing how we are justified before God, not by the works of the law but by the grace of the Lord Jesus Christ, and having a righteousness which is available for us only through His sacrificial death, he begins his fifth chapter with the declaration, "Therefore being justified by faith we have peace with God through our Lord Jesus Christ."[12] Elsewhere he writes to the Colossians that it was through the blood of His cross that the Lord Jesus Christ has made peace and reconciled us to God.[13] As a result of such a redemption, accomplished with such a sacrifice, the hearts and minds of Christians may forever be kept by the peace of God which passeth all understanding.[14] There is absolutely nothing in all the biographies of unbelievers, or rationalists, or modern skeptics, which can present any such testimony to the reality of peace and joy in the human heart as the New Testament proclaims. Professor Robert Flint was right when, years ago, he wrote in his famous work on Theism, "The heart can find no secure rest except on an infinite God. If less than omnipotent, He may be unable to help us in the hour of sorest need. If less than omniscient He may overlook us. If less than perfectly just, we cannot unreservedly trust Him. If less than perfectly benevolent, we cannot fully love Him. The whole soul can only be devoted to One who is believed to be absolutely good." [15]

A remarkable illustration of how men who, because of circumstances and doubt and disappointment find themselves in a mood of despair, can be brought into an experience of joy and peace, is revealed in the concluding verses of St. Luke's Gospel. On Easter day our Lord overtook two disciples, one by the name of Cleopas, walking toward Emmaus, concerning whom the Lord Himself said: "What communications are these that ye have one with another, as ye walk? And they stood still, looking sad." They told Him why they were sad: because of what had happened to the One they loved and adored, Jesus of Nazareth, a Prophet mighty in deed and word before God and all the people, who had been condemned to death and crucified three days before. They had hoped He was the One who would have redeemed all Israel, but now, apparently, He was not, for not only had He died, and not risen again, but actually His body had disappeared, and what had happened to Him none of them knew. Now when we come to the end of the chapter, we read that these very same people "returned to Jerusalem with great joy." [16] What changed the mood of their hearts? What has lifted this darkness, enabling them to rejoice and praise God? Three things, it seems: First, Jesus, rebuking them for not believing all that the prophets had spoken, began to expound the Scriptures to them, so that they came to realize not only what the Old Testament Scriptures meant, but that that which had been predicted of the Messiah had now come to pass. They had a new conviction of the truthfulness of the Word of God, and at the same time, the Messiahship of Christ. Furthermore, they had seen the Lord, for as He broke bread with them that night they recognized Him. In the evening He appeared to all the Eleven, in an upper room, and showed them His hands and His feet, when again they rejoiced. Finally, He gave them a great work to do—to preach repentance and remission of sins among all the nations, to be witnesses of the things they had seen, for which He promised them divine power. Seeing Him go up to heaven, and knowing He was the Son of God, knowing the Scriptures were true, knowing they had a great work to do by the power of God, they returned to Jerusalem with great joy. This is what we need today, an understanding of the Scriptures, a conviction that Christ is the Son of God, and a passion for doing the work which He has called us to do.

Turning from the New Testament Scriptures, may I bring to your attention the testimonies of a few of God's children in the seventeenth, eighteenth, and nineteenth centuries, which bear witness to the truth we are setting forth in this chapter and which Paul declared in his Roman epistle, mainly that there is peace and joy in believing. Take, for instance, these words of John Bunyan: "I see myself now at the end of my journey: my toilsome days are ended. I am going to see that head which was crowned with thorns, and that face which was spit upon for me. I have formerly lived by hearsay and faith; but now I go where I shall live by sight, and shall be with Him in whose company I delight myself. I have loved to hear my Lord spoken of; and wherever I have seen the print of his shoe in the earth, there I have coveted to set my foot too. His name has been to me a civet-box; yea, sweeter than all perfumes. His voice to me has been most sweet; and his countenance I have more desired than they that have most desired the light of the sun. His words I did use to gather for my food, and for antidotes against my faintings. He has held me, and hath kept me from my iniquities; yea, my steps have been strengthened in his way."[17] Crossing the English Channel over to France, this is the testimony of Madame Guyon after spending ten years in prison and suffering every conceivable indignity because of her loyalty to the Lord Jesus Christ, "I passed my time in great peace," she writes concerning these very years of imprisonment, "content to spend the rest of my life there if such were the will of God. I sang songs of joy, which the maid who served me learned by heart as fast as I made them: and we sang together Thy praises, oh my God! The stones of my prison looked in my eyes like rubies. I esteemed them more than all the gaudy brilliancies of a vain world."[18]

I doubt if many of our people today are acquainted with the remarkable biography of Harriet Beecher Stowe, written by her son, and perhaps many who know her only as the internationally famous author of "Uncle Tom's Cabin" are unaware that she was one who walked with God all the days of her life, and that the older she grew somehow the more wonderful the Lord became to her. In 1830, when only nineteen years of age, she wrote to her brother, Edward, "I have never been so happy as this summer. I began it with more suffering than I ever before have felt but there is One whom I daily thank for all that suffering since I hope that it has brought me at last to rest entirely in Him." When she was seventy-three years of age, she seemed more absorbed with the Lord Jesus than ever, after the whole world had recognized her literary genius, and she had been entertained by many of the great leaders of her century. "This winter I study nothing but Christ's life, it keeps my mind steady and helps me to bear the languor and pain of which I have more than usual this winter . . . As the true bond of union between the spirit world and our souls for one blessed hour in prayer when we draw near to Him and feel the length, the depth, the breadth, and the height of that love of His that passeth knowledge is better than all those incoherent, vain, dreamy glimpses with which longing hearts are cheated (she is referring here to Spiritism) . . . I thank God there is one thing running through all my thoughts from the time I was thirteen years old and that is the intense, unwavering sense of Christ's educating, guiding presence and care. It is *all* that remains now." When she was nearly eighty she wrote to a friend, "The inconceivable loveliness of Christ! It seems that about Him there is a sphere where the enthusiasm of love is the calm habit of the soul, that without words, without the necessity of demonstrations of affection, heart beats to heart, soul answers soul, we respond to the Infinite Love, and we feel his answer in us, and there is no need of words. All seemed to be busy coming and going on ministries of good, and passing each gave a thrill of joy to each as Jesus, the directing soul, the centre of all, 'over all, in all, and through all,' was working his beautiful and merciful will to redeem and save. I was saying as I awoke:—

'"Tis joy enough, my all in all,
At thy dear feet to lie.

Thou wilt not let me lower fall,
And none can higher fly.'

"This was but a glimpse; but it has left a strange sweetness in my mind."[19]

I challenge anyone in the world to produce a confession like this from any unbeliever, at the age of eighty, who all his life has kept away from God, has not known the Lord Jesus Christ, and has publicly and persistently denied the Christian faith. There is no such testimony to be found.

Probably no man in the nineteenth century, in Great Britain, preached to as many people, or with such power and blessing and results, as Charles H. Spurgeon. I think a testimony from such a one, who toiled incessantly, who held the greatest congregation in London for over twenty years, whose sermons are still printed by the thousands, and read and loved throughout the English world, I think the testimony of such a man, who stood up in the great city of London and lifted high the gospel, day after day, and year after year, is of some value. No rationalist in the whole nineteenth century spoke, in twenty years, to as many as Spurgeon preached to during his glorious ministry. This is his own confession to the reality of peace and joy, in the very prime of life, at the age of forty-three: "You come to know the God of hope through the Scriptures, which reveal him; by this you are led to believe in him, and it is through that believing that you become filled with joy and peace. It is not by working, nor by feeling, that we become full of joy; our peace does not arise from the marks, and evidences, and experiences which testify to us that we are the sons of God, but simply from believing. Our central joy and peace must always come to us, not as an inference from the internal work of the Spirit in our souls, but from the finished work of the Lord Jesus, and the promises of God contained in the Scriptures. We must continue to look out of self to the written word wherein the Lord is set forth before us, and we must rest in God in Christ Jesus as the main basis of our hope; not depending upon any other arguments than those supplied by the Bible itself. I will show by-and-by how we shall afterwards reach to a hope which flows out of the work of the Spirit within us; but at the first, and, I think, permanently and continuously, the main ground of the surest joy and truest peace must come to us through simply believing in Jesus Christ. Beloved, I know that I have been converted, for I am sure that there is a change of heart in me; nevertheless, my hope of eternal life does not hang upon the inward fact. I rest in the external fact that God hath revealed himself in Jesus as blotting out the sin of all his believing people, and, as a believer, I have the word of God as my guarantee of forgiveness. This is my rest. Because I am a believer in Christ Jesus, therefore have I hope, therefore have I joy and peace, since God hath declared that 'he that believeth in him hath everlasting life.' This joy can only safely come through believing, and I pray you, brothers and sisters, never be drifted away from child-like faith in what God hath said. It is very easy to obtain a temporary joy and peace through your present easy experience, but how will you do when all things within take a troublous turn? Those who live by feeling change with the weather. If you ever put aside your faith in the finished work to drink from the cup of your own inward sensations, you will find yourself bitterly disappointed. Your honey will turn to gall, your sunshine into blackness; for all things which come to man are fickle and deceptive. The God of hope will fill you with joy and peace, but it will only be through believing. You will still have to stand as a poor sinner at the foot of the cross, trusting to the complete atonement. You will never have joy and peace unless you do. If you once begin to say, 'I am a saint; there is something good in me,' and so on, you will find joy evaporate and peace depart. Hold on to your believing." [20]

The famous British cricketer, C. T. Studd, who joined the China Inland Mission in 1884, when paying his farewell visit to his own university (Cambridge), said to the men of that great school, shortly before he was to leave for China, "I want to recommend you to my Master. I have had many ways of pleasure in my time and have tasted most of the delights this world can give but I can tell you that these pleasures are as nothing compared with my present joy. I have had formerly as much love for cricket as any man could have; but when the Lord Jesus came into my heart I found I had something infinitely better. My heart was no longer set on the game, I wanted to win souls, to serve and please Him." [21] Many a rationalist, and many a skeptic, has voiced his own unbelief, at one time or another, in Cambridge, as in Oxford, and in many other of our universities, but none of them could ever stand up and give such a testimony as this—peace and joy they do not and cannot speak of.

I have not resorted in this volume to poetry, but I do not make an apology for doing so at the close of this chapter. Bishop Edward H. Bickersteth, in 1875, at the age of fifty, wrote a hymn of fourteen famous lines, which has since been sung in almost all the Protestant churches of the western world. We conclude this chapter with such words as these because they are the echo of the promises of the New Testament, and were a reality in the life of the Bishop who wrote them.

> "Peace, perfect peace, in this dark world of sin?
> The blood of Jesus whispers peace within.
>
> Peace, perfect peace, by thronging duties pressed?
> To do the will of Jesus, this is rest.
>
> Peace, perfect peace, with sorrows surging round?
> On Jesus' bosom naught but calm is found.
>
> Peace, perfect peace, with loved ones far away?
> In Jesus' keeping we are safe, and they.
>
> Peace, perfect peace, our future all unknown?
> Jesus we know, and He is on the throne.
>
> Peace, perfect peace, death shadowing us and ours?
> Jesus has vanquished death and all its powers.
>
> It is enough: earth's struggles soon shall cease,
> And Jesus call us to heaven's perfect peace."

In skepticism and unbelief there has always been, there cannot help but be, despair in the place of hope, a miserable unceasing restlessness in place of peace, and either an ever-deepening sorrow or a chilling stoicism instead of true and abiding joy. For all who have come to know and love the Lord Jesus Christ, no matter what their previous life was, no matter what their circumstances in life, there is available a peace that passeth all understanding and a joy the world can never take away. There *is* peace and joy in believing: there is neither in unbelief.

Chapter XI

SUGGESTIONS FOR AN IMMEDIATE VIGOROUS OFFENSIVE IN THE DEFENSE OF THE CHRISTIAN FAITH

To an unbelieving world which grows increasingly atheistic, and more and more profoundly ignorant of the most elementary truths of Holy Scripture, it is utterly useless for Christian believers, or even the church as an organization to insist that *mankind* must "return to the Bible," or "return to faith in God," or to urge the vowing of a new allegiance to something called religion. The "world" is not going to listen to such admonitions, for the "world" has already made up its mind that the Bible is not a divine book, and that the foundations of religion have about crumbled away. If the world is to be reached in its unbelief, it must be as individual men are dealt with, as the Church of Christ shows to the world its own implicit faith in the Word of God, and devotes itself to the work for which it was founded, the proclamation of the gospel of the Lord Jesus Christ. *What* the believing church is to do, and what individual Christians should do, in the deepening darkness of skepticism which is falling upon the world, with an increasing antagonism, not to "religion," but to the great fundamental truths of the New Testament, are difficult questions. I am compelled to write this chapter because I feel it is the only way to conclude the argument which I have attempted to construct in this volume. My own limitations are so many, and my knowledge so meager, that did I not feel some suggestions should be emphasized at this time, I would never undertake to write these final pages.

Exactly what course our civilization will take during the next thirty years, I do not know, of my own wisdom. According to the New Testament Scriptures, this age will end in a vast and deep apostasy, but whether or not this is the actual end of the age I cannot say, dogmatically. No one knew more truly how dark and unbelieving and skeptical the future would be than the Apostle Paul, and yet no one has spoken more frequently and vigorously of the necessity for fighting the good fight of faith, defending the gospel, and striving for the faith that we confess, than the same Apostle. We find in his epistles both the clear prediction of a coming apostasy, leading up to the return of Christ, and at the same time a constant exhortation to vigorously contend for the gospel. It will not then be counted a contradiction if believers to-day hold both these truths at the same time. One thing we can well believe, as was said years ago by Philip Schaff at the beginning of the first volume of his famous *History of the Christian Church,* "It is difficult to convert a nation; it is more difficult to train it in the high standards of the gospel; it is most difficult to revive and reform a dead or apostate church."[1] It is about this most difficult matter that I would like to speak in this chapter.

What All True Disciples of Christ Should Do for the Faith at This Time of Crisis. Nowhere in the New Testament are we told to assume an attitude of *laissez faire* in regard to attacks of infidelity, the efforts of false teachers to delude many, the denials of the faith within the church, the enemies of Christianity without. To the contrary, the New Testament epistles in describing the Christian life, among other things, continually set it forth as a life of conflict, of deliberate engagement in "the good fight of faith." It is to the phrases which are especially used by the Apostle Paul that I would like to direct our attention at the beginning of this chapter. The Apostle, writing at the close of his life, urges all faithful disciples, to "stand fast in the faith."[2] *The faith* is of course, as everyone recognizes, that body of truth which is elsewhere called the gospel, embracing belief in God, in Christ the Son of God, in Christ's death for sin, and His resurrection for our justification, in our own resurrection at the last day, eternal life in glory, and fellowship with the triune God. When this faith is being attacked, when enemies of every description, a vast host, with various and subtle devices, attempt to destroy confidence in this body of divine truth, or to deny the truthfulness of its precepts—what those must do who have been saved by this gospel, and have put their trust in Christ as Saviour, no matter what it costs, is to *stand fast in the faith,* i.e., we must never retreat from those great truths, without which there can be no saving gospel. It is not that in such a time of attack we are to stand fast in the theories of democracy, or to stand fast for some indefinite concept of "religion"; but that we are to stand fast *in the faith,* the faith set forth in the New Testament, and are not to allow men to push us back across the line of that conviction that embraces a supernatural Christ, into an area of indifference or denial. We are to stand for the Church, in its great creeds, which are bulwarks for us carved out of the rocks of divine revelation. If we leave these fortresses, we will find ourselves helplessly exposed to every device of the enemies of God, and will be driven step by step, and frequently league by league, back into the territory of agnosticism, if not absolute atheism, as many have experienced to their own sorrow. Well did Dr. Warfield express the necessity for such a firm stand on the part of all believers when, toward the close of the last century, he said: "We cannot mistake the fact that God's Word giving their meaning, their force and their value to His great redemptive action enters as vitally into our Christianity and hope as the acts themselves. As men we cannot let slip our faith in one without losing our grasp upon the other. The Word of the Living God is our sole assurance that there has been a redemptive activity exercised by God in the world. Just in proportion as our confidence in this interpretative Word shall wane, in just that proportion shall we lose our hold upon the fact of a redemptive work of God in the world. We all desire a Christianity which is secure from the assaults of the unbelieving world . . . but this security is to be sought and can be found only in a Christianity whose facts and doctrines are so entrenched against the inevitable assault that whatever else falls, they shall stand. What fatuity it is to seek it rather by yielding to the assault all it chooses to demand, contracting Christianity into dimensions too narrow to call out the world's antipathy and too weak to invite its attack. Such an eviscerated Christianity may no longer be worth the world's notice and by that same token is no longer worth the Christian's preservation. It has been reduced to a vanishing point, is ready to pass away."[3]

Not only are we to stand fast in the faith but we are to throw ourselves vigorously into "the defense of the gospel."[4] The word which Paul here uses is *apologia,* which means, first of all, a verbal defense, a speech in defense of what one has done or of a truth which one believes, e.g., Paul's defense before Agrippa. It is significant that this very form of Christian activity is urgently pressed upon the clergy of the Church of England, and those of the Protestant Episcopal Church of our own country, in their beautiful ordination service which, though I am not an Episcopalian, I have always felt is the most remarkable ordination service for the clergy of any communion in all of protestantism. In this service the bishop, among some other fine things, says to the one about to be ordained, "Seeing that you cannot by any other means compass the doing of so mighty a work pertaining to the salvation of man, but with doctrine and exhortation taken out of the Holy Scriptures, and with a life agreeable to the same: consider how studious you ought to be in reading, and learning the Scriptures, and in framing the manners, both of yourselves and of them that especially pertain unto you, according to the rule of the same Scriptures: and for this selfsame cause how ye ought to forsake and set aside (as much as you may) all worldly care and studies . . . and that you will continually pray to God the Father by the mediation of our only Saviour, Jesus Christ, for the heavenly assistance of the Holy Ghost, that by daily reading and weighing of the Scriptures ye may wax riper and stronger in your ministry . . ." Shortly after this, the Bishop asks the question, "Are you persuaded that the Holy Scriptures contain all doctrine required of necessity for eternal salvation through faith in Jesus Christ? And are you determined out of the said Scriptures to instruct the people committed to your charge? And to teach nothing (as required of necessity to eternal salvation) but that which you shall be persuaded may be concluded and approved by the Scripture?" The one being ordained answers, "I am so persuaded; and have so determined by God's grace." Shortly thereafter the bishop asks, "Will you be ready, with all diligence, *to banish and drive away all erroneous, and strange doctrines, contrary to God's word;* and to use both public and private monitions and exhortations as well as to the sick as to the whole within your Cures as need shall require and occasion shall be given?" Answer: "I will, the Lord being my helper."[5] This is what is meant by the defense and confirmation of the gospel. We may defend it with what we say; we may defend it by the life we live; we may defend it by challenging those that attack it; we may defend it by revealing in books, in our periodicals, in our local newspapers, from the pulpit, from a teacher's desk, from whatever position we hold in the business world, the falseness of the accusations that are brought against our faith, and the truthfulness of the great doctrines of the Christian religion.

Not only does the greatest of all the apostles lay upon every believer the obligation to "fight the good fight of faith," but when he himself comes to die, he could say without hesitation or fear of contradiction, "I have fought the good fight."[6] St. Jude, in his brief epistle, urges the same form of activity, when he admonishes believers that they should "earnestly contend for the faith."[7] The verb here translated "earnestly contend" is *epagonizomai* (found only here in the New Testament), and derives, as one immediately discovers, from the verb from which we have our English word *agonize*. The Greek verb was used to express the idea of contest in gymnastic games, the actual fighting against enemies of the state, and the struggling with those antagonistic to the gospel. The gospel, when these men were writing, was being threatened by teachers who denied its sufficiency, and would contaminate its purity, and it was necessary that men redouble their efforts to keep the deposit divinely given. In fact, it has been suggested that the word Jude uses here means "to fight standing upon a thing which is assaulted, and which the adversary desires to take away, and it is to fight so as to defend it, and to retain it."[8] This is what St. Paul means when, in writing to the Philippians, he says that we are all to unite "in one spirit with one soul striving for the faith of the gospel."[9]

In St. Paul's Second Epistle to the Church at Corinth there is to be found an exhortation which seemingly has almost dropped out of sight, certainly out of consideration on the part of contemporary Christianity. Conybeare's translation reads as follows: "For though living in the flesh, my warfare is not waged according to the flesh. For the weapons which I wield are not of fleshly weakness, but mighty in the strength of God to the overthrow of the strongholds of the enemies. Thereby can I overthrow the reasonings of the disputer and pull down all lofty bulwarks that raise themselves against the knowledge of God, and bring every rebellious thought into captivity and subjection of God."[10] Thayer defines the word here translated "strongholds" as "the arguments and reasonings by which a disputant endeavors to fortify his opinion and defend it against his opponent." Dr. G. Campbell Morgan, in the only satisfactory sermon I have ever seen on this verse, preached now nearly forty years ago, well said, "The purpose of the church's warfare is the capture of the inspirational centers of human life. Behind all our speaking is our thinking. The church's warfare is aimed at the capture of these inspirational centers, in order that they may be possessed by the ideals and purposes of Jesus Christ. The purpose for which the church fights, and must forever fight, is that she may bring the thinking of men into harmony with the thinking of Christ. . . . The church's business is to create opinion; to capture the thinking of men, and compel it to the thinking of Christ."[11]

There is one word, quite often found in the New Testament, expressing a fundamental duty of true followers of our Lord, which is seldom dwelt upon these days, even in evangelical circles, either in its literature or its preaching, a word that has direct relation to what we are setting forth in the early part of this chapter, and that is the word "confess." Our Lord urges the necessity for boldly confessing Him before men, and the Apostle Paul actually links the reality of our salvation with confessing with our mouth the Lord Jesus.[12] Antichristian spirits are characterized by the Apostle John as those who confess not that Jesus Christ is come in the flesh.[13] This matter of confessing Christ is something in which every believer, whatever be his training, and wherever he may be situated, can participate, and at no time in this century has such confession been so important as now. There is a vast conspiracy today in which the leaders of agnosticism and atheism unite to attempt to frighten Christians from confessing Christ, to persuade them that what they ought really to do is to remain silent, to let their "life" tell, to let the Christian religion "naturally" lay hold of the hearts of men, but not to talk about it publicly, nor intrude it into a conversation, nor to speak of it, for example, in a class-room. Thus, for instance, Dr. Durant Drake, for some years the professor of philosophy at Vassar College, in his widely used book, *Invitation to Philosophy,* says at the conclusion of his volume, "In the meantime we shall believe as our emotions and our hopes compel us, and no one can rightly condemn us, so long as we refrain from becoming dogmatic and trying to impose our beliefs upon others, and as long as we are honest enough to realize that the question remains open and that no man really knows."[14] Now to a subtle admonition like this we Christians should most emphatically object. This is contrary to everything that the New Testament tells us we ought to do with our gospel. Beginning with the end of the statement, Professor Drake is definitely wrong when he says, concerning the matter of religion and the problems it embraces, that "no man really knows." Well, the apostles knew; their epistles are filled with the phrase "we know." They knew because they were eye-witnesses of Christ, and His resurrection. They handled Him, they heard Him, they saw Him, they were convinced beyond all doubt of the great certainties of the faith; and so is every true Christian.[15] It is not only our privilege, but also our responsibility to know; to know Christ, to know that we have become the children of God, to know we are in-dwelt by His Holy Spirit, to know that we have a home in heaven, to know that we are delivered from the power of sin, to know that prayer is answered, to know a hope that fadeth not away. The question does *not* remain open. A Christian's life is not one filled with a continuous series of interrogations. Imagine St. Paul submitting to some threatening order that he was not to "impose his belief upon others"! Yet, that is exactly what the apostles were told, not to preach or teach in the name of Jesus, and those apostles went to prison rather than cease proclaiming Christ as the only Saviour among men.[16] If I saw a person going blind, and I knew of a doctor I thought could help him, I would every day urge him to consult that doctor, until he went, or blindness became total. If I knew that a friend's life was threatened, I would warn him. It is our business to talk about Christ who saves, and the Word of God which is a divine revelation, and the Father of our Lord Jesus Christ who loves men.

It is a strange thing, but these men who insist we should not impose our beliefs upon others, never hesitate to impose their disbeliefs on others. They write books to spread their wretched denials. They stand up in the class-room to impose their skepticism upon the plastic minds of their immature students. They go up and down the land, giving lectures, and writing articles in outstanding periodicals, to impose their agnosticism upon youth looking for something to believe. We need to be as dogmatic in our affirmations as they are dogmatic in their denials. If what we believe as the Christian faith is true, we ought to be terribly in earnest in telling people about it, and not frightened away by rreligious intellectuals, who say that to talk about these things with ıny conviction is an act of impoliteness, or discourtesy, or childishness. Dr. William Lyon Phelps tells us, in his fascinating *Autobiography,* hat he "was invited to teach in a certain college, and was asked if I ould keep my religion out of the class room; on my telling this to President Dwight he laughed and said: 'my own observation shows hat college teachers who are religious never mention it in the class oom; the pupils never find it out whereas those who are antireligious mpress their views on the students and talk about it constantly.'"[17]

What I am now going to say will probably shock many people; it s so contrary to everything that is being expressed in this age of an naemic toleration of every conceivable kind of heresy, in this age when eople are so glibly advocating a spineless universal religion, and earful of offending anyone by our own religious convictions. Let me ut it frankly, in one brief sentence: what we need today is some lownright, manly, courageous intolerance in the Christian church, f all those tendencies and humanistically-derived theories which, while hey may encourage the pride of man, are wholly destructive of anyhing bearing a resemblance to New Testament Christianity. Instead f speaking on the necessity of intolerance in my own words, may I ring to the attention of my readers, who may have come to look ıpon this word almost as something diabolical, a remarkable statenent by one of the greatest theologians of the beginning of our cenury, one whose influence was probably as wide as that of any other heological scholar in Great Britain, or America, thirty years ago. I efer to Professor James Denney. Before quoting the learned Profesor on the matter of intolerance, let us recall that in 1897 he succeeded Candlish as Professor of Systematic and Pastoral Theology in Glasgow Free Church College, and, two years later, on the death of Professor

Bruce, was appointed to the chair of New Testament Literature anc Theology, and in 1915, succeeding Professor T. M. Lindsay, was made Principal of the College, a position which he held until his death June 15, 1917. It was Denney who wrote the brilliant expositions or the Epistles to the Thessalonians and II Corinthians, in the *Exposi tors' Bible,* the commentary on Romans in the *Expositors' Greek Tes tament,* and one of the most remarkable books on the atonement o the last half century, *The Death of Christ.*

Professor Denney reminds us that, "immediately after Paul men tioned our Lord Jesus Christ as one *who gave Himself for our sins tha He might deliver us from this present evil world with all its evils* he says to the Galatians: 'Though we or an angel from heaven preach a gospel to you contravening the gospel which we preached, let him be anathema. As we have said before, so say I now again, if any mar is preaching a gospel to you contravening what you received, let him be anathema.' I cannot agree," says Denney, "with those who dis parage this, or affect to forgive it, as the unhappy beginning of re ligious intolerance. Neither the Old Testament nor the New Testa ament has any conception of a religion without this intolerance. Th first commandment is, 'Thou shalt have none other gods beside Me, and that is the foundation of the true religion. As there is only on God, so there can be only one gospel. If God has really done somethin in Christ on which the salvation of the world depends, and if he ha made it known, then it is a Christian duty to believe when he says 'Neither is there salvation in any other,' or John, when he says, 'He tha hath the Son hath the life; he that hath not the Son of God hath nc the life'; or Jesus Himself when He says, 'No man knoweth the Fathe save the Son, and he to whomsoever the Son willeth to reveal him.' In tolerance like this is an essential element in the true religion; it has th instinct of self-preservation in it; the unforced and uncompromisin defence of that on which the glory of God and the salvation of th world depends. If the evangelist has not something to preach of whic he can say, If any man makes it his business to subvert this, let hi be anathema, he has no gospel at all. Intolerance in this sense has i counterpart in comprehension; it is when we have the only gospe and not till then, that we have the gospel for all." [18]

Rarely do we hear these words of the Psalmist, but certainly they cannot be called vindictive, or vicious, or anti-Christian: "Do not I hate them, O Jehovah, that hate thee? And am not I grieved with those that rise up against thee? I hate them with perfect hatred: They are become mine enemies." Kirkpatrick refers to a relevant sentence from A. P. Stanley, by no means an ultra-conservative, in which the distinguished Dean of Westminster declared "the duty of keeping alive in the human heart, the sense of burning indignation against moral evil—against selfishness, against injustice, against untruth, in ourselves as well as others—that is as much a part of the Christian as of the Jewish dispensation." How quickly we have forgotten the Apostle's words, "Who is caused to stumble, and I burn not." "It was not to Paul a matter of indifference when any of the brethren, by the force of evil, for example, or by the seductions of false teachers, were led to depart from the truth or to act inconsistently with their profession. Such events filled him not only with grief at the fall of the weak, but with indignation at the authors of the fall." [18a] We need a zeal so fervent, such loyalty to the Lord, that we will not tolerate in our church, or in any group of which we have control, nor permit fellowship with, those who are betraying the truth, denying the Lord, and driving souls out into the darkness of unbelief and skepticism. We need to resent as quickly and with even greater indignation, insults cast at the Lord Jesus, whether it be in the name of scholarship, modernism, or compromise with the world, as when an insult is cast at one of our own loved ones.

The Urgent Need of the Church to Return to the Word of God. In this battle of increasing intensity, in an hour when the waves of unbelief are striking at, and have even broken through many of the doors of our churches, and have already overwhelmed too many of our more important educational institutions, the Church needs, for its own life, for the protection of its young, for power in meeting attacks upon her beliefs, for vigor and strength, for courage and hope, for power in winning souls, the Church needs to return to the Word of God. I do not know if it will; I do not know when it will; I do not know how it will do this. Certainly many sections of Christendom are deliberately and intentionally walking straight away from the

Word of God. That does not in any way alter the fact that what we need today, as a Church, is to go back into that divine revelation, to understand it anew, to believe it, to proclaim it.

Years ago there came a warning regarding this very matter from a most unexpected place, from one who himself did not always live up to what he then declared. I am referring to Dr. Charles Augustus Briggs, of Union Theological Seminary, who in his (in many ways remarkable book) *Biblical Studies,* declared: "Unless theology freshens its life by ever repeated draughts from the Holy Scriptures, it will be unequal to the tasks imposed upon it. It will not solve the problems of the thoughtful, dissolve the doubts of the cautious or disarm the objection of the enemies of the truth. She must beat out for herself a new suit of armour from biblical material which is ever new; she must weave to herself a fresh and sacred costume of doctrine from the Scriptures which never disappoint the requirements of mankind; and thus armed and equipped with the weapons of the Living One, she will prove them quick and powerful, convincing and invincible in her training of the disciple and her conflicts with the infidel and heretic . . . The history of the Church, and Christian experience, have shown that insofar as the other branches of theology have separated themselves from this fundamental discipline, and in proportion to the neglect of Exegetical Theology, the Church has fallen into a dead orthodoxy of scholasticism, has lost its hold upon the masses of mankind, so that with its foundations undermined, it has yielded but feeble resistance to the onsets of infidelity. And it has ever been that the reformation or revival has come through the resort to the sacred oracles for the organization of a freshly-stated body of doctrine, and fresh methods of evangelization derived therefrom. We thus have reason to thank God that heresy and unbelief so often drive us to our citadel, the Sacred Scriptures, and force us back to the impregnable fortress of divine truth, in order that, depending no longer merely upon human weapons and defences, we may use rather the divine. Our adversaries . . . can never contend successfully against the Word of God that liveth and abideth forever which, though the heavens fall and the earth pass away, will not fail, not one jot or tittle from the most complete fulfillment which will shine in new beauty and glory as its parts are one by one searchingly examined, and which will prove itself not only invincible, but all-conquering, as point after point is most hotly contested."[19]

Oh, the tragedy of hundreds of our pulpits today, in revealing a mysterious, determined avoidance of the proclamation of the truths of Holy Scripture. I love my fellow ministers, and listen to them preach, I trust, in the most sympathetic mood, but I must say that I have come out of the house of God again and again and again with a sad and bewildered heart, wondering what some men are doing all week, and what they believe in their hearts, and what they think will satisfy the hearts of men, when on Sunday morning they stand up before eternal souls, without a shred of divine truth, nothing relating to this holy revelation, nothing concerning the great, and powerful, the satisfying and transforming truths of the Christian religion. This book is not a place for recording personal experiences, but I hope I am forgiven for one illustration that comes before me as I write. A short while ago I went into a church of my own denomination, to hear one who has a congregation of over two thousand members. That morning he must have had at least twelve hundred people before him. He preached a sermon on the subject, "Indebtedly Yours." His primary exhortation was that we sign all our letters "indebtedly yours," because we were indebted to our government, and indebted to our parents, and to this and that. Neither the name of God nor the name of Christ was mentioned in the whole sermon, nor anything from the Word of God, until about the next to the last sentence, when something was said about Jesus in Gethsemane. There was no evening service in this church, and no prayer meeting: that was all those twelve hundred people had to live on that week—sawdust.

One of the greatest preachers of the last half century, as all of us will admit, was Joseph Parker, of City Temple, London. His bold opinion on this matter is too rare in our Laodicean age: "I can respect in some grim fashion the infidel, who blasphemes and who rejoices in his pillage; but the man in the pulpit who insults the very Bible on which he lives, and reviles the profession which he has claimed—I charge that man with worse crimes than blackened Barabbas or damned Iscariot."[20] Speaking of Joseph Parker, reminds me of a great paragraph in his chapter on the sending for Daniel at Belshazzar's feast. These are glorious words. "Preachers of the Word," said Parker, "you will be wanted some day by Belshazzar; you were not at the beginning of the feast, but you will be there before the banqueting hall is closed; the king will not ask you to drink wine, but he will ask you to tell the secret of his pain and heal the malady of his heart. Abide your time. You are nobody now. Who cares for preachers, teachers, seers, and men of insight, while the wine goes round, and the feast is unfolding its tempting luxuries? Midway down the programme to mention pulpit, or preacher, or Bible, would be to violate the harmony of the occasion. But the preacher, as we have often had occasion to say, will have his opportunity. They will send for him when all other friends have failed. May he then come fearlessly, independently, asking only to be made a medium through which divine communications can be addressed to the listening trouble of the world. . . . Every man, in proportion as he is a Daniel, has nothing to invent, nothing to conceive in his own intellect; he has no warrant or credential from the empty court of his own genius; he bears letters from heaven; he expresses the claims of God. O Daniel, preacher, thunder out God's word, if it be a case of judgment and doom; or whisper it, or rain in gracious tears, if it be a message of sympathy and love and welcome."[21]

It could be, may God grant that it might be, that this day of antagonism to the gospel may also prove a time when the word of God shall experience a phenomenal growth in the hearts of men throughout the world. It was when Paul was at Ephesus, where the Jews contended against him, where seven evil sons of a chief priest of the Jews attempted to imitate him, and when soon the whole city was in an uproar because of the power of this gospel, that we are told, "so mightily grew the Word of God and prevailed." The word *mightily* here means, with resistless and overpowering strength. "If we have Paul's vision, Paul's conception, we shall not say, There are many adversaries, therefore, we must abandon the work; but rather we must stay until Pentecost, and prosecute His great enterprises, 'buying up the opportunities, because the days are evil.' That is the spirit of this century. The days were evil days. Evil days created the opportunity for God-sent men."[22]

When St. Paul describes for believers the divinely prepared weapons they are to make use of, in the great struggle with the world-rulers of this darkness, he speaks of *only one offensive weapon,* the word of God, and, as Dean Howson said, many years ago, "When we strike we must strike only with the weapon which God puts into our hands—"[23]

The great Apostle Paul, on his last missionary journey, in bidding goodbye to the Ephesian elders, exhorted them to hold fast to the word of God, because of the tragedies that would in the future occur within the church itself regarding doctrinal matters. "I know that after my departing grievous wolves shall enter in among you, not sparing the flock; and from among your own selves shall men arise, speaking perverse things, to draw away the disciples after them. . . . And now I commend you to God, and to the word of his grace, which is able to build you up, and to give you the inheritance among all them that are sanctified." "As for the individual, so for the church, the written word is the guarantee for its purity and immortality," says Dr. Alexander Maclaren, "Christianity is the only religion that has ever passed through periods of decadence and purified itself again. They used to say that Thames water was the best to put on shipboard because, after it became putrid, it cleared itself and became sweet again. I do not know anything about whether that is true or not, but I know that it is true about Christianity. Over and over again it has rotted, and over and over again it has cleared itself, and it has always seen by the one process. Men have gone back to the word and laid hold again of it in its simple omnipotence, and so a decadent Christianity has sprung up again into purity and power. The word of God, the principles of the revelation contained in Christ and recorded for ever in this New Testament, are the guarantee of the Church's immortality and of the Church's purity. This man and that man may fall away, provinces may be lost from the empire for a while, standards of rebellion and heresy may be lifted, but 'the foundation of God standeth sure,' and whoever will hark back again and dig down through the rubbish of human buildings to the living Rock will build secure and dwell at peace. If all our churches were pulverised tomorrow, and every formal creed of Christendom were torn in pieces, and all the institutions of the Church were annihilated—if there was a New Testament left they would all be built up again. 'I commend you to God, and to the word of His grace.' "

"Let us learn from this passage," says Calvin, "that the more extraordinary the eagerness of wicked men to despise the doctrine of Christ, the more zealous should godly ministers be to defend it, and the more strenuous should be the efforts to preserve it entirely . . . having been told that men will thus despise and even reject the word of God, we ought not to stand amazed as if it were a mere speckle, when we see actually accomplished that which the Holy Spirit tells us will happen."

The Need for an Immediate Reaffirmation of Christ as the Son of God. The second great need in the Christian Church today is for a return to the reaffirming of the uniqueness, the pre-eminence and the supernaturalness of Jesus Christ, as the only begotten Son of God, in all the glory with which He is set forth in the New Testament: Divinely conceived, performing miracles, dying on the cross for sin, rising again from the dead, ascended into heaven, and sitting on the right-hand of God the Father, from thence He is coming to judge the quick and the dead. There are so many conferences today in which "religion" is being discussed, and in which it is continually insisted that we must get back to "spiritual" things, but unless we believe we have in the Bible a supreme revelation of God, and that there is salvation only through Jesus Christ His Son, we are going to do nothing but stumble about in the vagaries and insipidities born of this day of religious confusion, and of a lack of firm convictions and of faith in the New Testament.

In the issue of the *Atlantic Monthly,* that has appeared just as this chapter is being written, is an article by Dr. Bernard Idings Bell, in which he tries to warn the church that not only have men been brought up to give first and primary concern to the material things of life so that they have been trained to assume a materialistic attitude toward all problems, but that our men coming back from the war are going to have very little interest in things that we call religious or spiritual.[25] This may be so; we may be on the threshold of the most materialistic age which the world has known since the fall of paganism, but no matter what the future holds, this we must remember: there are certain things which men need, and in their better moments know they need, which only Christ as the Son of God can give. Only Christ as the Lamb of God can take away sin; only Christ as the Son of God can reveal God the Father to us—and without that revelation we must drift into utter agnosticism; only Christ can lead us into the presence of God; only He can reconcile men to God; only He can give us eternal life; only He has the truth which we need; only He can raise the dead; only Christ is preparing a home for His own above; only He will ultimately put down all war, and rebellion, and injustice. Only Christ offers a hope that never fadeth; only Christ can bestow a joy that the world can never take away; only Christ, and no one else, ever, can deliver from the power of sin. This is as true today as when the church was founded. Whatever be the attitude of men after the war to what we call spiritual truths, unless they are going to be content to go on as the most wretched of all creatures, their hearts will continue to need the things which Jesus Christ came to reveal, and provide, and make possible. That is why we must get back to this business of preaching Christ. For that the Church was instituted; for that we, as ministers, have been ordained; for that the power of the Holy Spirit is given; and through "the foolishness" of just that some are going to be saved.

Speaking as the moderator of the Free Church Assembly of Scotland, Dr. Alexander Whyte, in 1898 (and who in all Scotland could preach like Whyte at the close of the nineteenth century?), courageously spoke out his deep convictions on preaching Christ, in words that I wish could be heralded with power to ministerial students, and every man who stands in a Christian pulpit, in the whole western world today: "Is not the glory of God in the salvation of your hearers your main motive and chiefest end in setting out to be a minister? If we kept ourselves entirely true to that motive in our preaching, neither would the praises of men puff us up, nor would their blame embitter us and break us down. My sons in the service of our Lord Jesus

Christ, begin from the very beginning of your ministry, and before it is begun, to have your hearts clean and pure within you on the matter of your motives in your preaching. Preach our Lord; preach Jesus Christ—and Him crucified. And preach every single sermon of yours for the salvation of your hearers. Flee, like very poison—as it is—every other thought, every other motive and breath of a motive in your preaching. Preach your absolutely very best every returning Sabbath day. But no Sabbath day make good preaching your motive or your end. Preach your absolutely best, because the Lord of the day is your Lord and Master, and because He is the best master, and the best text, and the best praise, and the best reward for preaching. So enthrone and so exalt Jesus Christ in your heart that you will treat yourself on the spot, as a traitor to Him, every momentary delight you are at any time tempted to take in any man's praise of your preaching, as well as any resentment or depression at any other man's blame." [25a]

The late Professor Marcus Dods could not be accused of ultra-conservatism, and all of us must acknowledge that he is the author of some of the richest expositions of the last generation in the Christian church, and it is Dods who, in his inimitable volume on Paul's first epistle to the Corinthians regarding Christ as the center of all preaching, frankly says, and how true it is today, "Any teacher who professes to lay another foundation thereby gives up his claim to be a Christian teacher. If any one proceeds to lay another foundation than Christ, it is not a Christian Church he is meaning to build. He who does not proceed upon the facts of Christ's life and death, he whose instruction does not presuppose Christ as its foundation, may be useful for some purposes of life, but not as a builder of the Christian temple. He who teaches morality without ever hinting that apart from Christ it cannot be attained in its highest form may have his use, but not as a Christian teacher. He who uses the Christian pulpit for the propagation of political or socialist ideas may be a sound and useful teacher; but his proper place is the platform or the House of Commons or some such institution, and not the Christian Church." [25b]

There is no denying it that the convictions of the church are for the most part determined by the convictions of its clergy. The knowledge which Christian people of any one generation have of the Word of God will, for the most part, depend upon what they hear from the pulpit, and the interest the pastor of any church takes in seeing that in Sunday school classes the Word of God is really and truly taught. The blame for the impoverishment of most of our preaching today is to be laid at the door of our theological seminaries; even some of those that are sound neither train nor attempt to train their students in the preaching of the English Bible, and instructing them in its great and massive truths. Of course, in all those seminaries where the inspiration of the Scriptures and the deity of Christ and his atoning work are denied, there is being raised up and educated nothing but a group of men who, even unconsciously, and without determination, must be considered as enemies of the gospel and as copartners with all those forces and agencies which are today attempting to destroy the foundations of evangelical Christianity. Of course there are, all of us gladly acknowledge, a number of fine seminaries in our country, whose professors are true believers, and whose students are continually encouraged to preach the unsearchable riches of grace in Christ Jesus our Lord. But, as this volume has already shown, it is clear, from overwhelming evidence, that many of our larger seminaries are saturated with a Satanic antagonism to the Bible and the truths of the Christian Church, and are turning out literally hundreds of graduates, every decade, who have no experience of regeneration, who have no knowledge of or faith in the Word of God, and who do not and never can and never will preach a gospel that saves from sin and offers new life through an experience of regeneration, for the simple reason that these things they have long ago given up, or have never known.

I do not know if it is possible, but it would be a great thing for the church if every unbelieving professor in every theological seminary in this world could be dismissed from his position in that seminary. Of course, if the president of a theological seminary is himself an unbeliever, he will never desire to dismiss any member of his faculty, however agnostic and skeptical he may be known to be. If, however, the board of trustees of that seminary is composed of a group of men who have themselves been saved, who kneel down before Christ as the Son of God every day in prayer and confession, if they believe in the gospel, and in salvation through Christ, then they ought themselves to bring about such a cleansing of the institution over whose affairs they have been given charge.

During Israel's restoration, early in Nehemiah's ministry, we read: "But it came to pass, that when Sanballat heard that we builded the wall, he was wroth, and took great indignation, and mocked the Jews. And he spake before his brethren and the army of Samaria, and said, What do these feeble Jews? Will they fortify themselves? Will they sacrifice? Will they make an end in a day? Will they revive the stones out of the heaps of the rubbish which are burned? Now Tobiah the Ammonite was by him, and he said, Even that which they build, if a fox go up, he shall even break down their stone wall."[26]

Ten years had gone by, the temple had been finished, in spite of all opposition, ridicule, tragedy, lying, and some corruption. Nehemiah, after returning to Babylon for a period of time (not definitely designated) returned to Jerusalem, for the second time, and discovered a unique situation. "And before this, Eliashib, the priest, having the oversight of the chamber of the house of our God, was allied unto Tobiah: and he had prepared for him a great chamber, where aforetime they laid the meat-offerings, the frankincense, and the vessels, and the tithes of the corn, the new wine, and the oil which was commanded to be given to the Levites, and the singers, and the porters; and the offerings of the priests." In other words, Tobiah, who was one of the bitterest antagonists of the Israelites in rebuilding the temple of God, and re-establishing worship in Jerusalem, was then found not only a close friend of Eliashib, the priest, but *actually living in one of the chambers of the temple and supported, it would seem, by temple offerings.* So, said Nehemiah, "I came to Jerusalem, and understood of the evil that Eliashib did for Tobiah, in preparing him a chamber in the courts of the house of God. And it grieved me sore; therefore I cast forth all the household stuff of Tobiah out of the chamber. Then I commanded, and they cleansed the chambers: and thither brought I again the vessels of the house of God, with the meat offering and the frankincense."[27] Is it not true today that the Christian Church and Christian people are supporting men in their institutions who, by their own confession hate God, and do everything they can to destroy faith in the Christian religion?

A Program of Education That Centers in Christ. Never in the history of the Christian church has there been so much talk about, so much literature concerning, so much energy expended, so much promotion, as during the last thirty years the Christian church has devoted to the subject of what has been called "religious education." The tragedy of it all is that, with all our fine Sunday school buildings, our beautiful manuals, our attractive quarterlies, our teacher training courses, our supposed knowledge of the psychology of every age, and the development of discipline in the matter of teaching, the present generation of young people in this country may be called almost pagan in their ignorance of what the Word of God teaches, and of the great fundamental truths of the Christian faith. There are exceptions, especially in the southern part of the United States, where some fine teaching has been going on in the Sunday schools, and in many of the conservative churches of the north, particularly, I am afraid, in those that are today independent of our great denominations. What the Christian church needs in a time like this is the re-establishment, both in Christian homes and in Sunday schools, of a systematic instruction in the glorious truths of our eternal faith.

That the emphasis in too many of our influential circles of religious education in this country is not on the Word of God, one may judge, for example, by looking at the most recent issue of the *International Journal of Religious Education,* published by the International Council of Religious Education, a modernistic group indeed. On page three is the beginning of an article, "The World Church Is Here"; on page four begins an article, "We Must Get into Better Politics"; on page six begins a long article of four columns on "We Must Face Political Issues"; on page eight begins another article covering two pages, with the title "What Was Wrong with Our Peace Education"; on page ten the article is called, "The Churches and Public Opinion"; on page eleven begins an article in four columns on "They Teach Christian Citizenship"; on page thirteen, the article is "The Boys Built a Church." Passing over two or three brief items, we come to page fifteen, where the article, "Our Social Responsibility," is found; on page seventeen is the beginning of a play for the Christmas Season, called "He Who Walks in Love." [29] The rest of the paper concerns departmental suggestions, worship programs, etc There is not one single leading article in this entire issue of the journal of this international group that has anything to do with a knowledge of the Word of God, or with Jesus Christ our Lord, not one! Now if our teachers throughout the land are going to feed on such things as these, month after month, and devote their energies to political and economic subjects, to the advancement of the cause of international peace, to fellowship between capital and labor, etc., etc., where are they going to have the passion, the time, the desire, and the knowledge for teaching our young people that Jesus Christ died on the cross to save souls, that there was such a Person on earth as the Son of God, that believing in Him we have life in His name, and that there is such a book as the Bible, which contains rules from heaven for a life on earth, the secret of power and cleansing, strength and joy, and peace in the Holy Ghost? What a shame, what a crime, to starve the hearts of our young people today, on the froth of philosophical speculations, economic theories, and utopian schemes, when the divine bread for the human soul is here available for them in the Holy Scriptures!

The Training of a New Generation of Apologists. Has not the time come in the Christian church, particularly in the evangelical churches of America, to undertake, in the leading of God, the training of a group of gifted young men who can be used, in the generation immediately before us, when the battle for the Christian faith is undoubtedly going to be more severe even than today, for the powerful defense of the faith in the great citadels of unbelief of our country? We need a group of men such as the Roman Catholic church trains, e.g., the Paulist fathers, and the members of the Dominican order, who will remain in school long enough to know ancient and modern languages, to master the principles of philosophy, to have some acquaintance with modern science; who will at the same time have a thorough knowledge of the Word of God, and a discipline in the sacred and serious business of properly defending the faith before an unbelieving world. We do not need monasteries, but it is to the shame of protestantism that our clergy almost universally receive not more than half the training for their profession that many of these priests in the Roman church have received. If we could persuade a body of gifted, chosen young men to continue in their studies in divinity, in linguistics, and in philosophy, until they were about twenty-eight years of age, and during that time to acquire a thorough training in the history, the literature, and the methods of Christian Apologetics, we would have a body of men who could go from city to city, and, when the war is over, from one nation to another, powerfully, forcibly, logically, under the influence of the Holy Spirit, to present to multitudes the reason for the hope that beats in our hearts, and the great foundational truths upon which our faith forever rests. Why could not a number of protestant institutions which believe the Word of God, and believe in Christ as the Son of God, unite in the establishing of a seminary for these advanced studies, and prepare our young men to meet the increasing, vigorous attacks of an intellectual skepticism launched not alone from the atheistic universities of Russia, but even by the atheistic professors of many of our own greatest universities?

Some years ago, Dr. Robert Dick Wilson publicly declared, what needs to be affirmed even more today, "What we need in the Church today are more men that are able to follow the critics up to their lair, slaughter them in their den. It makes me sad to hear these old ministers of the gospel and Christians lament all the time about the attacks being made here and there upon the Bible, and they never do one thing to train the men to fight their battles for them. . . . I tell you, the day is at hand when the Church, instead of cowering and seeming, as many so-called Christians do, to rejoice in the supposed victories over the Bible truth, will demand that anyone who attacks the Bible will produce the evidence."[30] That great New Testament scholar, Dr. J. Gresham Machen, in a series of very important lectures on "The Importance of Christian Scholarship," which he delivered in London a few years ago (and which are, I am afraid, almost totally unknown to this present generation of American Christians), said some powerful things concerning the need for trained men in this field of Apologetics: "There are, indeed, those who tell us that no defense of the faith is necessary. 'The Bible needs no defence,' they say; 'let us not be forever defending Christianity, but instead let us go forth joyously to propagate Christianity.' But I have observed one curious fact—when men talk thus about propagating Christianity without defending it, the thing that they are propagating is pretty sure not to be Christianity at all. They are propagating an anti-intellectualistic, non-doctrinal Modernism; and the reason why it requires no defence is simply that it is so completely in accord with the current of the age. It causes no more disturbance than does a chip that floats downward with a stream. In order to be an adherent of it, a man does not need to resist anything at all; he needs only to drift, and automatically his Modernism will be of the most approved and popular kind. One thing needs always to be remembered in the Christian Church—true Christianity, now as always, is radically contrary to the natural man, and it cannot possibly be maintained without a constant struggle. A chip that floats downwards with the current is always at peace; but around every rock the waters foam and rage. Show me a professing Christian of whom all men speak well, and I will show you a man who is probably unfaithful to his Lord. . . .

"Some years ago I was in a company of students who were discussing methods of Christian work. An older man, who had had much experience in working among students, arose and said that according to his experience you never win a man to Christ until you stop arguing with him. When he said that, I was not impressed. It is perfectly true, of course, that argument alone is quite insufficient to make a man a Christian. You may argue with him from now until the end of the world; you may bring forth the most magnificent arguments: but all will be in vain unless there be one other thing—the mysterious, creative power of the Holy Spirit in the new birth. But because argument is insufficient, it does not follow that it is unnecessary. Sometimes it is used directly by the Holy Spirit to bring a man to Christ. But more frequently it is used indirectly. A man hears an answer to objections raised against the truth of the Christian religion; and at the time when he hears it he is not impressed. But afterwards, perhaps many years afterwards, his heart at last is touched: he is convicted of sin; he desires to be saved. Yet without that half-forgotten argument he could not believe; the gospel would not seem to him to be true, and he would remain in his sin. As it is, however, the thought of what he has heard long ago comes into his mind; Christian apologetics at last has its day; the way is open, and when he will believe he can believe because he has been made to see that believing is not an offence against truth."[31]

There is simply no limit to what a group of men like this could do, during the next few decades. And how they are needed! If such a trained body of men were available, could not *some* of our great schools, *some* of our great colleges, and a *few* universities, be persuaded to hearken to their message, or even perhaps to give them a place on their staff? If this is found impossible, these men of gifts, and power (and I mean spiritual power) could go into university cities, anyway, and, supported by believers in this country, could announce their subjects, and their purpose—to defend the faith, and secure audiences of restless, unbelieving, searching, bewildered students, in hired halls and auditoriums.

There is a remarkable page in the history of the University of Cambridge that bears directly on this matter. In the *Historical Register of the University of Cambridge to 1910* is the following record: "The Reverend John Hulse of St. John's College in this University, B.A. 1728, died in 1790, bequeathing his estates in Cheshire to the University, first, to maintain two Scholars at St. John's College; secondly, to found a Prize for a Dissertation; thirdly, to found and support the office of Christian Advocate, and fourthly, that of the Hulsean Lecturer or Christian Preacher. The Christian Advocate was required to be a 'learned and ingenious person of the degree of Master of Arts or of Bachelor or Doctor of Divinity, and of the age of thirty years or upwards,' and resident in the University, who should 'prepare some proper and judicious answer or answers every year to all . . . new and popular or other cavils and objections against the Christian or Revealed Religion, or against the Religion of Nature, such his written answer to be in English, and only against notorious infidels, whether Atheists or Deists, not descending to any particular controversies or sects amongst Christians themselves, except some new and dangerous error either of superstition or enthusiasm, as of Popery or Methodism, either in opinion or practice shall prevail.'"

Long ago this office of Christian Advocates was abandoned, or at least changed, for the same record tells us: "By a Statute confirmed by the Queen in Council August 1, 1860, the office of Hulsean Professor of Divinity was substituted for that of Christian Advocate; and the office of Hulsean Lecturer considerably modified. The Bishop of Ely is Visitor. The gross annual income from Mr. Hulse's Benefaction is about £1000."[32] Why could not prayer be undertaken now that God would create opportunities for Christian Advocates in a number of our great intellectual centres?

The Creation of a New Literature for the Defense of the Faith. With an adequately trained group of men, such as we have been considering, thoroughly disciplined in the fundamental arguments of anti-theistic philosophy and atheistic communism, acquainted at the same time with the important discoveries of biblical archaeology, and the conclusions of the best critical scholars in the western world, with a firm faith in the Scriptures as the inspired Word of God, we should also have what the church so badly needs today, a new body of apologetical literature. Aside from a heaven-sent revival, I doubt if there is anything which is so deeply and generally needed, both in the orient and in the western world today, as a number of powerful works, of the best scholarship, attractively written, which will present the great truths of the Christian faith in a manner that will demand the attention of our increasingly pagan younger generation. How we need such a literature today! We decry the influence, for example, of Dr. Harry Emerson Fosdick's widely circulated book *Understanding the Bible,* but what does the whole conservative Christian church have, equally attractive, and equally readable, to set up against it today?

Never has there been such a circulation of literature, such a multiplication of books, and abundant reading in every branch of knowledge, as at the present time throughout the world. One of the great agencies communism has so widely used in the propagation of its ideas is literature, even in Japan, China, and India. Many of the great books of the western world, in the field of philosophy, science, political economy, and law, were before the war being translated and published by the hundreds of thousands in the orient. Certainly the agnostic and atheistic works of John Dewey, Bertrand Russell, H. G. Wells, Julian

Huxley, Freud, etc., etc., have been avidly read by hundreds of thousands of educated persons in these countries. And what is the Christian church doing to produce a literature, of equal scholarship, that will present the reason for the hope that the church has held through these centuries?

At the Madras Conference, in 1938, some very sane words were said on this subject, from which we quote the following: "Hardly anywhere is the production of Christian literature keeping pace with progress in literacy and growth in the educated community. It is necessary to discover Christian writers native to each country, and give them training where required. Evangelistic literature must find the reader where he, or she, is. Writers and producers must be in close touch with the life of those for whom literature is intended. A new literature, rooted in the racial and cultural environment, is needed for the training and use of ministers, and lay workers. Literature is needed which deals with the fundamentals of the Christian religion in non-technical language, and in the thought-forms which people, steeped in modern culture, can understand."[33]

Mohammedanism is probably not going to grow, but atheism is already growing in Mohammedan countries; Buddhism is not growing, but atheistic communism is going to seize the minds of vast multitudes of men whose fathers and grandfathers were loyal Buddhists. *As communism and atheism grow, the true Christian faith, by which I mean, of course, faith in Christ as the Son of God, and faith in the Word of God, is declining.* There is no need of even doubting that Europe today is more pagan than it has been for a thousand years. False cults in our own country are springing up everywhere, and there is no reason for doubting that they will increase to an even greater number when the war is over; in fact, there are cities on the western coast of our country today where these cults have more people in their houses of worship, on Sunday nights, than have all the protestant churches of the same city put together.

There are vast multitudes of our men in colleges, or at least they were in our schools before the war fell upon us, who knew absolutely nothing of the Word of God, and would hardly know whether the Crucifixion of Jesus is in the book of Exodus or in the New Testament, who have never opened the Bible to see if Christ ever spoke of Himself as the Son of God; who have never examined the evidence of the Resurrection; who, though they have never honestly read the Bible, believe it is made up of superstitions and outworn myths. Our younger generation has had pounded into its ears sentences which imply that all of science is against the Bible, that history contradicts the Bible, that human nature is itself contrary to that which is set forth in the Holy Scriptures, that the Apostle Paul had a perverted mind, that the early church only laid hold of the Roman world because the people were superstitious and gullible, and that a really wise man knows better than to believe these sacred books in such a day as ours. It is time that this satanic spell is broken. It is time to inform our young men of the truth. I happen to know, as many others know, that there is a cry all over this country, from the hearts of men who believe, but are up against an organized system of unbelief, and from fathers and mothers who are seeing the faith of their sons disappear as they continue in their collegiate courses, there is a critical need for a great, powerful, scholarly, attractively-written literature in the field of apologetics. If this work is rightly done, there is no reason why these books cannot be translated into the languages of the great nations of the earth. I have just read a remarkable article, which carries the significant title, "The World Moves towards Literacy," in which it is stated, for example, that in Russia in 1914, 7,000,000 pupils were attending elementary schools, but by 1932 the number had risen to 19,000,000, and that in addition, "large numbers of untrained workers under the supervision of trained teachers, were enrolled to instruct the illiterate adults: children, too, were brought in to teach their elders." During the last twenty years in Turkey the number of people who can read and write has risen from seven per cent to forty per cent. In China, by July 1941, more than half of the boys and girls of school age in that great country, were actually in school—20,000,000 of them; and so, too, were more than thirty per cent of the illiterate adults up to the age of forty-five . . . "Dr. Yen has stated that, in the five years' period, 1935–40, new literates in China numbered about 30,000,000." In India are more than 300,000,000 illiterates, that is, about one-third of the total number of illiterates in the entire world, and yet in spite of the fact that more than 200 languages are spoken in that vast country, this problem is being successfully solved, or at least beginning to be solved, and it is believed by Dr. Laubach that theoretically it would be possible "to complete the task of making India literate within five years, if the slogan 'Each one teach one' were faithfully carried out." The author of this article, Mr. M. H. Faulds, concludes, "This world-wide movement towards literacy is of primary importance to the Christian Church. It will bring a tremendous demand for books in the years ahead, and it is the clear duty of the Church to see that an adequate supply is available of 'books that carry the message of our Lord.'

"In Europe generally, a shortage of books is certain after more than five years of war's devastation. In addition, the need for Christian literature is urgent in those lands where State paganism has been encouraged for many years by State-controlled publications. Dr. Laubach has pointed out that the opportunity which the Greek Catholic Church lost in Russia after the last war was seized by atheistic communism, and today the literate millions of that country are largely lost to the Church. History must not repeat itself. The Church must see and grasp the opportunity that awaits her of helping in the re-building of spiritual institutions in Europe through the power of the printed word. On the wider stage of the world, the Church faces opportunities on a scale unimaginable a few years ago. For 150 years, she has proclaimed the gospel in three main ways—by direct evangelism, by education, and by the ministry of healing. Today, in the providence of God, a new way of advance has opened up before the Church—evangelism through literature. Nothing approaching a sufficiency of books has ever existed in missionary lands, and the shortage grows more acute as literacy advances.

"Books are needed to save the new literates from a lapse into illiteracy and the inertia that accompanies it; to preserve the solid work of Governments and Missions; above all, to speed on the unfinished task of winning the world for Christ. The missionary Church, more than any other agency, has taught the people to read in the past, and today members of the Church are leaders everywhere in Mass Education movements. Surely, the Church will not lose the widened opportunities that await her now." [34]

The suggestion may sound fantastic, but what a hopeful day for the faith it would be if a group of men, capable of producing such a literature as this, could be brought together for a thorough discussion of the problems involved, and for the distribution of the labor. We need books for different ages, and books on different relevant subjects, books that will appeal to different peoples of the world. No doubt a volume defending the Christian faith to be used among the Mohammedans in Cairo would be, in parts, different from a work written in French for intellectual agnostics in the city of Paris. We need not only books, but we need a whole new group of conservative Christian scholars in the world who could be persuaded to contribute to a truly great journal established for the defense of the faith. I remember visiting a friend of mine at Princeton Theological Seminary, I think it was about 1924 or 1925, and during the brief visit the summer issue of the Princeton Theological Review came from the press. It was wonderful to hear these young men ask one another if they had read this article and that article, all within twenty-four hours after the periodical was in circulation. Some of those articles were like bombshells, not only at Princeton but throughout American protestant circles.[35] I am afraid there is not quite such a periodical today in the English language. All over America, especially in better-class restaurants, in railroad stations, we have all noticed attractively constructed racks on which are resting, for free distribution, the publications of the Christian Science Mother Church, including the daily *Christian Science Monitor,* and the *Christian Science Journal—for free distribution.* Why cannot conservatives, in some corporate way, produce attractive pamphlet literature in the defense of the Christian faith, for free distribution? The whole field is ripe. We hear some people talk about "the battle of the books." Well, you can only have a battle if you have strong forces on both sides. Let us not deceive ourselves by forgetting that the literature of communism, and books stamped with atheistic convictions, are going to be of *greater* number, and *more* widely circulated when the war is over, than ever before in modern history. There will not even be a "battle" of books, unless we produce some powerful literature, of an equal value, yes, of greater value, which can be used by those who believe, and which can be given to those who do not believe. We know that unbelief is unfair, in that it frequently will not read conservative literature, but *it is possible* to produce the kind of books that will have to be read, books that people will begin to talk about, that will compel some at least to ask their unbelieving leaders, including unbelieving ministers, what they think of this or that great Christian truth. What a great hour that would be if a new body of instructed laymen could confront unbelieving clergy, by asking why they have rejected the Resurrection, the Virgin Birth, and the inspiration of the Scriptures!

The Pre-eminent Prerequisites of Prayer and Spiritual Power. With all of our apologetic literature, which is very important, with all of the strong answers to criticisms made of the Word of God, replies to innumerable "reasons" for rejecting the Lord Jesus Christ, with all of our work, and the publication of literature, with preaching, and personal interviews, with the end of winning our skeptically minded youth back to Christ, and to faith in His Word, we should ever remember that for this type of work we need divine power, and if we do not have it, we will not accomplish anything worth talking about, and certainly nothing commensurate with the effort which is expended, and nothing at all like what needs to be accomplished *now*.

Our Lord promised the Church that on the day when it should be born, it would have an anointing of power from God.[36] I have heard a great many sermons, and read a great many pages on this promise of power through the Holy Spirit, but generally I feel that the meaning here has been missed. Men seem to pray for power in preaching, that they themselves might be dynamic, or unusually influential from the pulpit, capable of moving audiences, perhaps fluent in speech, etc., etc. Now, all this is all right, but the reason why the early church had to have *power,* divine power, was because of the many enormous powers which it had to overcome, powers which were holding the souls and minds and hearts of men in their fearful grip. There was, to begin with, the power of sensuality, the power of the flesh; there was the power of idolatry, with all of its show and appeal, its temples and priesthood, things that could be touched and seen and heard; there was the power of paganism, mastering the Mediterranean world for centuries; there was the power of the increasing tendency on the part of Roman rulers to be looked upon as God, and the determination of the

Roman government to enforce such deification; there was the power of false philosophy, and all the philosophic schemes which had been born and had flourished in the early Greek and later Roman world; there was the power of darkness, the sheer weight of despair and hopelessness; and, finally, there was the power of demons, and all the Satanic agencies which could be mustered by the arch-enemy of God and His gospel. If these early Christians had not had power, divine power, power greater than all the antagonistic powers in the world put together, the gospel would have been doomed from the first day of its declaration. It is this power that we need now, in the face of an increasing antagonism to Christian faith, an antagonism that is as powerful now as in the days of the early church—with this profound difference, that the ancient pagan world was weary of the failure and acknowledged futility and foolishness of its attempts to find God and to be delivered from sin, and was ripe for the proclamation of a divine message, whereas today, after 1900 years of the gospel, there is a mysteriously accelerated drifting away from the gospel, the truth of which can never be disproved, back into myths similar to those held in the ancient world at the time of our Lord's advent, or, into worse, an utter indifference to everything concerning God, even to the denial of the soul which can know God.

Have you ever noticed how many different powers there are arraigned against Christ and Christians in the New Testament, especially in the book of Revelation? We have already considered that galaxy of evil beings which Paul mentions in his last chapter to the Ephesians—principalities, powers, world rulers, spiritual hosts of wickedness. Elsewhere Paul talks about the "power of Satan," "the prince of the power of the air," "he that had the power of death, that is, the devil." [37] But in the book of Revelation notice the beings with whom power is always identified. There is, for example, the beast out of the sea to whom the dragon "gave his power and his throne and great salvation." We read of the power of the kings of the earth, the power of demons, the power of Satan himself, the power of the confederate enemies of God.[38] It is against these powers that anyone who attempts to do work for God will find himself set, and unless he has power from God in His service for Christ, he is doomed—he will be crushed.

Professor Robert Flint said a remarkable and true thing years ago, which I have never seen quoted anywhere, nor anything just like it expressed by others. "All the powers of the world above and of the world to come are needed to oppose the powers of the world below, and of the world which now is."[39]

We have almost forgotten to pray in this generation. We become alarmed, we say we will stand up for the faith, we testify, in part, but what the church needs right now is to drop on its knees and plead with God for a great victory in such a crisis as this. You will remember that at the end of his wonderful exhortation to put on the whole armour of God, the apostle concludes with an appeal for prayer to which he gives more space than to any other one aspect of the Christian's armour and warfare. These are his words: "Praying always with all prayer and supplication in the Spirit, and watching thereunto with all perseverance and supplication for all saints; and for me that utterance may be given unto me, that I may open my mouth boldly, to make known the mystery of the gospel." The finest exposition I have ever seen of these two verses is in what I believe to be the most remarkable volume devoted to an exposition of this entire passage concerning the warfare of believers that exists today in Christian literature. I refer to Dr. John Henry Jowett's masterly work, *The Whole Armour of God,* and without any comment whatever, I would like to bring to the attention of my readers some of the penetrating things which he has said for the entire church, in language more wonderful and gripping than I am able myself to command.

"Now why should the Christian warrior pray? He must pray as a suppliant for the robust health of his own spirit. Yes, but why should he pray for the maintenance of his own spiritual health? What is the vital relationship between the praying soul and the attainment of moral and spiritual robustness? How is prayer related to a man's moral force? This is the relationship. A praying warrior receives into his soul the grace-energies of the eternal God. The power of grace is just the holy love and strength and beauty of the holy Godhead flowing into the needs of the soul and filling them with its own completeness. Now we do not pray in order to make God willing to impart this grace, but in order to fit ourselves to receive it. We do not pray to ingratiate God's good-will, but to open our souls in hospitality. We do not pray in order to create a friendly air, but to let it in, not to propitiate God but to appropriate Him. We do not pray to turn a reluctant God toward ourselves, but to turn our reluctant selves toward a ready and bountiful God.

"But the Christian soldier is not only a suppliant for his own spiritual health. He is much more than this. The apostle counsels him to be a suppliant for the health of the entire Christian army. 'Praying always, with all prayer and supplication in the spirit, and watching thereunto with all perseverance and supplication for all saints.' That is to say, the Christian soldier not only prays for the health of his own spirit, but for a healthy 'esprit de corps' throughout the whole militant church of Christ. It is his duty and privilege to be prayerfully jealous for all the saints, and for the spiritual equipment of all his fellow-soldiers on the field.

"And then, just to finish it all, and by one example to show us how deep and wide is this ministry of supplication, the apostle Paul asks the young Ephesian soldiers to pray for him. 'And for me, that utterance may be given unto me.' Let us carefully note this, and let us observe its heartening significance. These young, immature Christians in Ephesus, trembling in their early faith, are asked to pray for the old warrior in Rome. He is now 'an ambassador in bonds,' held in captivity in imperial Rome, and the young soldiers in Ephesus are asked to be sentinel-suppliants for the stricken soldier far away. Do you believe this? And what does he want them to pray for? Listen to him again. 'And for me, that utterance may be given unto me.' Have you got the real inwardness of that appeal? A poor slave in Ephesus may, by his own prayer, anoint the lips of a great apostle with grace and power. What a vista of powerful possibility! Do all congregations realize that privilege and service concerning their ministers? 'For me, that utterance may be given unto me.' Do I realize that my prayers, obscure and nameless though I be, can give utterance to a Paul, a Livingstone, a Moffatt, or a Chalmers? Do I realize that I can pour grace upon their lips? What a brave and splendid privilege! Am I using it? I cannot get out of my mind the vision of some poor slave in Ephesus pouring grace and truth upon the apostle's lips in

Rome, and I cannot get out of my imagination the surprise which awaited the slave in glory, when Paul asked him, as a fellow-labourer, to share in gathering in the sheaves." [40]

In 1874, the outstanding apologete of Germany, Theodore Christlieb, author of one of the most influential books in the defense of the Christian faith of the nineteenth century, came to New York City for a series of lectures, and read a paper before the General Conference of the Evangelical Alliance on, "The Best Methods of Counteracting Modern Infidelity." In the midst of this remarkable address, he spoke in a most definite and uncompromising manner of the need for prayer in counteracting infidelity, and if any man could speak with the authority of success in this hard and necessary ministry, it was Professor Christlieb. From the report of this conference, I would like to place his words on this duty, in their entirety, before my readers.

"Amidst all this work, never let us forget the *personal preparation in secret.* If we are to conquer in our struggle against unbelief, it must be less exclusively than hitherto with word and pen, and more *on our knees.* Often while we fight hard we pray too little. Instead of at once fulminating *against* unbelievers, let us first wrestle *for* them with the power of intercessory prayer, that they may be enlightened by the Lord. No word or writing should go forth in this Holy War unaccompanied by prayer. Let no combatant enter the arena without putting on the spiritual as well as the intellectual panoply, that he may not fare as did the seven sons of Sceva. And let none who strive in the right spirit be left alone. Though we may not everywhere be able to succor and defend, yet the arms of our prayer can embrace the whole globe. Thus only can we become so filled with the Spirit that the image of Christ, the great Captain and Conqueror in the battle, shall shine out of every action and victoriously enlighten our opponents, when they see in our whole walk and conduct greater love and self-denial, greater self-sacrifice, greater quietness and firmness in distress and danger. *The Christian is the world's Bible,* and the only one which it reads. If we take care that in this book be plainly shown the loving spirit, the grandeur, and the winning friendliness of Christ, then we shall see many hearts open to receive this actual testimony of Christian life and suffering. For many of our opponents in secret envy us our

Christian comfort in misfortune and under heavy losses. Their hearts are often stirred by a deep yearning after the support which bears us up, and this superiority of Christian life can often drive the hardest heart to seek help of our Lord.

"In fine, *only life can beget life.* Where we wish to defend the Word of Life, our own life can not be separated from the Word. *The strongest argument for the truth of Christianity is the true Christian,* the man filled with the Spirit of Christ. The best means of bringing back the world to a belief in miracles is to exhibit the miracle of regeneration and its power in our own life. The best proof of Christ's resurrection is a living Church, which itself is walking in new life, and drawing life from him who has overcome death. . . .

"Before such arguments ancient Rome herself—the mightiest empire of the world, and the most hostile to Christianity—could not stand. Let us live in like manner, and then—though hell should have a short-lived triumph—eventually must be fulfilled what St. Augustine says, 'Love is the victory of the truth.'"[41]

Let me close this section of our chapter by referring especially to prayer for our colleges. Perhaps not many of my readers are acquainted with a remarkable book which was issued now nearly a century ago, by Dr. William Tyler, then the famous professor of Greek at Amherst College, a premium essay on, "Prayer for colleges written for the Society for the Promotion of Collegiate and Theological Education at the West." I must confess that this book itself was utterly unknown to me until last year, when I accidentally came upon it in a secondhand book store. It is one of the most stimulating volumes I have had in my hand for a long time. In the middle of this volume, Professor Tyler speaks of a *Concert of Prayer for Colleges,* which was born in 1823, in the following manner:

"There was a spirit of supplication among Christians in behalf of colleges and theological seminaries, created by statistical information in respect to them, published from time to time in the Annual Reports of the American Education Society. A concert of prayer was first established to be observed every Sabbath morning. Frequent and powerful revivals of religion in colleges followed, which seemed very much like answers to the supplications offered at these seasons of prayer. The children of God were encouraged to persevere, and finally, in consequence of a circular issued, with the knowledge and approbation of the directors of the American Education Society, the last Thursday of February, 1823, was set apart by many of the friends of Zion as 'a season of fasting and special prayer, that God will pour out his Spirit on the colleges of our country the present year more powerfully than ever before.'

"Subsequent to the establishment of the Sabbath Morning Concert, the Spirit of God was poured out, and cheering results witnessed. From 1820 to 1823 inclusive, there were revivals in fourteen different institutions; in 1824 and 1825, in five different colleges; in 1826, in six; in 1827, in five; and in 1831, in nineteen colleges, resulting in the hopeful conversion of between three hundred and fifty and four hundred students. In one of the colleges, the revival commenced on the very day of the concert. In 1832, some few institutions were blessed with the effusions of the Spirit; and also in 1833. A larger number were blessed with revivals in 1834, and no less than eighteen in 1835; and between one and two hundred students were brought hopefully into the kingdom of Christ. It has been estimated that fifteen hundred students were made the hopeful subjects of grace in thirty-six different colleges, from 1820 to 1835 inclusive.

"If any thing could make still more apparent the connection between this Concert of Prayer and the frequent revivals of religion that have occurred in our colleges since its appointment, it is the additional fact that these revivals have nearly all occurred during the winter term in which the concert is observed, and for the most part shortly after its observance. That is, perhaps, the most favorable season of the year for special attention to personal religion in colleges, as it is also in churches."

Later in the volume, Dr. Tyler suggests some reasons why we ought to especially pray for colleges. First of all he says:

"Our Lord has commanded it. Among the few special objects of prayer which Jesus enjoined upon his disciples, was the raising up and sending forth of preachers of the gospel. As he lifted up his eyes on the multitudes that flocked to hear him, and saw the field already ripe for the harvest, he turned to his disciples, and said, 'The harvest truly is great, and the laborers are few; pray ye, therefore, the Lord of the harvest, that he will send forth laborers into his harvest.' Here is our authority. Here, too, is our motive; it is the command of Jesus, who is our master and our friend. . . .

"The students need our prayers,—peculiarly need them. They are at a peculiarly susceptible and critical age. They are placed in peculiarly trying circumstances. Consciously or unconsciously, they are passing the most important four years of their existence,—deciding questions for themselves which it never will be in their power to decide again; exerting an influence on others, which they will never have the opportunity to exert anywhere else. Young men are *'strong'*; and now they are to decide the question, whether they shall be strong to do good, or strong to do evil. . . . The *pious students* need our prayers, that they may be living epistles of Christ, where so many eyes are constantly reading them that will not read the written Word of God; and that when they go forth into the world, they may go, not mere *'professors* of religion,' not ordinary Christians and commonplace ministers, but eminently holy and wise to win souls. The irreligious students need our prayers, that they may escape the many temptations incident to youth and college life; that they may not make shipwreck of themselves and many others for time and eternity; that they may not go out into the world educated and accomplished enemies of God and ministers of sin, but may be fitted by converting and sanctifying grace to serve God in their generation. . . .

"If prayer is the lever that is to raise this fallen world, here, *in our colleges,* is the place to apply it. If prayer is the engine that is to put in motion the whole train of redeeming influences, here is the point to which it should be attached. If prayer is the conductor, which is to convey divine influences from heaven to earth, these are the summits where especially it should be set up, and whence those influences will spread, like the electric fluid, through all the ranks and departments of society." [42]

The Place of Revival in Times of Spiritual Decline. Let me close this chapter with a word concerning the need for revival. If only America and Europe, and then the world, could be stirred once again with a mighty, heaven-sent movement, by the influence, the convicting and converting power of the Holy Spirit, then would great multitudes be truly brought out of the darkness of skepticism into the glorious light that radiates from Christ, the Son of God. I know it is unpopular now to talk about revival, about religious mass movements, and we often hear people say that we are never going to have again any great national religious experience, nor, it is said, can we expect thousands of people to crowd auditoriums to hear men preach and plead for the salvation of souls. I am not so sure. When revivals have fallen upon the western world, during the last five hundred years, from Savonarola in Florence, to D. L. Moody and Gypsy Smith in America and England, and huge crowds *have* gone to hear, to believe, to confess sin, and accept Christ, what is there about our generation that makes it so different from all preceding ones, that such scenes cannot be expected again, if God chooses to create them? Let us remember that a revival, among other things, means three things, if it is a real revival. It means salvation from sin, which in turn rests upon the preaching of the Word of God, and the presentation of the atoning work of Jesus Christ. There is no salvation from sin, no cleansing from sin, except in and through the Lord Jesus Christ, and His shed blood, and this precious truth can only be brought to men and women under the conviction of sin, by the preaching of the Word of God. In other words, no revival with permanent consequences, actually resulting in multitudes being truly redeemed, born again, united to the Lord Jesus Christ, confessing Him as their Lord and Saviour, can be expected, except the holiness of God, and the redemptive program of God, and the saving power of the Son of God, are clearly, powerfully unfolded to men. These truths are never found anywhere but in the Holy Scriptures. Every revival worthy of the name begins in the exaltation of the Word of God in the pulpit, its fearless proclamation by those anointed of God to preach the gospel. The revival under Josiah took place when "Hilkiah found the Book of the Law of the Lord." In the record of the revival under Jehoshaphat, there is a remarkable statement regarding the relationship of this revival of the Word of God, which could certainly serve as a perfect text for a charge to ministers: "And they taught in Judah, and had the book of the law of the Lord with them, and went about throughout all the cities of Judah, and taught the people." During the revival under Nehemiah, we read that "all the people gathered together as one man . . . and they spake unto Ezra the scribe to bring the Book of the Law of Moses which the Lord had commanded of Israel." [43]

In the particular revival under King Hezekiah, we come upon such phrases as "the word of the Lord," "the good knowledge of the Lord," "the law of the Lord," "the law of Moses the man of God," "as it was written," "his commandments which the Lord commanded Moses." As soon as Hezekiah announced his purpose to cleanse the city of Jerusalem from its abominations, we read that the Levites and others "gathered their children, and sanctified themselves, and came, according to the commandment of the king by *the words of the Lord,* to cleanse the house of the Lord." Later, when the Temple had been cleansed, and Hezekiah had begun to restore its neglected services, we are told that the king "set the Levites in the house of the Lord with symbols, with psalteries, and with harps, according to the commandment of David, and of Gad, the king's seer, and Nathan, the prophet, *for so was the commandment of the Lord by his prophets.*" [44] A revival which does not rest solidly upon the Word of God will ultimately either fade out, because there is no fountain of divine truth continually refreshing it, or it will run into dangerous and sensational emotionalism, which, after it has passed, will make those who have been the subjects of such an experience exhausted, and indifferent to the things of God, at times more easily accessible than ever to the inroads of Satan himself. There is something about the Word of God that men recognize as divine: when it is preached men know that they are hearing the Word of God, and nothing less will ever arouse a nation sunk in selfishness, self-satisfaction, and godlessness.

There is no greater example in the last century of the power of the Word of God rightly wielded than the ministry of Dwight L. Moody. Very early in his ministry, Moody visited a little mission chapel, a part of Theodore Cuyler's out-station work. So dead were the meetings that the congregation finally dropped to eighteen. In his fascinating *Bush Aglow,* Dr. Richard Ellsworth Day tells us that, "There was in that meeting a godly woman who said to Moody: 'We have plenty of preaching in Brooklyn; but if you will tell us something about the Bible, it will be blessed to us.' He wept in his room to think what a fool he had been, always letting his eyes run toward the pagan hills for help, forgetting *his* help should come from the Lord. 'God forgive him! and help him'—to 'go simple again.' The next afternoon, it was not an early sermonic peacock that he preened for a re-strutting, but a simple Bible reading. The ravishing sweet Fires of God at once came down, enveloping not only the little mission, but sweeping right up into Cuyler's home church. So mighty a visitation was it, that a church in Philadelphia invited him to hold meetings there. When he arrived in Philadelphia the idea of using old, sure-fire sermons was repugnant. He had a heart for nothing now but the glory of the Word."[45]

Let us never think that a real revival can ever occur unless it is characterized by a return to that great and final sacrifice of the Lamb of God, who is the eternal propitiation for our sins, and by whose precious blood atonement was forever provided for all who would confess their sins, and receive the gift of eternal life. As long as there is an ignoring of the Cross, or a perverted conception of the meaning of the Cross, or an abhorrence of the precious blood of the Son of God, as there is on the part of great multitudes today, even *in* the Christian church, a revival cannot come, at least a revival that saves the souls of men. Without the shedding of blood there is no remission of sins, and unless the blood of Christ is preached, and the Cross lifted high before the eyes of men, how can men ever be saved, and unless men are *saved,* in any great religious movement, what right have we to call such a movement a real revival? There is no forgiveness apart from the Cross, God is not reconciled apart from the Cross, eternal life will never be conferred apart from the death of Christ, and if there is no forgiveness, no reconciliation, no receiving of eternal life, then all our efforts are in vain, and whatever a religious movement accomplishes, it is not a revival.

Charles H. Spurgeon, after a very serious illness, in mid-life, came back to preach at the Metropolitan Tabernacle, London, on Sunday morning, November 16, 1873, with one great message burning in his heart—the preëminence of the blood of Christ. During his great sermon on this subject, Spurgeon said to the thousands of people who had gathered to hear him: "It is to Christ, then, this morning as the sin-bearer that I am about to direct your attention. It may not be many times longer that I may have the opportunity to preach the gospel, for bodily pain reminds me of my mortality. How soon are the hale and strong, as well as the sickly, carried off! and so many during the last few days whom we knew have been borne from among us to the silent tomb, that we are reminded how feeble our life is, how short our time for service. Let us, then, brethren, deal always with the best things, and attend to the most necessary works while yet our little oil suffices to feed the lamp of life. Rising newly from a sick bed, I have felt that if any theme in the Scriptures has an importance far above all the rest, it is the subject of the atoning blood, and I have resolved to repeat that old, old story again and again. Though I may be guilty of tautologies, I shall keep on sounding this silver trumpet, or ringing this golden bell again, and again, and again. So when I am dead, and gone the way of all flesh, you will perhaps say, his fault was that he dwelt too much on his favorite subject, the substitution of Christ. Ah, may I have no other fault to account for, for that shall be accounted to be one of my highest virtues! I would know nothing among men save Jesus Christ and Him crucified." [46]

It is possible for the most skeptical atmosphere to be broken into by the power of God, under the mighty ministry of some leader, to whom, by his very honesty and deep convictions, many will hearken. It has happened before, it can happen again. Nothing could be so religiously pitiful as, for example, the condition of Yale College toward the close of the eighteenth century, when one of its most distinguished presidents, and probably the greatest man in New England of his day, Timothy Dwight, came to be its president in 1795 at the age of forty-three, giant of intellect, and warrior of the faith. His latest biographer tells us, "He found the college in what some described as 'a most ungodly state with disorder, impiety, and wickedness rampant.' It was not a matter of a few mistaken notions as to doctrine, nor a suspicion of heresy here and there. The place was a hotbed of infidelity. Every up-to-date sophomore scoffed at the idea of divine revelation. Any Yale man worth his salt denounced organized religion and priestcraft as loudly as Voltaire has shouted down susperstition. The foe boring from within had gained full possession . . . There a pitiful minority, clinging desperately to an inheritage belief in Christianity, hardly dared to display its loyalty to a faith generally discredited and scorned. Student membership in the college church had sunk dangerously near extinct, most undergraduates avowed themselves skeptics. Intemperance, profanity, and gambling were common. If they neglected the classics they devoured Thomas Paine. Many in the first class which Dwight taught as president, had appropriated along with the ideas, the very names of favored French and English infidels, using them in preference to their own."

President Dwight was invited in pure deviltry to address the literary society of Yale on the question, "Are the Scriptures of the Old and New Testament the Word of God?" They thought he would decline to come before them to defend any such question, but here they were mistaken. Dwight urged them to collect every argument they could find against the Word of God—and how they took advantage of the opportunity! After he had allowed each one to state his case carefully, he entered the lists himself and after blasting their own statements of fact, "He presented positive proofs of the divine origin of the Scriptures in a torrent of irresistible arguments and animated eloquence which left the stoutest infidel in his audience confounded. His bolts had the effect of lightning upon the whole college. Shunning battle was not Dwight's way of winning a war. He struck in the open, full and hard, where all the world could see the foe fall. Almost before the campaign had opened, this decision at the outset started the rout of infidelity." With prayer offered every day for revival, men began to be saved; in 1802, one-third of Yale's 230 students had been converted, of whom over thirty entered the ministry. What a change in seven years, in fact, the change had been so great that it was said, "Yale College is a little temple." But somehow the doubts of unbelief came back and the number of professing Christians among the students at Yale in 1807 had dropped to fifteen.

One Saturday afternoon in April 1808, as President Dwight was conducting, as usual, the evening prayers, a change was noted in his manner. A revival was going on in the city of New Haven, but none in Yale. His prayer was more solemn and fervent than usual as he exalted the sovereignty of God in the dispensations of His grace. The next day he preached on Luke 7:11–15 and on that day there were great stirrings in the student body. One evening each week in the rooms of one of the tutors he met students who were seeking salvation and instructed them with wonderful kindness in the way of faith. Before the close of his administration (1817) Dwight saw a real revival breaking upon his school, hundreds of students were saved, the atmosphere of the college was changed; scores dedicated their lives to the Christian ministry, and we are told there were times when "nearly every room in the college contained at least one youth who was awakened to the corruption of his heart." From Yale the revival spread to other institutions of learning, to Dartmouth, and to Princeton, and schools of lesser size. What happened then could happen again and it is this that we need—a powerful presentation of the great doctrines of the Christian faith; a revealing of the way of salvation; an unfolding of the Word of God, all preceded by a fervent laying hold of God for such blessing upon the youth of our land.[47]

Let me close this chapter and bring to a conclusion this book, which should have been so much better written than it is, with a word of Horatius Bonar, of saintly memory, which he wrote after visiting western Europe, and especially France, at the age of seventy. His words are almost prophetic; with his deep knowledge of the Word of God and his spiritual insight into the conditions of western civilization, he seems to have so remarkably foreseen the dark days which are now upon us. "It may be that this last battle of the world is to prove the most terrible of all. Satan is evidently bringing up his reserves, and arming his hosts for the heaviest onset the Church has yet seen. Ancient Paganism fell before the gospel; mediaeval superstition gave way before it. But will not these new organizations of evil, in which the human heart is displaying its deadliest antipathies to God, prove too strong for it? Will it not have to retire discomfited before those 'armies of the aliens?' No. If this be the last battle, there must, out of it, come a last victory for the Book of God. Whether that victory may result in a wide acceptance of the truth over Europe is a question I do not undertake to answer; but that there will be victory of some kind for the Bible I believe,—victory which will show that there is no amount of antagonism to God which it cannot face, and no strength of human evil with which it cannot cope successfully, as 'the power of God unto salvation.' The Spirit, as at Pentecost, the Spirit of power, breaking down and upbuilding, dissolving and restoring, smiting and healing, overthrowing error, and giving truth the victory. That same mighty breath that swept through Antioch and Philippi and Colosse, destroying the idols and setting up the true God, can permeate Paris and Berlin and Vienna and Rome, with like irresistible potency as of old. The time may be short, the Divine judgments may be imminent; but the Bible and the gospel it contains will be displayed, in their power to contend with the last form of earth's wickedness as successfully as with the first." [48]

As we said once before, no one foresaw more clearly a great coming day of evil nor recognized more frankly the superhuman power of the enemies of our Faith than the Apostle Paul, but in the very passage where he describes them in detail and commends to us the whole armour of God, he concludes, as it were, with a shout of victory, with the acclamation of triumph, even before the battle is hardly begun, for, as Conybeare translates it (the vital truth here is rather lost in our own versions), Paul says that with all the power of the enemies against us, we are to "take up with you to the battle the whole armour of God, that you may be able to withstand them in the evil day, and having overthrown them all, *to stand unshaken.*"

Firmly convinced that only by the preaching of the gospel which is set forth in the Christian faith can men be saved from sin and the wrath to come, receive eternal life, and become the sons of God; persuaded that the facts of the world without, the data of history, the testimony of men's hearts in the experience of regeneration, and the revelation of the Holy Scriptures, unitedly witness to the truthfulness of the great affirmations of this faith; because this Christian faith is being wickedly betrayed from within, and assailed from without by enemies marshalled on every side, with strong indication that their attacks will become more powerfully organized and increasingly vicious; aware that vast multitudes of the peoples of the earth must be definitely classed as pagan, under the spell of the dual spirit of this age—blind unbelief and stolid agnosticism; all of us who believe must recognize this as the hour in which every true disciple of the Lord Jesus Christ should determine, and will, that, with the help of God, whatever the cost, for the sake of the Name, for the glory of God, for the strengthening of the wavering, the recovering of the doubting, and the salvation of the lost, as a soldier of Jesus Christ, equipped with the whole armour of God, we will

THEREFORE STAND.

NOTES

CHAPTER I

1. Luke 2:34, 35. The word is *antilego*. A most interesting study is that of the Greek words beginning with the prefix *anti*, which are used in the New Testament to express the idea of opposition to the Gospel, to Christ, and to Christians. Among these are, *antidikos* (I Pet. 5:8), *antithesis* (I Tim. 6:20), *antikeimai* (Luke 21:15; II Thess. 2:4, etc.), *antilogia* (Heb. 12:3), *antistrateuomai* (Rom. 7:23), *antichristos* (I John 2:22; 4:3, etc.).
2. Alfred Plummer: *A Critical and Exegetical Commentary on the Gospel According to St. Luke*. 6th ed. New York. 1903. p. 71.
3. Matthew 13:25–28, 39. It is significant that in the LXX version of Genesis 3:15, the word translated *enmity* is a form of the word our Lord uses here, *echthros*. Archbishop Trench quotes Chrysostom's apt comment, "After the prophets, the false prophets; after the apostles, the false apostles; after Christ, antichrist." *Notes on the Parables of Our Lord*, rev. ed. 1875. p. 93. On a related assertion of our Lord, found in Luke 8:12, see a remarkable sermon of Spurgeon's, "Satan's Punctuality, Power, and Purpose," in his *Sermons on Our Lord's Parables*. London. 1894. (No. 63.)
4. Matthew 21:33–44. See also Mark 12:1–9; Luke 20:9–19.
5. Matthew 23:31–37; Luke 11:47–51; 13:34. It is not without great significance that the first death in the Bible should be in the form of murder, actually fratricide, because one man was worshipping God *by faith*, and the other hated him for doing so.
6. Mark 14:27, 29. For other relevant uses of the verb see, e.g., Matt. 15:12; 11:6; 13:57; 26:31; Mark 6:3; Luke 7:27.
7. Mark 14:50.
8. Matthew 27:39; Mark 15:32.
9. Acts 4:11—*exoutheneo*.
10. Matthew 21:42; Mark 12:10; Luke 20:17—the word is *apodokimazo*. Also in I Pet. 2:4, 7.
11. John 15:20; 5:16; Luke 21:15. See note 1, above. On the subject of persecution, see a masterly article by T. Lewis, in James Hastings: *Dictionary of the Apostolic Church*. II. 168–186. His definition is worth repeating. Persecution is "the infliction of suffering, whether it be temporary discomfort or death, upon individuals for holding or advocating religious views, and adopting or propagating religious practices, which are obnoxious to the community, or to those in authority."
12. All these incidents may be found in Acts 4–12.
13. Acts 13:6–11. The two words are *diastrepho* and *anthistemi*, the latter having in it the idea of *anti*. "Bar-Jesus represented the strongest influence on

the human will that existed in the Roman world, an influence which must destroy or be destroyed by Christianity, if the latter tried to conquer the empire." Wm. M. Ramsay. *St. Paul the Traveller and Roman Citizen.* 1896. p. 79.

14. Acts 13:45. The word is *antilego.* See note 1, above.
15. I Thessalonians 2:15, 16. The word translated *contrary* is *enantios,* the root being *anti.* For a striking parallel, see the close of St. Stephen's address, Acts 7:51, 52. On Paul's terrible indictment of the Jews, one should consult the very full comments in John Eadie: *A Commentary on the Greek Text of the Epistles of Paul to the Thessalonians.* London. 1877. pp. 84–91.
16. I Corinthians 16:9. The word here is *antikeimai.* See note 1, above.
17. Philippians 3:18. The word is *echthros.* See note 3, above.
18. Romans 11:28.
19. Acts 28:22. The word, as in Acts 13:45, is *antilegeo.* See note 1, above.
20. II Peter 2:1–3a. cf. I Peter 4:14. The word translated *evil spoken of* is *blasphemeo.* Dr. John Henry Jowett, at the service designated as "The recognition of Dr. G. Campbell Morgan," on Wednesday, November 2, 1904, delivered a powerful message on a subject one would not generally think Jowett would ever undertake, "Destructive Heresies," based upon the opening words of this second chapter of II Peter. This originally appeared in the *Christian World Pulpit,* Vol. XLVI, pages 289–292, and is found reprinted in his *The Redeemed Family of God,* pages 279–295. Space allows for quoting only the concluding two sentences: "All the corruption of this chapter is traced up to unworthy conceptions of Christ, to the partial, if not entire, dethronement of 'the Lord of life and glory.' The immorality has its explanation in 'destructive heresy.' "
21. I John 2:22, 23. In view of the growing denial of the Deity of Christ in Christendom, the following comment on this verse by that great scholar Canon Westcott, should be pondered: "The denial of the Incarnation is in fact the denial of that which is characteristic of the Christian Faith, the true union of God and man. . . . Such a spirit, *whatever appearances may be,* is not of God. The antagonists regarded here are not mere unbelievers but those who knowing Christianity *fashion it into a shape of their own."* (The italics are mine.) Brooke Foss Westcott: *The Epistles of St. John.* 2nd ed. Cambridge. 1886. pp. 142–143.
22. Jude 4. The word for *deny, arneomai,* meaning *to disown,* is used with a greater frequency and sadness than is generally recognized; see, e.g., Matt. 10:33; 26:70, 72; Mark 14:68, 70; John 18:25, 27; Acts 3:14; I Tim. 5:8; II Tim. 2:12, 13, etc.
23. Revelation 1:9.
24. Revelation 6:9.
25. Revelation 12:17; 13:5, 6; 17:14; 19:19. Lange's comment on 19:19, written before 1870, is worth careful consideration—"It may only be gathered from the nature of the armies, that upon the side of Christ all the dynamic forces of spiritual humanity are concentrated, whilst upon the side of Antichrist demonic excitement may summon to its aid all the contrivances of craft and violence."

26. Revelation 2:13. Cremer, in a long discussion of the words *martus, marturia,* etc., says the idea of *martyrdom* cannot be said to be denoted in passages where they occur in the New Testament, but this is generally *not* the view held in reference to Rev. 2:13.
27. Luke 6:22. On the parallel passage, Matt. 5:10–12, not as detailed as the one in Luke, see some helpful remarks in F. B. Meyer: *"Blessed Are Ye,"* New York. 1898. pp. 117–130; F. W. Boreham: *The Heavenly Octave.* New York. 1936. pp. 105–115; J. H. Jowett, in the *British Congregationalist,* April 2, 1908. Farrar says, of Luke 6:22, that "we have here four steps of persecution increasing in virulence." F. W. Farrar: *Cambridge Greek Testament for Schools and Colleges. St. Luke.* Cambridge. 1891. p. 187.
28. Henry B. Smith: *Apologetics.* New York. 1881. p. 11. The missionary conference at Madras, December, 1938, agreed that, "There is more organized opposition to the Christian Church than at any time, within the past one hundred years." *The Madras Series* (Vol. III). *Evangelism.* New York, 1939. p. 378.
29. W. Windleband: *A History of Philosophy.* 2nd ed. New York. 1926. pp. 6, 7. See also Emile Boutroux: *Science and Religion in Contemporary Philosophy.* London. 1909. Eng. trans. pp. 1–3. Arthur Fairbanks: *A Handbook of Greek Religion.* New York. 1910. pp. 327, 328; "We must conclude that the dominant theories of knowledge in modern philosophy are incompatible with rational Christian belief." George F. Thomas, Prof. of Religious Thought, Princeton University—"Christianity and Modern Philosophy" in *The Vitality of the Christian Tradition.* New York. 1944. p. 248.
30. "He transcended the rationalism of his day and opened a new era in religious as well as in philosophical thought." Arthur Cushman McGiffert: *Protestant Thought before Kant.* New York. 1911. p. 250.
31. Immanuel Kant: *Religion within the Boundary of Pure Reason.* Tr. by J. W. Semple. Edinburgh. 1938. pp. 205–206. In a footnote strikingly revealing how difficult he found the resurrection of Christ to be when insisting on a rationalistic religion, Kant says that the death of Christ concludes His public life, "at least so much of it as can be held up as a fit example for general imitation," and then most significantly adds, "The more secret events—the Resurrection and Ascension—witnessed only by his immediate friends, cannot come within the sphere of a religion within the bounds of reason," although he seems to admit "their historical reality"! p. 170, note. The reason for the difference in the title of Kant's work in the text in this volume and in this footnote is due to the fact that I have used the generally accepted title in the text, but the exact title of the translation I have used in this footnote is the later translation by T. M. Greene, and H. Hudson Reid, *Religion within the Limits of Reason Alone.*
32. Kant, *ibid.* pp. 216, 217.
33. Clement C. J. Webb: *Kant's Philosophy of Religion.* Oxford. 1926. pp. 175, 176; see also John Oman: *The Problem of Faith and Freedom.* London. 1906. pp. 169–189.
34. Kant, *ibid.* pp. 228, 229.
35. J. H. W. Stuckenberg: *The Life of Immanuel Kant.* London. 1882. p. 354.

While fully recognizing the great importance of Kant, we should not forget that his type of religion, within the limits of pure reason, brought him none of the joy and peace that result from faith in Christ. "His life, as a whole, was a sad one, in spite of his intellectual pleasures and his great fame . . . Of inspiring faith and enthusiastic hope there is scarcely a trace, and, in reality, his religion was as emotionless practically as it was in theory . . . One of his friends and biographers said, 'Who has not read in his writings, and which of his friends has not heard him say frequently, that he would not be willing, for any price, to live his life over again on condition of living from the beginning just as he had done.'" *ibid.* pp. 423, 424.

36. Quoted in John Tulloch: *Modern Theories in Philosophy and Religion.* Edinburgh. 1884. p. 406.
37. R. Birch Hoyle: *The Teaching of Karl Barth.* New York. 1930. p. 71.
38. William Jackson: *The Doctrine of Retribution.* Bampton Lectures for 1875. New York. 1876. pp. 15, 16.
39. Otto Ruhle: *Karl Marx: His Life and Work.* Eng. trans. New York. 1929. p. 28.
40. Karl Marx, in Ruhle, as above, pp. 32, 33.
41. Ludwig Feuerbach: *The Essence of Christianity.* Eng. trans. New York. 1929. p. 28. On Feuerbach, one might profitably consult F. A. Lange: *History of Materialism,* Eng. trans. II. 246–256; and Etienne Gilson: *The Unity of Philosophical Experience,* 281–290.
42. Karl Marx: *Contribution to the Criticism of Hegel's Philosophy of Right.* pp. 12, 13.
43. *The Manifesto of the Communist Party* may be found in many different works on the history of socialism, and in separately-published form, and for this reason I have not given page-references for these easily located quotations.
44. Lenin's *Religion* is published in a pamphlet edited by International Publishers. New York. 1933. p. 48. In a recent book by Dr. James D. Smart, who has been called to be the head of all the publication work of the Presbyterian church, U. S. A., I came upon one of the most astonishing pages I ever expect to see in a work by an ordained Presbyterian minister, who, in the earlier pages of the same volume speaks of the necessity of the Word of God, etc., etc. These are Dr. Smart's words, and they need no additional comment whatever from me: "This was coupled with a perception that men never really get roused into passion against the evils which cripple and frustrate their life as long as they dream of a paradise the other side of death. That dream is like opium which deadens the pain caused by such evils and keeps men from reacting forcibly against them. Thus Karl Marx coined his phrase that 'religion is the opiate of the people,' a phrase which stuck in men's minds because there was so much in their religion that justified the criticism. Those social thinkers who still glibly use this phrase to dismiss religion fail, however, to realize that a criticism which was justified in Marx's day has lost all application to a Christianity in which other worldly dreaming has become a rarity and has been replaced by the passion for

social reform. The concentration of mind now in wide sections of the Church is, not upon a paradise beyond, but upon a paradise on the nearer side of death. Mention of the New Jerusalem suggests to a man of the present day, not some realm of bliss in another world, but a great new social order which he hopes may soon be brought into being among men." James D. Smart: *What a Man Can Believe*. Philadelphia. 1943. p. 240. Westminster Press, Philadelphia. Used by the kind permission of the publishers.

45. Ira Levisky, in, *Christianity and the Social Revolution*. New York. 1936. pp. 270–277.
46. Julian Hecker: *Christianity and Communism in the Light of the Russian Revolution*. London n.d., p. 527.
47. Voltaire: *Essai sur les Mœurs et l'Espirit des Nations*. part II. p. 205.
48. Benjamin Franklin Underwood, *Open Court*. (1887.) I. 213. Kirsopp Lake: *Immortality and the Modern Mind*. p. 21.
49. John Dewey: *A Common Faith*. New Haven. 1934. p. 80. Inasmuch as the name of Professor Dewey will often appear in these pages, we should remember that "the imprint of Dewey's thought is on all our normal schools. It shapes the lives of millions of school children here and overseas, though they may never hear his name." Harry Todd Costello, in, *Naturalism and the Human Spirit*. New York. 1944. p. 318. So also Max Nordau, in his *Interpretation of History*. "Religion has retarded, not advanced, civilization. It has injured knowledge. It has had no share in the softening of manners." New York. 1911. pp. 248, 249. This matter of the advantage or disadvantage of religion, and faith in God, in modern civilization, will be one of the crucial questions in the impending battle of supernaturalism *vs.* materialism, and for this reason I do not hesitate to add this supplementary note. In his Presidential address before the American Historical Association, December 26, 1906, on, "Religion still the Key to History," Justice Simeon E. Baldwin, for many years Professor of Law at Yale University, once President of the American Bar Association, etc., declared: "It may indeed be safely said that no single cause for the spread of religious liberty, and, by consequence, of civil liberty in modern times, has been so powerful as the circulation of the Bible in all languages." (*American Historical Review,* January, 1907, XII. 235.) Chief Justice Story, professor of law at Harvard for sixteen years, appointed associate justice of the U. S. Supreme Court, in 1811, at the age of 32, in his famous *Commentaries on the Constitution of the United States,* boldly affirmed that, "The promulgation of the great doctrines of religion, the being, and attributes, and providence of one Almighty God; the responsibility to Him for all our actions, founded upon moral freedom and accountability; a future state of rewards and punishments; the cultivation of all the personal, social, and benevolent virtues;—these can never be a matter of indifference in any well-ordered community. It is, indeed, difficult to conceive how any civilized society can well exist without them . . . It yet remains a problem to be solved in human affairs, whether any free government can be permanent, where the public worship of God, and the support of religion, constitute no part of the policy or duty of the state in any assignable shape."

(Vol. II. 2nd ed. Boston. 1851. pp. 591, 593.) "Having learned from the Holy Scriptures," declared Dr. Jonathan Mayhew, pastor of the West Church in Boston, in a sermon on "The Snare Broken," preached May 23, 1877, "that wise and brave and virtuous men are always friends to liberty, . . . and that, where the Spirit of the Lord is, *there* is liberty—*this* made me conclude that freedom is a great blessing" (p. 43). Lord Bryce, in his epochal work, *The American Commonwealth,* has a chapter on "The Influence of Religon" (Chap. CIII, toward the end of Vol. II, pagination varying with differenr editions), which he concludes with these words. "The more democratic republics become, the more the masses grow conscious of their own power, the more do they need to live, not only by patriotism, but by reverence and self-control, and the more essential to their well-being are those sources whence reverence and self-control flow." 2nd ed. London. 1891. p. 599. For further reading one might consult, R. H. Tyler: *The Bible and Social Reform,* Philadelphia. 1860; Oscar F. Strauss: *The Origin of Republican Form of Government in the United States.* 2nd ed. New York. 1901; B. B. Warfield: *The Book of Humanity.* New York. 1915; Julius F. Seebach: *The Book of Free Men.* New York. 1917. See also, the recent books by J. Wesley Bready, containing a great mass of incontrovertible evidence on the *social* benefits of the Christian religion, e.g., his *Wesley and Democracy;* and, *This Freedom—Whence?*

50. John Fiske: *The Beginnings of New England.* Boston. 1889. pp. 37, 45, 46.
51. The famous statements of Daniel Webster concerning the supreme importance of the Bible in the founding of our nation are now too seldom seen. One may find these for the most part in *The Writings and Speeches of Daniel Webster.* Boston. 1903. I. 224–226; IV. 223; XI. 142–148; XIII. 584–585; XVI. 655–657. His best statements, outside the Girard case, were given at various celebrations of the settlement at Plymouth, especially, December 22, 1820, and, December 22, 1850. The historian, G. P. Gooch, has said that the two great principles of the Reformation, the right of free inquiry, and the priesthood of all believers, have led respectively to liberty and equality. *English Democratic Ideas in the Seventeenth Century,* 2nd ed. 1927. p. 7.
52. Henry Campbell Black: *Handbook of American Historical Law.* 4th ed. St. Paul. 1927. pp. 514, 515.
53. In a message on "The Influence of the Bible," delivered before the Long Island Bible Society, in 1901. Quoted in Christian F. Reisner: *Roosevelt's Religion.* New York. 1922. p. 306.
54. Rudolf Eucken: *Main Currents of Modern Thought.* New York. 1912. p. 246.
55. Guglielmo Ferrero: *The Ruins of Ancient Civilization and the Triumphs of Christianity.* Eng. trans., New York, 1921, pp. 79, 80. On Christianity the greatest phenomenon of European history, see James T. Shotwell: *The Religious Revolution of Today.* New York. 1913. pp. 84–87. On Christianity the source of the conception of equality among men, see Rudolf Eucken: *Main Currents of Modern Thought.* pp. 348, 349.
56. William E. Gladstone: *Correspondence on Church and Religion.* London. 1910. II. 99. Frances Wentworth Knickerbocker: *Free Minds. John Morley and His Friends.* Cambridge. 1943. p. 239.

57. Ernest Gordon: *A Book of Protestant Saints.* Grand Rapids. 1940. pp. 90, 91.
57a. *Christian Counter-Attack: Europe's Churches against Nazism,* by Hugh Martin, etc. New York. 1944. pp. 15, 16.
58. This interesting passage is quoted in a volume by David G. Mears, *The Deathless Book* (Boston, 1888, pp. 296, 297), with no indication of the source. I have consulted the two leading authorities on Lowell in our country, and neither of them recognize it, but agree it could easily have appeared in some fugitive article of Lowell's.
59. Hurbert S. Box: *God and the Modern Mind.* p. 9.
60. Douglas C. MacIntosh: "Contemporary Humanism," in William P. King: *Humanism: Another Battle.* Nashville. 1931. p. 55.
61. Henry Nelson Wieman: *The Wrestle of Religion with Truth.* New York. 1927. p. 14. See also his words in *Christendom.* Fall, 1936. pp. 777, 778. For a summary of Wieman's conception of God, see Edwin A. Burtt: *Types of Religious Philosophy.* pp. 443 ff. Wieman's own confession shows how utterly irreligious he is—"I fear my religion has never been religious. . . . Since I was never led to identify religion with any particular set of beliefs or institution or program of action, I never felt any religious distress or perplexity when I had to make radical changes in my beliefs and programs. Whatever else God is, he is not a personality." In Vergilius Ferm: *Contemporary American Theology.* pp. 340, 341, 351. Yet without any "particular set of beliefs" he has been instructing hundreds of ministerial students in a *theological seminary* during the last seventeen years.
62. James Bisset Pratt, "Three Trends in the Philosophy of Religion," *Anglican Theological Review,* Oct., 1942. XXIV. 302. On the impersonality of God, see also George P. Conger: *The Ideology of Religion.* New York. 1942. pp. 247–251, who concludes, "whatever the extent to which, under modern criticism, personal qualities seem to disappear from the Object of religion, it may be recovered in another form in a heightened sense of the personal qualities of the founders and revealers," etc. Dr. Conger is the professor of philosophy in the University of Minnesota. I do not know any confession quite as pitiful regarding one's own personal religious convictions, or rather the absence of them, as the following statement by Professor Pratt, made in 1930, when he was fifty-five years of age: "My long study of mysticism and the religious consciousness reinforces, I suspect, the influence of Oriental thought; and I cannot say with the assurance I should have felt some years ago that Hindu and Buddhist Monism are quite mistaken. Is my personal realism necessarily incompatible with the ancient insight of the East? As yet I do not know. It may be that some day I shall have to resign one or both of them altogether. It may be that I shall yet find some kind of synthesis that shall transmute and save them both. Most likely of all I shall never come to any definite conclusion, but shall continue to wonder to the end of my days. . . . As I view the matter, Philosophy is a persistent attempt to get at the most probable explanation of our experience, to draw the most persuasive and inclusive picture of the world we live in. Just for this reason it is an investigation that can never be complete, a question that can never

be finally answered, a path that has no ending." J. B. Pratt, in *Contemporary American Philosophy,* Vol. II. 1930. pp. 218, 219.

63. Walter Marshall Horton: *Theism and the Scientific Spirit.* 1933. pp. 206, 218.
64. John Laird: *Mind and Deity.* London. 1941. p. 297; also his *Theism and Cosmology.* London. 1940. pp. 310, 319. "I incline towards the view that Nature is God's body, if there be a God." p. 301. "Surprise may be shown that anyone should seriously consider attempted demonstrations of theism in this twentieth century." p. 294. As an indication of how some leading theologians would radically disagree with Professor Laird's denial of the validity of theism, one might consider the following single sentence by Dr. John Wright Buckham, "Never before in the history of Christianity has Personal Theism been so widely questioned, yet never before have its philosophical foundations been so secure or its necessity for human need and spiritual progress so manifest." In Vergilius Ferm: *Contemporary American Theology.* 1932. p. 99.
65. Julian Huxley: *Essays of a Biologist.* New York. 1923. p. 295.
66. Sigmund Freud: *Psychopathology of Everyday Life.* Eng. trans. pp. 309, 310. In his volume, *The Future of an Illusion* (New York, 1929), he declares—"Religious doctrines . . . are all illusions, they do not admit of proof, and no one can be compelled to consider them as true or to believe in them." p. 55.
67. George Burnam Foster: *The Function of Religion in Man's Struggle for Existence.* Chicago. 1909. pp. 50, 73–76. For a sketch of his theological views, see John Horsch: *Modern Religious Liberalism.* 3rd ed. 1925. pp. 100–104.
68. *The Psychology of Religious Experience.* Boston. New York. 1910. p. 317. Ames has given us a full account of his conception of God, in *My Idea of God,* ed. by Joseph Fort Newton, Boston, 1926. pp. 237–250; which has been reprinted in *Contemporary Religious Thought,* compiled by Thomas S. Kepler. New York. 1941. pp. 180–184, in which he confesses, "My idea of Uncle Sam is of the same character." Shailer Mathews seems to make the same denial concerning the personality of God in the following words, "In the history of Christianity, as well as of every religion, while the term God was assumed to imply a personal existence, it was in reality an anthropomorphic conception of those personality-producing activities of the universe with which humanity is organically related." Shailer Mathews: *Is God Emeritus?* New York. 1940. p. 34.
69. John Morley, in *Encyclopaedia Britannica* 14th ed. VI. 194
70. For a brief account of the influence of this book, see Charles Howard Hopkins: *The Rise of the Social Gospel in American Protestantism. 1865–1915.* New Haven. 1940. p. 57.
71. Robert G. Ingersoll: *Works.* Vol. I. p. 89.
72. H. Shelton Smith: *Faith and Nurture.* New York. 1942. p. 27.
73. George Albert Coe, "My Own Little Theatre," in *Religion in Transition.* ed. by Vergilius Ferm. New York. 1937. p. 16. "If God is an omnipotent monarch who can do anything he pleases, he has no business to please to do some things he does and permit some things that he allows." Harry Emerson Fosdick: *Living Under Tension.* p. 219. "Since service of God is in

reality service of man, there will be sin in this new religion of democracy; it will be a failure to serve mankind." Charles A. Ellwood: *The Reconstruction of Religion.* pp. 139, 143.

74. G. A. Coe: *Educating for Citizenship.* New York. 1932. p. 143.
75. G. A. Coe, in *Religion in Transition.* pp. 97, 98.
76. G. A. Coe, in *Religious Education.* Oct. 1916. p. 379.
77. G. A. Coe: *The Psychology of Religion.* Chicago. 1916. p. 326.
78. G. A. Coe, in *Religion in Transition,* p. x.
79. G. A. Coe, *ibid.* p. 114.
80. Walter Rauschenbush: *A Theology for the Social Gospel.* 1917. p. 178. Such a conception accounts for the following (to many of us, blasphemous) declaration of Bosanquet, "When two or three are gathered together, cooperating for a social good, there is the Divine Spirit in the midst of them." *Essays and Addresses.* 1891. p. 121. For some important pages on the subject of the religion of humanity, see Ralph Henry Gabriel: *The Course of American Democratic Thought.* pp. 173–186.
81. A. C. McGiffert: "Democracy and Religion," in *Religious Education.* 1919. XIV. 161.
82. Gerald B. Smith, "Is Theism Essential to Religion?" *Journal of Religion,* July, 1925. V. 376. "Theism comes to be a matter of taste rather than a fundamental doctrine." p. 359.
83. R. W. Sellars: *The Next Step in Religion.* 1918. p. 217. One of the most blasphemous sentences that I have read in any book on religion by an American professor is found in this volume (182), "Paul's God was an Oriental Monarch; to the modern, He is a cad." In reading much of recent so-called religious literature, one is reminded of a word concerning Sennacherib, found in Israel's historical records—"he wrote letters to rail on Jehovah the God of Israel," II Chron. 32:17.
84. Edwin A. Burtt: *Types of Religious Philosophy.* New York. 1939. p. 293. See also pp. 453–455.
85. H. A. Overstreet, "The Democratic Conception of God," in the *Hibbert Journal,* 1912. XI. 408, 410. On the subject of humanity considered as God, there are a number of references to important statements in Douglas Clyde MacIntosh: *The Pilgrimage of Faith.* pp. 101–104. Aurel Kolnai in his profound work better known, I believe, in Europe than in this country, *The War against the West* (New York. 1938), quotes the German Philosopher Bergmann as saying, "Man himself shall rise up as God, as Christ; he shall become conscious of himself as such, and his essence shall take on the divine form" (p. 267). He also quotes the profession of faith of a group known as the "Völkische Aktion" announced on February 13, 1937, as follows, "I believe in our own divinity when millions of Germans are leagued around one Leader, I know God to be in the force of our blood alone." Kolnai's own statement deserves careful consideration and supports what is said concerning Satanic influence in other portions of this volume. "It is certainly a disconcerting and ominous symptom if a man refuses to believe either in God or in the Soul, considering himself to be a bundle of animal instincts justified in seeking gratification as best they can. However, it is incomparably

more Satanic and more deleterious to the moral order of the world if a man happens to believe both in God and the Soul, and also believes the Soul to be *the attribute of a Tribe, or a State, or himself to be God,"* pp. 230–231. Emmet John Hughes, in his much-eulogized work, *The Church and the Liberal Society* (Princeton, 1944, p. 144), alters our Lord's words to read, "For *ours* shall be the Kingdom, and the Power, and the Glory."

86. A. C. McGiffert: *The Rise of Modern Religious Ideas*. New York. 1915. pp. 240f.

87. Gerald B. Smith, in the *Biblical World*. May, 1918. p. 302.

87a. Luke 11:52.

88. James Rowland Angell, "Contemporary Youth and the World of Religion and Moral," in his *American Education*. New Haven. 1937. pp. 204, 205.

89. Charles Stelzle: *The Gospel of Labor*. New York. 1912. p. 81.

90. Robert Flint: *Theism*. 7th ed. rev. 1889. p. 51. Inasmuch as a large number of quotations, beginning with this one will be found in this volume, from the writings of Professor Robert Flint, it may not be out of place to say just a word here concerning the high place Flint held in theological circles at the close of the last century. Flint was the Professor of Moral Philosophy at St. Andrews University, 1864–1876; and Professor of Divinity, Edinburgh University, 1876–1903. Lord Acton gave instructions that unless Dr. Flint would write the chapter "The Philosophy of History" for *The Cambridge Modern History,* there was to be no such chapter. Professor John Dickie, in a fascinating work *Fifty Years of British Theology* (Edinburgh. 1927), has said "There was no position or honor in the gift of the church of Scotland which Dr. Flint might not have had, if he had had any desire for it, at any time during the last twenty-five years of his life. . . . So far as we still survive, we are all agreed that he is the greatest teacher we have ever known." (pp. 72–81).

91. Frances Wentworth Knickerbocker: *Free Minds: John Morley and His Friends*. Cambridge. 1943. p. 56.

92. John W. Bowman: *The Intention of Jesus*. Philadelphia. 1943. pp. 183, 184. It is not without significance that the Foreword of this book was written by Dr. Walter Marshall Horton, of Oberlin.

93. J. W. Bowman, *ut supra,* pp. 180, 181.

94. J. W. Bowman, *ut supra,* p. 186. The reference is Romans 1:4.

95. J. W. Bowman, *ut supra,* p. 184.

96. J. W. Bowman, *ut supra,* pp. 222, 224, 185.

97. J. W. Bowman, *ut supra,* p. 35. Dr. James D. Smart in the book we have already quoted, *What Can a Man Believe?* makes the astonishing statement (p. 134) that when we read that "at the baptism of our Lord, there was a voice from heaven saying, This is my beloved Son in whom I am well pleased," Jesus is quoting from the Second Psalm and Isaiah 42, and that "their coming together in the mind of Jesus indicates that He saw in Himself the fulfillment of Isaiah, the age-long expectation of the Messiah."

98. James Orr: *The Christian View of God and the World*. New York. 1893. pp. 235–238.

99. J. W. Bowman, *ut supra,* pp. 203, 204. These passages are quoted with the kind permission of the publishers, The Westminster Press, Philadelphia.
100. B. B. Warfield, "Jesus' Mission According to His Own Testimony," in his *Biblical Doctrines.* New York. 1929. pp. 323, 324.
101. Edwin Ewart Aubrey: *Man's Search for Himself.* Nashville. 1940. p. 216.
102. Henry Pitney Van Dusen, in *Liberal Theology. An Appraisal.* New York. 1942. pp. 220, 222.
103. Charles E. Eliot, in *Theology at the Dawn of the Twentieth Century.* Boston. 1900. pp. 514, 515.
104. Albert W. Palmer: *The New Christian Epic.* p. 187.
105. Douglas Clyde MacIntosh: *The Pilgrimage of Faith in the World of Modern Thought.* Calcutta. 1931. p. 284.
106. Hornell Hart, "Perfect Christ and Imperfect Jesus," in *Christian Century,* June 2, 1943. pp. 659, 661.
107. Paul W. Schmiedel: *Jesus in Modern Criticism.* London. 1907. p. 86.
108. John Herman Randall, and John Herman Randall, Jr.: *Religion and the Modern World.* New York. 1929. p. 219. This volume is used as a textbook in some of our state universities.
109. Albert Schweitzer: *The Quest of the Historical Jesus.* London. 1936. p. 399.
110. Douglas Clyde MacIntosh, "Is Belief in the Historicity of Jesus Indispensable to Christian Faith?" *American Journal of Theology.* pp. 368–372.
111. Douglas Clyde MacIntosh: *The Pilgrimage of Faith in the World of Modern Thought.* Calcutta. 1931. p. 267.
112. See p. 129.
113. Edwin A. Burtt: *Types of Religious Philosophy.* New York. 1939. p. 491.
114. H. G. Wells: *First and Last Things.* London. 1908. pp. 110, 111.
115. H. G. Wells: *The Outline of History.* New York. 1920. Vol. I. p. 574.
116. H. G. Wells: *Experiment in Autobiography.* New York. 1934. p. 46.
117. A. Tholuck: *Light from the Cross.* Eng. trans. Philadelphia. 1858. p. 12.
118. Robert S. Candlish: *The First Epistle of John expounded in a Series of Lectures.* Edinburgh. 1866. pp. 334–336. Candlish was Principal of New College, Edinburgh, and minister of Free St. George's Church.
119. H. G. Wells: *The Salvaging of Civilization.* New York. 1921. p. 104.
120. Julian S. Huxley: *Religion with Revelation.* New York. (c. 1927.)
121. James Bisset Pratt, "Religion and the Young Generation." In *Yale Review.* April, 1923. XII. 602.
122. George Albert Palmer: *The New Christian Epic.* pp. 29, 100, 101. "In this Bible of Humanity we ought to write," George Burman Foster: *The Function of Religion in Man's Struggle for Existence.* p. 292.
123. George Albert Coe: *A Social Theory of Religious Education.* New York. 1917. p. 65.
124. W. Macneile Dixon: *The Human Situation.* London. 1937. p. 22.
125. The titles of Dr. Dietrich's major works tell their own story: *The Gain for Religion in Modern Thought,* 1908; *The Religion of a Sceptic,* 1911; *Substitutes for the Old Beliefs,* 1914; *The Religion of Evolution,* 1917; *The Religion of Humanism,* 1919; *The Present Crisis in Religion,* 1923; *Humanism —A New Faith for a New Age,* 1925.

126. See, also, p. 40.
127. This four-page leaflet, "A Humanist Manifesto," was first published in *The New Humanist* (First Series), May–June, 1933, Vol. VI, No. 3; and is now reissued by the American Humanist Association. For an approving discussion of this document see Arthur Hazard Dakin: *Man the Measure*. Princeton. 1939. Chap. II. pp. 88ff.
128. Quoted in John Horsch: *Modern Religious Liberalism*. n.d. (c. 1921.) p. 158.
129. John Dewey: *A Common Faith*. New Haven. 1934. p. 71.
130. James T. Shotwell: *The Religious Revolution of Today*. New York. 1913. p. 151.
131. Wm. P. Montague: *Belief Unbound*. New Haven. 1930. pp. 21–25.
132. Wm. P. Montague, "Philosophy in a World at War," *Fortune,* March, 1942.
133. Will Durant: *On the Meaning of Life*. New York. 1932. p. 5.
134. H. L. Mencken, in *On the Meaning of Life,* pp. 33–35.
135. Carl Van Doren, "Why I am an Unbeliever," in the *Forum,* December, 1926. Vol. 76, pp. 864–869.
136. Alexander Meiklejohn: *Education between Two Worlds*. New York. 1942. p. 202.
137. Edwin A. Burtt: *Religion in an Age of Science*. New York. 1925. p. 145. For the same author's belief that a supernatural revelation is *not* necessary, see his *Types of Religious Philosophy*. New York. 1939. pp. 453–455.
138. Arthur Cushman McGiffert: *Christianity as History and Faith*. New York. 1934. p. 617.
139. E. S. Ames: *Religion*. New York. 1929. p. 177. See also his "The Validity of the Idea of God" in *Journal of Religion*. September, 1921. Vol. I. pp. 462–481.
140. A. Eustace Haydon: *The Quest of the Ages*. 1929. pp. 110, 115, 123, 124. See below, p. 128. In his more recent book, *Biography of the Gods* (1941), he concludes his final chapter "The Twilight of the Gods," with these words: "What the gods have been expected to do, and have failed to do through the ages, man must find the courage and intelligence to do for himself. More needful than faith in God is faith that man can give love, justice, peace and all his beloved moral values embodiment in human relations." (329). In reviewing the same author's *Biography of the Gods,* in which Dr. Haydon reiterates his idea that God is only the product of man's thinking, a Mohammedan journal, published in this country, *The Moslem Sunrise,* has well said, "What lends color to the significance is that Dr. Haydon happens to be the professor of Comparative Religion at the University of Chicago. No wonder the rising generations in the Western countries are rapidly being swept away by the turbulent stream of atheism and the western civilization is rocking to its very foundations." *The Moslem Sunrise*. 2nd Quarter. 1943. Vol. XV. 2. (Inside of back cover.) When the Mohammedans of this country have a truer conception of God than our professors of religion in our own universities, founded with Christian money, we are in a bad way.
141. Edward Grant Conklin: *Man Real and Ideal*. New York. 1943. pp. 201–203.

He adds, "The religion of science leaves to us faith in the worth and dignity and almost boundless possibilities of man."

142. This address of Professor Carlson's is reported, together with addresses by other speakers on religious beliefs at the University of Michigan, February–March, 1940, in mimeographed form, distributed by a student organization at the University. I am quoting from my own copy.

143. M. C. Otto: *The Human Enterprise*. New York. 1941. pp. 322–325, 334. It is strange to find Dr. Otto, an atheist, reviewing books in a publication of a theological seminary in this country, but he is the author of a long book review in the *Journal of Liberal Religion,* published by the Meadville Theological School, Winter 1945. VI. pp. 281–289.

145. W. M. Dixon: *The Human Situation*. New York. 1937. pp. 21, 14.

146. Herbert J. Mueller: *Science and Criticism. The Humanistic Tradition in Contemporary Thought.* New Haven. 1943. pp. 267–276.

147. D. C. MacIntosh, in *Humanism Another Battle Line.* ed. by Wm. P. King. Nashville. 1931. p. 55.

148. Quoted in Francis McCullagh: *The Bolshevik Persecution of Christianity.* New York. 1924. p. 359. See also A. Pinkevich: *Sciences and Education in the U.S.S.R.* London. 1935. pp. 34, 51. Beatrice King, in her *Changing Man: the Education System of the U.S.S.R.* (London. 1936), reports this incident—"At Easter-time in a school I visited the Russian lesson was used to disprove the existence of God. . . . The Soviet children are not just told there is no God and all religion is untrue. . . . They are told why religion was a necessity to primitive man, and why it is no longer a necessity but an obstacle to progress." (p. 42.) This is, we must remember, the teaching of Professor Dewey, in *our own* Columbia University, in New York City.

150. Quoted in Julius F. Hecker: *Religion and Communism.* London. p. 279.

151. Paul B. Anderson: *People, Church and State in Modern Russia.* New York. 1944. pp. 60, 89, 14, 145, 118, 119, 159. "What is obvious is that the religion of National Socialism, whether German or Nordic, must ever remain the supreme faith. . . . Under its sanctions the supreme end of all activity lies in the greater glory of the nation and its desire for biological development to the highest possible perfection." George Frederick Kneller: *The Educational Philosophy of National Socialism.* New Haven. 1941. p. 204. Gregor Ziemer, in his *Education for Death* (Oxford. 1941), has written some lines I cannot refrain from placing before my readers: "Courses 1–76 at the University are called Science of Religion. According to Dr. Leonard Rost, of the theological staff, whom I met frequently during my four years as postgraduate student at the University of Berlin, twenty-three of these courses prove the evil influence of the Hebrews on religion; eight are devoted to church architecture, and have nothing to do with religion as such; nine, labelled 'Philosophy of Religion,' prove that the faith of a nation in its leader is the best possible religion; eleven discuss the history of religion, a lamentable history indeed! Rost did not know what was going on in the others, but assured me that no old-fashioned theology was being taught anywhere in Nazi Germany." Gregor Ziemer: *Education for Death. The Making of the Nazi.* Oxford. University Press. 1941. p. 172.

152. On the entire subject of the attitude of Germany toward Christianity, particular reference should be made to the large sixteen-page pamphlet, *Watchman What of the Night,* by Stanley High; Wilhelm Hauer and Karl Heim: *The German Faith Movement,* 1937; "Rosenberg's Myth and Nazi Paganism," by Leonard de Moor, in *The Calvin Forum.* April, 1938. pp. 200–203.
153. Quoted in *Christian Counter-Attack,* etc., as below. p. 16.
154. Quoted in Hugh Martin: *Christian Counter-Attack Europe's Churches against Nazism.* New York. 1944. pp. 16, 17.
155. "Atheism and the Gospel in the Balkans," *Calvin Forum,* V. (July, 1940), 251, 252.
156. H. C. Armstrong: *Gray Wolf.* New York. 1933. p. 199.
157. Quoted in Monsignor M. D'Herbigny: *Militant Atheism. The World-Wide Propaganda of Communism.* London. 1930. p. 25.
158. See an article by Harold B. Hinton, in *New York Times.* December 4, 1934. "Dry, Atheist State Is Tobasco's Aim."
160. In House Report 2290, 71st Congress, 3rd Session. Investigation of Communist Propaganda. Jan. 17, 1931. p. 10.
161. Earl Browder: *What Is Communism?* New York. 1936. pp. 191, 192. See *Current Biography.* pp. 10–14. The following lines in the sketch of Mr. Browder in the 1944–45 *Who's Who in America,* is a good illustration of the destructive influence of atheism on ethical standards, "Sentenced to prison for four years for passport irregularity 1940 (sentence commuted by President Roosevelt after fourteen months in Atlanta prison)." Mr. Browder has been the general secretary of the Communistic party in the United States since 1930, and candidate for president of the United States on the Communistic ticket in 1936–40.
165. Fulton J. Sheen: *Seven Pillars of Peace.* p. 110.
166. Mowat G. Fraser: *The College of the Future.* New York. 1937. pp. 51, 52.
167. Lancelot Hogben: *Dangerous Thoughts.* New York. 1940. pp. 60, 143.
168. Wm. Ernest Hocking: *Living Religions and the World Faith.* New York. 1940. pp. 208, 284. Also, more recently, in *The Church and the New World Mind,* St. Louis. 1944, where we come upon such a subtle statement as this: "The inherent power of faith is that it directly undercuts the series of world envelopes with their diminishing intensities of loyalty" (p. 41). What Hocking thinks of the Bible of our faith, is not difficult to ascertain when we find him saying, "We cannot forget that Hinduism has given us, in the Vedanta, probably the strictest notion of the absolute unity of God that the race has achieved" (p. 56).
169. Hugh Miller: *Christian Truth in History.* New York. 1941. pp. 230–232. See also George P. Conger: *The Ideologies of Religion.* New York. 1940. pp. 257–258.
170. Edgar Sheffield Brightman: *The Future of Christianity.* New York. 1937. p. 80.
171. E. C. Raven: *Science, Religion, and the Future.* Cambridge. New York. 1943. p. 82.

172. Douglas Clyde MacIntosh: *The Pilgrimage of Faith in the World of Modern Thought.* Calcutta. 1931. p. 229.
173. Ralph Tyler Flewelling: *The Survival of Western Culture.* New York. 1943. pp. 26 ff., 243–244, 290–298, etc.
174. R. T. Flewelling, *ut supra,* p. 239.
175. R. T. Flewelling, *ut supra,* p. 252. It is nothing less than a mystery how these men who hold places of great influence in our contemporary intellectual world can be so utterly unaware of what is really happening on this earth, when, as our author here (p. 248), they can write, "The life of love . . . is the evangel which is already running out through the whole earth." I wonder how deep that river of love is today, e.g., among twenty million soldiers at each other's throats in Europe.
176. R. T. Flewelling, p. 29.
177. John 3:36; 5:24; 6:40; Matt. 28:18–20.
178. Harold J. Laski: *Reflections on the Revolution of our Time.* New York. 1943. pp. 3, 4.
179. Harold J. Laski: *Faith, Reason and Civilization.* New York. 1944. pp. 33–35.
180. The curse of atheism is not confined to the western world, but is fast eating into the spiritual vitals of the Orient. I am not in touch with much contemporary literature of the far East, but I have come upon two items, in such reading as I have been able to do, that are tragically indicative of this tendency. In the *Chinese Recorder* for January, 1938 (Vol. LXIX. p. 29), the well-known monk Tai Hsu makes this statement, "The majority of present-day scholars, on the basis of the truths of freedom and equality, advocate non-theism. In their desire to purify social customs they find the practical realization of the ideals of freedom and equality by means of conforming to nature. But still there are also some who use these same principles of freedom and equality as a basis for theism. Such are the religionists of the West. These religionists of the West consider all men to be beloved sons of God with no class or other distinctions. Thus they are held to be equal and to have the joy of freedom. As these theists consider God to be the creator of all things, all men are classed under one Supreme Being and all distinctions fade away." In *Pleasures of Publishing,* issued by the Columbia University Press, under date of September 25, 1944, there is a notice of a new work, *Readings in Modern Chinese,* edited by Chi-Chen Wang, which is described as "a collection of essays written in Chinese and for the Chinese, and discussing with complete frankness all the great movements of modern China." The notice seems to indicate that one passage alone appears in this book in English and these are the lines,

"I fight alone and win or sink
I need no one to make me free,
I want no Jesus to think
That he could die for me."

In *Collier's Weekly,* under date of November, 1943, is a most significant article by Robert Bellaire, called "'Christianity Must Go,' Says Japan," in which the following statement is made: "Today, Japan is as much at war with Christianity as with the United States. Christianity denies the Japanese claim of racial superiority and of the 'divinity' of their emperor, it urges social reforms which would lift the Japanese masses out of peonage, and it is a religion of hope which has given faith in eventual freedom to millions of helpless Orientals whom Japan intends to shackle eternally. 'The Chinese can never be subdued while Christians are able to preach their doctrine of faith and hope,' Jan Tsuchiya, Japanese propagandist chief in China, once told me. 'That is the nonsense we must silence.' . . . Their version of Christianity is this: Christ was an Oriental, born in Japan. He was a great prophet who gained His knowledge from Japan's god-emperors. He went to the West to spread His great teachings to the barbarians, but they rejected and crucified Him, misunderstood all He taught. After arising from the dead, Christ reappeared in Japan where He died again and was buried. The wisdom He acknowledged in the teachings of the god-emperors of His time is the same divine wisdom possessed by Emperor Hirohito today. The Japanese take hundreds of Chinese and Filipino Christians on free pilgrimages to Japan to visit the 'burial place' of the prophet Christ. (Such a shrine actually has been erected.) But the visitors are told that the important part of the trip is the opportunity to stand before the Imperial Palace in Tokyo and pay homage to the god-emperor. They are thus sent home with the thought that Christ is dead, but that the god-emperor is very much alive and is the rightful inheritor of the world." See also the remarks on the East Asia Religious League, in the *Atlantic Monthly*, Sept. 1943. p. 10.

CHAPTER II

1. Rudolf Eucken: *Main Currents of Modern European Thought.* New York. 1912. p. 469.
2. Edgar Shefield Brightman: *The Problem of God.* New York. 1930. p. 29.
3. Adolf Keller: *Christian Europe Today.* New York. 1942. p. 290.
4. Emil Brunner: "The Condition and Task of the Present-Day Church," in *Religion in Life.* Spring, 1943. p. 172.
5. E. Brunner, *ibid.* pp. 174, 175.
6. Alexander McLeish: *Europe in Transition. Part II. Churches under Trial.* London. n.d. pp. 15, 18.
7. A. McLeish, *ibid.* p. 26.
8. A. McLeish, *ibid., Part III. The Ordeal of the Reformed Church.* p. 31.
9. A. McLeish, *ibid. Part III.* p. 16.
10. A. McLeish, *ibid. Part II.* pp. 9, 10.
13. *The Guardian.* September 4, 1942.
14. J. T. Christie, in the London *Times,* September 28, 1942. I am indebted for this quotation and the one immediately preceding, to recent issues of a British periodical, edited by D. M. Panton, *The Dawn.*
15. Leslie Weatherhead, "Preaching in Wartime Britain," *Christian Century,* May 19, 1943. pp. 602–604.
16. My attention was drawn to this report by an article appearing in *Time,* May 3, 1943. p. 42.

17. Conrad Henry Moehlman: *School and Church: The American Way.* New York. 1944. p. 123.
18. C. H. Moehlman, *ibid.*, p. 139, summarizes this report. The amazing suggestion insisted upon with passionate pleading, and often with sarcasm, throughout this volume of Dr. Moehlman's, is that (1) because our country is now no longer predominantly Christian, and (2) because the Bible contains so many (he says) erroneous ideas and contradictions, confusing any teacher who is assigned the task of teaching it, the Bible should be entirely removed from our whole national system of public education! Dr. Robert W. Searle, General Secretary of the Greater New York Federation of Churches, informs me in a letter of Nov. 17, 1944, that in New York City, with a population of 7,500,000, there are approximately 2,000,000 *members* of all its Christian churches and Jewish synagogues. Of these, of course, thousands never attend any service.
19. The letter bears the date of July 14, 1944.
20. Ralph Henry Gabriel: *The Course of American Democratic Thought.* New York. 1940. pp. 14, 15.
21. R. H. Gabriel, *ibid.*, p. 407.
22. R. H. Gabriel, *ibid.*, p. 413.
23. Cyrus Northrup, in *Two Centuries of Christian Activity in Yale.* New York. 1901. pp. iii–vi.
24. Anson Phelps Stokes: *Memorials of Eminent Yale Men, Vol. II.* New Haven. 1914. pp. 375, 376.
25. Douglas Clyde Macintosh: *The Pilgrimage of Faith in the World of Modern Thought.* Calcutta, India. 1931. p. 267.
26. D. C. MacIntosh, "Is Belief in the Historicity of Jesus Indispensable to Christian Faith?", in *American Jour. of Theology.* XV. 1910. pp. 368, 372.
27. I am indebted for this quotation to Ernest Gordon's excellently documented study of Modernism, *The Leaven of the Sadducees.* Philadelphia. 1926. p. 116.
28. Harry Elmer Barnes: *The Twilight of Christianity.* pp. iv, v. His bitter hatred of everything cardinal in the Christian faith blazes forth on every page of this book.
29. James Henry Leuba: *God or Man?* 1933. pp. 272, 298.
30. *A History of Columbia University, 1754–1904.* New York. 1904. p. 444.
31. See pp. 33, 34, 65.
32. Edwin Grant Conklin: *Man Real and Ideal.* New York. 1943. p. 205.
33. "Religion in an Age of Secularism." The Inaugural Lecture of George F. Thomas, professor of Religious Thought on the Harrington Spear Paine Foundation, Princeton. 1940. p. 7.
34. G. F. Thomas, *ibid.* pp. 17, 21. The President of Princeton University, Dr. Harold W. Dodds, concludes an introductory word with this sentence: "We are most fortunate, in my judgment . . . to have our program inaugurated by a man of Professor Thomas' scholarship, teaching enthusiasm, and personal conviction."

35. Samuel C. Bartlett, in *Centennial Celebration at Dartmouth College. July 21, 1869.* p. 90.
36. Leon Burr Richardson: *History of Dartmouth College.* Hanover. 1932. p. 475.
37. Nathan Lord: *A Letter to the Alumni of Dartmouth College on Its Hundredth Anniversary.* New York. 1869. p. 5. Later in the same famous letter, he prophetically warns, "Christianity is most hindered where it should produce its best effects, and most dishonored where it should be most dignified—among learned men. It has been most obscured where it should have been most illustrated—in the schools, which had made the Word of God of no effect by their traditions" (p. 43).
38. *Centennial Celebration,* etc. pp. 90–99.
39. *Catalogue of Dartmouth College for the Year 1886–1887,* p. 24.
40. This pronouncement was given national circulation by receiving extended notice in the *Literary Digest.* May 14, 1927. Vol. 93, p. 31.
41. See *The Orozco Frescoes at Dartmouth College* (published by) Dartmouth College. Hanover. 1934.
42. *Essays Toward Truth,* New York. 1924. p. V.
43. *Essays Toward Truth.* p. 240.
44. *Essays Toward Truth,* pp. 211, 224–226.
45. Frank E. Gaebelein: *From a Headmaster's Study,* p. 20.
46. Dr. Nicholas Murray Butler, in his Annual Report as President of Columbia University, *Bulletin of Information.* 1934. p. 22. Dr. Walter S. Athearn, for many years Dean of the School of Religious Education in Boston University, frankly admitted, as long ago as 1914, "Our colleges are engaged in the work of shattering religious conceptions and either ignoring the consequences or . . . unloading their victims onto classes in religion where amateurs will attempt to rebuild what professionalism has destroyed." *The Church School.* Boston. 1914. pp. 256, 257. Dr. J. W. D. Smith, General Secretary of the Scottish Sunday School Union for Christian Education, a few years ago said, "The religious view of life may be represented in the curriculum of the state school, just as in Britain, but the intellectual presentation of it is inadequate and the weight of a humanistic culture is overwhelming," "The Crisis in Christian Education" in *Church Community and State in Relation to Education.* 1938. p. 139. It is very significant to note what is said and what is not said in the interim report of a committee appointed by the British Association for the advancement of science, in September 1941, "The last year would link together all the previous work, whether in natural science or the humanities, and bring it into relation with the best philosophic thought of the Western world, begun by Plato and Aristotle and continued by the greatest modern thinkers from Descartes to Whitehead. For the purpose of the present proposal, the chief problem of philosophy is not so much to explore ultimate reality as to construct in men's minds a working model that fits all kinds of human experience, not only of space and time but also of aesthetics, morals and religion." Quoted in the *American Scholar.* Summer, 1944. V. 13, p. 306. Granted that our education is for the most part pagan, the situation will be even worse if there is finally established that

for which so much agitation is observed at the present time, namely, an international society for education. Inasmuch as most of our outstanding educators and by far the greatest majority of our philosophers are agnostic and rationalistic, one may well judge how anti-theistic and anti-Christian will be the literature proceeding from such an organization, and the courses of subjects which they will be recommending for the entire western world. For excellent well-documented discussions of the entire question of religion in American education, see especially Howard Beale, *A Historic Freedom of Teaching in American Schools,* 1940; and Joseph H. Crooker: *Religious Freedom in American Education.*

47. J. F. Bethune-Baker: *The Miracle of Christianity.* 1914. pp. 15, 16.
48. Augustus Hopkins Strong: *A Tour of the Missions.* Philadelphia. 1918. pp. 189, 191.
49. Albert W. Palmer: *Paths to the Presence of God.* pp. 89, 90.
50. A. W. Palmer, *ibid.* p. 91.
51. Albert W. Palmer: *The New Christian Epic,* p. 30.
52. A. W. Palmer, *ibid.* pp. 100, 101.
53. A. W. Palmer, *ibid.* p. 194.
54. We need an encyclopaedic work which will thoroughly survey the religious and ethical teachings of textbooks used in our state universities, and denominationally supported colleges.
55. G. P. Conger: *The Ideologies of Religion.* New York. 1940. pp. 206, 207.
56. G. B. Smith: "Is Theism Essential to Religion?" *Journal of Religion.* July, 1925. V. 359.
57. Henry Nelson Wieman, in Vergelius Ferm: *Contemporary American Theology,* 1932, pp. 349–351. Elsewhere he defines God as "that character of events to which man must adjust himself in order to attain the greatest goods and avoid the greatest ills." *The Wrestle of Religion with Truth.* p. 14.
58. Edward Scribner Ames: *The New Orthodoxy.* 1925. p. 93.
59. A. Eustace Haydon, "The Theological Trend of Pragmatism," *American Journal of Theology.* 1919. XXIII. 409. See above pp. 75, 76.
60. See pp. 41, 42, 74.
61. Harry Emerson Fosdick, "The Peril of Worshiping Jesus." New York. 1931. This has been reprinted in so many different works, I refrain from giving pagination. Also, *The Hope of the World.* p. 96.
62. Harry Emerson Fosdick: *The Modern Use of the Bible.* p. 157. Also, *Living under Tension.* p. 122.
63. *Minutes of the General Assembly of the Presbyterian Church in the U. S. A.,* 1893, p. 161; 1894, p. 233; 1895, pp. 55, 160; 1896, p. 223.
64. Henry Sloane Coffin, in *Liberal Christianity, An Appraisal.* New York. 1942. pp. 234–237.
65. Henry Sloane Coffin: *The Meaning of the Cross,* 1931. p. 110.
66. Francis John McConnell: *The Christ-like God.* pp. 14, 15.
67. See, e.g., *Proceedings in the Trial of Charles A. Briggs on the Charge of Heresy* (1892–1894); and, *The Defence of Professor Briggs before the Presbytery of New York, Dec. 13, 14, 15, 19, 1892,* New York, 1893; *The Trial of the Rev. David Swing before the Presbytery of Chicago.* Chicago, 1874.

68. J. Gresham Machen, "The Present Situation in the Presbyterian Church," *Christianity Today,* May 19, 1930, p. 5.
69. Benedetto Croce: *The Conduct of Life,* London. n.d. pp. 190–193.
70. Sigmund Freud: *The Future of An Illusion.* New York. 1929, p. 55.
71. See pp. 61, 62.
72. While Mr. Julian Huxley hardly ever refrains from expressing his disbelief in the personality of God whenever he approaches religious subjects, his most extensive discussion of the nonexistence of God as a person will be found in his volume, *The Uniqueness of Man.* London. 1941. pp. 280–282.
73. Gilbert Murray: *Stoic, Christian and Humanist,* London. 1940. p. 179.
74. Carl Van Doren, "Why I Am an Unbeliever," in *Forum.* Dec., 1926. Vol. 176. pp. 865–868. "During the Middle Ages, practically all the philosophers were monks, priests, or at least simple clerics. From the seventeenth century up to our own day, very few churchmen have exhibited real creative genius in the field of philosophy. Malebranche and Condillac in France, Berkeley in Ireland, Rosmini in Italy can be quoted but as exceptions to the rule, and none of them is ever reckoned among the outstanding philosophical geniuses of modern times. Modern philosophy has been created by laymen, not by churchmen, and to the ends of the natural cities of men, not to the end of the supernatural city of God." Etienne Gilson: *God and Philosophy.* New Haven. 1941. p. 74. This matter of the unbelief of the intellectual leaders of our century deserves the most careful consideration, for it is exercising an enormous influence on the minds of our younger generation. One might add to the above statements Clemenceau's frank acknowledgment of atheism, toward the end of his life, "At last we are drawing near the day when the God who so long has been the absolute master of prostrate man, will crumble before the cross-examination of erect man and will leave behind only the ephemeral of a name without substance." G. Clemenceau: *The Evening of My Thought.* Boston. 1929. II. p. 522. Dr. Herbert Wildon Carr, the distinguished professor of philosophy in the University of London since 1918, and the author of a number of important volumes in the field of philosophical theory, in the work which he published when seventy years of age, *Changing Backgrounds in Religion and Ethics,* made this tragic confession, "Allegorise as we will the mythology of the Christian or of any other religion, we are confronted with the fact that the theory of evolution has completely altered the basis of traditional religious concepts and antiquated the venerable superstructure. No amount of genuine admiration for the intellectual eminence, moral force, saintly lives, and courageous self-devotion of the founders and apostles of the great historic religions can disguise the fact that our modern conception of man's origin, and of the progressive creative evolution which has determined his present commanding position, has rendered obsolete the whole class of ideas on which their teaching was based." When Professor Edgar A. Singer, Jr., of the University of Pennsylvania, wrote his work, *Modern Thinkers and Present Problems* (1923), his first six of seven names are: Bruno, Spinoza, Hume, Kant, Schopenhauer, Nietzsche. It is tragic that in almost all of the recent volumes which might be designated as "Anthologies of Faith,"

the writers are almost always rationalists. Thus, e.g., in *Whither Mankind, a Panorama of Modern Civilization,* edited by Charles A. Beard (1929), the chapter on science is done by Bertrand Russell, the one on religion by James Robinson, and the one on philosophy, by John Dewey. Prof. Carlton J. H. Hayes says much of the swift decline of religion in Europe is due to "the contemptuous if not hostile attitude toward it on the part of almost every first-rate literary man and almost every outstanding artist of the generation from 1871 to 1900." *A Generation of Materialism. 1871–1900.* New York. 1941. p. 151.

75. Luke 18:8.
76. J. C. Ryle: *Expository Thoughts on the Gospels, St. Luke.* Vol. II. p. 258; see also p. 255.
77. H. A. W. Meyer: *Critical and Exegetical Handbooks to the Gospels of Mark and Luke,* trans. from the fifth German edition, New York. 1884. p. 502.
78. Charles H. Spurgeon: *Sermons on Our Lord's Parables,* No. 41. This appeared originally in the *Metropolitan Tabernacle Pulpit.*
79. Alexander Whyte, in *Christian World Pulpit,* Oct. 24, 1900. Vol. 58. p. 264.
80. John A. Hutton: *The Fear of Things.* London. 1911. pp. 149, 150.
81. William E. Gladstone, in a letter to Sir Thomas Ackland. Bart. Dec. 3, 1893. *Correspondence on Church and Religion.* London. 1910. II. 122, 123.
82. II Thessalonians 2:7–12. On v. 11, Eadie has well said: "This unparalleled hallucination indicates a mysterious state of mind and of society—antichristian, antitheistic, credulous, with a fatal facility of being imposed upon by hellish masterv and subtlety." John Eadie: *Commentary on the Greek Text of the Epistles of Paul to the Thessalonians.* London. 1877. p. 288. A remarkable statement regarding Antichrist by Dostoevsky, written in 1880, in his *The Brothers Karamazov,* seems today as truly prophetic. "Oh, blind race of men who have no understanding! As soon as men have all of them denied God—and I believe that period analogous with geologic periods, will come to pass—the old conception of the universe will fall of itself . . . and everything will begin anew. Men will unite to take from life all it can give, but only for joy and happiness in the present world. Man will be lifted up with a spirit of divine titanic pride and the man-god will appear. From hour to hour extending his conquest of nature infinitely by his will and his science, man will feel such lofty joy in doing it that it will make up for all his old dreams of the joys of heaven." The Greek word in this famous passage of St. Paul's generally translated "falling away," is *apostasia,* meaning, in the Septuagint and the New Testament, "a *religious* revolt, from the worship of God or the law of Moses." Compare its use in the Septuagint version of Numbers 14:31; Joshua 22:22; I Kings 21:13; II Chronicles 29:19; 33:19; Isaiah 30:1; and Jeremiah 2:19 and 39:32. The most important New Testament parallel reference is Hebrews 3:12. For some strange reason our biblical encyclopedias and most commentaries on the New Testament almost totally ignore this subject of an apostasy in the end of the age; in fact, even the works on Pauline eschatology side-step a discussion of this important subject. One can quickly find scores of passages and long excursuses on the man of sin, mentioned in the same passage, but on apostasy

we can generally find nothing. Bengel says, "This apostasy is not determined in its extent by any particular place;—as widely as the faith extended, so widely, for the most part, does the apostasy extend." I have consulted practically every important commentary on the Thessalonian Epistles in our language and only once have I been able to find any comment worthy of note, "Such a defection is so sad and fatal that it opens the way for the daring and defiant revelation of the Man of Sin. He seizes the opportunity when all is asleep and fearless because faithless, to found his kingdom, diffuse his falsehood, and fortify his impious pretensions. This man would not be suffered to show himself, would not be permitted to gather strength and hardihood in a healthful and vigilant condition of the church (Luke 21:8)." John Eadie: *ut supra.* p. 266.

83. I Timothy 4:1.
84. II Timothy 3:7, 8.
85. Geerhardus Vos, "Eschatology of the New Testament," *International Standard Bible Encyclopedia,* II. 986.
86. H. C. G. Moule: *The Second Epistle to Timothy.* (Devotional Commentary series.) London. 1905. pp. 130–132.

During the one week preceding my first reading of proofs of the footnotes of this second chapter, for some strange reason, wholly unsolicited on my part and unsought for, three tragic confirmations of what is set forth in the first two chapters of this book were brought to my attention, all of them recent and each in a different way confirming the awful seriousness of the religious situation prevailing in our land.

While speaking at Oshkosh at a state Bible conference, I was told—and the name was given to me of both the college and the man participating, that a clergyman speaking at the chapel service of a college in Wisconsin, founded by Christian men, was told as he went to the platform to speak at that service, "Remember, no sermon and no prayer."

The day after I was told by a layman, who drove me in his car to a meeting in which he was interested, that in a college supposedly definitely Christian where his own daughter is now a student, the week before classes for a full day had been canceled that the students might listen to a man brought in who was supposed to be an expert in the problems of young people. His first message in the chapel that morning to the entire student body contained, among other things, a statement of his own disbelief in the virgin birth of Christ and his assertion that the matter of the resurrection of Christ was not important.

The same week a nationally known minister told me that in his own city a bishop of one of our great denominations had said before a great crowd in a pre-Lenten service that the novel, *The Robe,* was as inspired as the Word of God, and should be included in our Bible. I have checked each of these carefully and find that the statements were not exaggerated.

Since this chapter was composed, there has come to my desk a copy of *The Birmingham* (England) *Post* for May 8, 1944, on the front page of which is almost a column notice of a sermon delivered by the Bishop of Birmingham at a service held by the Guild of Undergraduates at Birmingham University on Sunday, the preceding day, which is one of the most tragic revelations of utter apostasy from the faith on the part of famous churchmen that I have seen for a long time. It should be remembered that the present Bishop of Birmingham is Dr. Ernest William Barnes, now seventy years of age, Bishop of Birmingham since 1924, and considered one of the great scholars of the Church of England in the field of scientific theory. Among other things, the bishop said this:

> "Today we are witnessing not the evangelization of the world, but the collapse of Christianity. . . . We do not believe in material happenings such as the nature miracles in the Gospels. Speaking for myself, I do not think that our Western civilization is ever going to return to such beliefs, and you can say this means that Christianity collapses so far as it is built on such beliefs. But the essence of Christianity is Christ's teachings. . . . If, as I think, the time has come when some repudiations are necessary, let us turn our attention to the things which remain unharmed by change and primarily on that which is fundamental, the witness of the Spirit of God to the soul of man."

Though the words still retain some semblance of a spiritual vocabulary, here is indeed a complete cutting loose from the great foundations of our supernatural faith. I wonder, but of course there is no way of ascertaining, how many churchmen, even churchmen in high authority today, think as the Bishop of Birmingham thinks. We are indeed in a very critical hour.

CHAPTER III

1. John 8:46. Strange there should be not one important printed sermon on this text in our language.
2. B. F. Westcott: *The Gospel According to John*. London. 1882. p. 137.
3. F. Godet: *Commentary on the Gospel of John*. Eng. trans. Vol. II.
4. R. C. H. Lenski: *The Interpretation of St. John's Gospel*. Columbus. 1931. pp. 636, 637.
5. Hebrews 4:12, 13.
6. William M. Ramsay: *The Cities of St. Paul*. n.d. pp. 16, 17.
7. William M. Ramsay: *Pauline and Other Studies*. n.d. pp. 4–6.
8. Romans 1:30. "*Hating God* is the highest manifestation of pride, which cannot brook the thought of this superior and judge." F. Godet: *Commentary on St. Paul's Epistle to the Romans*. American ed. New York, 1892, p. 111.
9. Romans 8:7.
10. Colossians 1:21.
11. Psalm 2:1–3.
12. Julius Müller: *The Christian Doctrine of Sin*. Eng. trans. Edinburgh. 1852. I. 182.
13. Robert Flint: *Agnosticism*. New York. 1903. p. 444.
14. Herbert H. Farmer: *Towards Belief in God*. New York. 1943. pp. 129, 130. Gibbon somewhere says, "The stubborn mind of an infidel is guarded by a secret incurable suspicion." I cannot, in discussing the antipathy of the

natural man to God, refrain from quoting the following profoundly true statement of America's greatest theologian, Jonathan Edwards: "The enmity appears in their judgments, their natural relish, their wills, affections, and practice. They have a very mean esteem of God. Men are ready to entertain a good esteem of those with whom they are friends: they are apt to think highly of their qualities, to give them their due praises; and if there be defects, to cover them. But of those to whom they are enemies, they are disposed to have mean thoughts; they are apt to entertain a dishonorable opinion of them: they will be ready to look contemptibly upon any thing that is praiseworthy in them. So it is with natural men towards God. They entertain very low and contemptible thoughts of God. Whatever honour and respect they may pretend, and make a shew of towards God, if their practice be examined, it will shew, that they certainly look upon him as a Being, that is but little to be regarded. The language of their hearts is, *Who is the Lord, that I should obey his voice?* Exod. v. 2. *What is the Almighty, that we should serve him? and what profit should we have if we pray unto him?* Job. xxi. 15. They count him worthy neither to be loved nor feared. They dare not behave with that slight and disregard towards one of their fellow-creatures, when a little raised above them in power and authority, as they dare, and do towards God. They value one of their equals much more than God, and are ten times more afraid of offending such, than of displeasing the God that made them. They cast such exceeding contempt on God, as to prefer every vile lust before him. And every worldly enjoyment is set higher in their esteem, than God. A morsel of meat, or a few pence of worldly gain, is preferred before him. God is set last and lowest in the esteem of natural men. . . . Natural men are greater enemies to God, than they are to any other being whatsoever. Natural men may be very great enemies to their fellow-creatures; but not so great as they are to God. There is no other being that so much stands in sinners' way, in those things that they chiefly set their hearts upon, as God. Men are wont to hate their enemies in proportion to two things, viz. their opposition to what they look upon to be their interest,—and their power and ability. A great and powerful enemy, will be more hated, than one who is weak and impotent. But none is so powerful as God. Man's enmity to others may be got over: time may wear it out, and they may be reconciled. But natural men, without a mighty work of God to change their hearts, will never get over their enmity against God. They are greater enemies to God, than they are to the devil. Yea, they treat the devil as their friend and master, and join with him against God. . . . One reason why you have not more sensibly felt the exercises of malice against God, is, that your enmity is now exercised partly in your unbelief of God's being; and this prevents its appearing in other ways. Man has naturally a principle of Atheism in him: an indisposition to realize God's being, and a disposition to doubt of it. The being of God does not ordinarily seem real to natural men. All the discoveries that there are of God's being in his works, will not overcome the principle of Atheism in the heart. And though they seem in some measure to be rationally convinced, yet it does not appear real; the conviction is faint, there is no strong conviction impressed on the mind, that there is a God: and oftentimes they are ready to think that there is none. Now this will prevent the exercise of this enmity, which otherwise would be felt; particularly, it may be an occasion of there not being sensible exercises of hatred." Jonathan Edwards: *Works*. London. 1817. V. pp. 287, 288, 293, 298.

15. Romans 1:21.
16. F. Godet, *ut supra,* p. 105.
17. II Corinthians 4:4.
18. Charles Hodge: *An Exposition of the Second Epistle to the Corinthians.* New York. 1859. pp. 85, 86.
19. Ephesians 4:18; 5:8.
20. Charles Hodge: *A Commentary on the Epistle to the Ephesians.* New York. 1857. p. 254.
21. T. K. Abbott: *A Critical and Exegetical Commentary on the Epistles to the Ephesians and to the Colossians.* New York. 1897. p. 131. On a closely related subject, the hardening of the human heart, see some profound observations in C. F. Keil: *Commentary on the Pentateuch.* I. 453–457.
22. John Eadie: *A Commentary on the Greek Text of the Epistle of Paul to the Ephesians.* London. 1854. p. 315. "A child in the lowest form of the Sunday School will answer questions with which the greatest minds of the ancient world grappled in vain." p. 314.
23. I Corinthians 2:14.
24. I Timothy 6:5.
25. Matthew 6:23.
26. Robert S. Candlish: *The First Epistle of John Expounded in a Series of Lectures.* Edinburgh. 1866. pp. 32–35. "Unbelief is not so much a dissent of the mind from any one particular truth or doctrine of revelation, as a darkness of the mind which intercepts a realizing view of all the truths and all the objects that lie spread over the region of spirituality." Thomas Chalmers: *Lectures on Romans.* I. 117. On the darkness of the mind of natural man, see also Theodore Christlieb: *Modern Doubt and Christian Unbelief.* p. 81; James Denney: *The Epistles to the Thessalonians.* pp. 191–192. On the general atrophy of the natural man in relation to spiritual things, see especially, Robert Flint: *Agnosticism.* New York. 1903. pp. 438–440. One brief passage must be quoted here. "Many are alive to the things of time and sense who are dead to things eternal and spiritual. The things, however, to which men are dead, they are apt to believe do not exist or cannot be known. And powers or apprehensions which men are unconscious of possessing they readily persuade themselves are not real powers."
27. II Timothy 3:8.
28. John Owen: *Nature and Causes of Apostasy from the Gospel.* London. 1676, pp. 227, 228.
29. John 5:44.
30. Henry Fairfield Osborn: *The Origin and Evolution of Life.* New York. 1917. p. ix.
31. The *New York Times,* Sept. 1, 1942, p. 17. How *can* a man with enough intelligence to hold a high position in one of our greatest universities, write

such a sentence as this?—"For the modern man, standing erect in his pride of power, the old ceremonial full of passivity and surrender is the symbol of a dying age." E. S. Ames: *The New Orthodoxy*, p. 117.

32. E. Brunner: *The Word and the World*. p. 16.
33. Jeoffrey Bruun, in Wallace K. Ferguson and Jeoffrey Bruun: *A Survey of European Civilization. 1500–the Present*. 1937. p. 645. On the contemporary spirit of self-sufficiency as a cause of unbelief, see M. L. Jacks: *God in Education*. London. 1939. pp. 9–11.
34. John Owen, *ut supra*, pp. 123, 134. The two passages quoted are II Cor. 10:5, and Eccl. 7:29.
35. Psalm 14:1; 53:1.
36. Robert South: *Sermons Preached upon Several Occasions*. New York. 1871. IV. 504, 505.
37. David Smith: *Man's Need of God*. London. 1910. pp. 98, 99.
38. Romans 1:28.
39. There is nothing in the pages of any modern British or American writer of world fame as blasphemous as Mr. Wells' foul and insulting sentences about God in his *Experiment in Autobiography*, e.g. pp. 28–30, 45, 150–152, 573–578.
40. Walter Marshall Horton, in Vergilius Ferm: *Contemporary American Theology*. 1932. p. 164.
41. Mark 9:21.
42. W. Macneile Dixon: *The Human Situation*. New York. 1937. p. 13.
43. W. M. Horton, in Vergilius Ferm: *Contemporary American Theology*. 1932. pp. 182, 183.
44. *ut supra*. p. 178.
45. Henry Nelson Wieman, in Vergilius Ferm: *Contemporary American Theology*. 1932. p. 345.
46. Edgar Sheffield Brightman, in Vergilius Ferm: *Contemporary American Theology*. 1932. pp. 56, 57, 62.
47. E. S. Brightman, *ibid*. p. 66. The words of the philosopher, A. J. Balfour, in his *Foundations of Belief* (1895. p. 210), should often be remembered: "The rationalist rejects miracles; and if you force him to a discussion, he may no doubt produce from the ample stores of past controversy plenty of argument in support of his belief. But do not therefore assume that his belief is the result of his argument. The odds are strongly in favor of argument and belief having both grown up under the fostering influence of his 'psychological climate.'"
48. Rudolf Eucken: *Main Currents of Modern Thought*. New York. 1912. pp. 44, 45.
49. Herbert H. Farmer: *Towards Belief in God*. New York. 1943. pp. 135–137.
50. Edward I. Watkin: *Theism, Agnosticism and Atheism*. London. 1936. pp. 23, 24.
51. Clement C. J. Webb: *A Study of Religious Thought in England*. Oxford. 1933. pp. 185, 186.
52. Luke 8:11–14. On the increasing dominion of material things in our modern world, see some very striking remarks in William E. Gladstone: *The Im-*

pregnable Rock of Holy Scripture, pp. 336–344. "Religion does not now engross the thoughts of mankind generally as it did in former generations; theology has ceased to be the favourite and dominant science; the sciences which deal with things seen and temporal are, on the contrary, those now held in highest honour and pursued with greatest zeal. But obviously the too exclusive cultivation of the physical sciences may be just as anti-religious in tendency, and as favourable to the spread of anti-theological agnosticism, as the too exclusive pursuit of bodily pleasure and material wealth." Robert Flint: *Agnosticism.* New York. 1903. pp. 437, 438.

53. James Jeans: *The Stars in Their Courses.* p. 152.
54. George Sarton: *The History of Science and the New Humanism.* Cambridge. 1937. p. 185. On, "The Religion of Science," see Edwin A. Burtt: *Types of Religious Philosophy.* New York. 1939. pp. 188–190.
55. Genesis 2:3.
56. E. Brunner: *Die Mystik und das Wort.* p. 224.
57. "The ceremony of the twentieth Brumaire was very important. The insignia of the Catholic religion in the Church of Notre-Dame had been covered up, and a mound had been heaped up, on which stood a Greek temple, with an inscription—'To Philosophy'—and with four busts of philosophers, no doubt those of Voltaire, Rousseau, Franklin, and, perhaps, Montesquieu. The 'Torch of Truth' flamed on an altar. . . . Then there emerged from the temple a beautiful woman, dressed in a mantle of blue and wearing the red cap. As the personification of Liberty she received the homage of the Republicans, who, stretching their hands toward her, sang a hymn by Marie-Joseph Chenier:

    " 'Come. Holy Liberty, inhabit this temple,
    Become the goddess of the French people.' "

    A. Aulard: *Christianity and the French Revolution.* Eng. tr. London. 1907. pp. 106, 107.
58. Romans 1:18.
59. Thomas Chalmers: *Lectures on the Epistle of Paul the Apostle to the Romans.* Vol. I. Glasgow. 1842. pp. 69, 70.
60. John 3:20.
61. Matthew 12:39; 16:4.
62. II Thess. 2:12; Col. 1:21. "He loves the deceit of unrighteousness, the falsehood which delivers him from God and from His law. . . . He believes the lie, just as a good man believes the truth; he becomes every day more hopelessly beclouded in error; and the end is that he is judged. The judgment is based, not on his intellectual, but on his *moral* state. It is true he has been deluded, but his delusion is due to this, that he had pleasure in unrighteousness. It was this evil in him which gave weight to the sophistries of Satan." James Denney: *The Epistles to the Thessalonians,* pp. 335, 336.
63. Hebrews 3:12.
64. Augustus H. Strong: *Miscellanies.* Vol. II. Philadelphia. 1912. pp. 370–372.
65. *Oxford English Dictionary.* Vol. V. p. 260.
66. Wm. G. Shedd: *Orthodoxy and Heterodoxy.* New York. 1893. p. 97. The

history of the word *libertine* is one of many testimonies to the relation of unbelief to immorality, "Full too of instruction and warming is our present employment of 'libertine.' A 'libertine' in earlier use was a speculative freethinker in matters of religion and in the theory of morals. But as by a process which is seldom missed free-*thinking* does and will end in free-*acting,* he who has cast off one yoke also casts off the other, so a 'libertine' came in two or three generations to signify a profligate especially in relation to women, a licentious and debauched person." R. C. Trench: *On the Study of Words.* 29th ed. New York. 1914. pp. 90, 91.

67. James Denney: *The Epistles to the Thessalonians* (in the Expositors' Bible). n.d. pp. 143–145.
68. Karl Pearson: *The Ethic of Free Thought.* London. 1888. pp. 426 ff.
69. Baker Brownell: *The New Universe.* New York. 1926. pp. 267, 268.
69a. "One of the most potent arguments against freethinkers was that they were naturally immoral and depraved. . . . In a list of nine reasons for opposing infidelity, six were on the grounds of immorality." Albert Post: *Popular Freethought in America.* New York. Columbia University Press. 1943. p. 200; see also pp. 185, 186, 201–203. One carefully reading through this fully-documented work will at least be forced to say, "One thing is certain: most of these freethinkers were coarse, and without moral standards." Even the late Professor James Moffatt admitted the definite relation of unbelief to "moral defects." "The objections to Christ, often paraded on intellectual grounds, are run back to moral defects, and failure to see the reality of God in Christ is attributed to some unreality of human character." Art. "Trust" James Hastings: *Dict. of Christ and the Gospels.* II. 768 (in referring to John 12:20 ff). One of the very best illustrations of this truth is told by a leading rationalist, John Morley. "One day, when present at a discussion as to the existence of a deity, in which the negative was being defended with much avidity he (Voltaire) astonished the company by ordering the servants to leave the room, and then proceeded to lock the door. 'Gentlemen,' he explained, 'I do not wish my valet to cut my throat to-morrow morning.'" John Morley: *Diderot.* Vol. 2. pp. 159–160. See, further, Robert Flint: *Agnosticism.* New York. 1903. pp. 284–286; Alexander J. Harris: *Problems of Christianity and Scepticism.* London. 1891. pp. 66–68.
70. H. P. Liddon: *Christmastide in St. Paul's.* 3rd ed. London. 1891. p. 12.
71. II Timothy 3:16.
72. This anecdote appeared some years ago in the columns of the *Saturday Review of Literature.* All my efforts to find it again have failed. If any reading these lines can give me the date of the issue in which it occurs, I would be deeply grateful.
73. Walter Lippmann: *A Preface to Morals.* New York. 1929. pp. 12, 21.
74. James Rowland Angell, in *New York Times,* June 16, 1930.
75. A. Harnack: *What Is Christianity?* Eng. trans. 2nd ed. New York. 1901. p. 30.
76. Goethe, quoted in R. M'Cheyne Edgar: *The Gospel of a Risen Saviour.* p. 233. Some of our modern philosophers are frank to acknowledge this place of *prejudice* in man's thinking. "Religion for most of us is so emphati-

cally a way of meeting personal need that when we try to reflect about it our reflection is exceedingly likely to be swayed by our eager individual concern; the results are partial to our own prejudices rather than objectively fair." Edwin A. Burtt: *Types of Religious Philosophy*. New York. 1939. pp. 2, 3.

77. Genesis 2:2.
78. Matthew 13:19.
79. John 8:44.
80. Ephesians 6:11. *Methodias tou diabolou.*
81. John Eadie: *A Commentary on the Greek Text of the Epistle of Paul to the Ephesians*. London. 1854. p. 441.
82. Ephesians 6:12. These world-rulers (*kosmokratoras*) are "not merely *rulers,* but *world-rulers,* powers dominating the world as such and working everywhere" (Salmond).
83. I Timothy 4:1. On this passage Lock aptly remarks—"As the Spirit of truth guides the Church aright, He is opposed in His beneficent ministrations by the spirit of error, who is 'the spirit of the world,' whose agents work through individuals." The apostolic fathers and early Christian apologists frequently referred to the influence of demons in pagan opposition to Christian truth. One paragraph from Justin Martyr will serve as a good illustration of this aspect of early Christian thought. "For we forewarn you to be on your guard, lest those demons whom we have been accusing should deceive you, and quite divert you from reading and understanding what we say. For they strive to hold you their slaves and servants; and sometimes by appearances in dreams, and sometimes by magical impositions, they subdue all who make no strong opposing effort for their own salvation. And thus do we also, since our persuasion by the Word, stand aloof from them (i.e., the demons), and follow the only unbegotten God through His Son—we who formerly delighted in fornication, but now embrace chastity alone; we who formerly used magical arts, dedicate ourselves to the good and unbegotten God; we who valued above all things the acquisition of wealth and possessions, now bring what we have into a common stock, and communicate to every one in need; we who hated and destroyed one another, and on account of their different manners would not live with men of a different tribe, now, since the coming of Christ, live familiarly with them, and pray for our enemies, and endeavour to persuade those who hate us unjustly to live comformably to the good precepts of Christ, to the end that they may become partakers with us of the same joyful hope of a reward from God the ruler of all. But lest we should seem to be reasoning sophistically, we consider it right, before giving you the promised explanation, to cite a few precepts given by Christ Himself. And be it yours, as powerful rulers, to inquire whether we have been taught and do teach these things truly. Brief and concise utterances fell from Him, for He was no sophist, but His word was the power of God." *The First Apology of Justin*. XIV. Someone should give us a careful study of the four important phrases of St. Paul and St. John, "the spirit of the world" (I Cor. 2:12); "the spirit that now worketh in the sons of disobedience" (Eph. 2:2); "the

spirit of error" (I John 4:6); and, "the *spirit* of the antichrist" (I John 4:3). Compare, "the Spirit of truth" (John 15:26; 14:17; I John 4:6).

84. James Denney: *The Second Epistle to the Corinthians.* (Expositors' Bible.) New York. 1903. p. 150.
85. I have been unable to recover the source of this quotation. Dr. Hutton has similarly been unable to recall in what work he wrote these words, but in a recent letter to the author he assures me this is still his firm conviction.
86. A. T. Robertson: *Word Studies in the New Testament.* New York. 1930. Vol. I. p. 260.
87. Edward Langton: "The Reality of Demonic Powers Further Considered," *Hibbert Journal,* July, 1937. pp. 605–615. See also Frederick A. M. Spencer, "Demonic Powers: The Case for Their Reality," the same, April, 1935. pp. 443–456.
88. Edwyn Bevan, in *The Kingdom of God and History.* Chicago. New York. 1938. pp. 52, 53.
89. Paul Tillich, in *The Kingdom of God and History.* New York. Chicago. 1938. pp. 117, 135.
90. Johann Warneck: *The Living Christ and Dying Heathenism.* pp. 74–76.
91. T. A. Gurney: *The First Epistle to Timothy* (*Devotional Commentary* Series). Philadelphia. 1907. pp. 183–184. Candlish, on the phrase, "the whole world lieth in the evil one" (I John 5:19), reminds us of a truth of which recent religious literature seems to be totally unaware. "The fall was a fall out of the arms of God into the embrace of the evil one. . . . The world listens willingly to its seducer as its comforter and guide; and frames its creed and constitution according to his teaching, and under his inspiration. He is its doctor of divinity; its faith, worship, discipline, and government are his." Robert S. Candlish: *The First Epistle of John Expounded in a Series of Lectures.* Edinburgh. 1866. p. 496. The entire chapter, pp. 494–503, should be read by every one who has any desire to know what the Apostle John here affirmed, by the inspiration of God.
92. Rudolf Eucken: *Main Currents of Modern Thought.* New York. 1912. p. 454.
93. William E. Gladstone: *The Impregnable Rock of Holy Scripture.* p. 347.
94. Acts 28:25–27.
95. R. B. Rackham: *The Acts of the Apostles. An Exposition.* 3rd ed. London. 1906. p. 505. See also some very remarkable paragraphs in C. J. Vaughan: *The Church of the First Days.* new ed. London. 1890. pp. 587, 597.
96. Ephesians 6:13, 14a. The only truly great exposition of St. Paul's description of the whole armour of God with which I am acquainted is that wonderful volume by John Henry Jowett, published during the First World War, *The Whole Armour of God.* We must resist quoting from his rich pages.

CHAPTER IV

1. John 15:11; 16:24; 17:13. We will have something further to say about joy in the teaching of our Lord, in Chapter X.

2. Quoted in John Cairns: *Unbelief in the Eighteenth Century*. Edinburgh. 1881. p. 141. The words are to be found in Voltaire's *Dialogues*. II. 194. This volume of Cairns is one of the *great* books of theological literature of the last quarter of the 19th century. So likewise, Voltaire's contemporary, Hume—"Where am I, or what? From what causes do I derive my existence, and to what condition shall I return? . . . I am confounded with all these quotations, and begin to fancy myself in the most deplorable condition imaginable, environed with the deepest darkness, and utterly deprived of the use of every member and faculty." David Hume: *Treatise of Human Nature*. Book I. p. 4, 7. Green & Grese edition. I. 548.
3. Quoted in Cairns: *Unbelief*, etc. p. 253.
4. L. Huxley: *Life and Letters of Sir G. D. Hooker*. Vol. I. p. 162. n. 1, and p. 39, n. 4.
5. J. R. Seeley: *Natural Religion*. pp. 261, 262.
6. John Morley: *Recollections*. Vol. II. New York. 1927. pp. 366, 367. John Stuart Mill chose as the epitaph for his tombstone the two words, "Most Unhappy."
7. Jean Jacques Brousson: *Anatole France Himself*. Philadelphia. 1925. pp. 70, 71.
8. Eve Curie: *Madame Curie. A Biography*. Eng. tr. Garden City. 1938. pp. 224, 225, 249, 251.
9. Eve Curie: *Madame Curie*. pp. 382, 383. These lines are reprinted with the kind permission of the publishers, Doubleday, Doran & Co., Inc.
10. *The Journal of Gamaliel Bradford. 1883–1932*. Boston. 1933. pp. 104, 105, 198. Under date of February 19, 1919 (p. 152), his soul cries out, "Who will tell me something of God? I know nothing about Him whatever." Similarly in his *D. L. Moody* (p. 95) "It is at any rate certain that those who have thought till they analyzed away sin and hell and reduced God himself to a shadow of a shade do not find their life of question a life of bliss."
11. Bertrand Russell: *A Free Man's Worship*. This essay, first published in 1918, has been so often reprinted in anthologies of contemporary literature, that I have not given page references for these paragraphs—the essay being brief, they can easily be found in any reprinted copy. See also his *Icarus, or the Future of Science*. New York. 1924. pp. 62–64.
12. H. G. Wells: *Experiment in Autobiography*. New York. 1934. pp. 12, 706, 631.
13. H. G. Wells: *The Fate of Man*. New York. 1939. pp. 230, 247.
14. Will Durant: *On the Meaning of Life*. New York. 1932. pp. 5, 8. See also, the famous discussion of the destructions of unbelief, in *The Modern Temper,* by Professor Josephy Wood Krutch, of Harvard University (New York, 1929), pp. XI, XVI, 9–13, 106, 247. A world-wide decline of moral authority, a spirit of contempt for law, and a disappearance of the sense of sin, is one of the most catastrophe-threatening characteristics of our age. Men of widely separated religious convictions, and men with no particular religious faith, write in sounding an alarm because of such conditions. Henry Truslow Adams, the historian, speaks of "the fear that we can no longer trust individuals or nations to act according to the ethical code on

which the whole of our civilization had been built. . . . We have had great economic depressions before but never in recent centuries such a complete abandonment of our traditional ethical code. It seems obvious to me that if we can no longer trust the plighted word or good faith of others, civilization must descend into anarchy" (in, *I Believe*. New York. 1939. pp. 343, 344). Eric Johnston, President of the United States Chamber of Commerce, in his much-discussed volume, *America Unlimited* (New York, 1944, pp. 232, 234), courageously declares: "A large portion of the globe is today under the bloody heels of men who apply oppression, terror, and methodical robbery with cold scientific precision; men who have made a religion of devious thinking and brutal action; men who consider the most repulsive means as justified by the end in view. . . . But this degradation has not been confined within the borders of totalitarian countries. In some degree it has tainted the whole world. Moral horror of this order cannot exist in any place without poisoning the whole earth with its polluted breath. Even among us in America there have been symptoms of moral weakness and decline. . . . To the extent that we have yielded to the wave of cynicism we have contributed to the great crisis of our epoch, which came to a head in the most destructive war of all time. It has clearly not been merely a political or economic crisis. It has been also a spiritual crisis. An evil wind has blown through the world and the havoc it has wrought in our souls is mirrored all around us in physical destruction."

15. David Alec Wilson: *Carlyle Till Marriage*. London. 1923. p. 147. Carlyle wrote to Jane Welsh (in 1825), words we all need to remember—"Depend upon it, Jane, this literature, which both of us are so bent on pursuing, will *not* constitute the sole nourishment of any true human spirit. Literature is the *wine* of life; it will not, cannot, be its *food*." (*ibid*. p. 368.)
16. George John Romanes: *A Candid Examination of Theism*. Boston. 1878. p. 114. John Fiske spoke with commendable frankness when he exclaimed, "If the world's long-cherished beliefs are to fall, in God's name let them fall, but save us from the intellectual hypocrisy that goes about pretending that we are none the poorer." *Through Nature to God*. 1899. p. 17.
17. James Orr: *Christian View of God and the World*. p. 52.
18. Guglielmo Ferrero: *Characters and Events of Roman History*. p. 4. "An inevitable fate, seen through the gloom of falling night, that indeed is the aspect of life which the literature of doubt displays to us. A grey shadow of melancholy spreads over this questioning, uncertain, disillusioned age." Henry van Dyke: *The Gospel for an Age of Doubt*. New York. 1896, p. 27;
19. P. T. Forsyth, in the *Christian World Pulpit*. Jan. 16, 1884. pp. 42–44. That our present pessimism is to be directly traced to our religious scepticism, is affirmed by many, e.g., Professor A. R. Reade, in his authoritative *Main Currents in Modern Literature*. (London, 1935.) "It is probably this prevailing rationalism, this ruling-out of the mystic consciousness of so many writers, that accounts for the very depressing character of a great deal of post-Victorian literature. For it is its hinterland that makes life mean or splendid." p. 105. "So fast and so far as God is unknown by any man," said President Noah Porter (1871–1886) of Yale, "so fast and so far does

hope depart from his soul." "Agnosticism a Doctrine of Despair," in *Present Day Tracts.* No. VIII. II. 31, 32.

20. James Orr: *The Christian View of God and the World.* p. 52.
21. H. P. Liddon, in John Octavius Johnston: *Life and Letters of Henry Parry Liddon.* London. 1904. p. 369.
22. Robert Flint: *Theism.* 7th ed., rev. Edinburgh. 1889. p. 301.
23. John 8:46. This verse has received extended treatment in Chapter III.
24. John 6:68.
25. Ephesians 2:12. "The Ephesians had no hope of any blessing which cheers and comforts, of any good either to satisfy them here, or to yield them eternal happiness. They had hope of nothing a sinner should hope for, of nothing a fallen and guilty spirit writhes to get a glimpse of. Their future was a night without a star. . . . The Gentile world were without a God to counsel, befriend, guide, bless, and save them. In this sense they were godless —no One to cry to, to trust in, to love, praise, and serve." John Eadie: *A Commentary on the Greek Text of the Epistle of Paul to the Ephesians.* London. 1854. pp. 55, 56.
26. Romans 15:13.

CHAPTER V

1. R. W. Livingstone: *The Greek Genius and Its Meaning to Us.* Oxford. 3rd impression. 1924. p. 11.
2. G. Otto Trevelyan: *The Life and Letters of Lord Macaulay.* New York. 1876. Vol. I. pp. 378, 379.
3. Sir Henry Moore: *Rede Lecture.* p. 38.
4. Sir Richard Jebb: "The Age of Pericles," in his *Essays and Addresses.* Cambridge. 1907. 104–126. For an authoritative survey of this period, see Arthur J. Grant: *Greece in the Age of Pericles.* New York. 1893.
5. P. B. Shelley: *A Discourse on the Manners of the Ancients,* in his *Works.* London. 1880. VII. 338.
6. Plato: *Protagoras.* 337. trans. by Jowett. I. 152.
7. Thucydides: *Peloponnesian War.* Book II. Chap. 37. For a convenient edition see note 36.
8. G. Lowes Dickinson: *The Greek View of Life.* New York. 1906. p. 105. (The second edition of this book was published in 1898; the 16th, in 1929. Pertaining to this one volume, I notice that the Harvard University Library has sixteen cards in its index.)
9. H. N. Couch: *Classical Civilization. Greece.* New York. 1940. p. 70.
10. J. B. Bury: *The Ancient Greek Historians.* New York. 1909. p. 79.
11. Paul Shorey, art. "Homer," *Encyclopaedia Americana.* 14th ed. Vol. XI. p. 337.
12. Barrett Wendell: *The Traditions of European Literature from Homer to Dante.* New York. 1920. p. 25. "Even the prose writers have the poetic gift of taking common words and making them seem as if they were newly minted, with edges unworn and their superscription still plain." S. H. Butcher: *Some Aspects of the Greek Genius.* 3rd ed. London. 1904. p. 16.
13. Herodotus: *The Persian Wars.* II. 52.

14. M. Rostovetzeff: *A History of the Ancient World*. Oxford. 1925. Vol. I. pp. 293, 294.
15. *Cambridge Ancient History*. V. 398.
16. J. B. Bury: *The Ancient Greek Historians*. 147, 148.
17. Ulrich von Wilamowitz-Moellendorff. p. 163. This remarkable statement from one of the greatest classical scholars of this century is quoted somewhere I think in the important writings of Greek science of Dr. Charles Singer of Oxford.
18. Plutarch: *Pericles*. XIII. from *Plutarch's Lives*. tr. by Bernadotte Perrin, in Loeb Classical Library. Vol. III. p. 41. London. 1916.
19. *Cambridge Ancient History*. V. 449. Ernest Arthur Gardner: *Ancient Athens*. London. 1907. pp. 321ff.
20. Sir T. L. Heath, in *The Legacy of Greece*. Oxford. 1921. p. 98.
21. *The Legacy of Greece*. p. 113.
22. *The Legacy of Greece*. p. 122.
23. *The Legacy of Greece*. p. 125.
24. Charles Singer, in *The Legacy of Greece*, p. 160.
25. Charles Singer, in *The Legacy of Greece*. p. 202.
26. John Burnet: *Greek Philosophy. Part I. Thales to Plato*. London. 1924. p. 4.
27. J. Burnet, in *The Legacy of Greece*. p. 58.
28. R. W. Livingstone: *The Greek Genius and Its Meaning to Us*. 2nd ed. Oxford. 1915. p. 248.
29. W. T. Stace: *A Critical History of Greek Philosophy*. London. 1934. p. 23.
30. Clement C. J. Webb: *A History of Philosophy* (Home University Library). London. n.d. pp. 30–32.

30a. Ernest G. Sihler: *From Augustus to Augustine*. Cambridge. 1923. p. 22. Students who expect to find ultimate truth in Aristotle, should remember the words of the distinguished philosopher and classical scholar, the late Professor John Burnet: "I never feel that I know what Aristotle really thought about anything." *John Burnet. 1863–1928*. p. 20.

31. W. T. Stace: *A Critical History of Greek Philosophy*. London. 1934. pp. 257–261, 298–300.
32. Aristotle: *Ethics*. in, *The Basic Works of Aristotle*. pp. 1, 2.
33. A. E. Zimmern, in, *The Legacy of Greece*. p. 331.
34. Aristotle: *Politics*. Book I. Chap. 1, in *Basic Works of Aristotle*. ed. by Richard McKeon. New York. 1941. p. 1127.
35. Aristotle: *Politics*. Book IV. Chap. 2.
36. This magnificent oration of Pericles is found in Thucydides: *Peloponnesian War*. Book II. Chaps. 35–36. It may conveniently be consulted in the new edition of *The Greek Historians*, ed. by F. R. B. Godolphin. New York. 1942. Vol. I. pp. 648–650.
37. S. H. Butcher: *Harvard Lectures on Greek Subjects*. London. 1904. p. 97. The same author, elsewhere—"The Greeks, before any other people of antiquity, possessed the love of knowledge for its own sake." *Some Aspects of the Greek Genius*. 3rd ed. London. 1904. p. 1.
38. R. W. Livingstone, in, *The Legacy of Greece*, p. 267.

38a. Ernest Renan, in *Nouvelles Etudes d'histoire Religieuse.* pp. 14ff. quoted in Cooper. p. 261.
39. George Foote Moore: *History of Religion.* rev. ed. New York. 1929. Vol. I. p. 469.
40. G. F. Moore, *ut supra.* p. 470.
41. G. F. Moore, *ut supra.* p. 442. See also p. 448.
42. Gerhard Uhlhorn: *The Conflict of Christianity with Paganism.* rev. ed. Eng. tr. New York. 1894. pp. 142, 143, 148, 149, 311.
43. George P. Fisher: *The Beginnings of Christianity.* p. 114.
44. G. L. Dickinson: *The Greek View of Life.* pp. 1, 2. See also Gilbert Murray, in, *The Legacy of Greece,* p. 16. Livingstone goes so far as to say the absence of a Bible was to the *advantage* of Greek religion! (pp. 54–61.)
45. Edwin Charles Dargan: *A History of Preaching.* New York. 1905. Vol. I. p. 18.
46. Xenophanes. quoted by Burnet: *Greek Philosophy.* p. 35.
47. Plato: *Republic,* p. 378. Jowett trans. III. pp. 250, 251.
48. Euripides: *Ion.* p. 429.
49. L. W. Farnell, in James Hastings: *Dict. of the Bible.* V. 145.
50. W. M. Ramsay, "Religion of Greece," in James Hastings: *Dict. of the Bible.* V. 150.
51. R. W. Livingstone: *The Greek Genius and Its Meaning to Us.* pp. 25–29.
52. E. G. Sihler: *From Augustus to Augustine.* Cambridge. 1923. p. 5.
53. Clement of Alexandria: *Exhortation to the Heathen.* Chap. IV. in *The Ante-Nicene Fathers.* Vol. II. pp. 188, 189. On the insignificance of moral genius among the ancient Greeks, see R. W. Livingstone: *The Greek Genius,* etc. 25–29. John Burnet: *Greek Philosophy.* Part I. *Thales to Plato.* p. 29.
54. Wilfred L. Knox: *St. Paul and the Church of the Gentiles.* Cambridge. 1939. p. 11, n. 2.
55. W. M. Ramsay, "Religion of Greece," J. Hastings: *Dict. of the Bible.* V. 150.
56. G. Lowes Dickinson: *The Greek Genius and Its Meaning to Us.* pp. 17, 18.
57. In Plato: *Charmides.* 155. Jowett trans. I. 12.
58. Uhlhorn. pp. 148–149. On this entire subject of failure to discover ethical power, one should consult *The Religion of Power,* by Harris E. Kirk, 1916.
59. John 17:17.
60. Philippians 4:8.
61. Plato: *Phaedo.* 85. Jowett's trans. I. 463. Even Gilbert Murray, never an advocate of Christian convictions, confesses that "A dialogue of Plato's hardly ever leads to a positive conclusion. It is always a discussion, not a pronouncement. It may reject many dogmas as demonstrably false; but it never claims to have reached the whole truth." *Stoic, Christian and Humanist.* London. 1940. p. 37.
62. Ephesians 4:21.
63. Pindar: *Olymp.* 11. *Ant.* 11.
64. Cicero: *Tusculanae Disputationes.* Bk. I. xi. 23.
65. Robert Flint: *Theism.* 7th ed. rev. Edinburgh. 1889. p. 307.
66. Xenophanes. These lines are quoted in F. M. Cornford: *Greek Religious*

Thought from Homer to the Age of Alexander. London. 1923. p. 87. See also, Aristotle: *Metaphysics.* I. 5.

67. Plato: *Timaeus.* 28c.
68. On Plato's conception of God, see especially, *Plato's Theology,* by Dr. Friedrich Solmsen, of Cornell University. Ithaca. 1942. For pre-Platonic writers, Roy Kenneth Hack: *God in Greek Philosophy to the Time of Socrates.* Princeton. 1931; and some very sane criticisms in Etienne Gilson: *God and Philosophy.* New Haven. 1941. pp. 25–29.
69. Aristotle: *Magn. Moral.* 11. 11.
70. E. G. Sihler: *From Augustus to Augustine.* Cambridge. 1924. p. 24. See also his *Testimonium Animae.* p. 243.
71. I Corinthians 1:21. "The eating of the tree of knowledge drove the Greeks from their paradise; but the vision of that Eden continues to haunt the mind of man." G. Loes Dickinson: *The Greek View of Life.* p. 64.
72. Ephesians 2:12.
73. Homer: *Odyssey.* XI.
74. *Oedipus Tyrannus.* 1186–1192. quoted by Fisher, *ut supra.* 108.
75. Theognis: *Elegies.* 425.
76. Euripides: *Oresphontes,* quoted in F. M. Cornford: *Greek Religious Thought from Homer to the Age of Alexander.* London. 1923. p. 153. (This is an invaluable anthology for the study of Greek religion.) So, Sophocles—"Not to have come into being at all, this is the triumphant position in the whole range of discourse; and the other, namely, when man has appeared, that he should go to that bourne whence he came, as speedily as possible, this is easily second . . . and by lot comes last old age, invalid, unsociable, unloved, where universal troubles are housed with troubles." *Oedipus at Colonus.* 1225ff.
77. Pindar: *Olympian.* XII. 1.
78. Cicero: *Ad Familiares.* XIV. 4. 1.
79. Pliny: *Natural History.* II. 7. (5). XXVIII. 1. (2).
80. S. H. Butcher: *Some Aspects of the Greek Genius.* 3rd ed. London. 1904. p. 162. In his *Harvard Lectures on Greek Subjects,* the same author asserts—"To the Greeks the future is dim and inscrutable; poets and prose writers repeat with many variations the sad refrain, 'Uncertain is the future!'" The last of the Latin historians, Ammianus Marcellinus (330–395 A.D.), summed up the mood of the last age of paganism when he wrote: "Nothing remained but tears and fears, the remembrance of the past being bitter, the expectation of the future still sadder." *Rerum gestarum.* XL. c 390. quoted in J. W. Thompson: *A History of Historical Writing.* New York. 1942. I. 95. "It is curious that a people like the Greeks should have faltered in their beliefs concerning the unseen world, and have believed so long in a state of cold and hopeless shadows when they might have constructed a realm of more glorious life. But the reason may have been that they so exhausted the vast possibilities of life on this side of the grave that the mind sank exhausted before the task of raising any structure of brilliant hopes as to the nature and conditions of existence beyond the grave." J. A. Macculloch: *Comparative Theology.* London. 1902. p. 285.

81. Galatians 4:4. "It was only after human wisdom had a lengthened and unembarrassed opportunity of showing what it could accomplish in the most favourable circumstances, and after it had clearly displayed its insufficiency, that Christianity appeared. Christ did not come till it was manifest that reason was wandering farther and farther away from God—that man had done his utmost with the unaided resources of his nature to devise a salvation, and had failed." Robert Flint: *Theism.* p. 310.
82. C. H. Moore: *Pagan Ideas of Immortality During the Early Roman Empire.* Cambridge. 1918. pp. 39, 40. See also his *Religious Thought of the Greeks,* p. 205.
83. Plutarch: *The Obsolescence of Oracles.* (*De Defectu Oraculorum.*) 17. Eng. tr. by F. C. Babbitt, in Loeb Classical Library. Plutarch's *Moralia.* Vol. V. pp. 401, 403. Milton's subsequent poetic version of the disappearance of the pagan gods brought about by the advent of Christ in his exquisite ode, *On the Morning of Christ's Nativity,* contains many true conceptions, and should be recalled at this time when so many hope for a *return* of paganism.
84. Justin Martyr, *Discourse to the Greeks.* V. Ante-Nicene Fathers. (ed. Roberts and Donaldson.) I. 272.

CHAPTER VI

1. William M. Ramsay: *Pauline and Other Studies.* n.d. pp. 53, 100. If you read this work a quarter of a century ago, you will be surprised, if you read it again, after these years, at the treasures still to be discovered in its pages. "Upon the whole," Schaff says, "St. Paul is, perhaps, the most remarkable man, and his Epistles, next to the Gospels, the most important literary production of all ages." P. Schaff, in J. P. Lange: *Romans.* p. 3. "St. Paul is spiritually the Great Power of the apostolic age; he laboured more, and not only laboured more, but created more than all the other." Adolf Deissmann: *St. Paul, A Study in Social and Religious History.* New York. 1912. p. 3.
2. Thomas Lewin: *The Life and Epistles of St. Paul.* London. 1890. Vol. II. pp. 244–249.
3. Horatio B. Hackett: *A Commentary on the Acts of the Apostles.* New ed. Philadelphia. 1882. pp. 204, 205. The various forms of this word appearing in the New Testament are important enough to be listed here. The verb *agnoeo, to be ignorant, not to know,* occurs in the following passages: Mark 9:32; Luke 9:45; Acts 13:27; 17:23; Rom. 1:13; 2:4; 6:3; 7:1; 10:3; 11:25; I Cor. 10:1; 12:1; 14:38; II Cor. 1:8; 2:11; 6:9; I Thess. 4:13; I Tim. 1:13; Heb. 5:2; II Pet. 2:12. *Agnoia,—want of knowledge, ignorance,* is found in Acts 3:19; 17:30; Eph. 4:18; I Pet. 1:14. *Agnosia,* with the same meaning, occurs twice, I Cor. 15:34; I Pet. 2:15; while the word *agnostos, unknown,* occurs only in Acts 17:23.
4. F. J. A. Hort: *The Way, the Truth, and the Life* (Hulsean Lectures for 1871). Cambridge. 1893. p. 64.
5. John Calvin: *Commentary upon the Acts of the Apostles.* Eng. tr. Edinburgh. 1844. Vol. II. pp. 146, 147.

6. John Calvin, *ibid*. p. 147.
7. R. J. Knowling: *The Expositor's Greek Testament. The Acts of the Apostles*. London. New York. n.d. pp. 365, 366. "The existence of gods, as ordinarily understood, must be denied, or at any rate that Epicurus would be justified in taking up an agnostic position. . . . The attitude of Democritus to popular conceptions of the future life may be gathered from a remarkable fragment preserved by Stobaeus: 'Some men who do not understand the dissolution of our mortal nature, but are conscious of the misery in human existence, painfully spend their allotted period of life in confusion and fear, inventing lies about the time after they are dead.'" R. D. Hicks: *Stoic and Epicurean*. New York. 1910. pp. 282–284.
8. R. J. Knowling, *ibid*. p. 366. On the relation of Paul to the Stoic religion see Maurice Jones: *St. Paul the Orator*. London. 1910. pp. 85–87, and Lightfoot's great essay, "St. Paul and Seneca," in his *St. Paul's Epistle to the Philippians*. pp. 270–333.
9. J. S. Howson, in W. J. Conybeare and J. S. Howson: *The Life and Epistles of St. Paul*. London. 1854. Vol. I. pp. 404, 410. "There is no greater apostolic word in the New Testament than this address on Mar's Hill." G. Campbell Morgan. "The Unknown God Made Known," p. 7. "For directness, for point, for application to his audience, for fervor, I doubt much whether it was ever surpassed, even by their own Demosthenes." James McCosh, in *Homiletic Monthly*. Feb. 1883. VII. 250. "In the metropolis of paganism, Paul has spoken words mightier and more beautiful than any which had ever fallen from the lips of philosophers or poets—words which will be a living power when temples and statues are in ruins. Their ruin is indeed already imminent. In preaching the true God, Paul has pronounced the death-doom of polytheism, and the sentence is without appeal." E. De Pressensé: *The Early Years of Christianity. The Apostolic Era*. Eng. trans. New York. 1882. p. 162. His incurable paganism Renan reveals with his usually brilliant style, when he must comment on this address of St. Paul—"Ah, beautiful and chaste images; true gods and true goddesses, tremble! Here is one who will raise the hammer against you. The fatal word has been pronounced: you are idols. The error of this ugly little Jew will be your death-warrant." Ernest Renan: *St. Paul*. Eng. trans. New York. 1869. p. 126. In addition to chapters on Paul in Athens, in the larger lives of the apostle, and the more important commentaries on the Book of Acts, the following may be consulted: Wm. Lindsay Alexander: *St. Paul at Athens*. Edinburgh. 1865. pp. ix. 322; Charles Shakespeare: *St. Paul at Athens* (Sermons). New York. 1878. pp. xvi. 167. Maurice Jones: *St. Paul the Orator*. London. 1910. pp. 80–106. John Eadie: *Paul the Preacher*. London. 1857. pp. 176–242; and, for articles on the Areopagus—W. J. Woodhouse in *Enc. Bibl*. I. cols. 294–96; J. E. Harry, in *ISBE*, I. 238, 239; F. W. Worsley, HDAC, I. 89, 90; J. R. Beard, in Kitto's *Cyclop Bibl. Lit*. I. 205–208; and, on Mar's Hill, H. B. Hackett, in Smith's *Dict. Bible*. III. 1807–1810. I have seen a reference to a work by J. R. Macduff, *St. Paul at Athens*, London. 1887, but apparently there is not a copy in any library in America. Prof. J. M. English has given us a valuable study of some of the less-frequently considered aspects of this

address in his, "Elements of Persuasion in Paul's Address on Mar's Hill at Athens," *American Journal of Theology*. 1898. Vol. II. pp. 97–109. Why we do not have some scholarly monographs on this inexhaustible passage, in English, I do not know. It would make, I should think, a perfect task for a doctoral thesis.

Note: After considerable research, I have been unable to come upon any important references to the use of this magnificent address, or at least its themes, in missionary preaching. I have seen it stated that Warneck, in *Paulus un Lichte der Leutigen Heidenmission* (3rd ed. 1922. p. 61) says that Paul's Athenian address is "an unsurpassable model for preaching to pagans, ignorant of Christianity," but I cannot find where it has been so used, to any notable extent. A few years ago, a well-known missionary in India, Dr. J. H. Maclean, of Conjeeveram, wrote that, "To one who has lived for many years in a sacred city of the Hindus no passage in the New Testament is more interesting than that which describes the visit of the prince of missionaries to a sacred city of the Greeks." "St. Paul at Athens," *Expository Times*. Sept. 1933. Vol. xliv. p. 550. I would deeply appreciate any communication regarding the use of this address of St. Paul's in the missionary preaching of modern times. Leading missionary authorities whom I have consulted in this country have been unable to recall *one* important reference.

10. Charles Merrivale: *The Conversion of the Roman Empire*. 2nd ed. London. 1865. pp. 1–3.
11. Philip Schaff: *History of the Apostolic Church with a General Introduction to Church History*. New York. 1854. p. 267. Rudolf Steir: *The Words of the Apostles*. Eng. tr. Edinburgh. 1869. p. 289.
12. A. Harnack: *The Expansion of Christianity in the First Three Centuries*. 1904. Vol. II. pp. 372, 373.
13. Matthew 13:58.
14. W. M. Ramsay, "St. Paul in Athens," in the *Expositor*, 5th series. 1895. Vol. II. pp. 275, 276. Unamuno, the Spanish philosopher, has caught the real meaning of the reaction of the Athenians to Paul's message, with his usual power of insight. "This admirable account plainly shows how far Attic tolerance goes and where the patience of the intellectual ends. They all listen to you, calmly and smilingly, and at times they encourage you, saying: 'That's strange!' or, 'He has brains!' or, 'That's suggestive!' or, 'How Fine!' or, 'Pity that a thing so beautiful should not be true!' or, 'This makes one think!' But as soon as you speak to them of resurrection and life after death, they lose their patience and cut short their remarks and exclaim, 'Enough of this! We will talk about this another day!' . . . And even if this belief be absurd, why is its exposition less tolerated than that of others much more absurd? Why this manifest hostility to such a belief?" Miguel de Unamuno: *The Tragic Sense of Life*. Eng. trans. London. 1931. pp. 49, 50. On why the Athenians interrupted Paul, when he began to speak of the resurrection, see Hermann Sasse, "Jesus Christ the Lord," in *Mysterium Christi*, ed. by G. K. A. Bell and Adolf Deissmann. London. 1930. pp. 100–102.
15. The Abbé Constant Fouard: *St. Paul and His Mission*. Eng. tr. London. 1894. pp. 155–157. There is nothing in English of real importance on the

early church at Athens. See, however, C. Baget: *De Titulis Atticae Christianis Antiquissimus*. Paris. 1878. Among those who are supposed to have been bishops of Athens are Dionysius, Publius, Quadratus. As late as 375, sacrifices were made publicly to Minerva. It was not the power of Christianity, but the invasion of the Goths, 396, that resulted in the destruction of the temple where Eleusinian rites were practiced. "The schools of philosophy at Athens continued to be centres of pagan teaching till the reign of Justinian (527–565), who issued a decree—addressed to the magistrates at Athens, forbidding the teaching of philosophy." Charles Henry Robinson: *The Conversion of Europe*. London. 1917. p. 236. For an account of the philosopher who came *from Athens* to tell Vladimir, Emperor of Russia, of Christianity, in 986, see later in Robinson's work, pp. 493–497; or, A. P. Stanley: *Lectures on the History of the Eastern Church*. 1861. pp. 388–409.

16. Etienne Gilson: *God and Philosophy*. New Haven. 1941. p. 122.
17. R. C. Trench: *Synonyms of the New Testament*. 9th ed. London. 1880. p. 222. See an interesting article by Dr. William T. Ellis, "Modern Athenians Gossip Much as They Did in the Time of Christ." *Literary Digest*. May 10, 1919.
18. Hermann Cremer: *Biblico-Theological Lexicon of the New Testament Greek*. 4th English ed. Edinburgh. 1895. p. 322.
19. Rudolf Eucken: *Main Currents of Modern Thought*. London. 1912. p. 271. Similarly, the Spanish philosopher, Miguel de Unamuno—"A rabid mania for originality is rife in the modern intellectual world, and characterizes all individual effort." *The Tragic Sense of Life*. Eng. tr. London. 1931. p. 53.
20. Sir William Hamilton: *Discourses*. p. 22. Herbert Spencer: *First Principles*. (1862.) pp. 67, 46, 100. T. J. Huxley: *Lay Sermons*. p. 20. Frederic Harrison, the positivist, not in any way a Christian, sarcastically exposed the folly of such a "belief," in his article, "The Ghost of Religion," in the *Nineteenth Century* (XV. [1884], pp. 494–506). "Where two or three are gathered together to worship the Unknowable, there the alegebraic formula (X^n) may suffice to give form to their emotions: they may be heard to profess their unwearying belief in X^n, even if no weak brother with ritualistic tendencies be heard to cry: 'O X^n love us, help us, make us one with thee.'"
21. George Santayana: *The Unknowable*. Oxford. 1923. p. 29. As in contemporary philosophical and religious thought, so in the realm of science, a sense of the unknown is being continually confessed. Thus, eg., in a new work on the philosophical aspect of science: "The mirror of nature that reason had endeavoured to build up through the ages is shattered, and we look for the first time out into an unknown world." George de Santillana: *Aspects of Scientific Rationalism in the Nineteenth Century, in the International Encyclopedia of Unified Science*. Chicago. 1941. Vol. II. No. 8, p. 47. "Man by the light of science can see his hands, and can catch a glimpse of himself, his past, and the patch upon which he stands; but around him in place of that known comfort and beauty he had anticipated, and in the first few moments falsely thought that he saw, is darkness still." C. E. M. Joad: *Philosophical Aspects of Modern Science*. See also A. J. Balfour: *Foundations of Belief*, pp. 71, 72.

22. Albert Schweitzer: *The Quest of the Historical Jesus.* Eng. tr. 2nd ed. London. 1936. p. 401.
23. Robert Henry Lightfoot: *History and Interpretation in the Gospels.* Bampton Lectures for 1934. New York. n.d. p. 225. (This forms the concluding paragraph of the volume.)
24. Arnold Toynbee, "The Menace of the New Paganism" in the *Christian Century.* March 10, 1937. Vol. 85. pp. 336–338.
25. Fulton J. Sheen: *Old Errors and New Labels.* New York. 1941. pp. 325–328.
26. On German pagan ideas in contemporary literature see e.g., C. L. Heymann, "The German God," in *Current History,* April, 1937, pp. 63–68; L. de Moor, "Rosenberg's Myth and Nazi Paganism," in the *Calvin Forum,* April, 1938. pp. 200–203; and "The German Paganism," in *Dawn,* March 15, 1938. As far back as 1910, the god Siegfried was being preferred by some German writers to Christ; see e.g. Otto Reuter: *Siegfried Oder Christus.* 1910. There is a good discussion of some aspects of this tendency in an article, "Greater than Hitler," in the *Catholic World.* Vol. 152. pp. 585ff.
27. See a very comprehensive article, "Neo-Paganism" in the *Quarterly Review,* April, 1891. Vol. 172. pp. 273–304. Walter Pater, in his famous work, *The Renaissance* (1873), bemoans the coming of Christianity. "The longer we contemplate that Hellenic ideal, in which man is at unity with himself, with his physical nature, with the outward world, the more we may be inclined to regret that he should ever have passed beyond it, to contend for a perfection that makes the blood turbid, and frets the flesh and discredits the actual world about us" (in the Modern Library edition, p. 185).
28. O. L. Reiser: *Philosophy and the Concept of Modern Science.* New York. 1935.
29. Julian Huxley: *What Dare I Think?* New York. 1931. p. 268.
30. Hilaire Belloc: *Essays of a Catholic Layman in England.* London. 1931. p. 26. Our leading classical scholar at the close of the 19th century, Dr. Basil Gildersleeve, foresaw this struggle. "Hellenism and Christianity are grappling now as they grappled seventeen centuries ago, and if the shape of the weapons has varied in the long struggle, the strategic points are unchanged." *Essays and Studies.* Baltimore. 1890. p. 252. Uhlhorn closes his epochal *Conflict of Christianity with Heathenism,* with this sentence, "Stronger almost than ever, the heathen spirit in modern guise is wrestling against Christian thought and life, and it almost seems as if the questions of the time should be gathered up into the question: 'Shall we remain Christian, or become pagan again?' " p. 479. Gilbert K. Chesterton, in his *Heretics* (1905), argues that inasmuch as the paganism of the ancient world was followed by Christianity, so it will again follow this neo-paganism. (See especially pp. 155, 170.) "Nobody in the nineteenth century, indeed nobody in the last five hundred years, thought that paganism had any future before it. . . . Today, however, in the most scientific age of the world's history, when the earth is yielding up all her secrets, and the cold clear light of science pierces into every human heart, there is not only a revival of a heathenish view of life, but also a cult of pagan rites in at any rate one great European country."

R. B. Mowat (Professor of History in the University of Bristol), "The Revival of Heathenism," *Hibbert Journal*. XXXIV. 1–9.

31. Joseph L. Hramadka, "The Modern Trend in European Protestant Theology. in, *Religion in the Modern World*. Philadelphia. 1941. pp. 24, 25.

CHAPTER VII

1. James McCosh: *The Supernatural in Relation to the Natural*. New York. 1862. p. 39. See also the author's *The Intuitions of the Mind*. new ed. London. 1865. pp. 165, 226–228, 236. "The human intellect is by its very constitution compelled to seek first causes for events, and final causes for order and adaptation; and it has no right to stop short, as the atheist would have it, when it cannot advance farther without rising to the apprehension of a Creative Reason." Robert Flint: *Anti-Theistic Theories*. Edinburgh. 1879. p. 20. "There is in every earnest thinker a craving after a final cause, and this craving can no more be extinguished than our belief in obstructive reality. Our belief in what we call the evidence of our senses is less strong than our faith that in the orderly sequence of events there is a meaning which our minds could fathom were they only vast enough." John Fiske: *Outlines of Cosmic Philosophy*. Boston. 1893. p. 193.
2. Julian S. Huxley, "A Biologist Looks at Man," in *Fortune*. December, 1942. Vol. 26. p. 138. "The nature of the sciences makes the question of creation for them (humanists) an idle question." A. H. Dakin: *Man the Measure*. Princeton, 1939. p. 60.
3. Asa Gray: *Natural Science and Religion*. 1880. p. 38.
4. T. H. Huxley, in *Nineteenth Century*. Feb., 1886. p. 202. Also, "To say, in the admitted absence of evidence that I have any belief as to the mode in which existing forms of life have originated, would be using words in a wrong sense." Presidential Address, British Assoc. for Advancement of Science. 1870. *Selected Works. Discourses Biological and Geological*. p. 259.
5. Ernest Haeckel: *The History of Creation*. Eng. trans. London. 1925. Vol. I. p. 8.
6. L. L. Woodruff, in *The Evolution of the Earth and Its Inhabitants*. Chap. III. "The Origin of Life," p. 107. George Sarton, in Isis. June, 1927. Vol. IX. pp. 232, 233.
7. Sir Oliver Lodge: *Man and the Universe*. 6th ed. London. 1909. pp. 19, 29.
8. Sir Arthur Keith, in *Westminster Gazette*. June 7, 1928.
9. J. Arthur Thomson: *Science and Religion*. New York. 1925. p. 14.
10. J. Arthur Thomson: *The Outline of Science*. New York. London. 1922. IV. p. 57. "I need scarcely say that the beginning and maintenance of life on the earth is absolutely and infinitely beyond the range of all sound speculation in dynamical science. The only contribution of dynamics to theoretical biology is absolute negation of automatic commencement or automatic maintenance of life." Lord Kelvin: *Popular Lectures and Discourses*. I. 198. The unanimous confession of modern science that it does not know, and cannot know, anything of the true origin of this universe, and of life, is so important, that I feel this extended list of additional statements will

prove of value. "We must halt at conditions of the beginning and the end. There is no standpoint from which to conduct investigations in either direction." W. Wundt: *Biological Problems.* p. 329. "The actual beginning of life remains an unsolved problem. The gap between earth materials and living matter has not been bridged." Rollin T. Chamberlin, "The Origin and Early Stages of the Earth," in, *The Nature of the World and Man.* Chicago. 1926. p. 53. "The question about the so-called primary origin of life is as incapable of being discussed as is the problem of death, in spite of the great number of popular works written about it. . . . Such remarks as I am able to offer about the origin and end of individual life, and the origin of life in general, can claim merely a subjective value. Materialists profess to know a good deal about all these eternal problems, but I confess that I know nothing at all about any of them." Hans Driesch: *The Science and Philosophy of the Organism.* Gifford Lectures. 1908. London. 1908. Vol. II. pp. 263, 260. "Evolution deals only with process, and does not touch the question of ultimate causation. What lies back of evolution no one knows. . . . Science cannot deal with this mystery; it is a matter of faith alone; but it is plain that Christian faith gives the largest value to human life and the greatest stimulus and comfort." E. G. Conklin, "Biology and Religion," in *Princeton Alumni Weekly.* March, 1925. "The first great crises in the evolution of organic beings was the origin of life. . . . Of this momentous event we have no record, nor does the geologic cause come either within the scope of our knowledge or conjecture, for the time was too remote and the first living substance too delicate to leave any decipherable record upon the rocks. All we can say of it is that in the fulness of time, when the earth had, in the physical course of its evolution, become adapted as the abode of life, living substances came into being." Richard Swann Lull, "The Pulse of Life," Chapter IV in *The Evolution of the Earth and Its Inhabitants.* p. 112. "Finally we may refer to the 'grand problem' of the origin of life itself. Any treatment of this question is bound to be wholly theoretical. We do not know a single thing about it. . . . All life comes from life." D. S. Jordan and V. L. Kellogg: *Evolution and Animal Life.* 1907. p. 41.

Henry Cotterill, "Primary Creation Beyond Science," in his *Does Science Aid Faith in Regard to Creation?* London. 1888. pp. 106–114. L. Franklin Grüber: *Whence Came the Universe?* Boston. 1921. pp. 292–293 (this volume, by the way, is one of superlative value, and the author would earnestly commend its careful study to all who are interested in the great subject of the Divine creation of the world).

11. Pasteur, in L. Descours: *Pasteur and His Work.* Eng. tr. London. 1922. p. 206.
12. John Calvin: *Commentaries on the First Book of Moses Called Genesis.* Edinburgh. 1847. p. 58.
13. Matthew 13:58.
14. For some of the more important passages in the Old Testament setting forth the truth that God created the world, see Job 38:4; Psalm 19:1; 24:1; 102:25; 104:2; Prov. 8:26–29; Isa. 40:26–28; Jer. 10:12, 16; 51:15, 16.

15. John 1:1–3; Romans 1:19, 20.
16. Hebrews 1:2.
17. Revelation 4:11.
18. L. Berkhof, *Systematic Theology*. 2nd ed. Grand Rapids. 1941. p. 129. On Creation a free act of the Divine will, see Hubert S. Box: *The World and God*. London. 1934. pp. 186, 187.
19. L. Berkhof, *ibid*. p. 132. In addition to the chapters on Creation in the well-known theologies, the following will be found of value (this list is only suggestive, not in any way exhaustive). Samuel Harris: *God the Creator and Lord of All*. Edinburgh. 1897. I. 463–490. Leander S. Keyser: *The Problems of Origins*. New York. 1926. p. 265. Bernard Boedder: *Natural Theology*. 2nd ed. London. 1927. pp. 119–148. J. S. Whale: *Christian Doctrine*. New York. 1941. pp. 11–34. John J. Colligan: *Cosmology*. Fordham University Press. New York. 1936. W. H. Dallinger: *The Creator, and What We May Know of the Method of Creation*. London. 1887.
20. Romans 4:17; Hebrews 11:3.
21. Colossians 1:16, 17.
22. On the creation of the world *ex nihilo,* one should first consult the profound chapters on the subject by Augustine, in Book XI of his *Confessions;* and especially Wm. G. T. Shedd: *Dogmatic Theology*. New York. 1888. pp. 464–472.
23. Charles Hodge: *Systematic Theology*. I. 558–561.
24. W. Lindsay Alexander: *A System of Biblical Theology*. Edinburgh. 1888. Vol. I. p. 132.
25. Wm. G. T. Shedd, *ibid*. pp. 472, 473.
26. Psalm 33:6; 148:5; Hebrews 11:3.
27. II Peter 3:5. "Here is the reason of their conduct, the root of all the evil. They forget because they wish to forget. . . . They are casting God out of all their thoughts: and so even to the things that are made, and by which He testifies to all men alike His eternal power and Godhead, they close their eyes, and refuse to read His wide-open lesson book." J. Rawson Lumby: *The Epistles of St. Peter*. p. 335.
28. John 1:1–3.
29. F. R. Tennant: *Philosophical Theology*. Vol. II. Cambridge. 1937. p. 125.
30. Auguste Comte: *Système de politique Positive*. Paris. 1851. Vol. I. p. 154.
31. Karl Pearson: *The Grammar of Science*. London. 1892. pp. 152, 153.
32. G. Watts Cunningham: *Problems of Philosophy*. New York. 1934. pp. 121–123. So also, Sir Arthur Eddington, in his Gifford Lectures, "Secondary physics can distinguish cause and effect, but its foundation does not rest on a causal scheme, and it is indifferent as to whether or not strict causality prevails. Whether or not there is a causal scheme at the base of atomic phenomena, modern atomic theory is not now attempting to find it, and it is making rapid progress because it no longer sets this up as a practical aim." Eddington then goes on to acknowledge, "A rather serious consequence of dropping causality in the external world is that it leaves us with no clear distinction between the Natural and the Supernatural." *The Nature of the Physical World*. New York. 1929. pp. 296, 309.

33. Etienne Gilson: *God and Philosophy*. New Haven. 1941. pp. 128, 129.
34. W. T. Stace: *A Critical History of Greek Philosophy*. London. 1934. pp. 6, 7.
35. Aristotle: *Physics*. Book II. Chap. 3 in *The Basic Works of Aristotle*. ed. by Richard McKeon. New York. 1941. pp. 240, 241.
36. Aristotle: *Metaphysics*. Book II. Chap. 2, as above, pp. 713, 714.
37. J. L. Stocks: *Time, Cause and Eternity*. London. 1938. p. 38.
38. Robert Flint: *Theism*. Edinburgh. 1884. pp. 123, 124.
39. Hubert S. Box: *The World and God*. London. 1934. pp. 143, 146.
40. Robert Flint: *Theism*. 7th ed. rev. Edinburgh. London. 1889. p. 130.
41. James Jeans: *The Mysterious Universe*. 1930. pp. 134, 136.
42. G. D. Hicks: *The Philosophical Bases of Theism*. New York. 1937. pp. 163–165. See also W. R. Matthews: *The Purpose of God*. London. 1935. pp. 35–37.
43. Hesiod: *Theogony*. 11. 211–239. Eng. trans. by Hugh G. Evelyn-White, in Loeb Classical Library. London. 1936. pp. 95, 97.
44. Hesiod: *Theogony*. 11. 510–530. *ibid*. pp. 117, 119.
45. L. T. More: *The Dogma of Evolution*. Princeton. 1925. pp. 87, 88.
46. W. Windleband: *History of Philosophy*. Eng. tr. 2nd ed. rev. New York. 1901. p. 54.
47. Plato: *Timaeus*. 29–32, in *The Dialogues of Plato*. trans. by B. Jowett, 2nd ed. Oxford. 1875. Vol. III. pp. 613–615.
48. Plato: *Timaeus*. 73, 74. *ibid*. pp. 657, 658.
49. W. R. Matthews: *God in Christian Experience*. New York. 1930. pp. 208, 209. "All things considered, we may say that the Unity of the Platonic system can only be established on the supposition that Plato in his own belief never really separated the efficient from the logical cause, the Deity from the highest Idea, that of the good. . . . He identifies them, he attributes efficient power and designing reason, sometimes to Ideas in general, sometimes to the highest Idea in particular." Eduard Zeller: *Plato and the Older Academy*. London. 1885. p. 285. "The word represented by *cause* has sixty-four meanings in Plato and forty-eight in Aristotle." William Kingdon Clifford: *Lectures and Essays*. 2nd ed. London. 1886. p. 103. Quoted in Ludurk Silberstein: *Causality*. London. 1933. p. 1.
50. W. R. Matthews: *Studies in Christian Philosophy*. London. 1921. pp. 194, 196, 204.
51. George Sarton: *The History of Science and the New Humanism*. Cambridge. 1937. p. 40.
52. Sir Isaac Newton: *The Mathematical Principles of Natural Philosophy*. trans. by Andrew Motte. New ed. rev. London. 1803. Vol. II. pp. 310–313. In a letter of January 17, 1693, Sir Isaac Newton wrote to Dr. Richard Benton, as follows, "Gravity may put the planets into motion, but without the divine power, it could never put them into such a circulating motion as they have about the sun; and therefore, for this, as well as other reasons, I am compelled to describe the frame of this system to an intelligent Agent." *The Works of Richard Benton, D.D.* Vol. III. *Theological Writings*. London. 1838. p. 210.
53. Johannes Kepler. Trans. by Charles Singer, in *Science, Religion and Reality*. New York. 1925. p. 141.

54. See the very informing article on Ray, by G. S. Boulger, *Dict. Nat. Biog.* XVI. 782–787.
55. John Ray: *The Wisdom of God Manifested in the Works of Creation.* Edinburgh. 1798. The preface is not paged.
56. Bence Jones: *The Life and Letters of Faraday.* 2nd ed. rev. London. 1870. Vol. II. p. 100.
57. Michael Faraday: "Lecture on Mental Evolution." quoted in Bence Jones *ut supra,* Vol. I. p. 298.
58. L. J. R. Agassiz: *Contributions to the National History of the United States.* Boston. 1857. Vol. I. pp. 10, 11, 135.
59. R. S. Dugan, in *Dict. of American Biography.* Vol. XX. 1936. p. 624. There is an interesting survey of the writings of American geologists of the nineteenth century in relation to the problems raised by the Genesis account of creation, by Conrad Wright, "The Religion of Geology," in *The New England Quarterly* (June, 1941), XIV. 335–358, which with unjustified dogmatism concludes, "It was Darwin who finally removed man from the center of the universe, and thereby crumbled the religion of geology to dust." George P. Merrill, in *Dict. of American Biography.* Vol. V. 1930. pp. 55, 56. James Dwight Dana, "Science and the Bible," in *Bibliotheca Sacra.* July, 1856. Vol. XIII. pp. 635, 636.
60. Charles Augustus Young: *God's Glory in the Heavens.* I have not felt it necessary to give separate pages for this twenty-page pamphlet.
61. James Clerk-Maxwell: in *Nature.* 1873. Vol. VIII. pp. 437–441.
62. Lord Kelvin, in *Nineteenth Century and After.* June, 1903. *LIII.* 1068, 1069. So likewise, Sir James Clerk-Maxwell, who spoke of "the image of Him who in the beginning created not only the heaven and the earth, but the materials of which heaven and earth consist." At the conclusion of his address, "On molecules," before the British Association, meeting at Bradford. From *Nature,* VIII. (1873), p. 431. "Purely mechanical reasoning shows a time when the earth must have been tenantless; and teaches us that our own bodies, as well as all living plants and animals and all fossil organic remains, are organised forms of matter to which science can point no antecedent except the Will of a creator, a truth amply confirmed by the evidence of geological history." Sir W. Thomson II. On Mechanical Antecedents of Motion, Heat, and Light. Mathematical and Physical Papers. Cambridge. 1884. pp. 37–38.
63. Arthur H. Compton, in the Magazine of the *Chicago Daily News.* April 12, 1936. The deliberate use of phrases found in the creation narrative by modern scientists must also be counted as a tribute to the accuracy and clearness of the biblical record. Thus, e.g., Sir Arthur Stanley Eddington has written—"Looking back through the long past we picture the beginning of the world—a primeval chaos which time has fashioned into the universe that we know. . . . The world was without form and almost void. . . . In the beginning was vastness, solitude and the deepest night. Darkness was upon the face of the deep, for as yet there was no light." *Science and the Unseen World.* London. 1929. p. 9.

64. Martin Luther: *A Critical and Devotional Commentary on Genesis.* Eng. tr. Minneapolis. 1904. Vol. I. p. 39.
65. Marcus Dods: *The Book of Genesis* in the series, *Handbooks for Bible Classes and Private Students.* Edinburgh. n.d. p. xvii. This is not to be confused with the same author's more famous volume on Genesis, in the *Expositor's Bible.*
66. S. R. Driver: *The Book of Genesis.* 8th ed. London. 1911. p. 33. Since writing this chapter I have reread some words of the late Dr. Keyser, which I believe should be fully quoted in our discussion: "If the Bible is God's revelation, it surely was intended to teach whatever it does teach. Therefore, when it recites history, it must tell the truth. When it touches on the realm of science, as it frequently does it must touch truly. The God of the Bible is represented in the Bible as the God of the whole universe—of the material as well as the spiritual realm. Biblical religion is of too wide a scope and too paramount a character to be set off in a corner. It touches life and experience at every point. Let it be admitted that the Bible is not a scientific textbook. There are many technical matters of science which God has wisely left man to discover for himself as a part of his mental, moral and spiritual discipline. But if the Bible is a divinely inspired book, it must tell the truth when it deals with other data. The critics who think they can go through the Bible and pick out its religious element, and separate it from the rest of its teaching, have an impossible task on their hands. They will inevitably shred its cloth of gold." Leander S. Keyser: *The Problems of Origin.* New York. 1926. p. 81.
67. James G. Murphy: *A Critical and Exegetical Commentary on the Book of Genesis.* Andover. 1868. pp. 30, 31.
68. Thomas Whitelaw: *Genesis.* (in the Pulpit Commentary series.) p. 4.
69. Arnold Guyot: *Creation.* New York. 1884. p. 33.
70. J. G. Murphy, *ibid.* pp. 34, 35.
71. II Peter 3:5. Prof. Bigg renders *di' hudatos* as "by means of water," and aptly adds, "Water is at once the material and the instrumental cause of the subsistence of the earth. It is made out of the sea below, and its life depends on the rain from above." Charles Bigg: *A Critical and Exegetical Commentary on the Epistles of St. Peter and St. Jude.* New York. 1903. p. 293.
72. Joseph Barrell, in *The Evolution of the Earth and Its Inhabitants.* New Haven. 1923. pp. 34, 35.
73. Charles Schuchert and Carl B. Dunbar: *Outlines of Historical Geology.* 3rd ed., in *Outlines of Geology,* by Longwell, Knoff, Flint, Schuchert and Dunbar. New York. 1937. p. 45.
74. Thomas C. Chamberlin and Rollin D. Salisbury: *Geology.* 2nd ed. New York. 1909. Vol. I. p. 8.
75. Thomas Whitelaw, *ibid.* p. 10.
76. James G. Murphy, *ibid.* p. 39.
77. James G. Murphy, *ibid.* p. 47.
78. Albert Perry Brigham: *A Text-Book of Geology.* imprint of 1911. (in Appleton's series of Twentieth Century Text Books.) p. 307.

79. Charles Schuchert and Carl O. Dunbar: *ibid.* p. 42.
80. R. T. Chamberlin, in *The Nature of the World and of Man.* Chicago. 1926. p. 52.
81. J. G. Murphy, *ibid.* p. 51.
82. Schuchert and Dunbar, *ibid.* p. 157.
83. J. G. Murphy, *ibid.* pp. 53, 56.
84. Thomas Whitelaw, *ibid.* p. 15.
85. Schuchert and Dunbar, *ibid.* p. 146.
86. S. R. Driver: *The Book of Genesis.* 8th ed. London. 1911. p. 13.
87. A. P. Brigham, *ibid.* p. 420.
88. Schuchert and Dunbar, *ibid.* Chart, p. 32. See some remarkable statements concerning this period on pages 210, 211.
89. A. P. Brigham, *ibid.* pp. 454, 455.
90. J. W. Dawson: *Origin of the World According to Revelation and Science.* London. 1877. p. 247.
91. J. Arthur Thomson: *What Is Man?* pp. 295, 296. "Man the summit of the series of living forms, and about to become the master of the organic and unorganic world." A. P. Brigham: *A Text-Book of Geology.* pp. 454, 455.

91a. Cuvier: *Discours sur les révolutions du globe.* Quoted by F. Godet, at the beginning of his essay, "The Six Days of Creation," in his valuable work, *Studies in the Old Testament.* Eng. tr. p. 65.

91b. L. T. More: *The Dogma of Evolution.* Princeton. 1925. p. 88. "The order of appearances of living and non-living things in the first chapter of Genesis corresponds in a most remarkable degree with the order of appearances as they are postulated by modern astronomy, and also by modern geology and modern biology. . . . In the days when the first chapter of Genesis was written Geology was an unknown science. . . . The possibility that the author of Genesis would manage to get the order correct merely by working it out from his knowledge of those sciences, or from guessing, would be as hundreds to one against. Surely, we may see in the remarkable correspondence between the order in Genesis and the order in nature the marks of a Divine revelation." pp. 10, 11. A. Rendle Short, M.D., B.S., F.R.C.S. Prof. of Surgery in University of Dublin. "The Christian and the Scientific Outlook," London. 1942. Inter-Varsity Fellowship of Evangelical Union.

91c. Arnold Guyot: *Creation.* New York. 1884. p. 136.

92. Quoted in L. T. More: *The Dogma of Evolution.* p. 143.
93. Francis Darwin: *Life and Letters of Charles Darwin.* II. 210.
94. T. H. Huxley: *Lay Sermons.* 1870. p. 322.
95. Vernon L. Kellogg in *Darwinism of Today.* p. 18.
96. J. Arthur Thomson: *Heredity.* 1908. p. 242.
97. D. H. Scott, in his address before the British Association for the advancement of Science. Edinburgh. Sept., 1921. A remarkable statement concerning this matter of fixity of species has recently come to my attention, which I believe many readers will appreciate having before them: "The individual is constituted of hereditary units . . . called genes, which are as supreme and unchangeable as the atoms of Chemistry. . . . Variation is caused by the

re-combination of the genes, not by their change. Variation is therefore restricted by the combination possibility of the genes. And these are limited by the crossing possibilities. Then again, since individuals belonging to different species of plant and animal cannot even be paired, much less produce offspring, the combination of variations is confined to the species. Variants are formed, out-crossed and arise anew in a kaleidoscopic sequence *within the species. But the species remains the same phere of variation.* The various species will remain like circles that do not intersect. *Species are constant.*" Heribert Nilsson (the Swedish plant-geneticist), "The Problem of the Origin of Species since Darwin." *Hereditas.* XX. 1935. Quoted in Douglas Dewar, "Dr. Julian Huxley on Evolution," *Evangelical Quarterly.* 1943. XV. 202, 203.

98. James Weir: *The Energy System of the Universe.* 1912. p. 200.
99. Sir James Jeans: *The Mysterious Universe.* new rev. ed. 1942. p. 91.
100. Alfred Russell Wallace, "Man's Place in the Universe," *Fortnightly Review.* March 1, 1903. pp. 396, 409, 411.
101. Leonard W. King: *Legends of Babylon and Egypt in Relation to Hebrew Tradition.* The Schweich Lectures for 1916. London. 1918. pp. 102–143; the same author's, *The Seven Tablets of Creation.* 1902; and *Babylonian Religion and Mythology.* London. 1903. pp. 53–120. See also, Robert William Rogers: *Cuneiform Parallels to the Old Testament.* New York. 1912. pp. 1–60; A. T. Clay: *Light on the Old Testament from Babel.* 2nd ed. Philadelphia. 1907. pp. 59–76.
102. Alexander Heidel: *The Babylonian Genesis. The Story of Creation.* Chicago. 1942. pp. 117, 118. (Dr. Heidel is Research assistant on the Assyrian Dictionary Project of the Oriental Institute, University of Chicago.) "It is in the work of the sixth day, however, that the biblical narrative rises to its greatest height, in its account of the creation of man endowed from the very beginning with the spirit of the divine Creator. A greater contrast between the statement in the impressive Hebrew narrative of the creation of man in the image of God, as against the Babylonian view of man's being created for the sake of the gods, to provide temples and worshippers for them, can hardly be imagined. The difference between the two points of view represents the wide gap between the matrialistic conception of the gods as powers of nature . . . and the conception of a Power expressed in spiritual terms who is the ultimate source of all life, etc." Morris Jastrow, Jr.: *Hebrew and Babylonian Traditions.* New York. 1914. p. 128.
103. S. A. B. Mercer, "A New Turning Point in the Study of Creation," in *Canadian Journal of Religious Thought.* June, 1924. I. 232. In the *New York Times,* December 13, 1941, there is quite an extended account of a report made to the Oriental seminar of the University of Pennsylvania, regarding some new translations from clay Sumerian tablets of about 2000 B.C., by Dr. Samuel N. Kramer, research associate of the Museum of the University of Pennsylvania. The item informs us that, "The Sumerian poem began with a description of the difficulties the gods experienced in obtaining their bread, especially after the female deities joined them. The goddess

of the primeval sea, 'The mother who gave birth to all the gods,' therefore aroused her sleeping son, Enki, the sea god and the god of wisdom, and asked him to 'fashion servants of the gods,' Enki, after considering the matter, leads forth his host of 'good and princely fashioners.'" One can quickly see what a chasm there is between such an absolutely unbelievable myth and the record in our Bible. For a more complete treatment of the subject see the author's subsequent work, *Sumerian Mythology*. Philadelphia. 1944. espec. pp. 30–40, 68–75.

106. Robert M. Brown, in *Dict. of American Biography*. Vol. VIII. 1932. p. 64.
107. Arnold Guyot: *Creation and the Biblical Cosmogony in the Light of Modern Science*. New York. 1887. pp. 2, 3.
108. William Cecil Dampier-Whetham: *Cambridge Readings in the Literature of Science. Being Extracts from the Writings of Men of Science to Illustrate the Development of Scientific Thought*. Cambridge. 1924. pp. 1, 2, and the Preface.
109. Louis Trenchard More: *The Dogma of Evolution*. pp. 242, 243.
110. Francis Bowen: *A Layman's Study of the English Bible*. New York. 1885.
111. C. Alphonso Smith: *Keynote Studies in Keynote Books of the Bible*. New York. 1918. pp. 34–46.
112. William Lyon Phelps: *Human Nature in the Bible*. New York. 1923. p. 3.
113. James G. Murphy: *A Critical and Exegetical Commentary on the Book of Genesis*. Andover. 1868. pp. 28–30.
114. W. Lindsay Alexander: *Biblical Theology*. Edinburgh. 1888. p. 130.
115. J. P. Lange: *Commentary on the Book of Genesis*. 6th ed. rev. p. 148. Early in his famous *Universal History* (Eng. trans. New York. 1885. pp. 21–23), Leopold von Ranke pays a glowing tribute to the value of the biblical record of creation in a passage which I fail to find referred to in contemporary apologetic literature: "The history of the creation in Genesis is not merely a cosmogonic account of primitive date, but above all else it is an express counterstatement opposed to the conceptions of Egypt and Babylon. The latter were formed in regions either naturally fertile or early animated by commercial intercourse; the Mosaic idea emerges upon the lonely heights of Sinai, which no terrestrial vicissitudes have ever touched, and where nothing interposes between God and the world. . . . The creation of man is the point in which all centres. With the Egyptians man is not distinguished in kind from the sun from which he issues rather as a product than as a creature, and the same is true of the Babylonian cosmogony, where the divine element in man is only revealed through the blood of a God chancing to fall down to earth. All creatures are generically the same with man. In the Mosaic cosmogony, on the other hand, the elements, plants, and animals are called into being by a supreme intelligent Will, which creates in the last place man after His own image. The divergence is immeasurable. God appears prominently as a Being independent of the created world; He appears to the prophet in the fire, but yet is not the fire; He is in the Word which is heard out of the fire. Speech is bestowed upon

man, who gives each created thing its name. In this his pre-eminence consists; for he alone, as Locke has remarked, possesses an innate faculty of framing an abstract idea of species, whereas other creatures can grasp nothing beyond the individual. While the descent of some from the sun and others from the stars establishes a difference between man and man, creation by the breath of God makes all men equal. Under the Godhead as independent of the created world the dignity thus implanted in men appears, it might also be said, as a principle of equality." *Universal History*. Eng. trans. New York. 1885. pp. 21–23. With such tributes as these to the accuracy and non-mythological origin of the Genesis record of creation, what a betrayal of the Christian faith, what a revelation of the unnecessary loss of confidence in the Scriptures is the statement of the famous report on Doctrine in the Church of England, which a few years ago, declared—"It is generally agreed among educated Christians that these (the creation narratives of Genesis 1 and 2) are mythological in origin, and that their value for us is symbolic rather than historical." *Doctrine of the Church of England. The Report of the Commission on Christian Doctrine appointed by the Archbishops of Canterbury and York in 1922*. London. 1938. p. 45.

116. James Orr: *The Christian View of God and the World*. 3rd ed. New York. 1897. p. 127.

117. James Clerk-Maxwell, "On Molecules," at a meeting of the British Association at Bradford. *Nature*. VIII. May–October, 1873. pp. 437–441.

118. A. H. Strong: *Systematic Theology*. Philadelphia. 1907. p. 389; see the entire discussion, pp. 386–389; also, L. Berkhof: *Systematic Theology*. 2nd ed. Grand Rapids. 1941. p. 131.

119. James Orr: *The Christian View of God and the World*. 1893. pp. 124–126. See also some excellent remarks in Walter T. Marvin: *An Introduction to Systematic Philosophy*. New York. 1903. pp. 300–301. "Everything points with overwhelming force to a definite event, or series of events, of creation some time or times, not infinitely remote. The universe cannot have originated by chance out of its present ingredients, and neither can it have been always the same as now." Sir James Jeans: *Eos, or the Wider Aspects of Cosmogony*. London. 1928. p. 55. Quoted in W. C. D. Dampier-Whetham: *A History of Science*. New York. 1931. p. 483. I deeply regret that I am prevented in this volume, from sheer lack of space, from discussing the complicated cosmological arguments of Kant and Hegel. If this volume were devoted exclusively to the doctrine of creation these subjects would be given considerable attention. Their omission here we believe does not weaken the argument of the chapter, and their inclusion would not change the argument. For a criticism of Kant's cosmological theories, see Edward Caird: *The Critical Philosophy of Immanuel Kant*. New York. 1889. II. 39–101; Robert Flint: *Agnosticism*. New York. 1903. pp. 224–227; for Hegel see McTaggart's *Helegian Cosmology*. For later discussions, especially the creation conceptions of Bergson, see Newton P. Stallknecht: *Studies in the Philosophy of Creation*. Princeton. 1934 (a volume I have found very difficult reading).

120. I am referring to *Theism and Cosmology* (Gifford Lectures, 1939), by John

Laird, Regius Professor of Moral Philosophy in the University of Aberdeen. London. 1940.

121. Theodore Christlieb: *Modern Doubt and Christian Unbelief.* pp. 161, 162.

122. Charles Harris: *Pro Fide.* 4th ed. London. 1930. pp. 12–15. On the inadequacy of pantheism, there are some good things in A. B. Bruce: *Apologetics; or Christianity Defensively Stated.* Edinburgh. 1892. pp. 71, 86–89.

123. Charles Hodge: *Systematic Theology.* I. 563, 564.

124. Charles Harris: *"Pro Fide."* 4th ed. London. 1930. pp. 7, 8. "A belief in more gods than one not only finds no support in the universe, but, as the very word universe indicates, is contradicted by it. . . . Everything counteracts or balances or assists something else, and thus all things proclaim their common dependence on One Original." Robert Flint: *Theism.* 7th ed., rev. Edinburgh. 1889. p. 125.

125. Stephen Charnock: *The Attributes of God.* Vol. II. pp. 281–292. See also Robert Flint: *Agnosticism.* New York. 1903. pp. 364–366; Henry Cotterill: *Does Science Aid Faith in Regard to Creation?* London. 1886. pp. 99–101. Herbert H. Farmer: *Towards Belief in God.* New York. 1943. pp. 17 ff.

126. Robert Flint: *Theism.* Edinburgh. 1884. pp. 127–129.

127. James G. Murphy: *A Critical and Exegetical Commentary on the Book of Genesis.* Andover. 1868. pp. 41, 42.

128. Robert Flint: *Sermons and Addresses.* New York. 1899. pp. 58, 59. See also James Denney: *The Way Everlasting.* pp. 74–87.

129. E.g., Psalm 104:24; 121:2; 124:8; 134:3; 136:5; 146:6. Rev. 4:11.

130. The passages are II Kings 19:15, 16; Jer. 32:17; Neh. 9:6.

131. Acts 4:24. I find *nothing* of any value on this verse in *all* the more important modern commentaries on the Book of Acts. It is here, as in hundreds of other places, that Calvin reveals himself as the preeminent commentator of the last three centuries. His words are worth quoting, as always: "Although this title and commendation of God's power be general, yet it ought to be referred unto the present matter, for they do in such sort acknowledge the power of God in the creation of the whole world, that they apply the the same therewithal unto the present use. In like sort, the prophets do oftentimes commend the same, to the end they may redress that fear which troubleth us when we behold the power of our enemies; secondly, they add thereunto the promise, and they make these two foundations of their boldness whereby they are emboldened to pray. And surely our prayers are such as they ought to be, and acceptable to God only then, when as staying ourselves upon his promises and power, we pray with certain hope to obtain that for which we pray, for we cannot otherwise have any true confidence unless God do will us to come unto him, and promise that he is ready to help us; and, secondly, unless we acknowledge that he is able enough to help us; wherefore let the faithful exercise themselves in this double meditation so often as they address themselves unto prayer. Furthermore, we gather hereby after what sort we ought to consider the creation of the world; to wit, that we may know that all things are subject to God, and ruled by his will, and when that the world hath done what it can, there shall no other thing come to pass but that which God hath decreed; yea,

that the wantonness of the wicked is monstrous, as if the clay should resist the potter; for this is the meaning of the faithful generally, that whatsoever dangers hang over their heads, yet can God prevent the same infinite ways, forasmuch as all things are in his hand, and that he is able to make all the parts of heaven and earth (which he hath created) to obey him." *Commentary Upon the Acts of the Apostles.* I. 182, 183.

132. Isaiah 40:25–31.
133. Isaiah 45:18–23.
134. Psalm 146:5, 6.
135. John Pearson: *Exposition of the Creed.* Vol. I. pp. 82, 83. The passage quoted is Isaiah 54:16, 17.
136. John Pearson, *ibid.* I. 80, 81. The verse quoted is Genesis 6:6.
137. Franz Delitzsch: *Commentary on the Epistle to the Hebrews.* Eng. trans. 3rd ed. Vol. II. Edinburgh. 1887. pp. 216, 217.
138. Robert S. Candlish: *The Book of Genesis Expounded in a Series of Discourses.* New ed., rev. Edinburgh. 1868. I. 6–8. Westcott reminds us that the word here translated *have been framed, katertisthai,* "expresses the manifoldness and the unity of all creation; and by the tense marks that the original lesson of creation remains for abiding use and application." B. F. Westcott: *The Epistle to the Hebrews.* 2nd ed. London. 1892. p. 352. "The system of which the first word is, In the beginning there was nothing except space and atoms, has for its last word, Eternal Death; as the system of which the first word is, In the beginning God created the heavens and the earth, has for its last word, Eternal life. What man who has a mind to think can hesitate to choose between Eternal Life and Eternal Death?" Robert Flint: *Anti-Theistic Theories.* Edinburgh. 1879. pp. 72, 73.
139. I Peter 4:19. Henry Alford: *The New Testament for English Readers.* rev. ed. Cambridge. 1872. II. 825. "We can scarcely doubt the example of the great Sufferer was present to the Apostle's mind, and his words were therefore echoes of those spoken on the cross, 'Father, into thy hands I commend my spirit' (Luke 23:46)." E. H. Plumptre: *The General Epistles of St. Peter, St. Jude.* Cambridge. 1899. p. 151.

CHAPTER VIII

1. Of 1071 verses in the English R. V. translation of Matthew's Gospel, 364 verses belong to the narrative of Passion Week, from the Triumphal Entry on Sunday, to the entombment on Friday, Matt. 21:1–27:61. In Mark's Gospel the proportion is 230 out of 667 verses, Mark 11:1–15:47. In Luke's Gospel the ratio is 231 out of 1053 verses, Luke 19:29–23:56. In John's Gospel the ratio is 275 out of 878 verses, John 12:12–19:42. Thus in the four Gospels 1100 verses are to be assigned to the last six days of our Lord's life, to the time of His burial.
2. Clifford Herbert Moore: *The Religious Thought of the Greeks.* 2nd ed. Cambridge. 1925. p. 357.
3. B. B. Warfield, "The Resurrection of Christ an Historical Fact, evinced by Eye-Witnesses," in *Journal of Christian Philosophy.* III. (1884.) p. 305.

One should be careful not to allow a supposed emphasis on the "spiritual" persuade one that the reality of the resurrection of Christ is not to be determined by historical evidence. Thus, e.g. (out of many), Hans Lietzmann, successor to Harnack at Berlin—"The verdict on the true nature of the event described as the resurrection of Jesus, an event whose significance for the history of the world cannot be measured, does not come within the province of historical inquiry into matters of fact, but belongs to the place where the human soul touches what is eternal." He himself accepts the vision hypothesis, to be discussed later in this chapter. *The Beginnings of the Christian Church*. New York. 1937. p. 77.

4. Luke 23:46.
5. James Denney: *Jesus and the Gospel*. 1909. p. 102. On the denial of the resurrection of the body in gnosticism, see Calvin Klopp Staudt: *The Idea of the Resurrection in the Ante-Nicene Creeds*. Chicago. 1909. pp. 50, 51.
6. Thomas James Thorburn: *The Resurrection Narratives and Modern Criticism*. London. 1910. pp. 142–144. There are some good thoughts on the meaning of a true resurrection in John Pearson: *An Exposition of the Creed*. Vol. II. p. 77. Doremus A. Hayes, in his excellent work, *The Resurrection Fact* (Nashville, 1932. pp. 200, 201), has some penetrating sentences concerning the difference between previous resurrections in the Bible, and the resurrection of Christ. In part, he says, "Every other resurrected man still was under death's power and had to face the possibility and the certainty of death again. Every other resurrected man still was liable to suffering and sin, still was in bondage to mortality and pain. Jesus was the first resurrected man to be released from the dominion of death into a life free from pain and infirmity and filled with glorious immortality. He is Death's Conqueror."
7. The References are: John 2:19, 21; Matt. 12:40; 16:21 (and parallels); 17:23; 20:19 (and parallels); 26:32. On Christ's predictions of His resurrection, see Joseph Clifford Fenton: *We Stand with Christ*, Milwaukee. 1942. pp. 353–356.
8. R. M'Cheyne Edgar: *The Gospel of a Risen Saviour*. Edinburgh. 1892. p. 32. "It has been often said, and surely with truth, that, if our Lord predicted His death, He must have predicted His Resurrection also: for only so could He reconcile His death with His Messianic claim. If Jesus claimed to be the Christ, and also anticipated with certainty His own death, the contradiction could only be solved by an equally confident certainty of His resurrection. Thus the prediction of His Resurrection seems confirmed by the requirements of His circumstances. If Christhood was His mission, and His death an absolutely essential condition of its fulfilment, the vindication of God's chosen must lie in reversing the death, that is in Resurrection. The Son of Man could not humanly go up to Jerusalem predicting His death unless He also predicted His Resurrection. Hence, most significantly, in keeping with the theological requirements of the position, every main prediction of His death is, in the earliest evangelical tradition, accompanied by an equally definite prediction by His Resurrection." W. J. Sparrow-Simpson: *The Resurrection and Modern Thought*. London. 1911. p. 12.
9. W. J. Sparrow-Simpson: *The Resurrection and Modern Thought*. London.

1911. pp. 230, 231. While the entire sermon occupies 23 verses in our English text (Acts 2:14–36), 12 of these, or more than one-half of the entire sermon are devoted to the evidence for and significance of Christ's resurrection.

10. John Mackintosh Shaw: *The Resurrection of Christ.* Edinburgh. 1920. p. 4. See also Alfred Barry: *The Manifold Witness for Christ.* New York. 1880. pp. 128, 129.
11. I Corinthians 15:14. "Faith in the resurrection is the very keystone of the arch of Christian faith, and, when it is removed, all must inevitably crumble into ruin. The idea that the spiritual teaching, that the lofty moral character of our Lord, will survive faith in His resurrection is one of those phantoms to which men cling when they are themselves, consciously or unconsciously, losing faith, and have not yet thought out the consequences of the loss. St. Paul knew what he was doing when he made Christianity answer with its life for truth of the resurrection. 'If Christ be not risen,' he said, 'our preaching is vain; your faith is also vain.'" H. P. Liddon: *Sermons.* (*Contemporary Pulpit Library.*) New York. 1888. p. 73.
12. Luke 24:46, 47.
13. The references are Acts 1:22; 2:32; 3:15; 5:32; 10:39; 13:31, 32; 26:16. The preëminent place assigned to the resurrection of Christ in the sermons recorded in Acts is often commented upon; I do not find notice taken, however, of the place of the truth of the resurrection in the trials of Paul. Before the Sanhedrin he declared, "touching the hope of the resurrection of the dead I am called in question" (23:6); and likewise before Felix (24:15). Festus in reporting Paul's case to King Agrippa, said questions had been raised concerning "one Jesus, who was dead, whom Paul affirmed to be alive" (25:9). Of Agrippa Paul asked, "Why is it judged incredible of you, if God doth raise the dead?" (26:8), and concluded by affirming that Moses and the prophets predicted that Christ must suffer, and that "He first by the resurrection of the dead should proclaim light both to the people and to the Gentiles." (26:23.) On the preëminent place given to the resurrection of Christ in the preaching of the Apostles, see Joseph Clifford Fenton: *We Stand with Christ.* Milwaukee. 1942. pp. 336–340.
14. Acts. 4:33.
15. The references are I Thess. 4:14; I Cor. 15:3, 4; Rom, 10:9; II Cor. 5:14, 15.
16. Romans 1:4; 4:25; Acts 17:31; I Thess. 4:14; I Cor. 6:14; 15:20, 21; II Cor. 4:14; Rom. 6:4, 5; 8:11.
17. Ch. Guignebert: *Jesus.* New York. 1935. p. 536. Even such a modernist as Prof. Shirley Jackson Case is compelled to acknowledge that the early Christians at least believed Christ rose from the dead: "The first Christians confidently believed that Jesus really died, was really buried, and actually rose from the dead and appeared to his disciples. The testimony of Paul alone is sufficient to convince us, beyond any reasonable doubt, that this was the commonly accepted opinion in his day—an opinion at that time supported by the highest authority imaginable, the eye-witnesses themselves." Shirley Jackson Case. "The Resurrection Faith of the First Disciples." *American Journal of Theology.* April, 1909. XIII. 171, 172.

18. H. D. A. Major, in *The Mission and Message of Jesus.* New York. 1938. p. 213.
19. Charles E. Raven: *Science, Religion, and the Future.* Cambridge. New York. 1943. p. 128. Streeter's pitifully weak attempt to account for the early power of the church is in the *Cambridge Ancient History.* Vol. XI. *The Imperial Peace. A.D. 70–192.* pp. 265, 266, 282.
20. J. S. Whale: *Christian Doctrine.* New York, Cambridge. 1941. p. 69.
21. The records of the entombment of Jesus and the later sealing of the tomb are—Matt. 27:57–66; Mark 15:42–47; Luke 23:50–56a; John 19:38–42.
22. Ch. Guignebert: *Jesus.* p. 500; see also, p. 535. Major, in *The Mission and Message of Jesus,* p. 215, believes this idea is historically acceptable. "Had the body of Christ merely been thrown into a common grave and left unattended, there would have been no possible reason for the anxiety of His enemies to spread the report that the body had been stolen." J. C. Fenton, *ut supra.* p. 346.
23. W. J. Sparrow-Simpson: *The Resurrection and Modern Thought.* pp. 21, 22. His references to Josephus are *Autobiography,* ch. 72; *Wars of the Jews.* IV. v. 2.
24. James Denney: *Jesus and the Gospel.* New York. 1909. pp. 130, 131. "The enemies of Jesus once placed a watch at His grave, that the body might not be stolen. Now, we ourselves stand before His empty tomb, to guard it with these arguments, and with the experimental proof of His resurrection power working in our hearts that none may again bury the Lord of glory." Theodore Christlieb: *Modern Doubt and Christian Belief.* p. 503.
25. The events of Easter Sunday are recorded in the following passages—Matt. 28:1–15; Mark 16:1–14; Luke 23:56b–24:43; John 21:1–25. The appearance to the Eleven, one week later, is found only in John 20:26–29. The appearance to seven disciples at the Sea of Galilee is recorded with considerable detail in John 21:1–24. Later appearances and the Ascension are referred to in Matt. 28:16–20; Mark 16:15–20; Luke 24:44–53.
26. Matthew 28:11–15.
27. Matthew 28:59–61; Mark 14:55–59.
28. Matthew 26:69–75; Mark 14:66–72; Luke 22:55–62; John 18:15–18, 25–27.
29. Justin Martyr: *Dialogue Against Trypho.* CVIII.
30. Tertullian: *Apology.* XXI.
31. Edward Gordon Selwyn, "The Resurrection," in, *Essays Catholic and Critical.* London. 1926. p. 318. "That without an exception *all* should have fallen asleep when they were stationed there for so extraordinary a purpose, to see that the body was not stolen . . . is not credible: especially when it is considered that these guards were subjected to the severest discipline in the world. It was death for a Roman sentinel to sleep at his post. Yet these guards were not executed; nor were they deemed culpable even by the rulers, woefully chagrined and exasperated as they must have been by failure of their plan for securing the body. . . . That the Jewish rulers did not believe what they instructed and bribed the soldiers to say, is almost self-evident. If they did, why were not the disciples at once arrested and examined? For such an act as was imputed to them involved a serious offence against the

existent authorities. Why were they not compelled to give up the body? Or, in the event of their being unable to exculpate themselves from the charge, why were they not punished for their crime? . . . It is nowhere intimated that the rulers even attempted to substantiate the charge." Richard W. Dickinson: *The Resurrection of Jesus Christ Historically and Logically Viewed.* Philadelphia. 1865. pp. 29, 31, 32. Hermann Samuel Reimarus (1694–1768), wrote a work entitled (in its translated form), *Concerning the Resurrection,* 1174 (which was brought out by Lessing), in which he proposed the theory that the disciples *did* remove the body of Jesus by stealth, and then proceeded to preach His resurrection. It is a clear indication of Albert Schweitzer's perverted conception of the historical value of the resurrection narratives, when he says of the rationalistic work of Reimarus—"His work is perhaps the most splendid achievement in the whole course of the historical investigation of the life of Jesus." *The Quest of the Historical Jesus.* 2nd ed. London. 1936. p. 23. R. McCheyne Edgar, *ut supra,* p. 104, concluding an excellent study of the testimony of the guards, finely says—"His enemies, led by their fears, posted witnesses at the very grave's mouth, whose utter defeat, either by the angelic manifestation or by that of the Risen One Himself, turns Christ's resurrection into a public and perfect triumph!"

32. Joseph Klausner: *Jesus of Nazareth.* Eng. tr. New York. 1925. p. 357. Klausner's words are—"We must assume that the owner of the tomb thought it unfitting that one who had been crucified should remain in his own ancestral tomb." And then he makes this astonishing admission—"it was, in the main, only the malicious invention of enemies unable to explain the 'miracle.'" The same theory was previously advocated by others, e.g., O. Holtzmann, in his *Life of Jesus.* Eng. tr. London. 1904. p. 499.
33. John 19:38
34. Mark 15:43; Luke 23:50. Studies of the character of Joseph of Arimathaea seem to be very scarce; there must be others, but the only one of any real importance I have found is by Dr. James Alexander Robertson, in his, *The Hidden Romance of the New Testament.* pp. 9–24.
35. Kirsopp Lake: *The Historical Evidence for the Resurrection of Jesus Christ.* New York. 1907. pp. 251, 252. P. Gardner-Smith: *The Narratives of the Resurrection.* London, 1926. pp. 134–139.
36. A. E. J. Rawlinson: *St. Mark. With Introduction, Commentary and Additional Notes.* 2nd ed. London. 1927. p. 243.
37. A. E. Morris: "The Narratives of the Resurrection of Jesus Christ" in *Hibbert Journal.* April, 1939. XXXIX. 319.
38. P. Gardiner-Smith: *The Narratives of the Resurrection.* London. 1926. "The body of Jesus may never have moved from its shelf in the rock-hewn tomb." (p. 190.) When he wrote this, the author was Dean and Fellow of Jesus College, Oxford.
39. David Strauss: *The Life of Jesus for the People.* Eng. trans. 2nd ed. London. 1879. I. 412. It is strange how some men, with such keen minds for scientific matters, should so quickly accept fantastic theories devised to discredit the supernatural. T. H. Huxley himself tried to revive this swoon theory, in a paper read before the Metaphysical Society, in 1876, but apparently he

thought it best not to subsequently publish it. See Leonard Huxley: *The Life and Letters of Thomas Henry Huxley*. London. 1900. I. 342.

40. William Milligan: *The Resurrection of Our Lord*. London. 1881. p. 76. The swoon theory seems to have been invented by Peter Annet, an English Deist, in 1768; was repeated in an anonymous work, *Ecce Homo,* appearing in Edinburgh, in 1799; and enthusiastically adopted by Paulus, in his *Das Leben Jesu*. 1828. It was, in part, adopted by Schleiermacher, and reissued by C. Voysey, in his *The Swoon Theory*. On the reality of the death of Christ, see, e.g., Christlieb: *Modern Doubt and Christian Belief*. pp. 455, 456.
41. Since writing this I have seen a reference in some volume to the "Santa Claus" idea in reference to the empty tomb, but I have been unable to recover it. Dr. Selby Vernon McCasland, after suggesting that the story of the empty tomb might be accounted for by (1) assuming it to be an historical incident; (2) by a vision experience; (3) as an inference from the resurrection faith; or (4), by the adoption of a grave story in one of the contemporary cults, reveals how indecisive and inadequate any of these theories are even for himself, by concluding that, "It is quite possible that neither one of the hypotheses stated is sufficient alone to account for the narrative, but that several influences worked together to give us the story of the empty grave," etc. *The Resurrection of Jesus*. New York. 1932. p. 176.
42. Quoted in Samuel H. Kellogg: *The Light of Asia and the Light of the World*. He has some excellent remarks on the late stories about a mythical resurrection of Buddha; see, especially, pp. 79, 80, 140–142. See also Thomas James Thorburn: *The Mythical Interpretation of the Gospels*. New York. 1916. p. 322.
43. Kirsopp Lake: *The Historical Evidence for the Resurrection of Jesus Christ*. New York. 1907. p. 253.
44. H. P. Liddon: *Sermons*. (*The Contemporary Pulpit Library*.) New York. 1888. pp. 71–73. Bishop Moule beautifully speaks of "the profound harmony of faith and reason at the door of Joseph's sepulchre." *From Sunday to Sunday*. New York. 1904. p. 94. W. Robertson Nicoll (*The Church's One Foundation,* New York. 1902. p. 150) quotes Pressensé as saying, "The empty tomb of Christ has been the cradle of the Church, and if in this foundation of her faith the Church has been mistaken, she must needs lay herself down by the side of the mortal remains, I say, not of a man, but of a religion." Nowhere is the untrustworthiness of Barthian theology so clearly revealed as in its astonishing denial of the importance of this fact. Barth himself says, "This tomb may prove to be a definitely closed or an open tomb; it is really a matter of indifference. What avails the tomb, proved to be this or that, at Jerusalem, in the year A.D. 30?" Karl Barth: *The Resurrection of the Dead,* Eng. trans. New York. 1938. p. 144. So, likewise, Dr. Richard Grover, a Barthian, in his *Primacy of Faith* (New York, 1943)—"From the historical point of view . . . the resurrection of Christ is a myth. . . . The historical fact is not the kind of fact which he believes." p. 213.
45. W. J. Sparrow-Simpson: *The Resurrection and Modern Thought*. London. 1911. pp. 83, 84.

46. W. J. Sparrow-Simpson: *Ibid.* pp. 92, 93, 95, 96.
47. W. J. Sparrow-Simpson: *Ibid.* pp. 98, 99.
48. E. Renan: *Les Apotres.* Paris. 1866. p. 13. Eng. tr. Boston. 1898. p. 49.
49. Joseph Klausner: *From Jesus to Paul.* Eng. tr. New York. 1943. pp. 255–258, 439, 440.
50. Theodore Christlieb: *Modern Doubt and Christian Belief.* pp. 462, 463; see L. de Grandmaison: *Jesus Christ,* etc. p. 212.
51. Joseph Klausner: *Jesus of Nazareth, His Life, Times, and Teaching.* Eng. tr. New York. 1925. p. 359. The most satisfying *definition* of a vision I have seen is the one by Weiss: "The scientific meaning of this term is that an apparent act of vision takes place for which there is no corresponding external object. The optic nerve has not been stimulated by any outward waves of light or vibrations of the ether, but has been excited by a purely inner physiological cause. At the same time the sense-impression of sight is accepted by the one who experiences the vision as completely as if it were wholly 'objective'; he fully believes the object of his vision to be actually before him." Johannes Weiss: *The History of Primitive Christianity.* Eng. trans. New York. 1937. I. 28.
52. E. Digges LaTouche: *Christian Certitude. Its Intellectual Basis.* London and Boston. 1910. p. 194. A perfect example of the abandonment of all laws of reason in attempting to escape the historical evidence for Christ's resurrection is this sentence from O. Holtzmann. "If it be objected that such visions could only come to one individual at a time, we need only to point to the indisputable witness of Paul, who says that on one occasion the risen Jesus was beheld by over five hundred persons at once." *Life of Jesus.* Eng. tr. London. 1904. p. 497. One of the most exhaustive examinations of the vision hypothesis will be found in Hilarin Felder: *Christ and the Critics.* London. 1924. Vol. II. 415–432.
53. John McNaugher: *The Resurrection of Jesus Christ.* Pittsburgh. 1938. pp. 9, 10. Among a large number of scholars who have adopted the vision hypothesis, is A. Seth Pringle-Pattison in his *Studies in the Philosophy of Religion.* Oxford. 1930. pp. 180–183.
54. Theodore Christlieb: *Modern Doubt and Christian Belief.* pp. 493, 494.
55. William Milligan: *The Resurrection of Our Lord.* London. 1881. pp. 79, 80. "By no normal person either in the apostolic age or in this would the mere appearance of the disembodied spirit or 'phantasm' of a dead man be regarded as evidence that the man in question has conquered death or was divine." Charles Harris: *Creeds or No Creeds?* London. 1922. p. 287.
56. This was first developed by T. Keim: *The History of Jesus of Nazareth.* Eng. tr. pp. 360–365.
57. William P. Armstrong, "The Resurrection and the Church." *Princeton Theological Review.* Jan. 1907. V. 22, 23.
58. Luke 1:3.
59. Edwin G. Selwyn: *The Approach to Christianity.* London. 1925. p. 199.
60. A. T. Olmstead: *Jesus in the Light of History.* New York. 1942. p. 251.
61. Harry Emerson Fosdick: *A Guide to Understanding the Bible.* 1938. p. 294.
62. William Milligan, *ut supra,* pp. 56, 57.

63. A. C. Headlam: *Christian Theology. The Doctrine of God*. Oxford. 1934 pp. 281, 282.
64. *The Beginning of Christianity*. Part I. *The Acts of the Apostles*. Vol. I. Prolegomena. London. 1920. pp. 321, 322. A similarly unfair repudiation of the validity of the resurrection narratives, from one high in ecclesiastical councils, co-author of one of the most comprehensive of recent works on Christ, is the following: "The belief in the Resurrection of Jesus was created, not by an objective experience of His disciples after His crucifixion, but by a subjective experience created by the impact of His personality upon their personalities in the preceding period. . . . If this psychological explanation of the origin of the faith in the Resurrection of Jesus be accepted, then our gospel narratives of the Resurrection are more of the nature of myth than history. Myth, let it be understood, is not falsehood, but truth which expresses itself in the form of imaginative narrative." H. D. A. Major, in *The Mission and Message of Jesus*. New York. 1938. pp. 217, 218. Dr. Major has been the Principal of Ripon Hall, Oxford, since 1919; for many years examining chaplain to the Bishop of Birmingham; founder of the *Modern Churchman*, 1911, and its editor since then.
65. John A. Scott: *We Would See Jesus*. Chicago. 1936. p. 134.
66. J. J. Van Oosterzee: *The Gospel According to Luke*. 1870. p. 398. On the resurrection body of our Lord, see also, Theodore Christlieb: *Modern Doubt and Christian Belief*. pp. 475, 476; W. J. Sparrow-Simpson: *The Resurrection and Modern Thought*. pp. 416, 417; E. Griffith-Jones: *The Ascent through Christ*. London. New York. 1899. pp. 342–344; J. A. Beet: *A Manual of Theology*. New York. 1906. pp. 216, 217; and some very sensible remarks in T. G. Bonney's Boyle Lectures for 1891, *Christian Doctrines and Modern Thought*. London. 1892. pp. 119–122.
67. Charles Gore: *The Body of Christ*. p. 129.
68. Theodore Christlieb: *Modern Doubt and Christian Belief*. pp. 475, 476.
69. A. Harnack: *What Is Christianity?* Eng. trans. 2nd ed. New York. 1903. pp. 173–176. On the relation of religion to history, especially in reference to Harnack's hypothesis, see W. J. Sparrow-Simpson: *Our Lord's Resurrection*. London. 1905. pp. 293–303.
70. "The Resurrection Fact," in the *Christian Century*. April 5, 1944. pp. 423–425.
71. Acts 9:1–9.
72. Acts 22:6–11; 26:12–19.
73. I Corinthians 15:5–8.
74. Doremus A. Hayes: *The Resurrection Fact*. Nashville. 1932. pp. 240, 241.
75. T. J. Thorburn: *The Resurrection Narratives and Modern Criticism*. London. 1910. pp. 84, 85.
76. A. C. Headlam: *Christian Theology. The Doctrine of God*. Oxford. 1934. pp. 278, 279.
77. J. Gresham Machen: *The Christian Faith in the Modern World*. New York. 1936. pp. 214, 215.
78. James Denney: *Jesus and the Gospel*. New York. 1909. pp. 110–113.
79. Calvin Klopp Staudt: *The Idea of the Resurrection in the Ante-Nicene Period*. Chicago. 1909. pp. 66–68. On the entire question of the resurrection

of Greek divinities, see, Lewis Richard Farnell: *The Cults of the Greek States.* V. Oxford. 1909. pp. 182–185, and his *Greek Hero Cults and Ideas of Immortality.* Oxford. 1921. pp. 390–401. On the relation of the idea of resurrection occurring on "the third day," in ancient Greek and Roman literature, see some interesting material collected in Johannes Weiss: *The History of Primitive Christianity.* New York. 1937. pp. 95, 96. On the resurrection of Osiris, see Charles H. Robinson: *Studies in the Resurrection of Christ.* London. 1909. pp. 158–162; J. G. Frazer: *Adonis. Attis. Osiris.* London. 1914. 3rd ed. rev. II. 15, 89–91. The following verdict by one of the greatest authorities of our century on ancient religions is particularly important: "There is nothing in the texts which justifies the assumption that Osiris knew he would rise from the dead, and that he would become the king and judge of the dead, or that the Egyptians believed that Osiris died on their behalf and rose again in order that they also might rise from the dead." E. A. Wallis Budge: *Osiris and the Egyptian Resurrection.* London. 1911. I., 312, 313. Grandmaison (*ut supra,* p. 345) approvingly quotes the conclusion of Boulanger that "the idea that the god dies and rises again to lead his worshippers to eternal life does not exist in any Hellenic mystery religion.

80. Clifford Herschel Moore: *Pagan Ideas of Immortality during the Early Roman Empire.* Cambridge. 1918. p. 23.
81. W. J. Sparrow-Simpson: *The Resurrection and Modern Thought.* London. 1911. p. 246. See also Leonce de Grandmaison: *Jesus Christ. His Person. His Message. His Credentials.* New York. 1934. pp. 345, 346.
82. Romans 1:3, 4. W. J. Sparrow-Simpson: *The Resurrection and Modern Thought.* pp. 287, 288. "If it be asked how the resurrection of Christ is a proof of his being the Son of God, it may be answered, first, because he rose by his own power. He had power to lay down his life, and he had power to take it again. John x. 18. This is not inconsistent with the fact taught in so many other passages, that he was raised by the power of the Father, because what the Father does the Son does likewise; creation, and all other external works, are ascribed indifferently to the Father, Son, and Spirit. But in the second place, as Christ had openly declared himself to be the Son of God, his rising from the dead was the seal of God to the truth of that declaration. Had he continued under the power of death, God would thereby have disallowed his claim to be his Son; but as he raised him from the dead, he publicly acknowledged him; saying, Thou art my Son, this day have I declared thee such." Charles Hodge: *A Commentary on the Epistle to the Romans.* new ed. 1882. p. 29. I wonder why our greatest preachers never preach on, or at least never publish a sermon on, this faith-assuring text? See, for two noteworthy exceptions, G. Campbell Morgan, in the *Westminster Pulpit.* IV. 129–136; H. P. Liddon: *Sermons on Some Words of St. Paul.* London. 1898. pp. 1–16.
83. Romans 4:25.
84. R. M'Cheyne Egar: *The Gospel of a Risen Saviour.* pp. 298, 299. See also J. H. Newman, "Christ's Resurrection the Source of our Justification," in his *Lectures on Justification.* Lect. IX, W. J. Sparrow-Simpson, *ut supra,* 302, 303.
85. John 5:25–29, etc.

86. Philippians 3:21.
87. Alfred Barry: *The Manifold Witness for Christ.* New York. 1880. p. 139. On the relation of the doctrine of rewards to Christ's resurrection, see R. M'Cheyne Egar, *ut supra,* pp. 314, 316.
88. John Locke: *A Second Vindication of the Reasonableness of Christianity. Works.* 11th ed. London. 1812. Vol. VII. pp. 339–342. Since reading Locke's essay, I have discovered a very comprehensive discussion of all the various aspects of Locke's understanding of Christ's Resurrection, and ours, in W. J. Sparrow-Simpson, *ibid.,* pp. 378–382.
89. H. W. H. Knott, in *Dictionary of American Biography.* Vol. VII. New York. 1937. p. 584.
90. Simon Greenleaf: *The Testimony of the Evangelists Examined by the Rules of Evidence Administered in Courts of Justice.* New York. 1874. pp. 28–31.
91. This statement by Lord Lindhurst was sent to Mr. E. H. Blakeney, of Winchester College, by the late Bishop H. C. G. Moule. Reference to the correspondence appeared in a British periodical, *Dawn,* some few years ago. I have since had it confirmed in a letter from Mr. Blakeney. In Marty Amoy's *The Domestic and Artistic Life of John Copley and Reminiscences of His Son, Lord Lindhurst, High Chancellor of Great Britain* (London. 1882. pp. 438, 439) occurs the interesting note—"A record of Lindhurst's belief in the truth of religion, and his view of the scheme of redemption, was found in his own handwriting after his death, in the drawer of his writing table." (Lord Lindhurst died October 11, 1863, at the age of 91.) I would presume that this statement concerning the resurrection of Christ would be a part of this document, but I have failed to find a printed copy of this record of his faith.
92. Thomas Arnold: *Sermons on the Christian Life. Its Hopes, Its Fears, and Its Close.* 6th ed. London. 1859. p. 324.
93. B. F. Westcott: *The Gospel of the Resurrection.* 4th ed. London. 1879. pp. 4–6.
94. Sir Ambrose Fleming: *Miracles and Science. The Resurrection of Christ.* London. n.d. pp. 11, 12, 15.
95. Howard A. Kelly: *A Scientific Man and the Bible.* Philadelphia. 1925. p. 20.
96. William Lyon Phelps: *Human Nature and the Gospel.* pp. 131, 132. R. M'Cheyne Egar, *ut supra,* pp. 241, 242 gives a remarkable testimony from the famous historian, Johann von Muller, in which he says that he relates, in a letter to his friend Charles Bonnet, in the year 1782, how he had been led to read the New Testament in his systematic perusal of ancient authors, and there discovered the historic key for which he had been long searching. "The light which struck Paul with blindness," he says, "on the way to Damascus was not more strange—more surprising to him, than it was to me, when I suddenly discovered the fulfillment of all hopes, the highest perfection of philosophy, the explanation of all revolutions, the key to all the seeming contradictions of the physical and moral world. . . . The whole world seemed to be ordered for the sole purpose of furthering the religion of the Redeemer; and if this religion is not Divine, I understand nothing at all. I have read no book on this subject; but hitherto, in all my study of ancient times, I have always felt the want of something, and it was not till I

knew our Lord that all was clear to me; with Him there is nothing which I am not able to solve. Pardon me for making to you the eulogy of the sun, as a blind man would do it, who all at once had received the gift of sight." The source he gives for this is Naville: *La Vie Eternelle*. Quatrième ed., pp. 211–213.

97. *Memoir of Sir James Y. Simpson, Bart., with an Account of the Funeral and Funeral Sermon*. Edinburgh. 1870. p. 31.
98. Martin Niemoeller: *God Is My Fuehrer*. New York. 1941. p. 191.
99. Sverre Norborg: *What Is Christianity?* Minneapolis. 1936. pp. 69, 70.
100. Acts 4:33.
101. James MacGregor: *The Apology of the Christian Religion*. Edinburgh. 1891. p. 319. It is amazing how in the vast literature of our generation on the subject of preaching and missionary activity, almost nothing is ever said about the pre-eminent importance of frequently and powerfully setting forth the great historic fact of the resurrection of Jesus Christ our Lord. The only notable exception with which I am acquainted is found in some words of Dr. H. Kramer of Java, uttered at the Jerusalem Meeting of the International Missionary Council. March 24–April 8, 1928. *The Christian Life and Message*. Vol. I. New York. 1928. p. 283: "One of the faults of the Church in the past had been that it had placed too exclusive emphasis upon the Cross and Reconciliation. Christianity had to find its central fact in the Resurrection. St. Paul said that without the Resurrection all our preaching was vain. Even preaching about the Cross and reconciliation was vain unless they were also glorious confessors of the Resurrection. The Resurrection was a deed of God in purely divine dimensions. The Cross was divine and human because it was impossible without the background of human wretchedness. The essence of Christianity was in the Resurrection. On the other hand, our emphasis upon the cross would thereby not become lessened, but rather would shine out more clearly."
102. R. M'Cheyne Egar: *The Gospel of a Risen Saviour*. p. 260. Warfield, nearly fifty years ago, foresaw that "in such vital facts as the resurrection of our Lord, and the miraculous context of the life of Christ generally . . . in this part of the apologetic field, probably, a new decisive battle will have to be fought in the interests of the possibility of theology."
103. John 20:27. The word is *apistos,* as in Matt. 17:17; Mark 9:19; Luke 9:41. "Faith in Jesus Christ is indeed faith in a Person. But it is faith in Him as what? If it be answered as Incarnate, as Mediator, these answers represent historic facts. Faith in His Person, in the Christian sense, cannot be separated from faith in His Incarnation and His Death and His Resurrection. For these facts are inseparable from the history of Redemption. They are of such a character that, without them, faith in Christ would be impossible." W. J. Sparrow-Simpson: *The Resurrection and Modern Thought*. London. 1911. p. 457.
104. B. F. Westcott: *The Gospel According to St. John*. London. 1882. p. 296. There is a remarkable statement concerning permanent doubt by the psychologist, Dr. Edwin A. Starbuck, in his article, "Doubt," in James Hastings: *Encyclopaedia of Religion and Ethics*. Vol. IV. p. 864, which should often

be repeated. "The danger of doubting is not only that it may become a fixed habit, but that interest may center in the process itself as severed from the complex of normal mental activities for healthy enthusiasms and become a mania. Pathologists have accepted this as a special type of insanity. Its symptoms are a state of persistent, intellectual unrest, a devouring metaphysical hunger, a morbid anxiety and mental dissatisfaction, accompanied not infrequently by a Hamlet-like paralysis of the will."

105. F. Godet: *Commentary on the Gospel of John*. II. 424.

106. Romans 10:9. I know of *nothing* of real significance that has been written on this verse—commentaries are totally inadequate. The following is the *only* comment I have been able to discover worth quoting: "Let that fact be apprehended in its momentous relations to God's justice and mercy, on the one hand, and to man's sins, sorrows, and hopes, on the other, and it will be found to have within itself all the elements of a grand ethical revolution in the soul and in the life. If Christ was really raised from among the dead by the glory of the Father (Rom. 6, 4), then assuredly the work, which received its consummation in the crucifixion, must, in its essence and its aims, have been, and must still be, well-pleasing to Him with whom we have to do; and therefore the adequate basis of spiritual security and peace to unrighteous men penitentially conscious of their unrighteousness." James Morison: *Exposition of the Ninth Chapter of the Epistle to the Romans*. new ed. London. 1888. pp. 231, 232. On the subject of the importance of Christ's resurrection, there are some worth-while pages in Harris E. Kirk's first and best book, *The Religion of Power*. New York. 1916. pp. 191–198.

107. Quoted by W. J. Sparrow-Simpson, "Adolf Harnack," in *Hibbert Journal*. April. 1938. p. 396.
Note: Canon Liddon, a painstakingly careful scholar, used in one of his sermons the remarkable illustration that follows, and his acceptance of it as genuine warrants us, I believe, in likewise accepting it as recording an actual episode: "During the years that followed the outbreak of the French Revolution, and the revolt against Christianity which accompanied it, there was an extraordinary activity in some sections of French society directed to projecting a religion that might, it was hoped, take the place of Christianity. New philanthropic enthusiasm, new speculative enthusiasms, were quite the order of the day. On one occasion a projector of one of these schemes came to Talleyrand. Talleyrand, you will remember, was a bishop who had turned sceptic, and so had devoted himself to politics. But, whatever else is to be said of him, Talleyrand possessed, in a very remarkable degree, a keen perception of the proportion of things, and of what is and is not possible in this human world. Well, his visitor observed, by way of complaint to Talleyrand, how hard it was to start a new religion, even though its tenets and its efforts were obviously directed to promoting the social and personal improvement of mankind. 'Surely,' said Talleyrand, with a fine smile, 'surely, it cannot be so difficult as you think.' 'How so?' said the friend. 'Why,' said Talleyrand, 'the matter is simple: you have only yourself to get crucified, or anyhow put to death, and then at your own time rise from

the dead, and you will have no difficulty.' " H. P. Liddon: *Sermons.* (*The Contemporary Pulpit Library.*) New York. 1888. p. 78. R. M'Cheyne Egar, in his *Gospel of a Risen Saviour,* p. 32, also records this incident, and says the party interviewing Talleyrand was Larevelliere-Lepeaux. See also, *Natural Religion,* by the author of "Ecce Homo" (Sir John Robert Seeley). 3rd ed. Boston. 1880. p. 173.

CHAPTER IX

1. Benjamin Ide Wheeler: *Dionysos and Immortality.* Boston. 1899. p. 21.
2. Quoted in C. H. Moore: *The Religious Thought of the Greeks.* p. 57.
3. Clifford Herschell More: *The Religious Thought of the Greeks from Homer to the Triumph of Christianity.* 2nd ed. Cambridge. 1925. p. 58. For Plato's conception of a future judgment of the soul, see his *Phaedrus,* 249 (Jowett, II. 125, 126), and the *Republic,* 614 (Jowett, III. 511–513). Also, Cicero: *Tusculam,* I. 30, 72; Virgil: *Aeneid* VI. 151, 152.
4. Rhadamanthus, a son of Zeus and Europa, was brother of King Minos of Crete. "In consequence of his justice throughout life, he became, after his death, one of the judges in the lower world." L. Schmitz, in Wm. Smith: *Dictionary of Greek and Roman Biography and Mythology.* London. 1839. Vol. III. p. 646. Aeacus, son of Zeus and Aegina, was also noted in Greece for his justice and piety. See the article "Hades," in *Harper's Dictionary of Classical Literature and Antiquities.* New York. 1827. pp. 760, 761; and Franz Cumont: *After Life in Roman Paganism.* New Haven. 1922.
5. For an illuminating discussion of "the weighing of the soul" in Egyptian eschatology, see George St. Clair: *Creation Records Discovered in Egypt.* London. 1898. pp. 474–479; Stephen Langdon, "Babylonian Eschatology," in *Essays in Modern Theology and Related Subjects.* New York. 1911.
6. *Oxford English Dictionary.* Vol. V. Oxford. 1933. pp. 617–621.
7. James Edwin Creighton: *An Introductory Logic.* 3rd ed. rev. and enl., New York. 1910. pp. 44, 45.
8. Deut. 16:18; cf. 1:16; Judges 2:16, 18; II Chron. 19:6.
9. Proverbs 20:8.
10. In reference to our Lord's trial, Matt. 27:19; John 19:13, in reference to a trial before Gallio, Acts 18:12–17; and, before Caesar, Acts 25:10, 20; 26:6.
11. Deut. 25:1.
12. Isaiah 33:22.
13. Genesis 18:25. It is strange how almost all modern commentators totally ignore this initial declaration of God's righteousness. Calvin is a welcome exception. His comment begins with this characteristically striking sentence —"He does not here teach God His duty, as if anyone should say to a judge, 'See what thy office requires, what is worthy, of this place, what suits thy character,' but he reasons from the nature of God, that it is impossible for Him to intend anything unjust."
14. Romans 2:16. The *secrets of men,* Hodge defines as "the things which have escaped the knowledge of others; those hidden deeds of the heart and life, which are the surest criterion of character. The searching character of this

judgment; its justice, as not guided by mere external appearance; and its contrast with mere human judgments, are all intimated by this expression." Charles Hodge: *A Commentary on the Epistle to the Romans.* new ed. 1882. p. 87.

15. On the subject of some of the great divine judgments of the past, see, especially a new book, *The Severity of God. A Study of Judgment Human and Divine,* by D. E. Hart-Davies, sometime Scholar of Corpus Christi College, Cambridge. London. n.d. (c. 1943). Also, an earlier work by Grant Stroh, *When God Comes Down to Earth.* Chicago. 1914. For judgments on Egypt, see Genesis 15:14; Exodus 6:6; 7:4; Acts 7:7; etc., on Moab, Ezek. 25:11, on Jerusalem, Ezek. 5:8, 10, 15; 14:21; 16:41; 28:22. How contrary to all evidence is a recent statement by a well-known writer on Biblical subjects—"So far as actual history attests the situation, it would appear that the Deity has not chosen to use violence to discipline mankind in the ways of righteousness." Shirley Jackson Case: *The Christian Philosophy of History.* Chicago. 1943. p. 212.
16. Job 19:29.
17. Rev. 19:11.
18. I Chron. 16:14; Psalm 105:7.
19. I Chron. 16:33; Psalm 96:13; 98:9.
20. For careful differentiation between the various judgments of the Bible, see, W. Trotter: *Plain Papers on Prophetic and Other Subjects* (new ed., rev.), pp. 564–577; William Evans: *After Death—What Then?* New York. pp 127–152. For a recent statement insisting that all these judgments occur at the same time, see L. Berkhof: *Systematic Theology.* 2nd ed. Grand Rapids. 1941. pp. 730–737; and, earlier, R. H. Charles: *A Critical History of the Doctrine of a Future Life.* London. 1899. pp. 336–339. There is a good chapter on "The Judgment and the Eternal State," in William Kelly: *Lectures on the Second Coming and Kingdom,* pp. 277–320.
21. The phrase "a day of judgment," occurs in Matt. 10:15; 11:22, 24; 12:36; in the Gospel of John we have "the last day" in 6:39, 40, 44, 54; 11:24; 12:48; and, elsewhere, "that day," Matt. 7:22; Luke 6:23; 10:12; 21:34.
22. Romans 2:5; cf. "the great day," Jude 6.
23. II Peter 2:9; 3:7.
24. I John 4:17; Rev. 11:18. On the phrase, "boldness in the day of judgment," Professor Robert S. Candlish says it refers not to "boldness prospectively when the day comes, but present boldness in the view of it now." *The First Epistle of John Expounded in a Series of Lectures.* Edinburgh. 1866. p. 379; see the entire discussion, pp. 379–383.
25. John 5:22, 23b, 27. "That the Father judges no one does not mean that while the Father quickens He does not judge, or that the Son alone, without the Father and apart from Him, does the judging. This would contradict that the Son does nothing of Himself. (v. 19.) The Father's giving the judgment to the Son shows that it is indeed the Father's. But he exercises it by giving it to the Son." R. C. H. Lenski: *The Interpretation of St. John's Gospel.* Columbus. 1931. p. 372.
26. Acts 10:42.

27. Romans 2:16; II Tim. 4:1.
28. William Milligan: *The Ascension and Heavenly Priesthood of Our Lord.* London. 1892. pp. 54–57.
29. Jonathan Edwards: *The Final Judgment.* In the *Works of President Edwards.* new ed. London. 1817. Vol. IV. p. 455.
30. Karl Barth: *Credo.* New York. 1936. pp. 124, 125. "The terrible doom of the wicked will therefore not be the ignorant stroke of one who does not know what life on earth is, but the calm decision of One who by His own experience has learned accurately to estimate all that extenuates guilt." Marcus Dods: *Christ and Man.* London. 1909. p. 258.
31. Willibald Beyschlag: *New Testament Theology.* Eng. tr. Edinburgh. 1899. Vol. I. p. 191.
32. Ecclesiastes 12:14. "All the doings of men, however private, however anxiously concealed from their fellow-creatures, performed in the dead of night, and far from any human eye;—and all their thoughts, and desires, and purposes, though studiously kept within their bosoms, and never whispered to human ear. Nothing shall escape detection and disclosure. The eye of omniscience having witnessed all, and the Mind that embraces present, past, and future with equal minuteness and equal certainty, having retained all; the sentence pronounced on each individual will be founded in a complete and unerring knowledge of all that he has been, and of all that he has done." Ralph Wardlaw: *Lectures Expository and Practical on the Book of Ecclesiastes.* Philadelphia. 1868. p. 416. Luther here is excellent: "The author does not speak here only of the judgment at the last day, but, of judgment in general. There is a judgment and an hour for everything with God, and no one can escape. Wherefore Arius and all heretics are already judged. But at the last day it will be made still clearer in the presence of all creatures, angels and men, that even now in the day of visitation, God the Lord has laid bare their sin and disgrace, that in a word, there is no more concealment."
33. Rev. 20:12, 13.
34. Hebrews 13:4.
35. T. W. Manson: *The Teaching of Jesus.* Cambridge. 1935. p. 271, 272.
36. John 3:18; also 5:24. "The standard of judgment is the revelation of God in the Son. Unbelief judges itself because it does not rest on the declaration of God's character and will, His love and grace, in the name of the Only-begotten Son. The revelation of the Father through the Son ought to carry a man's belief with it. He who does not believe is already judged in the fact that he does not believe." George Reith: *The Gospel According to St. John, with Introduction and Notes.* Edinburgh. n.d. p. 52.
37. John 12:48. "It is the whole presentation of Christ in His gospel which is meant. The hearing of this word, therefore, is not a mere incident in a man's life, it is the crisis of his history. . . . Jesus warns of the subjective judgment in conscience, when at the last the word of truth, which was set aside, shall come back armed with the scourged of evil memories. The unbeliever bears his judgment with him. It is written in himself, and will be inseparable from himself; he cannot escape from it." *ibid.* p. 78.

38. II Thess. 2:12.
39. I seem to have misplaced this reference, but similar ideas are to be found in his *Systematic Theology*. III. 847.
40. John 3:36.
41. I Cor. 16:22.
42. Psalm 9:8; 9:4; 50:6; 72:2; 96:10; 98:9; 119:7; Isa. 11:4; Jer. 11:20.
43. Psalm 119:137–44. This has been called "the hymn of God's righteousness." Each verse begins with the Hebrew letter *Tsadhe* which is the first letter of the Hebrew word *tsaddek*, meaning *righteousness*. See, e.g., Jehovah-Tsidkenu (Jer. 23:6), i.e., the Lord of our Righteousness.
44. Jer. 11:20.
45. II Timothy 4:8; Rom. 2:2.
46. I Peter 2:23.
47. Revelation 16:7; 19:2.
48. Revelation 19:11.
49. Hermann Cremer: *Biblico-Theological Lexicon of New Testament Greek*. 4th English edition. Edinburgh. 1895. pp. 183–190. pp. 184, 188. See the extensive treatment of the Greek New Testament vocabulary of righteousness in Ernest DeWitt Burton: *A Critical and Exegetical Commentary on the Epistle to the Galatians*. New York. 1920. pp. 460–474. "Neither justice nor righteousness is a matter of arbitrary will. They are revelations of the inmost nature of God, the one in the form of moral requirement, the other in the form of judicial sanction. As God cannot but demand of His creatures that they be like Him in moral character, so He cannot but enforce the law which He imposes upon them. Justice just as much binds God to punish as it binds the sinner to be punished. All arbitrariness is excluded here. . . . God can cease to demand purity and to punish sin only when He ceases to be holy, that is, only when He ceases to be God." A. H. Strong: *Systematic Theology*. Philadelphia. 1907. pp. 292, 293.
50. John 5:30.
51. Euripides: *Ion*. 429.
52. On the righteousness of Christ, see, e.g., Matt. 3:15; Rom. 3:21–26; I Pet. 2:23; I John 2:1, 29; 3:7.
53. I Cor. 1:30.
54. Rev. 16:5.
55. John Pearson: *An Exposition of the Creed*. Vol. II. p. 125.
56. Hebrews 10:27. The word translated *expectation* (*ekdoche*), occurs only here in the New Testament. The R. V. mg., instead of *fierceness*, reads *jealousy*, Westcott remarking, "the word suggests the thought of love which has been wronged." B. F. Westcott: *The Epistle to the Hebrews*. 2nd ed. London. 1892. p. 328. "A dread and shuddering anticipation of future punishment afflicts already the inmost soul of the apostate." F. Delitzsch: *Commentary on the Epistle to the Hebrews*. 3rd ed. Edinburgh. 1887. Vol. II. pp. 185, 186.
57. J. J. Greenough: *The Doctrine of the Last Things*. London. 1908. pp. 128–130. "It is certain matter of universal experience, that the general method of divine administration is, forewarning us, or giving us capacities to fore

see, with more or less clearness, that if we act so and so, we shall have such enjoyments, if so and so, such sufferings and giving us those enjoyments, and making us feel those sufferings, in consequence of our action." Joseph Butler: *The Analogy of Religion.* I. ii. 3 (ed. Gladstone. p. 50).

58. H. G. Wells: *Experiment in Autobiography.* New York. 1934. pp. 45, 322, 424. See also, pp. 29, 69, 126, 128–31, 146, 150, 267.
59. Hebrews 9:27. "After life is done, there is no living it over again a few more times; what awaits each one at death is God's verdict, either acquittal or condemnation." R. C. H. Lenski: *The Interpretation of the Epistle to the Hebrews.* Columbus. 1938. p. 323. The fact that there are almost no sermons by the great modern preachers of the Church on this text tells its own story.
60. C. H. Dodd, in, *The Kingdom of God and History.* Chicago. 1938.
61. H. P. Liddon: *Advent in St. Paul's.* new ed. London. 1896. pp. 18, 19. See also in the same volume, Sermons XXXV–XXXVIII. C. H. Dodd relates judgment to creation itself. "The prophetic view of God's dealings, as it looks back to creation, also looks forward to the consummation, the Day of the Lord." C. H. Dodd, in *The Kingdom of God and History.* Chicago. 1938. p. 21.
62. Robert Flint: *Theism.* 7th ed. Edinburgh. 1889. p. 220.
63. *Chicago Sun.* July 24, 1943.
64. A. A. Hodge: *The Atonement.* Philadelphia. 1867. pp. 62, 63.
65. See also, Christopher Dawson: *The Judgment of the Nations.* New York. 1942.
66. James Denney: *Studies in Theology.* New York. 1901. pp. 239–241.
67. William Caven: *Christ's Teaching Concerning the Last Things.* p. 60.

67a. Reinhold Niebuhr: *The Nature and Destiny of Man.* New York. 1943. p. 294. See also D. R. Davies: *On to Orthodoxy.* pp. 156–158.

68. Quotations are from *World Dominion.* Dec. 1942.
69. See, e.g., "The Challenge of International Lawlessness" by Robert H. Jackson, Associate Justice of the Supreme Court of the U. S., in *International Conciliation.* Nov. 1941. No. 374. pp. 683–691.
70. William F. Ogburn, "The Future of Man in the Life of his Past: the viewpoint of a Sociologist," in *Scientific Monthly,* April, 1931, pp. 296, 297. Dr. Ogburn was a Professor of Sociology in Columbia University, 1919–1927; and has held a professorship in the same subject in the University of Chicago since 1927. He served as President of the American Sociological Society in 1929.
71. Dean W. R. Inge: "Is Sin Obsolete?", in *Christian Century,* Nov. 22, 1923, p. 1511.
72. Bishop Chelmsford, in *The Church of England Newspaper,* Feb. 1943. "One day I think we shall return to these stern doctrines, realizing in them a truth more profound than we now know; and then we shall preach them with conviction, and being convinced ourselves we shall convince others." Roland Allen: *Missionary Methods: St. Paul's or Ours.* London. 1913. p. 102.
73. Matt. 11:21, 22; Luke 10:13, 14.
74. Acts 24:25. "O mighty truth that God is with the ministry, when the kings

of the earth that take counsel together are yet dismayed by it. Who is he that doth not see here something more than human eloquence, when a prisoner becomes the judge and the prince upon the throne becomes the criminal." Charles H. Spurgeon: *New Park Street Pulpit.* 1858. p. 52. "Think what the influences of time and sense are: think what it is to be surrounded by a gay and giddy world: think what it is to have every energy tasked to the uttermost in the discharge of business or in the pursuit of pleasure: think what it is to have passions clamouring within for their gratification, and making it the direct interest of a human soul to forget God, to deny Christ, to disbelieve eternity: and then wonder only, not that the Gospel has so little power, but that it has so much; wonder, not less that so many, who do not obey, fear the Gospel; that so many, as the minister of Christ reasons with them of righteousness and temperance and judgment to come, still, like Felix, tremble." C. J. Vaughan: *The Church of the First Days.* London. 1864. pp. 540, 541. A powerful sermon on this text is to be found in Gypsy Smith's: *As Jesus Passed By.* New York. 1905. pp. 139–150.

75. John Pearson: *An Exposition of the Creed.* Vol. II. pp. 137–138.
76. *ad Demetriadem,* ep. cxlii. My attention was drawn to this by its quotation in W. Lindsay Alexander's *St. Paul at Athens* (Edinburgh, 1865), pp. 264, 265.
77. John A. Hutton: *The Victory over Victory.* New York. n.d. p. 9.
78. Rudolf Stier: *The Words of the Apostles.* Trans. from the 2nd German ed. Edinburgh. 1869. p. 306.
79. II Cor. 5:11. On the *necessity* for an end of this age of man's history, the following is the most recent important affirmation: "From the Christian point of view the end of history is certain to come to pass—whether in connection with the physical end of mankind or previous to it, we do not know. . . . History needs an end which is itself beyond history, because thus alone can the purpose of God fully be carried out. Everything in history serves God's glory, but in most cases its particular meaning and function are not manifest as to most of the success and failures of history, we do not know how they are connected with the purpose of God. Similarly we know that in the body of Christ every individual member has eternal significance, and that we do not work merely for future generations. But if there were no opportunity of knowing exactly what our life was meant for, and contributed to, our historical existence would not differ from that of any plant or animal which serves to build up the life of this globe. Hence this earthly historical life must be followed by a timeless, yet conscious, communion with Christ." Otto Piper: *God in History.* New York. 1939. pp. 176–177. "It seems to me," Bishop Gore once wrote, "that any believer in the God of the prophets and of our Lord must believe with them in a Day of God, as bringing the present age, of human history, to its climax." Charles Gore: *Belief in Christ.* 1923. p. 149.

CHAPTER X

1. Thomas Carlyle: *The Life of Friedrich Schiller. Works.* (Crowell edition.) Vol. IV. pp. 42, 43.
2. Romans 15:13. All the more important, larger commentaries on the Epistle to the Romans strangely ignore this most pregnant phrase. In contrast with this see the very rich treatment of Thomas Chalmers in his inimitable *Lectures on the Epistle of Paul the Apostle to the Romans.* Glasgow. n.d. Vol. IV. pp. 390–397.
3. II Chron. 29:30, 36; 30:21, 23, 25, 26. The single exception is found in II Chron. 20:22.
4. Psalm 40:1–3.
5. A. W. W. Dale: *The Life of R. W. Dale of Birmingham.* New York. 1899. p. 319. The three preceding paragraphs I have taken verbatim from my *Glorious Revival under King Hezekiah.* (Grand Rapids. 1937.) pp. 43–45.
6. Luke 1:79; 2:14.
7. Luke 2:10.
8. John 15:11; 16:22–24; 17:13. On 15:11 see Andrew Murray: *Abide in Christ.* 173–179.
9. John 14:27; 16:33. P. T. Forsyth, shortly after the beginning of the First World War, in a characteristically profound sermon on John 16:33, concluded with these challenging sentences: "It is a bold thing to believe, in the midst of such a world of sin, with the memory of such a past as we feel, in the presence of such a holy God as from the cross makes sin so guilty and judgment so dreadful, with the wretched experience of the tough, invincible, recurrent power of sin in us. It is a bold thing in the face of the proud, progressive, aggressive, warlike world. It is an act of great courage, in the face of all that to-day to believe in the love and grace of God. For some who realize none of these things, it may even be an act of groundless audacity. But, if we do realize them, if we realize God's judgment, we need all the moral courage God can give us to believe in a thing so tremendous as the total victory over such a world already won, and already ours, even if we sometimes relapse. The cross of Christ was a thing more awful than even a European war. All things are ours, even that victory, that elevation over sin, and even our relapses cannot rob us of it. It is easy to believe with a poor sense of what the holy is, of what it makes sin to be, of what the world is, and can do. But it needs the courage of the cross to believe (at such an hour as this, say) in the completeness of the cross and its eternal victory. Our comfort is that it is the victory of the cross which reveals the true awfulness of our sin, and we realize evil truly only in the light of its conquest. The damning light is the saving light. Therefore, the more you fear, the more the cross is working in you—the cross' judgment is the effect of its grace. Therefore, be of good cheer. It is more than an individual calm; it is the Church's collective confidence on the scale of the world for the destiny of the world. The evil world will not win at last, because it failed to win at the only time it ever could. Be of

good cheer. It is a vanquished world. Christ has overcome it. It can make tribulation, but desolation it can never make." *Christian World Pulpit.* Feb. 17, 1915. Vol. 87. "Oh! what a confession are the rush and recklessness, the fever and the fret of this nineteenth century, and of this great, roaring, busy city in which we live! You go about our streets and look men in the face, and you see how all manner of hunger desires and eager wishes have imprinted themselves there. And now and then—how seldom! —you come across a face out of which beams a deep and settled peace. How many of you are there that dare not be quiet because then you are most troubled? How many of you are there that dare not reflect because then you are wretched? How many of you that are uncomfortable when alone, either because you are utterly vacuous, or because then you are surrounded by the ghosts of ugly thoughts that murder sleep and stuff every pillow with thorns? The world will bring you excitement; Christ, and Christ alone will bring you rest." Alexander Maclaren: *The Holy of Holies.* p. 142.

10. John 20:19–21, 26. "The two great blessings flowed together. In His wounds, He spoke the peace. Seeing Him, they knew the joy." H. C. G. Moule: *Jesus and the Resurrection.* 4th ed. London. 1905. p. 97. On v. 20, see a great sermon in James Iverach: *The Other Side of Greatness.* New York. 1907. pp. 85–101.
11. Romans 15:33; 16:20; II Cor. 13:11; Rom. 1:7; I Cor. 1:3; II Cor. 1:2; etc.
12. Romans 5:1.
13. Colossians 1:20.
14. Philippians 4:7.
15. Robert Flint: *Theism.* 7th ed. Edinburgh. 1889. p. 301.
16. Luke 24:17, 52. The experiences of the disciples which carried them from a mood of sadness to one of abounding joy, as recorded in the last chapter of Luke's gospel, is deserving of careful study.
17. John Bunyan quoted in David Smith: *The Pilgrim's Hospice.* p. 120. It seems to me that the entire life of Bunyan, after his conversion, is a living testimony to the abiding reality of the peace and joy that come with faith in Christ.
18. Thomas C. Upham: *Life, Religious Opinions and Experience of Madame Guyon.* new ed. n.d. pp. 381, 382.
19. Charles Edward Stowe: *Life of Harriet Beecher Stowe.* New York. Boston. 1890. pp. 48, 49, 418, 507, 508.
20. Charles H. Spurgeon: *The Metropolitan Tabernacle Pulpit.* 1877. XXIII. p. 644.
21. G. T. Studd, in Dr. and Mrs. Howard Taylor: *Hudson Taylor and the China Inland Mission.* 1934. p. 387.

CHAPTER XI

1. Philip Schaff: *History of the Christian Church.* Vol. I. p. 7.
2. Eph. 6:11, 13a; I Cor. 16:13; cf. I Tim. 6:20.

3. B. B. Warfield, "Christian Supernaturalism" in *Presbyterian and Reformed Review*. Jan. 1897. Vol. VIII. pp. 71, 72.
4. Philippians 1:16, 17. Referring to the latter, Vincent remarks, "the defense was made for establishment or confirmation, and resulted in it." M. R. Vincent: *A Critical and Exegetical Commentary on the Epistles to the Philippians and Philemon*. New York. 1897. p. 10.
5. This entire ordination service may be found in any Prayer Book of the Church of England or the Protestant Episcopal Church of our own country. Bishop Westcott, towards the close of his life, speaking to clergymen ordained with such solemn vows as these, gave an exhortation that seems almost prophetic, one we need to hearken to today even more than when the words were uttered: "I charge you, then, to prize and use your peculiar spiritual heritage which was most solemnly committed to you at your ordination. Our English Church represents in its origin and in its growth the study of the Bible. In the study of the Bible lies the hope of its future. For the study of the Bible in the sense in which I have indicated is a momentous importance at the present time, and it is rare; there is much discussion about the Bible, but, as I fear, little knowledge of it. . . . Our hearts again constantly fail us for fear of the things which are coming on the world. The Bible inspires us with an unfailing hope. We are yet further perplexed by conflicts of reasoning, by novelties of doctrines, by strange conclusions of bold controversialists. The Bible provides us with a sure touchstone of truth, while

   The intellectual power, through words and things,
   Goes sounding on, a dim and perilous way,

   and brings us back to a living fellowship with Him who is the Truth." Arthur Westcott: *Life and Letters of Brooke Foss Westcott*. London. 1903. II. 266, 267.
6. II Timothy 4:7.
7. Jude 3.
8. J. I. Mombert, in, G. F. C. Fronmüller: *The Epistle General of Jude*. Eng. tr. 1867. p. 13.
9. Phil. 1:27. "Here the metaphor seems to be drawn from the combats of the Roman amphitheatre. Like criminals or captives the believers are condemned to fight for their lives: against them are arrayed the ranks of worldliness and sin: only unflinching courage and steady combination can win the victory against such odds." J. B. Lightfoot: *St. Paul's Epistle to the Philippians*. London. 1896. p. 106. See also Robert Rainy's chapter, "Undaunted and United Steadfastness," in his *The Epistle to the Philippians* (1893). pp. 72–92.
10. II Cor. 10:4, 5. Plummer defines the strongholds as "the fortresses which hinder the success of the campaign, i.e., all the prejudices and evil practices which resist the influence of the gospel." Alfred Plummer: *A Critical and Exegetical Commentary on the Second Epistle to the Corinthians*. New York. 1915. p. 277.
11. G. Campbell Morgan, in *Westminster Pulpit*. Vol. III. (1908.) p. 148.
12. Romans 10:9. The primary place of oral utterance in the life of any Chris-

tian is indicated, e.g., by the frequent occurrence of such words as *tell, speak, say, declare, proclaim, preach, teach, confess, witness,* and the many passages in which occur such words as *lips, tongue, mouth,* etc. We need to testify boldly to the gospel (1) because of many who are speaking against it—see Luke 2:34; Acts 28:22; etc.; (2) because of such vast opportunities for speaking today, e.g., the radio, etc.; (3) because at the end of this age the arch-enemy of God will appear, *speaking* great swelling words against the Almighty, Dan. 7:8, 20; Rev. 13:5, 6. Note the prayer for boldness in such a ministry, on the part of the early Christians, e.g., Acts 4:29; 9:29; 18:9; Eph. 6:19.

13. I John 4:3; II John 7.
14. Durant Drake: *Invitation to Philosophy*. New York. 1933. p. 441.
15. See, e.g., I John 1:1; 2:3; 2:13, 14; 4:2, 6–8; Eph. 3:19; II Tim. 1:12; etc.
16. E.g., Acts 4:1–22; 5:17–42; 6:8–8:3; 12:1–19.
17. William Lyon Phelps, "As I Like It," *Scribner's Magazine*. July, 1929, p. 94.
18. James Denney: *The Death of Christ*. New York. 1903. pp. 109–111. The verses Denney quotes are, Gal. 1:4, 8; Ex. 20:3; Acts 4:12; I John 5:12; Matt. 11:27. See also a strong chapter, "The Anathema," in G. G. Findlay's *The Epistle to the Galatians*. pp. 34–49. "The intolerance of the Church does not involve any interference with liberty; on the contrary, it means the preservation of liberty. . . . A true Christian Church is radically intolerant. It presents the gospel of Jesus Christ not merely as one way of salvation, but as the only way. It cannot make common cause with other faiths. It cannot agree not to proselytize. Its appeal is universal, and admits of no exceptions. All are lost in sin; none may be saved except by the way set forth in the Gospel." J. Gresham Machen, "The Responsibility of the Church in our New Age," *Annals of the American Academy of Political and Social Science*. Jan., 1933. Vol. 165. p. 45.
19. Charles A. Briggs: *Biblical Studies*. 2nd ed. New York. 1844. pp. 11–13.
20. Joseph Parker, in the *Contemporary Pulpit*. 1884. Vol. II. p. 279.
21. Joseph Parker: *The People's Bible,* Vol. XVI. pp. 415, 416.
22. Acts 19:20. G. Campbell Morgan: *The Acts of the Apostles*. pp. 456, 457.
23. John S. Howson: *The Metaphors of St. Paul*. London. 1883. p. 15. Hodge rightly declares that all the triumphs of the Church "over sin and error have been effected by the word of God. So long as she uses this and relies on it alone, she goes on conquering; but when anything else, be it reason, science, tradition, or the commandments of men, is allowed to take its place or share its office, then the church is at the mercy of the adversary." Charles Hodge: *A Commentary on the Epistle to the Ephesians*. New York. 1857. p. 389.
25. Bernard Iddings Bell, "An American Forecast," *Atlantic Monthly*. December, 1944. Vol. 174. pp. 64–67.

25a. Alexander Whyte, *Record of Christian Work,* XVII. (1898.) p. 399.

25b. Marcus Dods: *The First Epistle to the Corinthians*. n.d. p. 87.

26. Nehemiah 4:1–3.
27. Nehemiah 13:4, 5, 7–9. Every student of American Christianity recognizes that the one who most frequently proclaimed the great truth of God's

love was Dwight L. Moody, yet it was this same Moody who declared, "God being my helper, I will never own fellowship with a man who denies the deity of my God and Saviour Jesus Christ, or sneers at His atonement." William R. Moody: *The Life of Dwight L. Moody*. p. 580.

28. "The desecration was the more pronounced as this was the very room which had been set apart for the offerings of the people, both those used for sacrifice and those for the support of the four groups of temple officers." Loring W. Batten: *A Critical and Exegetical Commentary on the Books of Ezra and Nehemiah*. New York. 1913. p. 288.

29. *International Journal of Religious Education*. October, 1944. A similar illustration of the larger amount of space given to secular subjects in religious periodicals may be found in *The Intercollegian,* which has for its subtitle, *A Monthly Journal of Student Christian Life*. The issue of July, 1940, is one of twenty pages, three columns to a page. On page 4 is some devotional matter under the heading, "Be Still and Know," with the following references for reading, I Cor. 12:31; 13; I John 4:7–12; 18:21. This is followed by a prayer by Dr. William Adams Brown, in which the name of Christ does not appear. The first article of length is called "The Church's Message to Labor," and here we have the astonishing statement, "They will express their discontent with any economic order wherein human worth and brotherhood are violated, etc. by the prayer—'Our Father . . . give us this day our daily bread and forgive us.' " On pages 5 and 6, is an article "Workers and the Church." On pages 7 and 9, is another article called "The Laborer Is Worthy," with some words from Mr. William L. Green, president of the American Federation of Labor; the column is headed, "Nobody is above unionism.' " Another column is given to words by John L. Lewis. On pages 10, 11, and 12, is material under the heading, "C.I.O. Publicist." On page 13, is a brief paragraph headed, "Worship and Social Action, ending with this sentence, "Not only may we look forward to new revelations of God as we shall come to worship Him after being reconciled with our brothers—after the abolition of race discrimination, economic injustice and war—but we may expect to meet God also as we strive in love to do His Will, as we undertake active programs to bring about social change, and are willing to pay the price to help bring the Kingdom of God on earth." There is nothing here at all for the growth of the soul of a college Christian —nothing to show him the way of salvation—nothing to reveal to him a way of holiness—nothing concerning the person and work of our Lord. Probably for many young college Christians this is the only so-called Christian periodical that comes to their dormitory room; if so, they are certainly starved for true spiritual food.

30. Robert Dick Wilson, in, the *Moody Bible Institute Monthly,* March, 1922. pp. 879, 880.

31. J. Gresham Machen, "The Importance of Christian Scholarship." These lectures first appeared in the *Bible League Quarterly,* c. 1930, and were reprinted in the same quarterly. January–March, 1940, and it is from this reprint I am quoting, pages 15, 16.

32. *Historical Register of the University of Cambridge to 1910*. Cambridge. 1917.

I notice that in the *History of the Christian Church during the Reformation,* by Charles Hardwick (1856; my edition, ed. by W. Stubbs, London. 1894), the legend under the author's name reads—"Late Fellow of St. Catharine's College, Divinity Lecturer at King's College, and Christian Advocate in the University of Cambridge." There was a time, early in our nation's history, when college authorities strove to *save* the faith of their students from the attacks of infidelity. Thus toward the close of the 18th century, Harvard College "actually presented gratis to every student," to counteract the writings of Tom Paine, a copy of Bishop Watson's *Apology for the Bible.* See Samuel Eliot Morison: *Three Centuries of Harvard, 1636–1936.* Cambridge. 1936. p. 185. Bishop Charles Pettit MacIlvaine, in the Preface to his famous *Evidences of Christianity* (1832, and later editions), informs us that he had lectured on the Evidences of Christianity, at the Military Academy at West Point. When the University of the City of New York was founded in 1831, Bp. MacIlvaine was invited to give the series of lectures that form the volume referred to.

33. See the entire section on "An Adequate Program for Christian Literature," Chapter VI in *The Life of the Church,* Volume IV of "The Madras Series." New York. 1939. pp. 276–371. "The theological seminaries, Christian colleges, universities and high schools have their part to play, as the Lindsay Commission on Higher Education in India has suggested. Full scope for the exercise of his gifts should be secured for any possible or actual literary genius. In many areas an editorial board should be formed to discover and develop natural gifts, to read manuscripts and to advise authors and publishing bodies. Such boards, with the help of the National Christian Councils, could secure from churches and missions the liberation for definite periods of church and mission workers who have a contribution to make to Christian literature. . . . We are convinced that a new literature for the training and use of ministers and lay workers is needed in most of the younger churches—a literature not borrowed from the West, but rooted in the racial and cultural backgrounds and the environment of the people among whom the work is to be done. . . . Above all, there should be literature for Christians and non-Christians which deals with the fundamentals of the Christian religion in simple and non-technical language and in thought forms which people steeped in modern culture can understand. Commentaries for the layman on books of the Bible have been mentioned as greatly desirable. In some countries where suitable writers and money are available, a power periodical to interpret current events and to introduce readers to the implications in modern life of Christian thought and practice will fill a very urgent and far-reaching need." At the Jerusalem Meeting of the International Missionary Council in 1928, the same need for literature was strongly emphasized, under the heading, "The Production, Publication, and Circulation of Christian Literature." "It is generally recognized and admitted that this is the most neglected part of the missionary enterprise. There is possibly no other missionary subject on which so many resolutions have been passed and so few put into effect. The need for literature, both for the rapidly growing indigenous churches and for the vast

number of literate non-Christians, is enormous, and is destined to increase greatly during the present decade. It is urgently necessary to supply this need, even on the negative grounds of counteracting or supplanting the ever-increasing amount of literature subversive of character and faith. It is still more important, however, on the positive grounds of developing intelligent churches and a well-furnished leadership for the Christian forces of to-day, and of supplying a modern apologetic for the present most-inquiring generation. The greater intelligence of both Christians and non-Christians, due to the marked recent expansion of the educational movement, both governmental and missionary, calls for a Christian literature far better in quality than that which now exists, and this, in turn, requires the services of more of the best-furnished scholars, thinkers, and writers. Possibly nineteen-twentieths of the volumes needed can better be produced by the Christian forces of different lands working in concert. In almost every mission field steps should be taken to bring together into an effective united scheme the various denominational and national literary enterprises. Wherever complete union cannot be brought about at once, there should be secured the closest possible cooperative arrangement." *International Missionary Cooperation.* Vol. VII, of the series reporting the Jerusalem meeting. New York. 1928. pp. 29–30.

34. M. H. Faulds. "The World Moves Towards Literacy," in *World Dominion,* November–December, 1944. pp. 349–357; see also, in the same valuable periodical, "Re-Education for Germany," by H. E. Friedeberg, and, "World Hunger for Books," by Cecil Northcott, both in the issue of May–June, 1944. One of the few books I have seen that are intended as *handbooks* for defenders of the faith, is *Catholic Evidence Training Outlines,* compiled by Maisie Ward and F. J. Sheed. The 4th edition, dated 1943 (1st ed. 1925), a volume of 362 pages, with a valuable bibliography, divided into two major divisions, "For Junior Speakers," and, "For Senior Speakers." So much of it is devoted to a defence of the primacy and doctrines of the Roman Catholic Church, that the volume can never serve as a manual for Protestants—but, as far as I know, we do not have a work of this kind for our younger Christians. See Edward J. Heffron: *The Catholic Evidence Guild.* Washington, D. C. 1935.
35. The particular issue referred to here, I discover, upon examining the files of this then powerful journal, was that of April, 1923.
36. Luke 24:49; Acts 1:8; cf. Luke 10:19.
37. II Thess. 2:9; Eph. 2:2; Acts 26:18; Heb. 2:14.
38. Rev. 9:3, 10, 19; 13:2; 17:3; 18:3; etc.
39. Robert Flint: *Theism.* 7th ed. p. 305. With this we should compare the words of Eucken, "We feel that we are face to face with forces which we dare not allow to overpower us; yet at the same time we do not seem to be able successfully to confront them." *Main Currents of Modern Thought.* p. 454.
40. John Henry Jowett: *The Whole Armour of God.* New York. 1916. pp. 131, 132, 138–141.

41. Theodore Christlieb: *The Best Methods of Counteracting Modern Infidelity.* New York. 1874. pp. 86–89. On the need of thorough preparation and adequate spiritual power for those who are to engage in the public defence of the faith, see Alexander J. Harrison: *Problems of Christianity and Scepticism.* London. 1891. pp. 219–221.
42. William S. Tyler: *Prayer for Colleges.* New and enlarged edition. Boston. 1877. pp. 149, 150, 187, 198–200, 208. (First ed. 1855; 3 editions published within six weeks; an enlarged edition, 1861. My own copy, of 1877, was published by the Congregational Publishing Society, Boston.) John Henry Jowett, in a powerful sermon on Acts 4:18–33 (which I wish space allowed for quoting entirely), well reminds us that, "These men of the early Church took their antagonisms into the presence of the great God, and they surveyed them there in the wealth and glory of adoring communion, and they saw things as they were, and that gracious, that exquisitely gracious promise that God made to men through the mouth of the Prophet Isaiah (Isa. 32:3), was redeemed in their experience: 'The eyes of them that see shall not be dimmed; they shall see things as they are.'" *Christian World Pulpit.* June 26, 1912. LXXXI. 403. It is not without close relation that the decision of the apostles, "We will give ourselves continually to prayer and to the ministry of the word" (Acts 6:4), is followed by the statement, "and the word of God increased." (V. 7.)
43. II Chron. 34:14; 17:9; Neh. 8:1; Gen. 35:1.
44. Accounts of the revival under Hezekiah are to be found in II Chron. 29, 30, and II Kings 18:1–7.
45. Richard Ellsworth Day: *Bush Aglow.* 1936. pp. 135, 136.
46. Charles H. Spurgeon: *Metropolitan Tabernacle Pulpit.* XIX. (1873.) p. 650.
47. Charles E. Cunningham: *Timothy Dwight: 1752–1817. A Biography.* New York. 1942. Chapter XI. "The Conquest of Infidelity." pp. 293–334. "Far more important than any counter-propaganda in weakening the influence of scepticism among the lower classes was the revival and its attendant camp-meeting. Beginning in the West toward the end of the eighteenth century, revivalism was spread by Methodist, Baptist and Presbyterian itinerants to the more settled parts of the country and even into the very strongholds of rationalism, the colleges. The new emotionalism was too much for the poorly organized freethinkers and the doubters were swamped as wave after wave of evangelicalism swept the countryside. In 1800 the Presbyterian Assembly reported 'a spiritual resurrection' as hundreds, among them avowed infidels and Universalists, were received into the Church." Albert Post: *Popular Freethought in America. 1825–1850.* New York. 1943. p. 27.
48. Horatius Bonar: *The White Fields of France.* London. 1879. pp. 320–324.

INDEXES

Note: In the following indexes, all material appearing in the body of this book, i.e., in the text, is supposed to be indexed. The author has compiled his own index, and if there are omissions, he alone is to blame. In addition, everything *new* appearing in the footnotes, in addition to all that is incorporated in the text proper, is here indexed, whether it be the names of additional authors, or new material on any one subject. When an author is quoted in the text itself, and a footnote connected with this quotation contains only the name of the author, and the book from which the quotation is made, together with the page, etc., the author's name appears in the index only in relation to the text. If, however, the footnote contains additional material from the same author, then he is given a double reference in the index, to the text and to the page on which the footnote occurs.

INDEX TO SUBJECTS

INDEX TO AUTHORS

SCRIPTURE PASSAGES COMMENTED UPON OR REFERRED TO